THE GHETTO IN GLOBAL HISTORY

The Ghetto in Global History explores the stubborn tenacity of "the ghetto" over time. As a concept, policy, and experience, the ghetto has served to maintain social, religious, and racial hierarchies over the past five centuries. Transnational in scope, this book allows readers to draw thought-provoking comparisons across time and space among ghettos that are not usually studied alongside one another.

The volume is structured around four main case studies, covering the first ghettos created for Jews in early modern Europe, the Nazis' use of ghettos, the enclosure of African Americans in segregated areas in the United States, and the extreme segregation of blacks in South Africa. The contributors explore issues of discourse, power, and control; examine the internal structures of authority that prevailed; and document the lived experiences of ghetto inhabitants. By discussing ghettos as both tools of control and as sites of resistance, this book offers an unprecedented and fascinating range of interpretations of the meanings of the "ghetto" throughout history. It allows us to trace the circulation of the idea and practice over time and across continents, revealing new linkages between widely disparate settings.

Geographically and chronologically wide-ranging, *The Ghetto in Global History* will prove indispensable reading for all those interested in the history of spatial segregation, power dynamics, and racial and religious relations across the globe.

Wendy Z. Goldman is Paul Mellon Distinguished Professor of History at Carnegie Mellon University, United States. She is a social and political historian of Russia, and her publications include *Hunger and War: Food Provisioning in the Soviet Union During World War II* (2015, ed. with Donald Filtzer), *Inventing the Enemy: Denunciation and Terror in Stalin's Russia* (2011), *Terror and Democracy in the Age of Stalin: The Social Dynamics of Repression* (2007), and *Women at the Gates: Gender and Industry in Stalin's Russia* (2002).

Joe William Trotter, Jr. is Giant Eagle Professor of History and Social Justice and past History Department Chair at Carnegie Mellon University, United States. He also directs Carnegie Mellon's Center for African American Urban Studies and the Economy (CAUSE) and is a past president of the Labor and Working Class History Association. His publications include *Race and Renaissance: African Americans in Pittsburgh Since World War II* (2010, co-authored with Jared N. Day), *Black Milwaukee: The Making of an Industrial Proletariat, 1915–45* (second edition, 2007), and *The African American Urban Experience: From the Colonial Era to the Present*, with Earl Lewis and Tera W. Hunter (2004).

THE GHETTO IN GLOBAL HISTORY

1500 to the Present

Edited by Wendy Z. Goldman and Joe William Trotter, Jr.

Routledge
Taylor & Francis Group

LONDON AND NEW YORK

First published 2018
by Routledge
2 Park Square, Milton Park, Abingdon, Oxon OX14 4RN

and by Routledge
711 Third Avenue, New York, NY 10017

Routledge is an imprint of the Taylor & Francis Group, an informa business

British Library Cataloguing in Publication Data
A catalogue record for this book is available from the British Library

Library of Congress Cataloging in Publication Data
A catalog record for this book has been requested

ISBN: 978-1-138-28229-2 (hbk)
ISBN: 978-1-138-28230-8 (pbk)
ISBN: 978-1-315-09977-4 (ebk)

Typeset in Bembo
by Deanta Global Publishing Services, Chennai, India

This book is dedicated with love to two strong, tough, and indomitable women:

Judith Trotsky Goldman and Eva Mae Trotter Powell

Judith (Yehudas) Trotsky Goldman (September 16, 1929–December 25, 2015) was born and raised in a tenement on the Lower East Side of New York, the quintessential ghetto for Jewish immigrants to America. Her father was a leatherworker, and the whole family joined the fight for workers' rights. She taught generations of children in the neighborhood at Seward Park High School and served as union chapter leader of the United Federation of Teachers. The neighborhood was poor, but she remembered when the line of children waiting to enter the Public Library on East Broadway stretched around the block, and the Garden Cafeteria was filled with communists, socialists, and anarchists arguing over politics. Scorning "white flight" to the suburbs, she raised her children on the Lower East Side. We grew up with Jewish, Italian, Chinese, Irish, African American, Puerto Rican, and Dominican neighbors. People sat outside on benches in the hot summer days and visited each other in the evenings. Women did laundry together and discussed what they would cook for dinner that night. They knew each other's children, celebrated the milestones of life together, and created an entire world.

Eva Mae Trotter Powell (August 12, 1937–) was born and raised in McDowell County, West Virginia. She is the second child of Joe William Trotter, Sr. and Thelma Odell Foster Trotter. She attended grade school in Hartwell and Berwind and graduated from Excelsior High School, near War, West Virginia. Following graduation from high school, she joined her older sister, Josie Lee Trotter Harris (1936–2016) in Massillon, Ohio. She worked a variety of jobs, married, raised her own three children, and provided consistent emotional and material support to me and my siblings among the "Trotter-14." As the city's industrial workforce downsized and laid off workers, she also joined her first husband Marvin Jones and operated a neighborhood restaurant and bar called "Eva's." The Jones bar and grill provided an important place for an entire generation of young men and women to weather the storm of hard times in the city's shrinking manufacturing economy. Eva also became a pillar of our spiritual community at Friendship Baptist Church. But this book is also a tribute to all my "10 Sisters" (Josie, Dee, Bobbie, Isalene, Doris, Mecca, Jessie, Voncille, and Sakina as well as Eva) who surmounted their own unique barriers and contributed to the well-being of the Trotter Family and the surrounding African American community.

CONTENTS

FIGURES

TABLES

CONTRIBUTORS

Tobias Brinkmann is the Malvin and Lea Bank Associate Professor of Jewish Studies and History at Penn State University, University Park, PA. Recent book publications include *Sundays at Sinai: A Jewish Congregation in Chicago* (2012) – Finalist for the National Jewish Book Award – and *Points of Passage: Jewish Transmigrants from Eastern Europe in Scandinavia, Germany, and Britain 1880–1914* (2013). He is currently working on a study about Jewish migration from Eastern Europe between 1860 and 1950.

Tim Cole is Professor of Social History at the Department of Historical Studies at the University of Bristol, and currently Director of the Brigstow Institute. He is the author of *Images of the Holocaust* (1999), *Holocaust City* (2003), *Traces of the Holocaust* (2011), and *Holocaust Landscapes* (2016), and co-editor of *Militarized Landscapes* (2010) and *Geographies of the Holocaust* (2014).

Bernard Dov Cooperman holds the Louis L. Kaplan Chair of Jewish History at the University of Maryland and has been Director of its Meyerhoff Center for Jewish Studies and its Miller Center for Historical Study. He is the author of numerous studies devoted to aspects of Italian Jewish history and has edited, among other relevant books, *Jewish Thought in the Sixteenth Century* (1983); *In Iberia and Beyond: Hispanic Jews Between Cultures* (1998); and (with Barbara Garvin) *The Jews of Italy: Memory and Identity* (2008).

Dawne Y. Curry is an Associate Professor of History and Ethnic Studies at the University of Nebraska-Lincoln. Curry, a US Fulbright scholar (2017–2018), is the author of *Apartheid on a Black Isle: Removal and Resistance in Alexandra, South Africa* (Palgrave, 2012). She is also a co-editor of *Extending the Diaspora: New Histories of Black People* (University of Illinois, 2009). Curry's research includes explorations into South African women's history, African-American Diasporic experiences in Africa, and resistance struggles before and during the era of apartheid.

Zvi Gitelman is Professor of Political Science and Preston Tisch Professor of Judaic Studies at the University of Michigan, Ann Arbor. Author or editor of sixteen books, including (ed.) *Bitter Legacy: Confronting the Holocaust in the Soviet Union* (1997), *A Century of Ambivalence: The Jews of Russia and the Soviet Union* (2001), and *Jewish Identities in Postcommunist Russia and Ukraine: An Uncertain Ethnicity* (2012). His current research focuses on World War II and the Holocaust in the Soviet Union.

Wendy Z. Goldman is Paul Mellon Distinguished Professor of History at Carnegie Mellon University, United States. She is a social and political historian of Russia, and her publications include *Hunger and War: Food Provisioning in the Soviet Union During World War II* (2015, ed. with Donald Filtzer), *Inventing the Enemy: Denunciation and Terror in Stalin's Russia* (2011), *Terror and Democracy in the Age of Stalin: The Social Dynamics of Repression* (2007), and *Women at the Gates: Gender and Industry in Stalin's Russia* (2002).

Jeffrey D. Gonda is an Assistant Professor of American History at the Maxwell School of Citizenship & Public Affairs at Syracuse University and a Faculty Associate in the Alan K. Campbell Public Affairs Institute. He is the author of *Unjust Deeds: The Restrictive Covenant Cases and the Making of the Civil Rights Movement* (2015). His research focuses on the intersections of race, law, and politics in the twentieth century.

Samuel D. Gruber is a Lecturer in the Jewish Studies program at Syracuse University and Visiting Associate Professor of Jewish Studies at Cornell University. He is the author of *Synagogues* (1999) and *American Synagogues: A Century of Architecture and Jewish Community* (2003), as well as numerous articles on art, architecture, and urbanism. Most recently, his work centers on Jewish settlement patterns in pre-modern Europe.

Alex Lichtenstein is Professor of History at Indiana University and Editor of the *American Historical Review*. He is the author of *Twice the Work of Free Labor: The Political Economy of Convict Labor in the New South* (1996); (with Christian Giuseppe De Vito) *Global Convict Labor* (2015); and (with Rick Halpern) *Margaret Bourke-White and the Dawn of Apartheid* (2016). He is at work on a history of South African industrial relations under apartheid.

Gali Mir-Tibon runs national programs in the field of education in Israel. She serves as CEO for the Institute for Excellence in the Humanities, a foundation for the promotion of liberal–humanistic values in the Israeli school system. Her PhD dissertation is titled "The Jewish Leadership of the South Bukovina Communities in the Ghettos in the Mogilev Region in Transnistria, and its Dealings with the Romanian Regime (1941–1944)" (Tel Aviv University). She is currently the head of the education board of "Lochamei Hagetaot" Ghetto Fighters' Museum. She is the author of the historical novel, *The Mothers' List* (2017).

Avigail S. Oren received her PhD in history from Carnegie Mellon University. During the 2014–2015 academic year, she participated in the A.W. Mellon Sawyer Seminar, "The Ghetto: Concept, Conditions, and Connections in Transnational Historical Perspective, from the 11th Century to the Present," as a pre-doctoral fellow. She specializes in twentieth-century US urban and American Jewish history.

Brian Purnell is Geoffrey Canada Associate Professor of Africana Studies and History at Bowdoin College. He is the author of *Fighting Jim Crow in the County of Kings: The Congress of Racial Equality in Brooklyn* (2013), which won the New York Historical Association best manuscript prize. His current research project is a history of people of African descent in New York City, 1626–present. He is the co-editor of the forthcoming anthology, *The Strange Careers of the Jim Crow North*.

Benjamin Ravid is Professor Emeritus in the Department of Near Eastern and Judaic Studies at Brandeis University, which he chaired from 1989–1992. His publications include *Economics and Toleration in Seventeenth Century Venice* (1978), and *Studies on the Jews of Venice, 1382–1797* (2003). He co-edited (with Robert Davis) *The Jews of Early Modern Venice* (2001), and over fifty articles on Venetian Jewry. He is currently working on a history of the Jews of Venice to 1797.

Stephen Robertson is Director of the Roy Rosenzweig Center for History and New Media, and Professor in the Department of History and Art History at George Mason University. He is author of *Crimes against Children: Sexual Violence and Legal Culture in New York City, 1880–1960* (2005); co-author (with Shane White, Stephen Garton, and Graham White), *Playing the Numbers: Gambling in Harlem Between the Wars* (2010); and one of the creators of the website, Digital Harlem, which won the AHA's inaugural Rosenzweig Prize for Innovation in Digital History and the ALA's ABC-CLIO Digital History Prize in 2010. He is currently completing projects on undercover investigators in American life from the Civil War to World War II, and a spatial history of the 1935 Harlem riot.

Helene J. Sinnreich is an Associate Professor in the Religious Studies Department and Director of the Fern and Manfred Steinfeld Program in Judaic Studies at the University of Tennessee, Knoxville. She serves as Editor-in-Chief of the *Journal of Jewish Identities*. She is the author of *A Story of Survival: The Łódź Ghetto Diary of Heinek Fogel* (2015). She is currently working on a book about the Krakow Ghetto.

Gavin Steingo is an Assistant Professor of Music at Princeton University. He is the author of *Kwaito's Promise: Music and the Aesthetics of Freedom in South Africa* (2016), and an edited volume (with Jairo Moreno), *Econophonia: Music, Value, and Forms of Life* (2016). His research interests include African music, music and materialism, labor and performance, and the anthropology of sound and listening.

Kenneth Stow is Professor Emeritus of Jewish History at the University of Haifa, Israel, and has been a visiting professor at Yale, University of Michigan, Smith College, and the Pontifical Gregorian University. He founded the journal *Jewish History* and served as its Editor for twenty-five years, until 2012. He is the author of many books, including *Alienated Minority: The Jews of Medieval Latin Europe* (1998), *Jewish Dogs, An Image and Its Interpreters: Continuity in the Jewish-Catholic Encounter* (2006), *Theater of Acculturation: The Roman Ghetto in the Sixteenth Century* (2015), and *Anna and Tranquillo: Catholic Anxiety and Jewish Protest in the Age of Revolutions* (2016). His current research focuses on the effects of legal change on de-confessionalization and Jewish emancipation in the early modern and modern periods.

Joe William Trotter, Jr. is Giant Eagle Professor of History and Social Justice and past History Department Chair at Carnegie Mellon University, United States. He also directs Carnegie Mellon's Center for African American Urban Studies and the Economy (CAUSE) and is a past president of the Labor and Working Class History Association. His publications include *Race and Renaissance: African Americans in Pittsburgh Since World War II* (2010, co-authored with Jared N. Day), *Black Milwaukee: The Making of an Industrial Proletariat, 1915–45* (second edition, 2007), and *The African American Urban Experience: From the Colonial Era to the Present* with Earl Lewis and Tera W. Hunter (2004).

Anika Walke is Associate Professor of Russian History at Washington University in St. Louis. She is the author of *Pioneers and Partisans: An Oral History of Nazi Genocide in Belorussia* (2015), and co-editor (with Jan Musekamp and Nicole Svobodny) of *Migration and Mobility in the Modern Age: Refugees, Travelers, and Traffickers in Europe and Eurasia* (2017). She is currently researching the long aftermath of the Nazi genocide in Belarus.

Lenore J. Weitzman has been a professor at Stanford University, the University of California, George Mason University, and Harvard University. She is the author of five books, including the award-winning *The Divorce Revolution: The Unexpected Social and Economic Consequences for Women and Children in America* (1985), which led to the passage of 14 new laws in California and reforms in national legislation on child support and pensions. Her current work focuses on Jewish resistance in the Holocaust. She co-edited *Women in the Holocaust* (Yale, 1999) with Dalia Ofer, a finalist for two Jewish Book Awards, and is now writing a book on the "*Kashariyot*", the young women who were secret couriers" for the Jewish resistance in the ghettos.

ACKNOWLEDGMENTS

It is a pleasure to thank our many colleagues, friends, sponsors, students, and family for helping to make this book possible. First and most importantly, we acknowledge the A. W. Mellon Foundation for its generous Sawyer Seminar Grant to explore the "Ghetto: Concept, Conditions, and Connections in Transnational Historical Perspective, from the 11th Century to the Present." The Sawyer Seminar grant enabled us to assemble an interdisciplinary and international roster of experts on the historical dynamics of spatial segregation in Europe, Africa, and North America from the early modern era through recent times. During the 2014–2015 academic year, we brought nineteen scholars to Carnegie Mellon University to analyze the ghetto in different times and places. Scholars from Africa, Great Britain, Israel, and the United States presented papers from multiple disciplines and methodologies, including history, musicology, anthropology, architecture, and digital humanities. Sixteen of the original eighteen essays from the Sawyer Seminar appear in this volume on the ghetto in global history.

The A. W. Mellon Seminar not only enabled us to bring together a broad cross section of scholars from a variety of disciplines and countries, it also supported a year-long international Postdoctoral Fellow, Gali Mir-Tibon, from Israel; four Predoctoral Graduate Student Fellows from Carnegie Mellon University (Alissa Bellotti, Susan Grunewald, Cassie Miller, and Avigail S. Oren); and extensive collegial interactions and intellectual engagement between faculty and graduate students at Carnegie Mellon University, the University of Pittsburgh, Pennsylvania State University, and West Virginia University. Participants represented a variety of disciplines and departments, including History, Political Science, Modern Languages, Sociology, Religious Studies, and libraries. We extend a special thanks to Caroline Acker, the former head of the Department of History; Adam Shear, Director of Religious Studies at the University of Pittsburgh; and Kwame Holmes, CAUSE Postdoctoral Fellow for 2014–2015. We would also like to thank the committed core of faculty who attended the Seminar regularly. Their contributions to our lively ongoing discussions over the course of the year allowed us to draw collectively on a growing fund of knowledge that deepened our approach to the subject.

The Seminar also drew regular participants from the larger, non-academic community, particularly members of the African American and Jewish communities, who helped us form a remarkably diverse group in terms of age, race, religion, nationality, and life experience. Attendance was high and conversation engaging at every meeting. Building upon the fruits of the Sawyer Seminar, in the spring of 2015 we launched a new graduate level course, "Transnational Spatial Confinement and Resistance." This course helped us to transform the collection of seminar papers into a cohesive volume on the transnational development of the ghetto across time and space. For their diligent engagement with issues in the Sawyer Seminar and later in the graduate seminar on the ghetto, we wish to thank our graduate students. In addition to the Predoctoral Fellows, these included David Busch, Christine Grant, Susan Grunewald, Mark Hauser, Amanda Katz, and Clayton Vaughn-Roberson. We are especially pleased with the results of the graduate student participation in this project, including most notably Avigail S. Oren's essay in this volume, based upon digital humanities research conducted under the auspices of the A. W. Mellon Sawyer Seminar.

From the beginning of our quest to carry out the aims of this project, we received strong and indispensable support from our department head, dean, provost, and president. For endorsing our proposal for a Mellon grant and for providing resources for its development, we wish to thank department heads Caroline Acker and Donna Harsch; deans John Lehoczky and Richard Scheines; provosts Mark Kamlet and Jahanian Farnam; and presidents Jerry Cohon and Subra Suresh. This book also benefitted from numerous other university administrators and technical support staff persons. We are grateful for the able assistance of Catherine Davidson, University Advancement Officer; Leslie Levine, Director of the Dietrich College Research Office; Gail Tooks and Natalie Taylor, Business Managers, Department of History; Jesse Wilson, the history webmaster and photographer; and Hikari Aday, Program Coordinator, the Center for Africanamerican Urban Studies & the Economy (CAUSE) and principal staff person for the Sawyer Seminar. We extend special thanks to Hikari for her efficient and effective work on this project from its inception as a proposal to A. W. Mellon through its completion as an edited volume. She has accompanied us every step of the way. Her initiative and organizational and technical skills lightened our burden considerably.

For her enthusiastic reception to our proposal to produce *The Ghetto in Global History*, we thank series editor Eve Setch at Routledge. Eve's early confidence in the potential of this volume is deeply appreciated. We are also grateful for the steady guidance and organizational assistance offered by assistant editor Amy Welmers. To our many supporters within and beyond the university, we offer sincere thanks, but we owe our greatest debt to members of our families. As always, we are grateful to our spouses, Marcus Rediker and H. LaRue Trotter, for their enduring love, support, and inspiration for completing this work. In the spirit of family, we also respectively dedicate this book to two beloved people, who experienced the ghetto in their own ways and taught us much about the meaning of community.

INTRODUCTION

The ghetto made and remade

Wendy Z. Goldman and Joe William Trotter, Jr.

The concept of the "ghetto," or the enforced spatial segregation of part of a population into a closed, demarcated space for habitation, work, and life, has a long and painful history. Indeed, "ghetto" as a name, a political and social practice, and as a lived experience has persisted for over half a millennium, surviving great transformations in economy, government, and the nation state. Few modes of control have been applied to so many different purposes and groups, from the walled enclosures of pre-modern Europe to the Nazi killing depots, the segregated communities of the United States, and the urban locations of South Africa. Deployed in different ways and invested with varied meanings, the concept has proved useful in maintaining social, religious, and racial hierarchies throughout centuries.

The Ghetto in Global History is the first book to compile the work of leading scholars with the aim of tracing the movement of the term and comparing ghettoization in widely different places and times.[1] The volume grew out of a Sawyer Seminar sponsored by the A. W. Mellon Foundation in 2014–2015. It includes the work of scholars from Israel, Europe, Africa, and the United States who study segregation in four historical periods and through a variety of disciplinary and methodological perspectives. The essays in the volume explore the remarkable tenacity of both the word "ghetto" and the multiplicity of practices it came to represent. They examine the uses of the ghetto for those in power, the lived experience of its inhabitants, the unique cultures it created, and the resistance it spawned.

Conceptual and definitional issues

Using a chronological and transnational approach, the volume examines the ghetto in four separate contexts. First, as a place for enclosing the Jewish urban population in Europe, which originated in Venice in 1516 and ended with the fall of the ghetto gates in Rome in 1870. Second, as a component of Nazi genocide against the

Jews of Europe and the former Soviet Union. Third, as a cornerstone of the racial segregation of African Americans in the cities of the United States. And fourth, as an implicit and sometimes explicit element in the residential and labor policies established by colonial and post-colonial authorities in South Africa.

In their efforts to delineate the "ghetto," scholars have crafted many definitions. Benjamin Ravid offers a pithy three-word definition in this volume that includes any space that is "compulsory, segregated, and enclosed." Other scholars offer alternative definitions more specific to period and place. And in some cases, definitions differ for the same time and place. The U.S. Holocaust Memorial Museum (USHMM) and Yad Vashem, in parallel projects to list and map the camps and ghettos of the Nazi era, used different definitions. The USHMM adopted the following criteria: "any place where the Germans concentrated Jews" by "ordering the Jews to move into a designated area, where only Jews were permitted to live," but made no stipulation as to duration. Dan Michman, the chief historian at Yad Vashem, used stricter criteria that specified both place and time: "Any concentration of Jews by compulsion in a clearly defined section of an existing settlement (city, town, or village) in areas controlled by Germany or its allies for more than one month."[2] Scholars of the African American experience use a looser definition, in keeping with a different context: "while the ghetto was an instrument of control and isolation," a neighborhood from which there were "serious barriers to exit," it was also a form of cultural and institutional empowerment.[3] Furthermore, in recent times, ghetto is used to describe a high concentration of any group segregated by class, sexuality, or other lines of social difference. People speak of "gay ghettos" and even "golden ghettos," or affluent, gated communities where people choose to segregate themselves from the less privileged. Its meaning, always mutable, has become ever more flexible and capacious.

Definitions are key to any efforts to systematically map or quantify ghettos. They are also critical to appreciating the often heated debates over the underlying sources of ghetto formation. Yet in compiling this volume and examining the ghetto as a global phenomenon, we are particularly interested in how the term and practice have traveled and changed over time. This volume takes a *historical* approach to the concept of the ghetto. As our contributors show, the ghetto has a long and fascinating etymology. The word, which initially described the early modern practice that spread outward from the Papal States, changed its meaning after the last ghetto gates fell before Napoleon's armies. Later, the word ghetto was applied to Jews in Poland and other parts of Eastern Europe, to Jewish immigrant neighborhoods in London as well as New York and other cities in North America, and to African American communities in the wake of the Great Migration of southern rural blacks into major metropolitan areas of the United States.[4] Chinatown, Little Italy, and other places where immigrants settled in large numbers also became known as "ghettos." At the same time, some scholars are beginning to reconceptualize the development of apartheid, South Africa's system of racial segregation, as a variant of ghetto formation.

One of the main contributions offered by the essays of this volume is precisely the variation, contingency, and mutability of the ghetto as a word, concept, and lived experience. Rejecting an emphasis on static definition, it is our contention that the ghetto in global history is best understood dynamically and historically. Indeed, we have based the volume on the argument that the practice, etymology, and meanings of the ghetto have shifted over time in conjunction with its circuits of transmission and its changing contexts. In choosing the four case studies highlighted in this volume, we worked with the simplest definition, that offered by Ravid: "compulsory, segregated, and enclosed." Three of our cases – early modern Jewish ghettos, Nazi ghettos, and African American ghettos – differed widely in purpose but were all known by the term. Our fourth case – urban segregated neighborhoods in South African cities – were not called "ghettos" by either their creators or their residents. Yet, as the essays in the African case show, the intended design of these areas and the lived experience of their residents meet the criteria of compulsory, segregated, and enclosed. Moreover, the practice of ghettoization has a significant place in colonial policy in Africa and in the Nazi-occupied territories, and further research may reveal new linkages between Nazism and colonial technologies of spatial control.

Circuits of transnational movement

Scholars agree that segregated quarters for Jews in Europe have a long history, but the *word* "getto" was first coined in 1516 when an old copper foundry ("getto") was enclosed as a site for Jewish settlement in Venice. The ghetto, both as policy implemented from above and as a structure shaped from below, has been repeatedly made and remade. Along with David Harvey, we begin with the premise that spatial forms contain social processes.[5] The ghetto has a long and dynamic history of imposition, developed by ruling elites with widely different aims and intentions. And it provoked an equally dynamic range of responses, which in turn reshaped its imposed structures. This dynamic between imposition and opposition is found in the very etymology of the word, which has traversed the world as a tool of control, a historical memory, a popular referent, and a conscious weapon in the struggle against segregation.

Separate quarters for Jews dated back to the pre-Christian Mediterranean, and existed throughout the medieval period. Separation of groups by ethnic, religious, or national origins was common. There was a "compulsory, enclosed and segregated" Jewish quarter established in Frankfurt in 1462, and in Spain before the expulsion of the Jews in 1492. Yet they were not known as "ghettos." The first ghetto was created in Venice in 1516 on the grounds of an old foundry, or, in Italian, "getto." In 1555, Pope Paul IV decreed that a ghetto be established for the Jewish population in Rome. The practice then spread throughout northern Italy and the Papal States, including those in France. (The Jews had been expelled from southern Italy, which was ruled by Spain, during the Inquisition.) By 1630, "getto" had lost its original meaning of foundry and come to mean a compulsory, segregated, and enclosed area for Jews. The purpose appeared threefold. First, to attract Jewish merchants into Italian city states as a way of promoting trade. Second, to respond to pressures on urban real estate by an increasing Jewish population. And third, to debase the Jews by forcing them to live separately from Christians in markedly poorer quarters. Jewish segregation thus had economic, social, and religious/racial components, all of which came to mark ghettos in other periods and places as well.

Throughout the eighteenth and nineteenth centuries, the system spread. Ghettoization became synonymous with urbanization as Jewish families, dispersed throughout rural villages, left the countryside and moved to the cities. The largest ghettos were centered in Venice, Frankfurt, Prague, and Trieste. Forced to live in special walled and gated quarters set aside within cities, Jews developed their own schools, civic institutions, and courts. The ghettos encompassed rich, middling, and poor Jews, who held a wide range of occupations. The compulsory living space contained a widely stratified population, a stable, multi-textured community, and strong Jewish institutions. The ghetto, to some degree, offered protection against the threat of expulsion and the powerful anti-Semitism of the outside world. The ghettos were crowded and unsanitary, but their conditions did not differ appreciably from those prevailing throughout early modern towns and cities. The streets were narrow, filthy, and subject to flooding, and the Jewish inhabitants were forced to pay an annual tax for the "privilege" of residing there. Fire was an ever-present danger. The entire Frankfurt ghetto, for example, was destroyed in Germany's largest known fire in 1711.

During the "long nineteenth century" that encompassed the struggle for civil rights, the Jews moved toward emancipation. After the French Revolution, the restrictions imposed by the ghetto became increasingly unsustainable. From 1789 on, the struggle for civil rights proceeded in fits and starts, advancing with Napoleonic conquest and the subsequent revolutions of 1848, and declining in periods of monarchical reaction. The ghettos were leveled and resurrected. In 1870, the gates to Europe's last remaining ghetto in Rome were removed. The ghetto system marked Jewish life in Western Europe for more than 300 years, affecting the relationship between Jews and the state, the local population, and reigning religious authorities. The fall of the ghetto, in the wake of the wave of revolutions sweeping Europe, was linked to the long struggle to enfranchise Jews as citizens within their respective nations.

Religious authorities abandoned the practice of a compulsory, segregated, and enclosed urban space for Jews, but the word did not die. By the late nineteenth century, it had become a synonym for "backward," "superstitious," and "unenlightened." Assimilating German Jews used the word to describe East European Jews who lived side by side with their Christian neighbors in small villages or *shtetlakh*, although these were neither segregated nor enclosed. The word "ghetto" also became a widespread synonym for exclusion and discrimination among European Jews still subject to fierce anti-Semitism. In Poland, in the mid-1930s, the government established anti-Jewish quotas in the universities and forced Jewish students to sit at the back of lecture halls on what became known as "ghetto benches."[6]

Having made its way into Eastern Europe, the word also made its way west, first crossing the Atlantic with the small number of German Jews who immigrated to the United States beginning in 1820. Concerned by the poverty, lack of education, and concentration of large numbers of Eastern European and Russian Jews who arrived later, toward the end of the nineteenth century, these German Jewish immigrants feared the growth of new ghettos. The Eastern European immigrants to the Lower East Side of New York and the East End of London imbued the word with their own meanings. Although these neighborhoods were neither compulsory nor enclosed, Jewish writers began using the term to describe any community where the Jewish poor lived in dense, segregated slums.[7]

Under the impact of World War I and the economic expansion of the 1920s, nearly two million blacks left the South for the urban North and West. The ghettoization of African Americans in the United States gained its sharpest expression in Northern cities during this moment of dynamic socioeconomic and demographic changes. As late as 1910, nearly 90 percent of the nation's black population lived in the South, and less than 22 percent of Southern blacks lived in cities. By the end of World War II, the African American population had become a predominantly urban population, largely segregated in the nation's major industrial cities. New York, Chicago, and Philadelphia absorbed the largest numbers, although the black population also increased dramatically in Detroit, Cleveland, Pittsburgh, and other cities of the Midwest and Great Lakes region. As the black urban population increased, residential segregation accelerated. In 1910, the city of Baltimore had passed municipal zoning legislation that divided the streets according to white or black occupants. After the US Supreme Court struck down this legislation in 1917, racial covenants began to replace explicitly racial street zoning ordinances.[8]

While southern cities figured prominently in legal efforts to create racially segregated neighborhoods, scholars of early twentieth-century southern and western cities eschew ghetto formation approaches to black urban life. Until World War II and its aftermath, African American homes remained closely interwoven with white ethnic and working class neighborhoods in the urban South and West.[9] While the new covenants, based on agreements used originally to exclude Asians and Jews, bound homeowners not to sell their property to African Americans across the nation, they had their most profound immediate impact on the urban Northeast and Midwest. By 1920, two-thirds of Manhattan's black population lived in Harlem, and similar patterns of housing segregation prevailed in Chicago and other cities of the Midwest. The World War I migration intensified this pattern of housing discrimination that was already well underway. Organizations like the Harlem Property Owners' Improvement Corporation and Chicago's Hyde Park Improvement Protective Club of Chicago pledged to keep their neighborhoods all-white. Formed in the years before World War I, the Hyde Park club exclaimed, "The districts which are now white ... must remain white. There will be no compromise."[10] During the Great Depression and World War II, high rates of black unemployment and the emergence of New Deal housing programs like the Federal

Housing Administration and the Works Projects Administration helped to deepen established patterns of spatial separation along the color line.[11]

As early as the 1920s, African American journalists, writers, and public speakers began to use the term "ghetto" to criticize discriminatory housing practices. Yiddish newspapers, too, referred to "black ghettos," making common cause between African Americans and Jews. The connection was soon grasped and disseminated by academics. In 1928, the sociologist Louis Wirth used the term to describe Jewish settlement in Chicago. Wirth's mentor, Robert Park, the founder of a pioneering group of sociologists known as the Chicago school, soon began to apply it to African Americans who came north to settle in cities. In a series of groundbreaking studies on black urban life in the years after World War II, the first generation of systematic historical studies of black urban life employed the notion of ghetto formation. Studies by Gilbert Osofsky, Alan Spear, Kenneth Kusmer, and others accented the development of the African American ghetto as a historical process that had deep roots in the transformation of race relations during the late nineteenth and early twentieth century.[12]

By the early 1980s, scholars of black urban life and history began to shift their focus away from an emphasis on segregation to the role of work and community. Examining the Great Migration, in which millions of men and women came north to take new industrial jobs, scholars focused on the contribution these new migrants made to the American economy and the robust communities they built. Emphasizing African Americans as agents rather than victims, researchers broadened their focus to encompass men and women at work, in unions, and within vibrant working-class neighborhoods.[13]

Yet, as deindustrialization demolished industrial jobs and black institutions declined, researchers began to revive the ghetto paradigm. In his influential study of late twentieth century Chicago, historian Arnold Hirsch coined the term "second ghetto" to underscore the spread of racially segregated neighborhoods into new areas of the urban environment during the years after World War II. The emergence of federally funded low-income public housing projects would provide a key popular image of the so-called second ghetto. Along with his emphasis on the pivotal importance of job discrimination and segregation in postwar Detroit, historian Thomas Sugrue also reinforced the salience of the ghetto in describing and explaining key features of the city's black community during the 1940s and 1950s.[14]

At the same time, other historians produced new studies of blacks in the postwar urban South and West. These scholars not only called attention to the increasing convergence of segregated housing patterns across regional lines, but also suggested that such processes had deep roots in earlier although less intensive forms of housing segregation in southern and western cities. Moreover, segregated housing in the Jim Crow South was not solely a product of racism in the urban housing market, it also entailed a substantial alliance between black economic elites and their white realtor counterparts and persisted through the heyday of the Modern Black Freedom Struggle. As historian Nathan Connolly noted about the Greater

Miami Metropolitan region, "Through a combination of tenant paternalism and savvy property management subcontractors, black and white landlords ... routinely exploited tenants to the point of destitution."[15] As the twenty-first century got underway, the ghetto remained a contested concept on the intellectual landscape of black urban history. One historian of the more recent past, observing the spread of racially segregated neighborhoods on the outskirts of the late twentieth-century city, deem these areas "surrogate suburbs" rather than "second ghettos."[16]

The term and the practice of "ghetto" thus traveled across the Atlantic, yet it continued to maintain a strong hold in Europe. As the last ghetto gates in Europe fell, European colonialists and their subjects employed the concept in old and new ways. In May 1899, Mahatma Gandhi published a letter in the *Times of India* concerning the segregation of Indians in South Africa. In order to dramatize the plight of his fellow Indian migrants, Gandhi turned to a word that had already gained some international recognition. Indian settlements, Gandhi noted, could be compared with "Jewish ghettos." In the years to follow, Gandhi repeatedly used the concept of the "ghetto" in order to shine a light on the spatial segregation in South Africa. In 1946, the South African government adopted the "Ghetto Act," designed to curtail Indian ownership of land and property in white "controlled" areas in Natal.[17]

The rise of racially segregated areas in South Africa was closely intertwined with the colonial transformation of the economy from indigenous herding and farming to new capitalist mining enterprises of diamonds and gold. The mines required waged workers and precipitated the incorporation of indigenous people into the larger processes of proletarianization and urbanization. With the emergence of an African industrial working class, government officials and employers structured the spatial division of the country. They aimed to separate the white city from the indigenous African rural areas while drawing heavily on migrant African labor. Nowhere else in the world was proletarianization, the process by which pastoralists and peasants were dispossessed and turned into waged labor, so deeply connected to racial segregation.[18]

At the turn of the twentieth century, the British High Commissioner for South Africa instructed white colonists to create distinctly separate racial zones in the cities. The colonists' efforts, aimed at the extraction of cheap labor, were soon encoded in legislation that came to encompass a native rural reserve system, pass laws, and urban locations, the legal scaffolding of the apartheid system that eventually developed. Race theorists, urban reformers, industrialists, and colonists all played significant roles in the expansion and embellishment of a racial system aimed to control African labor and eliminate competition from Indian merchants.[19]

Although colonial officials never used the term "ghetto," the practices they instituted were not unlike the compulsory segregation practiced in early modern Europe and more loosely, in the United States. As the Native Act of 1923 stated, "the town is a European area in which there is no place for the redundant Native who neither works nor serves his or her people."[20] At the same time, however, increasing numbers of rural Africans were needed to serve in mines and factories and as domestics in the towns. By insisting that African workers leave their families in the rural reserves, employers aimed to keep the cities "white," while shifting the cost of maintaining a family from the urban waged system to the increasingly impoverished native rural reserves. The wages that companies paid did not cover the cost of a family, and their profits increased accordingly.[21] Throughout the interwar period, eugenicists and racial theorists, strongly influenced by social Darwinism, provided an ideological justification for this system. Maintaining that the white race was "the fittest" to maintain global power and empire, they argued that segregation presented the only hope for white "preservation." As Carl Nightingale, a historian of transnational segregationist practices, notes, South Africa, the United States, and Nazi Germany "all drew heavily on the transoceanic trade in social Darwinist and eugenical ideas in the 1920s and 1930s."[22]

With Hitler's rise to power, Nazi theorists deliberately referenced and invoked colonial projects to support their claim for a German empire in the East. Hitler's colonial aspirations were also inseparable from a highly racialized understanding of modern and early modern ghettos on the European continent. The Nazi regime deployed a distorted racist perspective on the history of the Jewish ghetto in its quest to further Germany's quest for global military and political supremacy. One of the Nazi's earliest acts was to pass the Nuremberg laws, which created racial classifications based on "blood" and laws that barred Jews from the professions, civil service, schools, and civic life. Yet, until recently, scholars of the Holocaust split over the degree to which the ghetto, as a gateway to Nazi extermination camps, was the product of a master plan or an evolving consequence of wartime social and political pressures and imperatives.

In his path-breaking book, *The Emergence of Jewish Ghettos during the Holocaust*, historian Dan Michman advances a new argument that navigates between the so-called "intentionalist" and "functionalist" camps of Holocaust studies. In his view, early Nazi officials were divided over the development of a Jewish policy, some arguing as late as 1939 that the intensification of the spatial concentration of Jews would undermine rather than enhance control over the group. Throughout the late 1930s, the Nazis debated the advantages of concentrating the Jews into ghettos. In September 1939, after the invasion of Poland, the idea was finally adopted. The new policy of expulsion and control was formulated by Heinrich Heydrich, Chief of the Reich Main Security Office, in the Schnellbrief sent to the Einsatzgruppen on September 21, 1939. It instructed that Jews be expelled from German territories, moved from rural areas into cities, and contained in ghettos created in Jewish residential areas. Christians were to be removed from these areas, and Jews allowed to exit only under strict German control.[23]

Nazi-era ghettos were mapped roughly onto existing Jewish neighborhoods. According to Michman, the ghettos were only sealed because the Christians who remained in the newly demarcated Jewish zones were reluctant to abandon their homes and move to the "Aryan" side.[24] In an excellent essay reviewing the scholarship on Nazi ghettos, Christopher Browning, too, rejects the idea that the ghetto was a preconceived step in the Final Solution. He notes, "There is no single interpretative framework that encompasses ghettoization in the German-occupied east throughout the war years." Even after the Jews were herded into ghettos, Nazi officials continued to disagree over their purpose. "Productionists" argued that the ghettos could serve as a source of slave labor while "attritionists" maintained that the ghettos, filled with "useless eaters," should simply be allowed to starve to death. Jews from surrounding areas were forced to move into these spaces, which became ever more crowded with starving and dispossessed refugees.[25] In line with Herbert Backe's earlier "Hunger Plan" (1941), the Germans refused to provide more than starvation rations, and thousands of ghetto inhabitants began to die.[26] Attritionism was supplanted by productionism, which, in turn, was replaced in the summer of 1941 with liquidationism. Moreover, at various times, all three practices reigned at the same time in any one ghetto. People died of starvation, *aktionen* systematically murdered marked segments of the population, and the remainder continued to work.

With the invasion of the Soviet Union in 1941, the orders that accompanied Operation Barbarossa made the killing of Jews in and outside of the ghettos explicit. The Wehrmacht and the *Einsatsgruppen* (mobile killing squads) were instructed to murder all Jews, partisans, and Soviet officials in the occupied territories. The magnitude and complexity of ghettoization during the Nazi period were staggering. In total, the Nazis created over 1,100 ghettos, which swelled with Jews shipped from cities and rural areas throughout occupied Europe and the Soviet Union.[27] According to Gitelman and Weitzman, in eastern and western Belorussia alone, the Nazis established 257 ghettos while killing an estimated 2.2 million people and destroying nearly 210 cities. At its largest, the Warsaw ghetto housed 450,000 Jews in less than 1.3 square miles. The occupied Soviet territories were dotted with hundreds of smaller ghettos.

The number of ghetto inhabitants and ghettos was systematically reduced over time. Beginning in the fall of 1941, ghetto inhabitants were subjected to *aktionen* or mass round-ups aimed at their systematic liquidation. Workers received special passes or permits that exempted them from the killings, but over time, their numbers dwindled in the face of the continuing manhunts and transports to the death camps. Most of the Warsaw ghetto inhabitants, for example, were sent to the Sobibor and Treblinka extermination camps, where they were gassed. In July 1943, Himmler decided to transfer the last surviving inhabitants of the ghettos to concentration camps. The last ghetto on Polish soil, which had been created in Łódź in April 1940, was liquidated in August 1944. In the end, the Nazis were no longer interested in the skilled slave labor the ghettos afforded. All their inhabitants were subject to the "Final Solution."

By 1942, many inhabitants of the ghettos had come to understand that the ghetto was actually a prelude to murder. The people taken out were not headed to work camps as promised – they were going to their deaths. This realization dawned slowly, unevenly, and with great difficulty. It posed new and terrible questions for the starving, unarmed population, including how to resist without risking massive German retaliation against the children, women, and elderly members of the ghetto. Resistance movements were launched in the ghettos of Vilna, Warsaw, Bialystok, Baranovich, Pinsk, and other places. Possessing only the most rudimentary weapons, the young fighters were unable to prevent the ultimate liquidation of the ghettos and their inhabitants. Although a small number escaped to the forests to join the partisans, most did not survive. The Nazi ghettos provided the most "extreme" case: the forced segregation of a population as a prelude to mass murder. Yet they also served as part of a vast colonial project and labor system, elements that link them to other efforts at social segregation, exploitation, and control.

By the end of World War II, news about what had happened in the Nazi ghettos reached the United States. Historians, sociologists, and civil rights activists intensified their employment of the term "ghetto" to describe the overcrowded, impoverished, racially-segregated communities of urban African Americans. Activists regularly invoked the horrors of Nazi racial policies to challenge and break the boundaries of America's "ghettos." At the grassroots levels, the struggle for both "Jobs and Freedom," the key rallying cry of the renowned March on Washington in 1963, reinforced a focus on the labor as well as the racial basis of ghettoization.[28] As such, the increasing spatial concentration of African American workers fueled the rise of the Modern Black Freedom Movement that eventually demolished the old Jim Crow segregationist order in the United States. But deindustrialization of the nation's economy soon undercut this promising achievement in the lives of poor and working-class urban blacks.[29] Indeed, as the Modern Black Freedom struggle dissipated under the onslaught of global economic change, including the increasing movement of American manufacturing firms to overseas locations, African American activists joined the accelerating global condemnation and fight against the South African apartheid regime. By the late twentieth century, the transnational fight against apartheid and the remnants of Jim Crow in the United States had created a powerful cross-fertilization of ideas about "apartheid" and "ghettoization."[30] The confluence of these discussions and social struggles would spur new understandings of racialized forms of spatial segregation on both sides of the Atlantic.

Four case studies of ghetto formation

In using a transnational approach, we aim to uncover similarities, differences, and most strikingly, the human networks and connections in a practice that has spanned the globe. How does a word that initially denoted a "foundry" in sixteenth-century Italy come to encompass such a great diversity of practice, purpose, and meaning? Who are the human agents that carry the practice and the word from early modern Europe to the United States? Why and how did colonial officials and subjects seize on the practices of urban enclosure in Africa, if not the word itself? And what, if any, elements of lived experience were shared by those ghettoized in very different places and times? Scholars of delineated periods and places seldom trace the connections that might link one urban or national practice to another or notice the striking similarities between their own debates and those in other fields. By placing the ghetto in a comparative historical and transnational perspective, this volume seeks to remedy these gaps.

All four cases demonstrate that the ghetto was made by the elite and remade by its inhabitants in a dynamic process of contestation that unfolded over time. As David Harvey notes, planners "seek to promote a new social order by manipulating the social environment of the city," yet the social process possesses its own dynamic that achieves its own spatial form in spite of the planner.[31] And the converse of Harvey's statement is true as well: the dynamic within social processes is shaped in turn by policies and structural forces. Yet how much power did ghetto inhabitants have to shape their world? Where did the balance of power in this dynamic process of making and unmaking lie? All our contributors recognize that ghetto inhabitants at every time and place sought to survive and to create forms of community, but they differ, sometimes sharply, about the degree of external constraint residents of ghettos may have faced. Moreover, differences emerge not only among cases, which is to be expected given the different ghettos under examination, but also among the contributors within each case.

The early modern Jewish ghetto

The essays in this section show how the ghetto emerged from the European seg-regation of Jews during the early modern era. Ghettoization occurred at a time when Christianity struggled mightily to secure its independence and dominance over old-world Judaic beliefs and social practices. In the rhetoric and policies of the Catholic Church, the ghetto would serve as a holding ground for the conversion of nonbelievers to the Christian faith. Moreover, since ghettoization supplanted a previous history of Jewish expulsion from Christian-dominated territories, large numbers of Jewish people themselves deemed the ghetto a victory over earlier forms of exclusion and hostility in predominantly Christian cities and territories. Nonetheless, this section employs several overlapping but quite distinct definitions of what constitutes a ghetto. As noted above, historian Benjamin Ravid focuses on the spatial segregation of Jews in the early Italian peninsula (particularly Venice). He not only defined the early modern ghetto as "a compulsory, segregated, and enclosed Jewish quarter," but also shows how the ghetto gradually acquired this meaning during the sixteenth and seventeenth centuries. Based on the Jewish expe-rience in the early modern Polish city of Krakow, Bernard Dov Cooperman treats the ghetto "as an urban quarter *defined by law—and this in both a positive and negative sense.*" Official charters, grants, and licenses mapped the zones in which Jews were legally permitted to reside, including restrictions on their access to houses, trading opportunities, and cultural expression. Rather than a product of religious ideolo-gies and the conversion rhetoric of the Catholic Church, Cooperman argues that the ghetto responded to the rapid demographic, economic, real estate, and social transformations of the early modern city.

Similarly, historian Samuel Gruber defines the ghetto as part of a wider and growing pattern of social control (spearheaded by medieval and early modern elites) to regulate a variety of groups deemed a threat to the established urban order. Emphasizing urban geography and architecture, he notes that the enclosure of the Jews was not unique. Indeed, Venice was "a collection of enclosed spaces," a city of walled islands. Segregationist policies shaped the experiences of such widely different groups as nuns, fishermen, and prostitutes as well as German merchants and ethnic Albanians, Turks, and Jews. For his part, however, Kenneth Stow rejects such structural definitions of the ghetto. He conceptualizes the ghetto as a highly restricted living quarter that offered Jews few opportunities for escape. Based on anti-Jewish scriptures of the Roman Catholic Church as well as Roman law, he identified measures (prohibitions on intermarriage, certain forms of dress, dining, and bath-houses) that defined Jews as "polluters" of the new faith and justified their removal from contact with the larger Christian community. Although he acknowledges breaches in the wall that separated Christians and Jews, Stow none-theless reinforces images of the ghetto as set apart from the surrounding non-Jewish world and vulnerable to immanent violence and even threats of extermination by Christian authorities.

Diverse definitions of the ghetto entail different perspectives on the primary sources of ghettoization and its resulting impact on the lives, history, and culture of residents during the early modern period. Through a systematic application of his conception of ghetto formation as a coerced, segregated, and physically confined space, Benjamin Ravid concludes that the initial "impulse for segregating the Jews" came from the Christian church. Emphasizing the precise process by which the Catholic Church moved toward the segregation of the Jewish population, Ravid illuminates how the ghetto legitimized the Jewish presence in Venice under pres-sure from increasing numbers of Jewish refugees after the War of the League of Cambrai. Yet the ghetto by no means guaranteed Jewish residence in their confined corner of the city. In his view, Jewish residents owed the "privilege" of residing in the early modern ghetto to the precarious cycle of the "five-year charter of 1513." As he puts it, renewal of the charter always "hung in the balance, especially in the sixteenth century," and ghetto residents endured "the constant threat of potential non-renewal until the end of the Venetian republic in 1797."

Rather than ameliorating previous policies of Jewish exclusion from Christian areas, Kenneth Stow forcefully argues that the ghetto reinforced hostile Christian–Jewish relations. Deeply anchored in the language of the New Testament and Roman law, he concludes, "the problem of Jews polluting" the new faith not only gave birth to the ghetto, but also underscored "the centrality of religion as a determinant" of Jewish subordination in early modern Western culture, society, and politics.

Bernard Dov Cooperman and Samuel Gruber challenge cultural and religious interpretations of the origins and development of the early modern ghetto. In Cooperman's view, ghetto walls and other barriers to Jewish mobility were not impermeable. "Above all," as he succinctly notes, "ghettos were urban real estate and were inevitably shaped and reshaped by the same forces that affect cities eve-rywhere." As such, Cooperman clearly articulates the notion that the development of the early modern ghetto was a "negotiated space." It conceded something to the needs and demands of the Jewish people as well as reflecting the power of municipal authorities. Hence, the ghetto was "a compromise" between the deep hostility of the Catholic Church to a Jewish presence in the city and the need for the services provided by Jewish money lenders. Although he notes the uniquely discriminatory urban policies (gates, guards, and boat patrols) that greeted the Jewish population, Gruber emphasizes how a variety of early modern groups experienced the "cityscape of enclosed spaces," characterized by detailed injunctions on movement, residence, and behavior.

Stow's essay argues strongly against this perspective. In his view, the ghetto was not the mediated outcome of rivalries over trade and urban real estate, or a policy that resembled that toward other groups as well, but rather the culmination of a centuries-long animus of the Church. Pope Paul IV, "the arch exponent of the Catholic Reformation," aimed to segregate the Jews, purge what he perceived as a "pollutant," and then convert them. The decree to ghettoize the Jewish population was reinforced by Talmud burning and harsh economic pressure. Once the Jews were forced into ghettos, they were stripped of the rights to self-governance and to practice religious law.

The early modern case study raises questions that echo throughout the volume. Was the ghetto the culmination of the drive to remove Jews from society, motivated by Christian aims at conversion and fears of "pollution"? Or was the Venetian ghetto a form of inclusion, permitting Jews entry into a city that had formerly barred them? How much power were Jews in the ghetto permitted over their own affairs? Was the ghetto, in Cooperman's provocative words, "the birthplace of Jewish participation in the modern world" or did the restrictions imposed on the Jewish community systematically rob it of the right to adjudicate its own affairs? Did the ghetto nurture the development of a community or serve as an oppressive and humiliating barrier to its incorporation?

Nazi ghettos

Nazi ghettos are the only ghettos among our four cases that served as killing sites and way stations to extermination. The Nazis drew quite deliberately on early modern practices, yet these ghettos were never in existence long enough to constitute stable communities. As Zvi Gitelman and Lenore Weitzman point out, early modern ghettos aimed at conversion, Nazi ghettos aimed at annihilation. At the same time, as these five essays show, within a short time and under terrible duress, ghetto inhabitants did create rudimentary governments and social welfare services. Ghetto communities promoted culture, education, scholarship, and even entertainment. Their inhabitants used every possible means to survive, smuggled food, organized resistance, and in some instances, mounted armed uprisings. Scholarship on the Nazi ghetto also further complicates definitions of the ghetto and raises critical questions about the role of the ghetto in the Nazis' "Final Solution." Many consider ghettoization as one of several fixed steps leading toward the annihilation of the Jews. They contend that the "Final Solution" was imbedded in Nazi ideology, and that the ghetto was part of a central plan aimed at concentration, deportation, and death. Other scholars argue that the decision to adopt ghettoization was made locally as a contingent response to the problems that confronted the Nazis in their occupation of Eastern Europe and the Soviet Union.

Contributors to this section focus on food, spatial constraints, social differentiation, labor, and resistance. They demonstrate the great variation in Nazi ghettos: "closed" ghettos, where all movement was strictly monitored; "open" ghettos, where people were allowed to leave at prescribed times; and "destructionist" ghettos, where the inhabitants were concentrated solely for the purpose of murder. The essays also reveal that ghettos in Eastern Europe differed from those on Soviet soil. As Anika Walke points out, the former tended to be larger and to survive for longer periods. Located near rail lines, their inhabitants were brought from all over Europe and then transported by train to death camps. The latter, established after the invasion of the Soviet Union, were quickly subject to mass killing. Their inhabitants died by shooting in forests and pits, close to where the ghettos were created.

This section describes in careful detail the structures of daily life within the ghettos and how their inhabitants struggled to survive within extreme and deadly constraints. Until recently, for example, most studies focused on the larger Nazi ghettos established in Poland. In their innovative study of resistance in the smaller Belorussian ghettos of Baranovich, Bialystok, and Pinsk, Gitelman and Weitzman document local differences in Judenrat policies, access to arms, and proximity to partisan movements. These local circumstances, in turn, underlay the resistance strategies that Jews employed. Residents made collective decisions – to "escape" and participate in underground opposition efforts in Baranovich, to forge an ambiguous combination of resistance and acquiescence to regime orders in Bialystok, and to consider but abandon plans for armed resistance in Pinsk. In her analysis of the Minsk ghetto in the German-occupied Soviet Union, Anika Walke adds to our understanding of resistance strategies. She shows how the Nazi regime used work as part of a larger plan to decimate the Jewish population and as a form of "violence and humiliation." Even so, whereas other ghetto residents were exterminated by the spring of 1942, Minsk Jews used their access to labor camps to survive until October 1943, using the opportunity to leave the ghetto to smuggle food and weaponry back in, and when possible, to escape to the partisans.

Based upon a rich collection of records from the CNSAS (National Council for the Study of the Securitate Archives) secret service archive, the Carp Collection, and Yad Vashem, Gali Mir-Tibon underscores how German authorities provided Romanian officials a great deal of latitude to work closely with the Jewish committee to forge a policy that ultimately resulted in what she calls "selective rather than total annihilation." The Jewish committees in the Mogilev district forged a policy that ultimately protected their narrowly defined class and community interests. She argues that the groups that were sacrificed first were Jews from other areas, most often the Soviet territories, as well as the poorest and most vulnerable, mothers with small children. For her part, Helene J. Sinnreich offers a telling exploration of what she describes as the day-to-day mental, social, and cultural world of hunger. Sinnreich reveals the desperate struggle to survive on rations designed to impose slow starvation. She details the struggle within families and the ghetto at large as people coped with the effects of extreme hunger. Among a broad range of responses to hunger, she emphasizes how the search for sustenance moved people "to seek out a whole new range of foods and to invent new ways of cooking." In the larger scheme of Nazi power, however, she concludes that the quest for food also tragically underlay the decision of large numbers of Jews to comply with the forced labor demands of the Nazi regime, part with family property and keepsakes, and, "most dangerously," in the end to board deportation trains headed to the gas chambers. Finally, Tim Cole looks at ghettoization in Budapest, where Hungarian authorities established "ghetto buildings" and even "ghetto apartments." In calling these compulsory spatial units "ghettos," he notes that he "pushes the idea of the ghetto as a 'segregated and enclosed' space to the absolute limit."

These essays make important contributions to ghetto scholarship, bringing in the oft-neglected experiences of Jews in the occupied territories of the Soviet Union, challenging the notion of the ghetto as impermeable, and revealing the great range in Nazi policy as well as Jewish experience and response. At the same time, they share a common focus on the tragic dilemmas that confronted ghetto inhabitants as they struggled to survive within a world doomed to imminent annihilation.

US and African American ghettos

This case study traces the crucial link between the Jewish ghettos of Europe, both early modern and Nazi, and the African American ghettos of the United States. Tobias Brinkmann's essay establishes new conceptual groundwork for understanding the late nineteenth- and early twentieth-century spread of the ghetto to North America. He traces the movement of the word ghetto from Europe to Chicago as it was carried by a small group of German-Jewish immigrants who pioneered the religious Reform Movement in America. Alarmed at the great influx of Jews from Eastern Europe and Russia, they feared the creation of a new ghetto, filled with unassimilated Jews. Brinkmann shows how the first generation of German-American Jews disdained and then embraced their increasingly ghettoized counterparts from Eastern Europe. These shifting relationships were deeply rooted in emerging relations between German and Eastern European Jews on the continent. As their unity took hold on American soil, however, both groups distanced themselves from the massive in-migration of rural southern blacks, who increasingly inherited the label "ghetto residents." With the growth of Chicago's "Black Belt," a demarcated African American area abutting the older Jewish neighborhood, Jews began to leave, and the Southside was remade as an African American ghetto.

In his recent study of the transnational spread of the ghetto to North America, sociologist Mitchell Duneier underscores the impact of the Nazi ghetto on scholars of the twentieth-century black urban experience. According to Duneier, drawing almost exclusively on the scholarship of leading black urban sociologists (St. Clair Drake and Horace R. Cayton, Kenneth and Mamie Clark, and William J. Wilson),

the term ghetto may have surfaced among some early twentieth century observers of African American life in cities, but the abiding connection with the Jewish
ghetto (particularly its Nazi iteration) only gained currency in the years after World
War II. Avigail S. Oren, however, employing a new digital methodology of corpus
linguistics, documents extensive use of the notion of ghetto in the years before
World War II. Moreover, she shows how these uses of ghetto invoked medieval and
early modern European experiences at a time when the Nazi ghetto was more than
a decade away. The African American press was aware of Jewish segregation, and the
Yiddish press, too, emphasized the experiences that both groups shared. Specifically,
as early as the mid-1920s, a systematic examination of African American newspaper articles revealed the regular occurrence of such words as "black ghettos" and
"ghetto systems" to describe the increasing racial division of the industrial city.
Jeffrey D. Gonda's essay highlights another connection between the Jewish and
African American ghettos. Examining the famous Supreme court case, *Shelley v.
Kraemer*, that struck down the use of racial covenants, he describes how civil rights
attorneys crafted new and successful arguments that linked American segregation
to Nazi policies and introduced the emerging notion of human rights. In 1948, the
Court struck down the use of covenants that bound homeowners not to sell or rent
to African Americans.

Stephen Robertson examines Harlem in the 1920s, an area that contained one
of the largest concentrations of African Americans in the United States. He challenges many of our assumptions about Harlem as an enclosed space. Using digital
mapping tools, he shows that most of Harlem's residents worked and relaxed outside its boundaries and many whites worked, visited, and sought entertainment
within them. He concludes that black life was "constrained" but not "contained,"
and that Harlem was not a ghetto but a "racially variegated place."

Finally, Brian Purnell notes that if ghettos can be made, they can also be unmade.
Focusing on a bright moment in the 1960s and 1970s, he examines Community
Development Corporations and the millions of dollars in Ford Foundation and
federal funds they received. Based partly upon growing political and social awareness of profound modifications in the dynamics of housing segregation and ghettoization in mid-to-late twentieth-century America, Purnell underscores the need
for studies that move beyond notions of "ghetto-making" to ghetto "unmaking."
He argues that government- and foundation-funded Community Development
Corporations in Brooklyn, Watts, and Philadelphia achieved considerable success
during the 1970s. These organizations forged an agenda that moved toward unmaking some of the most debilitating aspects of the ghetto as a dilapidated, unhealthy,
and unsafe environment for its residents. These CDCs represented what Purnell
calls the "golden age" of community. They moved "to unmake the maldistribution
of power that defined ghettos with [both] bottom-up and top-down leadership."
Unfortunately, the community development groups soon lost their connection to
local organizing efforts. The government replaced the war on poverty with a war
on drugs that "focused more on jails, not jobs, for poor people." Poor and working-
class black women, pillars of grassroots efforts to demolish the most demeaning

features of ghetto life, were nudged to the side and treated "nationally as irritants rather than intellectuals and leaders" in the "unmaking" of ghettos. Passing of the dynamic CDCs also opened the door for the arrival of young, white, "moneyed," and "creative classes" who increasingly unmade the ghetto in the interest of capital rather than labor and established racially segregated black urban communities.

The essays in this section show how the word ghetto traveled from Europe and came to describe the experience of people in a new place. They also challenge easy unchanging assumptions about segregation and enclosure. Most importantly, they demonstrate how the ghetto is repeatedly made and remade in a dynamic process linked to employment, real estate values, and the changing politics of cities.

Urban locations, apartheid, and the ghetto in South Africa

The South African essays emphasize the intersection between colonial policies, proletarianization, racial ideology, and spatial segregation. They reveal strong similarities between the urban locations or townships in South Africa and ghettos in other places. With land for African urban dwellers limited by strict racial ideology and defined boundaries, the urban locations or townships were established to be segregated, compulsory, and enclosed. They experienced the same problems endemic to ghettos in other places and times: extreme overcrowding, repeated subdivision and sublet of ever smaller spaces, and an unsustainable strain on space, sewerage, water, and other basic necessities. Dawne Y. Curry examines Alexandra, a black township within Johannesburg, where tens of thousands of people sought living space after World War II. As Curry notes, landlords leased shacks to tenants, who in turn leased rooms to subtenants. Every bit of habitable space was filled with people desperate to gain a foothold in the city. Focusing on a squatters' movement within Alexandra, Curry describes its occupation of public space. The efforts to house squatters created a backlash from residents, who were angered at the loss of their public squares and the pressures the squatters placed on water, sanitation, and electricity. The squatters, in Curry's view, created a ghetto within a ghetto. The black residents of Alexandra met the squatters with the same objections that the white residents of Johannesburg had once voiced against them. Her essay reveals not only the enormous pressures on urban space created by capitalist development, but also the ways in which deep intra-ghetto conflicts and divisions are created by segregation and enclosure. As she notes, in addition to race, "other identity markers," including permanent and temporary, resident and squatter, and legal and illegal also became critical in shaping limited living space.

Alex Lichtenstein looks at the contradiction in Durban posed by the growth of manufacturing and the need for labor within a system that sought to preserve the city as white. He argues that the migrant labor system, which preserved the division between white cities and black Rural Reserves, began to break down under the need for labor. Factory employers disliked the fees they had to pay to tribal labor bureaus and considered migrant labor unreliable. In the mid-1970s, employers pressured the state to transform the peri-urban regions of Durban "into labor ghettos" for industries located in Durban. While employers preferred worker-commuters to long-distance migrants under contract, these commuting workers also posed new and unforeseen problems. Living with their families in close proximity to work, they came to understand themselves as workers with common interests rather than members of a rural native reserve. Indeed, the great strike wave of 1973 was based on the growing number of workers who lived in peri-urban areas, shanty towns, or native reserves that abutted the factories. Their militancy was rooted in a strong commitment to permanent urban living and their identification as workers. They had become, in Lichtenstein's words, "a ghettoized urban proletariat struggling for industrial citizenship in a segregated society."

Gavin Steingo turns to another city in South Africa, Soweto, the country's largest black peri-urban area. Steingo notes the further divisions created by apartheid policies after 1948, which included both "grand apartheid," which divided black Africans from white, and "petty apartheid," which further segregated black townships by ethnic groups. He wrestles with the larger question of location culture: do its constraints encourage creativity or impose "a kind of social death"? He argues that musical creativity is both encouraged by enclosed space and, at the same time, limited by lack of access to wider contacts and possibilities. His essay links to other contributors who pose the same question for ghetto inhabitants in other periods and places. Steingo looks at the lived experience of urban space that is not enclosed by walls, barbed wire, or fences, but rather by other more amorphous but no less real barriers to movement: lack of transportation and linking roads, and fear of crime. He sees post-apartheid Soweto as an area made from above and from below.

The South African case illuminates the utility of employing the ghetto to understand the history of segregated cities in another very different moment and place in time. It not only demonstrates how the ghetto interacted with "racial apartheid," another equally powerful frame for understanding the spread of the color line across the urban landscape, but also highlights the ways that ideas about the ghetto reached southern Africa via the European colonial project during the early twentieth century and via African American activists during the late twentieth century. This fruitful interchange of conceptualizations for understanding racialized spatial segregation in different places and times suggests fresh new possibilities for research on the ghetto in the years ahead.

The essays in this volume bring a rich store of expertise to bear on the ghetto. They share common themes, yet they are also at odds. They differ over the motivations of policymakers, definitions of the ghetto, permeability, and the weight of external oppression on internal development. Yet whatever the differences among our contributors, the essays, taken together, reveal one incontrovertible constant: the ghetto is continually being made and remade. Given its long history, multiple uses, and the persistence of segregation, we can expect the racialization of space to continue for many years to come. As contemporary politics in the United States show, walls appeal to both the ruling elite and privileged populations for many reasons. Yet we can also expect, if this volume is any indication, that the people contained within "compulsory, segregated, and enclosed" spaces will inevitably find ways to remake their world and to resist its dehumanizing boundaries.

Notes

1   Mitchell Duneier offers a synthetic overview of the history of the ghetto with a focus on African American ghettos, *Ghetto: The Invention of a Place, the History of an Idea*, New York: Farrar, Straus and Giroux, 2016. See also Ray Hutchinson and Bruce D. Haynes, eds., *The Ghetto: Contemporary Global Issues and Controversies*, Boulder, CO: Westview, 2011; Daniel Shwartz, *The Ghetto and Jewish Modernity*, Boston: Harvard University Press, in progress.

2   Martin Dean, "Editor's Introduction," in Martin Dean, ed., *Encyclopedia of Camps and Ghettos, 1933–45. Ghettos in German-Occupied Eastern Europe*, Vol. II, part A, Bloomington: Indiana University Press, 2012, p. XLIII; Dan Michman, *The Emergence of Jewish Ghettos During the Holocaust*, New York: Cambridge University Press, 2011, p. 4.

3   Duneier, pp. 38–40; Lewis Wirth, *The Ghetto*, Chicago: University of Chicago, 1928, p. 6; NPR interview with Richard Rothstein, Economic Policy Institute. http://www.npr.org/2015/05/14/406699264/historian-says-dont-sanitize-how-our-government-created-the-ghettos.

4   See Schwartz on the changing meaning of the ghetto for Jews. "The Ghetto: Metamorphoses of a Concept," presented at the University of Pennsylvania, February 7, 2016.

5   David Harvey, *Social Justice and the City*, Athens, Georgia and London: University of Georgia Press, 2009, pp. 10–11.

6   Israel Gutman, *Resistance: The Warsaw Ghetto Uprising*, Boston and New York: Houghton Mifflin, 1994, p. 14–48. On ghetto benches, see Michman, p. 30.

7   See, for example, the Anglo-Jewish writer Israel Zangwill, *Children of the Ghetto: A Study of a Peculiar People* (1892), *Ghetto Tragedies* (1893), and *Dreamers of the Ghetto* (1898); and later, Michael Gold, *Jews Without Money*, New York: Horace Liveright, 1930.

8   Duneier, pp. 29–32.

9   Earl Lewis, *In Their Own Interests: Race, Class, and Power in Twentieth-Century Norfolk, Virginia*, Berkeley: University of California Press, 1991; George C. Wright, *Life Behind a Veil: Blacks in Louisville, Kentucky , 1865–1930*, Baton Rouge: Louisiana State University Press, 1985; Albert S. Broussard, *Black San Francisco: The Struggle for Racial Equality in the West, 1900–1954*, Lawrence: University of Kansas, 1993; Quintard Taylor, *The Forging of a Black Community: Seattle's Central District from 1870 through the Civil Rights Era*, University of Washington Press, 1994; Shirley Ann Wilson Moore, *To Place Our Deeds: The African American Community in Richmond, California, 1910–1963*, Berkeley: University of California Press, 2000; Douglas Flamming, *Bound for Freedom: Black Los Angeles in Jim Crow America*, Berkeley: University of California Press, 2005.

10   Gilbert Osofsky, *Harlem: The Making of a Ghetto, Negro New York, 1890–1930*, Chicago: Ivan R. Dee Publisher, 1963/1996), pp. 106–107; Allan Spear, *Black Chicago: The Making of a Negro Ghetto, 1890–1920*, Chicago: The University of Chicago Press, 1967, pp. 17–23.

11   Arnold Hirsch, *Making the Second Ghetto: Race and Housing in Chicago, 1940–1960*, Chicago: University of Chicago Press, 1983.

12   Arvarh E. Strickland and Robert E. Weems, Jr., eds., *The African American Experience: An Historiographical and Bibliographical Guide*, Westport: Greenwood Press, 2001, pp. 9–10.

13   Joe William Trotter, Jr., *Black Milwaukee: The Making of an Industrial Proletariat, 1915–1945*, Champaign-Urbana: University of Illinois Press, 2006. This approach has also been supplemented by a new emphasis on popular culture. See, for example, Davarian Baldwin, *Chicago's New Negroes: Modernity, the Great Migration and Black Urban Life*, Chapel Hill: University of North Carolina Press, 2007.

14 Hirsch, *Making the Second Ghetto*; Thomas J. Sugrue, *The Origins of the Urban Crisis: Race and Inequality in Postwar Detroit*, Princeton: Princeton University Press, 1996, pp. 9–10.

15 Luther Adams, *Way Up North in Louisville: African American Migration in the Urban South, 1930–1970*, Chapel Hill: University of North Carolina Press, 2010, p. 46; N. D. B. Connolly, *A World More Concrete: Real Estate and the Remaking of Jim Crow South Florida*, Chicago: University of Chicago Press, 2014, quote, p. 9; Taylor, *The Forging of a Black Community*, 178–179.

16 Todd Michney, *Surrogate Suburbs: Black Upward Mobility and Neighborhood Change in Cleveland, 1900–1980*, Chapel Hill: University of North Carolina Press, 2017.

17 Cited in the *Collected Works of Mahatma Gandhi*, https://en.wikisource.org/wiki/The_Collected_Works_of_Mahatma_Gandhi/Volume_II/1899#Indians_in_the_Transvaal_.2817-5-1899.29, accessed April 8, 2017; Carl Nightingale, *Segregation: A Global History of Divided Cities*, Chicago and London: University of Chicago Press, 2012, pp. 283–284.

18 John Higginson, *Agrarian Origins of South African Apartheid, 1900–1948*, Cambridge: Cambridge University Press, 2014; William Beinert and Saul Dubow, eds., *Segregation and Apartheid in Twentieth Century Africa*, New York and London: Routledge, 1995, see especially essays by Harold Wolpe, "Capitalism and Cheap Labour Power in South Africa: From Segregation to Apartheid" and Martin Legassick, "British Hegemony and the Origins of Segregation in South Africa, 1901–1914."

19 George M. Fredrickson, *White Supremacy: A Comparative Study in American and South African History*, New York: Oxford University Press, 1981.

20 Fredrickson, p. 242.

21 Nightingale; Keletso Atkins, *The Moon is Dead! Give Us Our Money! The Cultural Origins of an African Work Ethic in Natal, South Africa, 1843–1900*, Portsmouth, New Hampshire: Heinemann, 1993; Kevin Beavon, *Johannesburg, The Making and Shaping of the City*, Pretoria: University of South Africa Press, 2004; Beinert and Dubow, eds.

22 Nightingale, p. 334.

23 Dan Michman, *The Emergence of Jewish Ghettos During the Holocaust*, Cambridge: Cambridge University Press, 2011, pp. 63–67.

24 Michman, pp. 61–89, 148.

25 Christopher Browning, "Introduction," in Martin Dean, ed., *Encyclopedia of Camps and Ghettos, 1933–45. Ghettos in German-Occupied Eastern Europe*, Vol. II, part A, Bloomington: Indiana University Press, 2012, p. xxvii. On the evolution of ghetto policy, see vvvii–xxxvii.

26 Adam Tooze, *The Wages of Destruction: The Making and Breaking of the Nazi Economy*, New York: Viking Penguin, 2006, p. 462. Michman, Gutman, and Samuel Kassow: *Who Will Write our History? Emanuel Ringelblum, the Warsaw Ghetto, and the Oyneg Shabbos Archive*, Bloomington: Indiana University Press, 2007.

27 Paul Shapiro, Alvin Rosenfeld, and Sara Bloomfield, "Preface," in *Encyclopedia of Camps and Ghettos, 1933–45. Ghettos in German-Occupied Eastern Europe*, p. xxv.

28 Will P. Jones, *The March on Washington: Jobs, Freedom, and the Forgotten History of Civil Rights*, New York: W.W. Norton, 2013, pp. ix, 163–200.

29 William J. Wilson, *When Work Disappears: The World of the New Urban Poor*, Chicago: University of Illinois Press, 1996, pp. xiii–xxiii.

30 Douglas S. Massey and Nancy Denton, *American Apartheid: Segregation and the Making of the Underclass*, Cambridge: Harvard University Press, 1993, pp. 15–19.

31 Harvey, pp. 44–45.

PART I

The early modern Jewish ghetto

View of Venice by Jacopo de' Barbari, 1500. Detail of the sestiere Cannaregio showing the area of the Ghetto, with the walled monastery of San Girolamo (left). Courtesy of Samuel Gruber

1

GHETTO

Etymology, original definition, reality, and diffusion

Benjamin Ravid

Introduction

At the outset, it must be acknowledged that the major impulse for segregating the Jews initially came from the Christian Church. Therefore, in order to understand that development, one must briefly consider the special attitude of Christianity toward Judaism. After the original Judeo Christians broke with Judaism by rejecting Jewish law and accepting pagans directly into their midst without first converting them to Judaism and thereby establishing Christianity as a separate religion, Christianity adopted a hostile "sibling rivalry" toward those who remained Jews. On a theological level, this was not – as is so often assumed – simply because the Jews were considered responsible for the death of Jesus according to the Gospels and especially the verse found only in the Gospel of Matthew 25:25, "His blood be upon us and on our children." Rather, it was because Christianity based itself and its legitimacy upon the Old Testament and claimed to be the true Israel, while condemning the Jews who were perceived as erring by stubbornly following the rabbinic interpretations of the Bible rather than the new true Christian exegesis. The classical Christian attitude to Judaism was summed up by the Witness Theory of the church father Augustine (354–430), which held that the Jews should not be killed but rather preserved in a position of inferiority in order to testify to their rejection by God, who had chosen Christianity as the true Israel and the inheritor of the biblical blessings while condemning the Jews to receive the curses enumerated in the Bible. With the expansion of Catholicism throughout Europe, this approach to the Jewish question came to be accepted by the secular authorities who, if they permitted Jews to reside in their realm, subjected them to a widely varying range of prohibitions and restrictions.

Jewish quarters had existed in the Hellenistic pre-Christian Mediterranean world, and as they spread throughout Christian Europe during the Middle Ages, they were designated various names in diverse languages. Some designations consisted of the local word for street, quarter, or district together with an adjective indicating that Jews lived there, while others did not reflect a Jewish presence.[1]

Although sometimes the origins of a Jewish quarter can be attributed to a specific act of legislation or administrative decree, often – especially in earlier periods – it remains veiled in the twilight zone of undocumented history. Various reasons have been proposed for the emergence of these Jewish quarters. The simplest explanations cite the natural tendency for groups of foreigners or individuals engaged in the same profession to settle together. Also, if the authorities of a given locale were trying to attract immigrants for commercial or economic reasons, as an inducement for them to come, they might be given a designated area in which to settle, sometimes even surrounded by a wall and perhaps also a gate or gates for their safety. More specifically, in addition to wishing to live close to relatives and friends, Jews also desired to be near the synagogue and other community institutions, as well as stores selling food prepared according to their religious rites and other items needed for their religious observances. And for their general solidarity and defense, Jews no doubt felt more comfortable living in close enclaves.

Yet the more that one looks at the phenomenon of the pre-modern Jewish quarter, the more one recognizes the validity of the astute observation of Haim Beinart, made over thirty years ago, that "more is unknown than known about the issue of Jews dwelling in separate quarters in the Middle Ages."[2]

Most basically, one must differentiate between the general term "Jewish quarter" and the term "ghetto," that originally indicated a very specific kind of Jewish quarter that we will define below as a compulsory, segregated and enclosed Jewish quarter. Modern scholars have very often employed the two terms indiscriminately without differentiating between voluntary areas of residence in which a substantial number of Jews lived together and compulsory, segregated, and enclosed Jewish quarters.[3] To complicate matters, in places where it is known that walls and gates existed, it is not always known when they were established, whether all Jews and only Jews were allowed to reside inside the enclosure, or whether the gates were locked for the entire night to segregate the inhabitants or rather for their security and could be opened when desired. To sum up, one can conclude that although compulsory, segregated and enclosed Jewish quarters were not completely unknown in Christian Europe before the sixteenth century, for some had been established in Christian Spain and one of the best-known ones was that established in Frankfurt in 1462, clearly they did not represent the norm, and one should not assume that any Jewish quarter belonged to that category without conclusive proof.[4] Certainly, the few that did could never have been referred to by contemporaries as ghettos, because the association of the word "ghetto" with a Jewish quarter commenced in Venice in 1516.

The word "ghetto" came into being to designate the copper foundry of the Venetian government, *il ghetto* (sometimes spelled *gheto*, *getto*, or *geto*) where bronze cannon balls were cast, from the root *gettare*, to cast or to throw, encountered in English words such as eject, jet, and trajectory. Eventually, an adjacent island was used to dump waste products from the ghetto, and it became known as the Ghetto Nuovo, the new foundry, to distinguish it from the area of the foundry that then became known as the GhettoVecchio, the old foundry.[5] However, in the fourteenth century, when the foundry was no longer able to meet the needs of the Venetian state, it was sold, and the area became the site of modest houses mainly inhabited by weavers and other petty artisans. Until the year 1516, the word "ghetto" was used only to refer to that area, and therefore all usages referring to ghettos as Jewish quarters prior to that date are anachronistic.

Subsequently, during the course of the sixteenth and seventeenth centuries, the word "ghetto" came to be used for all compulsory, segregated and enclosed Jewish quarters on the Italian peninsula. Then, in the nineteenth century, after those Jewish ghettos had been abolished (with the exception of that of Rome),[6] "ghetto" came to be used to refer in a new sense to designate dense areas of Jewish settlements in Europe and North America that were not compulsory, segregated and enclosed and often consisted of poor immigrants, and then by extension to such quarters of other minority groups. Although used to refer to Afro-American quarters in the United States before the Second World War, the usage of the term "ghetto" during the Holocaust led to a much greater awareness of the term, which then came to be used primarily to refer to Afro-American quarters, and then those of other minority groups.[7] Understandably, the simultaneous extended usages of the word "ghetto" in different senses created a blurring of the very important distinction between voluntary quarters and compulsory, segregated, and enclosed ones that reflected completely different attitudes on the part of the government.

The ghettos of the early modern Italian peninsula and Frankfurt

During the Middle Ages, the Venetian government acquiesced in the presence of a few individual Jews in the city of Venice, but except for the brief period from 1382 to 1397, never authorized Jews to settle as a group.[8] However, it allowed Jews to live on the Venetian mainland, especially in Mestre, across the lagoon from Venice. When in 1509 the enemies of Venice united and invaded the Venetian mainland and advanced to the edge of the lagoon in 1509, the government granted the inhabitants of the mainland, including Jews, refuge in the city. Then, in 1513, primarily because of the utility of the Jews as moneylenders since the Catholic Church prohibited Christians from lending money to fellow Christians at interest, the government issued a 5-year charter to a Jewish moneylender from Mestre, allowing him and his associate to operate small-scale pawnshops at controlled rates of interest in Venice itself. But many Venetians were bothered by the fact that Jews now resided freely all over the city. The clergy preached against the Jews, especially at Easter time when, due to the nature of the holiday, anti-Jewish sentiment tended to intensify, and demanded their expulsion. In 1515, around Easter time, the government proposed to relegate the Jews to the island of Giudecca (whose name, in this case, has nothing to do with Jews[9]) but no action was taken because of their objections. However, in the following year, 1516, again around Easter time, the Venetian Senate enacted, despite strong Jewish objections, a compromise between the new freedom of residence and the previous state of exclusion and required all Jews to dwell on the island called the Ghetto Nuovo.

The preamble to the legislation of 29 March recollected that in the past, various laws had provided that no Jew could reside in the city for longer than 15 days a year. However, out of necessity and because of the most pressing circumstances of the times, Jews had been permitted to live in Venice, primarily so that the property of Christians that was in their hands (i.e., the pledges in the pawnshops) would be preserved. Nevertheless, it continued, no God-fearing Venetian wished that they should live spread out all over the city in the same houses as Christians, going where they pleased day and night, and committing, as was known to all and was too shameful to relate, many detestable and abominable acts to the gravest offense of God and against the honor of the well-established Venetian republic.

Therefore, the legislation continued, all Jews then living throughout the city and those who were to come in the future were immediately to go to live together in the Ghetto Nuovo. In order for this to be done without delay, its houses were to be evacuated at once, and as an incentive for the owners to comply, the Jews (who since 1423 had been forbidden from purchasing or acquiring real estate in the Venetian state) moving in were to pay a rent one-third higher than the current rate, with that additional amount to be exempt from the *decima* tax. Furthermore, to prevent Jews from going around all night, gates were to be erected on the side of the Ghetto Nuovo facing the Ghetto Vecchio and also at the other end. These two gates were to be opened in the morning at sunrise and closed at sunset by four Christian guards who were to live there alone, without their families, and be paid by the Jews. The two sides of the Ghetto Nuovo that overlooked the small canals were to be sealed off by high walls, and all direct access from the houses to the canals, which served as the main route of communication and transportation in Venice, was also to be eliminated. Thus, the Jewish quarter known as the ghetto of Venice came into being.[10]

Now, to summarize, this Senate legislation contained three basic provisions:

- The new Jewish quarter was *compulsory* – every Jew had to live within it.
- It was *segregated* – no Christians were allowed to live inside it.
- It was *enclosed* by walls and a gate or gates that were locked at night and remained so until the morning.

Despite the attempts of the Jews to ward off segregation in the new compulsory area assigned to them, the Venetian government was adamant. While willing to make minor concessions on a few administrative details – such as extending the closing time of the gates by one hour in the summer and two in the winter when it got dark considerably earlier, allowing Jewish doctors to leave the ghetto after hours to treat Christian patients and eliminating the nocturnal boat patrol that the Jews were required to finance – it was unwilling to yield on the general principle that all Jews in the city had to live in the ghetto. While acknowledging that the presence of Jews in Venice was desirable because of considerations of *raison d'état* (reason of state), its religious concerns relegated them to their appropriate confined space in Christian society.

Nevertheless, although the establishment of the ghetto acknowledged the legitimacy of the Jewish presence in Venice, it did not ensure their continued residence, for that privilege was based on the 5-year charter of 1513. Consequently, it depended on the renewal of that charter, and although in retrospect the Jews resided in Venice until the end of the republic, nevertheless the renewal of the charter often hung in the balance, especially in the sixteenth century, and they lived under the constant threat of potential non-renewal until the end of the Venetian republic in 1797.[11]

Although a few compulsory, segregated, and enclosed Jewish quarters had existed prior to 1516, primarily in Spain and the Germanic lands, the best-known and longest lasting of which was that of Frankfurt am Main established in 1462, they were never called ghettos before the establishment of the Venetian ghetto in 1516. Thus, the oft-encountered statement that the first ghetto was established in Venice in 1516 is correct in a technical, linguistic sense but somewhat misleading in a wider context. It would be more concise and precise to assert that the compulsory, segregated and enclosed Jewish quarter received the name "ghetto" as a result of developments in Venice in 1516. In the felicitous formulation of Robert Bonfil, the city of Venice "retains the copyright for the semantically innovative term ghetto as defining the locus of the settlement of the Jews in the city."[12]

In 1541, some 25 years after all Jews in Venice had been compelled to live in the ghetto, visiting Levantine Jewish merchants complained to the Venetian government that they did not have sufficient space in the ghetto. In response, in the context of a larger plan designed to make trading in Venice more attractive to foreign merchants, the government acknowledged that those Jewish merchants were importing the greater part of the merchandise coming from the Ottoman Balkans, and therefore ordered that their complaint be investigated. Six weeks later, following the confirmation of their situation, the merchants were assigned twenty dwellings in the adjacent Ghetto Vecchio that was ordered to be walled up with two gates, one opening up to the pavement on the side of the canal of Cannaregio and the other, at the other end, to the wooden footbridge leading to the Ghetto Nuovo.[13]

Assigning the Ghetto Vecchio to Ottoman Jewish merchants further strengthened the association between the Jews and the word "ghetto," which did not remain confined only to Venice for long. At this time, the Counter-Reformation papacy adopted a more hostile attitude toward the Jews, and in 1555, Pope Paul IV, shortly after his inauguration, issued a bull that severely restricted the Jews.[14] Its first paragraph provided that henceforth all Jews in all places in the papal states were to live together on a single street, separated from Christians, and should it not suffice, then on as many adjacent ones as should be necessary, with only one entrance and exit.[15]

Consequently, in that same year, the Jews of Rome were required to move into a new compulsory, segregated and enclosed quarter in that city.[16]

In accordance with the papal bull, compulsory, segregated and enclosed Jewish quarters were also established in papal Bologna and Ancona, and in 1569 all Jews in the papal states were ordered to move to the compulsory, segregated and enclosed Jewish quarter of Rome or Ancona. Subsequently, other local Italian authorities instituted special compulsory, segregated and enclosed quarters for the Jews, and following the Venetian nomenclature, these new residential areas were given the name of ghetto already in the legislation that required the Jews to move into them. The major exception to ghettoization on the Italian peninsula was the case of Tuscan Livorno, because of the desire of the Grand Dukes of Tuscany to attract international Jewish merchants to develop their new port at Livorno (Leghorn).

Eventually, the word "ghetto" returned to Venice in its new sense of a compulsory, segregated and enclosed Jewish quarter with no connection whatsoever to the copper foundry that had given the Ghetto Vecchio and the Ghetto Nuovo their names. In 1630, the Jewish merchants requested that the ghetto be enlarged to house some wealthy new Jewish merchant families who would settle in the city if given suitable living space. In response, the Venetian Senate provided that an area located across a canal from the Ghetto Nuovo be enclosed and joined to it by a footbridge. Since areas called the old ghetto (the Ghetto Vecchio) and the new ghetto (the Ghetto Nuovo) already existed in Venice, it is understandable that this third ghetto almost immediately became known as the newest ghetto (the Ghetto Nuovissimo). However, the Ghetto Nuovissimo differed from the Ghetto Nuovo and the Ghetto Vecchio in one most important respect. While the two earlier designations had been in use prior to the residence of the Jews in those locations and owed their origin to the previous presence of a foundry in that area, the Ghetto Nuovissimo had no association with a foundry. Rather, it was called the Ghetto Nuovissimo because it was the site of the newest compulsory, segregated and enclosed Jewish quarter. The term "ghetto" had thus come full circle in the city of its origin: from its original specific meaning as a foundry in Venice, to a new generic usage in other cities to denote a compulsory, segregated, and enclosed Jewish quarter with no relation to a foundry, and finally to that generic usage also in Venice.[17]

Eventually, in May 1797, as the army of Napoleon Bonaparte stood poised at Mestre, across the lagoons from the city of Venice, the Venetian government dissolved itself in favor of a municipal Council influenced by the new French ideals of *liberté, egalité,* and *fraternité.* That Council ended the special restricted status of the Jews of Venice and ordered the ghetto gates torn down.

The French Revolution and Napoleon also extended the emancipation of the Jews, at least temporarily, to the areas that they conquered and permanently ended ghettos in places that became a part of France, such as Nice, Avignon and Carpentras. As for Frankfurt, in June 1796 the approaching French army, aiming its cannons at the Arsenal, struck the Judengasse instead, causing fires in many places with the result that most of it was burnt down. Despite immediate proposals to rebuild the Judengasse, it was never restored, although it should be noted that its

Jews did not gain permanent equality with the other inhabitants of the city.[18] This serves as a very important reminder that the presence of a ghetto constituted only one factor in determining the status of the Jews in any location. Significantly, it appears that never during its existence was the Judengasse referred to as a ghetto, for that word seems to have been confined to the Italian peninsula until sometime in the early nineteenth century.

The context of the early modern Italian ghetto and its social and cultural reality

Before moving on to a more detailed examination of the use of the word "ghetto" after the end of virtually all Jewish ghettos, one has to look at the context of pre-emancipation European society. Until at least the end of the eighteenth century, most of European society was basically corporate in nature, although signs of change could be discerned. No concept of universal citizenship with equal rights and participation in the governing authority existed. Rather, society comprised corporate bodies such as towns, clergy, guilds and universities with rights, privileges and obligations expressed in specific charters, and it was these corporate groups that the French revolutionary government and then other European governments sought to disband in order to create the modern sovereign state. In this context, pre-emancipation Jewish communities, whether or not confined to a ghetto, were treated as corporate bodies and granted internal autonomy. Jews were allowed to observe their religious rites and traditions, and to govern themselves internally. Accordingly, they developed forms of internal government, with assemblies and committees whose complexity depended on the size and nature of the specific community. These organizations administered the synagogue and other institutions required for the community to function, as well as confraternities to meet other needs, including those of the sick and the poor. They established a structured educational system to provide their children (primarily their sons) with the education necessary at least to read the Hebrew texts of their tradition to enable the community to function in an Italian-speaking environment. Thus, the community provided an organized framework that fulfilled the religious, social, philanthropic and other needs of the Jews as they waited patiently, prepared to endure their lot until the coming of the promised Messiah.

Since the early modern Italian ghettos enclosed all Jews in the city or town, they really constituted "the city of the Jews," a self-governing entity supported by the authorities because of its economic utility. Understandably, the individuals living in it varied greatly in wealth, although given the restrictions on the economic activity officially permitted to the Jews, a large number were not well off. Yet it must be recalled that the Rothschilds commenced accumulating their wealth within the Judengasse of Frankfurt. In short, the ghetto was not automatically synonymous with a broken-down society or with a slum, and those who had the means enjoyed a higher standard of living and furnished their apartments more luxuriously than others.

It must also be noted that the ghetto did not hermetically seal off the Jews from their environment. Indeed, it was never intended to eliminate all contact between Christians and Jews, for its creators constructed ghettos with holes, or more accurately, gates. To eliminate all contact, it would have been necessary to expel Jews from the entire area, as England had done in 1290, royal France in 1394, and Spain in 1492, following the failure of the program to isolate them in compulsory, segregated and enclosed quarters so that they could not influence New Christians to return to Judaism.[19]

The clearest indication that the ghetto was not intended to prevent all contact between Christians and Jews was that the ghetto gates were open during daylight hours, and sometimes, especially in winter, into the early evening hours. Jews could leave the ghetto during that time, and Christians could also enter it. Indeed, in some Italian ghettos, especially that of Venice, it was necessary for Christian borrowers to enter the ghetto to avail themselves of the basic moneylending functions for which Jews had been allowed to reside in the city or town, since the Jewish pawnshops were by law located in the ghetto. Once Christians had entered the ghetto, further contact of all sorts with all kinds of Jews was possible. Yet the establishment of the ghetto eliminated most contact during the dark and mysterious night when all sorts of undesirable things could occur, and also limited much casual contact that could have occurred in daytime between Jews and Christians had the Jews not lived in separate quarters. Generally, the privilege to be outside the ghetto after curfew time was granted only to very clearly defined groups such as, in Venice, doctors and merchants engaged in international maritime commerce, and also on an ad hoc basis to specific individuals for the benefit of the community or for their own benefit.

A consideration of the cultural life within the ghettos of cities such as Ferrara, Florence, Mantua and Venice and the extent to which external trends penetrated into them of necessity leads to a further re-evaluation of the widespread myth of the alleged negative impact of the ghetto in the Jewish intellectual and cultural spheres. Clearly, the Jews of the early modern Italian ghettos shared much of the general outlook and interests of their Christian neighbors, although they retained their own religious identity with all that it entailed, since for them the distinguishing feature of Judaism was not cultural but rather religious. Consequently, their cultural life was closer to the more open patterns that had characterized Spanish Jewry rather than to the more restrictive type characteristic of northern German-Polish Ashkenazi Jewry, which is often erroneously considered to constitute the norm rather than representing only one ethnic Jewish tradition among the many that evolved over time.[20]

Generally, the everyday spoken language of the Jews consisted of the local Italian dialect with some added Hebrew words taken from the Jewish religious and literary tradition. More educated members of the community could read Italian and some also Latin, and were well versed in both the classics of Greco-Roman civilization (although generally Greek culture was known through Latin translations) and contemporary Italian literature, and were even acquainted with patristic literature.

Thus, the decisive element determining the genres and modes of Jewish self-expression and creativity was not so much whether or not Jews were required to live in a ghetto, but rather the nature of the outside environment and whether it constituted an attractive stimulus to Jewish thought and a desirable supplement to traditional Jewish genres of intellectual activity, as was certainly the case on the early modern Italian peninsula where the afterglow of the Renaissance continued to shine.

Clearly, we must, as David Ruderman observed, "rethink our image of ghettos, particularly the notion that they inevitably lead to cultural isolation and stifling parochialism."[21] Along with the compulsory, segregated, and enclosed legal nature of the ghetto, Ruderman's "notion of open ghettos" in the wider cultural sense is simultaneously valid. Therefore, any attempt to characterize the nature and extent of the relationship between Jews and their Christian neighbors and the cultural-intellectual level inside the ghetto cannot merely assert that a ghetto existed and assume that constitutes an adequate explanation. Rather, one must take into consideration both the permeability of the ghetto walls in law and also the reality of everyday life. Although the ghetto involved a varying range of restrictions, ultimately it should always be kept in mind that the word "ghetto" itself only referred to a certain type of housing arrangements for Jews.[22]

Yet undeniably the compulsory, segregated and enclosed ghetto was very important in reinforcing the long-standing view that the Jew constituted an "Other" in Christian society from whom the faithful should stay away as much as possible. While the ghetto did not represent the beginning of a policy of marginalizing the Jews in Christian society, since discriminatory legislation of various kinds – such as the colored distinguishing marker – usually preceded the establishment of a ghetto, it did not constitute merely another manifestation of their already existing marginalization in Christian society but rather its ultimate phase. Still, the ghetto constituted an undeniable basic acceptance of the Jews within Christian society as they were assigned their own specific space integrated into the larger urban context.

The post-1800 usages of the word "ghetto"[23]

Initially, the word "ghetto" had been used only in connection with compulsory, segregated and enclosed Jewish quarters on the Italian peninsula. Interestingly, it does not appear in Shakespeare's classic *The Merchant of Venice* (written ca. 1596–1597). It seems to have appeared in print in the English language for the first time in the travelogue of the well-known English traveler Thomas Coryat, whose account, called *Coryat's Crudities*, was published in London in 1611. When introducing the ghetto in the course of his account of his visit to Venice in 1608, Coryat felt the need to explain the word as he wrote about "the place where the whole fraternity of the Jews dwelleth together, which is called the Ghetto."[24]

The question regarding when the word "ghetto" first appeared in the various European languages north of the Alps in the general sense of a compulsory, segregated and enclosed Jewish quarter, rather than referring to a specific Italian ghetto, still requires investigation. It must be stressed that any such investigation has to be undertaken on the basis of the sources in their original language and not based on translations. To give one example, the phrase " … durch die Einzwängung Frankfurter Judengassmauern" (through the compulsory Frankfort Jewish-street walls) of Heinrich Heine was translated into English as " … within the walls of the Frankfurt Ghetto," an anachronistic rendering that renders any philological investigation on the basis of translations futile.[25]

An examination of book titles reveals that until 1840 the word "ghetto" always referred to a specific Italian location.[26] It appears that the first books with the word "ghetto" in the title that did not refer to Italian ghettos were Berthold Auerbach's *Spinoza* (1837) and *Dichter und Kaufmann* (*Poet and Merchant*) (1840), published together as *Das Ghetto* (*The Ghetto*) (1840). However, the book of Leopold Kompert, *Aus dem Ghetto* (*Out of the Ghetto*) (1848), which opened with a sense of consciously standing "outside the ghetto," has been characterized as "the first collection of stories that carries a programmatic reference to the ghetto in its title. For this reason, Kompert can be regarded as the inaugurator of the ghetto story as a distinct genre within German literary history."[27]

Subsequent usages of the word "ghetto" reflect the paradoxical development that, as the few remaining compulsory, segregated and enclosed Jewish quarters of Europe were disappearing during the course of the nineteenth century, the word "ghetto" gained increasing international currency in a new sense. As a result of the attitude of assimilated European, and especially German, Jews toward the Jews of Eastern Europe, a new usage of the word "ghetto" developed in an extended meaning no longer confined to compulsory, segregated and enclosed Jewish quarters. As large segments of German Jewry strove to assimilate into the German middle class, they accepted the Enlightenment ideal of *Bildung*, stressing self-improvement on the basis of conceptions of rationality, enlightenment and culture. *Bildung* became the criterion for judging traditional Jewish culture, and it required the discarding of Jewish habits and ways of life that were considered superstitious, obscurantist and culturally backward.[28] Such a Jewish society was perceived as still existing to the immediate east of Germany, in Eastern Europe, especially in the lands that had formerly constituted Poland prior to the late eighteenth-century annexations by Russia, Prussia and Austria. The term "ghetto" began to be employed to refer not only to Jewish quarters of a compulsory, segregated and enclosed nature, but also to any Jewish settlement of a dense nature such as those in Eastern Europe and, by extension, as an adjective to refer to the separatist culture generated by such concentration.[29] Actually, of course, the word "ghetto" in its original pre-emancipation sense cannot be used in connection with Jewish life in Poland and Lithuania, and later Czarist Russia, which acquired a large number of Jews through the partitions of Poland. There, although Jews lived in small towns and rural villages that were often predominantly Jewish, often referred to as *shtetles* or *shtetlach*, they were never confined to compulsory, segregated and enclosed quarters separated from their Christian neighbors.[30] One looks in vain for a ghetto in "Fiddler on the Roof." Despite the general nineteenth-century Russian restriction whereby, officially, no

Jew could live outside the Pale of Settlement (basically, the Polish territory annexed by Russia), the Pale never possessed the one essential characteristic of the ghetto because within it the Jews were not segregated from their Christian neighbors. Furthermore, the requirement that all Jews were to live within the Pale was not always enforced, for at certain times, specific groups of Jews such as agriculturalists, holders of university degrees, merchants of the first guild, artisans, and army veterans were granted official permission to live outside the Pale.

Nevertheless, "ghetto" increasingly came to be used by many acculturated Jews as an adjective to characterize the now unacceptable way of life, mentality and culture created by the dense Jewish settlements in the East. Expressions such as "ghetto life" and "ghetto mentality" were intended to refer to the Eastern European pattern of Jewish life, and certain of its characteristic manifestations, usually in a hostile sense, and had little to do with the institution of the ghetto of the Italian peninsula. As German Jewry increasingly felt that it had overcome its own "ghetto past" and successfully entered modernity, the term "ghetto Jew" came to refer to the Eastern European Jew, the Ostjude who "became synonymous with *Umbildung*"[31] and was perceived as being beyond the bounds of civilization, indeed half-Asiatic, as in the title *Aus Halb-Asien* (*Out of Half-Asia*) of the novel of Karl Emil Franzos.[32] The central theme in the popular genre of "ghetto literature" that emerged in Central Europe toward the middle of the nineteenth century widely disseminated the stereotype of the ghetto throughout the German-speaking world and outside it through translations into other languages.[33] On the whole, the portrayal was generally negative, written from the point of view of a detached outside observer or former inhabitant who had managed to find the way "out of the ghetto." Nevertheless, there were also some who viewed the "ghetto" in a more positive light, especially as the "cult of the Ostjuden" emerged. As Steven Aschheim observed,

> The shtetl [small town]—affectionate synonym for the negatively loaded term *ghetto* functioned as a recognizable historical entity, nostalgic antithesis to the disenchantment of European life. It symbolized total and warm human community, *Gemeinschaft*, a counter-utopia to values lost in the world of impersonal *Gesellschaft*.[34]

The attitude of Zionism toward Ostjuden and the ghetto was complex and ambivalent. By affirming Jewish nationalism in its anti-bourgeois rebellion against that which it denounced as shallow, bourgeois middle-class Jewish life, the second-generation German Zionists challenged a basic belief of liberal assimilationist German Jewry in that they saw in the Ostjuden the maintenance of an authentic Judaism that required modernization just as emancipated Western Jewry needed to reclaim its national identity.[35] Yet, ultimately, the movement in favor of a new Jewish beginning in the national homeland perceived of Jewish residence outside that homeland as undesirable and abnormal as it strove to create in the homeland a new kind of Jew, often on the basis of physical labor, and held up the "ghetto" of the *luftmensch* in contrast to its new ideal. With this Zionist disparagement of Jewish residence outside the national homeland and its strong current of "the negation of the Diaspora," the word "ghetto" became a central element of the negative *galut* (Diaspora) existence that had to be transcended in the new rebuilt Land of Israel. As the New Year 1912 editorial of the Berlin *Jüdische Rundschau* asserted, "the whole *Golus* is the ghetto."[36]

By the later years of the nineteenth century, the word "ghetto" also came to be widely used in the English-speaking world in a completely different sense from its original pre-emancipation usage as a result of at least two major factors. The first was the immigration of Jews from Eastern Europe and their initial settlement in poorer urban neighborhoods in the West that were certainly not compulsory, segregated or enclosed, as for example in Berlin, Paris, London, New York, Philadelphia, Chicago, and Boston. The second was the increasing usage of the word "ghetto" in English fiction that portrayed Jewish life in an English-speaking environment. Certainly the prominent author Israel Zangwill did much to popularize the new, loose usage of the word "ghetto" in the general sense of a Jewish neighborhood rather than specifically as a compulsory, segregated and enclosed Jewish quarter through his popular novels and vignettes of immigrant Jewish life in London that were widely read on both sides of the Atlantic, especially since he used the word in the title of four of his widely read volumes: *Children of the Ghetto* (1892), *Ghetto Tragedies* (1893), *Dreamers of the Ghetto* (1898), and *Ghetto Comedies* (1907). Interestingly, the earliest example of the English usage of the word "ghetto" as not referring to an Italian ghetto cited in *The Oxford English Dictionary* is taken from Zangwill's *Children of the Ghetto*.[37]

Abraham Cahan, "one of Zangwill's early and abiding admirers,"[38] published his own novel, *Yekl: A Tale of the New York Ghetto* (1896), and later continued to portray Jewish immigrant life in New York in his epic *The Rise of David Levinsky* (1917). Between the appearance of the two works of Cahan, the "ghetto" was given further extensive exposure by the pioneering essays of Hutchins Hapgood, *The Spirit of the Ghetto: Studies of the Jewish Quarter in New York*, first published together as a book in 1902.

Yet probably no book did more to spread the usage of the word and of the concept of the ghetto in its extended meaning among social scientists and the educated public at large, especially in the United States, than did the classic study of 1928, *The Ghetto*, by the sociologist Louis Wirth.[39] Significantly, Robert E. Park, Worth's mentor and prominent member of the "Chicago School" of sociology, in his foreword to the book of Wirth made the important observation that

> "Ghetto," as it is here conceived, is no longer a term that is limited in its application to the Jewish people. It has come into use in recent times as a common noun – a term which applies to any segregated racial or cultural group.[40]

While initially associated with the settlement of Eastern European Jews primarily in Western European and North American urban centers in the later nineteenth century, the term "ghetto" became a popular and evocative expression of the negative consequences of the residential segregation of minorities.[41] It continued to gain wider currency as it came to be applied to an increasing number of situations outside the Jewish world. Jack London, in his *The People of the Abyss* (1903), observed that

> At one time the nations of Europe confined the undesirable Jews in city ghettos. But today the dominant economic class, by less arbitrary but none the less rigorous methods, has confined the undesirable yet necessary workers into ghettos of remarkable meanness and vastness. East London is such a ghetto, where the rich and powerful do not dwell, and the traveler cometh not. And where two million workers swarm, procreate and die.[42]

The Oxford English Dictionary, s.v. "ghetto," cites examples of the usage of the word in this new sense, no longer associated with the Jews but rather to refer to areas densely inhabited by other groups, as in the expressions the "working class ghetto" (1908) and "the London ghettos" (1909).[43] Furthermore, according to that source, by 1897 the word "ghetto" had already been used to refer not to living beings but to collections of inanimate objects, as in the sentence "The Farrington-road collection of barrows has become the vieriest ghetto of bookland."

Unquestionably, the word and concept of "ghetto" were given further prominence as a result of the Jewish quarters established by Nazi Germany during the Second World War.[44] Specifically, Mitchell Duneier pointed out that awareness of the Nazi ghettos led to an increase in the usage of the word "ghetto" to apply to Afro-American residential quarters before "finally overtaking the 'Jewish/Warsaw ghetto' usage in 1965."[45]

As noted, the word "ghetto" also came to be used as an adjective, and continues to be so used down to the present, as very loud cassette-tape recorders known as "boom-boxes" are also referred to as "ghetto blasters," and very often the music that they play as "ghetto music." The word "ghetto" of course here refers to contemporary "ghettos" and not to those in any aspect of the past Jewish experience.[46]

A comparison of early modern ghettos and Nazi ghettos

It must always be remembered that the twentieth-century ghettos of Nazi-occupied Western Europe differed fundamentally from those of earlier pre-emancipation ghettos in at least one crucial respect. Those earlier ghettos were intended to provide Jews with a clearly defined permanent space in Christian society in accordance with the traditional Christian theology that assigned to Jews the role of testifying to the validity of Christianity through their own abased condition until the second coming of Jesus, the Christian Messiah. However, the Nazi ghettos, after it was decided to embark on the final solution to the Jewish problem by their total elimination, eventually came to constitute merely temporary way stations on the road to its implementation. Thus, the two different kinds of ghettos highlight the difference between traditional religious anti-Judaism and modern racial antisemitism in its ultimate form. In the case of anti-Judaism, a Jew could escape from the ghetto by converting, while in the case of modern antisemitism, there was no way out, neither through one's own conversion nor even through that of both parents or of less than three grandparents. The different natures of the compulsory, segregated and enclosed ghettos of pre-emancipation Christian Europe contrasted with those of Nazi-occupied Europe lead to the conclusion that the experience of European Jewry during the period from 1939 to 1945 did not really constitute a return to the "Middle Ages" but rather signaled the advent of a completely new and far worse reality. Indeed, the statement – or better, misstatement – that the Holocaust represented a return to the Middle Ages is probably the biggest myth associated with the word "ghetto."

Conclusion

To summarize and conclude, the gradually extended simultaneous usages of the word "ghetto" have caused significant blurring of the very important distinctions between voluntary quarters and compulsory, segregated and enclosed quarters and obscured inherently different attitudes toward Jews and other minorities on the part of the governments under which they lived. In order to clarify the confusion, scholars have sought to differentiate between various kinds of living arrangements referred to as ghettos. For example, the twentieth-century Jewish historian Salo Baron distinguished between the "technical – or formal – ghetto" and the "non-technical ghetto."[47] Louis Wirth wrote about the "voluntary ghetto," which would have been considered oxymoronic by ghetto inhabitants of the early modern Italian peninsula. The literature on the ghetto includes formulations such as "'concrete ghettosation' refers to the *shtetl* in its original sense of a segregated place for Jews and 'mental ghettoisation' to the experience of a ghetto mentality in the Western countries to which the Jews fled."[48] Theodor Herzl employed the term "New Ghetto" to refer "to the social and cultural isolation experienced by assimilated Jewry after legal barriers had been replaced by a new informal type of segregation that from the 1870s onward was further fuelled by antisemitism."[49] Binary and other formulations may be useful within the framework of the presentation of their formulator, but when removed from that context, they become problematic. Perhaps somewhat more felicitous terms, at least for twentieth-century Eastern Europe, would be *Quasighettoisierung* and *Selbstghettoisierung* ("Quasi-ghettoization" and "Self-ghettoization"), suggested by Feliks Tych to refer to the pre-Second World War conditions in Poland as opposed to *Zwangsghettoisierung* (forced ghettoization).[50]

The basic problem is that "the word 'ghetto' has lived through more metamorphoses than any other word with such a long history."[51] So when one hears or reads the word "ghetto," one must ask: to which ghetto is the speaker or author intending to refer, and does the word evoke the intended image? If the compulsory, segregated and enclosed Jewish quarters of Venice, Rome and Florence were ghettos; if the Lower East Side of New York and Whitechapel of London were ghettos; if Warsaw,

Łódź and Bialystock were ghettos; if Westchester and Newton are "golden ghettos" – what exactly does the word "ghetto" mean? If our understanding of the word is unclear, how clear can our understanding of the Jewish experience be? And when we speak of non-Jewish ghettos in the cities of North America, South Africa and elsewhere in the world, to what are we referring? Is it a compulsory area established by the state, or rather by zoning laws or by red-lining? If so, is it enclosed and gated? Is there a curfew? Do we mean a voluntary area characterized by the residence of a certain ethnic group? Or … ? What image will arise in our minds, and does it correspond to the specific reality being referred to? We may encounter this important question when we read the morning newspaper or watch the evening news. Indiscriminate use of the word "ghetto" can lead to major distortions in our view of central aspects of both the history of the Jews and of our world.

Notes

1   On the situation in the Hellenistic and Moslem worlds, see B. Ravid, "All Ghettos Were Jewish Quarters but Not All Jewish Quarters Were Ghettos," *Jewish Culture and History*, 10: 2–3, 2008, p. 5 notes 2 and 1, respectively, reproduced in F. Backhaus, G. Engel, R. Liberlis and M. Schlüter (eds), *The Frankfurt Judengasse: Life in an Early Modern German City*, London–Portland, or.: Vallentine Mitchell, 2010, and on the names given to Jewish quarters, p. 5.

2   See H. Beinart, "Jewish Dwellings in Spain During the Fifteenth Century and the Edict of Separation" [Hebrew], *Tzion*, vol. 5, 1986, p. 61.

3   On the confusion between "Jewish quarter" and "ghetto," see A. Haverkamp, "The Jewish Quarter in German Towns during the Late Middle Ages," in R. Po-Chia Hsai and H. Lehmann (eds), *In and Out of the Ghetto: Jewish–Gentile Relations in Late Medieval and Early Modern Germany*, Cambridge: Cambridge University Press, 1995, pp. 13–16, especially pp. 14–15, note 7.

4   For details, see Ravid, "All Ghettos Were Jewish Quarters," pp. 6–14.

5   On the areas known as the Ghetto Nuovo and the Ghetto Vecchio prior to their association with the Jews in 1516 and 1541 respectively, see E. Concina, "Parva Jerusalem," in E. Concina, V. Camerino and D. Calabi, *La città degli Ebrei: Il ghetto di Venezia: Archittetura e urbanistica*, Venice: Albrizzi, 1991, pp. 12–24, summarized in B. Ravid, "The Venetian Government and the Jews," in R. C. Davis and B. Ravid (eds), *The Jews of Early Modern Venice*, Baltimore: Johns Hopkins University Press, 2001, pp. 9–10.

6   On the ghetto of Rome, see K. Stow, "The End to Confessionalism: Jews, Law, and the Roman Ghetto," in this volume.

7   On ghettos in the United States and also in Europe during the Holocaust, see the essays in this volume.

8   See Ravid, "The Venetian Government and the Jews," pp. 3–7.

9   See C. M. Sanfilippo, "Fra lingua e storia: note per una Giudecca non giudaica," *Rivista italiana di onomastica*, vol. 4, 1998, pp. 7–19.

10 For further details, see B. Ravid, "The Religious, Economic and Social Background and Context of the Establishment of the Ghetti of Venice," in G. Cozzi (ed.), *Gli Ebrei e Venezia*, Milan: Edizioni Comunità 1987, pp. 211–259, and B. Ravid, "Curfew Time in the Ghetti of Venice," in E. Kittell and T. Madden (eds), *Medieval and Renaissance Venice*, Urbana: University of Illinois Press, 1999, pp. 237–275, photo-reproduced in B. Ravid, *Studies on the Jews of Venice, 1382–1797*, Aldershot, Hants: Ashgate/Variorum, 2003.

11 See B. Ravid, "On Sufferance and Not as of Right: The Status of the Jewish Communities in Early-Modern Venice," in D. Malkiel (ed.), *The Lion Shall Roar: Leon Modena*

and His World, Italia: Conference Supplement Series, 1, Jerusalem: Hebrew University Magnus Press–Ben-Tzvi Institute, 2003, pp. 17–61.

12 See R. Bonfil, "A Cultural Profile," in *The Jews of Early Modern Venice,* p. 169.

13 See Ravid, "The Venetian Government and the Jews," pp. 12–15.

14 The Latin text of *Cum nimis absurdum* is readily available, with an English translation, in K. Stow, *Catholic Thought and Papal Jewish Policy, 1555–1593,* New York: Jewish Theological Seminary, 1977, pp. 291–298.

15 For the references in the remainder of this paragraph and the next two, see Ravid, "All Ghettos Were Jewish Quarters," pp. 15–16.

16 See K. Stow, "The End to Confessionalism: Jews, Law, and the Roman Ghetto," in this volume.

17 For details, see Ravid, "The Venetian Government and the Jews," pp. 19–20.

18 See A. Freimann and F. Kracauer, *Frankfort,* Philadelphia: Jewish Publication Society, 1929, pp. 180–212.

19 For details on Spain, see Ravid, "All Ghettos Were Jewish Quarters," pp. 13–14.

20 This important point has been stressed in R. Bonfil, *Jewish Life in Renaissance Italy,* Berkeley: University of California Press, 1994, pp. 120–121, 135, 153–154.

21 See D. Ruderman, "The Cultural Significance of the Ghetto in Jewish History," in D. N. Myers and W. V. Rowe (eds), *From Ghetto to Emancipation: Historical and Contemporary Reconsiderations of the Jewish Community of Scranton,* Scranton: Scranton University Press, 1997, p. 13.

22 See Haverkamp, "The Jewish Quarter," p. 13.

23 For a somewhat longer version of this section, see B. Ravid, "On the Diffusion of the Word 'Ghetto' and Its Ambiguous Usages, and a Suggested Definition," in F. Backhaus, G. Engel, G. Grebner and R. Liberles (eds), *Frühneuzeitliche Ghettos in Europa im Vergleich,* Berlin: Trafo, 2012, pp. 21–28.

24 See B. Ravid, "Christian Travelers in the Ghetto of Venice: Some Preliminary Observations," in S. Nash (ed.), *Between History and Literature: Studies in Honor of Isaac Barzilay,* B'nei B'rak: Hakibbutz Hameuchad, 1997, p. 120, photo-reproduced in Ravid, *Studies on the Jews of Venice.*

25 See R. Robertson, "Enlightened and Romantic Views of the Ghetto: David Friedländer versus Heinrich Heine," in A. Fuchs and F. Krobb (eds), *Ghetto Writing: Traditional and Eastern Jewry in German-Jewish Literature from Heine to Hilsenrath,* Columbia: Camden House, SC, 1999, pp. 36–37. See also the examples in E. Bourke, "The Frankfurt Judengasse in Eyewitness Accounts from the Seventeenth to the Nineteenth Century," involving Bettina von Arnim (p. 21), and Ludwig Börne's (pp. 23–24) in Fuks and Krobb, *Ghetto Writing,* pp. 21 and 23–24, respectively.

26 The only partial exception appears to be *Dell'influenza del Ghetto nello Stato,* by Giovanni Battista Gherardo d'Arco, published in Venice in 1782, but there the word "ghetto" was used in the collective sense of "the Jews," virtually all of whom on the Italian peninsula lived behind ghetto walls at the time; see G. Luzzatto Voghera, *Il prezzo dell'eguaglianza: il dibattito sull'emancipazione degli ebrei in Italia (1781–1848),* Milan: Franco Angeli, 1998, pp. 44–48.

27 See Fuks and Krobb, "Writing the Ghetto," in *Ghetto Writing,* pp. 4–6. See also F. Krobb, "Reclaiming the Location: Leopold Kompert's Ghetto Fiction in Post-Colonial Perspective," in *Ghetto Writing,* p. 45.

28 This paragraph and the following one are based on S. E. Aschheim, *Brothers and Strangers: The East European Jew in German and German Jewish Consciousness, 1800–1923,* Madison: University of Wisconsin Press, 1982; see especially pp. 3–12, 27–31, 80–84, 107–113.

29 See Aschheim, *ibid.,* p. 6. On the Jews of Eastern Europe, see essays in this volume.

30 See Ravid, "All Ghettos Were Jewish Quarters," pp. 16–18.

31 See Aschheim, *Brothers and Strangers,* p. 8; also p. 5: "by the second half of the nineteenth century, the expression *ghetto Jew* had become virtually synonymous with *Ostjude.*"

32 See Aschheim, *ibid.,* pp. 20, 28–31, 142, 221.

33   See Aschheim, *ibid.*, pp. 22–31.

34   See Aschheim, *ibid.*, p. 213.

35   See Aschheim, *ibid.*, pp. 81–84.

36   See Aschheim, *ibid.*, pp. 87–89, 96–97, 108–109, 111–113; quotation from the *Jüdische Rundschau* on p. 111. On this theme, see S. Rawidowicz, "On the Concept of Galut" (Yiddish), *Yivo Bletter*, vol. 21, 1943, pp. 165–188, published in English translation in B. Ravid (ed.), *S. Rawidowicz, Israel: The EverDying People and Other Essays*, Rutherford, NJ: Fairleigh Dickinson University Press, 1986, pp. 13–50, reissued in a slightly expanded paperback edition under the title *State of Israel, Diaspora and Jewish Continuity*, Hanover, NH: University Presses of New England, 1998.

37   *The Oxford English Dictionary*, second edition, Oxford–New York: Oxford University Press, 1989, VI: 492.

38   See M. Wohlgelernter, *Israel Zangwill, A Study*, New York: Columbia University Press, 1964, p. 91; for references to Cahan's reviews of Zangwill's writings, see p. 328.

39   See L. Worth, *The Ghetto*, Chicago: University of Chicago Press, 1928.

40   See Worth, *The Ghetto*, pp. vii–viii.

41   See P. I. Rose, "Introduction: The Ghetto and Beyond," in P. Rose (ed.), *The Ghetto and Beyond: Essays on Jewish Life in America*, New York: Random House, 1969.

42   See J. London, *The People of the Abyss*, New York: Macmillan, 1903, p. 210.

43   See *The Oxford English Dictionary*, VI: 492.

44   For the evolving usage of the term "ghetto" during that period, see D. Michman, *The Emergence of the Jewish Ghettos during the Holocaust*, New York: Cambridge University Press, 2011, partially summarized in Ravid, "On the Diffusion of the Word 'Ghetto'," pp. 29–32.

45   M. Duneier, *Ghetto: The Invention of a Place, the History of an Idea*, New York: Farrar, Straus and Giroux, 2016, see especially preface p. x, pp. 26–84, with the illuminating graph 1 on p. 83, and the concluding chapter, pp. 217–237; quotation on p. 84.

46   See F. Möbus and M. B. Münch, "Beyond the Ghetto: The Ghetto in Modern Punk and Rap Culture," in Fuchs and Krobb, *Ghetto Writing*," pp. 195–208, especially pp. 200, 207–208.

47   See S. Baron, *A Social and Religious History of the Jews*, 18 vols, Philadelphia: Jewish Publication Society, 1952–1983, 9:33. For Baron's general discussion of Jewish quarters and ghettos in general, see *A Social and Religious History* 9: 32–36, 11: 87–96 and 14: 114–120.

48   See E. Pederson, "Persecution, Exile, and the Mental Ghetto in Henry William Katz's novel *Die Fischmanns*," in Fuks and Krobb, *Ghetto Writing*, p. 156, note 1.

49   See Fuks and Krobb, "Writing the Ghetto – an Introduction," p. 3.

50   F. Tych, "Ghettos in Polen," *Wiener Jahrbuch für Jüdische Geschichte, Kultur und Museumswesen* 5, 2000–2001, p. 70.

51   "Das Wort Ghetto hat wie kaum ein zweites, das auf eine so lange Geschichte zurückblickt, Metamorphosen durchlebt," S. Mattl, "Walled Cities und die Konstruktion von Communities: Das europàische Ghetto als urbaner Raum," *Wiener Jahrbuch fur jüdische Geschichte Kultur und Museumswesen* 5, 2000–2001, p. 9.

2

THE END TO CONFESSIONALISM

Jews, law and the Roman ghetto

Kenneth Stow

Ghetto origins

The story of the ghetto, whether in Rome or those that followed, begins with
St. Paul in Galatians and Corinthians, where Paul warns against Judaizing, by which
he means participation in Jewish rituals, specifically circumcision, a practice he
deems to cast doubt on the efficacy of faith or, eventually, baptism. It was the
"little leaven" that soured the whole lump of dough, and, later, it was the source
of the pollution Paul abhorred. The believer must not, he said, in Corinthians (1,
10:16–18), be yoked together with the unbeliever, lest the believer be sullied. The
idea was perfected by the second-century Cyprian, as he condemned the priest
who, to escape persecution, served at pagan altars before returning to consecrate the
Eucharistic wafer, when in fact he desecrated it and passed on his pollution to those
who received the wafer at his hands. The same occurred through participation
in Jewish rites. The law *Christianorum ad aras* in Justinian's sixth century Code of
Roman law—not Church or canon law—repeats this idea. The anxiety underlying
such a law was reinforced by the many canons prohibiting close Jewish–Christian
contact, culminating in the demand that Jews wear a marker ("badge") on their
clothing, or in the rule of separate bath-houses in Spain, or the prohibition on
dining together, or having Christian servants lodge in Jewish homes. Roman Law
also forbids intermarriage. These laws were renewed constantly; their most rigorous interpretation was that of Pius VI in 1775. The ghetto must be seen as a step
along this long trajectory. This applies to Venice, to the Roman Ghetto ordered
established by Pope Paul IV in 1555 and to many other Italian ghettos, the last in
1782, and to which the *Juderias* of late medieval Iberia and even the *Judengasse* of
Frankfurt am Main, from 1462, were preludes.

The ghetto was the fruit of long development, not a *sui generis* early modern invention. Yet historians have not previously linked ghettos directly to the

longue-durée of Church–Jewish relations, just as they have ignored the theme of pollution and its avoidance as the principal driver of attitudes toward Jews. Ghettos culminated this drive by removing Jews from society, much as medieval kings had expelled them, from England, in 1290, and France, between 1306 and 1394; the Spanish, in 1492, argued that the problem of Jews polluting the tens of thousands of converts in the peninsula damaged the *res publica*, meaning the state viewed as a spiritual, Christian body. St. Paul had called this body the *unus panis, multi sumus*—the one body, though we are many, one in Christ. Only in the post-French Revolutionary world would the notion of the spirituality of the political state be divorced from the state's professing a unified confession (religion) that had to be defended, including by segregating or removing dissidence radically through conversion.[1]

Nonetheless, however much Paul preached about pollution, he also held that Jews were to be "loved." There was a need for the Jews because their conversion would signal the second coming of Christ. In Italy, more than elsewhere, and no doubt because the regnant *ius commune*—evolved from Roman law—granted Jews the status of civil *cives*, or citizens, Paul's teachings on allowing a Jewish presence were heard.

Before admitting Jews, in 1516, Venetians, especially lay leaders, argued that a permanent Jewish presence in the city would be an offense to God. Their presence would pollute the city which Venetians had come to perceive as a sanctified entity, a political *Corpus Christi*, or body of Christ, a metaphor frequently employed—and taken literally—by medieval and early modern towns.[2] The initial ambivalence of the lay leadership persisted, and Jews never gained permanent residence in the city. Because Venice privileged its own laws over those of *ius commune*, Jews there were not deemed *cives*, and their charters of admission had to be renewed every five or ten years, invariably preceded by a heated debate. In Rome, where Jews were *cives*, and where they had resided since ancient times, admission was never a question, nor was expulsion considered. Both politically and religiously, the popes (who from about 1350 through 1870 were the heads of a true political unit that occupied the entire center of the Italian peninsula) had been the Jews' constant protectors, as Jews themselves frequently acknowledged. Even during the ghetto period, the popes observed their commitment, at least to safeguard Jewish life. The popes were the consistent guardians of the equilibrium Pauline teachings promote: acceptance, in anticipation of the millennium, accompanied by firm steps to avoid pollution.

Events both internal and external in the early sixteenth century upset this consistency. Those events were not only the outbreak of Lutheranism and other heresies, paralleled by fears of Catholic disintegration along the lines of Henry VIII and England. There were also calls for internal reform that had been building throughout the previous century. Conversionary action, too, took center stage. The *Libellus ad Leonem Decem* of 1513, four years before the rebellion of Martin Luther, called for mass Jewish conversion, to be achieved, among other means, by ghettoization.[3]

In the early sixteenth century, the popes moved gingerly toward this end. Already in 1542–1543, a House of Converts was erected in Rome. In 1553, the

Talmud was burned; its supposed infamies were said to prevent Jews from seeing the light. The culmination came in 1555, when that arch-exponent of the
Catholic Reformation, the octogenarian Pope Paul IV, famed for his dedication
to rigid ecclesiastical discipline, decided to apply the same "disciplining" to Jews.[4]
Consolidating hundreds of years of canonical restriction, this pope issued the bull
Cum nimis absurdum, whose clauses denied Jews the right to have Christian servants
in their homes, forbade the erection of new synagogues, prohibited Jews from exer-
cising dominion of any kind over Christians and required them to wear a yellow
hat. Most of all, Paul IV ordered the Jews to live within closed quarters, originally
called the *serraglio* and, eventually, the Ghetto. The bull is explicit that the goal of
its legislative assault, over and above segregation and the control of Jewish behavior,
was *ad hoc ut*, to the very end, that Jews convert.[5] Until the time of Paul IV, papal
bull had said that Jews were accepted out of *caritas*: not charity, but fundamental
justice. The change to *ad hoc ut*, to the end they convert, was neither accidental nor
unnoticed. To argue, as Bernard Cooperman does, that *Cum nimis absurdum* does
not mention conversion, is to misread the text.

When, in 1442, in the bull *Super gregem*, Pope Eugenius IV insisted Jews in Iberia
live in *Juderías*, he was responding to a general social-religious crisis, the presence
in the Iberian realms of tens of thousands of untrusted New Christians (as converts
were called after 1391). His reasoning was blunt. Jews were corrupting the purity of
the faith, *fidei puritas*, and that alone justified segregation.[6] However, Eugenius was
preceded by Benedict XIII, who in his *Etsi doctoris gentium* of 1415 ordered Jews
(in Iberia) to live in designated precincts. And Benedict, anticipating Paul IV, linked
required Jewish quarters with harsh law and conversion. In Rome, it was Benedict's
policies that were revived with passion. Segregation would first purge the Jewish
pollutant and then, by conversion, eliminate it. The Roman ghetto was planned as a
holding area, a limbo that would limit pollution until the Jews converted.

Pious lashes

In Rome, rigorous legal application, in the spirit of Benedict XIII, was to serve
as the "pious lashes" first suggested by the late-sixth-century Pope Gregory the
Great as an effective mode to cure sinfulness, a motif reprised by the authors of
the *Libellus ad Leonem Decem* of 1513 in the form of punitive closure to hasten
conversion. The theme of *piis verberibus* was reiterated in the *De sola lectione* of
Francisco de Torres, who spoke of Jews converting when they "had to suck at
husks for sustenance."[7] Conversion is central in many other bulls issued by later
sixteenth-century popes. And it is the focus of the synthetic, comprehensive legal
tract of 1558 by the Venetian (Udinese) Marquardus de Susannis, which explains
how law, rigorously applied, will promote conversion. But so would special pressures. When Jewish loan banks, the backbone of an already deteriorating economy,
were closed in 1682, whole families rushed to the baptismal font (the greatest rush
of all occurred in the years following Mussolini's racial laws of 1938). Ghettoization
shattered the "tense intimacy" of Roman–Jewish relations.[8] *Cum nimis absurdum*

itself was reinforced by Talmud burning, forced preaching, economic pressure and, eventually, the mandatory transfer of Jews living in outlying settlements *into* the Roman ghetto.

The *raison d'être* of a conversionary policy as a mode of avoiding contamination is self-evident: complete purgation demanded the "recognition" of the "true religion." Conversions also convinced the Church that its ways were truth, challenged as they were not only by Luther and dissidence, but increasingly by modern polities that rejected ecclesiastical pre-eminence. It is no accident that conversionary policy hardened as modernity made itself ever more felt. *Houses of Converts*, the *Catecumeni*, as the Jews called them, were established in Bologna, Ferrara, Mantova, Pinerolo, Torino, Firenze, Ancona, Pesaro and Venice, and most powerfully, in Rome.[9]

Nonetheless, both Cooperman and Samuel Gruber ignore the *longue-durée* and modernity's social revolution, thus dehistoricizing the ghetto. Gruber argues that the Venetian ghetto was much like the special living quarters established for other groups in that city. Nevertheless, Benjamin Ravid has shown there were fundamental differences.[10] The *fondachi*, as these quarters were called (after a common Mediterranean usage for an "inn"), were small, located on the Grande Canale, and, most important, the *fondaco* of the Germans was not closed until 1531, sixteen years after the ghetto's founding, and that of the Turks did not fully exist before 1623, a time of great tension between Venice and the Ottoman Empire. By contrast, the Jews' ghetto was permanent, large and set in a corner of the city, on its own island. Moreover, the ghetto—and the *fondaco* of the Turks, was sealed, not only by gates, but by cementing in windows, preventing both sight and sound from the outside in, as well as from the inside out. By their special dress, Jews outside the ghetto, even in Venice, were compelled to carry the ghetto with them. As Pius IX noted in 1871, after the ghetto was razed and Jews moved freely throughout the city of Rome, the Jews were "barking up and down the streets" (*per le vie latrare*).[11] For him, the ghetto had been a kennel. Those wearing Jewish garb when venturing outside were little more than "dogs" on leashes.

Economics, or not

Economic concerns, the ones Cooperman designates as the cause of ghetto establishment, were at most secondary to anxiety about pollution. Cooperman ignores that relocation to a ghetto, intended, he says, to resolve issues of housing and commerce, always prejudiced Jewish standing. Jewishness lay at the roots of economic challenge, as events in Polish Kazimierz—the very example Cooperman brings to sustain his thesis—clearly demonstrate. In 1495, Jews were dismissed from Cracow and resettled in this (effective) suburb. Yet commercial differences between Jews and Christians in Cracow had been resolved a decade earlier through the contract drawn up in 1485 distinguishing Christian from Jewish spheres of commercial activity, retail from wholesale. Moreover, in 1485, Jews in Cracow were already living in a Jewish quarter. Separation was thus an issue unto itself, which only the Jews' removal from Cracow in 1495 (following a fire and an attack) settled.[12]

It was again the anxiety of contamination that led Paul IV, in 1555, to prohibit Jews from dealing in foodstuffs. Preventing the sale of food, especially meat, had long been a bone of contention and prohibitions on mixed dining go back to the fourth century.[13] These same anxieties had to have played a role in spatial questions, too, in negotiations that took place in cities like Modena about where to locate the ghetto.[14] Jewish economic issues were integral to, never divorced from, a spiritual dimension. This was even more so when the old "religious" base for economic discrimination was converted into a confessionally political one.

The Jewish economy was said to harm the *communis utilitas*. Jews must be made into agriculturalists. At about the time that Jewish banks were closed in Rome in 1682, it was being said that Jews, forced to become "diggers of trenches," would return to the status of Adam and Eve, whence they would be purified and accept Christ. In 1782, Count Giovanni d'Arco called all Jewish economic endeavor criminal and a threat to the political body. As put by Gavin Langmuir, a Jew was, uniquely, a Jew, *Iudaeus erat Iudaeus*, and all else followed from that premise. Jewish isolation and whatever flowed from that, economic restriction included, was unique.[15]

The need to ensure purity was ever present, in Venice as well as Rome. Has not Guido Ruggiero taught us that the Venetians perceived their city as an inviolable holy body? Cooperman asserts that those opposed to the Jews' entrance into Venice as permanent residents, regardless of the circumstances, including the compromise of the ghetto, were "old timers." Yet these so-called old-timers were among the city's most distinguished nobility, and to call them "old-timers" wrongly implies that negativity toward Jews was going out of fashion. Indeed, the limitations enacted in Venice by its lay heads, not the Church, were virtually identical to those imposed on Roman Jews after 1555.[16] Moreover, however much it focused on pollution, Venice, too, erected a House of Converts.

To be sure, Venice was not the Church. The Venetians had dominant commercial interests, but they sought to keep these interests in line with religious doctrine—the one complemented the other—and the same may be said of the many other Italian cities where ghettos eventually were established. The Grand Dukes of Tuscany took the ambivalent position of allowing Jews returning from Turkey (descendants of *conversos*, also known as New Christians, who, in Venice, came to live in the Ghetto Vecchio and especially the Ghetto Novissimo and were called Ponentines) to settle in Leghorn, uniquely without a ghetto. Jewish commerce *was* important. However, the justification in Venice for allowing the Ponentines to settle, free from prosecution for abandoning Christianity, was the defense that these people's baptisms had been absolutely forced (a technical definition) and, hence, was invalid. They had never been Christians. Pope Clement VII, supported by the great professor of canon law and Cardinal Pier Paolo Pariseo, had taken this position in the 1530s, hoping to avoid establishing an Inquisition in Portugal. The tactic did not succeed. Nonetheless, Clement's successor, Paul III, allowed former *conversos* to settle as Jews in Ancona in the 1540s.[17]

This compromise, as we may call it, points to the centrality of religion as a determinant. Jews residing in Florence, Siena and the small town of Pitigliano were obligated to live within ghetto walls; actually, the Florentine community was created by Jews from elsewhere in Tuscany, who were forced to come together in Florence about 1569, fifteen years after the founding of the ghetto in Rome and—I doubt coincidentally—in the same year that Pius V forced Jews out of all the small towns of the papal state. Only Leghorn was exempt. Moreover, in all ghettos, Jewish behavior was policed—sometimes more in theory than practice, because of objections by lay rulers—by the Papal Inquisition, a body wholly distinct from its Iberian counterparts, but which guided its actions by the rules of *Cum nimis absurdum* and the more stringent 1581 *Antiqua Judaeorum improbitas* of Gregory XIII.[18]

The absence of self-rule

One might think that Jews sought refuge from this papal assault by relying on what has often been called "Jewish autonomy": the ability of the Jews to act communally, as a self-regulating, self-protective body; indeed, as a formal, corporate group (much as the legally recognized corporations of the *ancien régime* in pre-Revolutionary France). Yet late ancient Roman law had declared that the Jewish community was not—and could not be—a true corporation, a statute that legal commentators affirmed repeatedly through early modern times. As late as 1733, Giuseppe Malatesta, the president of the Rione S. Angelo, where the ghetto was located, objected that a proposed census of the ghetto could not be left in Jewish hands. Unlike parish priests, he said, who are authorized legally to prepare the "status of souls" (roughly, a census) of their flocks, the heads of the Jews enjoy authority only through of the "consent" of their coreligionists.[19]

Theory and practice were consonant. Jewish communities rarely (if ever) enjoyed that most central quality of corporate life, primary jurisdiction, the possession of the formal judicial authority that obligated all corporate members to air disputes before corporate tribunals: in modern terms, the normal civil or criminal court system. Instead, Jews had only the option of agreeing to arbitrate among themselves. Otherwise, they might turn to non-Jewish courts, a practice communities sought to stifle. Criminal powers were exclusively in the hands of the "state." Jews, in other words, were fully, and directly, dependent on the will of their rulers. No intermediary, in the form of a collective, corporate structure (as in the case of so many others, even professional gilds) served as a buffer between the individual (Jew) and the state.[20]

Nonetheless, this direct relationship between individual and ruler, which would be the lot of all in post-Revolutionary Europe after corporate structures were eliminated, had a positive side. It emphasized the status Jews in Italy uniquely possessed of being legally *cives*, thanks to the *ius commune* that would continue to influence all continental legal systems until 1804, when it was abolished by Napoleon and replaced by the French *Code Civil*, to which I shall return.[21]

At the same time, Jewish status suffered from an internal contradiction. How could an entire group be considered *cives* in the civil law of *ius commune*, yet simultaneously suffer the discriminations originating in the laws of the Church, the canon law? The answer is that *ius commune* itself was religiously biased, perfected, as was its Roman Law ancestor, by the fifth- and sixth-century Roman Christian emperors: hence its prohibition of Jewish dominion over Christians and its affirmation that the Jewish community lacked corporate rights.[22] The conclusion of Marquardus de Susannis in his study of Jews in non-Jewish law was self-evident, stipulating that "full citizenship is gained only by regeneration at the baptismal font."[23] De Susannis's meaning was that in a confessional society, like Rome's, with an official religion and church, only adherence to the state religion entitles one to full civic rights. Jews thus were second-class citizens by legal definition; the only way out was through conversion. At the same time, should the confessional state come to an end and a system of law equal for all be installed, then Jews—in fact, members of any and all religious denomination(s)—would ipso facto be emancipated.[24]

Jews in their ghetto

Ghettoization, with its conversionary ends, had shattered the centuries-old "tense intimacy" of Jewish Christian relations in Rome, an "intimacy" that had enabled Roman Jews to be as Roman as they were Jewish, and as Jewish as they were Roman. Prior to 1555, and whatever the restrictions imposed by canon law, Jewish life was very much the life of all Rome, including language and food. Today, people go to "the ghetto" to eat "Jewish food," which is identified with historical Roman cuisine. Romans seem to have acculturated to Jewish ways as much as Jews did to Roman ones. Jews and Christians met each other daily in the markets and until the ghetto was erected, sometimes lived on the same streets. Business exchange was constant. Jews were prominent in wholesaling food, specializing in artichokes, fish and spices.[25] The ghetto did not seal off Jews and Christians hermetically from each other, but that which had once been unfettered was now surrounded by limitations and rules.

The ghetto as theater

Ghetto life created an ongoing, all-encompassing social theater. A sense of performance, especially repeated performance, in which Jews alternated roles as both actors and spectators, was, and always had been, integral to Jewish existence. The facilitator was the Jewish concept of sacrality, which was never bound up with place or epiphanies (sacred events), as was sacrality for Christians. Rather, for Jews, sacrality was (and is) achieved through engaging in tried (for them), true and oft-repeated ritual. A place becomes sacred by way of what is *done* in it, not through anything intrinsic to, or about, it.[26] Jews never separated holy from profane as hermetically as did Counter-Reformation Catholicism.[27] The synagogue itself was also the place of communal meeting and the venue of religious (civil) courts.

The ghetto in its entirety could become holy, its walls replicating those of ancient Jerusalem, whose legitimate residents were the true Jews.[28] Hence, however difficult ghetto life was, Jews could believe they were living in a place specially their own—and confirmed as their own—through the repeated performance of ritualized acts. This ritual has persevered even to modern times. A recent study of the house at 13 Via Portico d'Ottavia during the Nazi occupation of Rome (from September 1943 through June 1944), so many of whose residents were deported during, and after, the great *razzia* of October 16, 1943, highlights the ways in which these people achieved solidarity. All of them Jews, they acted as though they were living in a miniature, private ghetto, where one man's appearance on a balcony to pray on a Friday evening brought out everyone else (however observant) to the common courtyard to join together in this social act, or drama.[29]

The ghetto name

When Paul IV decreed the ghetto, it took eight months to see a first written Jewish response. As one woman put it: "the pope has ordered all the Jews to live together." Admittedly, the vast majority of Jews then in Rome, about 3,000—there would never be more than 4,000—already lived in the Rione S. Angelo, where the ghetto was to be located. But some had moved out, perhaps to the exclusive Via Giulia nearby, an act of the "pollution" Paul IV censured. Nonetheless, an order to live together so challenged the Roman Jewish past that it would take over thirty years until the meaning of this turn was comprehended.

The Venetian enclosure was called the ghetto from day one—which was the original name of the small island where a copper foundry had been located, from the Italian *gettare* (to throw), and where the Jewish ghetto would arise. The Roman enclosure was called the *claustrum Judaeorum* or, in Italian, the *serraglio*, the area or the cloister. Jewish notaries used the term *hazer*, or court(yard). In 1589, the notary Pompeo del Borgo, writing in Italian, spoke of *nostro ghet*. He was punning on the Hebrew (*get*) for a writ of divorce, which is always delivered by the man *to* the woman.[30] The Jews were the weaker woman, cut off (an idea the full name for the *get* embodies) from her erstwhile partner. The Latin, *libellum repudii*, is even stronger. The result could have been disaster. It was not. The *get* was duly noted, but mechanisms of preservation were also advanced. Roman Jewry survived.

Jewish notaries

The principal method of self-preservation was to contain disputes within the community, a goal achieved by persuading Rome's Jews to litigate through consensual arbitration; lacking any true jurisdiction, internal litigation could never be required. Of all the mechanisms the Jews of Rome used to convince themselves that, in some measure, they were the masters of their fate, the system of consensual arbitration was the most powerful. Arbitration among Jews was anything but novel, but in Rome it reached new heights, emphasizing a rituality of justice and acculturating to common Roman judicial practice. The mechanisms of arbitration in Rome were perfected by a small group of notaries, who were also rabbis, but whose rabbinic title and status as such had no real effect on their notarial skills. The acts they drew up rarely made use of *halakhah*, Jewish law.[31] I refer to Judah, but most his son Isaaco, Piattelli, who wrote in Hebrew, a Hebrew that was really Italian translated, reminding us of how Roman Rome's Jews intrinsically were.[32] It is important to note that the mechanisms of Jewish arbitration were developed a full generation prior to the ghetto, not as a hurried reaction to the dramatic changes of 1555. Apart from its immediate function of facilitating the settlement of disagreements, a durable system of internal justice also created what Nancy Struever has called a "public sphere," which translates as a sense that a community beyond the boundaries of the individual truly exists. One might also speak of a Roman Jewish "civil society." In the years between 1536 and approximately 1605, when Isaaco died, there was a total of 718 litigations. Between 1605 and 1640, when the Jewish notaries were suppressed by the popes, only about thirty disputes were recorded. It was not that the notaries had lost their skill. Rather, after 1621, the popes demanded that all Jewish litigation adhere to *ius commune*, meaning it was to take place before non-Jewish instances.[33]

Rarely were the arbiters rabbis. About 90 percent of the time they were laymen, occasionally a Christian. Formal rabbinic courts met but rarely, appointed by the communal heads, the *fattori*; rabbis were communal employees, lacking power, not communal heads. This structure of lay dominance persisted through the end of the eighteenth century. Even the one great rabbinic figure of the period, Tranquillo Corcos (d. 1730), was a communal dependent. His prestige otherwise derived from his social and economic status, but especially his knowledge of non-Jewish law, which he used time and again to respond to complaints and charges.

The *Universitas*

Theoretically, the public sphere of Jewish Rome should have been created by its community, the *Universitas*; pay no attention to the literal meaning of the Latin as corporation, or *societas*; the usage was so fluid that popes themselves sometimes designated individual synagogues as *universitates*. In fact, the *Universitas* constituted no more than a shadow government, although it did have a formal structure. Following the *Capitoli* of Daniel da Pisa, drawn up and papally ratified in 1524, there were three *fattori*, lay heads, who also on occasion nominated true rabbinic courts or *batei din*. Alongside the *fattori*, there was a restricted council of twenty and a larger one of sixty; seats were technically apportioned among Rome's Italian Jews and its Sephardim and Ashkenazim, although to no significant effect. These institutions, which functioned throughout the ghetto period, were unrelentingly set upon by papal officialdom and their prerogatives grindingly diminished. The *fattori* themselves charged that following new legislation in 1702, their very lives might be endangered should they make overly daring efforts on behalf of their fellows. They also petitioned that official acts not expose them to criminal charges or arrest. Toward the middle of the eighteenth century, there were long periods when nobody would take the job, and, in one year, a series of triumvirates was established, with three men serving alternately for three-month periods. The larger council of sixty met but a handful of times each year, always in the presence of a senior representative of the papal treasury, who pushed the council to do what it surely would not have done on its own, namely, levy taxes. Other than this, the council's actions were limited to appointing officers of the various confraternities formally under communal aegis, yet almost none of which had substance. Their principal function of succoring the poor and dowering brides was stymied by a severe shortage of funds. There was a modest school, the *Talmud Torah*, and, of course, people were buried, but that was about the limit.

The notaries and unity

Through sometime in the seventeenth century, the formal community was effectively overshadowed by the acts of the notaries and the informal civil society they created. Perhaps the definitive achievement of the notarial acts, beyond establishing a forum for handling disputes, was to create uniformity and, as a result, unity in the community by the simple but brilliant introduction of standardized forms and formulae. These acts, in turn, tell us a great deal about Jewish marriage, education, women's rights, economics and even public sanitation and language, and they throw light on the strategies Jews adopted to facilitate acculturation while remaining steadfastly Jewish. Like the notarial acts themselves, the vast majority of these strategies were in place before the ghetto's time.

The acts are especially informative about the varying groups of Jews who immigrated to early sixteenth century Rome and how they coalesced with those already there in the early decades of the sixteenth century. The small community, which in the year 1500 numbered only about 1,000, by mid-century had more than tripled; the population of the city as a whole doubled during the course of the sixteenth century, from about 50,000 to 100,000. Jews came from Iberia, from Sicily and from German lands. Others began to leave the many small towns around Rome where Jews had lived for centuries (or to which some of them traveled to do business). It is from these towns that Jews achieved the distinctive family names they still bear, for instance di Segni, di Cori, di Veroli and Anticoli.

But the praxis of these differing groups often conflicted, creating, as the traditional historical opinion has conveyed it, friction, and even active resistance to the newcomers. No doubt there was a period of adjustment, but hard evidence of strife is lacking. To the contrary, notarial acts show in black and white that within no more than two or three decades of their arrival, the immigrants were readily intermarrying with those already present, at a rate of over 22 percent. Two decades later, Jews were asked to choose Italian or Sephardi allegiance when joining the respective branches of the burial confraternity, to which almost every male belonged. Synagogue constitutions, too, point to amalgamation: notably, the Castilian–French synagogue, a mix that existed nowhere else. Sicilian Jews, who had lived under Aragonese rule and had their own rite, were listed as Italians. The Italian rite is unique, and is actually the ancestor of the Ashkenazi one.

A major achievement was the unification of marriage rituals, especially those touching on the return of the dowry upon divorce or death. All Roman Jews, regardless of origin, came to use a standard prenuptial contract, which also reveals Jewish accommodation to the general Roman practice. Jews elsewhere became engaged and then performed a formal betrothal and marriage ceremony simultaneously, which is the custom today. The giving of the ring and a statement by the groom of "you are dedicated to me (as my wife)," to which the bride signals assent, is the betrothal and the blessings under the marital canopy, the marriage. In Rome, imitating Christian practice, betrothal followed engagement by but a few weeks, while the marriage occurred months later. The terminology in the acts, however, is purely Hebrew, with the exception of a traditional judicial term that is employed as an intentional calque. The Italian *impalmamento*, signifying formal agreement to an engagement by handshake, became in Hebrew *teqi'at kaf*, which can accompany formal assent to a range of legal matters, but also translates as *impalmamento* literally.

Acculturation

Jews followed a distinct acculturational pattern, selectively taking a non-Jewish practice, and after a time of careful reflection, adopting it as their own, as in the case noted of *impalmamento-teqi'at kaf*. There was also originality, notably, with respect to the adoption of a child. Adoption as we know it today did not yet exist. Christians overcame this legal lacuna by bestowing on the adoptee an "irrevocable gift," known in Latin as a *donatio inter vivos*. Jews made the adopted child itself into such a gift, employing the Talmud term *matanah gemurah*, which translates as "a gift that cannot be taken back." Similar innovation occurred when one woman was falsely accused of not being a virgin at marriage. She was rewarded with a double marriage settlement, hers to keep forever; among Christians, a fine was paid to the father. Christian praxis might also be rejected. Jewish confraternities maintained self-leadership and were never transformed, as were parallel Catholic organizations, into clerically controlled ecclesiastical organs. The greatest Jewish act of borrowing and adaption was in the creation of the Hebrew notarial act.

Women had schooling as a matter of course, even as apprentices, where many learned the art of decorating tapestries, onto which they had to weave Hebrew liturgical phrases. Jewish women, distinctly unlike Christian ones, could swear in court or on contracts in their own names without being required, as, again, were Christian women, to have present an oath-helper, the *mundualdus*, just as Christians could not handle money by themselves, while Jewish women could. Finally, widows might remarry without losing custody of their children, a practice that had marked upper-class Italian women in places like Florence.

Where Jews did behave like everyone else was in the physical maintenance of the ghetto precinct. A series of texts shows applications made to extend sewer pipes from the communal school, where the majority studied (the better-off went to small private schools or had a private instructor), to the main sewage line into the Tiber. Rome, be it noted, had public drainage hundreds of years before other

European cities, a legacy from the Roman Empire, as are the aqueducts, and even the roads. To build, however, required approval by Rome's "masters of the roads," and plans had to show that no damage would occur to buildings under which the pipe would pass.

Jewish fate

Yet no matter how dutifully Jews occupied themselves with the ghetto's cleanliness or with that of their persons, whether in public baths, or in rental contracts that invariably specified the presence of toilets, or in ensuring the regular laundering of clothing, these facts were lost on Christians, who preferred to speak of the filth of the Jewish soul, which only the water of baptism could wash off.

The Jews' status was an intrinsic oxymoron: citizens with civil rights in law, yet highly regulated for religious reasons. As time passed, especially in the last two decades of the eighteenth century, Roman Jews could see how even their fellow Jews in other Italian cities were gaining rights. They could see the march to full equality, known as emancipation, in England, Holland, France and the American colonies. By contrast, in Rome, there was a growing realization that the decision of 1621 to have Jews air disputes before civil tribunals alone, which was also a death blow to the office of the Jewish notaries, destroyed the equilibrium that had held the Jews together for the ghetto's first seven decades. This decision was made even more fateful when it was complemented by the opinion of the leading contemporary canonist Antonio Ricciuli, who, echoing centuries of predecessors, said: "Jews are to exercise no jurisdiction, nor have internal resort to anything but Mosaic law." Mosaic law, in Ricciuli's terms, meant pure biblical law, without the rabbinic legal corpus on which *halakhah*, as applied in practice, depends. Theory soon became fact. In about 1700, Rabbi Tranquillo Corcos was forced to write a lengthy brief explaining why Jews were at all entitled to make a will rather than to follow precisely biblical ordinances on succession.

The legal conundrum

Yet Jews also learned to take advantage, in particular, by petitioning the popes when they felt these rights had been violated. One such petition, from 1793, reveals the depths of Jewish understanding. As *cives*, they queried whether the law should not work in their favor, as it did for others. As early as 1720, they asked why, as citizens, they should be forced to buy wheat for bread that would be offered to no others. Rather than solely weakening Jewish strength and resolve, as had been anticipated, it appears that depriving the Jews of the refuge of halakhic litigation had the sometimes potentially beneficial effect of fostering greater Jewish integration into the system of public law, such as it was in early eighteenth-century Rome. By eliminating Jewish self-jurisdiction almost entirely, the state may be said to have scored an "auto-goal," one which also revealed the state's inner contradictions that affected more than Jews alone.

On the one hand, the papacy was interfering in matters of Jewish marriage, sometimes even requiring a permit for a divorce, or taking charge in a possible case of (technical) adultery, which is to say that the papal civil government, by overseeing issues related to marriage, was acting perfectly in the mold of the modern, centralizing state. Nonetheless, typical of endless papal ambivalence, the idea that marriage might be a civil institution, controlled by civil authorities—as instituted by the Habsburg Emperor and then in France beginning in the 1780s—remained anathema. The Church was taking a small step forward and two large ones backward; Pius XII was still speaking forcefully against civil marriage in 1946.

The parallel deprivation of *halakhah* alongside integration into the norms of *ius commune* paradoxically gave birth to a Jewish civil status that was simultaneously deteriorating with respect to increasing control over Jewish behavior, exercised through ever greater canonically imposed restriction, and improving with respect to uniformity of justice within the state. The papacy chose to confront the challenge by ignoring it and by embarking, instead, on a three-pronged offensive that began in 1731 with a new confiscation of Hebrew books, including the financial records of the community, only some of which were ever returned. In the same year, a petition to enlarge the *Cinque scole* (the five synagogues housed in a single building) was not only denied, but in proceedings that dragged on for a decade, judges of the Roman Inquisition demanded that the synagogues be unified, since Jews in Rome, formally, had permission to have but one place of worship. Matters deteriorated further in 1755, when Pope Benedict XIV issued the unprecedented *Beatus Andreas*, beatifying a supposed victim of ritual murder, a charge previous popes had denounced.

A second step occurred in 1775, when Pius VI issued *Fra le pastorali sollecitudini*. Also known as "An Edict Against the Jews," this bull reiterated every past papal restriction, as well as emphasized the censorship and removal of suspect Jewish books, some of which, especially commentaries, Jews had managed to keep in their hands. The bull also reinvigorated the program of forced conversionary sermons begun in 1584. It forbade, as well, the entry into the ghetto of Christian washer women, whose work was essential because of the ghetto's limited water supply. This decree, the Jews lamented, endangered public health and could potentially cause a city-wide plague. Relatedly, partnerships between Jewish and Christian butchers were prohibited. Jews protested that without the Christian butchers to sell non-kosher hindquarters to Christians, the price would skyrocket and meat consumption would become prohibitive; a predicament that still exists today.

The third step was to stretch the legal limits with respect to conversions. The times were troubling ones for the Church. The Enlightenment, the initiative of states—even Catholic ones like Austria—to control marriage, the perceived dangers of Freemasonry all aroused grave fears, as bulls like *In iminenti* issued by Clement XIII in 1738 reveal. What better balm than a surge in conversions, which would be celebrated by elaborate ceremonies in the presence of high prelates as godparents? Conversion would confirm the ancient adage that the Church was a ship tossed on stormy waters, but would never sink.

As in the past, this conversionary drive persuaded few. The tactics were often desperate, including demanding those who converted "offer" family members, wives and children, who often balked and sometimes "escaped." Another ploy was to lure poor young men into being baptized, who would then "offer" young women to whom they claimed to have been betrothed, or at least "denounce" them as having expressed a will to convert. Offering, or oblation, was an old concept, applied normally to parents oblating children as monks or nuns. Moreover, doubtful offerings were often accepted on the grounds of *favore fidei*, for the sake of the faith, a legal, indeed supra-legal, principle at least six centuries old that all popes and canonists recognized.

Furthering this line were the adepts of the House of Converts, themselves converts, who knew no limits in bringing in a new neophyte. Just as the Church sought to prove itself through conversions, the adepts sought to justify their own actions, and perhaps, as well, to justify the institution's continuity, and assure their incomes.

The Jews mounted a spirited defense. To block chicanery by converted bachelors, the affective nuclear family was encouraged, building on the clearly enunciated right of Jewish women to refuse a match. Alongside affectivity, contraception, too, was apparently practiced, which had never been taboo in rabbinic literature. Small families meant fewer relatives, one of whom might "offer" another. The community also forbade the exporting of dowries without paying a large tax. The goal was to avoid a money drain, but, in the process, to also ensure a larger supply of eligible brides.

The stories are fearsome, but they also point to the end of the ghetto period. To defend children or wives who had been taken, as was the eighteen-year-old Anna del Monte in 1749, who spent thirteen days in the *Catecumeni* before being released, the Jews hired Christian lawyers, whose defense was rigorous, but whose concern was also the evolving nature of the modern state. These lawyers asked why the Jews' legal absorption into a state should end when it came to the *foro spirituale*, as it was called, why the spiritual forum and its laws should take precedence over the civil ones. Their questioning sometimes strained the permissible, notably that of Carlo Luti, who accused the pope of arrogance for privileging *favor fidei* over civil law. The response to Luti by the counselor of the papal Inquisition and Bishop Domenico Giordani confirmed Luti's suspicions. The pope, said Giordani (basing himself on a canon of Innocent III), is the arbiter of divine law on earth; "what he does is considered as though done by God."

Nevertheless, papal policies were inconsistent. By requiring Jewish civil conformity, the popes had inadvertently promoted proximity between the very groups they had striven to keep apart. One could go farther, and some did. They asked why, if it was correct for religious law to cede to civil statutes, "regeneration" through baptism should be the sine qua non for full citizenship. And why should the confessional element that so distinguished the pre-modern state not be discarded—those in the earlier eighteenth century could not yet have framed the question in just these words—and, in its place, a secular essence come into being? Should not the *corpus mysticum ecclesiae* be replaced by the *corpus mysticum reipublicae*: the mystical (unified) body of the Church replaced by the mystical (unified) body of the state? Should not Paul's *unus panis* be redefined in secular terms, to wit, *e pluribus unum* on United States currency? This, of course, was the spirit of the French Revolution, and it is certainly what George Washington intended when he wrote to the Jews of Newport, Rhode Island, saying that "the state demands no more of you than that you observe the law." Observing the law, reading Washington backward, creates the citizen.

The same message was broadcast by Napoleon's *Code Civil* of 1804, as it constitutionally abolished the *ius commune* that had sustained the confessional state and, consequently, legally put that kind of state to an end. In principle, the Code was going to fulfill the hopes expressed by the Roman Jew Antonio Pacifici on February 18, 1798, as he addressed fellow Jews and others while he stood under the *Albero della Libertà* placed in the *Piazza delle Scuole del Ghetto*. Reflecting on the reforms the French Republican army had initiated in newly conquered Rome, he said: "From here on," he said, "if you [Jews and Christians] are good citizens, ... [a single] law will judge us both; in civil life, all that will distinguish us one from another is virtue, and not religious belief."

Pacifici, of course, could not anticipate that his hopes would be dashed when the Napoleonic era ended and the ghetto was restored. In Rome, full rights would be achieved only when the 1,800-year-old framework that perceived the world in terms of purity and pollution was abandoned, which is to say, with the demise of the Papal State on September 20, 1870.

★★★

Where does this leave us? What do the Roman Jews and their ghetto experience teach us? The answer is twofold. First, from the perspective of the Jews who lived there, survival in a ghetto was a matter of careful strategy. Second, from the perspective of the historian and citizen, until a state or society comes to grips with systematic discrimination based on principle and rooted in law, the ghetto, in whatever form, will continue. For in the final analysis, how different is a confessional state from one grounded in racial ideology or the idea of the rightful superiority of any group over another? A perhaps obvious observation; however, one whose correspondence to fact the history of the Roman ghetto so amply confirms.

Notes

1 On the matters of purity, see Kenneth Stow, *Jewish Dogs, An Image and Its Interpreters: Continuity in the Catholic–Jewish Encounter* (Stanford: Stanford University Press, 2006) pp. 20–22; and David M. Freidenreich, *Foreigners and Their Food: Constructing Otherness in Jewish, Christian, and Islamic Law* (Berkeley and Los Angeles: University of California Press, 2011), *passim*; Angela Groppi, "Numerare e descrivere gli ebrei del ghetto di Roma," in Angela Groppi, ed., *Gli abitanti del ghetto di Roma 1733* (Rome: Viella, 2015); also Sandra Debenedetti-Stow, "'The Etymology of Ghetto': New Evidence from Rome," *Jewish History* 6 (1), 1992, 79–85. Recently, on Venice, Dana E. Katz, "'Clamber Not You Up To the Casements': On Ghetto Views and Viewing," *Jewish History* 24, 2010, 127–153. On earlier law, see Amnon Linder, ed., *The Jews in the Legal Sources of the Early*

Middle Ages (Detroit and Jerusalem: Wayne State and Israel Academy of Sciences, 1997). See also Kenneth Stow, "The Cruel Jewish Father: From Miracle to Murder," in David Engel, Lawrence H. Schiffmanm, Elliot R. Wolfson and Yechiel Y. Schur, eds, *Studies in Medieval Jewish Intellectual and Social History Festschrift in Honor of Robert Chazan* (Boston: Brill, 2012).

2 See Robert Bonfil, *Jewish Life in Renaissance Italy*, trans. Anthony Oldcorn (Los Angeles and Berkeley: University of California Press, 1994) pp. 38–44; and Guido Ruggiero, "Constructing Civic Morality: Deconstructing the Body. Civic Rituals of Punishment in Renaissance Venice," in J. Chiffoleau, L. Martines, and A. Paravicini-Bagliani, eds, *Riti e rituali nelle societa medievali* (Spoleto, Centro italiano di studi sul alto medioevo, 1994) p. 184.

3 See Kenneth Stow, *Catholic Thought and Papal Jewry Policy 155–1593* (New York: Jewish Theological Seminary, 1977) pp. 213–215, for a full discussion with citations.

4 See Antonio Prosperi and Paolo Prodi, eds, *Disciplina dell'anima, discipline del corpo e disicplina della società tra medioevo ed età moderna* (Bologna, Il Mulino, 1994).

5 Comparing *Cum nimis* with previous bulls, the introduction of the programmatic "to the very end that" announces something new. See Kenneth Stow, *Catholic Thought*, and *Taxation, Community, and State: The Jews and the Fiscal Foundations of the Early Modern Papal State* (Stuttgart: Hiersemann, 1984) pp. 55–70, on modifications in papal bulls and evolving conversionary policy.

6 *Super gregem* is found in Shlomo Simonsohn, *The Apostolic See and the Jews, 1394–1464* (Toronto: Pontifical Institute, 1989, no. 740) pp. 866–870.

7 Stow, *Catholic Thought*, pp. 211–220, 247–248.

8 See Kenneth Stow, *Theater of Acculturation: The Roman Ghetto in the Sixteenth Century* (Seattle: University of Washington Press, 2001), on Jewish life, with additions in Stow, *Anna and Tranquillo: Catholic Anxiety and Jewish Protest in the Age of Revolutions* (New Haven: Yale University Press, 2016).

9 Matteo Al Kalak and Ilaria Pavan, *Un' altra fede: Le Case dei catecumeni nei territori estensi (1583–1938)* (Florence, 2013); and Samuela Marconcini, *Tesi di perfezionamento in Storia Moderna, La storia della pia Casa dei catecumeni di Firenze (1636–1799)* (Florence, 2011); see Luciano Allegra, *Identità in bilico* (Turin, 1996) on events in Turin; Pierina Ferrara, "Lungo i percorsi della conversione: i neofiti romani nel XVIII secolo," in Gianluca Fiocco and Roberta Morelli, eds, *Città e campagna: un binomio da ripensare, Annali del Dipartimento di Storia* (Rome: La Sapienza, 2008) pp. 303–334.

10 See Benjamin Ravid, "Venice and Its Minorities," in Eric Dursteler, ed., *A Companion to Venetian History* (Leiden: Brill, 2014) pp. 449–485.

11 Kenneth Stow, *Jewish Dogs*, p. 31.

12 Bernard Weinryb, *The Jews of Poland: A Social and Economic History of the Jewish Community in Poland, 1100–1800* (Philadelphia: Jewish Publication Society, 1972) p. 65 shows 1485 was to get Jews out of retail trade, but tensions simmered, and an attack of 1484 after a fire was the excuse for the expulsion. We await further explorations by Anat Vaturi.

13 Stow, *Jewish Dogs*, pp. 153–155.

14 Federica Francesconi, "From Ghetto to Emancipation: The Role of Moisè Formiggini," *Jewish History* 24, 2010, 331–354.

15 See Kenneth Stow, "Jews and Christians, Two Different Cultures," in Uwe Israel, Robert Juette and Reinhard Mueller, eds, *Insterstizi, Culture ebraic-cristiane a Venezia e nei suoi domini tra basso medioevo e prima epoca moderna* (Rome: Edizioni di Storia e Letteratura, 2010) p. 33.

16 See Ravid, "*Cum nimis absurdum.*"

17 See Kenneth Stow, "Papal Power, the Portuguese Inquisition, and a Consilium of Cardinal Pier Paolo Parisco 6," *Journal of Levantine Studies* 6, 2016, 13–33.

18 On this subject, see Katherine Aron Beller, *Jews on Trial: The Papal Inquisition in Modena, 1598–1638* (Manchester: Manchester University Press, 2012).

19 See Groppi, "*Numerari*," for the full citation.

20   On Jewish corporate existence prior to the French Revolution, see Salo Baron, in "Ghetto and Emancipation: Shall We Revise the Traditional View," *The Menorah Journal* 14, 1938, 515–526.

21   See Adriano Cavanna, "Mito e destini del Code Napoleon in Italia," in Bernard Durand and Laurent Mayali, eds, *Excerptiones iuris: Studies in Honor of André Gouron* (Berkeley: University of California Press, 2000), and Raoul Charles Van Caenegem, *An Historical Introduction to Private Law* (Cambridge: Cambridge University Press, 1988).

22   See the Justinianic Code, *Corpus iuris civilis*, Paul Kreuger and Theodore Mommsen, eds, *Code* (Berlin, 1888), chapters 1, 9 and 8 with variations together with chapters 1, 9 and 1.

23   Marquardus de Susannis, *De iudaeis et aliis infidelibus* (Venice, 1558), composed to forward Paul IV's policies; on which see Stow, *Catholic Thought*. On "regeneration" in France reinterpreted in civil and social terms, see Jay R. Berkovitz, "The French Revolution and the Jews: Assessing the Cultural Impact," *AJS Review* 20, 1995, 25–86; Berkovitz, "Acculturation and Integration in Eighteenth-Century Metz," *Jewish History* 24, 2010, 271–294; and his *Protocols of Justice: The Pinkas of the Metz Rabbinic Court 1771–1789* (Leiden: Brill, 2014).

24   See on Siegmund Jacob Baumgarten, David Sorkin, *The Religious Enlightenment* (Princeton: Princeton University Press, 2008) pp. 152–163. See the summary and analysis of Baumgarten in Udo Arnoli, *Pro Iudaeis, Die Gutachten der hallischen Theologen im 18. Jahrhundert zu Fragen der Judentoleranz* (Berlin, 1993) pp. 173–185; I thank Anke Koeltsch for this text.

25   See Manuela Militi, "Gli ebrei «fuori dal Ghetto», Incontri e scontri con il Lazio durante la Repubblica romana (1798–1799)," *Archivi e Cultura* 40 2007, 195–215. See also Raffaele Pittella, "Labirinti archivistici e contesti istituzionali," in Groppi, *Gli abitanti*. See Irina Oryshkevitch, "*Roma Sotterranea* and the Biogenesis of the New Jerusalem," *RES, Anthropology and Aesthetics* 55/56, 2009, 174–181, contrasting Roman Baroque splendor with ghetto squalor.

26   Jonathan Z. Smith, *To Take Place: Toward Theory in Ritual* (Chicago: University of Chicago Press, 1987).

27   See Kenneth Stow, *Theater of Acculturation*, pp. 54–55, 96.

28   This concept is found first in the Books of Ezra, Nehemiah and Chronicles.

29   Anna Foa, *Portico d'Ottavia 13: Una casa del ghetto nel lungo inverno del '43* (Bari: Laterza, 2013).

30   See Kenneth Stow, "Sisto V, the Jews, and their Ghet," in David Ruderman, ed., *Essential Papers on Jewish Culture in Renaissance and Baroque Italy* (New York: NYU Press, 1992), and see again Debenedetti, "The Etymology."

31   The notarial acts, 6,000 and more, are housed in the Roman *Archivio Storico Capitolino, Notai ebrei*. See Kenneth Stow, *The Jews in Rome* (Leiden: Brill, 1995 and 1997) for 2,000 acts, summary, Hebrew texts and translation. See also the studies in Kenneth Stow, *Jewish Life in Early Modern Rome: Challenge, Conversion, and Private Life* (Aldershot: Ashgate, Variorum, 2007).

32   See Kenneth Stow, "Writing in Hebrew, Thinking in Italian," in Stow, *Jewish Life*.

33   The following pages recast findings in Stow, *Anna and Tranquillo*, with its full annotation, bibliography and textual citations.

3

THE EARLY MODERN GHETTO

A study in urban real estate[1]

Bernard Dov Cooperman

Urban perspectives on Jewry policy

In the study of Jewish history, the ghetto has been seen as a primary indicator of Christian Europe's hostility towards the Jews.[2] This approach, with its emphasis on the religious roots of a horrifying segregation, is itself the product of the circumstances that gave birth to modern Jewish historiography: from the late eighteenth century, European Jews were engaged in a constant struggle for legal equality and political enfranchisement, and they enlisted history to demonstrate the justice of their cause. From their perspective, enforced spatial segregation was the physical instantiation of everything that Jews were trying to overcome.[3] In the Jewish historical imagination, the ghetto became ubiquitous and its horrors magnified beyond all recognition. It was modern secularism and liberalism that had ended the Jews' physical isolation.

Ironically, ghettos have also become locations of Jewish "authenticity" for writers and artists.[4] Thus Israel Zangwill promoted his 1892 bestseller, *Children of the Ghetto*, as "a study through typical figures of a race whose persistence is the most remarkable fact in the history of the world, the faith and morals of which it has so largely molded."[5] Atavistic Jewish nostalgia and the demands of commercial tourism have combined to recreate and romanticize various Jewish ghettos.[6] In short, the ghetto described by modern Jewish writers, whether historians or novelists, was a hated institution and a deteriorated reality on the one hand, and the imagined site of a lost Jewish culture on the other. None of these factors contributed to an understanding of the ghetto reality.

I would like to suggest that we approach the ghetto as an urban phenomenon, an aspect of city life defined by the same topographic and functional considerations that shape the city generally in both time and space. If we contextualize the ghetto only in terms of "Jewry policy"—that is, the history of legislation specifically focused on Jews—we run the risk of missing what may be better seen within a broader set of urban phenomena. If we privilege religious categories of rhetoric and focus on formulaic Christian declarations about the dangers of contact with Jewish perfidy, we attribute causal significance to terminologies that may have actually served as convenient articulations or justifications for mundane economic or social tensions. Inevitably, the historian's conclusions are shaped by the questions he or she asks at the start.[7] By asking a different set of questions, we may be able to construct another view of the ghetto—one that will at least supplement that provided by the traditional surveys of Jewry policy.

What is the ghetto?

Ghettos existed on a spectrum of urban zoning arrangements that went from the organic neighborhood to the gated encincture, closed off and locked at night. Within this range, I will use the term ghetto to apply to a Jewish residential (and equally important, a commercial) space *defined by law*. This definition omits the spontaneous or "natural" Jewish neighborhood—Jews, like other ethnically or professionally defined groups, often chose to live in proximity to each other. But my approach intentionally includes zones *without* walls, and even those that might include a minority non-Jewish presence. Thus, in my understanding, the twin Jewish communities of Pisa and Livorno, established by an extremely liberal set of charters in the 1590s, were ghettoized even though the Medici grand dukes specifically refused to create a walled zone there.[8] Since their residential and commercial privileges were spatially defined, applying only to those who resided and traded in the two towns, these Jews must be understood as ghettoized despite the liberal terms under which they lived and despite the absence of walls around them.[9] I do not mean to ignore or trivialize the restrictive aspects of ghettos: by defining a space for Jews, the law was necessarily establishing both a *permitted* zone and a *prohibited* area where Jews might *not* live or trade. But no pre-modern ghetto was ever a prison, and spatial legislation was never a ban on all contact. Entry and exit were always permitted on some level. Ghetto guards might be, as in Venice, on the outside, charged with keeping Jews in at night, but they might also be inside, as in Cracow, charged with keeping thieves and vandals out.[10]

In order to understand the purpose of a ghetto, therefore, it is crucial to understand the circumstances under which zones were permitted or prohibited. The possible variations seem endless. Jews might, for example, be admitted to an area only for a limited term or only on certain days.[11] They might trade in a given market space on certain days. They might, or might not, store their goods there overnight, when they themselves were not allowed to be there. Livorno and Pisa, mentioned above, were special customs-free zones where Jews were granted extensive trading and residential rights, generous government loans, and a measure of self-governance—none of which were granted to Jews elsewhere in Medici territory.

Ghettoization, apparently so spatially fixed, can be, in my approach, best understood as part of a fluid equilibrium. Effectively, ghetto legislation might simply shift, or redirect, the pattern of Jewish residence and trade. Often, decrees of expulsion in fact required Jews only to move to a town or village just outside the jurisdiction of the zoning body. For example, Jews were not allowed to settle in Cologne from 1424, but they did live in the suburb of Deutz. Cologne residents of every class took regular advantage of the presence of the nearby "Jew-doctor," petitioning the government for a special license for the latter to ply his trade in the city.[12] Forbidden certain trades, Jews might engage in other, unregulated types of trade—whether at open fairs or by peddling in the countryside or by setting up their pawnshops just over a municipality's borders.[13] Like all zoning legislation, ghetto laws sought to fix spatially the competitive advantage of one group within what stubbornly remained a fluid reality. Each ghetto fit into a complex local market system, real, commercial, and personal. To properly understand the impact and function of a ghetto, we must include in our consideration those extramural zones where Jews lived beyond the jurisdiction of municipal authorities. Moreover, the wide range of variations in practice demonstrates, I would argue, that even though they were framed in religious (or ethnic) categories, ghetto laws are better understood as spatial compromises to resolve the local social tensions and economic rivalries that are typical of the urban context everywhere.

The ghetto as a Jewish city

Our image of the ghetto, and indeed the term itself, comes from Venice, the city that instituted a walled Jewish residential area from 1516. But it behooves us to remember that an older term, *vicus judaicus* (Jewish town), was the one first used in most legal documents, and it can properly be applied even in Venice where reference was made to *la città degli ebrei*.[14] This terminology reminds us once again that the ghetto was not only an isolating and limiting enclosure; it also represented the assignment to Jews of a municipal zone. They thus became responsible for its maintenance and governance. It has been pointed out by more than one Jewish historian that ghettoization led to the elaboration of a set of governmental norms among Jews, and indeed on some level to the development of a Jewish political theory.[15]

It would of course be simplistic to suggest that Jewish self-government developed only as a response to ghettoization. Obviously, diaspora Jews had organized themselves in various ways in previous centuries.[16] In Italy, Jews began meeting on an intercommunal basis already in the fifteenth century. In later decades, we see examples of elected, municipally based lay councils that challenged the autocracy of chartered Jewish bankers many years before the erection of ghetto walls. The new mercantile leadership claimed to represent the Jews of the city and, like the governments of the European city itself, claimed a measure of municipally defined autonomy, rejecting the right of outsiders—including even halakhic authorities—to interfere in their affairs.[17] Growing institutionalization is well-documented in sixteenth-century Italian Jewish communities and seems to be paralleled also in the new and ever larger settlements in east central Europe. The appointment of paid communal functionaries, insistence on formal election procedures, and systematic record keeping in *pinkasim* were all typical of the norms copied from the administrative practices of surrounding urban governments. We need not be surprised by a non-Jewish model for Jewish institutions. When they drafted their communal constitution in 1524, the Jews of Rome relied upon the non-Jewish authorities to authorize it. They necessarily devised rules of a sort that were intelligible and acceptable to papal bureaucrats, and framed them in Italian rather than Hebrew, using technical language and terminologies drawn from the institutional vocabularies of the surrounding municipal associations.[18] It seems to me not unreasonable, therefore, to suggest that the establishment of the "Jewish city" was possible because Jews had already gained considerable experience and fluency in the conventions of municipal self-government.[19]

But there is also a paradoxical implication to the close connection I have suggested between the ghetto and Jewish self-government. We know that the early modern period in Jewish Italy was marked by a shift in leadership from a few licensed bankers to a broader community of merchants. But the restrictions of ghettoization may have actually favored a concentration of power in a narrowing oligarchy based on property. To understand this, it is necessary to think about the way in which investors might be motivated to invest in ghetto buildings.

As is well known, by the end of the eighteenth century, Jewish ghettos in cities like Frankfurt, Venice, and Rome were overcrowded, and much of the housing stock badly deteriorated.[20] Though the dilapidation has contributed to the historically bad reputation of ghettos, in a sense we might also read it as an ironic indication of the success of the institution insofar as ghetto populations continued to grow, in some cases exponentially, for some two centuries at least. Frankfurt's *Judengasse*, for example, had been more than ample for an envisaged population of a little more than a hundred inhabitants when it was constructed in 1462.[21] Despite an intensive program of inbuilding, however, the closed quarter must have become badly overcrowded as thousands of Jews flooded into it over the following century. And yet the ghetto market generated real disincentives to capital investment in the buildings. Properties were actually owned by powerful local (non-Jewish) families—in Florence, for example, it was the Medici themselves—and they had little reason to put money into what was already a guaranteed and fixed source of income.

But strong Jewish control over ghetto housing may have been an equally powerful factor contributing to structural decay. Jewish conventions of rent control (*hazaka*) were recognized and enforced by state courts. While these legal arrangements gave Jewish renters a stake in their own housing, they simultaneously kept rents low even where Jewish population growth should have dictated otherwise. This arrangement favored those who already had apartments and protected them from normal market pressures. Jews clearly did improve their ghetto homes, and it would be too simple to label ghettos as slums, but the inflexible ghetto real estate market, constrained as it was by these powerful halakhic conventions, may well have contributed to a deterioration of the housing stock over time. It certainly also lent political strength to those already entrenched within the market.[22]

The ghetto as a merchant colony

From the point of view of early modern European cities, Jews were not only—and perhaps not even primarily—a religious group. Rather, they were a group of foreign merchants and tradespeople who competed for custom and markets with local non-Jews. The dynamics of each Jewish settlement depended therefore on the local specificity of this rivalry—the types and extent of commercial or financial activity in which Jews engaged in relation to the manufacturing, trade, and finance pursued by others in that locale. In frontier communities, for example, where urbanization was still underdeveloped, local non-Jewish merchants were not united or strong enough to object when the authorities (whether royal, noble, or ecclesiastical) welcomed Jewish rivals.[23] In more advanced commercial centers such as the communes of Renaissance Italy, however, powerful and well-organized merchant groups successfully limited or even blocked a competitive Jewish presence—that is, unless Jews provided direct benefits to the town government through the payment of taxes or long-term, low-interest loans.[24] When, as in Venice at the start of the sixteenth century, the economy changed and Jewish commercial services were too valuable to block, the best their local competitors could negotiate was to relegate Jewish trade to an inconvenient, enclosed part of town. Seen from this perspective, ghettoization reflects a compromise between the total exclusion that their Christian merchant rivals would have preferred and the total freedom that Jewish entrepreneurs sought. It is the task of the historian to track how interest groups played against each other, to identify the terms through which each group articulated its goals, and to follow the institutionalization of these interests in elaborate social institutions such as ghettos.

Understanding spatial segregation (ghettoization) as a process rooted in commercial competition rather than in religious ideology helps us to understand what happened in Cracow/Kazimierz, decades before the establishment of the ghetto in Venice. A medieval influx of German immigrants (including many Jews) had led to substantial town growth, a charter, and a measure of urban autonomy under so-called "Magdeburg Law." As part of its drive for autonomous jurisdiction and control, the emerging urban patriciate tried to drive Jews from the central market space. In 1485, the Jews collectively promised to encroach no further on the Christian trading area, but in practice, individual Jews often ignored the agreement and eventually it was repealed. Meanwhile, pressure on urban real estate increased because of spatial demands from the growing Akademia Krakowska. In 1469, Jews yielded their own communal buildings to the school in return for land elsewhere. Tensions continued to mount until finally, in 1495, Jews were given their own *vicus judaicus* across a short bridge in the separate urban jurisdiction of Kazimierz. Once established, Jews immediately began pressing for more space. They eventually were able to have all Christian residents expelled from their urban zone. The area was completely walled in only by 1627, and the gates were manned at night by Jewish guards. Historians, who often sum up the relocation as simply a response to popular riots in the city, have differed over whether or not to call the Jewish quarter of

Kazimierz a ghetto. But the dynamic was not different from processes common in urban settings even today. The give and take was far more complex, and the negotiated commercial-spatial solution far more nuanced, than the traditional narrative of Jewish expulsion would suggest. I would argue that similar negotiated settlements lie behind ghettoization in Germany and Italy as well.[25]

Considering the Jews as a merchant colony is important for another reason: it highlights an important legal precedent and structural model for the ghetto—namely the *fondaco*, a well-established mechanism for assigning trading rights, warehousing space, and a measure of extraterritorial legal autonomy to groups of foreign traders throughout the Mediterranean (and elsewhere). Of course, there were differences. In the merchant colonies, the consul was appointed by, and represented, a *foreign* ruler.[26] In Jewish merchant communities, on the other hand, the consul or body of governing stewards, even if elected by them, drew authority from the *host* government.[27] Thus the Jewish merchant community was obviously far less independent of its host country. Even so, the comparison with the *fondaco* reminds us that Jewish traders negotiated as a group for the settlement rights they received, and they operated under charters very much as a merchant company. The implications are twofold. First, we realize that the ghetto was a negotiated privilege as much as it was an imposed restriction. This should inspire further research to assess how Jews negotiated issues like the location and size of their space, specific trade rights, and the daily exigencies of urban life. And second, we can now understand better why there could be more than one charter for Jews in a given ghetto. In Venice, for example, there were three, each for a different group of businessmen/merchants. The groups negotiated independently of each other even though they also joined together as a Jewish community.

The functioning of Jewish "merchant companies" is highlighted in their control over membership (and therefore access to group privileges). Let me offer two examples from contemporary communities that were ostensibly far removed from the traditionally defined ghetto, but which were legally defined in a given space. In the Low Countries, in 1604, Alkmaar issued an invitation to "members of the Spanish and Portuguese nation." New settlers would, it was insisted, have to bring a certificate from the *parnacim et mamonim*—that is, the elected governors and council—of their last place of residence, attesting "that they were people of property who live properly."[28] The Jewish "trading company," in other words, was responsible for guaranteeing the activities of individual members. Similarly, the consul, and later the *massari*, of the new communities in Pisa and Livorno, were given the exclusive authority to accept or reject settlers. They soon developed legal procedures and formulae to accomplish this task, drawing for their models on the multilingual and transnational world of merchant practice rather than on any halakhic traditions. In making their decisions, the *massari* required evidence that the candidate was indeed a merchant who would participate honorably in the trade that provided the *raison d'être* of their community. Inevitably, resentments and conflicts arose, and dissatisfied individuals or groups took their complaints to the outside authorities who then had to decide how much to interfere in the affairs of the chartered community. Where necessary, individual licenses or second and even third group charters were issued, as mentioned. The existence of a licensed residential/commercial zone—what we know as the ghetto—inevitably sharpened internal conflicts, while giving Jewish leaders new experience in matters of "public law" and self-governance. It would also strengthen what we might call "sub-ethnic" Jewish identities, a feature of early modern and modern Jewish life. Historians usually attribute such distinctions to vestigial ethnic pride or liturgical distinctions. I would argue that exclusionary policies directed at "other" Jews were actually inspired by the legalized institutionalization of Jewish life we have been discussing.

The ghetto as a market space

Rich merchants aside, it is often assumed that most pre-modern European Jews made their living from pawnbroking and moneylending. Whether that is correct must be explored in another context. Suffice it to say here that focusing exclusively on moneylenders does not free us from the task of exploring how these Jews functioned within a market economy. Their credit activities were readily linked to currency exchange at fairs, and to financial management and estate stewardship on Polish latifundia.[29] But even more important for our topic is Jewish engagement in a broader "gray market" that functioned in parallel with the better-documented urban markets controlled by manufacturing guilds and elite long-distance traders. This secondary market was not limited to Jews, as we are now learning from the work of scholars such as Patricia Allerston on Venice and Laurence Fontaine more generally.[30] But it was a major area of Jewish specialization. The sale of pawns became trade in old clothes, and this soon included retailing "mill ends"—that is, pieces of yard goods that guild merchants sold off as "job lots" to unofficial retailers like the Jews. In some Italian cities at least, Jews were actually able to obtain guild licenses to market cheaper types of cloth such as linen. Jewish peddlers, who operated beyond the reach of urban regulations, undoubtedly sold a wide range of goods to their rural and small-town customers. And even the rag-trade (*strazzaria*), often explicitly assigned to Jews as in the Roman ghetto bull of 1555 (much to the frustration of their non-Jewish competitors), was not without market importance, a market that expanded, for example, with the increasing use of rag-based paper. We should also remember that pawnbroking shaded easily (and inevitably) into the trade in stolen goods, itself a complex phenomenon only partially defined by the rigid legal terminologies of ownership. Moneylending to farmers similarly led to speculation in agricultural "futures," a risky business in the sixteenth century as it is today, and one that often led to tension between Jews and Christian retailers.[31]

At least in Italy, there is a curiously self-contradictory relation between ghettoization and Jewish moneylending. On the one hand, Venice created its first Jewish ghetto for the bankers: their shops could be located only there, and the Jewish community's collective right to live in the *ghetto nuovo* depended on maintaining the shops, even though these were unprofitable.[32] *Cum nimis absurdum*, the famous papal bull of 1555 that ghettoized Roman Jewry, also included rules for how to manage the moneylending operations. Rome's Jewish banks would not be shut down for over a century.[33] On the other hand, in 1570, Tuscany went through considerable legal contortions in order to cancel all existing moneylending charters before allowing, and indeed encouraging, Jews to settle in the newly established ghetto in Florence.[34] Was the ghetto then a location for Jewish moneylending or its antithesis? The answer I would suggest lies in the larger economic reach of the Jewish pawnshops and the trades associated with them. Cities like Rome and Venice managed to force down the rates charged by Jews and so continued to tolerate the banks in their ghettos. Florence, on the other hand, opted to dispense with the Jews as providers of small-scale credit, but she allowed the other trades that were associated with the pawnshops to continue and to flourish. The implications of this for the local economy remain to be investigated.

In sum, we can only understand the ghetto when we realize that it was constructed in no small measure as an effort to distinguish between two parallel economies, to protect the privileges of licensed Christians who resented and perhaps feared competition from business rivals who were selling "inferior" or "questionable" goods.

The ghetto as a police zone and site of public discipline

Commerce aside, ghettos must certainly also be seen as expressions of the expanding social discipline, policing, and exclusion of undesirables characteristic of the early modern European city.[35] The pre-modern city was, after all, itself a walled enclosure with gates that were locked at night – gates that, as Daniel Jütte put it in a recent article, "function[ed] as a social filter … a crucial tool for the city's leadership to exert influence over the social life and demographic composition of the city."[36] Maria Boes, writing about Hamburg, notes that beginning in the fifteenth century, city gates were "increasingly used … not so much to admit, but to prevent people from coming to town."[37] How did this apply to Jews? Was the ghetto a way of keeping Jews out, or of letting them in? Was it only Jewish moneylenders who had to receive licenses to enter pre-modern cities? Could other Jews settle at will?[38] Certainly it has never been suggested that only the moneylenders were subject to ghettoization. The matter requires further exploration. But it would be instructive to look systematically at how early modern European cities attempted to use spatial controls vis-à-vis other social groups so as to contextualize the policies towards Jews.

Best studied in this regard are the control measures applied to prostitutes.[39] Both Jews and prostitutes were required to wear distinguishing marks on their clothing, were required to reside within certain areas of the city, and suffered from restricted access to public space. Historians who have dealt with early modern policies towards women have often decried the unfair gendering of public space in the same way that historians of the Jews have seen ghettoization as invidious and cruel.

This is more than an issue of similar policies. Jews' ghettos and assigned neighborhoods were often quite close to what today might be called "red light districts"; Jewish burghers complained that their wives and daughters were accosted by "johns." When such incidents are mentioned in the literature, they are usually understood as yet another example of oppressive anti-Jewish hostility, but the issue may be more complex. The links between Jews and prostitution may not have been as external, asymptotic, and artificially imposed as is often thought.

First, there was a business connection. Jewish shopkeepers in Rome, for example, were the regular suppliers of furnishings (beds, mattresses, draperies, clothing, even pictures on the walls) to prostitutes setting themselves up in business in the Eternal City.[40] Court records document many cases of Jewish men caught and punished for visiting Christian prostitutes, but we also have evidence for Jewish prostitutes who served both a Jewish and non-Jewish clientele. One fascinating case from Venice is that of Sarah Todesca, who was involved, at the very end of the seventeenth century, in a long-term affair with a Venetian lawyer named Alemante Angelo Nazari. The matter began when the Jewish Todesca was working as a prostitute in the ghetto. Nazari had represented her in a court case, but later snuck her out of the ghetto, had her baptized, and then kept her as a mistress, renting a room for her in a hotel/ brothel in the San Moise quarter. Alemante, in his own defense, asserted that his goal had been only to help the Jewess find Christ. Three points stand out about the quotidian reality of life in the ghetto. First: Sara continued to work as a prostitute to Jews; she was visited by Jewish clients from the ghetto even after she had converted (at least during Carnival, when disguises made this easier). Second, Sarah had daughters who moved into the House of Catechumens, the conversionary hostel. Third, Sarah's son remained a Jew in the ghetto, impoverished and living on the street unless some Jewish family was kind enough occasionally to take him in.[41] In short, Jewish quarters were not just located near red light districts. Jews could also be its customers, its workforce, and quite possibly also its owners and managers.

Let me end with one other aspect of the policing of Jewish zones. As mentioned already, Jewish economic activity certainly lent itself to various types of criminality – for example, the fencing of stolen property. The police chief of Livorno in the early seventeenth century was sure that Jews were responsible for most of the crime in the port. Leon Modena's son-in-law was among many Jews convicted of handling stolen property in Venice. Jews regularly ran card and dice games in the aristocratic courts of Ferrara and illegally in the back alleys of Rome, Venice, Pisa, and the like. Among the Jews who sought settlement rights in Livorno were convicted murderers and thieves, and the criminal records of the city include accounts of knife fights and brawls. Leon Modena bemoans the tragic fate of his sons: one died in a gang fight over a girl in the ghetto; another was exiled for gambling and theft; and a third seems to have been poisoned while conducting alchemical experiments together with a priest in a ghetto apartment. In short, the ghetto was not an ideal place to raise children. The famous Jewish criminal gangs of Germany were no doubt found in every Jewish urban zone.

The ghetto as a spatial expression of religious exclusivism

I have tried to outline ways in which the ghetto can productively be studied and understood as reflecting the same types of forces that determine the cityscape generally. Commerce and crime, crowding and competition were at least as important policy considerations as were religious doctrine and prejudice. Even if the establishment of the ghetto was justified in religious terminologies, I would argue that the immediate forces mobilizing such religious rhetoric rose up out of the world of the everyday. To ignore those forces is to misunderstand what was happening. The test case for my approach is certainly the ghetto of Rome, established in 1555 by the religiously severe Pope Paul IV Carafa. The long history of this enclosure (its gates would not be finally opened up until the fall of the papal government in 1870), its over-crowded conditions, and its unsanitary location in the capital city of Catholic Christendom combined to make this the archetypal ghetto. The pope's motives seem clear from the founding decree: Jews were condemned, it declared, to eternal servitude because of their great sin of deicide and were tolerated only out of Christian charity. Jews must therefore live together, separate from Christians. They must wear an identifying badge. They may not labor in public on the Christian Sabbath or on holy days. They cannot have Christian women as servants and nursemaids, nor may they allow poor Christians to address them as "sir" (*dominos*). And so on, invoking many long-standing Church positions regarding the Jews. The best-known interpretation of the bull, that by Kenneth Stow in 1977, argues that the bull was motivated by a new intensification of the Church's conversionary missionary: the overcrowded ghetto was part of a systematic campaign of negative pressure intended to make life as a Jew intolerable. Indeed, Stow reads the demand that Jews be restricted to *strazzaria* (the second-hand trade) and that they not trade in grains or other things needed for human use (article 9) as an absolute prohibition on any Jewish trade in foodstuffs. In a later essay, he describes the developing papal policy in this regard as an "issue of contamination" akin to rules about prostitutes and a harking back to late medieval French "laws forbidding Jews from touching food in the marketplace, lest what they touched and left unpurchased might later contaminate a Christian consumer."[42]

Stow's pioneering and influential interpretation has been challenged, not least over his reading of the Latin text.[43] But our interest is not just in the language but in the way the bull's provisions (unfortunately not always completely clear) may help us understand what led to the ghettoization in the first place. My own reading and contextualizing of this papal bull shows, I think, that the bull arose from the sort of immediate and practical issues of urban competition that we have already seen elsewhere. First, the population of Rome, both Jewish and non-Jewish, was growing, and Jews were seeking housing outside the traditional Jewish quarter in the *rione* Sant'Angelo. We have evidence that wealthier Jews had been seeking nicer homes for some time; even the "liberal" Pope Paul III had blocked them on several occasions. Now Paul IV took on the issue directly, justifying the restrictions by complaining of the effrontery and discordancy (*cum nimis absurdum et inconveniens*) of Jews who sought to live not just on Christian streets but "even in the more noble" parts of cities. Social order had to be reinforced, and markers of social status had to be maintained.

The bull also sought to better regulate a Jewish credit sector that had been licensed in the city from 1521 and was also expanding. We should not be surprised that the Roman government, like municipal authorities everywhere, sought consistently to lower the interest rates Jews might charge the poor.[44] With that goal, the bull forbade fraudulent contracts through which Jewish lenders might try to hide excessive or illegal loans (article 6). It demanded that Jews keep their record books in Italian, written in the Latin alphabet, so that the authorities might have better access (article 8). And Jews must limit themselves to the second-hand trade (that is, to lending money on used goods), and stop lending to farmers. As already mentioned, this last was effectively a form of speculation in grain futures, and frequently led to real tensions when a bad harvest left the loanbankers in total possession of a diminished but now much more valuable crop, and thus in charge of the city's vital supply of bread (article 9).[45]

In short, the immediate and declared instigation for walling Rome's Jewish neighborhood was competition for residential space caused by the expansion of the city's growing Jewish population into new neighborhoods. It was a logical part of the ongoing effort to control the Jewish credit sector and make it more open to government inspection. Conversionary ambitions and Counter-Reformation enthusiasms may have provided the rhetoric but not the motives. Of course, physical establishment of the ghetto made the rhetoric behind it ever more prominent in Church doctrine, a spatial expression of the Church's search for social discipline. It is significant that the Church knew of no other way to handle the presence in its midst of an industrious, literate, relatively well-off population of religiously "other."[46] The Church stubbornly insisted on ghetto walls, as on so many other aspects of an outdated papal secular rule, until the city was once and for all annexed into the nascent Italian State. In other words, what ended the ghetto was not a change in religious doctrine but a change in the authority structure and value system of the larger society, a society no longer content with government by an unqualified theological bureaucracy. Equally important, the urban tensions that required the ghetto in the sixteenth century were no longer relevant in the nineteenth. Both the city and the demographic and economic implications of a Jewish presence in it had changed as well. As the city (and its economy) changed, the walls of the ghetto disappeared.

What have we accomplished?

In this very rapid survey, I have bent customary definitions so as to include within the rubric of "ghetto" a far wider set of urban Jewries. I have compared the Jewish ghetto to other urban constellations: a residential neighborhood, a merchant colony, a market space, even a "red light" district. And I ended by suggesting, albeit very briefly, that ghetto walls fell because the economic functioning of the modern city no longer supported this type of spatial specialization. I have tried to move the discourse from the sphere of religious tolerance to that of urban zoning. The ghetto, in other words, is not a unique religiously inspired phenomenon born of

Christian dogma. It is the product of a well-known constellation in the history of the urban.

I am hardly alone in my approach to the ghetto phenomenon. Much recent work by local historians has contributed to our far more dynamic view of life behind ghetto walls. Equally important has been the contextualizing and comparative approaches that have explored spatial segregation in cities around the world. For example, Carl H. Nightingale's award-winning *Segregation: A Global History of Divided Cities* traces the links between capitalist interests, changing ideologies, and state power in various colonial regimes from the Indian Ocean to western North America. He acknowledges that boundaries between in- and out-groups have been a characteristic of urban society from the start. With Philip D. Curtin, moreover, he asserts that separating off urban "colonies" of foreign merchants and moneylenders was "one of the most widespread of human institutions." Even so, Nightingale did not see the obvious connection between Jewish ghettos and the patterns he was describing. In his introductory survey of "Seventy Centuries of City-Splitting," he relied on a few misleading popular histories for his information and coined a new term—"scapegoat ghettos"—to explain the Jewish case, arguing that the Serenissima invited the Jews into Venice only in order to make them seem ridiculous and to use "Jew-blaming" as a method of deflecting criticism of the government. This far-fetched rhetoric is its own refutation and contrasts sharply with the rest of Nightingale's analysis of urban segregation as a restriction of that very diversity vital to the city's prosperity and growth.[47] The Jewish ghetto was not an exception; it was a perfect model for segregatory practices that Europeans would carry with them throughout the world. And it was also, in many paradoxical ways, the birthplace of Jewish participation in the modern world.

Notes

1   This chapter expands upon an approach I first developed in "What If the Ghetto Had Never Been Constructed?", a contribution to Gavriel Rosenfeld, *What Ifs of Jewish History from Abraham to Zionism* (Cambridge: Cambridge University Press, 2016), pp. 81–102. In that paper, I tried to interrogate the historical evidence for the formation of major early modern ghettos and lay bare the assumptions of the traditional historiographical narrative.

2   This tendency can be seen already in Heinrich Graetz' foundational *Geschichte der Juden von den ältesten Zeiten bis auf die Gegenwart* (1853–1875); see, for example, vol. 7 (Leipzig: 1863), p. 106. Salo Baron's classic article "Ghetto and Emancipation: Shall We Revise the Traditional View?" *Menorah Journal* 14:6 (June, 1928), pp. 515–526 is the most often cited expression of the approach which contrasted ghetto oppression with emancipatory liberation, even though Baron himself intended to combat this polarized paradigm. On the Jewish quarter in an Islamic country, see Shlomo Deshen's study, *Mellah Society: Jewish Community Life in Sherifian Morocco* (Chicago: University of Chicago Press, 1989).

3   Thus, the social historian Jacob Katz sought to describe the modernization of "Jews isolated in ghettos on the fringe of society" in his influential *Out of the Ghetto: The Social Background of Jewish Emancipation, 1770–1870* (Cambridge, MA: Harvard University Press, 1973), p. 9. The view was preached to generations of American college students in Howard M. Sachar's popular textbook, *The Course of Modern Jewish History* (1958; revised edition, New York: Random House, 1990). The opening chapter on "The Jew as

Non-European" began with a stark contrast between Frankfurt's "majestic silhouette of spires and battlements" and the "little encincture—a hideous anomaly … the *Judengasse*, the ghetto of the Jews" (3).

4   For German literature, see *Ghetto Writing: Traditional and Eastern Jewry in German-Jewish Literature from Heine to Hilsenrath*, eds. Anne-Fuchs and Florian Krobb (Columbia, SC: Camden House, 1999).

5   "Introduction" (1893) reprinted in *Selected Works of Israel Zangwill: Children of the Ghetto, Ghetto Comedies, and Ghetto Tragedies* (Philadelphia: Jewish Publication Society, 1938), p. v.

6   For recent discussions of the (re-)invention of Jewish spaces, see Magdalena Waligórska, "Jewish Heritage Production and Historical Jewish Spaces: A Case Study of Cracow and Berlin," pp. 225–250, and Alla Sokolova, "Jewish Sights: Exoticization of Places and Objects as a Way of Presenting Local 'Jewish Antiquity' by the Inhabitants of Little Towns," pp. 261–280, both in *Jewish Space in Central and Eastern Europe*, eds. Jurgita Šiaučiūnaitė-Verbickienė and Larisa Lempertienė (Newcastle: Cambridge Scholars Publishing, 2007).

7   I allude, of course, to the insights of Hayden White, for example in the introduction to his *Metahistory: The Historical Imagination of the Nineteenth Century* (Baltimore: Johns Hopkins University Press, 1973) or "The Question of Narrative in Contemporary Historical Theory," *The Content of the Form: Narrative Discourse and Historical Representation* (Baltimore: Johns Hopkins University Press, 1987), pp. 26–57. But the general point is a matter of common sense and can be, I think, accepted, no matter our position on the relation between literary theory and historiography.

8   On the legal basis for this community, see my "Invitation to a Promised Land: The Medici, the Jews, and the Practice of Tolerance in Early Modern Europe" (PhD diss., Harvard University, 1976) and the many studies by Lucia Frattarelli Fischer now conveniently brought together in her *Vivere Fuori dal Ghetto: Ebrei a Pisa e Livorno (secoli XVI–XVIII)* (Turin: Silvio Zamorani, 2008).

9   Benjamin Ravid, the pre-eminent expert on the legislative history of the Venetian ghetto, has noted the multiple and varied meanings attached to the term ghetto. He chose therefore to define the word by "the three decisive characteristics" that applied in the Venetian case: "compulsory, segregated, and enclosed"; "All Ghettos were Jewish Quarters but not all Jewish Quarters were Ghettos," *Jewish Culture and History* 10:2–3 (2008), pp. 5–24:6, and see also his contribution to the present volume. My approach seeks to understand the forces at play in the admission and/or restriction of Jews as a group within the urban fabric, whatever the living arrangements.

10   See below, n. 25.

11   This was the case for Jews in Venice before the institution of the walled ghetto proper; Jews could enter the city for limited periods. Once their pass was up, they might leave and apply to return after the passage of a fixed amount of time. Similarly, Ashkenazi Jews moved to nearby Altona when they were expelled from Hamburg in 1648, but returned to trade there on short-term passes as mentioned in *The Memoirs of Glückel of Hameln*, trans. Marvin Lowenthal (New York: Schocken, 1977), p. 6 f.

12   Robert Jütte discusses a collection of over 300 such licenses that have by chance survived in the Cologne city archive from the years 1648–1667: "Patient und Heiler in der vorindustriellen Gesellschaft. Krankheits- und Gesundheitsverhalten im frühneuzeitlichen Köln" (Habilitationsschrift, Universität Bielefeld, 1989), pp. 116ff. I thank Professor Jütte for bringing his research to my attention and sharing the relevant material with me. The examples could easily be multiplied.

13   Jewish moneylenders settled, for example, in small towns nearby Rome, and sent runners or agents into the city searching for clients until 1521, when the popes licensed up to twenty Jewish banks within the city. See my "Licenses, Cartels, and Kehila: Jewish Moneylending and the Struggle Against Restraint of Trade in Early Modern Rome," in *Purchasing Power: The Economics of Modern Jewish History*, eds. Rebecca Kobrin and Adam Teller (Philadelphia: University of Pennsylvania Press, 2015), pp. 27–45:30. Similarly

in the case of Venice, before the institution of the ghetto bankers stored their pawns and maintained their "offices" in Mestre, even though they were allowed to come into the city to seek clients; Benjamin Ravid, "The Venetian Government and the Jews," in *The Jews of Early Modern Venice*, eds. Robert C. Davis and Benjamin Ravid (Baltimore: Johns Hopkins University Press, 2001), pp. 3–30:5. Admitting Jewish banks into the city proper was a lever with which to pressure Jews to lower their rate of interest.

14 This was the title chosen by architectural and urban historians Ennio Concina, Ugo Camerino and Donatella Calabi for their comprehensive study subtitled "Il ghetto di Venezia: architettura e urbanistica" (Venice: Albrizzi, 1991). Other terminologies for Jewish quarters such as *Judengasse* similarly range over a variety of Jewish spaces, from "organic" neighborhoods to legally imposed and restricted spaces.

15 Shlomo Simonsohn, "The Ghetto in Italy and Its Governance" [Hebrew], *Sefer ha-Yovel le-Yitzhak Ber* (Jerusalem: 1961), pp. 270–286. For an important exploration of the connection between Jewish spatial administration and the development of the early modern state, see Stefanie Siegmund, *The Medici State and the Ghetto of Florence: The Construction of an Early Modern Jewish Community* (Stanford: Stanford University Press, 2005).

16 Salo W. Baron was an enthusiastic advocate for the study of such Jewish organiza-tion. See his pioneering work on *The Jewish Community: Its History and Structure to the American Revolution* (Philadelphia: Jewish Publication Society, 1942), which of course can be supplemented by many subsequent anthologies of articles, especially in Hebrew. The ongoing series edited by Michael Walzer, Menachem Lorberbaum, et al., *The Jewish Political Tradition* (New Haven: Yale University Press, 2003) provides a convenient intro-duction to more philosophical and theoretical aspects of the issues involved.

17 Cooperman, "Theorizing Jewish Self-Government in Early Modern Italy," in *Una Manna Buona per Mantova. Studi in onore di Vittore Colorni per il suo 92° compleanno*, ed. Mauro Perani (Florence: Olschki, 2004), pp. 365–380, and Cooperman, "Political Discourse in a Kabbalistic Register: Isaac de Lattes' Plea for a Stronger Communal Government," in *Be'erot Yitzhak: Studies in Memory of Isadore Twersky*, ed. Jay M. Harris (Cambridge, MA: Harvard University Press, 2005), pp. 47–68 and 79★–93★.

18 Historians of the Jewish Early Modern have recently begun to investigate "record keep-ing" as a key to the sweeping changes of the era. The task is enormous since it requires addressing a wide range of Jewish governmental and legal texts, ranging from the for-mularies of *pinkasim* (communal record books) to the Hebrew notarial acts of Rome which often include a codicil to the effect that the parties agree that the document was to be considered as legally equivalent to one drawn up by a *notaio pubblico*—a Christian notary.

19 The sophisticated documentation of Jewish self-governments by no means implies that city and state authorities happily ceded all authority to them, even in matters regard-ing the Jews. See for example, the situation in Venice described by David Malkiel, "The Tenuous Thread: A Venetian Lawyer's Apology for Jewish Self-Government in the Seventeenth Century," *AJS Review*, 12:2 (Autumn, 1987), pp. 223–250.

20 For Venice, see Donatella Calabi, *Venezia e il Ghetto: Cinquecento anni del 'recinto degli ebrei'* (Turin: Bollati Boringhieri, 2016, originally published in French and soon, the author tells me, to appear in English), chapter 7.

21 On the Frankfurt enclosure, see Fritz Backhaus, Gisela Engel, Robert Liberles and Margarete Schliiter, eds., *Die Frankfurter Judengasse: jüdisches Leben in der Frühen Neuzeit*, 2nd edition (Frankfurt am Main: Societäts-Verlag, 2006), available in English as *The Frankfurt Judengasse: Jewish Life in an Early Modern German City* (London: Vallentine Mitchell, 2010), a collection already published as *Jewish Culture and History* 10:2–3 (2008). References are to that last publication. Fritz Backhaus explores "The Population Explosion in the Frankfurt *Judengasse* in the Sixteenth Century," ibid., pp. 25–44, tracing Jewish growth from some 150 to 2500 (from 1.5 to 15 per cent of the city population) between 1500 and 1600, at times despite the opposition of the municipal council and at times with its clear support.

22   The use of *hazaka* to shape the new ghettos and the objections of poorer Jews to these protectionist practices are already evident in the sixteenth century as I have tried to demonstrate in my paper "Regulating life within the urban ghetto," to be published in the proceedings of the conference "Les règles des lieux: Éspaces, institutions et société dans la ville moderne (XVIe–XVIIIe siècles)," held at the École Française de Rome, September 2016.

23   This does not mean that, as has been sometimes suggested, Jews automatically aligned themselves with central—as opposed to local—authorities. See for example Yosef Hayim Yerushalmi, "Servants of Kings and not Servants of Servants": Some Aspects of the Political History of the Jews" [Tenenbaum Family Lecture Series in Judaic Studies at Emory University] (Atlanta: Tam Institute, Emory University, 2007). The place of Jews between central and local powers varied with local political constellations. See for example the situation as Bologna was absorbed into the Papal States described by Maria Giuseppina Muzzarelli, "Ebrei, Bologna e sovrano-pontefice: la fine di una relazione tra verifiche, restrizioni e ripensamenti," in *idem*, ed., *Verso l'epilogo di una convivenza: Gli ebrei a Bologna nel XVI secolo* (Florence: Giuntina, 1996), pp. 19–53.

24   For examples of town councilors and representatives negotiating before the central authorities on behalf of Jews who sought lending licenses, see Anthony Molho, "A Note on Jewish Moneylenders in Tuscany in the Late Trecento and Early Quattrocento," in *Renaissance Studies in Honor of Hans Baron*, eds. A. Molho and John A. Tedeschi (Florence: 1971), p. 102; Bernard Dov Cooperman, "Portuguese *Conversos* in Ancona: Jewish Political Activity in Early Modern Italy," *In Iberia & Beyond: Hispanic Jews between Cultures*, ed. Bernard Dov Cooperman (Newark: University of Delaware Press, 1998), pp. 297–352:313. For Bologna, see the previous note.

25   Hanna Zaremska, "Jewish street (Platea Judeorum) in Cracow: The 14th–The First Half of the 15th C.," *Acta Poloniae Historica* 83 (2001), pp. 27–57; *idem*, "Crossing the River: How and Why the Jews of Kraków Settled in Kazimierz at the End of the Fifteenth Century," *Polin* 22 (2010), pp. 174–192; *idem*, *Żydzi w Średniowiecznej Polsce Gmina Krakowska* (Warsaw: Instytut Historii PAN, 2011), pp. 493–504; Majer Bałaban, *Tóldot ha-Yehudim be-Krakow u-ve-Kazimiez 1304–1868*, vol. 1 (Jerusalem: Magnes Press, 2002), edited by Jacob Goldberg from the expanded second Polish edition, especially chapter 12: "The Hundred Years War over the *Vicus Judaicus* and over Commercial Rights in Kazimierz (1533–1655)," pp. 148–163.

26   See for example Eric Dursteler's discussion of "The Bailo in Constantinople: Crisis and Career in Venice's Early Modern Diplomatic Corps," *Mediterranean Historical Review* 16:2 (December 2001), pp. 1–30. In his role as judge in disputes between merchants, the consul parallels the institution of a specially appointed "market judge" (*iudex fori*) that developed in central European cities; see, for example, Aleksander Gieysztor "Urban Changes in Poland in the 12th and 13th Centuries," *La Pologne au XIIe Congrès International des Sciences Historiques à Vienne* (Warsaw: Polish Academy of Sciences, 1965), pp. 7–30. In many cases in Italy, a special judge was appointed to provide summary justice for civil cases between Jews and non-Jews. These and other judicial arrangements all serve as models in the development of Jewish legal autonomy and require further study.

27   Daniel Jütte, "The Jewish Consuls in the Mediterranean and the Holy Roman Empire during the Early Modern Period: A Study in Economic and Diplomatic Networks (1500–1800)," in *Cosmopolitan Networks in Commerce and Society 1660–1914* [= *German Historical Institute London Bulletin*, Supplement 2], eds. Andreas Gestrich and Margrit Schulte Beerbühl (London 2011, pp. 153–186). On the consular activities of Magino Gabrielli Sarfatti in Livorno, see my "Trade and Settlement: The Establishment and Early Development of the Jewish Communities in Leghorn and Pisa (1591–1626)," (Cambridge, MA: Harvard University Ph.D., 1976), pp. 122 ff. On those of Daniel Rodriga in Venice and Spalato, see Benjamin Ravid, "Daniel Rodriga and the First Decade of Jewish Merchants of Venice," in *Exile and Diaspora: Studies in the History of the Jewish People Presented to Professor Haim Beinart*, eds. Aaron Mirsky et al. (Jerusalem: Makhon Ben-Zvi, 1991), pp. 203–223.

28   A. H. Huussen, "The Legal Position of Sephardi Jews in Holland, circa 1600," in *Dutch Jewish History*, Volume 3, ed. J. Michman (Jerusalem, Assen, Maastricht: 1993), pp. 19–41:31.

29   Serious study of how Jewish financial and marketing roles may have operated is still in its infancy, especially with regard to the pre-modern world. Michael Toch has begun to open up the topic in *The Economic History of European Jews: Late Antiquity and Early Middle Ages* (Leiden: Brill, 2013). For the implications of medieval moneylending, see Joseph Shatzmiller, *Shylock Reconsidered: Jews, Moneylending, and Medieval Society* (Berkeley: University of California Press, 1990) and *Cultural Exchange: Jews, Christians, and Art in the Medieval Marketplace* (Princeton, NJ: Princeton University Press, 2013).

30   Patricia Anne Allerston, "The Market in Second-Hand Clothes and Furnishings in Venice, c. 1500–c. 1650" (PhD, European University Institute, Department of History and Civilization, Florence, 1996); Laurence Fontaine, ed., *Alternative Exchanges: Second-Hand Circulations from the Sixteenth Century to the Present* (New York and Oxford: Berghahn Books, 2008).

31   For this issue in German lands see Manfred Gailus, "Die Erfindung des 'Korn-Juden': Zur Geschichte eines antijüdischen Feindbildes des 18. und frühen 19. Jahrhunderts," *Historische Zeitschrift* 272:3 (June, 2001), pp. 597–622, and Robert Jütte, "Das Bild vom 'Kornjuden' als Antifigur zum frühneuzeitlichen Prinzip der 'guten narung' und der 'moral economy,'" *Aschkenas* 23 (2013), pp. 27–52.

32   See David Malkiel, *A Separate Republic: The Mechanics and Dynamics of Venetian Jewish Self-Government, 1607–1624* (Jerusalem: The Magnes Press, 1991), especially chapter 5.

33   The text of the bull is conveniently available with English translation as Appendix I to Kenneth R. Stow, *Catholic Thought and Papal Jewry Policy 1555–1593* (New York: Jewish Theological Seminary, 1977), pp. 291–298. On Stow's readings, see below.

34   On the ghettoization decree of 1570 see Umberto Cassuto, *Gli ebrei a Firenze nell'età del Rinascimento* (Florence: Olschki, 1918), chapter 4, pp. 98–117 and Stefanie Siegmund, *The Medici State and the Ghetto of Florence*, part II, pp. 171–238. The text of the edict was published by Lorenzo Cantini, *Legislazione Toscana* 7 (Florence: 1803), pp. 376–378.

35   Herman Roodenburg and Pieter Spierenburg, eds., *Social Control in Europe: Volume I, 1500–1800* (Columbus: Ohio State University Press, 2004).

36   "Control over the gates was a crucial tool for the city's leadership to exert influence over the social life and demographic composition of the city … Apart from those who had been expelled or banned from the city, there were also two other groups of people who frequently sought entrance and were vigorously repelled by most cities: *vagabonds and beggars.* Entrance was also often barred to members of *religious minorities – particularly Jews.*" [emphasis added – BDC] Daniel Jütte, "Entering a City: On a Lost Early Modern Practice," *Urban History* 41:2 (2014), pp. 204–227:212.

37   Maria Boes, "Unwanted Travellers: The Tightening of City Borders in Early Modern Germany," in *Borders and Travellers in Early Modern Europe*, ed. T. Betteridge (Aldershot: 2007), pp. 87–111:92.

38   This has been suggested for Florence by Umberto Cassuto, though I know of no similar claim for other places; *Gli ebrei a Firenze*, p. 86: "Partiti i banchieri, gli altri ebrei che non esercitavano il prestito continuarono a dimorare in Firenze; nè, a quanto ci è dato sapere, alcun evento notevole venne a turbare la vita regolare della comunità …."

39   Diane Yvonne Ghirardo, "The Topography of Prostitution in Renaissance Ferrara," *Journal of the Society of Architectural Historians* 60:4 (2001), pp. 402–431 revised as "Marginal Spaces of Prostitution in Renaissance Ferrara," in *Phaethon's Children: The Este Court and Its Culture in Early Modern Ferrara*, ed. Dennis Looney and Deanna Shemek (Arizona Center for Medieval and Renaissance Studies, 2005), and see also "Women and Space in a Renaissance Italian City," [=Chapter 11 of] *InterSections: Architectural Histories and Critical Theories*, eds. Iain Borden and Jane Rendell (London: Routledge, 2000). Also useful to this discussion is Elizabeth S. Cohen, "Seen and Known: Prostitutes in the Cityscape of Late-Sixteenth-Century Rome," *Renaissance Studies* 12:3 (1998), pp. 392–409.

40 For example, Rome's Archivio di Stato, Notai Capitolini, Ufficio 30 contains scores of notarial contracts documenting the promises of *curiales* (courtesans) to repay Jewish businessmen for furnishings they had bought, so to speak, "on time." A comparison of entries in volumes 13, 14, and 15, covering the years leading up to, and immediately following, ghettoization, shows no change in this pattern of business. My thanks to Professor Thomas Cohen for bringing this series to my attention.

41 Adinah Miller, "Stopping Sex Crimes, Saving Souls: The Prosecution of a Jewish Prostitute in Early Modern Venice," unpublished paper, Renaissance Society of America annual conference (2009) based on Archivio di Stato, Venezia, *Esecutori Contro la Bestemmia: Processi*, Busta 2 (1697–1698). I thank Ms Miller for sharing her notes with me.

42 Stow, *Catholic Thought and Papal Jewry Policy*, above n. 33; *idem*, "The Consciousness of Closure: Roman Jewry and Its *Ghet*" in *Essential Papers on Jewish Culture in Renaissance and Baroque Italy*, ed. David B. Ruderman (New York: New York University Press, 1992), pp. 386–400:393 and n. 21 and 22; and, of course, his contribution to the present volume.

43 David Berger has questioned Stow's translation of the Latin, "Cum Nimis Absurdum and the Conversion of the Jews," *Jewish Quarterly Review* 70 (1) (1979), pp. 41–49, and see Stow's brief response in *Jewish Quarterly Review* 71 (4) (1981), pp. 251–252.

44 This perfectly reasonable approach to a real social issue has not been sufficiently highlighted by historians of the Jews, who have generally dealt with Jews' bank licenses as issues of tolerance, and have stressed, for apologetic reasons, that Jewish moneylenders generally charged lower rates of interest than did their (unlicensed) Christian competitors. For the traditional approach, see Léon Poliakov, *Les Banchieri juifs et le Saint Siège du XIIIe au XVIIe siècle* (Paris: SEVPEN, 1965), available in a partial English translation as *Jewish Bankers and the Holy See from the Thirteenth to the Seventeenth Century* (London: Routledge and Kegan Paul, 1977). For the pressures to lower interest rates specifically in Rome, see my "Licenses, Cartels, and Kehila," above, n. 13.

45 For a fuller analysis of real estate competition, the problem of speculating in grain futures, and other business practices in Rome and elsewhere, see my "What if the Ghetto Had Never Been Constructed?" (above, n. 1), p. 96 and the nn. ad loc. Stow's assumption that article 9 of *Cum nimis absurdum* was intended to prevent Jews from engaging in any food trade (above n. 42) seems to me untenable. The Jews' right to engage in all trade including foodstuffs was clarified immediately by papal officials. This was confirmed in the bulls *Dudum felices* (Pius IV, 1562) and *Christiana pietas* (Sixtus V, 1586), and by the facts of Jewish livelihood in the centuries that followed. I hope to deal with this issue in a separate paper. For now, the reader is referred to René Moulinas' portrayal of "un véritable petite guerre diplomatique" over this same issue a few years earlier in Provence; *Les juifs du pape en France* (Paris: 1981), 241ff. For a more detailed explanation of Jewish livelihoods in the ghetto period, see Serena di Nepi, *Sopravvivere al ghetto: Per una storia sociale della comunità ebraica nella Roma del Cinquecento* (Rome: Viella, 2013).

46 Trying to establish the urban dynamics of ghettoization does not obviate the need for continued investigation of Church attitudes. See for example the provocative arguments about canonists' positions towards usurers, both Christian and Jewish, offered by Rowan William Dorin, "Banishing Usury: The Expulsion of Foreign Moneylenders in Medieval Europe, 1200–1450" (PhD, Harvard University, 2015). He suggests that control over urban space and the decision whether to expel or tolerate, may not be determined by attitudes towards Jews per se. See the summary article, "'Once the Jews Have Been Expelled': Intent and Interpretation in Late Medieval Canon Law," *Law and History Review* 34:2 (May, 2016), pp. 335–362.

47 Carl H. Nightingale, *Segregation: A Global History of Divided Cities* (Chicago: University of Chicago Press, 2012). The quote from Curtin comes from *Cross Cultural Trade in World History* (Cambridge: Cambridge University Press, 1984), p. 3.

4

VENICE: A CULTURE OF ENCLOSURE, A CULTURE OF CONTROL

The creation of the ghetto in the context of the early Cinquecento city[1]

Samuel D. Gruber

Introduction

The creation of the Venice Ghetto in 1516 was a dramatic development in the distinction between Christians and Jews, but one that grew directly out of long-standing practices regarding the separation of Jews and other minority and often suspect groups from the mainstream. This study derives directly from questions posed about the broad context of the Ghetto by Professor Benjamin Ravid in 1986, and still only partly resolved.[2]

This essay looks at the Ghetto through an early sixteenth-century lens to ask how different and how unexpected was the enclosure of Venice's Jews. If the Ghetto was not so unexpected, then what was the historical, social, legal, and physical context that made the Ghetto mostly acceptable to Venetians – Christian and Jews?[3]

Venetian policies and statutes regulating life in the Ghetto differed from requirements imposed on social groups in other neighborhoods, but there were similarities, too. The distance between "normal" levels of control within the Renaissance city, and particularly in Venice, and the level of control in the sixteenth-century Venice Ghetto was simply a matter of degree. Unlike other Italian cities of the period, which divided space simply into public and private realms, Venice used spatial distinctions more assertively and these correspond in many ways to increased levels of social control, especially from the late fifteenth century through the 1530s.

Separating Jews: Prefiguring the ghetto

From the thirteenth century on, many Italian rulers and churchmen had talked about separating Jews from the population at large, but other than expelling all Jews from a locality, none had successfully carried out the threat. Jews had been forced from Angevin Naples in 1291 and the expulsions of ancient Jewish communities from Spain, Sicily, and southern Italy between 1492 and 1569 certainly helped focus the question in the early sixteenth century, when separation and enclosure became a viable alternative to full expulsion.[4]

Venice had, however, experienced and maintained separate Jewish quarters as it expanded power in the Eastern Mediterranean, where the separation of groups by tribal, religious, and national origin or affiliation was a custom of long standing. Jewish quarters existed in the colonies before Venetian rule. For example, the Jewish quarter of Candia, the capital of Crete, dated to the Byzantine period.[5] Venice accepted and expanded this policy and around 1325 imposed "residential segregation upon the Jews of her colonies, who were from then on to dwell exclusively within the boundaries of their respective *Judaiche*."[6] The employment of Jewish separation was an established practice by Venetians long before 1516.

Jewish quarters in most Venetian colonies were separated from Christian neighborhoods by walls and gates. When walls did not exist, other dividers were employed. In Rethymno in Crete, no physical boundary existed but the quarters were divided by crosses.[7] In those areas where Venice had outposts with trading privileges, but not total control, Jews to whom Venice had granted nationality (distinct from citizenship) often lived outside the Venetian areas of responsibility, instead residing in the Jewish streets of the host community. In Constantinople, however, Venetian Jews were eventually forced by imperial authorities to live in the Venetian section, where by 1343 they resided in a district called Cafacalea, where there was also a synagogue. This Jewish district does not appear to have been separated from the rest of the Venetian quarter.

In fifteenth-century Italy, spurred in large part by preaching friars, discrimination against Jews increased, anticipating the institution of the ghettos in Venice and then throughout the peninsula. In 1427, Giovanna II restricted the Jews in Lanciano in the Abruzzi to a single street. Similar efforts were made in Piedmont in the 1430s, and proposed in Bari, Cesena, and Ravenna during the 1400s. In Venice, laws enacted in 1423 and 1424 prohibited Jews from buying land or real estate anywhere in the Venetian state.[8] This was in line with policies throughout Europe where it was difficult for Jews to own immovable property or participate in many professions. In 1442, Pope Eugenius IV declared that "Jews shall not live among Christians but rather they ought to dwell among themselves, separated and segregated from Christians, within a certain distinction or place, outside of which they would by no means be allowed to own houses."[9] Meanwhile, with the establishment of church-sponsored small loan agencies (Monti de Pietà), many Jews found it more difficult to earn a living in mainland towns. By 1494, there were 30 *monti* in central and northern Italy.

In 1508–1516, in the War of the League of Cambrai, Venice was initially defeated when Pope Julius II aimed to curb Venetian mainland power. Thousands of refugees, including many Jews, retreated to the still-impregnable Venice itself. This rapid increase in the Jewish population upset the *status quo* which had allowed small numbers of individual transitory Jewish bankers, merchants and doctors to live and work in Venice in relative peace.

While, previously, individual Jews had been accused of various crimes, including sexual relations with Christians, the influx of refugees greatly increased the level of broad-based anti-Jewish sentiment, especially among the clergy. Calls for the expulsion of Jews from Venice, or at least for tighter regulation and separation, led directly to the compromise of establishing the Ghetto in 1516. Jews could still reside and do regular business in Venice, but they had to live separately, under curfew, and with other controls.

Around Easter 1516, Zacaria Dolfin proposed to "send all of them [the Jews] to live in the Ghetto Nuovo which is like a castle, and to make drawbridges and close it with a wall; they should have *only one gate*, which would enclose them there and they would stay there, and two boats of the Council of Ten would go and stay there at night, at their expense, for their greater security." In 1516, it was officially decreed that "The Jews must all reside together in the houses in the court within the Ghetto near San Girolamo, where there is plenty of room for them to live. And in order to prevent their roaming about at night, let there be built two gates."[10]

The Ghetto as a Venetian institution

The Venetian Ghetto, however, should not be understood solely in the tradition of isolation and control of Jews; it also legitimized their presence. Benjamin Ravid has written that "paradoxically, when viewed in historical perspective, the establishment of the ghetto marked a positive development in the history of the Jews of Venice. Previously, Jews as a collective group had been authorized to live in the city only for a brief 15-year period from 1382 to 1397, although the presence of individual Jews in fifteenth-century Venice is well documented."[11]

The Ghetto's creation was also about the separation of Venetians, particularly *good* Venetians, from any outsider or undesirable group. While extreme, the Ghetto was part of a wide range of customs, laws, and policies (often state-sponsored) to monitor and control differences in class, gender, religion, place of origin, and legality. The Ghetto was not a natural development, and certainly not a necessary one, but in the context of the era, it was neither entirely *unnatural* nor unexpected.

Two important and detailed accounts of the Venice at the turn of the sixteenth century allow us to place the Ghetto's establishment into a broader physical, cultural, and legal context. The superb view-map of the city drawn by Jacopo de' Barberi and printed in 1500 presents every neighborhood in the city in considerable detail.[12] We see the Ghetto as part of a cityscape of enclosed spaces. The massive diary of Marin Sanudo, a participant and observer of everything Venetian at the end of the fifteenth and beginning of the sixteenth century, allows us to see how the creation of the Ghetto and other contemporary events looked through contemporary Venetian eyes.[13]

In Venice, the need for protective measures for Jews was advocated from the late fifteenth century. In 1475, Fra Bernardino da Feltre stirred up anti-Jewish passions on the mainland, including inflammatory sermons in Trent denouncing Jews for the practice of ritual murder, charges that led to the arrest, torture, and execution of leading Jews and the expulsion of the rest of the community. Bernardino also instigated the expulsion of Jews from Brescia and the Umbria towns of Perugia and Gubbio. At the same time, there were anti-Jewish riots in Florence and Forli and Ravenna's synagogue was burned down. Venice's government, as well as the Duke of Ferrara, acted to ban such anti-Jewish sermons and put Jews under their protection. Thus, already 40 years before the ghetto, the Venetian state intervened as a protector of Jews. This action alone suggests that, although there were onerous restrictions placed on Jews within the Ghetto and imposed regulating behavior outside the Ghetto, too, these restrictions should be understood as part of overall Venetian social policies and in light of what was allowed to Jews in places outside the city. If we view the Ghetto in the worst light, we fail to understand what must have been a real attraction of the place, and of Venice. Indeed, over time, more and more Jews moved to Venice, often preferring the increasingly crowded Ghettos to residential options in other places.

Organization of the city

Long-standing rivalries and hostilities set Venice at odds with competing Mediterranean trading states in the fifteenth century, stimulating an official posture of Venetian superiority and even invincibility. Following Constantinople's fall to the Turks in 1453, Venetian political and artistic rhetoric grew increasingly strident and triumphalist. While Venice celebrated its singularity, it also intensified its condescension to non-Venetians in expressions sometimes bordering on xenophobia. With a series of political and economic setbacks culminating in the War of the League of Cambrai, but including an outbreak of plague in 1497 and the Rialto fire of 1514, there was a tendency by the Venetian state to assert control over a wide range of social groups whose actions or beliefs were seen to run counter to norms. In the late fifteenth and early sixteenth centuries, the political and religious leadership of Venice sought new ways to control the many different social, economic, national, and religious groups within the city and even strove to tighten control over the behavior of the nobility – the very families that made up the state. These efforts met with mixed success, but provided valuable lessons in controlling Jews.

Venetian state actions included efforts to enclose and control many segments of the population, including nuns, prostitutes, criminals, arsenal workers, fisherman, Greeks, Albanians, Germans, Turks, and others. These policies of separation and enclosure, already inherent in Venice's form of distinct and often scattered islands, can be found in religious leaders' fulminations, in Venetian statutes, and by examining the city's physical form. Special buildings were erected. Gates and walls were common. Separation and enclosure were essential qualities of both Venetian urbanism and social policy.

In the pre modern era, separation was not thought to be inherently bad. Separation of hermits from society and of religious from secular institutions was as old as Christianity. Venice was renowned for its monasteries, and Francesco

Sansovino wrote in his 1581 guidebook that there were 59 monasteries, 31 friaries, and 28 nunneries.[14] While the friaries tended to be in populated districts, many monasteries and some nunneries were scattered on tiny islands of the lagoon, which were in turn celebrated for and closely identified with their inhabitants. One of these monasteries, San Girolamo, was located on an island so close to the Ghetto that without enclosure walls, one could almost jump from one enclave to the other. Many more monastic and charitable institutions were located near the Ghetto in the Canareggio *sestiere*.

This culture of separation was not unique to Venice. It was manifest in many areas of medieval life, and was frequently an important feature of architecture and urban design. Still, in late medieval Italy, there was a strong communal aspect to urban development which militated against too much spatial separation or specialization. In the communes of central and northern Italy, urban and social unity were tied together, and distinct neighborhoods or *rioni* often bordered a shared central space.[15] Elsewhere throughout the Mediterranean, however, from the Levant to Spain, the culture of separation and enclosure was much stronger. Separation and enclosure were expressions of hierarchical and often authoritarian regimes of Christian Byzantium (until the fifteenth century), the Muslim Middle East, and Reconquista Spain. Venice, more than other Italian cities, was linked to these.

Physical separation of many sorts was an accepted part of the Venetian urban experience. Both at home and abroad, the Venetian state burnished an image of *La Serenissima* as a timeless unity, an essentially unchanging and stable construction of a physical and social order that emerged from the lagoon waters. In fact, Venice was a city of parts. These parts were often distinctive and separate, literally isolated, since the city was made of a series of islands, which often developed and functioned alone. Both unity and hierarchical separation were articulated in the great processions in Saint Mark's Square.

In 1494, Canon Pietro Casola described Venice, from where he was embarking on a Holy Land pilgrimage: "I cannot give the dimensions of this city, for it appears to me not one city alone but several cities placed together."[16] This view is repeated by Francesco Sansovino in 1581. Even after most of the islands had been connected by bridges, he still considered Venice "not one but many separate cities, all conjoined together."[17] It is commonly stated that there were seventy islands which corresponded to the seventy city parishes. More than half of these probably were not connected to any others through the fifteenth century, but afterward, the pace of bridge building accelerated, knitting disparate neighborhoods of Venice more tightly together. Corresponding to this, many confraternities increasingly drew membership from across the city. Many specialized charitable institutions replaced more local parish-based initiatives. Scattered about the islands were enclosed religious communities in ever growing numbers. There was a rash of cloister building in the late fifteenth and sixteenth century, suggesting a new urge to define and enclose space. In the early 1500s, tensions ran high over the obligations and expectations of *clausura*, the confinement of religious orders.

The Ghetto and other contemporary urban developments

Where and what was the "Ghetto near San Girolamo?" In the fifteenth century, speculators and entrepreneurs were developing the outer islands of the *sestiere* Cannaregio, including older industrial sites, for housing. The Ghetto was developed by the merchant brothers Costantino and Bartolomeo de Brolo in the mid-fifteenth century. They apparently adapted a foundry site (of which we know little) into a housing complex with a cistern beneath a campo, three well heads, and a row of modest two-story houses around the perimeter. This is what we see in the Barberi view. By 1500, there were already several large religious institutions in Cannaregio, including the fifteenth-century Church of S. Maria dell'Orto with its impressive cloister. Also nearby were San Giobbe, founded as a hospice for the poor; S. Geralamo; Sant'Alvise; S. Maria dei Servi; and the Misericordia. The Ghetto was set within this constellation of religious foundations, many of which had been founded to deal with the *Serenissima's* dispossessed, or those least integrated into the larger social order.

Many of the principles applied to organize and discipline the Venetian poor had already been formulated by the mid-1520s in the permanent Magistrato all Sanità. Venice also implemented state policy against vagrants and the desperately ill.[18] A decree of the *Provveditori all Sanita* of 22 February 1521 (Venetian style) describes the suffering and care of those afflicted with "French pox" in a hospital at Spirito Santo, but decrees that "if from henceforth any men or women sore of the French pox or other ill are called upon by the agents of the aforesaid hospital to go and enter the place to be nursed and looked after, and yet refuse and will not go, even in response to a further summons from the constable or servants of our office, they shall be, and shall be known to be, banished from this our city."[19]

Cannaregio's northern edge and the western edge of *sestiere* Dorsoduro served in some ways as the city's frontier, with the largest amount of undeveloped "land" in reserve. This periphery district was used similarly to *sobborghi* in other Italian towns; land situated just inside or out of town walls. To this zone could be sent (or exiled) those necessary evils to the maintenance of a successful economic and social order. Interspersed with convents, monasteries, hostels, and hospitals were slaughterhouses, brickyards, boat yards, tanners, and dyers, etc.[20] In the Barberi view, we see many sites surrounded by wooden fences or brick walls.

Cannaregio was convenient for shipping and, especially, the transport of materials in small boats from the mainland. Nowhere else in Venice was there so much open land, except on the Giudecca (where it was first proposed to send the Jews, but the idea was rejected after Jews' complaints about the safety of the place). The exile of the Jews to their Ghetto, itself a former industrial site, was part of this process. Throughout the sixteenth century, Cannaregio continued to be filled.[21] Thus we see in the sixteenth century a process that will be repeated in subsequent ghettos in centuries to come: the least desirable or least empowered populations are provided marginal accommodations (often at inflated prices).

The Ghetto Nuovo is an island surrounded by canals, with buildings arranged around a trapezoidal courtyard with entrances by bridges at opposite corners.

Sometime after its establishment in 1516, three sides were filled with ever taller and increasingly crowded buildings, creating a castle-like enclosure around the campo which still served as the public cortile. Though notable in Cannaregio, such structures were not uncommon in older parts of the city.

To modern eyes, it seems as if the Jews were cut off from the rest of Venice. But canals, bridges, gates, walls, and the inner court were, in fact, ways in which all Venetians defined their urban space. Many examples of similar walls can be seen on the Barberi plan and the walled enclosure of San Geralamo, which occupies the island immediately adjacent to the Ghetto, and close by, one still sees walls at the old Servite convent. All these walls provide the same type of division: keeping people in and water out.

During the day, there was much coming and going from the Ghetto. As Bernard Cooperman suggests elsewhere in this volume, the Ghetto location and condition was more advantageous than punitive. Jews had secured a large segment of open space with easy access to the Rialto area for trading, but close to boats to the mainland. They were about as far from the government and ceremonial center of San Marco as they could be in the city, a considerable blessing in the Jewish community's daily life. Coming and going in the ghetto was monitored by a small number of appointed observers, but life in the Ghetto, like in many small parishes and enclosed private palaces and residential courts, was beyond the scrutiny of most Venetians. Jews were located far from major public and Christian processions, most of which began or ended at San Marco.[22]

Enclosed spaces of all types filled much of Venice. To make civil, market, religious, or agricultural space work, Venetians often walled it in. The wall – sometimes solid, occasionally porous – represents the atomization of Venice almost as much as does the canal (technically, the process of canal and wall building are often related). The Ghetto is one example of this; another is the Arsenal, a huge 60-acre expanse surrounded by two and a half miles of walls and moats.[23] An enormous number of enclosed spaces existed throughout the city, and the Barbari view-plan allows a review of these spaces in the very years when the separation of Jews in the Ghetto was discussed and enforced. Physical remnants of some of these spaces remain, including many traces of gates and other mechanisms of enclosure.

Enclosed courts were common in Venetian residential and religious architecture. These could be as small as light wells or as ample as small piazze. Some were primarily family courtyards, but often properties opening onto a single space were owned by different individuals or families. Some Venetian families amassed adjacent properties, but others spread throughout the city, renting space to others within their own building and on their court.

In the fifteenth and sixteenth centuries, charitable institutions built housing for the needy and other clients. These complexes included residential spaces with individual, numbered entrances on a common wide street (*calle*) or court (*corte*), usually entered through a gate and sometimes through a narrow passageway (*sottoportego*). Entering such secluded enclaves as the Corte de la Tana or the Corte Nova was an experience similar to entering the Ghetto.

Venetian Jews called the Ghetto's campo their "courtyard," common parlance for the open spaces within many Venetian housing blocks, both for the very wealthy and less affluent. For Jews, their "courtyard" also had to serve as a city in miniature, combining many traditional functions of the parish campo – the market or religious center – with ceremonial space for specifically Jewish needs. Thus, the paved courtyard of the campo with its cistern, wellheads, and scores of windows that looked out onto it was similar in form to many of the parish campi of Venice. In this sense, the Ghetto was the "Jewish parish." Even the limited access was similar to the norm, since many campi had only two or three points of entrance and egress. Ghetto shops lined the ground floors of buildings and some loggie projected from the building line. But there was no dominant building, like a church. Synagogues and community buildings were mixed within, mostly on upper floors.

From the mid-fifteenth century, Venice's government coped with the population rise by sanctioning large-scale housing developments. Like the de Brolo development at the Ghetto, these were typically arranged around courtyards. The previously mentioned Corte Nova alla Tana was developed behind the rope works of the Arsenal in *sestiere* Castello by the Procurators of San Marco as almshouses in 1429. According to Richard Goy, "The site was a substantial rectangular plot, one short side of which faced the Rio della Tana while the other end faced another canal, the Rio di Castello," now reclaimed as the Via Garibaldi. It was broad enough to allow the construction of two rows of cottages, "with a spacious courtyard in the centre." A high brick wall with crenellations and a single portal for access was built at each end. Such features were common in similar projects.[24] Nearby, a similar development, built at the end of the century by the Ospedale di Santi Pietro e Paolo, was known as the Corte dei Preti.[25] More such complexes are seen in the Barberi Plan.

These projects resemble the arrangement of Venice's Armenian and Albanian neighborhoods, which were each compressed into a few small *calle*, *sotoprotegi*, and *corte*, entered through once-gated narrow passages which could be locked from within. Even without gates, however, the narrow openings leading to the city's many closed courts limited all but the most local traffic.

One still-functioning complex is Corte San Marco, built in 1538–1542 (the Ghetto itself was expanded in 1541). An inconspicuous gate is the sole entrance to the central court, from where all houses are entered. Opening inward, it was presumably locked from the inside. The gate and *sottoportego* passage were off-center from the court itself, a deliberately skewed approach to open spaces common in private and public spaces throughout Venice, including the Ghetto.

At the Ghetto, gates were locked from the outside with guards at the bridges and gates. Like many other Venetian entryways, the Ghetto gates were unobtrusive (in contrast to the gates to the Roman Ghetto built much later in the century).[26] Boats circled the Ghetto to ensure there was no escape during lock-down hours, a "service" for which Jews had to pay. Despite the fact that Jews themselves had previously pleaded vulnerability to pillage if settled on the Giudecca, the notion of Ghetto policing as a form of protection for Jews was clearly a justification for separation rather than a response to Jewish fears. But other groups and classes in Venice also were similarly, if not identically, restricted and surveilled. German merchants were confined in their Fondaco, which was locked tight at night, with punishments for those who ventured out after curfew. And some types of workers, particularly those at the Arsenal, were guarded and also locked in.

Foreigners in Venice

Jews lived in Venice before the Ghetto was created, but were forbidden permanent settlement. A modest Jewish community existed on the mainland at Mestre, so the coming and going of Jews was not unusual. In 1515, when the Ghetto was being considered, however, Jews resided in the Venetian neighborhoods of San Boldo, Sant'Agustin, Santa Maria Mater Domini, San Cassian, and San Polo, all in the *sesitieri* of S. Polo and Santa Croce.[27] They were one of many groups who migrated to and from Venice according to economic needs. These included national, ethnic, and religious groups that came to Venice on an itinerant or permanent basis. In the fifteenth century, Greeks were the most prominent outsiders.

Greeks have a special place in Venice due to years of Venetian sovereignty over the Adriatic and the Peloponnese, and in Crete.[28] Cardinal Bessarion, Patriarch of Constantinople, presented his library to Venice and in a letter of 1468, wrote "Though nations from almost all over the earth flock in vast numbers to your city, the Greeks are most numerous of all: as they sail in from their own regions they make their first landfall in Venice, and have such a tie with you that when they put into your city they feel they are entering another Byzantium."[29]

Greeks and Christian groups including Albanians, Dalmatians, and Armenians migrated to Venice in sizable numbers in the centuries after the Fourth Crusade in 1204. Corfu fell to Venice in 1386. Even more Greeks arrived after the Ottoman conquest of Anatolia and the Balkans and the fall of Constantinople in 1453. Greeks were then allowed to celebrate the Eastern Orthodox rite at altars in several Venetian churches (as Catholics, Albanians, and Dalmatians had less difficulty fulfilling religious needs). San Biagio became the religious home to Greeks in 1470 and the community opened a scuola dedicated to San Nicolo in 1498. But for Venice's early sixteenth-century Patriarch and others, Greek rites were considered heretical. In 1504, the Patriarch spoke out against the Greeks at San Biago for practicing Orthodox rites, but they were defended by the Doge. Perhaps strengthening the Patriarch's position, the Greeks petitioned in 1511 for their own church, arguing that Jews had synagogues and Armenians had mosques.

In 1526, a new permanent site was allocated for Greeks in the parish of Sant'Antonin. Housing for expatriate residents, a hospital, the scuola, a "university", and a burial ground developed around the church. All this happened more or less simultaneously with the establishment of Venice's Jewish community in Cannaregio. The compact, well-defined Greek district lies between two parallel canals, the Rio dei Greci and the Rio della Pieta. Greeks were better integrated into Venetian society than Jews, and some prominent Greek families from Venice's overseas empire, such as the Cypriot Flangini, were admitted to the nobility. Still, the

Greek enclave functioned as a distinct national, religious, and linguistic quarter, much as did the Ghetto.[30]

The Albanians first concentrated at San Severo, and moved at the end of the fifteenth century to San Maurizio where they had a small scuola attached to the parish church.[31] Like the Albanians, Dalmatians had close ties with Venice, which controlled Dalmatian towns. Known in Venice as Schiavoni (Slavs), they were closely tied to the Greeks, and their enclave was close to the Greek center. The Dalmatian community, largely comprising sailors and traders, established a small scoula by 1461 on land belonging to the Knights Templar. In 1502, when a relic of Saint George was obtained, the community also commissioned a painting cycle from Carpaccio. The façade of the hall was built in 1551 by Giovanni de Zan. There was also a small affluent Armenian community, based since the thirteenth century at San Zulian, where Armenians owned houses and there was a hospice and small Armenian rite oratory. More Armenians arrived after the Ottoman conquest of 1453.

These "eastern" quarters developed as distinct cultural and physical neighborhoods with recognizable architectural features and tightly organized residential spaces. Though not required, strong traditions, group dynamics, particularities of language and dress, and economic ties created these ethnic-religious enclaves. Although these enclaves do not meet the definition of Ghetto as "compulsory, segregated, and enclosed," put forth by Benjamin Ravid, to the people of early sixteenth-century Venice, the distinction between Greek, Albanian, Armenian, and Jewish neighborhoods/ghettos might not have been too obvious. As the Jewish Ghetto grew in the sixteenth century, with new sections to accommodate different Jewish "national" groups, the distinction between ethnic-national neighborhoods and Ghetto would have blurred even more.

Fondaci

For Europeans, and especially Venetians, separation was clearly evident in the ways foreign merchants' communities were treated. It was normal, first in Byzantium and then in Muslim port cities, for foreign traders to be isolated in their neighborhoods and often in their own enclosures. This was practiced in Venice, too. The creation of the Ghetto drew on earlier Italian calls for the separation of Jews into controlled areas, Venetian experience of being separated in Muslim cities in enclosures known as *fondaqs* or *fondaci*, and Venetians' own construction of *fondaci* for visiting merchants in their midst. Though we cannot verify these claims, the Fondaco degli Arabi (warehouse or enclosure of the Arabs) is said to have been located near Santa Maria dell'Orto on the far western edge of Cannaregio, and some writers have accepted a Persian fondaco dating from the early thirteenth century.[32]

Several historians draw the connection between *fondaci* in the Arab world and the Venice Ghetto.[33] Ironically, in the Muslim world, Jews were much less likely than Christians to be confined to enclosed areas. An indigenous Jewish population could be found in most Muslim cities, and it was usual for large numbers of Jews to live close together. Still, such settlement was mostly voluntary and customary, based on self-interest rather than law. In Morocco, however, Jews were already living in walled *mellahs* in the fifteenth century. Merchants traveled frequently, too. Venetians were known for their extensive network of commercial, military, and diplomatic outposts throughout the Mediterranean and increasingly on the Terrafirma. Similarly, transience in Jewish communities, including Venice before 1516, was not uncommon.

The original separation of German merchants within Venice was strictly for economic reasons. Germans visiting Venice for other reasons – personal, religious, artistic, etc. – were not restricted. As early as 1314, legislation of the Great Council required that merchants who were to live in the Fondaca dei Tedeschi were to go directly to the Fondaca and deposit and register all their goods there. This was long before the Reformation, so that act was not aimed at non-Catholics, but was solely to force all goods brought in by Germans to be accounted for, for reasons of customs duties and taxation. Similar institutions probably existed elsewhere in the Venetian maritime empire. The fifteenth-century pilgrim Felix Faber stayed in the house of the Teutonic lord (*domus dominorun teutonicorum*) in the Greek port of Modon, and this may have been a German fondaco. Jews, however, such as Rabbi Meshulam of Volterra, were able to find lodging with fellow Jews in the *burgus* of Modon.[34]

Religious conflicts of the sixteenth century added another reason for separation – the isolation of corrupting religious ideas. An ordinance of the *Sette Savi* of the Rialto in "1528 reiterated that all Germans and other foreigners from the northern lands who were required to reside in the Fondaco dei Tedeschi do so, while those not required to live there were to stay in the other specific houses set apart for them under penalty of a fine of twenty-five ducats to be paid by both the foreigner and the Venetian host for each violation."[35] As the Protestant Reformation continued to make advances, the aim of this and similar legislation may have been more religious and moral than economic. The possibility of northern merchants importing these new ideas, and the printed materials that helped disseminate them, was a real concern for Venetian leaders. From a religious perspective, after Luther's Reformation, Germans were more dangerous than Jews.

The purpose and nature of these rules of separation were not unlike those imposed upon Jewish merchants. The Germans, however, were technically visitors to the city, so their settlement was really a hostel, not a neighborhood. Though the Fondaco, like the Ghetto, might be seen as restrictive, Venetians would not have seen it that way. The Fondaco dei Tedeschi had stood near the southern end of the Rialto Bridge since the fourteenth century, and when the mix of buildings burned down in January 1505, rebuilding became an immediate priority. Since German trade was economically important, it took only a week for the decision to rebuild the Fondaco "quickly and beautifully." The result was an impressively large building block left simple to speed up construction work.[36]

Other foreign groups, including those from throughout Italy, lived in S. Polo and areas near the Rialto. Some, like the Bergamaschi (from Bergamo), were the butt of jokes and became standard stereotyped characters in Venetian literature. The satirical poet Andrea Michieli (Strazzola) (d. 1510) called them a "stinking, cursed and iniquitous race."[37] The description might have been used by some against Jews, too.

Large numbers of pilgrims from across Italy and Northern Europe also came to Venice for embarkation to the Holy Land, since from about 1380 to 1530, Venice was the sole port for voyaging to the East. English, German, French, and Spanish pilgrims were plentiful every spring, before the departure of the Jaffa galleys. Pilgrims initially had free reign in the city, but mostly stayed with their national group. The Venetian government sought to control lodging to provide standards of accommodation, track revenue, and better monitor visitors. Friar Felix Fabri (1441–1502), who wrote of his month-long stay in Venice in 1483 before embarkation, stayed at St. George's, the public but almost exclusively German hostel. "The entire household spoke German ... which was a great comfort to us, for it is very distressing to live with people without being able to converse with them."[38] Pilgrims frequently lodged with members of the own "nation." In 1500, this was to be expected: like stayed with like. This notion is epitomized in Felix Fabri's story of a big, black dog at the inn that wagged his tail and showed how pleased he was with all Germans, but raged, "barking loudly, leap[ing] furiously ... upon Italians or Lombards, Gauls, Frenchmen, Slavonians, Greeks, or men of any other country except Germany."[39]

Prostitutes, nuns, and nobles

Venetian women comprised the one social group that was closest to the Jews in the type of separation and enclosure they experienced. Half the population faced a wide variety of social, political, religious, and territorial restrictions that often made the general situation of the city's Jews seem normal, if not benign. In recent years, there has been increasing research on the role of women in the Renaissance, and especially in Venice, regarding "the geography of gender" and "gendered space."[40] Three groups of women during the fifteenth and sixteenth centuries – nuns, noble women, and prostitutes – have received considerable scholarly attention. Looking at these women's regulated lives provides a wide and deep look into the city's culture of enclosure and separation. Most restrictions imposed on other groups, including the Jews, had already been applied to the lives of women. These include forced enclosure, special areas for habitation and display, limited freedom of movement, limited interaction with others, defined appearance and dress, and other regulations and restrictions.

It has been noted by Ravid and others that similarities in legislation concerning Jews are found in Venice's treatment of prostitutes – a necessary population in a port city, but one reviled by churchmen as much as they reviled Jews.[41] Because prostitution was ingrained socially and economically, restrictive measures, as with Jews, were aimed at control rather than eradication. But the association of Jews and prostitution was an old one, dating to early Christianity. Saint John Chrysostom (c. 347–407), in his disparagement of Judaism, likened the synagogue to a brothel. "Where a harlot has set herself up, that place to a brothel. But the synagogue is not only a brothel and a theater; it also is a den of robbers and a lodging for wild beasts …"[42]

Robert C. Davis has written that prostitutes occupied a special place – or perhaps one should say many places – in the cities of Renaissance Italy, and nowhere more so than in Venice. As early as 1358, the Venetian government attempted to confine prostitutes to particular locations, and (as with the Jews) to have them wear a distinctive article of yellow clothing. As they did with Jews, however, all levels of society engaged with prostitutes, whether the oft-mentioned common whores of the street or their higher class sisters, the courtesans.[43]

In 1423, the Council of Forty required *sestieri* heads to find places in the Rialto appropriate for prostitutes. Prostitutes had to stay in their alleys and were only allowed to go elsewhere in the city on Saturdays. That same year, a group of houses[44] known as the Castelletto, or "little castle," in the Rialto area was chosen as the site for prostitutes to live under government supervision. One is reminded of the Ghetto legislation, which specifically said the Ghetto was "like a castle." The Castelletto was apparently part hostel and part prison, likely similar to charitable hospices for orphans and the poor that operated with firm discipline and high expectations (sometimes forced) that beneficiaries remain home at most times, and certainly in the evening. In 1486, prostitutes were required to live in a place near the Rialto and such regulations continued well into the 1500s. Penalties included fines and whippings.

In 1423, a law was passed requiring prostitutes to live in Castelletto, but allowing them to ply their trade elsewhere during the day (between the *marangona* bell in the morning until the first ringing of the evening San Marco bell – when they were to return to Castelletto to be locked in by the ringing of the third bell). This, too, is echoed in the Ghetto legislation. Additional moves to restrict the prostitutes were made in 1460, 1486, and 1490.

The language of separation for Christian religious communities and Jews was often similar, especially so in regard to the *clausura*. In the early 1500s, the government initiated actions to keep both Jews and nuns from unnecessary contact with the larger population. For the ancient convent of S. Zaccaria, this meant pressuring the nuns into stricter *clausura*, much tighter than anything imagined or enacted for the Jews. San Zaccaria had developed as a cloistered space within a larger gated enclosure, its layout fixed by 1500. Like the future Ghetto, the S. Zaccaria complex was entered from three points: two on land and one from the water. All three entrances were protected by gates, one of which, probably the one entered during processions from S. Marco, was marked by a significant sculpture. One can still trace, in these gate's door jambs, how they could be shut and bolted.

As part of a general reform of convents in 1509, stricter laws were enacted against nuns who left the convent for any reason and those who assisted them. Wayward nuns would be consigned to the patriarch "who the Signoria prays and entreats to punish them so as to make them a most significant example to others." Anyone who took a nun into a home would be banished from Venice for five years. Boatmen who helped in escapes and those that rowed people around the convents would be flogged.

Enclosure for nuns, of whom many were noblewomen confined against their will, was much stricter than for Jews in the Ghetto. Within the San Zaccaria compound, however, was an even stricter enclosure, including two internal courtyards, and further separation within the convent spaces. Actual fighting over the nuns' freedom in their own church took place in 1514, when nuns threw stones at the Patriarch and his officials. Nonetheless, new grilles were installed within the church, further separating the nuns from what had been their traditional space. New rules forced the nuns into an even more confined part of the complex and the convent church.[45]

Part of the movement to reform convents was aimed at diluting the resistance of the older, affluent convents favored by the nobility, which were seen as morally lax, with the insertion of observant nuns, who would remake the culture. The Patriarch pushed for these reforms in the convents of San Zaccaria, Santa Anna, Santa Maria la Celestia, and Santa Maria delle Vergini (Verzene). At the latter, the Patriarch actually partitioned the space by building walls and closing doorways to allow new observant nuns of Santa Justina to enter and further enclose the nuns of the "Verzene." These latter nuns then tore down the wall rather than submit, but by November 1519, the Patriarch received approval for his actions from the Pope, over the objections of many noble relatives of the nuns. Thus, more dividing walls went up at Celestia, Santa Chiara, and Santa Anna, as well.

Conclusions

By the late sixteenth century, Venice was widely considered a wonder of the world. Its proponents extolled its many virtues, but they were not unaware that wealth and splendor required strong controls. Is it coincidental that Francesco Sansovino, describing Venice and its institutions in his *Venetia città nobilissima et singolare descritta in XIIII libri* of 1581, consecutively places his passages about three geographically and functionally distinct urban centers: the Fondaca dei Tedeschi, the Arsenal, and the Jewish Ghetto? Sansovino's descriptions suggest that he, too, recognized in the urban topography and the international economy of sixteenth-century Venice a culture of enclosure and control.

By law, guards were required to be posted at the gates of the Ghetto, and boat patrols circled the Ghetto to make sure there was no escape during lock-down hours. This was an imposition on Jews, and also a punishment. Any justification of this policy as "protection" is just an excuse. But in this context, it is still important to remember that other groups and classes in Venice were similarly, if not identically, restricted. The German merchants, too, were confined in the locked Fondaco dei Tedeshi and there were serious punishments for those who ventured outside after curfew.

Indeed, the memory of the construction of the Germans' new home was fresh in Venetian minds when the future of Jews in the city was debated. The importance of Jews to the economy was emphasized, though there was never any consideration of such a state-sponsored enclave to hold or house them. Still, the area to which they were assigned – the ghetto – wasn't entirely unlike the Fondaco dei Tedeschi. While not located on the Grand Canal or at the Rialto Bridge, neither was it very far. Nor was the Ghetto far from the city's business center. The Ghetto was not a hodgepodge of buildings or anything resembling what we would consider a slum. In fact, it was a housing development with abundant light and air and low buildings ringing a spacious, public, well-watered campo.

Efforts were regularly made to confine prostitutes to particular neighborhoods, and to buildings which could be locked and guarded. While the "Castellato" near the Rialto was established for this purpose as part hostel and part prison, we also still need to investigate the rules and regulations of many charitable hospices which most likely operated on similar principles, namely firm discipline and high expectations (perhaps forced) that beneficiaries remained home, inside, at most times, and certainly in the evening. Other groups, including the city's women and its large working-class population, were also subject to restrictions and controls.

In sheer numbers, the majority of Venetians experienced state controls on a daily basis, and a large number of these took the physical form of walls and gates, guards and patrols, and badges and special passes. Because no one class of Venetian (except perhaps nuns) faced as many restrictions as Jews, we must consider the Ghettoization of the Jews as exceptional. With hindsight, when we think how Jewish life would be further restricted in many places in subsequent centuries, and how the term "Ghetto" would be widely applied, we tend to recoil at the word and the institution of the Venetian Ghetto. Looking through the eyes of ghetto contemporaries, however, and placing the Jewish experience within its wider historical context, the Ghetto appears exceptional in its totality but hardly extraordinary. At that time, Venetian Christians and Jews would have viewed and accepted the decision of the Senate to allow Jews to reside in the Ghetto, under specific terms, as normal, acceptable, and perhaps even fair. The ghetto was a compromise. No one group got everything it wanted, but the Jews succeeded in escaping their earlier fate of expulsion and in arriving in Venice to stay.

Notes

1 This chapter continues a subject I first addressed in 2006 at a National Endowment for the Humanities (NEH) Seminar on "Shaping Civic Space in a Renaissance City: Venice, c. 1300–c. 1600. I thank Professors Gary Radke and Dennis Romano for their advice and support during that seminar and subsequent encouragement. An early version of this topic was presented as "The Creation of the Ghetto in the Context of Early Cinquecento Venice: A Culture of Enclosure, a Culture of Control," at the annual meeting of the Renaissance Society of America (Chicago, April 2008). I thank the Gladys Krieble Delmas Foundation for a travel grant that allowed me to continue research in 2009.

2 Ravid, B., "The Religious, Economic and Social Background and Context of the Establishment of the Ghetti of Venice," in G. Cozzi (ed.), *Gli ebrei e Venezia*. Milan, 1986, pp. 211–259.

3 To answer this, I draw on the important work of Prof. Ravid as well as of Robert Davis, Donatella Calabi, and Ennio Concina, and my own work on Venice's urban form and features.

4   Gruber, S. D., "Selective Inclusion: Integration and Isolation of Jews in Medieval Italy," in S. Bronner (ed.), *Framing Jewish Culture: Boundaries, Representations, and Exhibitions of Ethnic Difference, Jewish Cultural Studies*, Vol 4 (2013), pp. 97–124.

5   Jacoby, D., "Venice and the Venetian Jews in the Eastern Mediterranean," in G. Cozzi, (ed.), *Gli ebrei e Venezia*. Milan, 1986, p. 29.

6   Ibid., p. 29.

7   Ibid., p. 37.

8   Ravid, B., "Between the Myth of Venice and the Lachrymose Conception of Jewish History: The Case of the Jews of Venice," in Cooperman, B. and Garvin, B. (eds), *The Jews of Italy: Memory and Identity* (Bethesda, MD: Univ. Press of Maryland, 2000), p. 152.

9   Cited in Richards, J., *Sex, Dissidence and Damnation: Minority Groups in the Middle Ages* (London: Routledge, 1991), p. 108.

10   Ravid, op. cit. 1986, pp. 213–222.

11   Ravid, op. cit. 2000, p. 152.

12   Schulz, J., "Jacopo de' Barberi's View of Venice: Map Making, City Views, and Moralized Geography before the Year 1500," *Art Bulletin* 60:3, 425–74.

13   Labalme, P. H. and White, L. S. (eds.), *Venice Cita Excelentissima, Selections from the Renaissance Diaries of Marin Sanudo* (Baltimore: Johns Hopkins University Press, 2008).

14   Sansovino, F., *Venetia città nobilissima et singolare descritta in XIIII libri* (Venice: Giacomo Sansovino, 1581).

15   Gruber, S. D., "Ordering the Urban Environment: City Statutes and City Planning in Medieval Todi, Italy," in Warren Ginsberg (ed.), *Acta*, 15 (1988, published 1990), *Ideas of Order in the Middle Ages*, 121–35.

16   Pietro Casola, Canon, *Pietro Casola's Pilgrimage to Jerusalem in the Year 1494*, trans. M. Margaret Newitt, 125–26, cited in Wilson, B., *The World in Venice: Print, the City, and Early Modern Identity* (Toronto, Univ. of Toronto, Press, 2005), p. 24.

17   Sansovino, op. cit., cited in Brown, P. F., *Private Lives in Renaissance Venice: Art, Architecture, and the Family* (New Haven: Yale University Press, 2004), p. 189.

18   Pullan, B., *Rich and Poor in Renaissance Venice: The Social Institutions of a Catholic State, to 1620* (Cambridge, MA: Harvard University Press and Oxford: Blackwell), p. 238.

19   Chambers, D. and Pullan, B. (eds.), *Venice: A Documentary History, 1450–1630* (Oxford: Blackwell, 1992), pp. 308–9.

20   Wheeler, J., "Neighborhoods and Local Loyalties in Renaissance Venice," in A. Cowan (ed.), *Mediterranean Urban Culture 1400–1700* (Exeter: Univ. of Exeter Press, 2000), p. 38.

21   Braunstein, P., "Cannaregio, zona di transito?," in Calabi, D. and Lanaro, P. (eds), *La Città Italiana e I Luoghi degli Stranieri, XIV–XVIII Secolo* (Rome-Bari: Laterza, 1998), pp. 52–62.

22   Muir, E., *Civic Ritual in Renaissance Venice* (Princeton: Princeton University Press, 1981).

23   Davis, R. C., *Shipbuilders of the Venetian Arsenal: Workers and Workplace in the Preindustrial City* (Baltimore: Johns Hopkins University Press, 1991), p. 3.

24   Goy, R., *Building Renaissance Venice: Patrons, Architects and Builders c. 1430–1500* (New Haven and London: Yale University Press, 2006), pp. 47–8.

25   On this and similar projects built through the eighteenth century see Maretto, P., *La Casa Veneziana nella storia della città* (Venice: Marsilio Editori, 1986).

26   Gruber, S. D., "Mapping Jews: Cartography and Topography in Rome's Ghetto" in Verstegen, I. and Ceen, A. (eds.), *Giambattista Nolli and Rome: Mapping the City before and after the Pianta Grande* (Rome: Studium Urbis, 2014), p. 124.

27   Wheeler, op. cit., 31–42.

28   On the Greeks in Venice, see Tiepolo, M. F. and Tonetti, E. (eds), *I Greci a Venezia, Atti Convegno Internazionale di Studio, Venezia 5–7 novembre 1998*, Venice, Istituto Veneto di Scienze, Lettere ed Arte, 2002.

29   Quoted in Chambers and Pullan, op. cit. pp. 357–58. For full Latin text, see Mohler, *Kardinal Bessarion* 3:541–43. Also cited in Rosand, *Myths of Venice*, p. 104.

30 Tiepolo and Tonetti, 2002.
31 Goy, op. cit., p. 235.
32 Concina, E., *Fondaci: architettura, arte e mercatura tra Levante, Venezia e Alemagna* (Venice: Marsilio, 1997).
33 Howard, D., *Venice and the East* (New Haven and London: Yale University Press, 2000), pp. 8–9.
34 Gertwagen, R., "Venetian Modon and Its Port, 1358–1500" in A. Cowan (ed.), *Mediterranean Urban Culture 1400–1700* (Exeter: Univ. of Exeter Press, 2000), pp. 125–48, 248–54.
35 Ravid, op. cit. 1986, p. 230.
36 Goy, op. cit., pp. 45–7.
37 Wheeler, op. cit., p. 38.
38 Davis, R. C., "Pilgrim-Tourism in Late Medieval Venice," in Findlen, P., Fontaine, M. M., and Osheim, D. J. (eds), *Beyond Florence: The Contours of Medieval and Early Modern Italy* (Stanford, CA: Stanford Univ. Press, 2003), p. 129.
39 Davis, op. cit, p. 162.
40 Davis, R. C., "The Geography of Gender in the Renaissance," in Brown, J. C. and Davis, R. C. (eds.), *Gender and Society in Renaissance Italy* (London: Longman, 1998), pp. 19–38.
41 Ravid, op. cit., 1986, pp. 230–234.
42 Saint John Chrysostom, *Adversus Judaeos*, Homily I.
43 Labalme, P. H., "Sodomy and Venetian Justice in the Renaissance," *Legal History Review*, 52 (1984), pp. 217–54; and Labalme, P. H. and White, L. S., "How To (and How Not To) Get Married in Sixteenth-Century Venice: Selections From the Diaries of Marin Sanudo," *Renaissance Quarterly*, 52 (1999), pp. 43–72.
44 For a listing of laws regarding the confinement of prostitutes, see Ravid, B., op. cit., 1986, pp. 231–4.
45 LaBalme and White, op. cit., 2008, pp. 380–92.

PART II
Nazi ghettos

Photograph of Łodź ghetto showing the entrance and a sign forbidding non-Jews to enter the ghetto. © United States Holocaust Memorial Museum, courtesy of Antonii Marianowicz

5

"THERE WAS NO WORK, WE ONLY WORKED FOR THE GERMANS"

Ghettos and ghetto labor in German-occupied Soviet territories

Anika Walke

When an interviewer asked Maria Boiko (Maria Abramovna Akselrod) whether she had worked while she lived in the ghetto of Minsk during World War II, she exclaimed, with some exasperation: "There was no work, we only worked for the Germans!"[1] Many things may have prompted her strong reaction. Most likely, it is related to her perception of the German occupation as a period that stands in sharp contrast to a life free of coercion where categories such as "work" have meaning and where work determines a person's place in the world. The way we understand work is often associated with notions of freedom and unfreedom, its creative potential, and its contribution to producing the means of existence.[2] Boiko's statement evokes the specter of violence associated with labor during the Nazi regime: ghetto labor may have deferred the worker's violent death, but otherwise had no value for the worker's life and community.

The role of labor is central to analyses of the Nazi regime's use of coercion, specifically in labor and concentration camps. I suggest extending the focus on labor to a study of ghettos established in German-occupied territories during World War II. This lens reveals the distinct purpose of ghettos in various regions, and it adds depth to analyzing the practice of ghettoization as a central element and indicator of the Nazi genocide of thousands of Jews in Eastern Europe, specifically in Soviet territories. In particular, ghetto labor reflects the German goal of extermination, starting with the use of people's ability to work to define who lives and who dies, to using labor as a form of humiliation in preparation for mass murder. Boiko's statement, from such a perspective, signals that ghetto inmates recognized that activities usually considered productive had become part of a destructive agenda that removed individuals from the larger society in order to kill them.

Ghettos and the Nazi genocide in Eastern Europe

What is a ghetto? As this volume shows, definitions have changed over time, reflecting the different purposes and circumstances of a residential district for a particular population, circumscribed by material or immaterial boundaries. For an analysis of ghettos' role in German-occupied territories during the Nazi regime, Dan Michman's definition is useful: "Any concentration of Jews by compulsion in a clearly defined section of an existing settlement (city, town, or village) in areas controlled by Germany or its allies for more than one month."[3] In simpler terms, the editors of the *U.S. Holocaust Memorial Museum Encyclopedia of Camps and Ghettos, 1933–1945* defined a ghetto as "a place where the Germans concentrated the Jews," taking into account that, especially in the Soviet territories, this included not only specific town districts, but also individual streets or buildings. They further qualify this place as one that housed larger family units rather than individuals separated by gender and was located close to the original location of the Jewish community.[4] The closeness of ghettos to, or even location within, prewar home-towns is a crucial marker. Rather than being subjected to deportation to concentration or extermination camps, many Eastern European Jews were rounded up, held, and killed locally. Whereas the mass murder of Polish Jews was still largely centered in the extermination camps of Bełzec, Chełmno, Treblinka, or Sobibor, Soviet Jews more often than not were killed close to home, in the forests and fields where they had once worked or walked for relaxation.[5] What we know as the "Holocaust" in this region did not take place in the death factories. The genocide was implemented in face-to-face interactions, between Germans and their often local auxiliaries, and Jews who were shot at anti-tank ditches or hastily dug pits that turned into mass graves. Therefore, the mere existence of the ghettos and their particular use, both in Poland and the Soviet Union, are indicators of the distinct ways in which the German occupation regime implemented its goal to eradicate European Jewry.

The ghetto of the Nazi period was first explicitly proposed by Reinhard Heydrich, Chief of the Reich Main Security Office, i.e., the leader of the Gestapo, Criminal Police, and Security Service (SD), in September 1939. Then suggested as a facilitator of control and expulsion, the ghetto would later become central to preparing for mass murder, either by way of deportation to the aforementioned killing facilities—as in Poland, beginning in early 1942—or mass shootings and asphyxiations in gas vans just outside of town. The latter marked the beginning of the systematic extermination program and took place, first, in German-occupied Soviet territories in summer and fall 1941. For the purpose of this chapter, I focus on the ghettos in this region, and the way ghetto labor was used or not used. This perspective demonstrates why the Soviet territories ought to be considered as one of the central loci of the Nazi genocide of European Jewry, and which role ghettos played here as well as in the larger context. Alongside, I hope to identify questions for further research on the role of unfree labor for the experience and perception of regimes of violence.

What is different about Soviet ghettos? Looking for the use of labor in these ghettos shows that they were primarily a convenient, if not necessary, instrument to prepare for genocide.[6] Ghettos in occupied Poland underwent distinct stages and, often for years, fueled the illusion that to labor would save someone's life, before they turned into death traps. Ghettos in Soviet territories show a convergence of ghettoization and destruction.[7] Internal German debates about the use of ghettos such as the one in Łódź pitted "productionists" against "attritionists," i.e., officials attempting to yield profit from ghetto labor against those who hoped that disease and starvation would decimate the ghetto population.[8] In the Soviet territories, the conflict might best be defined as one between productionists and eliminationists. Here, we can observe ongoing disagreements between civilian and SS administrations as to whether Jews' labor skills should be used to help provide for military and civilian needs or whether Jews should be murdered as racial enemies, with the SS clearly favoring swift killings.[9] "Ghettos," or "Jewish districts"—the terms were used interchangeably by German authorities, but survivors usually use "ghetto" to describe their confinement—were a familiar and helpful way to separate Jews from others and keep them in place, available for further intervention such as labor duty or extermination, but also helped to regulate access to food supply.[10] Many ghettos in Soviet territories were not surrounded by a fence or a wall but remained so-called "open ghettos," marked by signs warning non-Jews not to enter and Jews not to leave, by threat of (usually) capital punishment. Lastly, the first Polish ghettos, established between 1939 and early 1941, were located near railroad junctions to enable mass transportations—originally, to places "further east." Ghettos in the Soviet area were often, though not exclusively, within walking or short driving distance from where Soviet and other Jews would be killed. The invasion and occupation of Soviet territories marked the point of no return toward, and a central site of, systematic extermination.

Ghetto labor in German-occupied Soviet territories: Belorussia

Belorussia and its capital Minsk serve as important case studies for understanding the impact of the German war of annihilation on Soviet society and the destruction of Jewish people and communities by the Nazi regime. Both the quick military advance as well as the beginning of the systematic killing of Jews reflect the strategies and goals of the war: to occupy Soviet territories so as to capture "living space" and appropriate resources, enslave parts of the population, and exterminate those who were considered sub-human, including Jews, Roma, mentally and physically disabled persons, or enemies such as Communists, Red Army officers, and Soviet professionals.

Maria Boiko was 18 years old when her husband was drafted into the Soviet Army at the beginning of "Operation Barbarossa," the German invasion of Soviet territories in June 1941. Like thousands of other Soviet citizens, she was surprised by the attack and tried to leave the city. The majority of the population, however, was caught behind the frontline.[11] Minsk was fully captured and occupied by German troops on 28 June 1941. Immediately, party functionaries, members of the so-called intelligentsia, i.e., professionals, and many Jews, were arrested. Up to 10,000 male civilian prisoners, among them many Jewish men, were killed in early July.[12] The German Field Commander Karl Schlegelhofer ordered the establishment of a "Jewish district" on 19 July 1941, long before the city became the headquarters of the German civilian administration of the Generalkommissariat Weißruthenien.[13] Over a period of five days, ending on 24 July, Maria Boiko, her newborn daughter, and about 50,000 other Jews had to leave their homes, cramming into a space of less than a square mile in size.[14] All Jews over the age of ten had to wear a Yellow Patch of ten centimeters in diameter on their chest and back.[15] The patch stigmatized Jews who would try to move about freely: many were thrown in jail or worse when they were discovered on their own and outside the ghetto or without the patch.[16]

The Minsk ghetto was located in the part of the city that was badly hit by air raids and combat during the invasion. Often housed in damaged properties, ten to 12 people shared rooms that used to house three. As one interviewee recalled, "we slept underneath and on the table."[17] Residents had to leave behind much of their moveable property such as furniture, bedding, pots, or food supplies when they moved into the ghetto, and they subsequently suffered from hunger, cold, and illnesses that went untreated. The territory of the ghetto was surrounded by barbed wire. As elsewhere, this flexible enclosure testified to the use of the ghettos in Belorussia as holding pens in preparation for genocide.[18] After killing actions in Minsk, the barbed wire fence and some guard posts were moved, adjusting the ghetto territory successively downward to match the ever-shrinking number of inhabitants.[19]

Ordered by the German authorities, the *Judenrat*, a Jewish leadership body, was established.[20] This committee was designed to help implement plans for exploitation and extermination by registering all ghetto inhabitants and organizing work details. Yet the Minsk Judenrat, especially the first under Ilya Mushkin, also used its position and authority to assist those in need. A ghetto hospital, an orphanage, and a soup kitchen supported inhabitants of the ghetto unable to work, mostly elderly people and children.[21] First and foremost, however, the Judenrat functioned as a labor office. All males older than 14 years and females over 16 were considered fit for work and were required to report to the Judenrat for work every day.[22] It was crucial to labor for the Germans, either in one of the workshops located within the ghetto or at sites in the Russian district such as the printing shop and the buildings and factories appropriated by the Generalkommissariat or the German military, in order to access regular, if meager, food rations. Boiko worked on a construction site, clearing the rubble at administrative buildings that had been severely damaged during the invasion. The "backbreaking work," as she described it, provided her with a daily, if minimal, food ration. Similarly, Mikhail Treister recalls that he received a bowl of watery soup and 150 grams (5.2 oz) of bread for the day when he worked as a cobbler.[23] Non-working ghetto inmates were to receive half of the workers' rations.[24]

Mass killings overshadowed the search for food, heating supplies, or medical supplies. Members of the Einsatzgruppe A, the Security Service (SD), German Police, Latvian and Ukrainian militias, and others killed ghetto inmates either directly in the ghetto or took them to execution sites on the outskirts of Minsk in Drozdy, Blagovshchina, Trostenets, or Tuchinka, where they shot them in trenches and ravines.[25] Other victims were herded into gas vans, the so-called *dushegubki* (soul killers), and asphyxiated while the vans were driven from the town to prepared mass graves.[26] Archival documentation and eyewitness testimony reveal a chronology of death for the Minsk ghetto, with estimates of the overall number of victims varying between 56,000 and 63,000.[27] Between July and September 1941, up to 7,000 Jews were murdered. During a pogrom on 7 November 1941, between 12,000 and 18,000 people were killed, largely in an attempt to vacate housing for Jews from Germany and other European countries who were deported to Minsk and held in the so-called "Sonderghetto," a restricted space within the ghetto.[28] On 2 March 1942, between 5,000 and 8,000 inmates of the ghetto were killed, many of them unemployed; others were children who had been rounded up in the ghetto orphanage. In the summer of 1942, the Nazi leadership again ordered the killing of so-called "non-productive" Jews, i.e., people who were not employed in producing goods essential for the war effort. Within three days, from 28 July to 1 August 1942, up to 25,000 Jews from the Minsk ghetto were murdered. Spring 1943 saw an increase in random killings of Jews that took place daily, both inside and outside the ghetto.[29] Fearing for their lives, Maria Boiko and hundreds of Jews fled the ghetto to join partisan detachments in the surrounding forests. Between 21 and 30 October 1943, the Jews remaining in the ghetto—approximately 2,000 in number—were murdered, marking the end of the Minsk ghetto.[30]

Maria Boiko's experience of German occupation, ghettoization, and eventual rescue by joining a group of guerilla fighters exemplifies the experience of Soviet Jews during the Nazi regime.[31] Though there was no consistent policy or pattern, within weeks German military or civilian authorities established ghettos nearly everywhere.[32] In smaller towns and villages, the ghettos often existed only for a few months, sometimes weeks or even days, serving merely the purpose to concentrate the local Jewish population in preparation for mass murder. Overall, there were more than 90 ghettos in the Generalkommissariat Weißruthenien, the western parts of the Belorussian Soviet Socialist Republic that were part of the Reichskommissariat Ostland, and about 101 ghettos in the eastern parts that remained under the direction of Army Group Center for the duration of the occupation.[33] The elderly, women, and children constituted the bulk of ghetto inmates in the summer and fall of 1941, as men of draft age had either been mobilized into the Soviet army or arrested or executed as potential resisters in the first days of the war.[34] The execution of professionals, party functionaries, and other male Jews in leadership positions in July and August 1941 was then quickly followed by mass killings in the Eastern parts of Belorussia that targeted women, men, children, and the elderly alike.

The immediate turn toward mass murder may be explained by the fact that, for the Germans, the territories that had been part of the Soviet Union before the annexations of 1940 were home to the personification of Judeo-Bolshevism and thus "required" immediate action.[35] Simultaneously, we ought to note the confluence of several factors that marked the shift from plans to expel Jews from Europe to kill them in October 1941: the borders around German-occupied Europe were sealed, making emigration impossible; German authorities decided to deport German Jews to the East; and gassing facilities in Bełzec and Chełmno were being built.[36] The mass killings in the summer and fall of 1941 and spring of 1942 that targeted the majority of Soviet Jews that had come under German rule were thus the first step in a series of murderous assaults against German, Polish, and other European Jews.

Despite the killings that decimated the Jewish population, the Minsk ghetto was an exception; located in the capital of the Generalkommissariat Weißruthenien and the seat of multiple administrative and production facilities, it existed for over two years and throughout two major killing waves in the second half of 1941 and 1942. Only the ghettos in Lida, Nowógrodek, and Głębokie existed till spring of 1943 and thus longer than most other ghettos in the area. The waves of ghettoization and mass murder highlight the connection and conflict between the Nazi regime's economic considerations and genocidal plans. The Minsk ghetto reflects this logic in some detail, showcasing the use of Jewish labor over a prolonged time. It also sharpens the view for the difference between eastern parts of Belorussia, where genocide took precedence over exploitation.

Before the invasion, Alfred Rosenberg, *Reichsminister für die besetzten Ostgebiete* (Reich Minister for the Occupied Eastern Territories), had proposed the removal of Jews in the Occupied Eastern Territories from public life, their confinement to ghettos, and that they be forced to work on construction sites and in agriculture.[37] Soon after the invasion and after an occupation regime had been established, these guidelines were implemented. Jews were called upon to clear roads from rubble or collect the dead bodies left behind during the fighting. In winter months, Jews had to clear the roads of snow.[38] Often, work assignments had little value other than to humiliate and degrade those subjected to it: for example, in Rogachev, a town east of Minsk, the inmates of the Jewish ghetto were forced to perform tasks that lacked clear purpose, such as moving piles of sand at the banks of the river from one place to another, and they received no food.[39] Overall, in Eastern Belorussia, i.e., the area that remained under military administration, already in 1941 only 75,000 of 150,000 Jews were working, half of the Jewish population.[40] The low number of workers partially results from the fact that most heavy industry had been evacuated or destroyed during the invasion and labor power needs were lower than elsewhere.[41] In the area further west, Jewish labor was more prominently used. In the Generalkommissariat Weißruthenien, 100,000 of 250,000 Jews worked in the summer of 1941; by the summer of 1942, 94,000 (i.e., 75%) of 125,000 Jews labored.[42] But even so, by the beginning of 1943, only 9,000 workers were left in the Minsk ghetto.[43]

Where Jewish labor was used, this took place in highly constrained and limited forms. In Minsk and a few other places such as Białystok, Nowógrodek, Slutsk, or Bobruisk, Jews were regularly marched out of the ghetto or toiled in workshops within the ghetto. As a rule, they produced or repaired military equipment, including uniforms, shoes, tanks, radios, watches, or ropes. Hundreds of Jews worked at the railroad yard in Minsk, where they unloaded equipment for front troops or loaded trains with property or foodstuffs that the Germans had confiscated and which were now transported to Germany. Others worked in army vehicle depots, or were sent to forests to log wood, dig peat in the swamps, or help collect the harvest. Many Jews worked for the civil administration under Generalkommissar Wilhelm Kube, heating or cleaning buildings and offices, preparing food, or doing the laundry for employees.

Typically, Jewish workers did not receive wages, but were given meager food rations.[44] In keeping with the ideological premise that only workers were eligible for food, the German administration in Slutsk and Słonim created special sections within the ghetto where workers were housed; this segregation enabled the quick selection of people to be killed.[45] In Minsk, workers received ID cards that helped them to evade selection for the murder round-ups. Elena Drapkina, who worked at the railroad yard, was able to produce one of these during a large selection in March 1942 and thus managed to escape execution. She points out that most specialists, workers with ID cards, were male, i.e., the chances to survive were deeply gendered, as war-related jobs were often reserved for men capable of hard physical labor.[46]

From the perspective of the occupation regime in the Soviet territories, Jewish labor was beneficial for the maintenance of administrations and to support the German war effort, but not much else, which distinguishes these ghettos from other forms of forced labor utilized by the Nazi regime. The labor performed by non-Jewish populations of occupied territories, after their deportation to Greater Germany or to labor camps, or by Jewish and non-Jewish concentration camp prisoners, played a significant role in the German war economy (and for postwar West Germany as well).[47] By 1944, forced laborers made up more than 25% of the German work force; the production of weaponry and other industrial goods, construction and repair of roads and bridges, mining coal and ore, but also farm work relied on forced labor.[48]

The labor performed by Jewish men and women in Eastern European ghettos largely fulfilled other functions. Ghetto labor contributed comparatively little to the overall output beyond supporting troops stationed locally or engaged in nearby front battles.[49] Labor in the ghettos in the Warthegau (Litzmannstadt [Łódź]) or the Generalgovernment (Lublin, Kraków), where Jews worked in workshops in the ghetto or were rented out to German firms, filled the coffers of German ghetto commanders, civil administrations, or the SS.[50] When Jews in the Soviet territories worked in the short period between ghettoization and mass murder, one might speak of a "windfall gain," but not a systematically planned use of labor force.[51] Work for the Germans in ghettos in the Soviet Union's Belorussian or Russian republics, which were administered by the German military, signified largely a form of discrimination and punishment and enabled a system of selection that condemned more and more ghetto inmates to death.[52] Here, ghetto labor was essential for the establishment of a system of discrimination and terror, in which racially defined groups were made to work and were exploited in a specific way.[53] The quality and purpose of this labor, in turn, confirmed the place of the workers within the Nazi racial hierarchy.

Jewish workers and forced labor

For Soviet Jews who were forced to work for the Germans, the work sites assumed an ambiguous role. They were sites of humiliation and segregation as much as sites of survival, because to work meant to eat and live. At the same time that food rations and meals enabled survival, they continuously marked the segregation of Jews from their non-Jewish coworkers. In other instances, work sites turned into sites of rescue or resistance, especially when they were located outside of the ghetto boundaries. Labor, here, made the ghetto boundaries porous and helped undermine the occupation regime.

Mikhail Treister vividly describes the difference between Jews and non-Jews, here identifiable in the difference between watery soup given to Jewish workers and Russian workers' lunch packages:

> While we were eating our so-called soup, the Russians brought bread, lard, pickles, and on the side chewed on these unimaginable delicacies. We tried not to look at each other. They were also paid for their work. And we went home differently: they went to their families, we—in a column, toward our netherworld where most of us had already lost their family.[54]

This tension symbolizes a precarious role of ghetto labor. The ghetto workers were caught in a contradiction: to work was the only way to prove that one was worth keeping alive, but to work also helped maintain the occupation regime and its violent policies. The different ways in which the Judenräte across Eastern Europe responded to German orders is indicative of this tension: some, most notably Mordechai Rumkowski in Litzmannstadt (Łódź), or Ephraim Barash in Białystok, egged on the ghetto inmates to work as hard as possible and obey orders, hoping to save the "productive" segments of the ghetto population.[55] Others, like Ilya Mushkin in Minsk, fulfilled German orders to a minimum and put much effort into supporting an underground movement that emerged quickly, notably driven by inmates of the ghetto.[56] Mushkin, certainly because of the mass killings in the summer of 1941, recognized that the Minsk ghetto was not supposed to last but functioned merely to control the Jews' movement and separate them from the remainder of the population.

Nevertheless, employment within and outside of the ghetto also helped undermine the starvation, isolation, and, ultimately, extermination pursued by the German regime. Take, for instance, Rita Kazhdan. Kazhdan, a 14-year-old teenager at the time, had lost both parents; her father was killed during one of the first raids in August 1941, her mother during a round-up of women and children in March 1942. Assisted by a former classmate, young Rita found employment in the tank factory (*Panzerwerk*) run by the German company Daimler Benz. Cleaning the repair shop and offices of German administrators, she received a piece of bread and a bowl of soup every day. Her friend Lidia Parfimchuk worked in the workshop kitchen and often put an extra portion of food into a container that Rita left near the kitchen. At the end of the workday, Rita picked up this container and took it home to her younger brother Grisha, who was too young and too weak to work himself. In the summer of 1942, after another major killing action in the ghetto, Rita asked her supervisor to employ Grisha, as she was afraid he would be caught during another raid while she was at work during the day. As a messenger boy, Grisha was able to "legally" leave the ghetto with Rita every day, and received his own bowl of soup.[57]

Rita Kazhdan regularly interacted with Russian POWs and Jewish men working in the boiler room of the tank factory. Soon enough, she was asked to collect bullets or other useful things when she was cleaning the upstairs offices.

> One of the guys made a container that had a double bottom, and I put the bullets, or carbide, in the lower part, covered it, and on top of it Lidia ladled soup or whatever food was available. I hid the bullets at home until I was able to pass them on to a young man, Iuzik, who took them to partisans; in return he had promised that he would make sure my brother and I would be able to join them.[58]

Ekaterina Tsirlina and Mikhail Treister, who both worked for the air force, albeit in different workshops, also used their work placement to support the underground. Ekaterina and her friend Tsilia Botvinnik smuggled a number of weapons out of the weapons workshop where they worked, and Mikhail retrieved leather or complete shoes to sell or pass on to underground members.[59]

Elena Drapkina benefitted from interactions with coworkers. As part of a column of 16 women, she would clean arriving trains, remove snow from the tracks, and receive a daily food ration. In addition, she said, "whatever people had left, we took it to work and exchanged it with Russian workers for flour, pearl barley—anything, really."[60] In 1942, two Russian workers offered to obtain a passport for Elena that would identify her as a Polish woman and enable her to leave the ghetto. Drapkina did not go immediately, because she was afraid that she would endanger her housemates or coworkers. Frequent controls and marks on people's coats that identified a person's residence and the number of housemates helped the ghetto command detect any unexplained absences. If an absence was discovered, all residents of the building were taken hostage and killed.[61] Elena thus waited for a suitable moment, which came after the cruel pogrom in July 1942, when the high death toll set all data and registration records in disarray. Drapkina left the ghetto, passing as a gentile woman, and found refuge in a farmer's household west of Minsk before joining a partisan unit.

Labor, designed as a form of exploitation, humiliation and as part of an extermination program, opened up spaces for resistance when workers undermined these functions of labor and appropriated it as a site of agency, acquiring resources including food and information, or planning escape and sabotage. These "alternative ways of knowing and using [...] space" conflicted with the ideals and demands of the occupation regime.[62] Such a "rival geography," in which the purpose of restricted spaces is redefined, is a central form of overcoming alienation and challenging authority and was an important way to reclaim dignity and a sense of self-determination.[63]

Nonetheless, ghetto labor was work for the occupation regime. Survivor narratives indicate that ghetto inmates saw their work as highly problematic.[64] Maria Boiko, quoted at the beginning of this chapter, exclaimed that "there was no work, we only worked for the Germans." At first glance, we may assume that she cannot identify as labor what was, in postwar Soviet society, considered to be treason: work during the occupation.[65] I believe that she poses a more complex question. Boiko argues that working for the Germans was not work, not an activity or an effort directed at the production or accomplishment of something. Did she, then, see it as the opposite? As a destructive, or meaningless activity? There are surely different answers, but it is worthwhile to consider labor in terms of the value attached to it: Is it work when I am forced to do things that I am physically barely able to survive, and which have no relation to my personal aspirations? Work may be productive in the sense that something is created or accomplished—shoes are produced, rubble is cleared, trains are moving—but it may not have meaning because it has no relevance for the worker's future or her place in the world. To work meant not to be killed immediately. This, of course, was immensely relevant at the time, though Boiko's statement suggests that the knowledge of the role of employment to defer one's death removed any other meaning from her activity.

Nina Romanova was fully aware of the role of work to place her in a racist hierarchy that, eventually, foresaw her death. Having narrowly escaped a mass execution in her hometown of Gusino, a small place near Smolensk, Romanova was eventually deported to a labor camp in Bodenbach (Bynov), Southern Bohemia. There, Nina had to toil in a workshop where zippers for German uniforms were produced. In an interview in 2001, Romanova said, "but after all that I had gone through, I did not want to work for them."[66] At least once, she managed to injure herself and thus escaped producing clothes for those who had killed most of her family. In a ghetto, such behavior was inconceivable, and it is likely that Romanova survived her defiance only because she disguised her Jewish identity and pretended to be a Russian. Regardless, her approach indicates an effort to refuse to work for the Germans. Working for them, she argues, she would have supported, or at least not challenged, the Germans' violence and rule over occupied Europe, but also over herself. Refusing to work offered her an opportunity to regain a sense of self and agency that was otherwise lost. Because of its nexus with race, ghetto labor was a form of oppression that continuously reinforced the marginalized status of Jewish workers and relied on their marginalized status. Nina

Romanova's self-injury is a protest against the use of labor as a tool to reproduce this marginalization.

The notion of being able to choose who to work for, and in which way, determines how individuals perceive their labor, and I suggest taking it as a starting point for further analyses of perceptions of work under force, including ghetto labor and forced labor more generally. They are structurally related, conjoined by the worker's lack of affirmation for their activity and the lack of a broader social function of the work.

Ruth Klüger, in her memoir *Still Alive*, for instance, describes and explains her feelings about work she had to perform in the concentration camp Groß-Rosen:

> We were assigned to do men's work: we cleared the forest, excavated, carried the trunks of trees, and laid railroad tracks. Obviously something was supposed to go up in Gross-Rosen, but I was not interested in what it might be. *It is the nature of slave labor that the worker either ignores or hates the purpose and end product of his work.* Karl Marx would have appreciated us and, I hope, turned in his grave if he could have seen us prove his thesis.[67]

Klüger's comparison to slave labor is notable, as it places her experience of alienation in a larger framework of unfree labor and thus opens up the possibility for further analyses. We can compare the workers' perception, for instance, not only to those of other workers at the same time or in different time periods, but also to other periods of their lives in which they may have toiled. In the case at hand, the role of Soviet prewar experiences for understanding labor during the Nazi regime presents itself as a useful starting point, notably because the Soviet Union is frequently presented as a system similarly reliant on violence and coercion. A major challenge to gauge the perceptions of Soviet Jewish ghetto laborers, whether they saw their work for the Nazi regime as a distinct form of violence, is a generational one: many survivors quoted here did not (or did only briefly) join the Soviet labor force prior to the German invasion, due to their age. At the same time, this generation was most likely to survive the Nazi genocide and forms the core of those who we can ask. Either way, even those who did not work but were students observed their parents' and other family members' participation in the Soviet economy, and will have noted various regulations of labor that determined Soviet citizens' lives.

Shortly after the Russian Revolution in 1917, employment was compulsory; the late 1920s increased pressure on the Soviet population as the fulfillment of the so-called Five Year Plans required extraordinary efforts.[68] By 1932, employment was closely related to limitations of freedom of movement as Soviet citizens received internal passports that made it impossible for them to move from one place to another of their own volition.[69] Furthermore, the Stalinist economy of the 1930s was in a permanent state of emergency and reflected the militarization of society, i.e., work was heavily disciplined: workbooks documented tardiness or early leave from work and were the basis for various forms of punishment. By 1940, workers and employees were prohibited from missing work or quitting their jobs on their own accord, offenses that were punishable by imprisonment or corrective labor.[70] Soviet citizens', Jews and non-Jews, ability to encounter labor as free and as a means to appropriate and produce the material means of existence was potentially marred by these experiences.[71]

Was work thus always considered to be an activity directed at the submission and restraint of the worker? Did it ever have the potential to bring human nature to blossom? The physical violence exerted by German authorities against ghetto laborers, and the function of employment to determine one's right to live, clearly distinguish ghetto labor in the German-occupied Soviet territories from prewar labor. Albeit restricted and restrictive, Soviet workers' labor was conceived as a contribution to Soviet society, as constitutive of communal life, a value of labor that the Nazi regime clearly denied to Jews toiling in the ghetto. Work, as a result, did not appear as "work," was consciously denied, or redefined to allow for other actions. The extent of these responses is yet to be uncovered, but the few examples given here suggest a clear awareness of the assault on humanity, norms, and culture that the Nazis committed in the ghettos.

Labor as violence

The nexus of labor and violence is productive for investigating ghettos in German-occupied Soviet Belorussia, specifically in Minsk, as distinct historical phenomena that are, nonetheless, reminiscent of other forms of segregation, exploitation, and violation, even and especially when they vary. Ghetto labor not only forced people to work but also stripped work of its meaning and larger social function. Rather than being creative, ghetto labor further segregated Jews from other populations and facilitated the destruction of Jewish life and community. In this way, the ghettos acquired meaning as the sites where the surplus population—not working, ill, half-dead—was produced. This role of ghettos of the Nazi period as the site of "factual propaganda" placed them within a larger history of ghettoization, where the ghetto is home to somehow backward, uncivilized, unworthy populations.[72] The endpoint of the segregation, mass murder, however, surely distinguishes these ghettos.

As Hannah Arendt pointed out in her analysis of the Nazi regime, the absolute breakdown of all moral norms is located in the fact that the concentration camps "offend … our common sense … by the complete senselessness of a world where punishment persecutes the innocent more than the criminal, where labor does not result and is not intended to result in products …"[73] Labor in the camps—and much of the ghetto labor described above—did not result in products, but was a means to humiliate, hurt, and kill people or, in the negative sense, separate those who live from those who die.

Ghetto labor in the German-occupied Soviet territories was a central element of a violent terror regime. The exploitation of ghetto labor here, similar to the larger ghettos of Poland, relied on the segregation of Jewish populations from their non-Jewish compatriots. The difference is that the ghettos in the Soviet region were often established at the same time that executions were prepared, sometimes even afterwards. The spatial concentration of Jews enabled the occupation regime to conduct killing actions during which the non-working population—children, the elderly, many women—were divided from workers and marched to execution sites. For those who survived this murder, ghetto labor had the potential to undermine the segregation from non-Jewish populations, when workers who were employed in workshops, factories, or railroad yards toiled alongside non-Jewish workers and received support or information. Nonetheless, the ghetto reached into these spaces as well: differences in payment, appearance, and mood between the ghetto Jews and those who lived outside the ghetto fence marked the difference.

Ghetto labor was instrumental in securing Nazi domination: as in Minsk, it supported the German administration and the war effort by providing supplies for fighting troops. Here, but especially where ghetto labor had no economic value and no productive outcome but was used to humiliate, it helped reinforce a racist hierarchy where Jews were considered sub-human and unworthy of living. In this vein, ghetto labor placed workers in an impossible position, asking them to support the regime that humiliated them. Ghettos in Nazi-occupied Europe established conditions under which people's productive activity was emptied of meaning for the worker; it was aimed at creating and sustaining a society to which the worker ultimately did not belong. Ghetto labor thus was a central element of, and enabled by, the segregation and separation of European Jews from society.

Studying the meaning of forced and specifically ghetto labor during the Nazi regime has political relevance, as two recent instances have revealed. First, in the late 1990s, German society broadly debated, and finally allocated, financial compensation for people who had been deported to Greater Germany or labor camps from their home countries where they were forced to toil for German enterprises, farms, private households, or welfare institutions.[74] Secondly, a discussion about the role and value of labor during the Nazi regime unfolded when, in 1997, Jewish survivors of Nazi ghettos claimed pensions based on the work they had performed during World War II.[75] Both of these debates triggered numerous scholarly projects that revealed the extent and impact of forced and ghetto labor under the Nazi regime. The perceptions of former workers, however, remain largely understudied; only projects foregrounding the narratives (oral histories) of former forced laborers provide some insight here.[76] Such a study is, of course, a difficult undertaking, but as Paul K. Eiss has pointed out, one that would greatly enrich our understanding of free and unfree labor.[77] In addition, understanding how the fundamental way in which humans acquire consciousness of themselves as individuals and as members of a community—through work—is impacted by particular policies, practices, and conditions will allow us to better gauge the impact of ghettos and other spaces of constriction.

Notes

1   Boiko, Maria. Interview 32128. Visual History Archive. USC Shoah Foundation Institute, 1997. Accessed 12 July 2010.

2   On the notion of labor in relation to freedom, see Karl Marx, "Economic and Philosophical Manuscripts of 1844: Estranged Labour," in Robert C. Tucker, ed., *The Marx-Engels Reader*, New York: Norton, 1978, pp. 66–125; Alfred Schmidt, *Der Begriff der Natur in der Lehre von Marx*, Frankfurt/Main: EVA, 1993.

3   Dan Michman, *The Emergence of Jewish Ghettos During the Holocaust*, New York: Cambridge University Press, 2011, p. 4.

4   Martin Dean, "Editor's Introduction," in Martin Dean, ed., *Encyclopedia of Camps and Ghettos, 1933–1945*, Vol. II: *Ghettos in German-Occupied Eastern Europe*, Bloomington: Indiana University Press, 2012, p. xliii.

5   Tim Cole, *Holocaust Landscapes*, London: Bloomsbury, 2016, p. 49.

6   Michman, *Emergence*, p. 120.

7   Browning, "Introduction," in Dean, ed., *Encyclopedia*, p. xxxvii.

8   Ibid., p. xxvii.

9   Christian Gerlach, *Kalkulierte Morde: Die deutsche Wirtschafts- und Vernichtungspolitik in Weißrussland 1941–1944*, Hamburg: Hamburger Edition 1999, ch. 7.2–7.4; Christoph Dieckmann, *Deutsche Besatzungspolitik in Litauen, Vol. 1–2*, Göttingen: Wallstein Verlag, 2011, pp. 793–802, 1047–1194.

10   Martin Dean, "Eastern Belorussian Region," in Dean, ed., *Encyclopedia*, p. 1641; Michman, *Emergence*, p. 120.

11   On the failed evacuation plans and attempts, see Hersh Smolar, *The Minsk Ghetto: Soviet Jewish Partisans against the Nazis*, New York: Holocaust Library, 1989, p. 17; Inna Gerasimova, "Evrei v Partizanskom Dvizhenii Belorussii, 1941–1944: Obshchaia Kharakteristika," in Iakov Basin, ed., *Uroki Kholokosta: Istoria i sovremennost'*, Minsk: Kovcheg, 2009, p. 138; Rebecca Manley, *To the Tashkent Station: Evacuation and Survival in the Soviet Union at War*, Ithaca: Cornell University Press, 2009, p. 48.

12   V. I. Adamushko et al., eds., *Svidetel'stvuiut palachi: Unichtozhenie evreev na okkupirovannoi territorii Belarusi v 1941–1944gg.*, Minsk: NARB, 2011, p. 171.

13   Yitzhak Arad, *The Holocaust in the Soviet Union*, Lincoln: University of Nebraska Press, 2009, p. 152. See also Raisa Chernoglazova, ed., *Judenfrei! Svobodno ot evreev! Istoriia Minskogo getto v dokumentakh*, Minsk: Asobny Dakh, 1999, pp. 31–32, for the full text of the order.

14   Estimations of the actual number of Jews who entered the ghetto in the summer of 1941 range from 30,000 to 100,000; recent calculations show that between 45,000 and 55,000 Soviet Jews were trapped in occupied Minsk; see Petra Rentrop, *Tatorte der Endlösung: Das Ghetto Minsk und die Vernichtungsstätte von Maly Trostinez*, Berlin: Metropol Verlag, 2011, p. 114; D. Romanovskii, "Minsk," in Il'ia Al'tman, ed., *Kholokost na Territorii SSSR: Entsiklopedia*, Moskva: ROSSPEN, 2009, p. 591; Anne Speckhard, "Minsk," in Dean, ed., *Encyclopedia*, p. 1234.

15   Romanovskii, "Minsk," p. 591; "The Minsk Ghetto," in Ilya Ehrenburg and Vasily Grossman, *The Complete Black Book of Russian Jewry*, transl. and ed. by David Patterson, New Brunswick, USA/London, UK: Transaction Publishers, 2002, p. 114.

16   Oral Testimony of Lisa Gordon, Yad Vashem Archives, YV 4047, p. 5. See also *Daily Journal of Police Battalion 322*, 30 Sep. 1941, Natsional'nyi Arkhiv Respubliki Belarus' (NARB) f. 4683, op. 3, d. 936, l. 43–45, published in Chernoglazova, ed., *Judenfrei!*, p. 163, for a report on the murder of 64 Jewish women who were caught without the patch.

17   Elena Drapkina, interviewed by author, St. Petersburg, April 2001.

18   Wendy Lower, "Facilitating Genocide: Nazi Ghettoization Practices in Occupied Ukraine, 1941–1942," in Eric J. Sterling, ed., *Life in the Ghettos during the Holocaust*, Syracuse: Syracuse University Press, 2005, p. 12.

19   For more on ghettoization practices in German-occupied Belorussia, see Al'bert Kaganovich, "Voprosy i zadachi issledovania mest prinuditel'nogo soderzhania evreev na territorii Belarusi v 1941–1944gg.," in Ia. Z. Basin, ed., *Aktual'nye voprosy izuchenia kholokosta na territorii Belarusi v gody nemetsko-fashistskoi okkupatsii: Sbornik nauchnykh rabot* (Minsk: Kovcheg, 2005), electronic document, <http://www.homoliber.org/ru/kg/

kg020108.html>, accessed March 8, 2012; Martin Dean, "Life and Death in the 'Gray Zone' of Jewish Ghettos in Nazi-Occupied Europe: The Unknown, the Ambiguous, and the Disappeared," in Jonathan Petropoulous and John K. Roth, eds., *Gray Zones: Ambiguity and Compromise in the Holocaust and Its Aftermath*, New York: Berghahn Books, 2005, pp. 205–221.

20 Order No. 31 of the Security Police and Security Service on the Formation of a Judenrat, NARB, f. 4683, op. 3, d. 943, ll. 88–89, published in Chernoglazova, *Judenfrei!*, p. 33. See also Romanovskii, "Minsk," p. 591.

21 Smolar, *The Minsk Ghetto*, pp. 18, 53.

22 Rentrop, *Tatorte*, p. 127.

23 Mikhail Treister, Interview 2324, VHF/USC Shoah Foundation Institute; Mikhail Treister, interviewed by author and Eva Determann, Minsk, March 2003; Mikhail Treister, "Probleski pamiati," in Z. Tsukerman, ed., *Katastrofa: Poslednie svideteli*, Moscow: Dom Evreiskoi Knigi, 2008, p. 303.

24 Romanovskii, "Minsk," p. 593.

25 Romanovskii, "Minsk," pp. 594, 596; Rentrop, *Tatorte*, pp. 139–140.

26 A German prisoner of war confirmed in interrogations in 1945/1946 that such vehicles were used between fall 1941 and fall 1943; "Iz Protokola doprosov Karla Bukhnera ob unichtozhenii evreev v g. Minske, 26.4.1945–6.2.1946," in V. I. Adamushko et al., eds., *Svidetel'stvuiut palachi*, pp. 83–84.

27 Marat Botvinnik, *Pamiatniki genotsida evreev Belarusi*, Minsk: Belaruskaia Navuka, 2000, pp. 13–21; V. I. Adamushko et al., eds., *Svidetel'stvuiut palachi*, pp. 171–172.

28 Rentrop, *Tatorte*, pp. 159–184 offers a detailed account of non-Soviet Jews' situation in Minsk.

29 "The Minsk Ghetto," in Ehrenburg/Grossman, *Black Book*, pp. 132–138; Smolar, *The Minsk Ghetto*, pp. 139; Botvinnik, *Pamiatniki*, p. 19.

30 Botvinnik, *Pamiatniki*, p. 20; V. I. Adamushko et al., eds., *Svidetel'stvuiut palachi*, p. 171; Romanovskii, "Minsk," p. 597.

31 For a more detailed account and analysis of this trajectory, please see my book: Anika Walke, *Pioneers and Partisans: An Oral History of Nazi Genocide in Belorussia*, New York: Oxford University Press, 2015.

32 Browning, "Introduction," xxxii; Michman, *Emergence*, pp. 107, 114.

33 Martin Dean, "Weissruthenien Region (Generalkommissariat Weissruthenien)," in Dean, ed., *Encyclopedia*, p. 1160, and Dean, "Eastern Belorussia Region," p. 1640.

34 Christoph Dieckman and Babette Quinkert, "Einleitung," in Christoph Dieckman and Babette Quinkert, eds., *Im Ghetto, 1939–1945: Neue Forschungen zu Alltag und Umfeld*, Göttingen: Wallstein, 2009, p. 25.

35 Gerlach, *Kalkulierte Morde*, p. 606.

36 Christopher Browning, *Nazi Policy, Jewish Workers, German Killers*, New York: Cambridge University Press, 2000, p. 39.

37 Martin Dean, "Generalkommissariat Weissruthenien and the Military Occupied Territories of Eastern Belorussia and Russia," in Jürgen Hensel and Stephan Lehnstaedt, eds., *Arbeit in den nationalsozialistischen Ghettos*, Osnabrück: Fibre Verlag, 2013, p. 259.

38 Ibid., p. 263–264; see also Elena Drapkina, interviewed by author, St. Petersburg, April 2001; Frida Ped'ko, interviewed by author, St. Petersburg, May 2005.

39 A. Zamoiskii, "Rogachev," in Al'tman, ed., *Kholokost*, pp. 861–862; Smilovitsky, "Rogachev," in Dean, ed., *Encyclopedia*, p. 1723.

40 Dean, "Generalkommissariat Weissruthenien," p. 263.

41 Gerlach, *Kalkulierte Morde*, p. 606; Dean, "Eastern Belorussian Region," p. 1641.

42 Dean, "Generalkommissariat Weissruthenien," p. 263.

43 Bernhard Chiari, *Alltag hinter der Front: Besatzung, Kollaboration und Widerstand in Weißrussland, 1941–1944*, Düsseldorf: Droste, 1998, p. 240.

44 Gerlach, *Kalkulierte Morde*, p. 661; Dean, "Generalkommissariat Weissruthenien," p. 261.

45 Dean, Generalkommissariat Weissruthenien," p. 261.

46 Elena Drapkina, interviewed by author, St. Petersburg, April 2001.

47 Karl Heinz Roth, "Unfree Labor in the Area under German Hegemony, 1930–1945: Some Historical and Methodological Questions," in Tom Brass and Marcel van der Linden, eds., *Free and Unfree Labor: The Debate Continues*, Bern: Peter Lang, 1997, p. 141; Herbert Schui, "Zwangsarbeit und Wirtschaftswunder," *Blätter für deutsche und internationale Politik* 2, 2000, pp. 199–203.

48 Ulrich Herbert, *Arbeit, Volkstum, Weltanschauung. Über Fremde und Deutsche im 20. Jahrhundert*, Frankfurt/M.: Fischer, 1995, p. 121. For the (still most) comprehensive account of forced labor under the Nazi regime, see Ulrich Herbert, *Fremdarbeiter: Politik und Praxis des "Ausländereinsatzes" in der Kriegswirtschaft des Dritten Reiches*, Stuttgart: Dietz, 1999. On trajectories of forced labor during the Nazi regime, see Roth, "Unfree Labor," pp. 127–144.

49 See Dieckmann, *Deutsche Besatzungspolitik*, 1530–1531; Ingo Loose, "Die Bedeutung der Ghettoarbeit für die nationalsozialistische Kriegswirtschaft," in Hensel/and Lehnstaedt, eds., *Arbeit*, p. 88.

50 Andrea Löw, "Warthegau. Und diese Stadt wird leben, weil sie so leidenschaftlich leben will," in Hensel and Lehnstaedt, eds., *Arbeit*, pp. 113–138; Stephan Lehnstaedt, "Generalgouvernement. Organisierung und Formen von Beschäftigung der jüdischen Bevölkerung (1939–1943)," in Hensel and Lehnstaedt, eds., *Arbeit*, pp. 159–180; Katrin Reichelt, "Generalkommissariat Lettland. Ghettoisierung und jüdische Zwangsarbeit 1941–1943," in Hensel and Lehnstaedt, eds., *Arbeit*, pp. 233–256.

51 Frank Golczewski, "Reichskommissariat Ukraine und Ostukraine. Ghettoarbeit während des Massenmords," in Hensel and Lehnstaedt, eds., *Arbeit*, p. 296.

52 Dean, "Generalkommisssariat Weissruthenien," p. 272.

53 I borrow here from Lisa Lowe's analysis that challenges Marx's concept of abstract labor by highlighting the role of racial difference for the functioning of capitalism and, conversely, the role of labor market segmentation for the social, political, and legal status of particular workers; see Lisa Lowe, *Immigrant Acts: On Asian American Cultural Politics*, Durham: Duke University Press, 1996, pp. 27–28. See also Karl Marx, "Chapter on Capital," in *Grundrisse*, transl. by Martin Nicolaus, New York: Penguin, 1973, p. 296.

54 Treister, "Probleski Pamiati," p. 310.

55 See Sara Bender, *The Jews of Bialystok During World War II and the Holocaust*, Worchester: Brandeis University Press, 2008.

56 Romanovskii, "Minsk," p. 591.

57 Rita Kazhdan, interviewed by author, St. Petersburg, April 2001.

58 Rita Kazhdan, interviewed by author, St. Petersburg, May 2005.

59 Mikhail Treister, Interview 2324, Visual History Archive, USC Shoah Foundation Institute, 1995. 25 June 2010; Mikhail Treister, interviewed by author and Eva Determann, Minsk, March 19, 2003; Ekaterina Tsirlina, interviewed by author, Minsk, October 13, 2002; Ekaterina Tsirlina, Interview 28012, Visual History Archive, USC Shoah Foundation Institute, 1997. Accessed 13 July 2010.

60 Elena Drapkina, interviewed by author, St. Petersburg, April 2001.

61 Smolar, *The Minsk Ghetto*, p. 87.

62 Stephanie M.H. Camp, *Closer to Freedom: Enslaved Women and Everyday Resistance in the Plantation South*, Chapel Hill: University of North Carolina Press, 2004, p. 7.

63 Ibid.

64 Of course, in working with personal accounts we face a complex web of ways to make sense of past historical experience that includes multiple layers of social and political discourses on the past. For the sake of space, I refer the reader to Anika Walke, "Memories of an Unfulfilled Promise: Internationalism and Patriotism in Post-Soviet Oral Histories of Jewish Survivors of the Nazi genocide," *Oral History Review* vol. 40, no. 2, 2013, pp. 271–298; Anika Walke, "Pamiat', Gender, i Molchanie: Ustnaia Istoria v (Post-) Sovetskoi Rossii i Prizrachnaia Gran' mezhdu Privatnym i Publichnym," *Laboratorium: Zhurnal Sotsialnykh Issledovanii*, 1, 2011, pp. 72–95.

65 Tanja Penter, "Zwangsarbeit: Arbeit für den Feind. Der Donbass unter deutscher Okkupation (1941–1943)," *Geschichte und Gesellschaft*, vol. 31, no. 1, 2005, 70; Laurie R.

Cohen, *Smolensk Under the Nazis: Everyday Life in Occupied Russia*, Rochester: University of Rochester Press, 2013, p. 78.

66 Nina Romanova-Farber, interviewed by author, St. Petersburg, April 2001.

67 Ruth Kluger, *Still Alive: A Holocaust Girlhood Remembered*, New York: The Feminist Press, 2003, p. 119 (my emphasis).

68 Penter, "Zwangsarbeit," p. 97; Marcel van der Linden, "Forced Labour and Non-Capitalist Industrialization: The Case of Stalinism," in Brass and van der Linden, eds., *Free and Unfree Labour*, p. 354.

69 Wendy Goldman, "The Internal Soviet Passport: Workers and Free Movement," in Marsha Siefert, ed., *Extending the Borders of Russian History*, Budapest: CEU Press, 2003, pp. 315–331.

70 Van der Linden, "Forced Labour," p. 354. See also Dieter Neutatz, *Die Moskauer Metro. Von den ersten Plänen bis zur Großbaustelle des Stalinismus*, 1897–1935, Köln: Böhlau, 2001, esp. p. 13.

71 Penter, "Zwangsarbeit," p. 97.

72 I borrow the term "factual propaganda" from Hannah Arendt's analysis of the emergence and production of the stateless Jew in interwar Europe who would be rejected not only by the Nazis, but by the whole world; Hannah Arendt, *The Origins of Totalitarianism*, New York: Harcourt, 1976 [1948], p. 269.

73 Hannah Arendt, "Social Science Techniques and the Study of Concentration Camps," in *Essays in Understanding, 1930–1954* by Hannah Arendt, ed. by Jerome Kohn, New York: Harcourt, 1994, p. 241.

74 On the debate, see Dieter Schröder and Rolf Surmann, "Entschädigung im Jahrhunderttakt," *Blätter für deutsche und internationale Politik* 3, 1999, 292–295; Klaus Barwig and Günter Saathoff, eds., *Entschädigung für NS-Zwangsarbeit: Rechtliche, historische und politische Aspekte*, Baden-Baden: Nomos, 1998.

75 For a broad discussion of ghetto labor and pensions, see Jürgen Zarusky, ed., *Ghettorenten. Entschädigungspolitik, Rechtsprechung und historische Forschung*, München: Oldenbourg, 2010; Hensel and Lehnstaedt, eds., *Arbeit*.

76 Alexander von Plato, Almut Leh, and Christoph Thonfeld, eds., *Hitler's Slaves: Life Stories of Forced Labourers in Nazi-Occupied Europe*, New York: Berghahn Books, 2010.

77 Paul Eiss, review of *Free and Unfree Labour: The Debate Continues*, ed. Tom Brass and Marcel van der Linden, New York: Peter Lang, 1997, in *Journal of Social History* vol. 34, no. 1, 2000, p. 220.

6

HUNGER IN THE GHETTOS

Helene J. Sinnreich

Imagine, if you will, an impoverished people living in a defined geographical area with limited places to purchase food. The food available is more expensive, limited in quantity, and of lower quality than the food available outside the area or ghetto. For the people in this area or ghetto, food costs more inside the ghetto than outside the ghetto. I am writing about Jews living in ghettos in Nazi-occupied Europe during World War II. However, there are clear parallels to contemporary ghettos where inhabitants may live in a state of food insecurity and food deserts – places where there is not abundant fresh food available. While the experiences of the Jews in the Nazi ghettos were ultimately vastly different from those in contemporary ghettos, there are pieces to the contemporary and past experience that are potent fodder for comparison. For example, the two share households living in a state of food insecurity, where illness or any other setback could create a food crisis; techniques to "stretch food" and make it last until the next time it could be purchased; and social and family relations impacted by hunger.

Hunger and starvation in the modern era should not exist. Nobel Prize-winning economist Amartya Sen's entitlement theory explains that lack of food is not necessarily the result of insufficient food, but rather an individual's ability to obtain that food through one's endowment bundle (that which one can use to purchase food – money, goods, or labor). However, food insecurity is not only about the value of specific objects, the exchange rate of currencies, or the value of particular types of labor. One's endowment bundle's value can be impacted by "race." Nazi racial theory denied Jews their humanity, and ultimately, their right to live. Their ideology labeled Jews as "worthless eaters," which enabled the Nazis to withhold from them access to food.

This article outlines the experiences of Jews in the ghettos whose lack of food was an overwhelming daily concern, consuming all aspects of existence. Thoughts, actions, and even dreams were devoted to food and its acquisition. Hunger affected social, and particularly family, relations as starving people sought to feed themselves, at the expense of larger society or even loved ones. Others deprived themselves by giving up their meager food rations for the benefit of loved ones. The dire nature of hunger in the ghetto led residents to seek out a whole new range of foods and to invent new ways of cooking. For those with access to food and the mechanisms of its distribution, food became a means of control. The hunger of the ghetto population compelled ghetto inmates to engage in forced labor for the Nazis, to hand over their valuables, or most dangerously, the most significant effect of starvation on ghetto inhabitants was death. Those who did not succumb to hunger diseases found themselves compelled to board the deportation trains to the extermination camps.

Historians examining ghettos have often looked at the Nazi oversight of ghettos and Jewish leadership in ghettos with the aim of determining its purpose within Nazi policy and extermination plans. However, uncovering the functions of the ghetto within early Nazi policy remains elusive, as ghettos were created in different times, places, and forms for a variety of purposes. No matter the original intent of the creation of a ghetto – whether ghettoization served as an experiment in the destruction of Jews or was just a by-product of ghetto conditions – by 1942, Nazi policy ultimately condemned all ghettoized Jews to death. What ghettoization did accomplish was to strip most Jews of their valuables, engage them in forced labor, and/or decimate them through ghetto conditions. Additionally, this focus on leadership does little to examine the experiences of the ordinary ghetto dweller from their own perspective. Often the ghetto leadership, through its elite status, was able to avoid hunger and starvation in the ghettos. The widespread experience of hunger by those in the ghetto is primarily revealed through analysis of the writings and other documents created by those without leadership positions and provides a window onto the experiences of the ordinary ghetto dweller – a type of history from below.

In the large-scale closed ghettos such as Warsaw and Łódź, the German authorities had more control to limit the amount of foodstuff entering the ghetto in order to extract valuables and labor from ghetto inhabitants. These were ghettos where hunger and starvation were most widespread. Food allotments for those in the ghetto were below subsistence levels: if food arrived in an edible condition in the ghetto and was distributed perfectly equally, it came to approximately 800 calories per day in Warsaw and from 1,000–1,200 calories per day in Łódź.[1] This amount was grossly inadequate, as a healthy person doing no labor needs 1,680 calories per day while a person doing light work should receive 2,400 calories per day, and someone doing hard labor in a cold climate should receive from 4,000 to 5,000 calories per day.[2] In 1938, the average daily caloric intake for individuals in Germany was 3,040 calories.[3] During World War II, the Germans "considered 1,800 calories a day an absolute minimum."[4] Even the meager amount of food allotted by the Germans to the Jews of the ghetto never reached its dwellers due to embezzlement all along the food supply lines. For example, David Kahane reports in his diary that corruption in the food supply department in Lvov was so bad that, aside from 70 grams of bread per day, there was not much else available for the Jews.[5] Moreover, the food that did reach the ghetto was often of inedible quality. These factors combined to the effect that the food dispensary often ran out of products before the ghetto population was able to obtain them. The failure of food to arrive became a regular feature of life in the ghetto.

Faced with limited foodstuff entering the ghetto, the Jews created various licit and illicit means of internal food distribution, acquisition, and use, at both the communal and individual level. Licit distribution methods varied between ghettos and often changed over time. In many ghettos, private shops and restaurants were initially the distribution points of foodstuffs purchased by the Jewish ghetto administration, who was able to purchase limited amounts of food from the German authorities at prices which were significantly higher than those outside the ghetto. A problem that quickly arose with private sellers of food in the ghetto was that they often exploited their position through price gouging and speculation. In Łódź, the most inferior meat was sold to people in queues while good quality meat was sold secretly at exorbitant prices.[6] A similar practice was also in use during World War I, when shopkeepers in Imperial Russia were accused of denying having food in stock and then selling it to the well-to-do at exorbitant prices.[7] In response, many ghettos such as Łódź established ration-card systems whereby individuals could purchase food directly from the Jewish ghetto administration (which in turn obtained food from the Germans) but in limited quantities. In many communities, in addition to food available for purchase, there were soup kitchens which served meals for purchase or for the poor. In many ghettos, there was also some sort of social welfare distribution of food.

Employment, whether in the ghetto administration, in a factory or workshop manufacturing goods for the Germans, or through engagement in some other type of labor which provided services to the ghetto dwellers, was one of the most important means of obtaining food. Payment for labor in money, ration coupons, or in kind as well as being served meals at work were licit ways of obtaining food through work. Another form of work which provided food was the private production of food such as growing vegetables, which some people did even on the little strips of dirt in front of apartment buildings. Unfortunately, in the ghettos, the majority of official work positions gave the worker a ration or payment on which starvation was certain. For example, Krakow ghetto survivor Halina Nelken worked as a technician in a pharmacy making 29.04 zloty per month, which had the purchasing power of two loaves of bread.[8] Many ghetto dwellers would take poorly paid employment for a short period in the hope of eventually finding something with higher remuneration, or they would turn to illicit means to supplement their intake. In the meantime, for those who were able to obtain these positions, hunger and imminent starvation were staved off with the meager food allowance the job offered. Only through additional means could the overwhelming majority of ghetto dwellers avoid starvation; even fewer avoided hunger. Ultimately, many remained in poor-paying positions as this served as protection from deportation to a concentration camp.

The second factor that affected the ability of ghetto dwellers to obtain food was the quantity and value of movable goods a family or individual had in their possession that could be sold or traded. Furniture was traded for use by other families, as well as for firewood. Linens, clothes, lamp wicks, and other goods were traded for food. Many ghetto families traded the last of their possessions for food, medicine, or firewood but were still unable to avoid starvation. The most common type of exchange was food items. Many people traded the more valuable portions of their food ration allowance, such as meats and fats, for a larger quantity of less valuable items, such as vegetables. Other items sold on the black market were those that were in some way produced through labor. A meat allowance became more valuable by processing it into horse meatballs, or a saccharine allotment into candies. Found items such as the bits of coal that children dug or often "mined" in the ghetto garbage could be sold for use in cooking or heating. Unfortunately, for many in the ghetto, the licit acquisition of food via trade often depended on having been affluent or well-to-do prior to the war. As Sarah Rosen writes of Murafa ghetto,

> By the summer of 1942, many of the deportees had parted with most of the clothes, valuables, and money they had brought from home, having exchanged them for food and heating during the difficult winter of 1941–42 … Those who had survived joined the growing circle of impoverished deportees in the ghetto, having exhausted whatever meagre means they had, while the gap between the affluent and the poor widened.[9]

Those without pre-war assets to sell off – or personal connections to transform into the rare job which provided enough food to avoid hunger – were often driven by desperation for nourishment into less-than-optimal work situations. The Jewish ghetto administration would use food as leverage to compel ghetto inhabitants to take this unsavory work. In Rymanow, for example, assistance from the self-help organization was only available to those who registered with the employment office.[10]

A third important source of food was social welfare. Many ghettos—large and small—created various forms of social welfare. In Baranow, a communal kitchen was started; it began by serving only a few hundred and eventually served thousands.[11] A more informal mutual aid system began to evolve in Murafa, whereby "It became known that on a certain day a slice of bread could be found at a certain house, while on another day a bowl of soup or a potato could be obtained from another family. The donating families did so anonymously."[12] In Łódź, relief took the form of a formal network of soup kitchens, special food distributions, and/or money payments. The largest to the smallest ghettos were plagued by the question of how to provide necessary social welfare, now needed not only by the pre-war impoverished but those rapidly becoming impoverished as well. Emanuel Ringelblum, writing from within the Warsaw ghetto, noted:

> The well-established fact is that people who are fed in the public kitchens are all dying out, subsisting as they do only on soup and dry rationed bread … One is left with the tragic dilemma: being that no one will survive? Or

are we to give full measure to a few, with only a handful having enough to survive?[13]

It may seem strange to speak of the poor of the ghetto, as it is generally understood that ghettoization and the extraction of wealth from the Jews of Nazi-occupied Europe led to their impoverishment as a whole. Yet there was a gradation of wealth in the ghetto. The poor and those unable to find employment were the first to suffer from Nazi policies, as they were the least buffered, the least able to save themselves from the starvation enforced on the ghetto as a means of drawing out wealth, and thus the first to be left with no wealth with which to feed themselves. In fact, a large number came to the ghetto with nothing to protect them from starvation.

In the pre-war period, Eastern Europe had a large group of Jews living in poverty who relied on extensive relief from foreign funds such as the American Joint Distribution Committee. Soup kitchens and other means of support had been part of a large-scale relief system keeping poor Jews from starvation before the war. With the outbreak of the war, many who were already living on the brink of starvation were put in a perilous situation. Shortly after the sealing of the Łódź ghetto, the ghetto population as a whole began starving and during July and August of 1940, 1.5 percent of the ghetto population perished.[14] Despite the fact that the German authorities were receiving reports of the massive mortality rate in the ghetto, and that in August 1940, only 52.2 percent of the ghetto population purchased food rations, in September food deliveries to the ghetto were stopped for several days to see if this produced more valuables, which the German authorities believed were being hidden by the incarcerated ghetto Jews.[15] The ghetto dwellers, however, had run out of goods, money, and valuables and without income were unable to purchase food. In October 1940, after a system of relief had been created to provide money for the unemployed to purchase foodstuffs, 96.7 percent of the ghetto population purchased food rations.[16] Welfare eventually proved perilous. In Łódź, in July 1941, there was a mass registration of welfare recipients for work in the ghetto and on labor details.[17] In January 1942, deportations bound for Chelmno began and those on the welfare rolls were among the first to be deported, and by spring 1942, it was clear that the ghetto was largely devoid of welfare recipients.[18] Similarly, those Jews receiving assistance in the Lvov ghetto were amongst the first to be deported.[19]

On the opposite end of the spectrum were the elite of the ghetto. These included high-level ghetto administration officials, those with sufficient pre-war resources to sell off items and sustain themselves, those with personal connections adequate to obtain a good position within the ghetto, and those who profited from war-time circumstances. Sarah Rosen notes that the elite, "Unlike the poor ... did not know hunger."[20] From within the Warsaw ghetto, Stephan Ernst wrote:

> There are twenty thousand, perhaps thirty thousand, people who really have enough to eat; they are the social elite. They contrast with the quarter-of-a-million-strong mass of beggars and paupers who are only struggling to

postpone death by starvation ... And in between these two is a group of about two hundred thousand "ordinary people" who more or less manage, and retain some sort of human face. They are still clean, dressed, their stomachs are not swollen from starvation.[21]

The elite of the Warsaw and Łódź ghettos were notorious for enjoying private dining halls, such as the Adria or Adas restaurants, where high-ranking administration officials, smugglers, and other notables of the ghetto could be found.[22] The elite also had means to create their own benefits. For example, "The deportees from South Bucovina had the resources to launch various economic ventures in order to meet their needs for food, heat, and medicine. Those who had the initiative opened small bakeries and pastry shops; a cantina was opened by 11 partners from South Bucovina."[23] The ghetto elite also often had access to additional rations. This could be through unofficial access, such as gifts from other members of the elite. In the Łódź ghetto, for example, the manager of food supplies, Reingold, sent extra food to dignitaries as a means of currying favor.[24] These elite, however, were the exceptions. The vast majority of those in the ghetto did not have these advantages.

Lastly, in the ghetto, the most important means of obtaining food was through theft and other illicit means. This took all forms, from large-scale operations to smuggling to petty pilfering, but it was essential for nearly all ghetto inhabitants to survive in a place where the food supply was inadequate to ensure the survival of all ghetto inhabitants. In Warsaw and Krakow ghettos, where there were multiple entrances to the ghetto or where ghetto dwellers were able to leave the ghetto for work, there was rampant smuggling. Smuggling created not only an elite class of those able to get food into the ghetto but also dramatically increased the number of calories available for consumption.

The culture of hunger

Post-war survivor testimonies and diaries relate the persistent hunger of the ghettos and its effects. In her immediate post-war testimony in June 1945, survivor Flora Herzberger stated that during her time in the ghetto, she had "practically nothing to eat ... swollen from hunger and marked by death, mentally no longer alert ... even fist fights broke out."[25] She described how, just 10 months after her arrival in the ghetto, her husband, emaciated beyond help, died of hunger.[26] Ghetto chronicler Zelkowicz lamented, "... a Jewish mother in the ghetto, crying without end, hungry, her children hungry, and with nothing to give them, because the Jewish children in the ghetto are always hungry ..."[27] One mother who survived the war related, "I can tell you, I pulled my hair from my head, many, many, many times, on account [of] the children[,] they ask for bread and there was not to give them anything! What could a mother do! Just to kill yourself This was all you could do, to kill yourself."[28]

The response of many who were watching their children or relatives die was to sacrifice what little they had for family members. Siblings, spouses, and particularly parents would forgo food or share what they had with their loved ones. Usually the issue of how much to sacrifice arose when a family member fell sick. If each person ate their own rations, it would not usually be enough food for the sick person to recover, in which case, the sick family member would probably be doomed to die. If family members gave up part of their meager rations, they would then be susceptible to illness. This was a tragic situation for families in the ghetto. Since forfeiting ones' own food to save a sick family member might lead to illness, possibly even death, families often would sell their last possessions—blankets and beds and other basic necessities (that also shielded family members from susceptibility to illness due to cold) to purchase additional food and/or medications. In his July 27, 1942, sketch, "Litzmannstadt Death," Osker Singer recorded the trials of a woman who forfeited her food in an effort to save her husband, Mordechai K., from death by starvation.[29] As Mordechai's body swells from hunger, he tries to lie to his wife about the cause but she knows the truth. She skims some from her own food to add a little to his. As Mordechai begins to recover, and his wife is deteriorating, he realizes what has happened. He confronts her and she denies it. Eventually he gets sick again and succumbs to his illness.[30] Aliza Pionka tells the tragic story of two sisters in the ghetto. When one fell ill, the other filled in, working a double shift, so her sister could continue to remain on the work register and receive her supplemental soup.[31] Soon the one who had been working a double shift also fell ill and eventually both sisters died.[32]

Not every story of family relations in the face of hunger was one of sacrifice. One ghetto chronicler wrote of two women who accused their father of denying their dying mother food and medical attention. When they bought food for their mother, the father ate it himself.[33] Oftentimes individuals were overcome by their hunger. An anonymous girl wrote in her diary on March 11, 1942, that she ate all the honey. She was traumatized by her own hunger and its effect on her family. Of her actions, she wrote, "I am selfish. What will the family say? I'm not worthy of my mother, who works so hard ... I have no heart, I have no pity. I eat anything that lands near me ..."[34] On another occasion, she tells of how she stole a spoonful of noodles from the family ration, which ended in a terrible fight with her father. She wrote of the incident:

> My father complained ... I got excited and cursed my father. What did I do! I am sorry for what happened, but what is done cannot be undone. My father will never forgive me. I will not be able to look him straight in the eye. He stood at the window and started crying like a small child.[35]

Similarly, another ghetto diarist wrote of the shame of having consumed his sister's bread:

> I finished up my loaf of bread ... [in] three days, that is to say on Sunday so I had to wait till the next Saturday for [a] new one. I was terribly hungry ... I was lying on Monday morning quite dejectedly in my bed and there was the

half loaf of bread of my darling sister … I could not resist the temptation and ate it up totally … I was overcome by a terrible remorse of conscience and by a still greater care for what my little one would eat for the next five days. I felt a miserably helpless criminal … I have told people that it was stolen by a supposed reckless and pitiless thief and, for keeping up appearance[s], I have to utter curses and condemnations on the imaginary thief:"I would hang him with my own hands had I come across him."[36]

It was not only siblings and spouses who ate the rations of family members. The *Chronicle* reported that "an eight-year-old boy filed a police report against his own parents, whom he charged with not giving him the bread ration due him.The boy demanded that an investigation be conducted and the guilty parties be punished."[37] The fighting over food in the ghetto was not limited to families but extended to a variety of social interactions.The doctors researching hunger in the Warsaw ghetto noted that victims of hunger could become aggressive, particularly at the sight of food. Oskar Rosenfeld recorded multiple incidents of individuals fighting as a result of hunger. He described a blind rabbi standing near two men who were fighting: "He feels his way to the two of them. His whole body shakes. 'Oh, how hunger has brought down my poor people. A piece of bread, a few decagrams of fat could help you. And there father stands again son, brother against brother, friend against friend.'"[38] The irritability in part came from the physical discomfort of hunger. Those who experienced hunger wrestled with the pains of their body and the rebellion of their stomachs.Yehuda Elberg recorded in his Warsaw Diary that "A dybbuk [spirit] has entered my belly. My belly talks, shouts, even has complaints[,] and drives me mad."[39]

Mental alertness is reduced in persons experiencing hunger. Scientists conducting starvation experiments at the University of Minnesota noted that "In the case of famine … coherent and creative thinking is impaired."[40] They additionally cite research on the famine in Russia from 1918 to 1922, in which intellectuals noted a decrease in their mental abilities.[41] The doctors of the Warsaw ghetto noted that victims suffering from starvation were, "depressed, and uninterested in everything around them until they saw food …"[42] David Sierakowiak recorded in his diary, "I descend lower and lower. I find even reading difficult. I can't concentration on anything for any length of time. I count the time from meal to meal."[43] Ultimately, extreme hunger reduced people to basic animal instincts. Scientists of hunger studies at the University of Minnesota noted that, among those suffering from famine, "… the usual social amenities and graces are dropped …"[44] Rosenfeld made note of this in the ghetto, stating that, "People became coarsened, their manners less fastidious, their tastes less squeamish, their disgust for certain foods overcome by the intensity of their hunger."[45]

In the mental life of the victims, one of the most significant manifestations of hunger was fantasies about food. In their experiments on starvation, the University of Minnesota scientists found that "[i]n the case of famine, food becomes the central topic of conversation and writing …"[46] For the Jews in the ghetto, lack of food was the overwhelming concern of daily life. Viktor Frankl discussed prisoners' reactions to the lack of adequate food, noting that "[b]ecause of the high degree of undernourishment which the prisoners suffered, it was natural that the desire for food was the major primitive instinct around which mental life centered."[47] Food consumed all aspects of existence for the starving ghetto dwellers. Their thoughts, actions, and even dreams were devoted to food and its acquisition. In trying to understand why the Jewish masses were passively going to their deaths due to hunger, Ringelblum recorded the following: "Recently I talked with one of these refugees who had been starving for a long time. All he thinks about is food, particularly bread: wherever he goes, whatever he does, he dreams of bread; he stops in front of every bakery, in front of every window. At the same time, he has become resigned and apathetic; nothing interests him anymore."[48] Food fantasy and food obsession in the ghetto could be so overwhelming that they were tormenting.[49] Ruth Gold, in her memoirs of her time spent in a Romanian ghetto, remembered how hunger tormented her. Of her family's bread, she noted that her "... senses were consumed by the loaf of bread dangling from the side of the crib ... It was neither greed nor selfishness that corrupted me, but that ferocious hunger which I had endured for so many weeks, a tormenting hunger I will never be able to describe in words ..."[50] Soon after the closing of the Krakow ghetto, Halina Nelken reported that she and her family were suffering from hunger. [51] Her complaints of hunger are repeated in a stanza of a poem she wrote in June 1941, which read, "In vain I try with my wish of a villa under a blue sky to kill my hunger and my wish for a piece of gray wartime bread." [52]

The hunger of the ghetto population led them to eat a whole new range of foods. Jean Soler, in his article "The Semiotics of Food in the Bible," states that "the mere fact that a thing is edible does not mean it will be eaten."[53] In the ghetto, people began to discover that many things they had not eaten before were in fact edible. In *Whose Hunger? Concepts of Famine, Practices of Aid*, Jenny Edkins notes that

> It is not possible to read accounts of famines and the hardships and inhumanities to which people are driven during such periods without coming across accounts where things are eaten that under normal circumstances would in no sense count as food. During famines, people search the land for wild fruits, berries, etc., which serve as famine foods. If circumstances become more extreme, bark is stripped from the trees, grass is eaten, even the dirt is consumed ...[54]

Things that were not consumed prior to the war not only entered the ghetto diet but became quite commonplace and in fact desirable. Many items such as rotting vegetables, vegetable peels, and other items that had been thrown in the trash prior to the war became sought-after items. For example, Jakub Poznanski records paying nearly half a day's salary for ten dekagrams of rotten radishes in December 1942.[55] Other items that were usually thrown away, such as the outer leaves of cabbages, radishes, and carrots, soon found their way not only into the ghetto-dwellers diets but were even sold on the black market.[56] One anonymous diarist recorded, "There is a lot of cabbage on the Rynek Balucki, but it has gone bad. People started to fight for those rotten leaves as if they were some kind of treasure." [57] Famine conditions often lead to anything vaguely edible being sold. During the Chinese famine of 1942, vendors sold leaves for the starving to consume.[58]

In the ghetto, "[p]eople invaded the fields in search of edible grass, leaves and roots."[59] Łódź ghetto survivor Herzberger related how children would gather grass that would be cleaned and eaten with vinegar.[60] Potato peels, which had previously been discarded, became so coveted as to require a doctors' prescription to obtain them.[61] Bella Karp, a survivor of the ghetto, described eating patties made from ground-up potato peels.[62] The March 20, 1944, diary entry of Rosenfeld recounted the strenuous effort it took to prepare potato peels into dumplings, including washing them and running them through a meat grinder.[63]

The change to eating what had previously been considered garbage was a slow development. In the first months after the closing of a ghetto, smuggling still existed and people still had food reserves, and thus those who still had resources could obtain food. Those whose resources had already run out were forced to discover methods of survival soon to be adopted by the vast majority of the ghetto population. A ghetto welfare worker making an inspection a few months after the closing of the ghetto learned of the new eating habits that had developed and which were to become commonplace in all ghetto households. Her discovery was made when she inquired after a bad smell. She asked the man why there was so much trash in his apartment, to which he responded that the pile causing the smell was not trash. Rather, he explained, that for the poor of the ghetto who could not afford cabbages, radishes, kohlrabi, and beets, the rotting "leaves of cabbage, of radishes, of kohlrabi or beets" served, despite the bad smell, as food.[64] Interestingly enough, Avraham Hasman recorded that he began selling beet leaves to a poor neighbor whom he had caught stealing from his garden. Hasman noted that he had been throwing out the beet leaves because not only were they bitter but they also caused swelling.[65] But his logical connection was faulty: he assumed that the desperately poor who were swelling were doing so because of the beet leaves, but in fact they swelled with hunger and were only eating beet leaves to try to stave it off. Those who were fed well enough to avoid swelling had the luxury of being able to eat only the beets themselves. In these early days, it was still possible for those desperate enough to search garbage dumps to find potato peels, rotting vegetables, and moldy bread with which to make a meal.[66] Similarly, during the Irish famine of the mid-nineteenth century, starving people were found digging through garbage heaps in search of potato peels.[67]

Soon the hunger in the ghetto was such that one of the most remarkable inventions of the ghetto, described by ghetto historian Singer, arose—the ghetto "salad." Having run out of milk, the ghetto dairy gathered scraps left over from ghetto kitchens and turned them into an edible "salad." Scraps such as wilted vegetable leaves were soaked and cleaned until they appeared regenerated, the edible bits of rotten vegetables that could be cut off and saved were soaked until the smell diminished, and unblemished pieces of moldy bread were added, and it was all mixed together, then seasoned with spices to mask the smell. This ghetto salad was served to inhabitants "fortunate" enough to have a ration coupon for it.[68] Not only edible things made their way into the ghetto diet. When oil could not be found, machine oil was used for cooking.[69] The reasons for the consumption of these dangerous and novel food items was best articulated by Eichengreen, who wrote of herself and her family after one year in the ghetto: "We no longer cared what we ate …"[70] As historian and Łódź ghetto survivor Marian Turski writes of the diaries of the Łódź ghetto, they "… provide much information about everyday life in the ghetto, including how to deceive the stomach by making a cake out of potato peels or a so-called bread soup composed of water, a slice of bread, and a morsel of turnip."[71]

Not only new foods as ingredients appeared in the ghetto, new ways of cooking appeared as well. Shortages of flour, meat, and even potatoes forced women to create ways of stretching their food; some of them might have had experience from the food shortages of World War I or from a lifetime of poverty. There were, however, ways of stretching food that were unique to the ghetto. For example, ersatz coffee, made from grains, became a popular substitute to be used in lieu of flour for making cakes. A cake recipe from the Łódź ghetto calls for three potatoes, 12–15 spoons of (ersatz) coffee, two spoons of flour, ten saccharine tablets, one spoon of drinking soda, and a little salt.[72] A cake could be made with even fewer ingredients by adding vegetable leaves. Beet leaves, cooked and ground up, could be added to the above recipe, and a cake could be made using one less potato. This recipe had an advantage—as noted by the survivor who recorded the recipe—in that the water used to cook the beet leaves could then be used to make soup.[73] Beet leaves could also be salted and fried and thus turned into "herring."[74] Ersatz coffee could also be used to stretch traditional dishes when ingredients were missing. For example, potato latkes, a traditional Eastern European Jewish dish normally made of flour, potatoes, and egg, was made by adding 12–15 spoons of ersatz coffee to three potatoes and a little flour; less flour and less potato were needed for this type of coffee pancake than the traditional potato pancake.[75] Ghetto homemakers had to be extremely creative to stretch the food products they were given. They contrived ways of making soups out of radish and stretching their small meat allotments by mixing in vegetables.[76] One recipe from the ghetto called for making five big cutlets from two hundred grams of horsemeat (which required grinding the horsemeat), adding two shredded potatoes, some rye flour, and seasoning with salt and pepper. The cutlets formed from this recipe were then fried in a little oil.[77]

When even meat or vegetables could not be found, other things were ground up to make a meal. Cutlets of ersatz coffee, potato peels, and radish leaves were fried and eaten.[78] The strategy of using potato peels for food was not limited to the Łódź ghetto. In the Minsk ghetto, pancakes and other foods were made from potato peels.[79] Łódź ghetto fiction writer Isaiah Spiegel noted in his story "Ghetto Kingdom" that

A master chef has discovered that leftover potato peels washed and ground can be transformed, as if by sheer magic, into flat cutlets; this sticky, cloying delicacy is as sweet as a piece of fine cake, though the sand that hasn't been washed away by the water grates between the teeth. But who cares about that? The demon hunger renders the delicacy a savory meal to the sick and swollen, magically converting it into the wheat bread they have been dreaming of.[80]

This desperation for food, interestingly enough, did not lead, as far as is known, to widespread cannibalism. Edkins notes that in times of famine, "people may resort to eating each other's children or even their own children. Such practices of cannibalism are well documented. They appall the imagination and make one wonder precisely in what sense food *exists.*"[81] While there were cases of cannibalism which were known to have occurred in the Warsaw ghetto, I was unable to find any such documented cases in other ghettos.

Starvation physically transforms its victims. During the first phases of starvation, the body will compensate for a lack of calorie intake by consuming body fat. Victims of starvation may first take note of rapid weight loss when their clothing becomes too big for their bodies. Rosenfeld stated that people took notice of their weight loss "Only when they noticed that their clothes were getting looser, the shirts around the neck became wider, skirts, blouses, hung loose around the body."[82] A sign of this physical transformation of ghetto inhabitants was an advertisement in the *Chronicle* stating "Men's collars taken in at the barbershop at 13 Lutomierska Street."[83] In his work about the Warsaw ghetto, Charles Roland also related how, in the first stages of hunger, the Jews joked about the lack of food. He referred to a woman who joked about how she no longer needed to diet.[84] The weight loss in this early stage, however, was dangerously substantial. According to the Łódź ghetto chroniclers, weight losses of 20 or 30 kilograms became frequent.[85] The result was a noticeable decrease in body volume, leaving sagging skin. The loss of fat and resulting sagging skin in the abdomen area is often one of the first places that weight loss is noted in victims of starvation. Rapid fat loss also left hunger victims with hollow eyes: "the eyes ... sunken in the sockets like dried nuts in their skins."[86] The sunken eyes of the starving are apparent in numerous ghetto photographs. This loss of body fat was followed by a loss of muscle. As Viktor Frankl, a physician imprisoned at Auschwitz, noted: "[t]he organism digested its own protein."[87] The body was capable of even further energy conversion and after consuming muscle, if the body was still denied adequate nutrition, would begin to consume organ tissue.[88] In children, this extended malnutrition results in stunted growth, which was noted by doctors in the Warsaw ghetto of the starving children there.[89] In women, menstruation ceased.[90]

As testified to in the Eichmann trial, in the last stages, "People either swelled up from hunger or became emaciated."[91] The doctors of the Warsaw ghetto, who studied the starvation disease in the Warsaw ghetto, noted that at this point victims required hospitalization. They describe the victims as pale and bluish-looking, with faint pulses, poor lungs, swollen limbs, and aged appearance.[92] Kahane described the Lvov ghetto masses as having "… blue swollen faces … their bodies are simply bloated by hunger."[93] Other observers of starvation victims noted the change in skin color just before dying from starvation. Zelkowicz described people with "sunken black or gray cheeks."[94]

There were numerous other physical transformations endured by those suffering from starvation. One major effect of the lack of food is the inability of the body to keep warm. Maintaining body temperature requires calories. As Nazi scientists were aware, cold weather requires more calories to keep warm.[95] Hunger victims, however, often felt chilled even in warm weather.[96] There were many instances of ghetto inhabitants being described as bundled up in their blankets and warm clothes, even in the middle of summer. Another effect of the lack of food, which was observed by the clandestine researchers in the Warsaw ghetto, was tremendous thirst and an increase in the amount of urination. The need to go constantly to the toilet was a difficulty in the ghetto when less than one percent of the apartments there had indoor toilets.[97] Those experiencing hunger had to then use scant resources to go outside into the cold to relieve themselves (or at least to empty chamber pots). Ghetto survivor Eichengreen related in her memoirs that "[i]ndoor toilets belonged to another life; here, the outhouses were three flights down. As hunger weakened us, it became an ordeal to go up and down the stairs …"[98]

Lack of calories eventually takes its toll on movement, as all physical activity requires calorie expenditure. Roland wrote that hunger resulted in "profound weakness and the inability to sustain even the smallest physical effort."[99] Additionally, movement was made even more difficult due to swollen limbs. The hungry were also described as shuffling along. "Weakness in the limbs took over. For many it was torture to climb one or two flights …"[100] Eventually, "the knees no longer support … the weight …"[101] Zelkowicz recorded that "[s]uch a [starving] person does not 'walk' but drags along like an accursed specter."[102] Eventually, lack of energy and swollenness would lead a person to bed rest. Large numbers of ghetto residents took to their beds when exhaustion from hunger set in. There was a hope that a few days of bed rest would allow the person to regain their strength.

Ultimately, hunger and hunger diseases took a terrible toll on the health and lives of many ghetto dwellers. The most common diseases in the ghetto were hunger diseases and hunger-related diseases. For example, writers in the *Chronicle* stated that the rise in tuberculosis and lung diseases in the ghetto was the direct result of malnutrition.[103] Lung disease was particularly rampant among the hungry. Korczak, writing his diary from the orphanage he oversaw in the Warsaw ghetto, related that he asked his charges to smile. He noted, "They are ill, pale, lung-sick smiles."[104] Hunger and disease further aggravated one another, as "[d]isease impairs absorption and utilization of nutrients, raises nutritional needs and may also reduce appetite."[105] Ultimately, the most significant effect of starvation on ghetto inhabitants was death.

Death from hunger took many forms. Some succumbed to hunger diseases. Others, driven by hunger, boarded deportation trains. Some volunteered for backbreaking work that would contribute to eroding their health. Others died in pursuit of food, whether it was being caught smuggling food or engaging in food riots. For almost all ghetto dwellers, the struggle against hunger was a central part of ghetto existence.

Notes

1   Calculations based on Bundesarchiv NS 19/2655/26, also see from the Jewish Historical Institute of Warsaw, or Zydowski Instytut Historyczny (hereafter referred to as ZIH); 301/634, testimony of Israel Tabaksblatt; and for Warsaw, see Elie Cohen, *Human Behavior in the Concentration Camp*, M.H. Braaksma (trans.), New York: The University Library, 1953, p. 73. Israel Gutman also reports the incredibly low number of 184, see: Israel Gutman, *The Jews of Warsaw, 1939–1943: Ghetto, Underground, Revolt*, Bloomington: Indiana University Press, 1982, p. 66.
2   Cohen, *Human Behavior*, pp. 56–57.
3   Hans Jurgen Tueteberg and Jean-Louis Flandrin, "The Transformation of the European Diet," *A Culinary History of Food*, New York: Penguin Books, 2000, p. 455.
4   William Moskoff, *The Bread of Affliction: The Food Supply in the USSR during World War II*, Cambridge: Cambridge University Press, 1990, p. 53.
5   David Kahane, *The Lvov Ghetto Diary*, Amherst: University of Massachusetts Press, 1990, p. 20.
6   YIVO RG-241, doc. 883.
7   Barbara Alpern Engel, "Not by Bread Alone: Subsistence Riots in Russia during World War I," *The Journal of Modern History* 69.4, December 1997: 715.
8   Diary Entry of January 1941, Halina Nelken, *And Yet, I Am Here!* Translated by Halina Nelken and Alicia Nitecki, Amherst: University of Massachusetts, 1986, p. 68.
9   Sarah Rosen, "Surviving in the Murafa Ghetto: A Case Study of One Ghetto in Transnistria," *Holocaust Studies: A Journal of Culture and History* 16.1–2, Summer/Autumn 2010, 168–169.
10   *Gazeta Żydowska*, July 8, 1942.
11   *Sefer yizkor shel kehilat Dzialoszyce*, p. 37.
12   Rosen, "Surviving in the Murafa Ghetto," p. 171.
13   Zoe Vania Waxman, *Writing the Holocaust: Identity, Testimony, Representation*, Oxford: Oxford University Press, 2006, p. 30. See Emanuel Ringelblum, *Notes from the Warsaw Ghetto*, Schocken, 1974, pp. 181–182.
14   Christopher Browning, "Nazi Ghettoization Policy in Poland, 1939–1941," in *The Path to Genocide*, New York: Cambridge University Press, 1992, p. 35. Alan Adelson and Robert Lapides (eds.), *Łódź Ghetto: Inside a Community Under Siege*, Penguin Books, 1991, p. 92.
15   Browning, "Nazi Ghettoization Policy in Poland," p. 35.
16   YIVO RG-241, doc. 883.
17   *Chronicle*, July 5–12, 1941.
18   United States Holocaust Memorial Museum (USHMM) RG 02 *127; Zelkowicz, *In Those Terrible Days*, 199–201; *Chronicle*, January 1–5, 1942; YIVO RG 241, doc. 927.
19   Eliyahu Yones., *Smoke in the Sand: The Jews of Lvov in the War Years 1939–1944*, New York: Geffen Publishing House, 2004, p. 164.
20   Rosen, "Surviving in the Murafa Ghetto," p. 169.
21   Waxman, *Writing the Holocaust*, p. 27. See also Barbara Engelking, *Holocaust and Memory*, Leicester: Leicester University Press, 2002, p. 104 for long block quote.
22   *Chronicle*, June 7–8, 1941.
23   Rosen, "Surviving in the Murafa Ghetto," p. 169.
24   Adelson, *Łódź Ghetto*, p. 445.
25   USHMM RG-02 *162.
26   Ibid.

27 Zelkowicz, *In Those Terrible Days*, pp. 112–113.
28 Lillian Kranitz-Sanders, *Twelve Who Survived: An Oral History of the Jews of Łódź, Poland, 1930–1954*, New York: Irvington Publishers, Inc., 1984, p. 85.
29 YIVO RG-241, doc. 868.
30 Ibid.
31 Anna Eilenberg-Eibeshitz, *Preserved Evidence: Ghetto Łódź*, Haifa: H. Eibeshitz Institute for Holocaust Studies, 1998, p. 241.
32 Ibid.
33 Zelkowicz, *In Those Terrible Days*, 89.
34 Michal Unger, "The Status and Plight of Women in the Łódź Ghetto," *Women in the Holocaust*, Dalia Ofer and Lenore J. Weitzman (eds.), New Haven: Yale University Press, 1999, p. 134.
35 Marian Turski, "Individual Experience in Diaries from the Łódź Ghetto," *Holocaust Chronicles: Individualizing the Holocaust through Diaries and other Contemporaneous Personal Accounts*, Robert Moses Shapiro (ed.), New York: Ktav Publishing, 1999, pp. 120–121.
36 Robert Moses Shapiro, "Diaries and Memoirs from the Łódź Ghetto in Yiddish and Hebrew," *Holocaust Chronicles: Individualizing the Holocaust through Diaries and other Contemporaneous Personal Accounts*, Robert Moses Shapiro (ed.), New York: Ktav Publishing, 1999, pp. 109–110.
37 *Chronicle*, January 12, 1941.
38 Adelson, *Łódź Ghetto*, p. 183.
39 Lucy Dawidowicz. *The War against the Jews 1933–1945*, New York: Bantam Books, 1986, p. 210.
40 Ancel Keys et al., *The Biology of Human Starvation*, University of Minnesota Press, 1950, p. 784.
41 Ibid., p. 789.
42 Charles G. Roland, *Courage Under Siege: Starvation, Disease, and Death in the Warsaw Ghetto*, New York: Oxford University Press, 1992, p. 115.
43 Turski, "Individual Experience in Diaries from the Łódź Ghetto," pp. 119–120.
44 Keys, *Biology of Human Starvation*, p. 785.
45 Dawidowicz, *War against the Jews*, p. 211.
46 Keys, *Biology of Human Starvation*, p. 784.
47 Victor Frankl, *Man's Search for Meaning: An Introduction to Logotherapy*, New York: Simon & Schuster, 1984, p. 48.
48 Leon Poliakov, *Harvest of Hate: The Nazi Program for the Destruction of the Jews of Europe*, New York: Holocaust Library, 1979, originally published 1954, p. 96.
49 Lucille Eichengreen, *Rumkowski and the Orphans of Łódź*, San Francisco: Mercury House, 2000, p. 6.
50 Ruth Glasberg Gold, *Ruth's Journey: A Survivor's Memoir*, iUniverse, 2009, pp. 66–67.
51 Diary entry of March 25, 1941, Halina Nelken, *And Yet, I Am Here!* Halina Nelken and Alicia Nitecki (trans.), Amherst: University of Massachusetts, 1986, p. 74.
52 Diary entry of June 9–17, 1941, Halina Nelken, *And Yet, I Am Here!* Halina Nelken and Alicia Nitecki (trans.), Amherst: University of Massachusetts, 1986, p. 82.
53 Jean Soler, "The Semiotics of Food in the Bible," *Food and Drink in History: Selections for the Annales Economies, Sociétés, Civilisations*, Robert Forster and Orest Ranum (eds.), Elborg Forster and Patricia Ranum (trans.), Baltimore: Johns Hopkins University Press, 1979, p. 126.
54 Jenny Edkins, *Whose Hunger? Concepts of Famine, Practices of Aid*, Minneapolis: University of Minnesota Press, 2000, p. 63.
55 Jakub Poznanski, *Dziennik z Łódźkiego getta*, Warsaw: Dom Wydawniczy, 2002, p. 21.
56 *Chronicle*, August 1, 1941; *Chronicle*, July 22, 1941.
57 ZIH 302/9, anonymous girl's diary.
58 David Arnold, *Famine: Social Crisis and Historical Change*, Oxford: Basil Blackwell, 1988, p. 18.

59   Eilenberg-Eibeshitz, *Preserved Evidence*, p. 235.
60   USHMM RG-02 ★162.
61   Zelkowicz, *In Those Terrible Days*, pp. 193–197.
62   Letter of March 11, 2000 from Bella Karp to Helene Sinnreich in response to questions sent.
63   Unger, "The Status and Plight of Women in the Łódź Ghetto," p. 135.
64   Zelkowicz, *In Those Terrible Days*, p. 43.
65   Eilenberg-Eibeshitz, *Preserved Evidence*, pp. 236–238.
66   Oskar Rosenfeld, *In the Beginning Was the Ghetto: Notebooks from Łódź*, Chicago: Northwestern University Press, 2012, p. 170.
67   Gerard MacAtasney, *Leitrim and the Great Hunger 1845–50: A Temporary Inconvenience?* Leitrim: Carrick on Shannon and District Historical Society, 1997, p. 98; testimony of James McGrath.
68   YIVO RG-241, doc. 872.
69   Eilenberg-Eibeshitz, *Preserved Evidence*, p. 235.
70   Eichengreen, *Rumkowski and the Orphans of Łódź*, p. 19.
71   Turski, "Individual Experience in Diaries from the Łódź Ghetto," p. 118.
72   S. Glube, "Meachlim in Łódźer Ghetto" [Meals in the Ghetto of Łódź], *Fun Lectn Churban: Tzytschrift fur geshichte yidishen laben beten Nazi Rezim* [From the Last Extermination: Journal for the History of the Jewish People During the Nazi Regime], no. 9, Munich: Eucom Civil Affairs: September 1948, p. 80.
73   Ibid, p. 80.
74   Eilenberg-Eibeshitz, *Preserved Evidence*, p. 235.
75   Glube, "Meachlim in Łódźer Ghetto," 80.
76   Ibid, p. 81.
77   Ibid.
78   Eilenberg-Eibeshitz, *Preserved Evidence*, p. 235.
79   Moskoff, *The Bread of Affliction*, p. 66.
80   Isaiah Spiegel, *Ghetto Kingdom: Tales of the Łódź Ghetto*, David H. Hirsch and Roslyn Hirsch (trans.), Evanston: Northwestern University Press, 1998, p. 96.
81   Edkins, *Whose Hunger?*, p. 63
82   Rosenfeld, *In the Beginning Was the Ghetto*, p. 17.
83   *Chronicle*, August 4, 1941.
84   Roland, *Courage Under Siege*, p. 98.
85   *Chronicle*, August 4, 1941.
86   Piero Camporesi, *Bread of Dreams: Food and Fantasy in Early Modern Europe*, David Gentilcore (trans.), Chicago: University of Chicago Press, 1989, p. 27.
87   Frankl, *Man's Search for Meaning*, p. 49.
88   Laurie DeRose, Ellen Messer, and Sara Millman, *Who's Hungry? And How Do We Know? Food Shortage, Poverty and Deprivation*, New York: United Nations University Press, 1998, p. 7.
89   Roland, *Courage Under Siege*, p. 115.
90   Adelson, *Łódź Ghetto*, p. 377.
91   State of Israel Ministry of Justice. The Trial of Adolf Eichmann: Record of Proceedings in the District Court of Jerusalem. Jerusalem: Trust for the Publication of the Proceedings of the Eichmann Trial, in cooperation with the Israel State Archives and Yad Vashem, the Holocaust Martyrs' and Heroes' Remembrance Authority, 1992–1995, p. 379.
92   Roland, *Courage Under Siege*, p. 116.
93   Kahane, *The Lvov Ghetto Diary*, p. 52.
94   Adelson, *Łódź Ghetto*, pp. 128–129.
95   NS/19/54.
96   Roland, *Courage Under Siege*, p. 115.
97   Adelson, *Łódź Ghetto*, p. 36.
98   Eichengreen, *Rumkowski and the Orphans of Łódź*, p. 2.

 99 Roland, *Courage Under Siege*, p. 115.
100 Adelson, *Łódź Ghetto*, p. 180.
101 Camporesi, *Bread of Dreams*, p. 27.
102 Adelson, *Łódź Ghetto,* pp. 128–129.
103 *Chronicle,* July 20, 1941.
104 Janusz Korczak, *Ghetto Diary*, New York: Holocaust Library, 1978, p. 188.
105 DeRose et al., *Who's Hungry?*, p. 4.

7

"AM I MY BROTHER'S KEEPER?"

Jewish committees in the ghettos of the Mogilev district and the Romanian authorities in Transnistria, 1941–1944[1]

Gali Mir-Tibon

"A small group of people – sometimes one single person – were capable of creating a community from the mass of uprooted, exhausted suffering and persecuted people, through initiative, courage, strong will, stamina, and the power of respect as well as Jewish solidarity."[2] This is how Matatias Carp, a historian who lived through the Holocaust in Bucharest, Romania, described the work of the Jewish committees in the ghettos of the Mogilev district in Transnistria, which was the killing ground for Romanian Jews during the Holocaust. Is this an accurate description or an idealization of the brutal reality?

Transnistria was an artificial geographic term created by the Germans in World War II, referring to the southwest part of the Ukraine that was given to Romania in the summer of 1941. Romania did not annex the region, but included the territory as "Guvernământul Transnistriei" under the Romanian governor. Before the war, this area was under Soviet rule.[3] On June 22, 1941, as the Soviet Union was invaded, two Romanian armies joined the German forces, and Marshal Ion Antonescu, the fascist dictator of Romania, personally headed the advance on the Ukrainian front. Before fighting had even ended, special forces of the Ministry of the Interior, assisted by the gendarmerie[4] and Romanian military forces, began expelling Jews in July 1941 from the provinces of Bessarabia and North Bukovina, in October 1941 from South Bukovina,[5] and in December 1941 from Dorohoi.[6] These Jews were sent to a territory called Transnistria, which literally means "beyond the river Nistru" (Dniester) (Figure 7.1). The name Transnistria was used to designate the province only from 1941 to 1944.[7] A total of 195,000 Jews were deported to Transnistria. Only 45,000 survived and returned to Romania at the end of the war.[8]

This chapter explores how the Jewish committees operated vis à-vis the Romanian governorate within the unique circumstances in the Mogilev district during the Holocaust, and how they took advantage of the conditions that developed in the region to benefit members of their original Romanian hometown

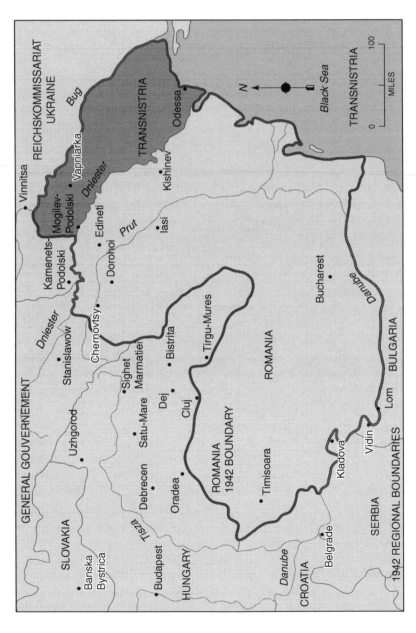

FIGURE 7.1   Romania 1942, Transnistria indicated. After map © United States Holocaust Memorial Museum, Washington, DC

Jewish communities. The conduct of the Romanian authorities in the Mogilev district created unique circumstances for the Jewish committees – a reality that does not always coincide with the common historiographical perceptions regarding the Jewish councils in the ghettos of Poland and Eastern Europe.[9] This variance is due to the fact that the committees of the Mogilev district, unlike the Polish and Eastern European councils, were not dealing with a Romanian plan for the total annihilation of the Jews in the district. Therefore, the actions of these committees to save the Jews of their hometowns were of great value. The Jewish leadership of the Mogilev district is referred to as *Jewish committees* rather than *Jewish councils*, in order to distinguish them from the Jewish councils in the Eastern European ghettos and how the latter were perceived. The term *Judenrat*, commonly used for these Jewish officials in the ghettos, was rarely used in Transnistria.[10] The term predominantly used was *Coordonarea* (coordinator), which was short for *Comitetul Evreiesc penrtu Coordonarea Muncii*, i.e., Jewish Committee for Coordinating Labor. As the name suggests, the Romanian regime expected the Jewish committee to comply with the regime's forced labor demands.[11] This chapter focuses on the heart of the conflict rooted in the actions of the Jewish committees: the expulsion of thousands of Jews from the ghettos in the Mogilev district to German-controlled forced labor camps near the Bug River and to the starvation death camps of Scazineti and Pechora.[12] These camps were vacant Soviet headquarters that had been converted by the Romanians into annihilation-through-starvation camps. Surrounded by barbed wire, with armed Romanian gendarmes and Ukrainian police positioned around the perimeter, the Jews in these camps were imprisoned and no food or sustenance was provided. Out of 3,000 Jews who were sent to Pechora from the Mogilev ghetto in the fall of 1942, only 28 were still alive several months later.[13]

The term *ghetto*, as used in the Mogilev district, had a different meaning from its common use in Poland. Benjamin Ravid's definition of ghetto as "compulsory, segregated, and enclosed" applies only to the segregated nature of the Mogilev ghettos established in the former Jewish neighborhoods in which Jews were first set apart. But those ghettos were not closed until September 1942, and even then, Jews who could afford to pay for housing in the Ukrainian neighborhoods were able to live outside the ghetto walls.[14] Martin Dean determines three critical elements to define a ghetto: (1) the resettlement of Jews in a defined residential area; (2) their separation from the general population; and (3) imposing sanctions on the Jews for leaving that defined area.[15] Transnistria was dotted by more than two hundred such ghettos of Jews forcibly concentrated into defined spaces. Due to the fact that the Romanian occupation forces had not planned for the Jews of Romania to stay in the Mogilev district, no areas had been outlined for them when they arrived in the fall of 1941.[16] Therefore, they were required to find their own housing in the villages and towns they passed on their journey. Naturally, many settled in previously Jewish-owned houses that had been ruined in bombings or were left empty when the Jewish residents were murdered in the German-Romanian invasion of the USSR.[17] The ghettos in the Mogilev district were not called *Ghettos* by their inhabitants, but *lager* (camp), *quarter*, or *neighborhood*. Most of them were not sealed off with barbed wire or fences but had obvious boundaries, since they had been Jewish neighborhoods for generations. In the fall of 1942, some of the Jewish neighborhoods were demarcated by barbed wire and the Jews who were renting houses in the Ukrainian neighborhoods were transferred into the area that was now fenced off and officially declared a Jewish neighborhood. Only then did the Jews start using the word *ghetto* for the fenced-off Jewish sites.[18]

The unique circumstances in the Mogilev district under Romanian occupation

Transnistria province had been built as a military and economic colony with two essential purposes: to provide protection against the Soviet eastern front, and to offer cheap labor for mining, rebuilding war damage, and constructing roads and bridges for use by military forces.[19] Operated under dual military and civil rule, the Romanian forces could treat any of the Jews in Transnistria as an enemy or a spy and execute them without trial. The Romanian authorities viewed the 200,000 Jews deported to the province as a financial burden on the occupying power, particularly in the Mogilev district, where a quarter of them were settled.[20]

Due to the size of the area occupied by the Romanians and Germans and ongoing battles in Eastern Europe, the Romanian authorities in the Mogilev district of Transnistria exerted a high degree of sovereignty and independence in their decision-making. There was no clear and consistent policy of the Romanian central government concerning the future of the Jews expelled from Romania. This gave the local forces great leeway in making decisions.[21] For example, Ion Baleanu, Prefect of the Mogilev district, proposed to deport the Jews from Mogilev to Scazineti in February 1942,[22] and Prefect Constantin Nasturas initiated and implemented the expulsion of 3,000 Chernowitz Jews from the Mogilev ghetto to the forced labor camps in Ladyzhyn.[23] Dimitrie Ştefănescu, the general administrative inspector of the gendarmerie in the district, described the province: "Transnistria, an area rife with battles and war, was in a state of emergency, and the reign of the motherland stopped at the Nistru."[24]

In November 1941, Transnistria's governor Gheorghe Alexianu issued Order No. 23 to determine the temporary settlement arrangements of the Romanian Jews in the Transnistria province.[25] The Romanian notion that Transnistria was the focus of Romanian colonialism was manifested in the order: the areas in which Jews were settled were called *Colonii*.[26] According to the fifth clause of the directive, "The 'colony' will be headed by *Sef (head)de Colonie* –a Jew approved by the authorities."[27] There were two advantages to reestablishing the Jewish committees with their chairmen. It provided the Romanian government a way of delegating tasks to a Romanian-speaking internal Jewish body, and it gave the Jews who had been expelled from Romania a way to influence the Romanian authorities, to mitigate their demands, to manage limited financial resources, and to leverage the most significant resource at their disposal to help the deportees: medical and technological education.[28]

The relationship between the chairmen of the Jewish committees and the Prefects and Pretors in the district differed from the role of the Judenrat in the Warsaw ghetto and others: Baleanu allowed a Jewish committee representative, usually Siegfried Jägendorf, chairman of the Jewish committee in the Mogilev ghetto, to participate in the meetings of the Romanian authorities in the district, and even voice his views.[29] Meir Teich, chairman of the Shargorod Committee, was granted permission to establish a Jewish police force in the ghetto, which was also responsible for Shargorod's Ukrainian residents.[30] The chairmen of the committees could resign from their posts and some, such as Jägendorf and Yossef Shauer, did so, and the Romanian governorate did not harm them by way of reprisal.[31] In contrast, in Nazi ghettos in Poland, most attempts to avoid the position of Judenrat were severely punished by execution.

The Romanian attitude towards the Jews in the Mogilev region changed over time. From November 1941–February 1942, the ghettos were "open" and Jews lived in the former Jewish Ukrainian neighborhoods and rented rooms in other neighborhoods in towns. Until February 1942, the Romanian authorities avoided direct involvement in the affairs of the Jewish population in the ghettos and left the Jews almost completely in the hands of the Jewish committees. Carp summed up that initial period under Romanian rule in Transnistria as follows: "Within a period of six months, despite coping with various kinds of deaths, starvation, disease and suffering, the independent authority of the Jews took on the form of a state."[32] In March 1942, the Romanian policy regarding the Jewish population shifted. This change had two main causes. First, as Soviet forces gathered strength in 1942 along the eastern front, and the partisan movement expanded, the Romanian forces were less assured of their victory. They frequently felt threatened and sought to limit the movement of the Jews.[33] Second, no less than their fear of the Russians, the Romanians dreaded an outbreak of typhus.[34] In the winter of 1941–1942, thousands of Jews died of typhus in the Mogilev district's ghettos; and in March 1942, when gendarmes started to show signs of contamination, the Romanians began to understand the connection between overcrowding, poor sanitary conditions, and the outbreak of the epidemic.[35] Baleanu's concern that overcrowding would bring about a typhus epidemic led him to a plan for the gradual deportation of half of the Jews from the town of Mogilev. The first stage of this plan included an order by Prefect Nasturas for the deportation of 4,000 Jews to Scazineti in May 1942, and the second stage was an order for the deportation of 3,000 Jews to the camp at Pechora in October 1942.[36]

In addition, the Romanians sought to isolate the Jews because of their Romanian nationalism and anti-Semitism.[37] Nasturas was the one to express this ideology best.[38] In the summer of 1942, he ordered the closing of the ghettos in the Mogilev district.[39] Ştefănescu also proposed to rid the Mogilev district of its Jews.[40] We have no information on whether these officials sought an overall annihilation plan for the Jewish population of the district. However, they clearly did take significant steps towards reducing the number of Jews under their jurisdiction by imprisoning them in closed ghettos during the summer of 1942, further distancing the

Jews from the possibility of a viable life, and expelling Jews to the starvation death camps of Scazineti and Pechora. Despite statements made by the Romanian Chief of Staff, and even by Antonescu himself, concerning the general Jewish population in Transnistria, it appears that unlike the policy towards the Jews in Poland, the actual steps taken by the Romanian authorities in the Mogilev district led to selective rather than total annihilation.[41] This approach determined, to a large degree, the methods adopted by the Jewish committees for coping with the Romanian authorities in the district.[42]

Methods adopted by the Jewish committees for coping with the Romanian authorities

The unique status of the Jewish committees in the Mogilev district's ghettos during the Holocaust was based on the fact that the committees combined a headship, appointed by the ruling authorities, with an authentic leadership. Headship refers to an administrative body appointed by the ruling authority that determines its objectives and selects its chiefs who, out of fear of punishment from an external power, serve the ruler's interests. By contrast, leadership develops spontaneously; it motivates people to act of their own volition, serves the interests of the group, and unites it.[43] The roots of the leadership in the Mogilev ghettos can be found in the period before the Holocaust. Certain modes of action were dictated by long-standing traditions while others were adapted to the new reality. This stability was apparent in the identity of committee members and in their tactics. Most of the members and chairmen of the Jewish committees were well-known public figures in the South Bukovina province before the war, serving from a sense of duty toward their hometown communities. This phenomenon was common in Polish Nazi ghettos as well.[44] This fact had a decisive influence on the fate of the communities they headed, compared with the communities from North Bukovina and Bessarabia who lost their leadership as early as 1940, when the Soviets entered these provinces. As a result, the Jewish communities sustained a continuity of coping methods, including bribery and persuasion, two practices that were implemented before the war in Romania to release detainees and cancel decrees handed down by the authorities. These practices were used even more extensively in the Mogilev ghettos. Romanian commanders viewed their postings in the distant and hostile province of Transnistria as difficult and dangerous, yet lacking the prestige that accompanied battle. These officers sought to establish themselves financially during the war and therefore were easier to sway through bribery.[45] The many cases in which Romanian officials were paid off to breach or alleviate commands in the Mogilev district attest to the widespread culture of bribery. Some officials even issued receipts for the bribes they received.[46] Like the Mafia demands for protection money, they ruled by intimidation, threats, and monetary blackmail.[47] This attitude created leeway for the Jewish leadership to negotiate and help its communities. The committee chairmen also worked to establish support and welfare institutions which addressed the needs of the ghetto populations. The need for such institutions was far greater than that of any Jewish community in pre-Holocaust Romania.

In addition to the prewar practices employed by the Jewish leadership, it adopted new approaches, including the establishment of enforcement agencies, such as the department for coordinating Jewish labor and the Jewish police. It also implemented rescue through work, which essentially meant providing a flexible Jewish workforce, appropriately trained, with almost no demands in terms of remuneration, thereby presenting itself as valuable to the Romanian authorities and worth maintaining.

Due to the extreme circumstances, the ghetto leadership had greater authority than it had before the war in South Bukovina. The Mogilev district ghetto leadership was responsible for the very existence of its community members. The broad responsibilities of the Jewish leadership – providing work, creating lists of Jews for forced labor, or erasing names from lists and sending the Jewish police force to gather Jews intended for expulsion to the starvation death camps – created a situation whereby the Jews were almost entirely dependent on their Jewish committee leaders. The committees had a broad power base, which was unprecedented in terms of determining the fate of others and was restricted only by the Romanian authorities.[48]

Although they operated under similar historical conditions, interpreted situations in a similar fashion and shared assumptions, the decisions and conduct of committee chairmen were based also on their personalities and on the unique situation in each of the ghettos in the district.

Siegfried Jägendorf, chairman of the Mogilev ghetto, was an entrepreneurial leader. He focused on assuming control over the ghetto's economic activities, and even those of the entire district. Jägendorf coped with the most fundamental problem in the Mogilev district: the right of Jews to exist. To this end, he created a vital service based on an interest shared by the Romanian governorate and the Jewish public: using Jewish labor to renovate the power station and reinstate the *Turnatoria* (the foundry), thereby ensuring the Jews were an invaluable force for the Romanian authorities.[49] Meir Teich, chairman of the Jewish committee in the Shargorod ghetto, was a conservative leader. He chose to operate by implementing familiar practices from the period of his leadership in South Bukovina prior to deportation, including bribing officials and forging personal connections with officials who represented the Romanian authorities.[50] The only novelty he introduced to the ghetto was the establishment of a Jewish police force to impose the committee's authority. Max Rosenstrauch, chairman of the Jewish committee in the Djurin ghetto, was a formalist leader. He placed great importance on carrying out every command of the Romanian authorities to the letter, proving loyalty and obedience and in return, being able to provide some relief to Djurin's Jewish residents. Any initiatives that deviated from the orders were, in his view, deceitful and therefore dangerous, and undermined his authority and approach.[51]

All committee chairmen of the ghettos in the Mogilev district, including Shauer and Danilov, who both served briefly as chairmen of the Mogilev ghetto Jewish committee, acted out of the conviction that they understood the Romanian authorities' mindset, motives, and concerns, and therefore knew how to deal with them. They formed alliances with the Prefects and with the Romanian gendarmerie, usually through bribes, and negotiated with them on almost every matter to try to ease the living conditions in the ghettos and prevent the expulsion of Jews to the work camps and annihilation sites in Transnistria.[52] They did in fact successfully reverse some of the decisions of the occupying forces. They reduced the numbers of persons deported from the ghettos, postponed deportations, obtained approvals for assistance and contact with the Jewish community in Romania, opened stores and small businesses, gained permission to live outside the ghetto, received temporary travel passes for individuals within the region, and ran welfare institutions and hospitals.[53] The ability of these chairmen to make decisions, despite the daily threat of death, under conditions of existential uncertainty and insecurity, gave the Jewish population a sense that its leadership knew what to do and could navigate them towards a safer future. This was one of the reasons why, despite the criticism and anger leveled at the Jewish leadership, the Jewish population in the district continued to accept its leadership and obey it.

Jewish leadership in the ghettos of the Mogilev district operated on the basis of two premises. The first was that a reasonable possibility existed for a large part of the Jewish population in the Mogilev district ghettos to survive to the end of the war, as they were not facing a total annihilation. They did not know what was happening to the Jews in Poland and Eastern Europe. The news of the genocide that was taking place in the German-occupied areas of Europe did not reach the deportees in the Mogilev district and their ghetto leaders until the end of the war.[54] Fragments of information concerning mass murders in the south of the Transnistria province were believed to be part of a different set of events, namely the miserable fate of the Jews of Bessarabia and North Bukovina, who were marched to death sites.[55]

At the same time, the leadership was no less assured of the second premise – that not all the Jews in the ghettos could be saved. By February 1942, it became clear to the Jewish committees and their chairmen that they would not be able to save all the Jews. This fear was grounded in the explicit command in May 1942 to send 4,000 Jews from the Mogilev ghetto to Scazineti,[56] and the command in July 1942 to send 1,000 Jews each from the Djurin and Shargorod ghettos and 3,000 Jews from the Mogilev ghetto to Pechora. The leaders knew those Jews were sent to death and had to make tough decisions.[57]

Based on these two premises concerning the chances of survival of the Jews in the Mogilev district, the Jewish committees and their chairmen decided to cooperate with even the most brutal orders of the Romanian authorities. This cooperation included being involved in consolidating the lists of Jews to be deported from the Mogilev district to the Scazineti and Pechora starvation camps. When preparing these lists, they took into consideration economic status and the hometowns from which the Jews in the ghettos had come.[58]

Social and financial status

Among the South Bukovina Jews arriving at the Nistru transit point in Ataki on November 1941 by train, and despite harsh conditions, there were those who succeeded in bringing money, jewelry, and other belongings with them.[59] Property of this nature could be sold – especially items of clothing and footwear – guaranteeing its owners food and shelter and helping them survive the first few months. By contrast, families from Bessarabia and North Bukovina arrived in convoys in the summer of 1941 by foot, with no property or extra food or clothing, partly because of the economic circumstances and partly because they were robbed in the course of their journey. There were noticeable differences in the living conditions between the haves and the have-nots and in the chances of survival of their families and communities, triggering personal conflicts and rivalry between groups that were competing for the few resources available. This rivalry in turn brought about clashes led by the leadership of the district's Jewish committees, some even involving the Romanian authorities to suppress opposition.

Difference in financial status constituted, in part, the difference between life and death in the Mogilev ghettos. Shlomo Arbenstahl testified: "Only those who had no money and no contacts were sent to forced labor."[60] On the eve of the deportation of a large number of Jews from the Djurin ghetto in the summer of 1942, the poorer ghetto dwellers forced the wealthier ones to open their pockets by invading their homes and refusing to leave until they received enough money to bribe the authorities and revoke the deportation order.[61] Binyamin (Benno) Brecher testified: "Former professors, professional people, and others who had no connections roamed the streets of Mogilev like beggars and asked for bread."[62]

In 1943, the situation improved slightly. Parcels of food and clothing arrived from the Jewish aid committee in Romania and the Joint Distribution Committee (JDC).[63] Yet many Transnistrian deportees still strongly felt the disparities between the various groups in the ghetto: while most Jews from South Bukovina, Chernowitz, and Dorohoi received assistance from the Bucharest Aid Committee and relatives and friends in Romania, this was not true for the deportees from North Bukovina or the local Ukrainian Jews.[64] Yetty Bartfeld wrote in her diary: "The aid is given to them [the rich], and they do not share it with the poor."[65] On November 24, 1943, Kunstadt wrote: "In Transnistria there are places where the Jews wish they were dead, but there is also another Transnistria, where the wealthy sit day and night playing poker, and their hands are not empty."[66]

The Romanian policy of reducing the Jewish population in the ghettos also had an underlying financial basis. On October 12, 1942, General Ion Iliescu, Transnistria's Gendarmerie Inspector, suggested that the quota of 3,000 Jews for deportation to the Pechora camp be filled with the poorest. His reasoning was that they would die sooner anyhow, and that that was the purpose of the starvation camp.[67] Danilov, who executed the actual deportation in the Mogilev ghetto as the head of the Jewish police, testified: "Wealthy Jews enjoyed the protection of the authorities. It was clear that the committee could not touch them, so the bad luck fell on others."[68] Among the weak and poor were a large group of single mothers; married women whose husbands were absent, either because they were serving in the Red Army or they had died in Transnistria. These mothers and their children were regarded as non-productive. Burdened with the care of young children, they could not participate in the forced-labor duties or go to the neighboring villages to look for work. When the chairmen of the Jewish leadership in the ghettos were required to cull the population, they selected single mothers with young children.[69]

Considerations based on origins

The experience of the Jews of North Bukovina and South Bukovina in the year prior to Germany's invasion of Russia had a clear impact on the fate of Jews in each of the two provinces during the Holocaust and in Transnistria. The Romanians ascribed significant meaning to the year 1940, when the Soviets seized the province. North Bukovina was part of the Soviet Union for one year and socialist and communist ideas were favorably viewed by a small part of its Jewish residents. As a result, the Romanians were hostile towards Jews in North Bukovina, suspecting them of supporting communism and the Soviet Union. South Bukovina, on the other hand, had remained in Romania's control since the end of World War I.[70] After their deportation to the Mogilev district in Transnistria, South Bukovina's Jewish communities acclimated and coped with the harsh situation far better than the Jews of Bessarabia and North Bukovina or the local Ukrainian Jews. South Bukovina's Jews had several advantages: they came with their leaders, brought part of their assets with them, and had language skills that allowed them to communicate easily with the Romanians. Cultural and economic disparities that had existed prior to the war among individuals, families, and communities were more evident in Transnistria, particularly when the communities were compelled to deal with each other. These differences played an important role in the decision-making of the Jewish committees established in the Mogilev district.

The South Bukovina Jews identified strongly with their hometown communities and less so with Jews in general. In the testimonies of survivors, the Romanian hometown almost always appears alongside the individual's name as an inseparable part of the person's identity.[71] This identity was so strong that in many cases, members of one community refused to assist Jews of another. Zecharia Pitero of Dorohoi gave an account of his experience in Shargorod: "A mother asked for bread for her starving child from the Câmpulung cooperative, [...] the South Bukovinians said that the money received from the Jewish aid agency in Romania was intended to help Jews from their hometown and not from other places."[72] In the Shargorod ghetto, Jews from Suceava set up a bakery and a soup kitchen supplying 200 bowls of soup and a small store for "their own folk only."[73]

Differences and discrepancies existed not only between the various communities of deportees from Romania, but also between Romanian and local Ukrainian Jews. The Ukrainian Jewish communities that survived the German invasion of the Soviet Union were poor and without means,[74] and among them were old people, children, and women who were left alone after the men were drafted, murdered, or evacuated.[75]

The Romanian authorities in the Mogilev district accepted these class and financial divisions and even encouraged them, since they allowed for a divide-and-rule policy and guaranteed the cooperation of the stronger communities. For example, the gendarmerie report of September 1943 listed the Jews in the Shargorod ghetto according to the province from which they arrived.[76] The Romanian governorate imposed a strict hierarchy: "The authorities separated the Jews who were to stay in Mogilev, who were seen as trash, from the Jews who were actually scum and intended to be deported further [...] these were poor Ukrainian Jews, who did not speak German or Romanian and had lived under Soviet rule for a year before 1941."[77] Jews from South Bukovina were considered Romanian, even if their mother tongue was German, as were Jews from the Dorohoi province whose mother tongue was Romanian and who were municipally affiliated prior to deportation with the *Regat* – the Romanian Old Kingdom. These Jews were similar to the occupying Romanian forces in appearance, language, and customs, and the Romanian forces allowed them to live in colonies in Transnistria. Other Jews – from the North Bukovina communities, Bessarabia, and the local Ukrainian communities – were considered to be lower on the hierarchy, making them the first to be listed for expulsion to Scazineti and Pechora. This phenomenon could be compared to the attitude of Vichy France towards "our Jews" and "newcomer Jews."[78]

Kunstadt also outlined the order of entitlement to life as viewed in the district, based on the province of origin in Romania: "The highest in the hierarchy are those from northern Moldova [Dorohoi province], who are absolutely kosher. They are not suspected of being Bolsheviks. Then are the South Bukovinians, who remained in the realm of the Kingdom up to the Siret River. Then comes North Bukovinians, who were under Soviet occupation for a year, under the hammer and sickle, and last, the remainder of Jews from Bessarabia who were considered 'red'."[79] The Department of Registration in the ghettos played an important role in the capacity of the Romanian authorities to distinguish between the different origins of the Jews. Simcha Zeidenstein testified: "The Jewish committee in Mogilev comprised primarily Jews from South Bukovina [...] the Jews from North Bukovina were thought to be communists."[80] When the Romanian authorities wanted to rid the province of large numbers of Jews, they took these divisions into account, for their own reasons. This approach further reinforced the disparities, to the degree that cultural differences determined the fate of certain communities, as Jews destined for deportation from the Mogilev district were selected based on their community of origin. Or as Carp put it: "If they could not discriminate the Jews on the basis of race, they could discriminate them on the basis of status. Conditions were created that nurtured a mental and spiritual climate of separation."[81]

The Romanian authorities could have implemented a random policy for reducing the Jewish population in the district's ghettos by deporting Jews to Scazineti and Pechora and beyond the Bug River without the cooperation of the Jewish committees. And occasionally, they did: when one hundred Jews were required to make up the quota for the first deportation from the Mogilev ghetto to Scazineti, the gendarmerie randomly rounded up Jews from the ghetto's streets.[82] However, the Romanian authorities preferred a policy of selectively ridding themselves of the Jews, selecting and sending the poorest Jews as well as those who were perceived as lacking affinity to the Romanian people. The Romanian authorities would not have been able to choose the poorest or the 'least Romanian' without the cooperation of Jewish committees.

The Jewish leadership in the ghettos had an understanding with the Romanian authorities that certain people would not be deported to Scazineti, Pechora, and the Bug camps. The two main criteria to be met, accepted by both the Romanian authority and the Jewish leadership, were (1) having a job in the ghetto or the ability to pay for a work exemption, and (2) belonging to certain provinces in Romania.[83] The examples below show the importance of origin in deciding the identity of deportees. On May 25, 1942, a special memorandum from Ştefănescu made clear what was expected from the Mogilev ghetto committee regarding the identities of deportees, and detailed the priorities: "Lists of all Jews from Chernowitz shall be given to the gendarmerie. Should the Jews from Chernowitz not fill the quota, it shall be filled with Jews from other provinces of occupied Bukovina [i.e. North Bukovina]."[84] Selecting the Chernowitz Jews for deportation meant that the gendarmerie had to access the files of the Jewish committee's Department of Registration.[85] On June 28, an order was given to deport an additional 500 Jews specifically from North Bukovina.[86] Kunstadt noted that the Romanian deportation plan of July 1942 for the entire Mogilev district not only set a quota of Jews to be deported, but also provided guidelines to the Jewish committee for selection: "First the Ukrainian Jews will be sent (like a sacrificial atonement), [and then] the Jews of Bessarabia and North Bukovina who enjoyed the 'Garden of Eden' in Stalin's period."[87] Rosenstock's diary also shows that selecting the deportees from the Djurin ghetto was not random, but was linked to the Jews' Romanian hometown: "One thousand Jews will remain in Djurin, all from South Bukovina."[88] Most of the deportees to Scazineti were the poor and those who came from Chernowitz and North Bukovina. Clearly, the deportees were not selected at random. The identities of those destined for expulsion were determined by committees where Jewish community representatives convened with representatives of the Romanian authorities. The assistance provided by committee members to the authorities on the day of deportation is also detailed.[89] Without this assistance, the Romanian authorities would not have been able to make selective deportations of 2,900 Jews to Scazineti.[90]

The interests of the Jewish committees and the Romanian forces in the province were coordinated: Romanian authorities were interested in selectively ridding themselves of the Jews in the ghettos by deporting them to the starvation camps, indicating that they preferred to send the weak, the poor, and those suspected of being disloyal to Romania. The objective of the Jewish committees was at first to save as many Jews as possible. But as conditions worsened, and the danger of death grew greater, this ambitious goal quickly proved to be unfeasible. It was replaced by a more modest and self-serving one: to save the Jews of their own hometowns. Therefore, Danilov focused chiefly on saving Jews from Dorohoi; Jägendorf focused on saving Jews from Rădăuți; Yonnas Kessler, on Jews from Vatra Dornei; and Teich primarily assisted Jews from Suceava. This target was impressively achieved: over 70 percent of the Jews from South Bukovina's communities (25,000 at the outset of the German-Romanian attack on the Soviet Union) were still alive when the Red Army liberated the Mogilev district.[91]

These divisions between the communities allowed for the South Bukovina Jews to take part in organizing the deportations to Pechora and Scazineti, knowing that the Jews destined for deportation were not "real Romanians" like the Jews from Dorohoi or South Bukovina. It also created a sense of relative immunity among the Jews of Dorohoi and South Bukovina, which helped the Romanian authorities achieve cooperation from the members of these communities, as well as the desired conduct inside the ghettos.[92] In preparation for the deportation to Scazineti towards the end of May 1942, for example, the Jewish committee in Mogilev appealed to the ghetto population to maintain order for its own benefit, and to approach a special committee if a designated deportee felt they should not have been selected for deportation because they held a job and therefore belonged to the "right" group in the ghetto.[93]

The Jewish committees applied this strategy for two and a half years to cope with the Romanian authorities. The greater the chances of survival of their hometown communities, the more they were willing to cooperate. The willingness of the Jewish committees to be involved in the deportations to Scazineti and Pechora enabled them to determine who would be deported from the ghetto and who would stay, but it also allowed them to bargain with the authorities and reduce the quotas by 25 percent.

Conclusion

The Jewish leadership in the ghettos of the Mogilev district was compelled to function under grave conditions. The community had been removed from its homeland and culture, and had very few resources in comparison with its needs. It lived in crowded conditions with poor sanitation amid constant outbreaks of disease and widespread death. The Jewish committees assumed that the Romanian authorities in the Mogilev district did not seek the total annihilation of its Jewish population. Rather, they thought, the governorate sought to take maximum advantage of the Jews as a work force with total disregard to the fate of the population. Not all the Jews in the ghettos in the district could work, which was the basic way of saving them, nor could they all pay bribes, as many had very little means. Unlike the Jewish Councils in the ghettos of Poland and East Europe, the Jewish committee leaders and members of Mogilev survived the holocaust. Some later penned their perspective of brutal events, insisting that their conduct and decisions were the only way to save many of the Jews in the Mogilev region.[94] The Jewish Councils in Poland and other areas faced a total annihilation of the ghetto so the selections they made did not save anyone, but the selections made by the Jewish committees in the Mogilev region proved to be effective. Fully 70 percent of the South Bukovina Jewry was rescued. At the same time, their strategy sharply poses the moral questions: Am I my brother's keeper? and: Who are we to consider as "brothers"?

In order to protect their hometown communities, the Jewish committees maintained ongoing contact with the Romanian authorities. The relationship was also founded on similar perceptions regarding hierarchic identity and the sense of belonging among the diverse Jewish communities in the ghettos of the Mogilev district. Jewish committees negotiated with the Romanian regime over deportations to the Scazineti, Pechora, and Bug camps; they exerted tremendous efforts in preventing the deportation of those close to them, such as affluent Jews or members of their hometown communities from South Bukovina; and participated in registering the Jews of North Bukovina, Bessarabia, and Ukraine, and even assisted in rounding them up.[95]

The representatives of the ghetto population, most of whom were from South Bukovina, assessed their behavior based on their success in saving the Jews from their hometowns. They believed their fellow community members understood and accepted the price: the loss of other communities in the ghetto. Despite the harsh conditions with which they coped, they did not perceive themselves as agents of the Romanian governorate but as leaders of their communities. Community leaders believed that, given the circumstances under which they operated, their approach was optimal. In his trial after the war, Danilov wrote: "It was crucial that we sacrifice some people to save the other 17,000 who remained in Mogilev. Without our intervention the entire ghetto was under risk of evacuation."[96] Teich wrote after the war: "We believed that this was the only way to clear the conscience of our heavy hearts."[97] Yet, the words of Kunstadt resound in our ears, reminding us of the human cost of this strategy: "The committee arranged generous amounts of food and beverage with the head of the gendarmerie, and there was a celebration that the money used to pay for could have been enough for a whole week in the public kitchen. That very night, in an attic, a young man from Rădăuți hanged himself because his wife had been nagging him for a week to get some milk for a sick toddler, costing half a mark, and he could not find half a mark."[98]

Notes

1   This essay was prepared on the basis of my Ph.D. dissertation, supervised by Dr. Raphael Vago. See: G. Tibon, *The Jewish Leadership of the South Bukovina Communities in the Ghettos in the Mogilev Region in Transnistria, and Its Dealings with the Romanian Regime, 1941–1944,* Tel Aviv University, 2013. I would like to thank the History Department of Carnegie Mellon University in Pittsburgh, PA, where this article was written in the framework of the Sawyer Seminar Postdoctoral Fellowship; a different version of this article was first published in *Dapim: Studies on the Holocaust*: G. Tibon, 'Am I My Brother's Keeper? The Jewish Committees in the Ghettos of Mogilev Province and the Romanian Regime in Transnistria during the Holocaust, 1941–1944,' *Dapim: Studies on the Holocaust,* vol. 30 (2) 2016, 93–116. I thank the Yoran Schnitzer Foundation and the Goldstein-Goren Diaspora Research Center at Tel Aviv University and the

Hannah Ha'Elyon Foundation of Yad Vashem for their support of my study. The paper is based, to a large extent, on the interrogations, personal files and punitive files of the Jewish leaders and Romanian officials, which are located in the Consiliul National pentru Studierea Arhivelor Securitatii (CNSAS) archive, the secret service archive in Bucharest, Romania, together with documents found in the Jägendorf and Carp collections and testimonies in the Yad Vashem and United States Holocaust Memorial Museum (USHMM) archives.

2 M. Carp, *Holocaust in Romania: Facts and Documents on the Annihilation of Romanian Jews 1940–1944* (Trans. Sean Murphy), Harbor, FL: Safety & Simon Publications, 2000, p. 157.

3 J. Ancel, *Transnistria, 1941–1942: The Romanian Mass Murder Campaigns*, 2003, Tel Aviv University, vol. 2, p. 15.

4 Jandarmeria (Gendarmerie) – a military body involved in policing and assisting the police force.

5 David Sha'ari counted 25,923 Jews in South Bukovina in 1940. See: Raphael Vago & Libiu Rotman (eds.), *History of the Jews in Romania, Between the Two World Wars*, Tel Aviv: Diaspora Research Center, 1996, vol. 3, p. 241 (Hebrew).

6 The district was administratively annexed to Bukovina in 1938. In the summer of 1941, the Jews were expelled to other districts within Romania and returned to Dorohoi to be expelled again – to Transnistria.

7 Romanian and German forces completed the occupation of the province on July 15, 1941. Odessa was seized several weeks later and became the capital of the province and the seat of government. See: Radu Ioanid (ed.), *History of the Jews in Romania, The Holocaust*, vol. 4, 2002, pp. 113–122, Tel Aviv: Diaspora Research Center.

8 On the expulsion from Romania's different regions, see: Tuvia Friling, Radu Ioanid & Mihail E. Ionescu (eds.), *Final Report: International Commission on the Holocaust in Romania*, Bucharest: Polirom, 2005, p. 138. Vladimir Solonari claims that the anti-Jewish policy and expulsion of Jews from Bessarabia and Bukovina in 1941 were part of Antonescu's comprehensive vision of Romania's future after the war, as a country free of foreigners. See: Vladimir Solonari, "Model Province": Explaining the Holocaust of Bessarabian and Bukovinian Jewry, *Nationalities Papers*, vol. 34 (4), 2006, 472. See also: Ronit Fisher, Between Ethnic Cleansing to Genocide: An Alternative Analysis of the Holocaust of Romanian Jewry, *Yad Vashem Studies*, vol. 40 (1), 2012, 133–164. See also: Dennis Deletant, Transnistria and the Romanian Solution to the "Jewish Problem," *The Shoah in Ukraine: History, Testimony, Memorialization*, Ray Brandon & Wendy Lower (eds.), Bloomington and Indianapolis: Indiana University Press, 2010, pp. 156–159.

9 Simon Geissbuhler, "What we know now about Romania and the Holocaust – and why it matters?" *Romania and the Holocaust, Events-Contexts-Aftermath* (ed. Simon Geissbuhler) Ibidem-Verlag, Stuttgart, 2016, pp. 243–244.

10 Bianca Rudich Gassner's testimony is one that uses the term *Judenrat*. Her testimony was given in 1961, and may have been influenced by the discussion in Israel. B. Rudich Gassner, Yad Vashem Archive, O-3/1751 (Hebrew).

11 Z. Sherf, *Yad Vashem Archive*, O-3/1526; Y. Yalon, *Yad Vashem Archive*, O-3/1238; S. Freiling-Avivi, *Yad Vashem Archive*, O-3/13014.

12 Public Prosecutor Constantin Mocanu's speech after the war trials in June 1945: "Two sites will remain blackened forever: Scazineti and Pechora. They are the most predominant stain on Antonescu's government [...] tens of thousands of expelled persons died of starvation as a result of a blanket prohibition against supplying food." [Trans. from Romanian]. See: Punitive File of Botoroaga and Others, CNSAS Archive, vol. 1, 7795.

13 Deportations to the starvation death camps were known as *descongestionarea*, i.e., thinning the crowd or reducing the density, in much the same way as the expulsion of the Jews from the north-eastern parts of Romania was called *evacuation*. The Romanian word *deportati*, used by the Romanian forces for Jews deported from the provinces of Bukovina, Bessarabia, and Dorohoi, meant both immigrants and deportees. By referring

to these Jews as *immigrants* or *evacuees*, the Romanian authorities could assume involvement in a process of voluntary immigration rather than forced deportation. See: Letter to the Governor of Transnistria dated December 12, 1942: Jean Ancel, *Transnistria, 1941–1942*, 2003, vol. 2, 481.

14   Lipman Kunstadt, *traybt men yidn ibern dnyester: togbukh funem transnistrishen giheynm* (The Persecution of Jews beyond the Dniester: A Diary from the Transnistria Hell), 1980, Haifa: Self-Published, p. 47.

15   Martin Dean, "Life and Death in the 'Gray Zone' of Jewish Ghettos in Nazi-Occupied Europe: The Unknown, the Ambiguous, and the Disappeared," in *Gray Zones: Ambiguity and Compromise in the Holocaust and Its Aftermath (Studies on War and Genocide)*, Jonathan Petropoulos & John Roth (eds.), Oxford: Bergham Books, 2005, pp. 209–210.

16   The intention of the Romanian General Staff was to deport the Jews to the eastern side of the Bug River, to German territory, and hand them to the Einsatzgruppen. However, the German murder units were occupied exterminating the Jews of western Russia, and refused to take on any extra work at the time. See: D. Deletant, "Transnistria and the Romanian Solution to the Jewish Problem," in *The Shoah in Ukraine: History, Testimony, Memorialization*, B. Ray & W. Lower (eds.), Bloomington and Indianapolis: Indiana University Press, 2010, pp. 156–159.

17   Most of the original Jewish population of the Transnistria province, about 300,000 people, had been murdered by the Einsatzgruppen, assisted by Romanian military units and militias from the local Ukrainian population. Dennis Deletant and Ottmar Trasca (eds.), *Al III-lea Reich si Holocaustul din Romania, 1940–1944, Documente din Arhivele Germane* (Romanian) (The Third Reich and the Holocaust in Romania, 1940–1944, Documents from German Archives), Bucuresti: Institutului pentru Studierea Holocaustul din Romania, 2007, p. 30; M. Kerner, *Yad Vashem Archive*, O-3/915.

18   E. Lustig, *Strochlitz Archive*, R3H22. Y. Rand & Sha'ari, *Memorial Book of the Jewish Community in Vatra Dornei and Surroundings*, p. 163 (Hebrew); Fisher, "Between Ethnic Cleansing to Genocide," p. 87: Nasturas' Order No. 147, 2001.

19   Transnistria 1941–1942, *The Romanian Mass Murder Campaigns, History and Document Summaries* (3 vols). Tel Aviv: The Goldstein-Goren Diaspora Research Center, Tel Aviv University, 2003, vol. 2, p. 15; J. Ancel, *The History of the Holocaust, Romania*, Jerusalem: Yad Vashem, 2002, vol. 2, p. 765 (Hebrew).

20   Nasturas wrote after the war: "The presence of 50,000 Jews expelled to this [Mogilev] district caused many difficulties to the administrative authorities." [Trans. from Romanian] Letter to Jägendorf, April 13, 1945, Jägendorf Collection, *Yad Vashem Archive*, p. file 10.

21   Punitive File of Botoroaga and Others, *CNSAS Archive*, vol. 2, p. 7795.

22   *Prefect* was the district commander, equivalent in rank to colonel. The district was known as *prefecture*. *Pretor* was the commander of a sub district, equivalent to a major. The word *pretor* in Romanian also means judge, and the pretors, like the prefects, had legal authority and could sentence the subjects in the area under their control. The deportation planned in February took place in May 1942. J. Sigfried, *Jagendorf's Foundry, Memoir of the Romanian Holocaust 1941–1944* (Hit-Manheimer Aron [edited with commentary]), 1991, New York: Harper-Collins, p. 69.

23   Punitive file of Botoroaga and Others, *CNSAS Archive*, vol. 2, p. 7795.

24   Court file of Dimitrie Ştefănescu, *CNSAS Archive*, vol. 1, p. 8279.

25   A. Shachan, *Ba-kefor ha-lohet lochamai-hagetaot*, 1988, pp. 382–383. The occupying Romanian governorate decided to replace the *Obshchina*, the local Jewish committee appointed by the Germans, with a committee made up entirely of Romanian-speaking Jews. Shlomo Kleiman, Yad Vashem Archive, O-3/5245 (Russian). Shmuel Spector, "Ghettos and Judenrats in the Occupied Areas of the Soviet Union," in *Proceedings of the Tenth World Jewish Congress on Jewish Studies*, D. Assaf (ed.), Jerusalem: Magnes, 1990, p. 453.

26   Regarding the common use of the word *colony* to describe concentrations of Jews in the Mogilev district, see: Yitzhak Yalon, Yaacov Rand and David Sha'ari (eds.). *Memorial*

Book of the Jewish Community in Vatra Dornei and Surroundings, Bukovina – Romania, Tel Aviv: The Association of Survivors from Vatra Dornei and Surroundings, 2001, p. 142 (Hebrew). The irony in the use of the term *colony* is emphasized in Mirjam Korber's diary: "Indeed, some settlers we are, without any land, without a home." See: Korber, Mirjam, *Deportiert: Judische Uberlebensschicksale, 1941–1944,* Ein Tagbuch: Hartung-Gorre, Konstanz, 1993, p. 90 (German).

27 For the English translation of the directive, see: Avigdor Shachan, *Burning Ice: The Ghettos of Transnistria (East European Monographs)* (Translated by Shmuel Himelstein), New York, Columbia University Press, 1996, pp. 480–481. Based on the expulsion routes, four areas of camps and ghettos formed unintentionally between the Bug and the Nistru (Dniester) rivers: in Tulchin; in Balta – south of the Bug; between Berezovka and Golta – near the Bug; the fourth area, which is the focus of this chapter, was the Mogilev district in northwest Transnistria. The Prefect of Mogilev controlled five sub districts: Mogilev, Shargorod, Kopaygorod, Zhmerynka, and Stanislavski. Transnistria was declared an administrative unit on August 30, 1941, with the signing of the Tighina Agreement. The agreement determined the authorities given to the Romanian regime and Germany's rights in this territory. See: Dennis Deletant, "Ghetto Experience in Golta, Transnistria, 1942–1944," in *Holocaust and Genocide Studies,* 2004, vol. 18 (1), p. 2.

28 Wherever the deportees themselves did not initiate establishing a new committee, the establishment of the Jewish committee was delayed until spring of 1942. See: Wolf Rosenstock, *Dachauer Hefte, Die vergessenen lager 5, Die Chronik Von Dschurin* (The Dachau Books, The Forgotten Camps 5, The Chronicles of Djurin), Verlag Dachauer Hefte, 1989, p. 6. (German).

29 Jägendorf Collection, *Yad Vashem Archive,* File 6, p-9.

30 M. Teich, "The Jewish Self-Administration in Shargorod Ghetto (Transnistria)," in *Collection of Studies on Chapters of the Holocaust and Heroism II,* Yad vashem, Jerusalem, 1958, pp. 213–214.

31 Despite Jägendorf being left out of committees headed by Mihai Danilov, Yosef Shauer and Moshe Katz, he nonetheless remained involved in the Ghetto's public activities, and claimed responsibility for the Ghetto's shop area and public institutions, including the Mogilev orphanage. See: Jägendorf Collection, File 8, p-9. See also: Jägendorf, p. 164.

32 Carp, *Cartea Neagră, Suferintele evreilor din Romania, 1940–1944* (The Black Book of the Sufferings of Romanian Jews), 1947, Bucuresti: Societatea Nationala de Editura si Arte Gratice "Dacia Traiana" (Romanian), vol. 3, pp. 15–16.

33 Ancel, *Transnistria 1941–1942,* 1941, vol. 2, p. 112. By September 1941, a center for combating local espionage was set up in the Gendarmerie Control Center of each district. Nonetheless, the concerns of the Romanian authorities continued to grow. In a circular ordering the closure of the Ghettos and limitation of travel permits, the central command also requested all possible information on Jews in the Ghettos: "Day and night, the activities of the detained Jews (illegal and open), the number of support organizations, threats to the official organization of the State, trends and ambitions" (Romanian). See: Carp, *Cartea Neagră,* 1942, p. 377. See: Gendarmerie Bulletin of January 9, *Matatias Carp collection Yad Vashem,* O–11, file A-8-99.

34 Similar to the outbreak of the epidemic in Transnistria's Balta and Yampol districts. See: Gendarmerie Bulletin of October 15–31; Ancel, *Transnistria 1941–1942,* 1941, vol. 2, pp. 220, 400. See also: punitive file of Botoroaga and Others, CNSAS Archive, vol. 1, P-7795. Pretor Romeo Orasanu, who was accused of sending Jews to Scazineti, claimed this was an order received from higher ranks (from Ion Iliescu, the gendarmerie inspector of Transnistria), and explained that he was compelled to take this action to try to avoid the spread of typhus in the province.

35 The Gendarmerie Bulletin addressed the daily dangers inherent to the existence of the Jewish public in Transnistria as perceived by the Romanian regime: espionage and typhus contamination. See: Gendarmerie Bulletin of January 9, 1942, *Matatias Carp collection Yad vashem,* O–11, File A-8-99.

36   Ştefănescu testified that the deportation to Scazineti was an attempt to avoid typhus from spreading to the Romanian forces. *CNSAS Archive*, vol. 1, File P-8279. On June 3, 1942, a command was given by the governor of Transnistria Alexeanu to Prefect Nasturas, as follows: "As it has become clear that in most of the towns and villages, the Jews constitute a permanent source of physical contamination [for typhus] and spiritual contamination [referring to their alleged support for communist ideals and Russia's success], and that they are not isolated as commanded [in Order No. 23 of November 23, 1941], steps must be taken to gather the Jews from your district into Ghettos and assign them to work in factories and agriculture" (Romanian). See: Carp, *Cartea Neagră*, p. 357.

37   As Dan Michman writes: "To restore the Jews to their deserved status" (Hebrew). See: Dan Michman, *The Jewish Ghettos in the Holocaust: How and Why Did They Emerge*, p. 118. Nasturas indeed worked endlessly to replace Jägendorf, the manager of the foundry, and the Jewish laborers. See: Jägendorf Collection, *Yad Vashem Archive*, File 1-9, p. 9. This tendency to spread the idea of Romanian national sentiment in the province when Nasturas held office manifested itself not only in the efforts to replace Jewish industrial workers with Ukrainians under Romanian supervision, but also in replacing the Ukrainian mayor of Mogilev, Ivanov, with the Romanian Captain Nicolae Botta, who assumed his position in April 1942. The desire to establish a pure Romanian society sans foreigners was clearly there. See: Washington Archive USHMM R-G-31.011M Reel 7 (Romanian). See: Personal file of Constantine Nasturas, CNSAS Archive, I-329788.

38   Personal file of Constantine Nasturas, CNSAS Archive, I-329788. His personality and ideological path integrated religious anti-Semitism. He admired Romanian intellectuals and poets such as Eminescu and Iorga, who were notorious xenophobes in general, and anti-Semite in particular. Nasturas himself was an admired poet in Romania. See website: www.referatele.com/referate/romana/Nasturas-Volbura-Poiana.

39   Carp, *Cartea Neagră*, p. 361: a classified circular dated July 5, 1942, sent by the administration of the Mogilev district to the central command authorities.

40   In a letter dated February 11, 1942, sent by Ştefănescu to Colonel Constantin Tobescu, head of the gendarmerie service in the Transnistria Government (Romanian). See: CNSAS Archive, File P-8279. Ironically, the letter notes the tension between the headquarters and the forces in the field, and ends: "We ask that you also inform this Inspector General on the steps you agree to take." From this remark, and the entire letter, it seems that Ştefănescu felt he was not included in central decision-making concerning basic issues in Transnistria, nor were his views on these issues accepted. See also: Ancel, *Transnistria 1941–1942*, vol. 2, p. 150.

41   Dennis Deletant, "Transnistria and the Romanian Solution to the Jewish Problem," p. 189.

42   Punitive File of Botoroaga and others, CNSAS Archive, vol. 1, P-7795; also, court file of Dimitrie Ştefănescu, CNSAS Archive, vol. 1, P-8279; and personal file of Constantine Nasturas, CNSAS Archive, I-329788.

43   See Michman's distinction between *headship* and *leadership*: Dan Michman, *The Holocaust and Holocaust Research: Conceptualization, Terminology and Basic Issues*, Tel Aviv: Moreshet/ Sifriat Poalim, Yad Vashem and Ghetto Fighters' House, 1998, pp. 108–109 (Hebrew).

44   Israel Gutman and Rachel Manbar (eds.), *Patterns of Jewish Leadership in Nazi Europe, 1933–1945*, Jerusalem: Yad Vashem, 1979 (Hebrew). See also: Lucy Dawidowicz, *The War Against the Jews, 1933–1945*, New York: Holt, Rinehart and Winston, 1975.

45   Colonel Nasturas had retired from the Romanian career army on March 26, 1941, but was recruited as a reservist from the outbreak of war until its end. See: personal file of Constantine Nasturas, CNSAS Archive, I-329733. Pretor Botoroaga was a major in the reserves; the third prefect, Constantin Loghin, was a colonel in the reserves. See: punitive File of Botoroaga and Others, CNSAS Archive, vol. 2, P-7795. Dimitrie Ştefănescu was called up for reserve duty despite having retired in May 1941. See: court file of Dimitrie Ştefănescu, CNSAS Archive, vol. 1, P-8279.

46 Mayor of Mogilev, Botta, took bribes regularly. Jewish survivors who testified at his trial presented his actions in a positive light. Jägendorf collection Yad Vashem, File 7, p. 9.

47 Some Romanian officers and soldiers were put on trial during the war for disobeying orders and taking bribes. Most senior among them were Prefect Baleanu and his two deputies. For the testimonies and the trial protocol, see: Matatias Carp, *Cartea Neagrǎ*, vol. 3, pp. 190–192. Summary of Baleanu and his deputies' investigation (Romanian), ibid., p. 361.

48 F. E. Fiedler, *A Theory of Leadership Effectiveness*, New York, NY: McGraw-Hill, 1967, pp. 22–25 on how much influence the leader has on power factors such as employment, dismissal, discipline, promotion and rewards. In the Jewish committees, the "power of position" was measured by life and death factors that could determine a person's fate. On the power of Judenrats in occupied Poland, see: Raul Hilberg, "The Ghetto as a Form of Governance," *Yalkut Moreshet: Holocaust Documentation and Research*, 1975, p. 94 (Hebrew).

49 Jägendorf Collection, *Yad Vashem Archive*, File 24, p. 9. Lipman Kunstadt, *Traybt men yidn ibern dnyester: togbukh funem transnistrishen giheynm* (The Persecution of Jews beyond the Dniester: A Diary from the Transnistria Hell), Haifa: Self-Published, 1980, pp. 14–15 (Yiddish).

50 Court file of Meir Teich, CNSAS Archive, P-50678 (Romanian). See also: Teich, *The Jewish Self-Administration in Shargorod Ghetto* (Transnistria), Yad Vashem, 1958, pp. 218, 233.

51 Emma Lustig, Strochlitz Archive, R3H22; Kunstadt, *Togbukh* (Diary), pp. 279, p. 244.

52 Ioanid, *History of the Jews in Romania*, p. 189. See also: J. Ancel, *History and Document Summaries, 1941–1942*, Tel Aviv: Goldstein-Goren Diaspora Research Center, Tel Aviv University, vol. 2, 2003, pp. 509–539.

53 Teich, *The Jewish Self-Administration in Shargorod Ghetto (Transnistria)*, pp. 209–210; see also: Ioanid, *History of the Jews in Romania*, p. 191.

54 M. Fox, *Yad Vashem Archive*, O-3/6350723 (Hebrew).

55 Ancel, *The History of the Holocaust, Romania*, vol. 2, p. 1027. Referring to the mass murders that took place in south Transnistria, in Domanovka and Obodovka, among other locations: Y. Yalon, *Yad Vashem Archive*, O-3/1238.

56 In a letter to Prefect Baleanu, Jägendorf stated that the conditions in Scazineti were unlivable. See: report of the delegation to Sczineti, 1942, Jägendorf Collection, *Yad Vashem Archive*, File 6, p-9.

57 Rabbi Karelnik, who organized a fund to redeem Jews deported from the Djurin ghetto, estimated that he would only be able to save half of them. Kunstadt noted that eventually the decision was to deport five percent of the ghetto's Jews, and nobody believed that they would fall into that very small percentage. Kunstadt, *Togbukh*, pp. 104–105.

58 E. Shturper, *Strochlitz Archive*, R3H22. Jägendorf had already prepared the lists for deportation, but he had done it by elimination – he had actually made a list of those who were to stay in Mogilev. See: Jägendorf Collection, *Yad Vashem*, 1942, File 9, p-9. See also: Jägendorf, pp. 117–118; and Rosenstock, *Die Chronik Von Dschurin*, p. 60.

59 Matatias Carp, *Transnistria le'ben, leiden un umkuft fon Bessarabise, Bukoviner, un Rumanishe yeden* (Yiddish) (Transnistria, the Life, Suffering and Death of the Jews of Bessarabia, Bukovina and Romania), Buenos Aires: St. Martin, 1950, p. 215. See also: Erwin Shturper, Strochlitz Archive, R3H22: "The Dorohoi Jews had money, while others were destitute" (German).

60 Shlomo Arbenstahl, Yad Vashem Archive, O-3/1485 (Hebrew).

61 Kunstadt, *Togbukh*, p. 87. See also Yitzhak Artzi, Feibish Herman and David Sha'ari, *Our Siret: The Story of a Jewish town*, The Association of Survivors from Siret, 2003, p. 187: "Approximately 120 families of means, most of whom were from Suceava and Gura Humora, succeeded in obtaining permission from the Romanian authorities to live outside the ghetto. They rented rooms in the lower neighborhood from the Ukrainians."

62 Binyamin Brecher, *Lo Eshkah Otakh Mogilev*, Holon: Private Publication, 2002, p. 15 (Hebrew).

63 The Joint Distribution Committee, colloquially called *The Joint* – a worldwide Jewish relief organization, established in 1914.

64 Some 12,000 Ukrainian Jews remained in their villages throughout the Mogilev district after the mass murders at the start of the German-Romanian occupation of Ukraine. These Jews lived in central towns in Shargorod, Djurin and Mogilev and in remote villages. See: Christopher R. Browning, *The Origins of the Final Solution: The Evolution of Nazi Jewish Policy, 1939–1942*, Jerusalem: Yad Vashem, 2004, p. 334. See also: Yitzhak Arad, The Holocaust of Soviet Jews, *Three Million – Massuah* 29, 2001, pp. 22–23 (Hebrew).

65 Yetty (Yehudit) Bartfeld, *Yoman Ahava Betransnistria* (Hebrew) (Love Diary in Transnistria), Tzvi Avni (Nelo) (ed.), Tel Aviv, Eked, 1998, p. 37 (Hebrew).

66 Kunstadt, *Togbukh*, p. 340.

67 Carp, *Holocaust in Romania*, p. 218. Theodor Lavi and Jean Ancel, *Encyclopaedia of Jewish Communities in Romania*, Jerusaelm, Yad Vashem, 1969, p. 465; Jägendorf Collection, Yad Vashem Archive, p. 9, File 14. Orashenu, Commander of the Gendarmerie Legion, was also accused of sending poor Jews when conducting the deportation to Scazineti. CNSAS Archive, vol. 2, P-7795.

68 Court file of Danilov, CNSAS Archive, vol. 1, P-7795. Israel Gutman wrote about the perception of the Judenrat in Poland's Ghettos: "Deportation to death applies to Jews who have no vital efficacy; it is necessary to accept this partial sacrifice in order to save from this fate the laborers and those fit to work" (Hebrew). See: I. Gutman, "The Judenrat as a Leadership", *Leader and Leadership*, I. Malchin and Z. Tzachor (eds.), Jerusalem: Zalman Shazar Center for the History of Israel, the Israeli Historical Society, 1992, p. 284.

69 G. Tibon, "Women and Teenage Girls in the Holocaust of the Jews of Bessarabia and Bukovina", M.A. thesis, Haifa University, 2010, pp. 60–62 (Hebrew).

70 Lavi and Ancel, *Encyclopaedia of Jewish Communities in Romania*, p. 429.

71 B. Brecher, *I Will Not Forget You, Mogilev*, pp. 17–18; 22 (Hebrew). Lists of those who died in the Ghetto all detail hometown in Romania, as do the lists documenting the distribution of clothing sent by Romania's Jews. See: Jägendorf Collection, File 24, p. 9; Jägendorf Collection, File 6, p-9.

72 Z. Pitero, *Yad Vashem Archive*, O-3/2469.

73 Teich, *The Jewish Self-Administration in Shargorod Ghetto* (Transnistria), p. 213.

74 Y. Bauer, "The Reaction of Jewish Groups to Nazi Policy During the Holocaust," in *The Holocaust in Jewish History: Historiography, Consciousness, Interpretations*, Dan Michman (ed.), Jerusalem: Yad Vashem, 2005, p. 114 (Hebrew).

75 J. Ancel, "The German-Romanian Relationship and the Final Solution," *Holocaust and Genocide Studies*, 2005, vol. 19 (2), 252–275.

76 Ben-Zion Fuchs (ed.), *The Book of the Jews from Suceava (Shotz) and the Surrounding Communities*, Haifa, The Association of Former Residents of Suceava (Shotz) and Surroundings, 2007, p. 119 (Hebrew).

77 Kunstadt, *Togbukh*, p. 79.

78 M. R. Marrus and R. O. Paxton, *Vichy France and the Jews*, New York: Basic Books, 1981.

79 L. Kunstadt, *Ztwaishen Dniestr un Bug, Die Zukufunt* (Between the Dniester and the Bug) (Yiddish), vol. 82, 1979, pp. 139–142.

80 S. S. Zeidenstein, *Yad Vashem Archive*, O-3/10799 (German).

81 Matatias Carp collection, *Yad Vashem*, O-11, File A-8-99.

82 According to Danilov's testimony: "They took the old-age home and the sick, grabbed some 80 Jews in the ghetto, women without men and men without women, children without parents, all taken without any of the property that they still owned, in order to make up the 100 who were missing from the group" (Romanian). See: Danilov's defense statement at his trial, CNSAS Archive, vol. 1, File P-7795.

83 Jägendorf offered his own criteria for deciding which Jews would remain in Mogilev: "necessity, output, discipline, labor and respect". Document of April 8, 1942, Jägendorf Collection, *Yad Vashem Archive*, File 6, p-9.

84 Carp, *Cartea Neagră*, p. 252.
85 S. Zeidenstein, *Yad Vashem Archive*, O-3/10799.
86 For various orders and deportation commands, see: Carp, *Cartea Neagră*, pp. 351–352; 377–378. See also: Jägendorf Collection, *Yad Vashem Archive*, File 14, p. 9, dated September 29, 1942. A. Koch, *Yad Vashem Archive*, O-11, File 150 (Romanian and Hebrew). E. Shturper, *Strochlitz Archive*, R3H22. See also: testimonies of Ukrainian Jews born in the Mogilev district, in Y. Kogan (ed.), *Live Historical Testimony: Memoirs of Prisoners in Ghettos and Labor Camps*, Tel Aviv: Golan, 2003, pp. 19–20 (Hebrew).
87 The order called for the deportation of 4,000 Jews from the Shargorod region, including the Djurin ghetto. Half of these Jews were either Ukrainian or from North Bukovina and Bessarabia. The oral order was given verbally on June 12, 1942, to Katz and Rosenstrauch by Pretor Dindelgan at the region headquarters. See: Kunstadt, *Togbukh*, p. 94.
88 Rosenstock, *Die Chronik Von Dschurin*, p. 61. Ştefănescu testified that his role was "chairman of the committees established by the authorities to select Jews to send to Scazineti." Declaration by Ştefănescu, undated (from his re-trial, 1955), CNSAS Archive, vol. 1, File P-8279. Orashenu claimed after the war that it was the Jewish committee in the Mogilev Ghetto that introduced the approach of selective deportation and that the list of deportees was compiled by a joint committee of the Jewish committee and the Romanian authorities, headed by Ştefănescu. Furthermore, he claimed that the authority to determine who would return either from the Scazineti camp to Mogilev and who would be sent from Scazineti to labor camps in the Bug area was that of the Jewish committee of the Scazineti camp, headed by Dr. Gadel Preminger. CNSAS Archive, vol. 2, P-7795. Erwin Shturper, Strochlitz Archive, R3H22.
89 In a special meeting of the Jewish committee of Mogilev, held on the night of May 27, 1942, in preparation for the deportation to Scazineti planned for two days later, it was decided that "five to ten people would operate on every street, to distribute the announcement and identify those who need to be informed." Jägendorf Collection, *Yad Vashem Archive*, File 6, p-9 [trans. from Romanian].
90 Carp, *Cartea Neagră*, pp. 253–255. The deportation order was eventually executed only in October 1942.
91 By comparison, of the 200,000 Jews in the Bessarabia community prior to the mass murders and deportations of 1941, 40,000 fled to the Soviet Union, and in 1944 only some 11,000 remained. Of 70,000 Jews from North Bukovina and some 30,000 Jews expelled from Chernowitz to Transnistria, less than half survived. See: Raul Hilberg, *The Destruction of European Jewry*, Jerusalem & Beer Sheva: Yad Vashem & Ben Gurion Institute, 2012, p. 736 (Hebrew). See also: Ioanid, *History of the Jews in Romania*, p. 189; and Ancel, *History and Document Summaries*, pp. 509–539.
92 Gali Tibon, "Two Front Battle: Opposition in the Ghettos of the Mogilev District in Transnistria 1941–4," in *Romania and the Holocaust, Events-Contexts-Aftermath*, Simon Geissbuhler (ed.), Ibidem-Verlag, Stuttgart, 2016, pp. 155–163.
93 "The interest of the Jews remaining in the town is to maintain order in the procession." Jägendorf Collection, *Yad Vashem Archive*, File 6, p-9 (Romanian).
94 Meir Teich, "The Jewish Self-Administration in Shargorod Ghetto (Transnistria)," in *Collection of Studies on Chapters of the Holocaust and Heroism II*, Sigfried Jagendorf (ed.), Yad Vashem, Jerusalem, 1958. *Jagendorf's Foundry, Memoir of the Romanian Holocaust 1941–1944* (Hit-Manheimer Aron [edited with commentary]), New York: Harper-Collins, 1991.
95 The list of local Jews at Shargorod was prepared by the local Rabbi Shlomo Kleiman. Shlomo Kleiman, Yad Vashem Archive, O-3/5245.
96 CNSAS Archive, File P-7795, vol. 1.
97 Teich, *The Jewish Self-Administration in Shargorod Ghetto* (Transnistria), pp. 220–221.
98 Kunstadt, *Togbukh*, p. 283: "The neighbors found him in time and cut the rope" (Yiddish).

8

JEWISH RESISTANCE IN GHETTOS IN THE FORMER SOVIET UNION DURING THE HOLOCAUST

Zvi Gitelman and Lenore J. Weitzman[1]

The Nazi ghettos and Jewish ghettos in historical context

In sharp contrast to the ghettos described by other contributors to this volume, the primary purpose of the Nazi ghettos in the former Soviet Union was the annihilation of the Jews. For example, Benjamin Ravid, who characterizes the pre-modern ghetto as a place that was "compulsory, segregated and enclosed,"[2] sees the primary purpose as religious, in that Catholic doctrine held that "Jews should not be killed but rather kept in a position of inferiority in order to testify to their rejection by God, who had selected Christianity as the true Israel ..."[3] Medieval authorities eliminated the presence of the Jews by segregation, conversion, or expulsion, but not by annihilation.[4]

Similarly, Bernard Cooperman, who defines the ghetto as "an urban quarter defined by law — in both a positive and a negative sense," also sees a more benign motivation in arguing that the ghetto was primarily constructed for economic and urban planning.[5]

In contrast, although the Nazi ghettos of World War II were also "compulsory, segregated and enclosed," their purpose was neither religious nor economic. It was, ultimately, annihilation. While pre-Nazi ghettos were animated by hatred of Judaism, Nazi ghettos were set up out of hatred of Jews. Another important difference was that Jews who converted to Christianity could leave the pre-modern ghetto, but the Nazis classified Jews who converted to Christianity as Jews if they had a Jewish parent or three Jewish grandparents. They were neither recognized as Christians nor allowed to leave the ghetto. Religious texts that had defined Jews were replaced by racist theories that determined who was a Jew by "blood" or descent. For example, Sister Teresa Benedicta of the Cross, born as Edith Stein, the daughter of a German Jewish family, was murdered at Auschwitz. In sixteenth-century Europe, she would have lived freely.

Nazi rationales for ghettoization

The conventional wisdom is that the primary function of the Nazi ghettos was to gather Jews in one place in order to facilitate their murder en masse. As Dan Michman observed, "Scholars assumed that such a significant phenomenon must have been the outcome of deliberate forethought and planning."[6] But Michman argues strenuously against this:

> The central authorities of Nazi Germany never elaborated a clear and unequivocal definition of what a ghetto was or should be (from their point of view). Moreover, we do not have a single major document that points to the sources of the ghetto concept, its essence, and the ways for implementing and managing it.[7]

Ghettos were not set up everywhere, even in Poland, nor were they set up at the same stage of conquest. According to Michman, the Nazis took note of what we call "Jewish neighborhoods" and redefined them as "ghettos." "The Germans merely *demarcated their boundaries* and forced those Jews who had moved elsewhere in the city to return 'home.'"[8]

Along the same lines, Christopher Browning argued that "Ghettoization was not a conscious preparatory step planned by the central authorities to facilitate the mass murder ... **Ghettoization was ... carried out at different times in different ways for different reasons on the initiative of local authorities**."[9]

The fact that the Germans did not consistently use the term "ghetto" lends credence to arguments that the ghettos were not part of a master plan. The first ghetto was established in October 1939 in a small Polish city, Piotrkow-Trybunalski. It was first referred to by Germans as a *Judisches Wohnviertel*, but within three weeks, "signs bearing the German word '*Getto*' were posted around the designated neighborhood."[10] Initially, at least, the most infamous/famous ghetto of all, in Warsaw, was called the "*judischer Wohnbezirk*," and the ghetto that lasted longest and perhaps is best documented, in Łódź, was called "*Wohngebiet der Juden*."[11] Though all these German terms mean "a Jewish quarter," the lack of consistent terminology is significant.

Were ghettos designed to gain Jewish property, exploit Jewish labor, facilitate mass murder, or all of these at once? Some in the Nazi regime appreciated the economic potential of Jews working for no wages in ghettos and argued for not killing at least the skilled workers, but they eventually lost out to those who saw the ghettos as facilitating the mass murder of Jews, no matter their skills and contributions to the war effort.[12] Somewhat in parallel, Jewish leaders in some ghettos, such as Chaim Rumkowski in Łódź, believed that if the Jews worked hard enough, they would make themselves indispensable to the Nazis and avoid deportation to death camps. While that strategy was successful for a while, in the end the orders for the murder of the Jews came from Berlin. None of the local Jewish leaders and none of the local German authorities (who may have themselves wished to continue to profit from the productivity of these ghettos) could refuse those orders. The tactics of these Judenräte heads may have enabled some Jews to survive longer (and even survive the war), but they themselves were all murdered in Majdanek or Auschwitz.

Ghettoization in West Belorussia

According to Soviet sources, during World War II the Germans killed more than 2.2 million people in Belorussia and destroyed a total of 209 cities and 9,200 villages. One out of every four people in Belorussia was killed,[13] over half a million of them Jews.[14] During the war, the Nazis set up 106 ghettos in eastern Belorussia (Soviet territory since ca. 1921) and 151 ghettos in western Belorussia (formerly Polish territory that became Soviet in 1939)[15] (Figure 8.1).

This chapter is a comparative study of how and why Jewish "resistance" took different forms in three of these ghettos in West Belorussia: Baranovich and Pinsk in present-day Belarus, and Bialystok, today in Poland.

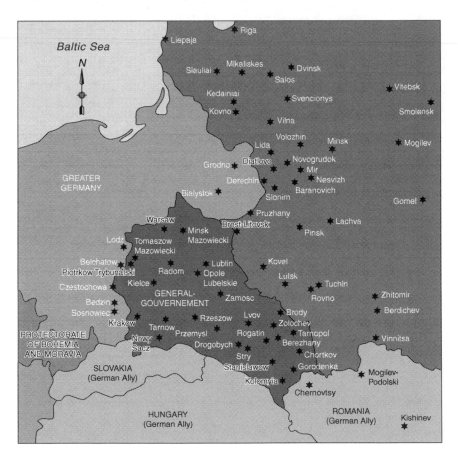

FIGURE 8.1 Nazi ghettos in Eastern Europe. Courtesy of the U.S. Holocaust Memorial Museum, *Historical Atlas of the Holocaust*, p. 54

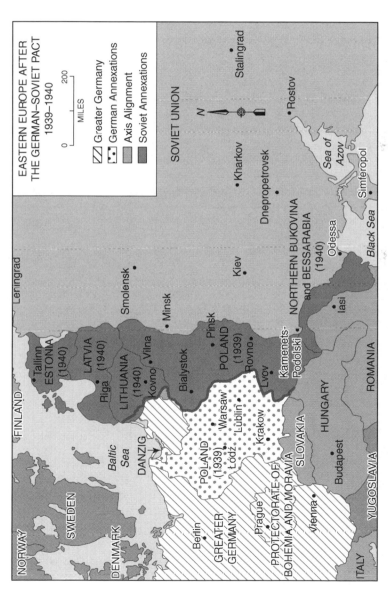

FIGURE 8.2 Eastern Europe after the German–Soviet pact, 1939–1940. Courtesy of the U.S. Holocaust Memorial Museum, *Historical Atlas of the Holocaust*

The most important difference in the ghettoization process in Belorussia (today, Belarus) was that between areas that were in Poland before 1939 and areas that were in the USSR before 1939. Figure 8.2 shows this divide graphically.

Christopher Browning notes that among the Nazis, "'productionists' attempted to harness and profit from ghetto labor" and often prevailed over "'attritionists' who were eager to decimate the incarcerated Jews through starvation and disease."[16] In the newly acquired Soviet areas, however, "ghettoization was ... both simultaneously and inextricably connected with the implementation of the Final Solution. Here ... ghettos served as holding areas for Jews who could not be killed immediately in mass executions by gunfire, and exploitation of ghetto labor—though not absent—was often peripheral."[17]

Despite the differences in these two patterns, there was still considerable variation within both areas in the timing of the first killings, the establishment of ghettos, and the liquidation of ghettos. As Table 8.1 shows, in Belorussia the first killings and the establishment and liquidation of ghettos did not occur at a uniform time. We are unable to say with certainty why this was so. The data may bear out the supposition that local German authorities had discretion in these matters, and that their actions were influenced both by the degree of their intent to kill Jews and by objective local circumstances. Thus, in Grodno, the killings were delayed by the late arrival of the murder "specialists," the Einsatzgruppen charged with "eliminating Jews and Commissars [Communists]." They had not arrived in Grodno when Reinhard Heydrich and Heinrich Himmler visited there on June 30, 1941. A German official admitted that "In Grodno and Lida in the first days only [sic!] 96 Jews were killed. I ordered that this be significantly increased."[18] On July 11, Himmler and Heydrich returned to Grodno and an *Aktion* was launched in which a larger number of Jews were killed, though figures are not available.[19]

Table 8.1 shows that there was considerable variance in the time elapsed between the capture of the city and the first killings, and between the killings and the establishment of ghettos. The first killings of large numbers of Jews began on the very day the Germans captured Bialystok, but not until two months after capturing Czyzewo and Gomel. A survivor from Czyzewo asserts that "the fate of Czyzewo Jews was comparable—with certain nuances—to that of Jews in the other shtetls in Poland." But, she recalls, "In the beginning all was quiet. The Germans did not bother people on a large scale. They shaved the beard of one man, hit another. Somewhere outside of town they even shot a Jew and found some reason for doing so. The people [*oilem*] calmed down and began to think, 'the devil is not as bad as depicted ... .' People ... said that they would not slaughter a community of Jews."[20]

Table 8.2 shows that there is also considerable variation in *when* ghettos were established, even within the same German administrative unit, indicating that the decision to do so was not made at the level of that unit but locally, in the cities and towns themselves.

Thus, ghettoization occurred between 2.5 weeks and 40 weeks after the Germans captured a town. Though in the two towns in the *Reichskommissariat Ukraine* (RKU) that we list, each of the ghettos was established nine months after

TABLE 8.1 Ghettos in West and East Belorussia[21]

City	German district	Date captured in 1941	First killings in 1941[22]	Time between capture and killings	Ghetto established	Ghetto liquidated	Approximate duration of ghetto
Baranovich	GKW*	June 25	July 9	2 weeks	December 12, 1941 (sealed off)	December 17, 1942	53 weeks
Slonim	GKW	June 25	July 17	3 weeks	September 1941	Late June 1942	ca. 36 weeks
Bialystok	Distrikt Bialystok	June 27	June 27	same day	July 26, 1941	August 16, 1943	107 weeks
Czyzewo	Distrikt Bialystok	June 22	August 20	ca. 8 weeks	September 1941	November 2, 1942	56 weeks
Grodno	Distrikt Bialystok	June 23	Late June	ca. 1 week	November 1, 1941	March 12, 1943	62 weeks
Lachwa	RKU**	July 7–8	September 3, 1942	60 weeks	April 1, 1942	September 3, 1942	20 weeks
Pinsk	RKU	July 4	July 6	2 days	April 30, 1942	October 29, 1942	24 weeks
Minsk	GKW	June 28	July 2	5 days	July 19, 1941	October 21, 1943	117 weeks
Gomel	Army Group Center	August 19	October	ca. 8 weeks	mid-September, 1941	November 3–4, 1941	7 weeks
Mogilev	Army Group Center	July 26	August	ca. 2 weeks	August 13, 1941	October 23, 1941	9 weeks
Vitebsk	Army Group Center	July 11	July 20	1 week	July 25, 1941	October 8–10, 1941	10 weeks

*Generalkommissariat Weissruthenien

**Reichskommissariat Ukraine

TABLE 8.2 Time from capture to establishment of ghettos

GKW (Generalkommissariat Weissruthenien)	
Baranovich (P)	22 weeks
Minsk (SU)	3 weeks
Slonim (P)	10–12 weeks
Bialystok (P)**	4 weeks
Czyzewo (P)	10 weeks
Grodno (P)	17 weeks
RKU (Reichskommissariat Ukraine)	
Lachwa (P)	36 weeks
Pinsk (P)	40 weeks
Army Group Center	10–12 weeks
Gomel (SU)*	4 weeks
Mogilev (SU)	2.5 weeks
Vitebsk (SU)	4–8 weeks

*=in the Soviet Union before 1939
**In Poland before 1939

capture; by contrast, in the Bialystok area, ghettoization was undertaken between one and (over) four months.

Yet, if there was no master plan for creating ghettos and no single formula for organizing them and conducting "operations" in them, there were, nevertheless, important similarities among the ghettos.

Generally, the operations of the Germans followed the following pattern:

1. First, they killed a number of Jews soon after the town was captured. In many places, the first victims were community leaders, the intelligentsia, and religious leadership, who might organize resistance, as well as the young and strong, who might offer physical resistance.
2. Then they established a ghetto, almost always in the poor part of town. Ghettos ranged in size from one street in smaller towns to a large neighborhood, as in Minsk (two square kilometers, about 40 streets and 273 residential buildings).[23] As people were deported or died, the area of the ghetto would shrink. Some ghettos were sealed off by walls (Minsk), some by barbed wire (Pinsk, Baranovich), and some were "open."
3. At the same time, the Germans might begin sending Jewish men and women to forced labor, either in or beyond the ghetto—to build roads, work in factories, clean German houses—and to repair and make ammunition.
4. Then they carried out a series of *Aktionen*, often mounted on or in close proximity to Jewish holidays, in which they would kill several hundred or thousands of Jews in or near the ghetto. In many places, the elderly, ill, children, and others who were not working were the first people killed.

5. In some ghettos, the "useful" laborers (craftsmen, repair workers) were spared and even sent to live in a separate ghetto.
6. Finally, the ghetto was "liquidated": the Jews who were left, typically the "useful" laborers, were killed and the ghetto was destroyed.

Even if there was no standard formula for establishing and running the ghettos, the overall pattern may indicate a general understanding among German authorities of what was to be done and how to do it. We do not know whether this was the result of consultations or observation by one group of Germans of what others had done. In any case, on July 19, 1942, Heinrich Himmler ordered all ghettos in the *Generalgouvernement*[24] to be liquidated by the end of the year.[25] On June 21, 1943, he ordered the liquidation of all ghettos in the *Reichskommissariat Ostland* (the Baltic States and Belorussia). Remaining Jewish inhabitants able to work were to be sent to concentration camps.

Jewish resistance: The dilemma of *Amidah*

While German policies varied somewhat, the final outcomes were the same: all Jews were slated for death. Jewish responses to the Nazis also varied, and in some (usually small) ways they could make the difference between life and death, or in the amount of time one lived before he or she was killed.

We now turn to the question of how and why Jewish "resistance" took different forms in three West Belorussian ghettos: Baranovich (with a population of 12,000 Jews in 1939), Bialystok (43,000), and Pinsk (27,000).[26] These micro-histories illuminate how specific environments influenced individual actions and, in turn, how individual decisions and actions cumulatively determined or heavily influenced individual and collective outcomes.

In this analysis, we draw on interviews with survivors of the Baranovich and Bialystok ghettos; published and unpublished memoirs; *yizker bicher* (memorial books); Soviet government investigations; German reports; and oral testimonies and books in Hebrew, Yiddish, Russian, and German. They illustrate how specific circumstances, subjective perceptions, and individual decisions differentiated what happened in these three ghettos. They also illustrate the complexity and contingency of resistance. By "resistance" we mean revolt, escape, joining the partisans, and what Yehuda Bauer calls "*amidah*," standing up to the Nazis in one form or another.

In general, German tactics were devastatingly effective in limiting potential resistance, not only among Jews, but also among entire nations in Nazi-occupied Europe. It is important to underscore just how successful the Nazi policy of reprisals was in limiting resistance. For example, in Yugoslavia, according to some, Drazha Mihailovic and the Serbian Chetniks stopped fighting the Germans when the latter killed large numbers of Serbs in reprisal for Chetnik assassinations of German soldiers.[27] In Czechoslovakia, following the mass killings and deportations from the small towns of Lidice and Lezaky (June 1942) in reprisal for the assassination of Reinhard Heydrich (May 27, 1942), there was no effective Czech resistance. On the other hand, if it is true that during the occupation, for every German killed by a Pole, 100–400 Poles were shot in retribution,[28] this did not deter the Home Army or Communist resistance from continuing their fight against the Nazis. Nor did the atrocity at Oradour-sur-Glane in June 1944 deter the French Resistance. But since Jews in ghettos were not fighting a general war against the Germans or seeking national liberation, the possibility of German reprisals was localized and brought into sharper focus. The reprisals would be made against them and their families, and there would be no one else who would take up their struggle. In contrast to anti-Nazi resistance groups in Europe, the Jews had no allies and no hope of defeating the Nazis.

Nevertheless, Jews in each ghetto thought about how they could resist. They wrestled with life-and-death dilemmas of the consequences of evasion, flight, and rebellion for themselves and for the weaker members of their family and their community. They also struggled with how to forge consensus among the disparate elements in the ghettos. Our interviews with survivors reveal their deep differences over these strategies and tactics at the time, and the long-term resentments they fostered.[29]

It is generally believed that once the Jews were incarcerated in ghettos, they did not resist the Nazis, except in Warsaw in 1943. That ghetto uprising, the subject of historical studies, memoirs, novels, and plays in several languages, is considered exceptional.[30] A smaller, "attentive public" may be aware that uprisings or escapes occurred in and from other ghettos such as in Vilna (Vilnius), Minsk, Krakow, and other places in Eastern Europe. As the editors of the *Holocaust Encyclopedia* note,

> Well before the famous April uprising in the Warsaw ghetto, Jews revolted in many of the ghettos of Belorussia, including Nesvizh (20 July 1942), Kletsk (22 July), Derechin (24 July), and Lachva (3 September). The Jews of the Bialystok ghetto took up arms on 16 August 1943 and … fought … for five days…. [Ghetto] inmates succeeded in daring escapes from a series of ghettos – 300 people from Mir, 233 from Novogrudok, 100 from Kobrin, about 80 from Miory, and 208 from the concentration camp in Novy Serzhen …[31]

These exceptional acts of resistance in no instance forced a German retreat from or abandonment of the ghetto. At most, they allowed a relatively small number of people to escape to the "Aryan" side of town where they might have found hiding places with non-Jewish protectors or to the forests where some were able to join partisans. But the decision to resist or escape was never unambiguous. It was entangled with moral and practical dilemmas.

Resisting the Nazis in Baranovich, Bialystok, and Pinsk: Comparing outcomes

By comparing these three ghettos, we seek to explain why resistance in Baranovich yielded some results, why it was planned but was not as successful in Bialystok, and why it was considered but not undertaken in Pinsk. Two kinds of considerations influenced the different responses in the three ghettos. The first was objective circumstances: environment, such as local topography and access to the forest, access to arms, the attitudes of local populations, and access to partisan groups. The second was human decisions and people's "subjective" views of the situation, which included the influence of peer groups and membership in political movements, personalities, decisions of local Judenräte, and personal experiences.

In Baranovich, after considerable debate, a group that had armed itself chose to escape from the ghetto to the partisans, rather than mount an uprising within the ghetto, as some had urged. In Białystok, after similar agonizing debates over resisting or escaping, different groups in the ghetto made different choices about these options. Some escaped while others stayed to fight in the ghetto. In Pinsk, a group prepared to mount an uprising, but was ultimately persuaded not to do so because their action could bring about the liquidation of the entire ghetto.

Some critical factors that we believe help explain the relative success of resistance in Baranovich were:

1. Access to arms: Jewish laborers from the Baranovich ghetto worked in a German munitions repair factory and were able to steal guns and ammunition from the factory. That not only gave them access to arms they could smuggle into the ghetto for their planned revolt, but also increased the probability that they would be allowed to join the partisans because weapons were usually required for acceptance by the partisans. In Pinsk, by contrast, the Jews had no access to arms, and little contact with the partisans, even though the Polesie region was a major area of partisan operations.
2. Support from the Judenrat: Many (but not all) members of the Baranovich Judenrat were sympathetic to the idea of active resistance, and were willing to help the resistance. Some were themselves active in the resistance. In contrast, in Pinsk, the Judenrat was strongly opposed to resistance and actively discouraged the potential resisters because they were afraid of reprisals.

Białystok falls somewhere in between, and presents a more complex picture of the variables we consider significant. While it resembles Pinsk in the lack of access to arms and in the Judenrat's discouragement of active resistance, it is complicated by the fact that the head of the Judenrat, Efraim Barash, maintained close ties to the head of the united Jewish resistance movement, Mordechai Tenenbaum. Barash provided Tenenbaum's group with social services, office space, passes to leave the ghetto, and other assistance that facilitated their plans for armed revolt.[32]

In all three ghettos, potential resisters faced the same critical dilemma: should they remain in the ghetto to fight—and die—"for Jewish honor," or could they actually thwart the Germans—and avenge the deaths of their families and friends— by escaping from the ghetto to fight with the partisans?

There were anguished debates about this question in all three ghettos. In the end, potential resisters in Baranovich escaped to the partisans, those in Pinsk neither escaped nor fought, and the Bialystok youth split: the Communist resisters left for the partisans, and the Zionist resisters stayed to fight for Jewish honor.

In the following pages, we provide a closer look at each ghetto to highlight the specific constellation of factors that facilitated resistance in Baranovich, deterred it in Pinsk, and undermined it in Bialystok.

The German occupation and the Holocaust

Following the general pattern outlined above, in each of these three cities the Germans began their occupation by trying to eliminate the likelihood of resistance. In Bialystok, they did it on the very first day. After capturing the city on the evening of July 26, 1941, three companies of *Polizeibataillon* 309 began rounding up Jews the next day. They shot several hundred Jews in various locations around the city and locked up about 800 Jews in the Great Synagogue, set it on fire, and burned alive almost all of them. "On this day, an estimated 2,000–2,200 of the city's 50,000 Jews were burned, shot, or tortured to death."[33]

The Germans followed a similar pattern in Pinsk and Baranovich. In each city, they first murdered young men and the intelligentsia, terrorizing the Jewish population, though most did not perceive it as a prelude to mass murder. In all three cities, the second step was to require Jews to work in forced labor, accompanied by beatings and punishments for real or imaginary infractions. After that, or simultaneously, came ghettoization, moving the Jewish population into a geographically defined and eventually closed-off area. That was followed by a series of *Aktionen*, in which large groups were killed in stages, as outlined above.

Pinsk: The failure of resistance[34]

In Pinsk, over the course of three years (July 1941–July 1944), about 25–30,000 Jews were murdered in and around the city: only 17 Jews survived in Pinsk to see the liberation. There were two waves of mass executions. The first was in August 1941, when about 8,000 men were shot. Thus, within a month of the German occupation, most able-bodied men, those most active in Pinsk's public life, were gone.[35] The second mass execution took place on October 29, 1942, when German Police Battalion 306 and other units murdered about 20,000 Jews.[36] The remaining 143 craftsmen and doctors, who were performing "useful work," were shot on December 23, 1942.

Despite the early elimination of most people who could have mounted resistance, a resistance group of about 50 did form in the ghetto and managed to obtain some arms and ammunition. The Judenrat[37] got wind of the group and asked them not to leave for the forest to join the partisans, because that would endanger the entire ghetto, as the Germans were likely to engage in reprisals. The group was persuaded. As one said: "From day to day we postponed the breakout[38] [because] we did not want to be directly responsible for causing ... the destruction of thousands of Jews."

When the potential resisters sensed that a final *Aktion* was in the offing, they planned ways of resisting by force, including burning down the ghetto and then fleeing. But Alfred Ebner,[39] deputy civilian commander of the ghetto, persuaded the Judenrat that "nothing will happen to the Jews of Pinsk ... [because] they were working for the German war effort."[40] The Germans also spread rumors that all who were working would remain in the ghetto.[41] Most ghetto inmates believed this. The underground's plans for action were "frustrated by the calming declarations the Germans disseminated through the Judenrat."[42] The underground was caught unprepared when the final destruction came. They never took action.

The Germans used a similar ploy in Bialystok and placed large orders for work in the ghetto factories. This convinced Jewish workers that they were secure. The Judenrat itself took the initiative and opened a furniture factory, tailoring and milliner's workshop, and a chemical factory. Sarah Bender observes that the Judenrat tried to promote a work ethic. "The Judenrat's emphasis on the importance of work was based on two assumptions: first, that work was a passport to safety, and second, that work would supply the minimum requirements for survival under occupation conditions."[43] The chairman of the Judenrat, Ephraim Barash, "sincerely believed that Jewish labor was a safe—albeit difficult—prescription for survival. For many months, he tried to persuade others (and perhaps himself, too) that the benefit the Germans reaped from the labor of the ghetto Jews had softened their attitude toward them."[44] Indeed, according to Bender, "Most of the ghetto residents ... not only failed to realize the enormity of the danger awaiting them but also appeared to believe that they would survive the war intact."[45]

Baranovich: Why was it different?

What was different about Baranovich? At first glance, the German occupation in Baranovich followed the standard pattern. Within two weeks of the German occupation, in early July 1941, the Germans targeted and killed over 400 young men, shocking and terrorizing the Jewish population. They established a ghetto about five months later, in December 1941, and murdered most of the 12,000 Jews imprisoned there in three separate actions—in March 1942, September 1942, and in December 1942, when they liquidated the ghetto.

However, there were two important differences between Baranovich and Pinsk. First, early on in Baranovich, as men were being picked off the streets for labor, a member of *Agudas Yisroel*, an Orthodox religious party, initiated a meeting in a synagogue in which a committee was chosen to represent them to the Germans. The Germans made this committee a Judenrat, so that unlike in Pinsk, the Judenrat was actually chosen by Jews.[46]

In Bialystok, the Judenrat was also chosen by Jews, but at the command of the Germans, not on the initiative of Jews. On June 29, 1941, the Germans ordered Chief Rabbi Gedalyah Rosenman to set up a Judenrat within a day. The Germans accepted a list of 12 well-known public figures that the Jews presented to them.[47] After the Judenrat complied with an order to deport 10,000 (of 43,000) Jews from the ghetto, the largest in the area, to Pruzhany (September–October 1941), relations between the Jews and the Judenrat soured, especially when it became apparent that the Judenrat was favoring the wealthy. Chairman Barash was well aware of this. On November 2, 1941, he said, "The Judenrat acts as a kind of shield that protects the ghetto from trouble. However, the ghetto does not behave toward the Judenrat as it deserves … we do not deserve the curses and slander that are being leveled at us."[48] But by 1942, when life in the ghetto had "stabilized," many were employed, and the food supply and health services were reasonable, Barash seems to have gained the confidence of most ghetto inmates.[49] In fact, when a few young women from the Jewish underground in Grodno escaped to Bialystok, the inhabitants turned on them for "spreading false rumors about the Germans killing the Jews, and for trying to incite discord in an otherwise happy and productive ghetto."[50]

The Judenrat in Baranovich was different because it was formed by the Jews, and its leader, Yehoshua (Owsiej) Izykson, and his assistant Genia Mann, had the respect and support of the Jewish community. In addition, the Judenrat made every effort to resist the Germans and help the Jews, including those trying to organize resistance. Finally, the Judenrat in Baranovich was unusual in that some Judenrat members were themselves in the Jewish resistance. In fact, most of the Jewish policemen they appointed—15 out of 22 policemen, according to one participant—were part of the resistance.[51]

The second important difference in Baranovich was that many Jewish slave laborers were employed in "Feldzug [probably Feldzeug] B," a workshop where captured Soviet weapons were repaired. This gave members of the underground a chance to steal rifles, grenades, and bullets from their workplace. Though it was dangerous and risky, it provided a rare opportunity for ghettoized Jews to acquire weapons.[52]

Noach Roitman, employed in Feldzug B and an active member of the resistance,[53] describes how the arms were obtained and hidden, and smuggled into the ghetto with the help of the Jewish police:

> Members of the underground who worked in those shops would dismantle the barrels of rifles, hide them on their persons, and bring them back to the ghetto at the end of the day's work … The Jewish police would inform the underground members at which entrances to the ghetto there would be bodily searches and the arms smugglers would bring in grenades wrapped around parts of their bodies and bullets hidden in their shoes or boots. The weapons parts were put in a hiding place, and then wooden stocks, smuggled separately, would be attached and the weapons inspected by several young men who had served in the Polish army …
>
> The men would shorten the butts of guns and hang them around their necks while the women would smuggle hand grenades, bullets, and unassembled gun parts. The Germans would permit us to bring 5–6 foot long wooden logs home to heat our houses. During work hours the Jews would hollow out the logs and hide whole rifles in them. Within a few months we had amassed 70 rifles, two machine guns, thousands of hand grenades

and bullets and around 50–70 handguns. Moshe Topf, David Winter, and [Eliyahu/Aliosha] Zarickiewicz had all been in the Russian Army so they knew how to reassemble the arms.[54]

Another group of workers—young women who were working in German homes and offices— also played an important role in smuggling weapons or parts of weapons into the ghetto. Their job was to clean the Germans' offices, wash their laundry, and perform other menial tasks.

> The Germans became accustomed to these pale, frightened, shivering girls who trembled at every sound, fearing that they would soon be led to their deaths. The girls acted dumb, as if they understood nothing, and looked at the armed police with fright … And thus the Germans grew to trust these girls over whom a sentence of death hung.[55] But when some of these 16 and 17-year-old girls saw the atrocities, they resolved to steal arms, which they hid or buried until such time they thought they could smuggle them into the ghetto.[56]

By the time of the second *Aktion* in Baranovich, in September 1942, the underground had a significant store of arms and ammunition they planned to use against the Germans as soon as they started the *Aktion*. But, as in Bialystok and Pinsk, the Germans deceived the Jews. In the fall of 1942, on the day after Yom Kippur, the Germans told the Judenrat that *Todt* (labor force) inspectors would be coming to the ghetto for a "routine inspection." A Judenrat member persuaded the resistance not to interfere and not to resist with grenades because "it was just a routine inspec tion" and that resistance would condemn the entire population to death.

The German forces entered the ghetto wearing Todt uniforms, hiding their guns under the uniforms. "They then took out their weapons and began shooting … and carried out the 'slaughter.'" Members of the resistance later wrote that they "felt the burning shame of being tricked and being helpless in the face of a *shechiteh* [slaughter]."[57]

Both during and after this time, there were fierce and sometimes violent debates among the members of four distinct groups in the resistance: these groups, weakly linked to prewar youth or political movements, together totaled about 200 members, including about 50 women. They debated whether to mount armed resistance in the ghetto or flee to the forest.

Some were determined to remain in the ghetto to organize a future revolt and thereby take a stand for Jewish honor. Others were equally intent on escaping from the ghetto to join the partisans, who were just 17 kilometers away in the forest. Still others urged restraint to avoid reprisals.[58] One can imagine how difficult and tense these deliberations were in the absence of any information about German plans, and in conditions of great secrecy and uncertainty.

Heated arguments between these groups culminated in one particularly ugly confrontation in which one faction of the resistance forcibly prevented another group from escaping from the ghetto by threatening to inform the authorities on the night of the planned escape.[59] But later on, many of those who were initially prevented from leaving managed to escape to join the partisans. In addition, after the second *Aktion*, when it became clear that the Jews had been tricked by the Germans and there was no hope of mounting resistance in the ghetto, many more decided to escape. It should be noted that most of them escaped from their work places—not from the ghetto itself—to the forests.[60] Eventually, they were joined by most of those who had originally opposed their escape.[61]

The determination of these Jews in the resistance is the third important factor that differentiates Baranovich from Pinsk, and both from Bialystok. Even though there were voices urging restraint in both ghettos, Baranovich's Jews were emboldened by having weapons and were not deterred by the kinds of arguments that restrained the Jews in Pinsk.

In Bialystok, the situation was more complicated. In late 1941, Communists and two Zionist groups tried to organize resistance. In 1943, after an *Aktion* in February that sent about 8,000 Jews to Treblinka and Auschwitz, and 2,000 were killed in the city, the Communists tried to escape to the forest and link up with the partisans. The Zionist groups, He-chalutz Ha-Tzair-Dror, led by Mordechai Tenenbaum, and Ha Shomer Ha-Tzair, led by Chaika Grossman, refused to leave the ghetto and fought the Germans and their Ukrainian auxiliaries in the ghetto itself.

On August 16, 1943, after large forces of Ukrainians and Germans had surrounded the ghetto, the underground prepared for action. But three things hampered their planned attack: (1) they had not been warned by Barash of the impending *Aktion*, though he had promised Tenenbaum he would do so; (2) they were very poorly armed; and (3) their appeals to the population to join them fell on deaf ears. They had posted stirring appeals, "Do not go willingly to your deaths … fight for your lives, attack your executioners with you [sic] teeth and your nails, with axes and knives, with acid and iron rods … Except for our honor we have nothing left to lose." But, admitted Chaika Grossman from Ha-Shomer Ha-Tzair, who survived and later became a member of the Israeli parliament, Jews read the posters or leaflets "and turned away quietly, each to his own home … We had no masses behind us."[62] Their battle was over quickly. The underground lost 200 of its members; the only surviving member of its command was Chaika Grossman.

Sarah Bender comments that although the uprising began as soon as the Germans entered the ghetto, as did the Warsaw Ghetto revolt (April 20, 1943), the initial Warsaw revolt in January 1943 took the Germans by surprise; it was much more carefully planned, and it had "the backing of the masses." Moreover, the Warsaw uprising "could count on assistance from the Aryan side."[63] To be sure, it was minimal, but the Bialystok resistance apparently had no such assistance at all. Why the Warsaw uprising had more support among the ghetto inmates and the Polish resistance is a matter for further research. But Bender explains the lack of mass support for the resistance in Bialystok as due to the fact that most Bialystok Jews believed Barash's dictum that their work would save them because the Nazis needed their labor and their productivity.[64] She suggests that Barash's assurances, his faith in their productivity, and his hopefulness became their wish and faith. They believed he would ensure their survival. With that belief, they had no interest in risking their lives by joining the resistance and/or undertaking any activities that would upset the Germans."[65]

Finally, perhaps counter-intuitively, one individual could make a crucial difference. For example, in the Baranovich area, Edward Chacia [Chacza],[66] later recognized as a "righteous Gentile" by Yad Vashem, risked his life and his family's to serve as an active liaison between escaping Jews and the partisans. Chacia had a remote house in the woods that served as a hiding place, for information gathering, and as a transfer point for ghetto Jews and partisans.[67] Moreover, Chacia's help enabled men who originally escaped to the partisans to return to the ghetto to rescue others who might not have been able to make it to the partisans on their own.[68]

Yehuda Bauer believes that "between 500 and 750 Jews must have managed to escape from the [Baranovich] ghetto." Only about 250 of the escapees survived the subsequent years with the partisans or in the forests.[69] We do not know how many survived by hiding in the city. In Pinsk, there were only 17 survivors in the city. In Bialystok, "On July 22, 1944, the day Bialystok was liberated by the Red Army, the only Jews left in the city were several dozen who survived by hiding on the 'Aryan' side of the city[70] and a small group of women (from the resistance) who were living on false papers."[71]

In summary, our comparison of Pinsk, Baranovich, and Bialystok leads us to conclude that the more organized resistance to the Nazis and the larger number of survivors in Baranovich was due to six factors:

1. The attitudes of the Judenrat and its direct support for the resistance;
2. The ability of Jews to obtain arms and ammunition;
3. The determination of a group of young people to escape from the ghetto and join the partisans;
4. The ability of the Baranovich resisters to ignore pre-war differences between secular and religious, Zionist, Communist and socialist, and among Zionist movements; to join forces, steal and hide weapons, and to escape to the partisans;
5. The willingness of the Baranovich resisters who escaped to the partisans to come back to the ghetto and lead them to the partisans;
6. The singular importance of one non-Jew who sheltered, protected, and advised Jews moving between the ghetto and the partisans made the difference between survival and death.

Finally, we believe that chance or luck must always be added to any explanation for individual and collective survival during the Holocaust. That may be hard for social scientists and historians to accept, but the evidence seems to point in that direction.

Notes

1 Gitelman's research was funded in part by the Conference on Material Claims Against Germany, Grant Number S028; Yad Vashem Institute, Israel; the United States Holocaust Memorial Museum, Washington, DC. Weitzman's research was also supported by the

US Holocaust Memorial Museum. We are grateful to these institutions for their support. We wish to thank Claudia Lahr at the University of Michigan for her research assistance.

2 Benjamin Ravid, "Ghetto: Etymology, original definition, reality, and diffusion," ch. 1 in this volume, 23.

3 Ibid.

4 Ibid.

5 Bernard Cooperman, "The Early Modern Ghetto: A study in urban real estate," ch. 3 in this volume, 58.

6 Dan Michman, *The Emergence of Jewish Ghettos During the Holocaust*, New York; Cambridge University Press, 2011, p. 8.

7 Ibid., p. 3.

8 Ibid.

9 Emphasis ours. "Nazi Ghettoization Policy in Poland, 1939–41," *Central European History*, 19, 4 (1986), 343–344. Quoted from Michman, 17.

10 Ibid., p. 79.

11 See Isaiah Trunk, *Łódź Ghetto*, Bloomington, IN: Indiana University Press, 2008; Andrea Low, *Juden im Getto Litzmannstadt: Lebensbedingungen, Selbstwahrnehmung, Verhalten*, Göttingen: Wallstein, 2006; Alan Adelson and Robert Lapides, eds, *Łódź Ghetto: Inside a Community Under Siege*, New York: Viking, 1989; Michal Unger, *Łódź: aharon ha-getdot be-Polin*, Jerusalem: Yad Vashem, 2005; and the diary, Jakub Poznanski, Pamietnik z Getta Łódzkiego, Łódź: Wydawnictwo Łódzkie, 1960.

12 See Adam Tooze, *The Wages of Destruction: The Making and Breaking of the Nazi Economy*, London and New York: Allen Lane, 2006. Hermann Goring, chief of the Luftwaffe, advocated the exploitation of Jewish labor, while Reinhard Heydrich, head of the SS, advocated mass murder. At the Wannsee Conference, January 20, 1940, Heydrich established the control of the SS of all anti-Jewish operations and brought various Nazi administrations together to cooperate in them.

13 A. A. Kovalenia, *Belarus '1941–1945 Podvig. Tragediya. Pamiat'*. vol. II. Minsk: Belaruskaya navuka, 2010.

14 Yitzhak Arad estimates that between 556,000 and 582,000 Jews were killed on the territory of Belorussia. *The Holocaust in the Soviet Union* (Lincoln, NE and Jerusalem: University of Nebraska Press and Yad Vashem Institute, 2009), p. 525.

15 Personal communication from Dr. Martin Dean, U.S. Holocaust Memorial Museum, to Zvi Gitelman, January 15, 2015. Dr. Dean points out that these figures includes 16 ghettos in GK Litauen, now north-eastern Belarus, and 22 ghettoes in GK Wolhynien-Podolien (RK Ukraine) that were in western Belorussia after World War II. We are very grateful to Dr. Dean for this information.

16 Christopher Browning, "Introduction," in Dean, *Encyclopedia*, xxii.

17 Ibid.

18 Quoted in Tikva Fatal-Knaani, *Zo lo otah Grodno*, Jerusalem: Yad Vashem, pp. 120–121.

19 Ibid., p. 121. Fatal-Knaani speculates that the Einsatzgruppen may have simply passed Grodno by as the army, which they followed, was advancing so swiftly.

20 Yentl Kitai, "Veise teg un necht," in *Yizker-buch noch der khorev-gevorener Yidisher kehileh Chizheve*, pp. 863–864.

21 The information is taken from Ilya Al'tman, ed., *Kholokost na territorii SSSR: Entsiklopedia* (Moscow: Rosspen, 2011); Geoffrey Megargee and Martin Dean, ed., *Encyclopedia of Camps and Ghettos, 1933–1945*, Bloomington, IN: Indiana University Press and United States Holocaust Memorial Museum, 2012, vol. II, part B; Israel Gutman, ed., *Encyclopedia of the Holocaust*, New York: Macmillan, 1990; Robert Rozett and Shmuel Spektor, eds., *Encyclopedia of the Holocaust*, New York: Facts on File, 2000; Tikva Fatal-Knaani, *Zo lo otah Grodno*, Jerusalem: Yad Vashem, 2001, pp.120–121; E. Rozenblat and I. Elenskaia, *Pinskie Evrei, 1939–1944*, Brest, 1997; Nachman Tamir (Mirski), *Pinsk: Sefer edut ve-zikaron likhilat Pinsk-Karlin*, Tel Aviv: Irgun yotsai Pinsk-Karlin bimdinat Yisrael, 1966, vol. II; Shimon Kantz, ed., *Yizker-buch noch der khorev-gevorener Yidisher*

kehileh Chizheve, Tel Aviv, 1961; Nachum Alpert, *The Destruction of Slonim Jewry,* New York: Holocaust Library, 1989; Kopel Kopalnitsky, *Sentenced to Life,* London:Vallentine Mitchell, 2007; and other sources.

22 By "first killings," we mean not necessarily the first *Aktion,* but the first recorded killing of a group of Jews for purposes of intimidation. For example, 96 Jews were killed in June in Grodno and Lida, 80 of the intelligentsia in Grodno in July 1941, and 73 in Baranovich. "Killings" were of relatively narrowly defined groups, whereas *Aktionen* were carried out against larger groups (e.g., women, elderly, children). Both were planned. Note that in Lachwa, significant numbers were killed only on the day of the uprising, September 3, 1942.

23 D[aniel] Romanovskii, "Minsk," in Ilya Al'tman, ed., *Kholokost na territorii SSSR: Entsiklopedia.* Moscow: Rosspen, 2011, 592.

24 This was the German designation for the parts of Poland that had not been incorporated into the Third Reich. It included the districts of Warsaw, Krakow, Radom, Lublin, and Lwow (Lvov, Lviv). The ghetto in Łódź was not destroyed until summer 1944.

25 Browning, "Introduction," in Dean, *Encyclopedia,* xxxiv.

26 These towns had several things in common: (1) they were part of historic "Liteh" and shared the Litvish cultural tradition; (2) they were in the same general geographic area; (3) the cities were near forests and/or swamps; (4) having all been in Poland in the interwar period, all had become part of Soviet (west) Belorussia in 1939; (5) each had a vibrant, rich Jewish political, religious, and cultural life before the Soviet occupation of 1939; (6) all three were enclosed ghettos.

27 Jozo Tomasevic, *The Chetniks,* Stanford: Stanford University Press, 1975, p. 351. See also Matteo Milazzo, *The Chetnik Movement & the Yugoslav Resistance,* Baltimore: Johns Hopkins University Press, 1975.

28 Richard Lukas, Forgotten Survivors: Polish Christians Remember the Nazi Occupation, Lawrence: University Press of Kansas, 2004. Online. <http://www.projectinposterum.org/docs/survivors_print.htm> accessed January 18, 2015.

29 Lenore J. Weitzman, "Dilemmas and Decisions in the Ghettos," paper presented at the "Lessons and Legacies" conference, Claremont College, November 4, 2016.

30 An early study by a Polish Jewish Communist, who headed the Jewish Historical Institute in Warsaw until his death in 1966, is Ber Mark, *Der ufshtand in varshever geto,* Moscow: Der emes, 1947. This appeared one year before the Soviet regime closed down all Yiddish publications. The book appeared in a Polish translation a few years later, and then again in Yiddish in Poland. A comparison of the editions might be enlightening. See Bernard Mark, *Powstanie w getcie warszawskim na tle ruchu oporu w Polsce, geneza i przebieg* Warszawa: Zydowski Instytut Historyczny, 1954 (Yiddish edition, *Der oifshtand in varshever geto* [Warsaw:Yidish bukh, 1955]). A novel (1950), and a play based on it (1961, 1964), were written by John Hersey, *The Wall,* New York: Knopf, 1950. The best-known scholarly study in English is Israel Gutman, *Resistance: The Warsaw Ghetto Uprising,* Boston: Houghton Mifflin, 1994. An earlier Hebrew version is *Yehudai Varshah, 1939–1943: geto, mahteret, mered,* Tel Aviv: Sifriat Poalim, 1977.

31 Walter Laqueur, ed. *Holocaust Encyclopedia,* New Haven:Yale University Press, 2001.

32 For different perspectives on the Białystok ghetto and the resistance, see Sarah Bender, *Mul mayet orev:Yehudai Byalistok be-milhemet ha-'olam ha-sheniyah, 1939–1943,* Tel Aviv: Am Oved, 1997 translated as *The Jews of Bialystok during World War Two and the Holocaust,* Waltham: Brandeis University Press, 2008; Chaika Grossman, *The Underground Army: Fighters of the Bialystok Ghetto,* New York: Holocaust Library, 1987; Freia Anders, Katrin Stoll and Karsten Wilke, eds., *Der Judenrat von Bialystok: Dokumente aus dem Bialystoker Ghetto 1941–1943,* Paderborn: Schöningh, 2010.

33 Bender, p. 92–93.

34 A comprehensive overview of the Holocaust of Pinsk Jewry is found in E.S. Rozenblat and I.E. Elenskaya, *Pinskie evrei, 1939–1944,* Brest: Brestskiĭ gosudarstvennyĭ universitet, 1997. Another rich source is Nahom Boneh (Mular), "Hashoah ve-hameri," in N. Tamir (Mirski), ed., *Pinsk: sefer edut ve-zikaron le-kehilat Pinsk-Karlin,* Tel Aviv: Irgun

yotsai Pinsk-Karlin be-Yisrael, 1966, vol. II, pp. 323–360. See also the brief "Afterword" by Zvi Gitelman, in Azriel Shohet, *The Jews of Pinsk, 1881 to 1941* (edited by Mark Jay Mirsky and Moshe Rosman), Stanford: Stanford University Press, 2012. This is an edited and translated version of *Toldot Kehilat Pinsk: 1881–1941*, Tel Aviv, 1977.

35 Boneh describes them as "the best of the population from a physical and spiritual point of view. Among them were almost all of the working and studying youth, teachers and school administrators, and all the intelligentsia except doctors," p. 330 (Hebrew).

36 Katharina von Kellenbach, Nahum Boneh, and Ellen Stepak, "Pinsk," in Geoffrey Megargee and Martin Dean, eds., *Encyclopedia of Camps and Ghettos, 1933–1945*, Bloomington, IN: Indiana University Press, 2012, vol. II, Part B, p. 1445. According to Rozenblat and Elenskaia, "24–25,000 people were killed in the city of Pinsk in 1941–42." *Pinskie evrei*, p. 205.

37 The first head of the Judenrat in Pinsk was David Alper, formerly principal of the Tarbut gymnazium. He is said to have resigned after two days. (Boneh [Moliar], p. 326). Binyamin Boksztanski succeeded Alper, but all who have written about the subject agree that the real chairman was Motl Minski, who had lived in Danzig and knew German well. The Judenrat employed about 4–5,000 people. See also Rita Margolin, "*Hakamat yudenrat be-Pinsk: efsharuyot khipus*," Jerusalem: Yad Vashem, 2001–2002, unpublished. Ms. Margolina is an invaluable source for the history of Pinsk and lived there until the mid-1990s. She has been most generous to Zvi Gitelman and every other researcher of Pinsk.

38 Testimony of David Gleibman-Globe, New York, 1962, quoted in Boneh, pp. 341–342.

39 On Ebner, see Katherina von Kellenbach, "Vanishing Acts: Perpetrators in Postwar Germany," *Holocaust and Genocide Studies*, 17, 2, Fall 2003, pp. 305–329. Ebner told the Jews that the pits being dug at Dobrovolia airfield were to hold oil tanks and phoned the engineer at the field to have him confirm it. Boneh, p. 342. See also Donald McKale, *Nazis After Hitler*, Lanham, MD: Rowman and Littlefield, 2012, pp. 215–216.

40 After the war, Alfred Ebner was tried twice for war crimes (1964, 1966). Von Kellenbach notes that "According to an official statistic produced by the German justice ministry in 1986, of the 90,921 criminal investigations opened by prosecutors between 1945 and 1986, 83,140 ended without a conviction." Ebner was judged to have "pseudo dementia," and in 1973 was declared unfit to stand trial, though he was a successful businessman. "He died peacefully in 1987, his involvement in the genocide unacknowledged, unrepented, and unpunished." "Breaking the Silence: Ordinary Germans and the Holocaust," *ReVision*, 22, 1 (Summer 1999), pp. 33–34.

41 A 1942 German report said that 4,150 Jews were working every day and 8,000 others worked roughly every third day. Tikva Fatal-Knaani, "The Jews of Pinsk, 1939–1943, Through the Prism of New Documentation," *Yad Vashem Studies*, XXXIX, 2001, p. 166.

42 Boneh, p. 343.

43 Bender, p. 107.

44 Ibid., p. 124.

45 Ibid., p. 127.

46 According to Rita Margolina, in Pinsk, 18 of 31 prewar communal leaders remained in the city under German occupation but none of them was on the Judenrat. See p. 11.

47 Bender, p. 93.

48 Quoted in ibid., p. 114.

49 Ibid., p. 151–153.

50 Lenore J. Weitzman interview with Hasia Bornstein-Bielicka, June 14, 1994, Kibbutz Lehavot ha-Bashan, Israel. See also Weitzman interviews with Lisa Chapnick, June 1994, Tel Aviv, Israel, and with Lisa Chapnick and Anya Rod on October 19, 2003, and December 18, 2003, Beer Sheva, Israel.

51 Eliezer Lidovskii, "Vidershtand organizatsie," in *Baranovich – sefer zikaron*, Tel Aviv: Irgun yotsai Baranovich beYisrael, 1953, p. 469.

52 The Jews had to acquire arms, whether for a revolt within the ghetto or for escape to the partisans, where they would be turned away if they showed up unarmed. The

penalty for possessing anything remotely resembling a weapon was death, so this was an extremely dangerous operation.

53 Noach Roitman says that he, Moshe Topf, and Eliyahu Zarickiewicz organized a group of about 60 "who brought arms to my uncle's house where I lived in the ghetto (101 Orla Street)." (Noach Roitman's Story, unpublished mss., p. 33) … "The great majority of the underground groups members were under 30 years old, the rest mainly people who had lost their families in the first *Aktion/shchiteh* and felt they had nothing more to lose." Zvi Gitelman and Lenore Weitzman interviews with Noach Roitman, December 12, 2010, and January 17, 2011, in Rockville, MD, tape 4.

54 Zvi Gitelman and Lenore Weitzman, interviews with Noach Roitman, December 12, 2010, and January 17, 2011, in Rockville, MD, tape 4 and Noach Roitman's Story, mss., p. 31.

55 Avraham Lidovskii, *Ba-yearot: reshimot shel partizan yehudi*, Tel Aviv: Hakibutz hameukhad, 1946, p. 44. Avraham Lidovskii, born 1901, was the older brother of Eliezer (b. 1908) (thanks to Marlene Gitelman, University of Michigan Library, for this information). Curiously, neither Eliezer nor Avraham mention in their writings that they were brothers. They are both mentioned in Dina Porat, *The Fall of a Sparrow: The Life and Times of Abba Kovner* (Stanford: Stanford University Press, 2010), pp. 193–194, 196.

56 Ibid.

57 *Baranovich – sefer zikaron*, p. 493.

58 Within the underground, Kopelovich and Zarickewicz urged a strategy of escape to the forests (about 17 kilometers from Baranovich) and the partisans, while Lidovskii advocated an armed uprising before the Germans could mount a second *Aktion/shchiteh*. A third proposal was "not to arouse the bear in the forest," and stage a revolt only when the Germans would start another mass killing.

59 Some members of the Judenrat, with whom Eliezer Lidovskii and others were in contact, counseled against resistance because German reprisals would be so harsh. One, who had a religious background, thought that a martyr's death (*al kidush Hashem*) was the only solution, while the young Slonimer rebbe (Shlomo Weinberg) was enthusiastic about resistance. According to Noach Roitman, a group led by Moshe Topf wanted to leave the ghetto before the second *Aktion*, but Eliezer Lidovskiii, a pre-war left-wing Zionist who had his own resistance group, prevented them from doing so and informed on them to an uncooperative Judenrat member. In the course of the debates, Topf fired a gun, alerting the Germans to the fact that some Jews had arms. The Germans then deported 700 Jews to a labor camp at nearby Koldychevo and to the small town of Molodechno.

60 The escape is summarized in Bauer, "Jewish Baranowicze," *Yad Vashem Studies*, pp. 136–140.

61 They could do so because they had arms and the partisans accepted them, albeit often reluctantly. Second, Noach Roitman and others had pre-war business and social relations with some of the local population which served them in good stead in obtaining food, weapons, support, and cover.

62 Grossman, *The Underground Army*, p. 276.

63 Bender, p. 263.

64 Ibid., p. 287.

65 Ibid., p. 304.

66 Since all references we have to this man are in Hebrew or Yiddish, we do not know the actual Polish spelling of his name and offer the two likely alternatives.

67 Bauer calculates that Chacia/Chacza saved "between sixty and 150 persons." "Jewish Baranowicze," p. 142. Chacia was recognized by Yad Vashem in 1962 as a "Righteous among the Nations." He survived the war and visited Israel as the guest of some of the people he saved. Lenore Weitzman and Zvi Gitelman interview with Noach Roitman, Rockville Md, December 12, 2010. The encyclopedia *Kholokost na territorii SSSR* erroneously calls him "Khotya" and says he died in the Koldychevo camp in 1944 (p. 52).

68 One was a sympathetic German supervisor who helped them smuggle arms to the ghetto.
69 Bauer, pp. 120–130.
70 Sarah Bender and Teresa Prekerowa "Bialystok" in Israel Gutman, ed., *Encyclopedia of the Holocaust*, New York: Macmillan, 1990, p. 214.
71 Sara Bender, "Bialystok," in Megargee and Dean, eds., *Encyclopedia of Camps and Ghettos 1933–1945*, vol. II, Part A, p. 870. These data are corroborated by Lenore Weitzman's interviews with the following members of the Bialystok resistance who survived on false papers on the "Aryan" side: Hasia Bornstein, Lisa Chapnick, and Anya Rod, cited in note 50 above, and Bronka Klibanski in Jerusalem, Israel, on June 12, 1995 and December 19, 2003.

9

WHEN (AND WHY) IS A GHETTO NOT A "GHETTO"?

Concentrating and segregating Jews in Budapest, 1944

Tim Cole

The question when (and why) is a ghetto not a "ghetto" comes to the fore when examining the concentration and separation of Jews in the Hungarian capital, Budapest, in the second half of 1944. In the late spring and early summer of 1944, the municipal authorities responded to national ghettoization legislation that ordered officials in those towns and cities with a total population of more than 10,000 to determine which "parts, or rather specified streets, or perhaps designated houses" Jews were to live in.[1] In the second half of June 1944, Budapest's Jews were ordered to move into close to two thousand houses – marked with a large yellow star – spread across the city. Implementing concentration and segregation at the scale of individual buildings, rather than streets or sections of a city, was something that national legislation explicitly made provision for and it is clear that it was not only in Budapest that local officials chose to concentrate and segregate Jews in "designated houses."[2] However, this practice of dispersed ghettoization – especially when considering, as this chapter does, what it meant in practice – pushes definitions of the wartime ghetto to their very limits.

The impetus on precise definitions of what the Nazi-era "ghetto" was, and was not, emerged in particular during two large-scale projects undertaken by the Israeli and American Holocaust research and memory institutions, Yad Vashem and the United States Holocaust Memorial Museum (USHMM), respectively. In parallel, both research institutes began the massive task of developing encyclopedias of all the ghettos created by Germany and their wartime allies. For the editors, there was a pressing and practical need to develop a watertight definition of the "ghetto" in order to determine which places to include in, and exclude from, these volumes. However, this was extremely challenging given the lack of a single German definition and the variety of practice on the ground. The USHMM team worked with the core principle that "a ghetto is a place where the Germans concentrated the Jews" before making individual decisions on a case-by-case basis, paying particular attention to how this place was referred to by contemporaries – whether that was the German authorities or their Jewish victims. This focus on considering each individual place in turn was driven by a concern with compiling "as comprehensive and accurate a list as possible."[3]

In contrast to USHMM concerns with inclusion framing their definition of the ghetto, the Yad Vashem project adopted their definition with a view to exclusion. As they developed their encyclopedia, Yad Vashem worked with a definition of a ghetto as "any concentration of Jews by compulsion in a clearly defined section of an existing settlement (city, town, or village) in areas controlled by Germany or its allies, for more than one month."[4] In many ways, the Yad Vashem definition drew upon, and shared much with, Benjamin Ravid's simple three-word description of the early modern ghetto as "compulsory, segregated, and enclosed."[5] However, it differed in important ways, given that it both specified the scale at which the ghetto was implemented as well as the temporal duration of the ghetto's existence. This was intentional. As Dan Michman, chief historian at Yad Vashem who wrote the introduction to the encyclopedia noted, this definition, while including "various patterns of residential concentration – neighborhoods, streets, groups of buildings," purposefully excluded "single buildings, such as the Judenhäuser [Jewish houses] in Germany" as well as non-residential buildings such as "barracks."[6] This decision to limit the scope of the encyclopedia project through specific acts of exclusion shaped the working definition of "ghetto" both in terms of scale and longevity in significant ways.

However, as this essay shows, the rather narrow Yad Vashem definition, as well as Ravid's broader concept of the ghetto, is challenged when considering the story of the concentration and segregation of Jews in Budapest in the second half of 1944. The ghettos established here do fit with ideas of ghettoization as the compulsory relocation of Jews within German-controlled space. Hungarian Jews were forced into ghettos following the German occupation of their somewhat reluctant ally in March 1944. But it is here that narrow definitions of the ghetto start to break down. At this late point in the war, anti-Jewish measures were implemented with lightning speed. The country's 600,000 Jews, who had been spared from mass deportation and murder up until this point, were quickly marked with a yellow star in early April and placed into ghettos in larger towns and cities during April, May, and June. For most, these ghettos ended up being highly temporary living places – in some cases, close to or even less than the one-month minimum that the Yad Vashem team somewhat arbitrarily assigned. Between May and July 1944, over 430,000 Hungarian Jews were deported, mostly to Auschwitz Birkenau. In early July, deportations were halted following the intervention of the Hungarian Regent, Miklós Horthy. This meant that rather than being deported, Jews in Budapest continued living in a series of different urban ghettos until the end of the war. While these ghettos in the Hungarian capital had the temporal duration demanded by the Yad Vashem definition, during the summer and fall of 1944 the Budapest ghetto operated at the scale of individual buildings – and indeed, as this essay shows, in practice, the scale of the individual apartment – pushing ideas of the ghetto as a "segregated and enclosed" space to the absolute limit. Of course, one option is to see what happened in Budapest in the summer and fall of 1944 as something other than the creation of a "ghetto." However, rather than getting bogged down in discussions of terminology, it is more productive to use the tensions between what happened on the ground in Budapest and continent-wide definitions of the "ghetto" to ask why such an unusual form of ghetto was initially created in the Hungarian capital and what this meant for the city's Jewish and non-Jewish population.

The first section of this chapter uncovers the series of ghettos imagined and implemented in Budapest between April and June 1944. Here, it brings the importance of non-Jewish neighbors into the story of ghettos that has tended to be approached solely from the perspective of the dominant Holocaust binary of perpetrators and victims.[7] Not only were city officials well aware that the building of ghettos impacted non-Jews as well as Jews, but in Budapest, non-Jewish neighbors were active agents who not only shaped the ghetto but also dramatically influenced the scale at which ghettoization was implemented. The second part of the chapter shifts to explore lived experiences of dispersed ghettoization in Budapest during the summer and fall of 1944, drawing on collaborative interdisciplinary research undertaken with geographers and geographical information scientists. Working with digital mapping highlights the significance of physical distance and suggests that "invisible walls" and not simply the more visible walls of the official ghetto boundaries shaped the daily experience of Jews living in the Budapest ghetto in the summer and fall of 1944. The final part of the chapter examines the later period, in November 1944, when new ghettos were established in the city, arguing that this amounted to the implementation not only of "hyphenated ghettoization," or different ghettos for different categories of Jews,[8] but also what can be seen as a form of "hypersegregation"[9] in the wartime Hungarian capital. It was only during this final stage that the Budapest ghetto approached the Yad Vashem definition of a "ghetto." However, as this chapter argues, we do well to recognize and seek to understand the multiple forms that the ghetto assumed across time and space. The questions of why this was the case and the impact of this on Jewish lived experiences of the Budapest ghetto lie at the heart of this chapter.

Planning and building the Budapest ghetto: April–June 1944

As they drew a series of lines, oftentimes firstly on a map and then on the ground, separating out Jews from non-Jews in the city, urban planners encountered problems.[10] Ghettos, as the Yad Vashem definition highlights, were not created in *terra nulla*, but rather within "an existing settlement" with its own longer histories and geographies of Jewish and non-Jewish residential patterns. Jews and non-Jews tended to live on the same streets and indeed in the same apartment houses, not in separate places in the city in the way that ghettoization imagined and demanded. This meant that in many places, determining the precise location of the ghetto was a contested and drawn-out process with myriad plans drafted and then either tweaked or rejected.[11] Budapest was no exception to this. During the spring and summer of 1944, ghetto planners worked through a number of different schemes and responded to the opposition of non-Jewish neighbors.

But while Budapest shared the more general problems of identifying the precise place of the ghetto in the city, there were also – like elsewhere – city-specific contexts that shaped the emerging ghetto plans. In Budapest, building the ghetto coincided with the start of Allied bombing of the Hungarian capital. In the first week of April, Budapest was bombed for the first time, and hundreds of Jewish apartments were requisition for use by non-Jewish bomb victims.[12] For Bernard Klein, these evictions marked "the beginning of the ghetto, since the Jews were evicted from certain sections of the towns."[13] The right-wing press certainly shared this view of what was happening. Although these relocations predated the issuing of national ghettoization legislation on 28 April, the right-wing press challenged the shape of this emerging "Jewish quarter" or "ghetto." Adopting what became a widely shared discourse across the spring and early summer of 1944, the press saw Jews as fifth columnists in cahoots with the Allies. Working with these assumptions, the press challenged plans to concentrate Jews into a single quarter on the grounds that it would expose the rest of the city to Allied bombing.[14]

These press concerns were responded to by one of the secretaries of state in the Interior Ministry, László Endre. In an interview, he reassured readers that the city's Jews would not be concentrated in a single ghetto but in a number of closed Jewish quarters, "close to everywhere we expect to be attacked by the terror bombers, for example factories, railway stations …"[15] These principles of dispersing the ghetto and using the city's Jews as a human shield do appear to have shaped, at least in part, the initial set of ghetto plans drawn up in early May 1944. In their initial efforts at the local implementation of national ghetto legislation, urban planners identified seven ghetto areas across the city – three on the Buda side and four on the Pest side of the river Danube. Two of these seven sites were in areas of traditional Jewish residence in the city, but the other five made little sense in terms of where Jews lived. Rather, they were sited either within the industrial ring of the city which had been bombed so consistently throughout April or close to the Castle Hill which was home to government buildings and by the city's southern railway station.[16]

But there was more to these initial ghetto plans than simply the intentional dispersion of the city's Jews so that ghettos could provide a protective shield for the capital. City officials were concerned not only with where Jews were to be placed (Jewish presence), but also where they were to be removed from (Jewish absence).[17] Central to the May 1944 ghetto plans was the goal that 13 main streets and five squares on the Buda side of the river Danube, and 19 main streets and eight squares on the Pest side would be "completely cleansed" of Jews. Moreover, Jews were to be removed from high-quality housing stock and relocated into poorer quality housing. Not only was the city to be "cleansed" from what was seen to be the dirtying presence of Jews, but also the perceived unfair distribution of housing was to be remedied by the relocation of Jews from what was assumed to be privileged living space into second-rate accommodation. This was nothing less than seizing on ghettoization as an opportunity to implement a spatial revolution in Budapest along anti-Semitic lines.[18]

However, during the course of May, these radical plans were shelved and replaced with plans for a much more dispersed form of ghettoization. Rather than creating seven ghetto areas, officials decided in late May to designate houses throughout the entire city on the basis of majority occupation, determined through a door-to-door survey. After this survey had been completed, a long list of buildings where Jews were to move into immediately was published on 16 June. The list contained 2,639 houses and apartment buildings spread across all of the city's fourteen districts, including on those streets and squares that had been identified for clearing of Jews less than a month before.[19] This decision was applauded by the right-wing press that even went as far as claiming some role within the decision, arguing that "from the beginning" their "point of view was that the Budapest Christian and Jewish populations must take their share of the Anglo-Saxon air terror …"[20]Although the press interpreted the highly dispersed form of ghetto ultimately adopted in the city as being shaped primarily by the opportunity to utilize Jews as a human shield, it is clear that city planners also had other concerns. As they implemented ghettoization in June 1944, concerns with the potential impact of ghettoization upon the city's non-Jewish population and the practicalities of enacting ghettoization as quickly and straightforwardly as possible came to the fore. One attraction to ghetto planners of a policy of dispersed ghettoization implemented at the scale of the individual apartment building was that it took the ghetto to where Jews already lived, and thus where non-Jews did not, which would limit the number of forced relocations of both Jews *and* non-Jews. The adoption of a highly dispersed form of ghetto in Budapest ultimately amounted to a decision to take the ghetto to the Jews, rather than the Jews to the ghetto, and built upon – and hardened – the existing patterns of Jewish residence (or presence) in the city.[21]

Although identifying those apartment buildings where Jews formed the majority of tenants limited the number of non-Jews that would have to relocate as a result of creating such a dispersed ghetto, the right-wing press still estimated that some 12,000 non-Jewish families would be forced from their homes and it is clear that some of these were not happy with having to move.[22] In the days following the issuing of the 16 June list of ghetto houses, hundreds of residents – both Jewish and non-Jewish – petitioned the mayor, mostly with requests that they be permitted to remain in their homes. Within the city archives, some 600 or so of these petitions survive. Many (just over 200) were written by non-Jews arguing for the cancelation of ghetto designation for the house where they lived. Another large group (just over 150) came from Jews asking for the opposite – that their houses be designated ghetto houses. In both cases, non-Jews and Jews shared a concern with staying where they were. However, a smaller number of petitions were rather different. For some non-Jews, ghettoization was not something to be avoided, but seized upon as an opportunity to leave their current homes and move into better-quality apartments previously occupied by Jews. Other petitioners – both Jews and non-Jews, and sometimes a coalition of the two – challenged the scale at which ghettoization was being implemented, calling for "mixed" house status for their property.[23]

The sheer number of petitions submitted meant that not only were the specific properties where designation was contested checked to see what proportion of Jewish and non-Jewish tenants lived there, but it seems that the entire ghetto list was rechecked in a rapid door-to-door survey of the city. The results of this survey shaped the definitive ghetto list issued on 22 June. This saw a reduction in the total number of ghetto houses from 2,639 to 1,948, through a mixture of cancellations (840) and additions (149). There was a clear shift away from the Buda side of the Danube to the Pest side; 582 properties in Buda had been designated on 16 June. On 22 June, this was reduced to 220. In comparison, Pest saw less of an overall fall in the numbers of ghetto houses (2,057 down to 1,728), but there were more marked reductions in the outer suburbs of Pest where, for example, the fourteenth district saw more than a halving of the number of properties included in the dispersed ghetto (500 down to 207).[24] The reduction of properties in the Buda and Pest suburbs reflected an explicit policy of ensuring that Jews would no longer live in small family dwellings (a specific absence), but rather would be concentrated in larger apartment buildings. This meant both that desirable properties were made available for non-Jews and that Jews were more tightly controlled, which was critical given that the ghetto was still being imagined at this point in mid to late June as a temporary gathering point prior to deportation.[25] However, unlike Jews living in the more than 150 other ghettos created across the country, Budapest's Jews were ultimately not deported in the summer of 1944. With the halting of deportations in early July, Jews continued to live in the dispersed ghetto throughout the remainder of the summer and into the fall of 1944.

The geography of everyday life in the dispersed ghetto in Budapest: June–October 1944

A few days after the second definitive list of ghetto houses was published, a series of regulations was issued on 25 June, laying out the details of day-to-day life in this dispersed ghetto. One regulation stands out, given its acknowledgment that non-Jews were permitted – in practice – to remain living in apartment buildings on the ghetto list. The stipulation that "Christians" were forbidden from hiding Jews or allowing Jews admission "for no matter how brief a period into either Christian houses *or the Christian-tenanted portions of Jewish houses*" points to the placing of the ghetto boundary, not at the front gate of individual apartment buildings, but at the front door of individual apartments *within* those buildings.[26] In short, it seems that the category of "mixed" house, argued for by a number of petitioners, was officially tolerated. How many non-Jews stayed put is hard to state with any confidence. Randolph Braham, following the early post-war writings of Jenő Lévai, claimed that around 12,000 non-Jewish neighbors remained living within the ghetto, although it is hard to tell where Lévai got these figures from.[27] What can be said with more confidence is that in the area of the seventh district that later became the Pest ghetto, which forms the focus of the third section of this chapter, 144 of the 162 ghetto houses that were incorporated into the ghetto were partially occupied by non-Jews in November 1944.[28] If we can extrapolate from these figures, it would suggest that the vast majority of the close to two thousand ghetto houses across the city were, in reality, "mixed" houses where significant numbers of non-Jewish neighbors stayed put. This forces a reframing of our understanding of the scale of ghettoization in Budapest that was enacted not at the scale of area of the city, street, or individual building but ultimately of the individual apartment, as well as the nature of segregation within this highly unusual ghetto.

By officially tolerating the presence of non-Jewish neighbors within ghetto buildings, the ghetto implemented in Budapest was not simply dispersed across close to two thousand apartment buildings across the city, but in thousands of individual apartments within just under two thousand apartment buildings. Given the last minute compromise as a result of non-Jewish petitioning that permitted them to stay living within ghetto buildings, Michman's definition of a ghetto as a "clearly defined section of an existing settlement" was pushed to its limits in Budapest in the summer and fall of 1944. Although the 25 June legislation sought to define and police the boundaries within what were in reality "mixed" apartment buildings by forbidding Jews from entering the apartments where their non-Jewish neighbors lived, on the ground this depended on the position taken by caretakers within individual ghetto buildings.[29] Moreover, shared spaces within apartment buildings – the stairways, balconies, and courtyards – were far less "clearly defined." This shared space within what were in reality "mixed" houses extended, at least in part, to the city as a whole, given the problems of supplying such a dispersed ghetto.

In order for individuals living within the dispersed ghetto to access foodstuffs and other essentials, a curfew was introduced that allowed the city's Jews to leave their homes for a limited number of hours each afternoon. Initially set at 2–5 pm, these hours were extended and then underwent a series of minor adjustments throughout the summer and fall of 1944, although it seems that even when Jews could leave their homes for longer periods, in practice they sought to leave and return within as short a period of time as possible. Working with these notions of temporal constraints, Alberto Giordano and I – as part of a broader project creating a geographic information system (GIS) of the Budapest ghetto – mapped the critical places that Jews sought to visit when they were permitted to leave their homes. Most significant in oral accounts were the city's market halls (access to foodstuffs). We also mapped the Swedish and Swiss legations (access to protective paperwork) that were increasingly important during the late summer and fall of 1944, as well as hospitals (access to healthcare) that Jews were permitted to use. Hospitals and other Jewish institutions were also sites to be visited – like other ghetto houses – in order to see family members and friends. Given that Jews were not permitted to use private transport during the ghetto period, and appeared reluctant to use the final tram car designated for Jews, we calculated distances between locations by time, using an average walking speed for a healthy adult of 1.3 meters per second. We then used network analysis to calculate the shortest distance (the "least-cost" route) between each Jewish residence and the nearest market hall, the nearest hospital, and the Swedish legations (Figures 9.1, 9.2 and 9.3). The GIS produced maps as the result of each of these calculations, showing either the estimated travel time from a given street segment to a given destination or the estimated cumulative density of Jewish pedestrians along each segment during the non-curfew period on a typical afternoon.[30]

Such mapping is highly speculative. There are too many unknowns. For example, to give just one, did Jews use the most direct routes to get to their destinations in order to arrive as quickly as possible and avoid the long lines that survivors recall, or did they choose to use side streets to avoid non-Jews and officials? Moreover, while GIS analysis can show where Jews *could* physically walk within the confines of the curfew, it cannot show us where Jews *did* in fact go in the city, or how non-Jewish neighbors were a vital resource in going further and earlier. Regardless of the unknowns, we were interested in what more abstract modelling of the spatialities of everyday life in the ghetto might suggest. One thing that emerged was a sense that physical distance from people and resources mattered in the context of the temporal restrictions of the curfew in a city where a dispersed ghetto meant that it was physically impossible to get all the way across the city and back within the timescale of the curfew. Mapping out 30-minute and 60-minute walking distances from market halls, the offices of the Swedish legations, and the hospitals permitted for Jewish use (Figures 9.1, 9.2 and 9.3) prompted us to imagine the existence of "invisible walls" within this highly dispersed ghetto where, in practice, distance separated out Jews from key resources as well as from other Jews.

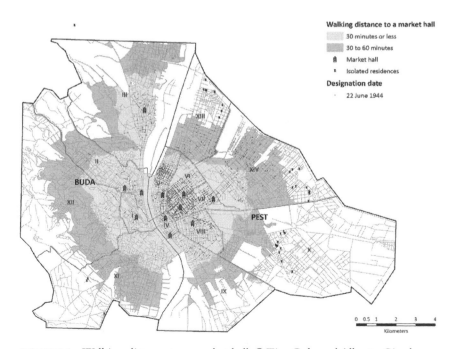

FIGURE 9.1   Walking distance to a market hall. © Tim Cole and Alberto Giordano

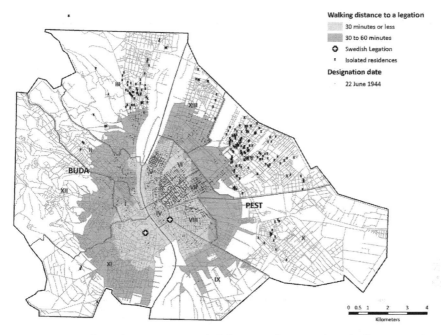

FIGURE 9.2　Walking distance to a Swedish legation. © Tim Cole and Alberto Giordano

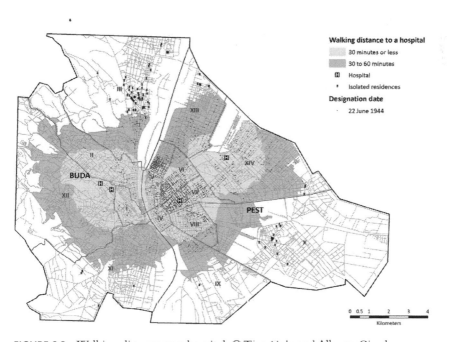

FIGURE 9.3　Walking distance to a hospital. © Tim Cole and Alberto Giordano

This experimental mapping led us to reconceptualize dispersed ghettoization in Budapest. Ghettoization during the Holocaust is generally imagined as a simultaneous process of both concentration and segregation: Jews were placed in increasingly physically concentrated living quarters *and* separated from the non-Jewish population through the creation of closed and guarded boundaries.[31] While concentration appears to be the norm, the extent and nature of segregation varied.[32] In Budapest, the dispersed ghetto functioned as a place where Jews were not only segregated from non-Jews but also from other Jews, and from the means of survival, through the creation of invisible walls of distance. Each of the 1,948 ghetto houses designated on 22 June 1944 was a discrete ghetto whose boundaries were permeable – initially at least – for only three hours each day. There were legislative limits to where Jews could go: they were, for example, forbidden from entering apartment buildings that were not on the ghetto list. But there were also physical limits to where Jews could go given the temporal limits on when Jews could leave their apartments. There are parallels here with Gavin Steingo's essay in this volume, which introduces the spatial limits of those he memorably dubs the "walking class" in Soweto. The "walking class" of Jews living in Budapest similarly experienced limits to where they could and could not go within the dispersed ghetto adopted in the city.

Given the spatio-temporal limits to accessing both resources and people, social networks within apartment buildings became all the more important as ghettoization was enacted. In a sense, dispersed ghettoization shrank the space of daily life and caused a turning inward as the apartment and apartment building became the operational scale at which day-to-day life was lived for the majority of the day. In this context, it mattered enormously whether Jews remained living in their previous apartment building or had to move in June 1944. Staying put not only meant hanging on to material things such as furniture. More critically, it meant having a pre-existing set of social networks with non-Jewish neighbors. In the words of one survivor from Budapest whose family remained living in their own apartment, staying put meant "everything." Continuities of contact between her mother and market stall owners that had been built up over a number of years were particularly important, as they made shopping for non-rationed goods during the curfew far easier. A long-time, non-Jewish neighbor who remained living in his apartment next door "helped find someone who was willing, for payment of course," to take her to hide in the countryside.[33]

The importance of non-Jewish neighbors living within "mixed" houses was heightened by the fact that, given their freedom of movement throughout the city, they were able to broach the "invisible walls" within the dispersed ghetto. For example, another survivor who managed to get hold of Swedish protective paperwork in the early summer recalled that she "was the first who got these Swedish papers from Wallenberg in my building. And after the other people find it out, and everybody rush to Mr. Barat [a non-Jewish neighbor living in the building] and asked him to get it, and they got [them]."[34] As this interview suggests, the limits posed by distance could be and were navigated by coalitions of Jews and non-Jews within "mixed" houses. Non-Jews in the city were an important part of the story of ghettoization, not only as it was planned and contested in the spring and early summer of 1944, but also as it was implemented and lived in the summer and fall. By dint of the fact that ghettos were constructed in the heart of the city, non-Jewish neighbors were intimately involved at every stage and need to be taken more seriously within the historiography as active participants in the story of ghettos.

The shift to "hyphenated ghettoization": November 1944–January 1945

The ghetto was created in Budapest at the moment that pressure was mounting to halt the deportation of Jews from Hungary. Horthy's decision to stop deportations at the outskirts of the capital meant that Budapest's Jews continued to live in the dispersed ghetto throughout the summer and fall. The ghetto changed shape in minor ways, with small numbers of ghetto houses vacated, for example, for the use of German soldiers in September and October.[35] However, more significantly, the meaning of the ghetto changed in the new circumstances. By the end of August, it appeared that the city's Jews had weathered the storm, especially when the more moderate government headed by former military chief General Géza Lakatos took power in late August. Rather than ghettoization as a prelude to deportation, the dispersed ghetto became home to a mass labor force. On 7 September, all able-bodied 'Jews', both male and female, between the ages of 14 and 70, were called up to report for "defence work."[36]

However, this situation of relative normalization proved short lived. After a bungled attempt to withdraw from the Axis side of the war, Regent Miklós Horthy was forced to nullify his proclamation of the end of the war on 16 October and formally entrust Ferenc Szálasi with forming a new government.[37] The next day, Adolf Eichmann returned to Budapest with demands for the delivery, on foot, of 50,000 able-bodied Jews, with any remaining able-bodied Jews to be mobilized for labor in Hungary and those unable to work to be concentrated in camps close to Budapest. In this changed context, ghetto houses in the city were sealed for ten days and thousands of Jewish men and women were mobilized for labor and marched out of the city. Those Jews who remained in the city experienced a new set of ghettos that marked a shift from dispersed ghettoization to "hyphenated ghettoization" and, in the case of one of the ghettos, the adoption of "hypersegregation."

Rather than seeing all Jews in the country as a homogenous whole, the new Arrow Cross government divided the remaining Jews into a number of distinct categories, each of which was to experience distinct territorial solutions. This "final plan," issued on 17 November, resulted in the development of two different ghettos in Budapest in late November 1944 for two different groups of Jews in the capital – those with and without the protection of the neutral powers.[38] These two ghettos – in the interwar middle-class area of Újlipotváros in the fifth district and the traditional Jewish quarter around the Dohány u. synagogue in the seventh district, respectively – built upon both pre-histories of Jewish residential patterns in the city and also earlier histories of ghetto planning and implementation. However, both differed from the earlier dispersed ghetto, with this particularly marked in the case of the closed Pest ghetto established in the seventh district in the heart of the city.

The so-called "International ghetto" created in the fifth district in northern Pest, close to the Danube shore, included just over 120 apartment buildings spread over a handful of streets.[39] In short, it was ghettoization at the scale of the individual building – as the June ghetto plans had originally been imagined. Working at the scale of individual buildings meant that, more or less, those houses in the area that had been part of the ghetto since late June could now be repurposed for inclusion in the International ghetto. For example, all the buildings that had been designated on Pozsonyi út on 22 June were now re-designated for the use of "protected Jews" – in the main, those with Swedish papers – although this was not the case with all buildings included in the ghetto area.[40] This shift from housing Jews to housing "protected Jews" meant that those Jews without protective paperwork issued by the neutral powers had to leave their homes. But also on the move were non-Jews, who had been tolerated in living within what were in practice "mixed" houses during the summer and fall. As one survivor recalled, "anyone who did not belong, these had to go whether he was a gentile person or a person with a Jewish – but did not have the passport …"[41] Ghettoization was no longer to be tolerated at the scale of the individual apartment, but at the scale of the individual apartment building in the case of the International ghetto, and the scale of the "section of an existing settlement" in the case of the so-called "Pest ghetto."

In late November, a large contiguous walled-ghetto was created in the heart of Budapest, following meetings between the city's police and Jewish leaders. Mapped out on 29 November, the ghetto lay within the traditional Jewish district in Pest, and fitted squarely with one of the seven ghettos drawn up by city officials on 9 May, 1944 as well as the area "between Dob u. and Podmaniczy u.," which had been rumored as a potential ghetto site in the press as early as April 1944.[42] Around half of the apartment buildings within this area had been part of the earlier dispersed ghetto of houses marked with a yellow star. This was another case of a longer-running story across 1944 of the choice of location for the ghetto being shaped by where Jews already were (and non-Jews were not). However, the decision to create a single, walled ghetto at the scale of a part of the city rather than the scale of the apartment building, let alone the individual apartment, meant that, as the authorities themselves were well aware, large numbers of non-Jews would be forced to move. This impacted not only non-Jewish residences, but given the central location, also business premises.[43] Unlike the earlier toleration of non-Jewish neighbors remaining within the dispersed ghetto, non-Jews were now ordered to leave the ghetto "with understanding and in a self-sacrificing spirit, thereby helping to solve finally the hitherto neglected Jewish question," although those who refused to vacate their homes were threatened with internment.[44] By November 1944, state-sanctioned violence was to be used against Jew and non-Jew in the pursuit of state aims, with little in the way of effective means of appeal. The opportunity for popular contesting of the shape of the ghetto had disappeared.

Moreover, non-Jews moving out of the new ghetto area were not free to go anywhere in the city, but were explicitly restricted to moving to former Jewish homes within Pest, unless they owned an apartment in a former dispersed ghetto house in Buda. Rather than being made available for non-Jews moving out of the ghetto, it is clear that others had their eyes on former Jewish homes on the Pest side of the Danube. Before plans for the Pest ghetto were finalized, officials were already working out what to do with former dispersed ghetto houses in Buda. In the third district in northern Buda, 74 of the 119 soon-to-be-vacated ghetto houses had already "been reserved for the army, the German army and the *Nyilas* party," complete with sufficient fuel to heat these apartments during the winter months.[45] The attraction of Buda was obvious, given the rapid advance of the Red Army from the East in the final weeks of the war in Hungary.

With Buda cleared of Jews, along with the suburbs of the city, Budapest's Jews were now (at least officially) confined to two places in the city – either the protected houses in the northern part of Pest, or the closed ghetto in the center of Pest. In the case of the latter, the right-wing press saw – and celebrated – this as the final act of separating out the "Pest Jewry" who had now returned to their place in the traditional Jewish quarter of the city.[46] This built on long-standing pragmatic concerns with taking the ghetto to the Jew, rather than taking the Jew to the ghetto, but it also drew on anti-Semitic ideas of the Jewish place in the city. However, this final act of ghettoization that brought Jews into the heart of the city is perhaps somewhat surprising given, as David Sibley suggests, that imaginary landscapes of exclusion tend to push the minority to the periphery or off the very edge of the earth. Sibley points to

> a history of imaginary geographies which cast minorities, "imperfect" people, and a list of others who are seen to pose a threat to the dominant group in society as polluting bodies or folk devils who are then located "elsewhere": This "elsewhere" might be nowhere, as when genocide or the moral transformation of a minority like prostitutes are advocated, or it might be some spatial periphery, like the edge of the world or the edge of the city.[47]

Certainly, within the geography of apartheid, the racialized Other was restricted to the spatial periphery in South Africa. And yet in Budapest, the final acts of ghettoization brought Jews to the very center of the city. The city's Jews were given two hours to gather what they could carry from the apartments that had formed their homes within the dispersed ghetto and move into the ghetto. On 7 December, the ghetto was sealed.

Conclusion: Ghettos, segregation and "hypersegregation"

The closed ghetto constructed in central Pest in the winter of 1944 comes closest to the Yad Vashem definition of the "ghetto," given its implementation at the scale of a distinct section of the city covering a number of adjacent streets. However, rather than identifying this moment as the point when the ghetto became the "ghetto" in Budapest, this chapter has argued that there was a shifting pattern of ghetto making across 1944 in Budapest. Rather than getting drawn into debates over definition, it is more productive to explore how and why these variously shaped ghettos were implemented and what the implications were for the city Jews and their non-Jewish neighbors. As the chapter has argued, non-Jewish neighbors are clearly a part of the story of ghetto making and ghetto experience and need to be better integrated into historiographies of urban segregation.

Reflecting on the moment in the winter of 1944 when the ghetto in Budapest radically changed shape and was implemented on a markedly different scale, it is potentially fruitful to work with Massey and Denton's ideas of "hypersegregation" to distinguish between differing degrees of concentration and segregation across the evolving ghetto. Although developed in a very different context – urban segregation in the United States – Massey and Denton's concept of "hypersegregation" is potentially a useful tool for differentiating between the wide varieties of forms that Nazi-era ghettos took. According to Massey and Denton, the experience of "hypersegregation" – which they identify as distinctive to African Americans – represents the coming together of five spatial dimensions of segregation – "evenness, exposure, clustering, centralization, and concentration." A number of these spatial dimensions of segregation can be seen in both the highly dispersed ghetto, operating in practice at the scale of the individual apartment in the summer and fall, as well as the sealed ghetto created across a number of streets in central Pest in the winter of 1944. Both were characterized by degrees of segregation identified through what Massey and Denton dub "evenness" – "the degree to which the percentage of minority members within residential areas equals the citywide minority percentage" – and "concentration" – "the relative amount of physical space occupied by a minority group" – although these were more marked in the case of the Pest ghetto. However, the other three spatial dimensions – "exposure" or "the degree of potential contact between minority and majority members," which "reflects the extent to which groups are exposed to one another by virtue of sharing neighborhoods in common"; "clustering," which "is the extent to which minority areas adjoin one another in space" and so "is maximized when minority neighborhoods form one large, contiguous ghetto and minimized when they are scattered"; and "centralization," or "the degree to which minority members are settled in and around the center of an urban area, usually defined as the central business district" – were distinct to the Pest ghetto established in winter 1944.[48]

While both dispersed and concentrated ghettoization in Budapest in 1944 can be seen as the construction and experience of Nazi-era ghettos, there were important differences between these two different phases. The hyper-dispersed ghetto created in June 1944 that not only was spread throughout close to 2,000 apartment buildings across the city, but also in practice operated at the scale of the individual apartment, pushes existing definitions of the ghetto to the limits. Although moving into these different ghettos was "compulsory" across the period June–December 1944, the idea of the ghetto as both "segregated" and "enclosed" varied markedly as the ghetto changed shape, and both ideas are challenged by experiences of everyday life within this ghetto during the summer and fall of 1944. However, rather than rejecting the idea that this highly dispersed local response to national legislation was indeed a "ghetto," it is more productive to consider varying degrees of segregation across ghettos and the impact of this on those living within them. It is clear that in Budapest a very different ghetto was created in central Pest in December 1944 that radically changed the experience of both Jews and non-Jews in the city. This hypersegregated ghetto was implemented in a different political context, with changed imaginings of the relationship of the state vis-à-vis both Jewish and non-Jewish citizens.

What both ghettos shared, however, perhaps ironically, is that they turned out to be equally anachronistic. Although radically different in the form and degree of segregation, both were created right on the cusp of changing circumstances. In June 1944, the dispersed ghetto was built at the same time that calls were mounting to halt the deportations. Rather than being a way-station to Auschwitz, as other Hungarian ghettos were, the ghetto in Budapest became home to a domestic labor force through the summer and fall of 1944. In December 1944, the Pest ghetto was created as the Soviet advance gained pace. Two days after the Pest ghetto was sealed, the Red Army broke through the Friesner Line and by the end of December had laid siege to the city. As the German and Hungarian military fled westwards, the Soviets entered deeper into Pest, liberating the Pest and International ghettos in mid-January. Unique to ghettos across Hungary and beyond, the evolving "ghetto" in Budapest was liberated rather than liquidated.

Note on figures

These are taken from Tim Cole and Alberto Giordano, "Bringing the Ghetto to the Jew: Spatialities of Ghettoization in Budapest" in Anne Kelly Knowles, Tim Cole, and Alberto Giordano (eds.), *Geographies of the Holocaust* (Bloomington: Indiana University Press, 2014) 120–157. They were developed through a collaborative research project made possible by National Science Foundation Awards nos. 0820487 and 0820501. Maps not to be reproduced without the authors' permission.

Notes

1 T. Cole, *Holocaust City: The Making of a Jewish Ghetto*, New York: Routledge, 2003, pp. 77–9; T. Cole, *Traces of the Holocaust. Journeying in and out of the Ghettos*, London: Continuum, 2011, pp. 57–59.
2 Cole, *Traces of the Holocaust*: pp. 56–70.
3 M. Dean (ed.), *The United States Holocaust Memorial Museum Encyclopedia of Camps and Ghettos, Volume II: Ghettos in German-Occupied Eastern Europe*, Bloomington: Indiana University Press, p. xliii.
4 D. Michman, *The Emergence of Jewish Ghettos during the Holocaust*, New York: Cambridge University Press, 2011, p. 4.
5 B. Ravid, "All Ghettos were Jewish Quarters but not all Jewish Quarters were Ghettos," *Jewish Culture and History* 10: 2–3, 2008, pp. 5–24.

6 Michman, *The Emergence of Jewish Ghettos*, p. 4.
7 T. Cole, "Geographies of Ghettoization: Absences, Presences, and Boundaries" in P. Giccaria and C. Minca (eds.), *Hitler's Geographies: The Spatialities of the Third Reich*, Chicago: Chicago University Press, 2016, pp. 266–281.
8 Cole, *Holocaust City*, p. 204.
9 D.S. Massey and N.A. Denton, "Hypersegregation in U.S. Metropolitan Areas: Black and Hispanic Segregation along Five Dimensions," *Demography* 26:3, 1989, pp. 373–391.
10 Cole, *Traces of the Holocaust*, pp. 65–70.
11 C.R. Browning, "Nazi Ghettoization Policy in Poland, 1939–1941," *Central European History* 19, 1986, pp. 343–363; Cole, *Traces of the Holocaust*, pp. 41–55.
12 Cole, *Holocaust City*, pp. 81–83.
13 B. Klein, "The Judenrat," *Jewish Social Studies* 22: 1, 1960, p. 32.
14 Cole, *Holocaust City*, pp. 82–84; 115–125.
15 Cole, *Holocaust City*, pp. 84, 88.
16 Cole, *Holocaust City*, pp. 84–93.
17 T. Cole, "Ghettoization" in D. Stone (ed.), *The Historiography of the Holocaust*, Houndmills: Palgrave Macmillan, 2004, pp. 65–87.
18 Cole, *Holocaust City*, pp. 88–91.
19 Cole, *Holocaust City*, pp. 101–115.
20 Cole, *Holocaust City*, p. 119.
21 T. Cole and A. Giordano, "Bringing the Ghetto to the Jew: The Shifting Geography of the Budapest Ghetto" in A.K. Knowles, T. Cole, and A. Giordano (eds.), *Geographies of the Holocaust*, Bloomington: Indiana University Press, 2014, pp. 120–157.
22 Cole, *Holocaust City*, p. 125.
23 Cole, *Holocaust City*, pp. 131–156.
24 Cole, *Holocaust City*, pp. 156–159.
25 Cole, *Holocaust City*, pp. 155–167.
26 R. L. Braham, *The Politics of Genocide: The Holocaust in Hungary*, New York: Columbia University Press, 1994, p. 856.
27 Braham, *Politics of Genocide*, p. 735; J., Lévai, (1946) *Fekete Konyv a Magyar Zsidosag Szenvedeseirol*, Budapest: Officina, 1946, p. 156.
28 Cole, *Holocaust City*, p. 155.
29 M. Rigó, "Ordinary Women and Men: Superintendents and Jews in the Budapest Yellow Star Houses in 1944–1945," *Urban History* 40: 1, 2013, pp. 71–91; T. Cole and A. Giordano, "Rethinking Segregation in the Ghetto: Invisible Walls and Social Networks in the Dispersed Ghetto in Budapest, 1944" in H. Earl and K. Schleunes (eds.), *Lessons and Legacies XI. Expanding Perspectives on the Holocaust in a Changing World*, Evanston: Northwestern University Press, 2014, pp. 265–291; I. Adam, *Budapest Building Managers and the Holocaust in Hungary*, Houndmills: Palgrave Macmillan, 2016.
30 Cole and Giordano, "Bringing the Ghetto to the Jew."
31 R. Hilberg, *The Destruction of the European Jews*, 3rd edition, New Haven: Yale University Press, 2003, pp. 236–237.
32 T. Cole, "Contesting and Compromising Ghettoization, Hungary 1944" in J.K. Roth, J. Petropoulous, and L. Rapaport (eds.), *Lessons and Legacies IX: Memory, History and Responsibility*, Evanston: Northwestern University Press, 2010, pp. 152–166.
33 Cole and Giordano, "Rethinking Segregation."
34 Cole and Giordano, "Rethinking Segregation."
35 Cole, *Holocaust City*, p. 193.
36 Cole, *Holocaust City*, p. 194.
37 N.M. Nagy-Talavera, *The Green Shirts and the Others: A History of Fascism in Hungary and Rumania,* Stanford: Hoover Institution Press, 1970, pp. 226–232.
38 Cole, *Holocaust City*, pp. 197–210; T. Cole, *Holocaust Landscapes*, London: Bloomsbury, 2016, pp. 151–169.
39 Á. Ságvári, *A Budapesti Zsidóság Holocaustja 1944*, Budapest: The Jewish Agency for Israel, 1994, p. 9.

40   Cole, *Holocaust City*, p. 210.
41   Cole, *Holocaust City*, p. 209.
42   Cole, *Holocaust City*, p. 82.
43   Cole, *Holocaust City*, pp. 212–213.
44   Cole, *Holocaust City*, p. 215.
45   Cole, *Holocaust City*, p. 216.
46   Cole, *Holocaust City*, pp. 216–217.
47   D. Sibley, *Geographies of Exclusion: Society and Difference in the West*. London: Routledge, 1995, p. 49.
48   Massey and Denton, "Hypersegregation," p. 373.

PART III

U.S. and African American ghettos

Crawford Grill, Pittsburgh. Photograph by Charles "Teenie" Harris, *Crawford Grill No. 1 and Crampton Drug Store Seen from Opposite Side of Street, 1401 Wylie Avenue, Hill District, c. 1943.* Courtesy of the Carnegie Museum of Art, Pittsburgh; Heinz Family Fund, 2001.35.2227

10

SHIFTING "GHETTOS"

Established Jews, Jewish immigrants, and African Americans in Chicago, 1880–1960

Tobias Brinkmann

In 1928, the sociologist Louis Wirth (1897–1952) published his dissertation titled "The Ghetto." The book, an immediate success, was in print until the late 1960s and was widely used in courses in urban sociology. In the concise and well-written study, Wirth compared the early modern Jewish ghetto in the German city Frankfurt am Main with the Jewish immigrant neighborhood in Chicago known as "ghetto." Wirth tried to assess whether the legacy of forced Jewish segregation in early modern Italy and Central Europe influenced the clustering of Jewish immigrants from Eastern Europe in run-down inner-city neighborhoods in the United States and Western Europe at the end of the nineteenth century. Chicago's Jewish "ghetto" developed during the 1880s in the wake of the mass immigration of Jews from Eastern Europe. Already in the 1870s, similar Jewish immigrant neighborhoods emerged in New York and London. By 1910, the "New York Ghetto" on the Lower East Side was one of the most densely settled urban areas in the United States and home to over 350,000 Jews. The public perception of these neighborhoods as "ghettos" was influenced in no small part by the works of Jewish authors. In his 1892 novel *Children of the Ghetto*, the respected Anglo-Jewish writer Israel Zangwill popularized the name for the area settled by Jewish immigrants in London's East End. Four years later, journalist Abraham Cahan published *Yekl: A Tale of the New York Ghetto*, a collection of short stories about Jewish immigrants in New York. Both Zangwill and Cahan aimed at a general readership, trying to raise sympathies for Jewish immigrants. Opponents of immigration exploiting widespread anti-Semitic stereotypes pointed to the immigrant ghettos as proof that Jewish immigrants were inassimilable. In an 1896 article on "Chicago's Ghetto," a local reporter depicted Jewish immigrants as "unique people [living] in our midst, and yet no more of us than are the people of the South Sea islands." The general *and* Jewish public in the United States and in Western Europe widely associated Jewish immigrant neighborhoods with the early modern ghettos for Jews. As Zangwill put it: "People who have been living in a ghetto for a couple of centuries are not able to step outside merely because the gates are thrown down … The isolation from without will have come to seem the law of their being." Wirth quoted this passage to emphasize that the ghetto continued to "linger[s]" in the "Jewish mind" long after it had been dissolved.[1]

Locating the ghetto in time and space

Louis Wirth himself was an immigrant and a Jew who grew up in rural Hesse as the son of a cattle dealer. Rural Jews in Germany still spoke Yiddish around 1900, and Wirth probably acquired some knowledge of the language, which was closely related to his native German. In 1911, when Wirth was 14 years old, he and his sister moved to relatives in Omaha, Nebraska. A fellowship took the high-school graduate to the University of Chicago. After graduation, he briefly found employment as a social worker before resuming his studies. After completing his dissertation at the University of Chicago in 1924, he struggled to find a position for several years. In 1930, Wirth returned to his alma mater, emerging as a widely respected urban sociologist who served as president of the American Association of Sociology in the late 1940s. In his path-breaking 1938 article "Urbanism as a way of life," Wirth analyzed the multiple relationships between "urbanites," arguing that the modern city constituted "a mosaic of social worlds." Frequent and continuous encounters between strangers of different backgrounds in the dense urban space, Wirth argued, promoted the "secularization of life." While not disavowing his dissertation, Wirth never returned to the subject of Jewish life in the city before his untimely death of a heart attack in 1952. Historian Hasia Diner speculates that anti-Semitic discrimination in the academy may have been a factor.[2] Wirth did, however, speak up publicly against the discrimination of African Americans, in particular against attempts by his employer, the University of Chicago, to prevent the settlement of African Americans in the wider vicinity of the campus in the Hyde Park neighborhood.[3]

Like other students of the influential sociologist Robert Park at the University of Chicago, Wirth ventured into the city, conducting interviews with immigrants. Park and his students used Chicago as a laboratory to understand the forces transforming the modern American city. Between 1840 and 1900, Chicago had expanded from a small town on the western frontier to the fifth-largest city in the world. In 1890, immigrants from Europe and their American-born children represented a staggering 80% of the city's population, an unusually high proportion compared with other rapidly growing American cities at the time. Between 1870 and 1920, mass immigration (and natural growth) pushed the number of Jews in Chicago from a few thousand to over 300,000. Only New York and Warsaw had larger Jewish populations. After 1880, Chicago also attracted sizeable groups of other Eastern and Southern Europeans, joining older communities of German and Irish immigrants. The post-1880 immigrants settled in adjacent neighborhoods surrounding the inner city, often in close proximity to industrial jobs.[4] Members of the Hull House Settlement already published detailed maps of the West Side immigrant area in

1895, highlighting the ethnic diversity of districts that were perceived as exclusively Jewish or Italian. Wirth discussed only in passing that many non-Jewish immigrants had settled in the ghetto area, while a significant number of Jews found housing in areas dominated by other immigrant groups. In his view, this reflected already the dissolution of the ghetto neighborhood.[5] Immigration restrictions passed by the United States Congress in the aftermath of the First World War sharply reduced immigration from Eastern and Southern Europe. The sharp decline of immigration from Europe that had begun already during the war coincided with the first phase of the Great Migration from the South. Between 1910 and 1920, over 50,000 African Americans moved to Chicago. This migration continued during the 1920s, even after a notorious race riot in August 1919 and even though discrimination, informal settlement restrictions, and violence occurred on a daily basis.[6]

The research of Wirth and other young Chicago sociologists occurred in the early 1920s when most of the post-1880 migrants from Eastern and Southern Europe in Chicago were on the move, leaving densely settled inner-city neighborhoods for areas further west and north, often acquiring small bungalow-style houses. Indeed, as Wirth was conducting interviews in the early 1920s, thousands of Jews had already left what he described as the "vanishing ghetto" for North Lawndale on Chicago's far West Side. Many Czech immigrants headed from the Pilsen area on the West Side to South Lawndale.[7] At the same time, the steady migration of African Americans into Chicago continued. However, not all post-1880 immigrants and their descendants were relocating. Catholics, especially, stayed put, notably Poles. They remained attached to the parish system that was tied to neighborhoods.[8] In contrast, Jewish and Protestant congregations followed their members to new neighborhoods. Arriving African American migrants partly moved into areas that were vacated by the bungalow belt migrants. They faced a serious obstacle that was not immediately apparent to the sociologists researching immigrant neighborhoods in transition. Many white landlords refused to rent or sell to African Americans. Before 1900, the relatively small African American community was located on the Near South Side, but many African Americans found housing in other neighborhoods. As more newcomers arrived from the South in the years before the First World War, violence and open discrimination increased. Most African Americans settled in the so-called Black Belt, a clearly (albeit informally) demarcated area on the South Side that developed around the older African American settlement core and was inhabited almost exclusively by African Americans. The gradual expansion of the Black Belt on the South Side and into the West Side during and especially after the First World War was accompanied by violent attacks directed against the African American newcomers, especially in areas on the South Side. Catholic Poles "defended" their invisible parish boundaries against African American newcomers. Fierce resistance by white landlords and residents, violence, and a racist white police force explain why new arrivals were forced into in a tightly segregated and neglected area on the city's South Side, sharing quarters with longer-settled African Americans who could not move out.[9]

Almost in passing, Wirth alluded to the transition of the West Side during the early 1920s: "the Negro has drifted to the near West Side for precisely the same reason that the Jews and the Italians came there." He explained that unlike other whites, Jewish landlords did not discriminate against African Americans. Indeed, Wirth described the ghetto as "another haven of refuge in a city" for African Americans.[10] The latter point highlights an ambivalence that Wirth associated with the early modern and the immigrant ghetto. Both ghettos offered a degree of protection and familiarity for their residents, even serving as hubs of a flourishing community life. At the same time, they increased the isolation of the residents and thus obstructed assimilation. Like his mentor Park and other members of the Chicago School of sociologists, Wirth was a proponent of assimilation. He quoted the Cincinnati Reform rabbi and historian David Philipson who described Jewish immigrant ghettos in the United States as "a result of the instituted ghetto of the Middle Ages," calling for a break-up of the "constant menace."[11]

"The Ghetto" is still widely referenced. While the empirical material presented in the study is valuable, Wirth's analysis is flawed. His discussion of the early modern ghetto suffered from a focus on general works rather than specific studies. Admittedly, detailed studies about different ghettos in the German lands and Italy had not been published in the mid-1920s. As sociologist Mitchell Duneier has recently emphasized, Wirth's assumption that the "voluntary" Jewish neighborhoods of the medieval period had brought about the imposition of "involuntary" ghettos of the early modern period is mistaken. This point matters because Wirth hinted that, like the early modern ghetto, the voluntary immigrant ghetto might become a permanent institution, separating Jews from the rest of society.[12] It is also questionable whether the *Judengasse* in Frankfurt am Main or indeed any other early modern Jewish ghetto in Central Europe or Italy can be described as "typical." The same applies to the Jewish immigrant ghetto in Chicago. Wirth's teacher Robert Park and his colleague Ernest Burgess proposed that the residential mobility of immigrants correlated with different stages of assimilation. The immigrant ghetto served as an area of first settlement. According to this explanatory model, the move to an area of secondary settlement corresponded with a shift from the native language to English and a weakening of ancestral religious and cultural ties.[13] Beginning in the 1960s, sociologists and historians questioned the linear assimilation model proposed by Park and his collaborators. The empirical results of studies by Wirth and his fellow researchers simply could not be applied to other cities such as New York, where immigrants moved from ethnically mixed neighborhoods to the Lower East Side rather than in the opposite direction. Today, assimilation is defined as an open-ended, non-linear process that can correspond with different stages of dissimilation. Instead of gradually conforming to an opaque majority or mainstream society, members of different immigrant groups and members of longer-settled groups are influencing each other, creating new groups which can overlap, with some individuals belonging to several groups at the same time.[14]

Most important, the linear Chicago School assimilation concept cannot be applied to African American migrants moving to northern cities. Ironically, that was already a result of studies conducted by two students of Wirth and Park in the 1930s, Horace Cayton and St. Clair Drake. The detailed research of Cayton and Drake showed that, unlike adjacent immigrant neighborhoods, African American city migrants could not move easily from the Black Belt to a neighborhood of secondary settlement. However, the "color line" was not impermeable. Although frowned upon by most African Americans living in the Black Belt, intermarriage and "passing" did occur frequently. Cayton and Drake emphasized that "passing" did not simply depend on being mistaken for a member of another group, such as South Asians, but also on patterns of behavior and dress perceived as "white" outside of the Black Belt.[15]

The discussion of Wirth's study raises the question of how different ghettos were connected, how the concept "moved" across the Atlantic and within the United States, and how connections between different ghettos emerged. To highlight the gap between perception and actual residential patterns, and between formal and informal residential segregation, it is worthwhile to look at a small immigrant group that most authors discussing the ghetto concept in the American context overlook, even though its members were closely tied to early modern Jewish ghettos, American Jewish immigrant neighborhoods, and the segregated African American residential districts as they emerged in the 1920s: Jews from Central Europe who arrived before 1880 and who, together with their American-born descendants, represented the small Jewish establishment in most American cities before the First World War.

Rejection and nostalgia

As Napoleon's troops moved into the western part of the Holy Roman Empire and northern Italy in the late 1790s, ghettos and settlement restrictions for Jews were abolished. In annexed areas west of the Rhine, Jews became fully emancipated French citizens. Most German states under French control passed emancipation laws that gave Jews far-reaching (albeit not full) civil rights, such as the Prussian 1812 emancipation edict. With its demise, the ghetto became a highly ambivalent symbol among German Jews. Different Jewish views of the ghetto were a result of the prolonged emancipation process in the German states, which lasted to the early 1870s. German state bureaucrats tied the granting of civil rights to proof of modernization. Jews were expected to leave the traditional Judaism of "the" ghetto behind. In 1781, Prussian bureaucrat Christian Wilhelm von Dohm, an acquaintance of the Jewish philosopher Moses Mendelssohn, acknowledged in an influential text that Jewish difference was a consequence of enforced isolation rather than inherent in the Jewish tradition or "character." Outside the ghetto, Dohm argued, Jews would become "normal" if they were subjected to an extensive process of bourgeois "improvement" or education.[16] The connection between Dohm's demand and the approach of the Chicago School over a century later is striking. Most Jewish community leaders embraced the bureaucratic modernization project because they associated modernization with universal and pluralist Enlightenment principles rather than exclusionary concepts of a German "Volk" or conversion to Protestantism. The rise of the Jewish Reform movement in the early decades of the nineteenth century in the German states illustrates this transition. Reformers did not want to sacrifice Jewish specificity, let alone convert, but rather wanted to redefine and modernize Judaism by critically evaluating its core texts.[17] In their view, ghettos symbolized Jewish tradition and social isolation – the "medieval" past. The advocates of Jewish modernization used negative images of the ghetto as a foil but overlooked that the Jewish ghetto was not a medieval institution, that ghettos had not been completely closed-off spaces, and that the few cities with ghettos in Central Europe were sites of encounters and dialogue between Jews and others.

At the same time, Jewish modernizers were also beholden to romanticized, even nostalgic, notions of a disappearing Jewish life-world. During the first half of the nineteenth century, the ghetto emerged as an influential genre in German Jewish literature. Writers such as Berthold Auerbach and Leopold Kompert promoted nostalgic views of a Jewish past and *Gemeinschaft* that found wide acclaim among Jewish readers in a period of rapid social transformation. As Richard Cohen has emphasized, for modernizing Jews, the ghetto represented Jewish authenticity.[18] Nineteenth-century German Jewish ghetto nostalgia needs to be differentiated from the romanticized image of the Jewish *shtetl* that can be traced to Jewish writers and artists in late nineteenth-century Eastern European cities, resurfacing as part of American (Jewish) popular culture during the 1960s. The "imagined *shtetl*," as it was depicted in the successful 1964 Broadway play "Fiddler on the Roof," was a symbol of the Jewish life-world in Eastern Europe that had been destroyed in the Holocaust and at the same time a powerful affirmation of Jewish identity in a pluralist American society.[19]

After 1850, nostalgic German Jewish views of the ghetto were sidelined but not completely marginalized by increasingly negative depictions of the Jewish "ghetto" in Eastern Europe, where it had not existed in the early modern period. Jewish emancipation and modernization did not take place in a vacuum. With the founding of the German nation state in 1871, the last German Jews were fully emancipated. The demand to revoke Jewish emancipation was a rallying point for the rising anti-Semitic movement in Germany and Austria in the 1870s. The emergence of modern anti-Semitism in Germany coincided with the early stages of the Jewish mass migration from Eastern Europe to and through Central Europe to the United States. On the eve of the mass migration in 1870, 70% of the world's Jewish population lived dispersed in several regions across the Russian and Austro-Hungarian Empires and in Southeastern Europe, mostly in small towns.[20] Germany bordered Eastern Europe and fears of a (Jewish) mass migration were widespread in the decades before 1914. As Steven Aschheim has shown, many German Jews subscribed to negative and distorted views of Eastern European Jews as "ghetto Jews," even though many had themselves grown up in a rural and traditional Jewish milieu. The rejection of the *Ostjude* really illustrates the disassociation of many German Jews from their own tradition. Anti-Semitic agitators linked calls for returning German Jews to the "ghetto" with distorted images of Eastern European "ghetto"

Jews who were "invading" Germany. However, toward the end of the nineteenth century, German Jewish images of the ghetto as a center of Jewish spirituality and authenticity also shifted east. A growing number of younger Zionists, for instance the philosopher Martin Buber, embraced an image of *Ostjuden* as authentic Jews.[21]

Chicago's Jewish ghetto

How did images of the ghetto propagated by Jewish writers and scholars in Central Europe during the nineteenth century come to the United States? Between 1820 and 1880, more than 100,000 Jews moved from Central Europe to the United States. Their number was small, if compared to the millions of other German-speaking immigrants arriving in the same period, and to the over two million Jews who immigrated between 1880 and the early 1920s, but since very few Jews had settled in the United States before 1800, Central European migrants represented the Jewish establishment. They were socially mobile, becoming part of the urban bourgeoisie by the 1870s, especially in Midwestern cities such as Chicago where informal anti-Semitic discrimination was less common than in cities on the East Coast before the 1890s. Central European Jewish migrants took significant cultural capital across the Atlantic – at a time when cultural Germany enjoyed great renown in the United States – and they retained close links with their co-religionists in Central Europe as even a superficial look at Jewish community papers reveals. The Jewish Reform movement, which faced many obstacles in Europe, flourished in the United States. Reform Jews in Chicago and several other northern cities strongly opposed slavery in the South. During the Civil War, Jewish and German immigrant leaders in Chicago linked calls for the emancipation of slaves in the South with demands for the full emancipation of Jews in the German states.[22]

The rising Jewish immigration from Eastern Europe became a matter of great concern to the small communities of longer-settled Jews in the United States in the 1880s. Just as they had joined the urban bourgeoisie, large numbers of new immigrants who were visibly Jewish and poor appeared to pull them back in time and space to a place they had left behind when they moved to the United States and Britain earlier in the nineteenth century. The initial rejection of the immigrants by established Jews was driven by fears about the loss of social status and of power over the (loosely organized) Jewish community. Jewish leaders were concerned that anti-Semitism would spread from Europe to the United States.[23] Established American Jews began to encounter informal exclusion more frequently after the mid-1870s. Jewish leaders blamed Eastern European immigrants for the rise of anti-Semitic discrimination, even though established Jews were the main target of this discrimination, not the new immigrants. Jews were caricatured as nouveau riche parvenus who lacked the appropriate forms of behavior. Other "outsiders" – Catholics, Chinese immigrants, and African Americans – encountered more open discrimination, even violence. Low social mobility and, in the case of Chinese immigrants, strictly enforced racial segregation and immigration restrictions excluded them from social spaces established Jews, as whites, could enter. Whiteness and high social mobility made established Jews particularly suspicious in the eyes of self-declared defenders of the old order.[24]

It is hardly surprising that most established Jews in Chicago watched the rise of the Jewish immigrant neighborhood on the West Side uneasily. The directors of the United Hebrew Charities, the social arm of the established Jewish community, declared in 1897, "If you could give to your board $50,000, they would expend it well. They could take a first step toward clearing out the ghetto and preventing our applicants from huddling together in one corner of the city." The Hull House settlement, located in the heart of the West Side immigrant neighborhood, also took a strong line against the ghetto. Settlement worker Charles Zeublin stressed that the "annihilation" of the ghetto was its "greatest need."[25] As in other cities, established Jews in Chicago launched a number of Americanization projects for the new immigrants that closely echo Dohm's concept of civil "improvement." The most ambitious project was the state-of-the-art "Jewish Training School," which was erected in the heart of the West Side neighborhood in 1890.[26] As thousands of Jewish immigrants were pouring into the ghetto on the West Side, Emil G. Hirsch, the prominent rabbi of the city's leading Reform temple, Chicago Sinai Congregation, described the ghetto, "this new *Judengasse* west of the river," as a "heavy burden on our communal institutions."[27] Hirsch was appalled by "the men and families now huddled together in these streets plastered all over with Hebrew lettered signs." In his view, the ghetto was "the root of the trouble … this piece of Russia and Medieval Germany here on the soil of America." Hirsch, a declared opponent of Zionism, associated the ghetto with one particular "danger," the rise of a Jewish "nationality" in America.[28]

These harsh comments should not be taken out of context. Hirsch's strong reaction in the first half of the 1890s betrays his struggle to accept that Reform Judaism represented a shrinking minority of American Jews as more and more traditional Jews were arriving from Europe. Instead of a post-ethnic universal Judaism in America, the ghetto raised the specter of the dark European past, of a "closed" traditional Judaism and of a Jewish "nationality." Soon after the turn of the century, Hirsch publicly acknowledged defeat: "These hordes from the East of Europe will determine the character of the Judaism of tomorrow in the United States. We have ceased to be the dominant factor. We are now in the minority."[29]

Some established Jews embraced the new immigrants. Not surprisingly, they personally knew immigrants and recognized the gap between perception and reality. Earlier than most established Jews, Chicago judge and Sinai member Julian Mack took issue with the widespread arrogance towards the immigrants. "The caste feeling is strong amongst us, even in the younger generations. Wealth and culture are too apt to beget a sense of superiority and, all-forgetful of the moral truth that character, not wealth or birth, is the criterion of rank, we, who have had the greater opportunity and have too often abused it, look down upon the struggling foreigner because, forsooth, he was reared in a wretched hovel of a Russian ghetto."[30] This self-critical assessment reflected the beginnings of a wider shift and gradual opening to the immigrants. Even Hirsch became aware of the potential pitfalls of his hostile rhetoric. Around the turn of the century, the leaders of Chicago's established Jewish community began to reach out to the new immigrants. At the same time, Hirsch and his congregation began to interact with members of Chicago's (still) small African American community.

Established Chicago Jews and African Americans before and after 1917

After a brutal race riot in Springfield in 1908, on the eve of the Lincoln centennial, Hirsch joined the signers of a declaration calling for an end to racial inequality and discrimination. Jane Addams, W. E. B. DuBois, and Rabbi Stephen S. Wise also signed the declaration. This call led to the founding of the National Association for the Advancement of Colored People. Although Hirsch is regarded as a cofounder of the NAACP, he did not play a serious role in its organization. In 1912, the NAACP held its fourth annual meeting in Chicago. Sinai's imposing new temple was chosen as the opening venue under the banner "Our Common Humanity."[31] Soon after the founding of the NAACP, one of Hirsch's congregants, Sears & Roebuck executive and philanthropist Julius Rosenwald, turned his attention to the situation of African Americans in the South. A key influence was Booker T. Washington, who became Rosenwald's friend after their first meeting in 1911. When Washington died in 1915, Hirsch contributed a personal tribute to the founder of Tuskegee to the *Chicago Defender*.[32] Following a suggestion by Washington, Rosenwald helped to set up more than 5,300 public schools across the American South for African American children between 1912 and 1932.[33] Education and schools were a crucial legacy of the prolonged emancipation discourse in the German context and thus had a special meaning for Jews in – and Jewish immigrants from – Central Europe. It is highly likely that the Jewish Training School on Chicago's West Side served as inspiration for the Rosenwald schools.

Rabbi Hirsch repeatedly spoke up against racial injustice; on a few occasions, he addressed African American audiences. At a 1911 luncheon at the Republican Club in New York, where he shared a panel with W. E. B. DuBois, Hirsch questioned whether race had any scientific basis. If all people were "descended from one ape," nobody could make a serious case for the supposed superiority of one race over another. Race was not biologically determined, he argued – racial prejudice had sociological causes. Hirsch singled out slavery as a major culprit. This institution had corrupted societies, because individuals were treated and gradually began to behave as "members of a class." The notion of a "chosen class with privileges that can't be taken away" was, in Hirsch's view, "essentially un-American." And he continued, "the American who harbors race prejudice is committing a crime against his Americanism."[34] In November 1912, Hirsch, who according to the African American daily *Chicago Defender* was the "greatest living American Hebrew" (an assessment he certainly shared), addressed 1,200 congregants at Chicago's African Methodist Episcopalian Bethel Church. Bethel, one of the most vibrant African American churches in Chicago, served upwardly mobile members of the African

American community. Bethel was, as Hirsch freely admitted, an inspiration for Sinai as an "institutional synagogue." Bethel's spiritual founder Reverdy C. Ransom, an African American minister and social gospel advocate, was, like Hirsch, an early member of the Hull House circle.[35]

During the First World War, race emerged as a new and powerful source of tension over the ownership of urban space in Chicago – in addition to labor conflicts, interethnic turf wars, and the rise of machine politics.[36] Sinai was drawn into the conflict over the Black Belt, in part because it was locked into a quickly changing neighborhood. This was a new experience for a hitherto relatively sheltered congregation. Within a few years, the sharply segregated Black Belt grew into America's second largest center of African American life, after Harlem in New York.[37] By 1919, African Americans began moving into the Grand Boulevard neighborhood, home to many Sinai members and its large temple. Rather abruptly, the congregation found itself on the front lines of a conflict over the shifting boundary of the Black Belt. In April 1919, the *Chicago Tribune* reported that Bethel Church (African Methodist Episcopal [AME]) was close to acquiring Sinai's temple. When contacted by the paper, representatives of both congregations would not confirm the story. However, according to the executive director of the Sinai Social Center, Samuel D. Schwartz, "the influx of Negro residents" drove many members further south into Kenwood and Hyde Park. One was none other than Sinai's ailing rabbi, who had moved to an apartment building in Hyde Park.[38]

The decision of Sinai's leaders not to follow their members to Hyde Park and Kenwood when the congregation still had the option to do so was certainly understandable. Its temple and the state-of-the-art social center were just a few years old, and Kenwood and Hyde Park were within walking distance from the temple. Serving thousands of congregants and their families in rented quarters seemed impossible; completing a new building would have taken several years. And Sinai had long opposed race discrimination. Following the notorious August 1919 race riot, white homeowners formed the Kenwood and Hyde Park Property Owners Association. In the fall of 1919, the association pressured local real estate agents to join "our fight against the Negro." In November 1920, the Kenwood and Hyde Park Property Owners Association called on Sinai to become a corporate member. After a long discussion, the board refused because "it would be improper for Sinai Congregation to join such an organization." Thus Sinai did not relocate, even when almost all Jews in Chicago – including its own members – were on the move.[39]

Apart from the occasional interfaith meeting, Sinai did not use its location to build deeper ties to its African American neighbors. In a report to a February 1927 meeting of the congregation, Sinai's new rabbi, Louis Mann, did not mince his words: Sinai was now "in the very heart of the colored district." The service attendance, though still strong, was lagging because people had had the "most unpleasant experiences" in the vicinity of the temple.[40] At the annual meeting two months later, it was resolved to sell the temple and the center and to move to Hyde Park. Now, the situation had apparently become intolerable. "The intrusion of undesirable elements into our neighborhood," had forced the congregation to cancel many of its programs. Mann's comments from the February meeting were printed as part of the annual report. But the text was carefully edited: the word "colored" was replaced by the word "new." The board did not want to publicize the fact that race was the driving factor behind the decision to relocate. Sinai entered into negotiations with Bethel Church about the sale of the temple. The board bought a plot in Hyde Park. But the talks with Bethel dragged on without result. The congregation still had not found a solution by October 1929.[41]

The coverage of the main daily for African American readers, the *Chicago Defender*, also points to the withdrawal of Sinai Congregation from its African American neighbors during the 1920s. The paper rarely mentioned Sinai, even though its temple was located on the southern edge of the vibrant Bronzeville entertainment district, whose new residents mostly belonged to the upwardly mobile members of the African American community. Sinai's silence on the issue of segregation is revealing, especially since several African American leaders pointed to parallels between the enforced isolation and persecution of Jews in early modern and post-1918 Europe and present-day Chicago. Following the 1919 race riot, Reverend Archibald J. Carey of Bethel AME Church – with which Sinai had cordial relations – spoke up against the Kenwood and Hyde Park Property Owners Association, accusing especially Jewish but also German, Irish, Italian and other immigrant members of the Property Owners Association of hypocrisy. He wondered how they could deplore the violence against members of their respective groups in Europe in the aftermath of the war if, at the same time, they were backing the segregationist Property Owners Association.[42] It is not unlikely that Carey's public condemnation influenced Sinai's decision in the following year not to back the Property Owners Association. An important exception within the congregation was philanthropist Julius Rosenwald, who continued his support for African Americans in Chicago after the war. He especially backed the Chicago Urban League, a branch of the National League on Urban Conditions among Negroes, which promoted social reform and was backed by white progressives and African American community leaders.[43]

The Great Depression almost led to the dissolution of the erstwhile wealthy Sinai Congregation and relocation plans were shelved. In 1944, when it left its temple in Grand Boulevard, Sinai had almost completely cut its ties to African Americans.[44] After renting temporary quarters for several years, the congregation moved into a new temple in Hyde Park in 1950. Its new home forced Sinai to take a position in that neighborhood's complex racial politics. The congregation openly backed the controversial "urban renewal" scheme promoted by the University of Chicago and the city's new mayor Richard S. Daley that was designed in part to push African American residents out of Hyde Park. Aggressive policing of building code violations was used to condemn buildings, most of which were occupied by African Americans. "Urban renewal" saved the university and became a model for other inner-city universities that bordered segregated and crisis-ridden neighborhoods. As Arnold Hirsch has shown in his study *The Making of the Second Ghetto*, this policy did little to address the worsening racial segregation, let alone its causes.[45]

More noteworthy than Sinai's role in the ambiguous neighborhood politics of Hyde Park was its passivity in the struggle for civil rights in the 1950s and 1960s.[46] Particularly striking is the silence of Rabbi Mann, whose predecessor was, after all, one of the founders of the NAACP. Instead, Rabbi Weinstein of KAM (Kehillat Anshe Maarab – Congregation of the Men of the West), Sinai's neighbor in Hyde Park, emerged as an outspoken critic of the hidden agenda behind the renewal policy. He criticized residential segregation soon after his arrival at KAM in the late 1930s, arguing that Jews could not deplore anti-Semitic discrimination if they did not fight racism. Throughout the 1950s, Weinstein made no secret of his fierce opposition to segregation. He supported the fight against crime and slumlords, a serious issue for KAM and its members. However, Weinstein accused the city and Mayor Daley of promoting segregation rather than integration, betraying the legacy of Lincoln: "People who live differently come to think differently and a city, like a house, divided into rich and poor, black and white, cannot stand." In the 1960s, Weinstein gained national recognition for his support of civil rights, and he emerged as an early critic of the Vietnam War.[47] Thus Weinstein continued the tradition of social action and dissent in the name of universal ideals that once had been the hallmark of Sinai.

New African American ghettos?

Members of the established Jewish community in Chicago frequently used the term "ghetto" for the Jewish immigrant neighborhood on the West Side but not for the Black Belt area. This raises the question of when the term "ghetto" was employed to describe segregated African American residential districts in the Black Belt. Did African American leaders use the term, and did they reflect on its Jewish origins? The digitization of the *Chicago Defender* makes it possible to trace how often the term "ghetto" was mentioned in the pages of the main African American daily. The analysis shows that "ghetto" was only used up to three times annually during the 1920s. After 1932, the number increased to about eight or nine times before shooting up in 1943 to 40 and 71 in 1946, and before reaching an average of almost 30 annually for the rest of the 1940s. Before the mid-1920s, ghetto usually referred to the Jewish area on the West Side but sometimes also to other neighborhoods settled by "foreigners" (i.e., immigrants).[48] In a 1926 article reprinted from "The Nation," the later NAACP leader Walter White denounced the rise of "Negro ghettos" in northern cities.[49]

In the 1930s, "ghetto" was used to describe segregated neighborhoods in Chicago and American cities. In some cases, authors drew comparisons with the situation of Jews in early modern Europe. The author of the 1937 opinion piece "Building Ghettos" attacked a Jewish judge in Chicago who had upheld an injunction against a black family who had been expelled from a home outside the Black Belt. Pointing at the contemporary situation in Nazi Germany and the history of early modern Jewish ghettos, the author stressed: "If any people in the world know the horror of the ghetto, it is the Jews." A Jewish judge should be "the last one to try to force the black man into a ghetto in America."[50] In the late 1930s, authors began referring not to Jewish or other immigrant ghettos when discussing the segregation of African Americans but to the persecution of Jews in Nazi Germany. A 1938 editorial compared the treatment of Jews in Germany with that of African Americans in the United States, warning that the latter were socially and economically placed in "indefinite ghettos."[51]

An extensive quantitative analysis by Duneier confirms this observation. Based on an analysis of all books published between 1920 and 1975 and digitized by Google Books, he has observed a close correlation between the use of the term "black" or "Negro" ghetto and of the term "Warsaw" or "Jewish" ghetto. In 1940, when the Nazi regime established the Warsaw ghetto, the frequency of both terms increased significantly and remained high for "black" ghetto for decades, while the use of "Warsaw" or "Jewish" ghetto declined after the war. Based on this analysis, Duneier argues the term "black" ghetto was occasionally used to describe neighborhoods but had not developed into a fully formed concept before 1940. Its use was triggered by the discussion about Nazi ghettos in Poland in the early 1940s, just when the situation in inner city neighborhoods in the North seemed increasingly hopeless.[52]

For Chicago, there is no compelling evidence to prove that the term ghetto shifted from immigrant "ghettos" to segregated districts for African Americans as they emerged during the First World War. Rather, it appears that African Americans looked across the Atlantic to Jews in Nazi Germany and later Nazi-occupied Poland, and to a lesser extent to Jewish ghettos in early modern Europe to make sense of the segregation they experienced in northern cities.

Conclusion

The discussion of shifting ghettos in Chicago highlights the powerful impact of perceptions on the use of the term ghetto and thus the need to historicize the concept and use it cautiously. Especially in regard to late nineteenth-century Jewish immigrant neighborhoods, the gap between perception and the actual residential settlement patterns was wide. American immigrant neighborhoods were (and continue to serve as) gateways. These neighborhoods are often ethnically diverse and experience a high degree of fluctuation. They are not, as Wirth argued, "transplanted" communities from the old world but shaped by the conditions of the "new world."[53] Networks pull(-ed) new arrivals into neighborhoods dominated by other immigrants from the same place of origin with affordable housing, proximity to work places, and familiar cultural activities. Residents had (and have) the choice to leave for other neighborhoods, depending on their means and available incentives. Whiteness studies have highlighted that in the case of Jewish and Irish immigrants, the processes of assimilation, social mobility, and social acceptance were closely intertwined. In sharp contrast, by the 1920s, longer-settled and socially mobile African Americans with the means to relocate could not leave segregated neighborhoods in northern cities, as more migrants from the South were moving into these areas and were kept out of other neighborhoods. One important exception in the American context was larger settlements of Chinese immigrants who experienced massive discrimination and frequently were restricted to segregated "Chinatowns," notably on the West Coast. However, unlike Jews and internally moving African Americans, Chinese faced severe immigration restrictions after 1882. In Chicago, Chinese immigrants experienced relatively little discrimination, largely because their number remained very small until the 1970s.[54]

The depiction of Jewish immigrant neighborhoods in America as ghettos owed much to the view of established Jews who were largely immigrants from Central Europe. The inner-Jewish perception of Jewish immigrants from Eastern Europe betrays a close connection to the image of the ghetto in Germany. Members of the established Jewish community in Chicago associated Jewish immigrants in Eastern Europe early on with the term ghetto, viewing them through the lens of their own past in traditional Jewish communities in Central European villages and towns. The Americanization projects designed for the new immigrants closely echo the modernization schemes propagated by state bureaucrats and Jewish communities in the German states during the first half of the nineteenth century. Established Jews, Progressive reformers affiliated with the Hull House settlement led by Jane Addams, and, later, the sociologists of the Chicago School regarded the Jewish and other immigrant ghettos as obstacles to assimilation.

Established Jews in Chicago also interacted with members of the African American community. Like other German-speaking immigrants, leading Jews in Chicago supported the abolition of slavery in the 1850s and continued to criticize the discrimination of African Americans in the South after the Civil War. In the first decade of the twentieth century, Chicago Sinai, the main Reform congregation in the city, reached out to members of the small African American community. Together with Progressive reformer Jane Addams, Sinai's rabbi was one of the founders of the NAACP. Yet the onset of the Great Migration during the First World War constituted a turning point. While not openly backing segregationist groups like the Kenwood and Hyde Park Property Owners Association, Sinai refused to engage with its new neighbors. After it had relocated to Hyde Park in 1944, the congregation even backed the controversial urban renewal scheme led by the University of Chicago and the City of Chicago, while other Jews such as Rabbi Weinstein of KAM sharply criticized urban renewal as a thinly veiled attempt to keep Hyde Park "white." During the 1920s and 1930s, leading Jews in Chicago did not use the term ghetto for the emerging Black Belt. One obvious reason was that the term was rarely employed to describe the residential segregation of African Americans before the early 1940s. The use of the term ghetto for the Black Belt by Jews would only have made sense if Jewish leaders had taken a strong position against segregation. In the aftermath of the First World War, established Jews were increasingly feeling the impact of anti-Semitic discrimination. Only a few figures such as New York rabbi Stephen S. Wise continued to speak up against racism and segregation and to foster ties with African Americans. Rabbi Weinstein's engagement in the early 1950s, and that of many other Jews who supported the Civil

Rights struggle, occurred at a time when Jews were increasingly regarded as part of the American mainstream.[55]

There is little evidence pointing to a shift in the ghetto concept from Jewish immigrant ghettos (as they were perceived by established Jews, social reformers, and even scholars) and the segregated districts for African Americans as they emerged after the First World War in northern cities like Chicago. Rather, as African American leaders recognized that segregation would not be overcome, they looked for other models. The coverage of the *Chicago Defender* indicates that, already before the Nazi regime established closed districts for Jews in occupied Poland in 1939–1940, editorial writers drew parallels with the persecution of Jews in Nazi Germany.

Notes

1   L. Wirth, *The Ghetto*, Chicago: University of Chicago Press, 1928, pp. 117–118; M. Rischin, "Toward the Onomastics of the Great New York Ghetto: How the Lower East Side Got its Name," in H. Diner, J. Shandler, B. Wenger (eds) *Remembering the Lower East Side: American Jewish Reflections*, Bloomington, IN: Indiana University Press, 2000, pp. 13–27; A. Cahan, *Yekl: A Tale of the New York Ghetto*, New York: Appleton, 1896; M. Rischin, "The Megashtetl/Cosmopolis: New York History Comes of Age," *Studies in Contemporary Jewry* 9, 1999, 171–178; *Chicago Tribune*, 2 February 1896 ("In Chicago's Ghetto").

2   L. Wirth, "Urbanism as a Way of Life," *The American Journal of Sociology*, 44, 1938, 1–24 (quote: 15); H. Diner, "Louis Wirth and the Making of the Ghetto," in L. Wirth, *The Ghetto: With a New Introduction by Hasia Diner*, New Brunswick: Transaction Publishers, 1998, pp. ix–lxix.

3   M. Duneier, *Ghetto: The Invention of a Place, the History of an Idea*, New York: FSG, 2016, pp. 48–49, see also *Chicago Defender*, 2 October 1937 ("Building Ghettos").

4   D. Pacyga, *Chicago: A Biography*, Chicago: University of Chicago Press, 2009, pp. 184–189; T. Brinkmann, *Sundays at Sinai: A Jewish Congregation in Chicago*, Chicago: University of Chicago Press, 2012, p. 124.

5   Residents of Hull House (eds) *Hull House Maps and Papers: A Presentation of Nationalities and Wages in a Congested District of Chicago*, New York: T.Y. Crowell, 1895; Wirth, *Ghetto*, pp. 226–231.

6   J. R. Grossman, *Land of Hope: Chicago, Black Southerners, and the Great Migration*, Chicago: University of Chicago Press, 1989; T. L. Philpott, *The Slum and the Ghetto: Neighborhood Deterioration and Middle-Class Reform, Chicago, 1880–1930*, New York: Oxford University Press, 1978.

7   Pacyga, *Chicago*, pp. 204–224.

8   J.T. McGreevy, *Parish Boundaries: The Catholic Encounter with Race in the Twentieth-Century Urban North*, Chicago: University of Chicago Press, 1996, pp. 7–28.

9   A. H. Spear, *Black Chicago: The Making of a Negro Ghetto 1890–1920*, Chicago: University of Chicago Press, 1967, pp. 201–222; Philpott, *The Slum and the Ghetto*, pp. 115–145.

10 Wirth, *The Ghetto*, p. 231.

11 Duneier, *Ghetto*, pp. 39–40; Wirth, *The Ghetto*, p. 280.

12 Duneier, *Ghetto*, p. 43.

13 Wirth, *The Ghetto*, pp. 241–261; J. Gurock, "Time, Place and Movement in Immigrant Jewish Historiography," in L. Landmann (ed.) *Scholars and Scholarship: The Interaction Between Judaism and Other Cultures: The Bernhard Revel Graduate School Conference Volume*, New York: Yeshiva University Press, 1990, pp. 169–185; C. Hoffmann, "From Heinrich Heine to Isidor Kracauer: The Frankfurt Ghetto in German-Jewish Historical Culture and Historiography," in F. Backhaus et al. (eds) *The Frankfurt Judengasse: Jewish Life in an Early Modern City*, London: Valentine Mitchell, 2010, 41–58; Duneier, *Ghetto*, pp. 38–44.

14 R. Kazal, "Revisiting Assimilation: The Rise, Fall, and Reappraisal of a Concept in American Ethnic History," *American Historical Review* 100, 1995, 437–471; E. Morawska, "Defense of the Assimilation Model," *Journal of American Ethnic History* 13, 1994, 76–87.

15 St. Clair Drake and Horace R. Cayton, *Black Metropolis: A Study of Negro Life in a Northern City*, New York: Harcourt, Brace and Co., 1945, pp. 174–213.

16 C.W. von Dohm, *Über die bürgerliche Verbesserung der Juden*, Berlin: Friedrich Nicolai, 1781.

17 M. A. Meyer, *Response to Modernity: A History of the Reform Movement in Judaism*, New York: Oxford University Press, 1988.

18 K. H. Ober, *Die Ghettogeschichte. Entstehung und Entwicklung einer Gattung*, Göttingen: Wallstein, 2001; J. M. Hess, "Leopold Kompert and the Work of Nostalgia: The Cultural Capital of German Jewish Ghetto Fiction," *The Jewish Quarterly Review* 97, 2007, 576–615; R. I. Cohen, "'Nostalgia and 'Return to the Ghetto': A Cultural Phenomenon in Western and Central Europe," in J. Frankel, S. Zipperstein (eds) *Assimilation and Community: The Jews in Nineteenth-Century Europe*, Cambridge: Cambridge University Press, 1992, pp. 130–155.

19 S. Kassow, "Introduction," in S. T. Katz (ed.) *The Shtetl: New Evaluations*, New York: NYU Press, 2007, pp. 1–28, esp. 17–23; D. Miron, "The Literary Image of the Shtetl," *Jewish Social Studies*, 1, 1995, 1–43.

20 A. Ruppin, *Soziologie der Juden*, Berlin: Jüdischer Verlag, 1930, Vol. 1, pp. 67–86.

21 S. Aschheim, *Brothers and Strangers: The East European Jew in German and German Jewish Consciousness 1800–1923*, Madison: University of Wisconsin Press, 1982.

22 Brinkmann, *Sundays at Sinai*, pp. 31–62; *Illinois Staatszeitung* (Chicago), 20 August 1862.

23 Brinkmann, *Sundays at Sinai*, pp. 148–169.

24 H. R. Diner, *A Time for Gathering: The Second Migration 1820–1880*, Baltimore: Johns Hopkins University Press, 1992, pp. 191–193.

25 *Ninth Annual Report of the United Hebrew Charities [of Chicago] 1896/97*, Chicago: Ettlinger, 1897, p. 7; Charles Zeublin, "The Chicago Ghetto," in *Hull House Maps and Papers*, pp. 91–111 (quotes on pp. 94, 96, 103, 105, 110); for background: K. Sklar Kish, 'Hull House Maps and Papers: Social Science as Women's Work in the 1890s,' in M. Bulmer, K. Bales, and K. Sklar Kish (eds) *The Social Survey in Historical Perspective 1880–1940*, Cambridge: Cambridge University Press, 1991, pp. 111–147.

26 Brinkmann, *Sundays at Sinai*, pp. 162–169.

27 *Reform Advocate* (Chicago), 14 April 1894.

28 Emil G. Hirsch, "A Great Danger," *Reform Advocate*, 13 April 1895.

29 *Reform Advocate*, 30 August 1902.

30 *Sixth Annual Report of the United Hebrew Charities 1893/94*, Chicago: Privately Published, 1894.

31 P. M. Ascoli, *Julius Rosenwald: The Man Who Built Sears, Roebuck and Advanced the Cause of Black Education in the American South*, Bloomington: Indiana University Press, 2006, pp. 160–161; *Chicago Defender*, 20 January 1912 ("Rabbi Hirsch Offers the Use of His Mammoth Temple Free of Charge").

32 Ascoli, *Rosenwald*, pp. 83–92; *Chicago Defender*, 20 November 1915 ("Appointed by Providence, Says Rabbi Hirsch"); M. S. Hoffschwelle, *The Rosenwald Schools of the American South*, Gainesville: University Press of Florida, 2006, pp. 28–35.

33 Ascoli, *Rosenwald*, p. 217; Hoffschwelle, *Rosenwald Schools*, pp. 225–238.

34 *New York Times*, 5 March 1911 ("Danger to Nation in Race Prejudice").

35 *Chicago Defender*, 16 November 1912 ("The Institutional Church"); C. S. Morris, *Reverdy C. Ransom: Black Advocate of the Social Gospel*, Lanham, MD: University Press of America, 1990, p. 105.

36 J. Higham, *Strangers in the Land: Patterns of American Nativism 1860–1925*, New York: Atheneum, 1977, pp. 264–277.

37 Grossman, *Land of Hope*, pp. 123–160; A. Hirsch, *Making the Second Ghetto: Race and Housing in Chicago, 1940–1960*, Cambridge: Cambridge University Press, 1983, p. 16; L. Cohen, *Making a New Deal: Industrial Workers in Chicago 1919–1939*, Cambridge: Cambridge University Press, 2008, pp. 34–51.

38   D. Pacyga, *Polish Immigrants and Industrial Chicago: Workers on the South Side, 1880–1922*, Columbus: Ohio State University Press, 1991, pp. 224–228; *Chicago Tribune*, 20 April 1919 ("Bethel Church Moves to Buy New Property").

39   E. Goldstein, *The Price of Whiteness: Jews, Race, and American Identity*, Princeton: Princeton University Press 2006, p. 68; *Chicago Tribune*, 21 October 1919 ("Hyde Parkers Swear to Hold on Color Line"); Kenwood Property Association to Sinai Congregation, 29 November 1920, in Sinai Papers, American Jewish Archives, Cincinnati, Minute Book, Box 11, Folder 3.

40   Report by Louis Mann, 6 January 1926; Special Meeting, 22 February 1927, in Sinai Papers, Chicago Sinai Congregation Archive.

41   66th Annual Meeting, 10 April 1927 (papers regarding acquisition of land in Hyde Park), in Sinai Papers, Chicago Sinai Congregation Archive.

42   *Chicago Defender*, 1 November 1919 ("Rev. Carey Denounces Hyde Park Protective Association").

43   Spear, *Black Chicago*, pp. 104, 169–170, 173.

44   Brinkmann, *Sundays at Sinai*, pp. 283–286.

45   Hirsch, *Making the Second Ghetto*, pp. 135–170; *Chicago Tribune*, 28 March 1952 ("Vote Hyde Park Council Aid in Fight on Crime"); *Chicago Tribune*, 20 May 1952 ("2,500 at Rally Draft Drive to Fight Crime in Hyde Park"); *Chicago Tribune*, 20 June 1952 ("District Chairmen Chosen for War on Crime on South Side"); *Chicago Tribune*, 6 February 1964 ("Decide High Rise Co-Op Soon"); *Chicago Tribune*, 26 May 1968 ("In Hyde Park Residents Fight Renewal Plan"); Board Meeting, 6 May 1968, in Sinai Papers, Chicago Sinai Congregation Archive.

46   *Chicago Tribune*, 1 February 1965 ("Rabbi Karff Urges School Race Control"); *Chicago Tribune*, 17 May 1965 ("Rabbi Cautions Negro Leaders on Flare-Ups").

47   Quoted from an address Weinstein gave to the Committee on Planning and Housing of the City Council of Chicago on 22 September 1958, in J. J. Feldstein (ed.) *Rabbi Jacob J. Weinstein: Advocate of the People*, New York: KTAV, 1980, 115; *Chicago Tribune*, 19 February 1953 ("Rabbi Decries Decay of Ellis Av. Residence"); *Chicago Tribune*, 24 February 1963 ("Rabbi, Negro Will Discuss Racial Unity"); *New York Times*, 3 November 1974 (Weinstein's obituary).

48   *Chicago Defender*, 4 June 1921 ("Defender to Give Prizes for Best Kept Lawns").

49   W. White, "Segregation Moves North," *Chicago Defender*, 31 October 1926.

50   *Chicago Defender*, 13 August 1932 ("The Failure to Make the Most of Segregation"), 2 October 1937 ("Building Ghettos").

51   *Chicago Defender*, 8 October 1938 ("Merit Must Count").

52   Duneier, *Ghetto*, p. 83.

53   Wirth, *Ghetto*, p. 202.

54   H. Ling, *Chinese Chicago: Race, Transnational Migration and Community Since 1870*, Stanford: Stanford University Press, pp. 24–57.

55   On coverage of Wise, see for instance *Chicago Defender*, 13 January 1923 ("Jews and Race Must Be as One").

11

"IS A NEGRO DISTRICT, IN THE MIDST OF OUR FAIREST CITIES, TO BECOME CONNOTATIVE OF THE GHETTO … ?"

Using corpus analysis to trace the "ghetto" in the black press, 1900–1930[1]

Avigail S. Oren

Introduction

At the 500th anniversary of the Venetian Ghetto's establishment, "ghetto" remains a globally popular term to describe urban segregation and poverty. Despite this, popular memory rarely links the global "ghettos" of the present with the original sixteenth-century *geto* of Venice, instead associating the term with a nearer past— the segregated neighborhoods of twentieth-century industrial American cities. Over five centuries, "ghetto" became a global metaphor, a label so distanced from its origin as a religiously segregated neighborhood of Jews in early-modern Italy as to be applied to any poor racial or ethnic enclave. To trace the dissolution of the term's precision and distinction through popular usage, it is critical to understand how "ghetto" migrated from the Jewish to the African American context and how it came to be used in black discourse in the early twentieth century.[2] Was "ghetto" used in black discourse in the early twentieth century, when immigration and the great migration brought large communities of African Americans and Jews together in northern cities? If so, to make what point or comparison?

African American newspapers provide a simple way to assess black discourse, as newspapers were written for a broad audience and were the product of a diverse authorship. The increased digitization of newspapers by databases such as ProQuest presents new opportunities for historians to apply digital methodologies to answer questions of change over time. Although a close reading of articles could identify the first uses of "ghetto" by African American writers or about African American neighborhoods, as well as the implications and meanings of the term in its discursive usage, the vast amount of information contained within a large set of articles obscures broader patterns from the vision of any individual researcher. The digital methodology of corpus linguistics augments the qualitative analytical expertise of a close reader with the quantitative capability of computers to identify patterns in language. Historians have already used more traditional historical methodologies to trace the migration of the term "ghetto" to the United States. The question I pose within this chapter is different. What additional insight can a quantitative analysis of a set of articles from African American newspapers yield about how the term "ghetto" transitioned from the Jewish to the African American context?

In this chapter, I will review the most recent scholarly literature that explains how the term "ghetto" came to describe African American urban neighborhoods after World War II. I then trace the development of a corpus analysis project from beginning to conclusion in order to model how the methodology can be used to answer historical questions, and I will show how the findings of my corpus analysis qualify the argument that the concept of the "black ghetto" arose in the post-World War II era. I argue that "ghetto" was used in black discourse in the 1920s, before the Nazi ghetto injected the term into popular discourse. The black press captured and published incidences of speechmakers, interviewees, and journalists using the term "ghetto" to pointedly describe segregated urban areas. My analysis of articles from black newspapers throughout the United States demonstrates that in the 1920s, writers and speakers—for the press often published transcripts of spoken lectures and quotes from public officials—described segregated neighborhoods in American cities as "black ghettos" and "ghetto systems" in order to draw a political parallel between the early-modern European Jewish ghetto and new legalized forms of discriminatory residential housing restrictions. Protesting the northward spread of Jim Crow policies, the "ghetto" evoked an institution that was clearly un-American, un-enlightened, and medieval.

The ghetto: From the Yiddish press to sociological scholarship

Jewish immigration to the United States peaked in 1906, and between 1881 and 1910 more than a million and a half Jews arrived in the country.[3] This immigration overlapped with the first Great Migration of black southerners seeking employment and safety in burgeoning industrial cities. Between 1900 and 1930, over 1.3 million African Americans moved northward.[4] In large cities like New York, Boston, Baltimore, Cleveland, Pittsburgh, and Chicago, communities of Jews and African Americans had ample opportunity to interact and observe one another. Black workers often found employment in and shopped from Jewish businesses, and the communities often lived in overlapping or adjacent neighborhoods.[5] Both communities were heterogeneous and diverse in terms of the class, religious, political, and ethno-racial identity espoused by individuals within them, but what African American and Jewish leaders shared was continuous internal debate about the place of their minority group within pluralistic, "egalitarian" American society.

Jews saw black oppression as the defining paradox of American democracy. Historian Hasia Diner, in her 1977 study of Jewish engagement with African Americans in the interwar period, argued, "for many American Jewish leaders black issues provided an attractive forum in which to work out certain tensions of acculturation."[6] The Yiddish press was the mouthpiece for this forum. Jewish writers' sympathy for the plight of black Americans drew them towards historical comparisons with their European past.[7] These writers discussed the parallels between the historical oppression of black people in America and Jews in Europe and debated how the United States could overcome this past and begin to respect, enfranchise, protect, and yield prosperity for its minority peoples.[8] Diner found that in the 1910s and 1920s, Jewish writers referred to the "ghetto" conditions of segregated black neighborhoods at least eight times, across four different Yiddish newspapers: "The newspapers noted that, in the realm of housing, blacks suffered as much where no legally established 'ghettos' existed. Blacks paid exorbitant rents for shoddy apartments, and when they moved into better neighborhoods, they faced the hostility and violence of their neighborhoods."[9] The Yiddish press therefore brought "ghetto" as a descriptor of black conditions into not only Jewish popular discourse, but also the discourse of a multiracial and multiethnic group of socialists, workers, and unionists. Diner did not trace this comparison in the black press. Her study focused on the ways that Jewish leaders used the plight of African Americans to argue for the betterment of Jewish life in the United States, but did not extend to how African Americans may have used the comparison for their own betterment.

New scholarship on the translation of the ghetto concept from Jewish to black discourse has focused on how the meaning and power of the concept evolved along with this shift. Sociologist Mitchell Duneier and historian Daniel Schwartz have recently written about the history of the term "ghetto," a history that both scholars view as a "conflict over meaning, replete with shifting notions of, and recurring arguments over, what constitutes a ghetto."[10] Their discussions of the ghetto are predicated on the definition of "ghetto" established by historians of early modern Italy, particularly Benjamin Ravid. In his examination of the Venice ghetto, Ravid argues that despite the existence of similar Jewish quarters before 1516, it was in Venice where the term "ghetto" was first used and thus the original and authentic definition of "ghetto" is that of the Jewish neighborhood of Venice, one that is "compulsory, segregated, [and] enclosed." It was later that the term began to be applied to "any area densely populated by Jews, even in places where they had freedom of residence and could and did live in the same districts and houses as Christians."[11] Ravid left the tracing of this "looser sense" of the ghetto to other scholars.[12]

Schwartz, a historian of modern Jewry, examines how American Jews in the nineteenth century feared the emergence of "ghettos" in the United States, a pattern of segregation they perceived as anti-modern, old-world, and unenlightened. They did not fear the establishment of compulsory European-style ghettos, but rather the association of Jews with clannishness, poverty, and outmoded traditionalism. By the early twentieth century, "ghetto" was used to define the difference in class, language, and religious observance between two generations of Jewish immigrants to America. The more established, affluent, and Americanized members of the Jewish community—predominantly those who arrived from Germany in the mid-nineteenth century—framed the "ghetto" as a neighborhood and a mindset from which the wave of newly arriving Eastern European Jews, temporarily trapped, should and would leave.[13] In the 1920s, urban sociologists such as Robert Parks and Louis Wirth codified and universalized this paradigm into a race relations cycle wherein all minority populations began as a voluntary, unified, ghettoized group in a standoff against the dominant culture before, in the cycle's final stage, assimilating and leaving the ghetto behind.[14]

In *Ghetto: The Invention of a Place, the History of an Idea*, Duneier examines the genealogy of the term from this point, when it was adopted by the social sciences to explain immigrant acculturation and the opposite phenomenon—why African Americans were not experiencing the same rates of upward mobility, residential dispersion, and social integration as white ethnics. Duneier draws his readers into the lives, careers, and scholarship of three emblematic African American social scientists—Horace Cayton, Kenneth Clark, and William Julius Wilson—to show how each tried to highlight the discrimination, powerlessness, and pathologies of African American urban neighborhoods by evoking the persecution of Jews in Nazi ghettos. Duneier argues that the term and metaphor of the "ghetto" lost its symbolic power in contemporary discourse because these scholars helped divorce the ghetto from its origins in modern Jewish history.[15]

Duneier notes that although social scientists saw the Nazi ghettos as a "crucial reference," they did not make important historical distinctions between the regime of separation and control that characterized the early modern European ghettos and the scheme of expulsion and annihilation that motivated the creation of Nazi ghettos.[16] In *Ghetto*, Duneier traces how the evolving scholarship of urban sociologists carried the concept further and further from its origins. Examining *Black Metropolis*, published in 1945, Duneier argues that Horace Cayton and his co-author St. Clair Drake "dispensed with the ghetto as a historical concept." Although they viewed the ghetto as the result of white repression more akin to that imposed on the Jews by the Catholic Church than by the Nazis, Drake and Cayton "regarded the ghetto as a metaphor for both segregation and Caucasian purity in the Nazi era."[17] They also argued that segregation was not a function of *national* policies or social institutions, but a "local phenomena." In 1965, Kenneth Clark intensified *Black Metropolis*'s emphasis on external forces in his book, *Dark Ghetto*. As Duneier shows through a close reading of Clark's work, Clark characterized the ghetto as a colony "controlled by forces outside the community" and saw the ghetto as a place of powerlessness, pathology, and degradation that resulted from the reflection and magnification of white ostracism.[18] By the 1980s, when William Julius Wilson published *The Declining Significance of Race*, differentiation between the black middle class and the poor black "underclass" pulled sociologists towards a more class-based definition of the ghetto.[19] Duneier argues that "for the first time since the Nazi and civil rights eras, the ghetto was now being defined without reference to either race or power," signaling a clear break with the ghetto's Jewish history in both Europe and the United States.[20]

Duneier bases his claims in close readings of Cayton, Clark, and Wilson's work, but to bolster his claim that the adoption of "black ghetto" in the American context is directly related to Hitler's resuscitation of the term "ghetto," he examines a sample of the Google Ngram corpus, made up of books digitized by Google in order to track changes in the frequency of word or language usage over time. The sample Duneier analyzed consisted of 800,000 books published in the United States between 1920 and 1975 that include the phrase(s) "Jewish ghetto," "Warsaw ghetto," "black ghetto," or "Negro ghetto." From this data, Duneier argues that scholars cannot "take it for granted that black and others would have called their restricted neighborhoods 'ghettos' in the absence of the Nazi reference" because there is "a rise in references to black ghettos only *after* the rise of Nazi ghettos in popular consciousness." Duneier leaves open the possibility that "ghetto" could have entered black discourse in reference to early-modern European Jewish ghettos, but argues that because "clearly the use of the term 'black ghetto' did not spike in response to the restrictive covenants of the late 1920s," it was only the Nazi-style ghetto that had the metaphorical and symbolic power to catapult the term into popular usage in the African American context.[21]

The term's flexibility ensured its power, until its flexibility was overextended and "ghetto" was used to describe everything and nothing. Duneier argues that social scientists *should* have made this distinction between early-modern European ghettos and Nazi ghettos because, in addition to demonstrating "the amount and consequences of segregation," they could have shown "variations in human flourishing and control that are found wherever people are restricted in space."[22] It was the ubiquity of the Nazi referent in popular discourse, Duneier claims, that made these scholars use the ghetto comparison at all. And yet, the legacy of the "ghetto" in Jewish and then black discourse proved resilient, as Duneier shows that the metaphor of the early modern ghettos also appeared in the writings of these social scientists.[23]

Ironically, however, in making this critique, Duneier ignores the scholarship produced by a cohort of urban historians in the 1960s and 1970s who *did* make a clear historical comparison between American and early modern European Jewish ghettos as a way of explaining the rise of segregated black neighborhoods. "Ghetto synthesis" scholars such as Alan Spear, Gilbert Osofsky, David Katzman, and Kenneth Kusmer argued that the color line was the modern incarnation of Jewish ghettoization; just as Jews were compelled to live together and apart from their Christian neighbors, it was white hostility that caused the residential separation of black urban citizens.[24] From its inception," Spear concluded that

> the Negro ghetto was unique among the city's ethnic enclaves. It grew in response to implacable white hostility that has not basically changed. In this sense it has been Chicago's only true ghetto, less the product of voluntary developments within than external pressures from without. Like the Jewries of medieval Europe, Black Chicago has offered no escape.[25]

These historians, unlike their sociologist peers, foregrounded the compulsory nature of the Jewish ghetto—even if they did ignore the "human flourishing" of agency and autonomy that occurred in both Jewish and African American ghettos.

While the spike in usage following World War II is incontrovertible, I argue that the incorporation of quantitative analysis of a corpus newspaper data from the 1920s tempers this claim and provides some evidence that journalists and intellectuals writing for (or quoted in) the black press did draw a direct connection to the early-modern European Jewish ghetto. The term was used in the black press to draw a parallel between the systemic nature of the early modern Jewish ghetto and black urban residential neighborhoods in the United States; the Jewish ghetto, as a product of bureaucratic and social control, was a powerful analogy that could be harnessed to critique attempts to implement Jim Crow-style legislation outside of the American South.

When used in black discourse, this analogy also extended beyond particular locales to identify a national pattern of legal and social acceptance of race-based housing discrimination. Duneier points out that Cayton and Drake's use of "ghetto" in *Black Metropolis* in 1944 was a turning point in social scientists' understanding of the term, when it became a signifier of the differences between local black neighborhoods and white ones.[26] Drake and Cayton "were content to find the idea of the ghetto useful for understanding their own city and society," particularly the race restrictive covenants that consolidated black Chicagoans into exclusively African American neighborhoods.[27] "Beyond their reference to the concrete conditions caused by the covenant," Duneier claims "Drake and Cayton did not invoke the ghetto to refer to any of the ways in which the ghettoized were controlled by external institutions … they also mostly wrote as if once a residential area was enclosed, its problems stemmed from local neighborhood conditions."[28]

Black Metropolis did focus on one city and one black community, but Drake and Cayton saw the "Midwest Metropolis" as a representative case study to explain the persistence of a *de facto* color line in Northern cities despite the absence of *de jure* Jim Crow laws.[29] The black residents of Chicago that Drake and Cayton interviewed and quoted in the book also reflected an understanding of segregation as legally sanctioned and very much a product of translocal patterns of racial discrimination. A chauffeur told an interviewer that "I have thought of ways to break down this segregation, but when I think that anything you do makes you a lawbreaker, you then cease to fight individuals, for then it becomes a war with the law." Another woman implied that government and moneyed interests were ultimately responsible for restrictive covenants, arguing that "What the government should do, or somebody with money, is to fight restrictive covenants and let our people move where they want to." Reflecting on these interviews, Drake and Cayton concluded, "Negroes do not accept this definition of their 'place,' and … they believe that *enforced* segregation is unjust."[30] The authors viewed the "black ghetto" as the product of the public sanctioning of restrictive covenants and racial violence, external forces common to many Northern cities.

Before Wirth's *The Ghetto* or Horace Cayton and St. Clair Drake's *Black Metropolis*, the use of the term "ghetto" *was* used to imply national or broader forces—it wasn't just a local condition. It was an attempt to draw connections between the regime of legalized discrimination that extended from the American

South to the American North. It was not widespread in the discourse—nothing like what ghetto would become after World War II, as Duneier demonstrates—but its usage *was* slowly increasing, indicating that readers recognized and responded to its symbolic power.

Methodology

Corpus linguistics is a methodology for analyzing a body of texts in order to understand how written and spoken language is used at a particular time, in a particular place, or by particular people. The methodology is especially useful for revealing rare or exceptional cases *or* patterns of typical language use. Although this analysis *can* be done without a computer, as scholars have long done through the close reading of texts, conducting corpus linguistics with computational software allows for researchers to review a much larger body of texts than the human mind can handle otherwise. Even more helpfully, this software can apply mathematical principles to written texts and identify patterns otherwise invisible to the human eye.[31] Historians have used this methodology to examine such disparate questions as how descriptions of English beggars in books changed over the course of the seventeenth century or how British perceptions of Cuba were depicted in periodicals during the Victorian period.[32]

Although there are many diachronic English-language corpora that historians can access for free online, there are no extant corpora of black newspapers or periodicals.[33] To create a historical corpus of articles from the early twentieth century, I consulted the ProQuest Historical Newspapers database of black newspapers. Six of the nine black newspapers digitized as part of this collection were published prior to the 1930s—*The Baltimore Afro-American, Chicago Defender, New York Amsterdam News, Norfolk Journal and Guide, Philadelphia Tribune*, and *Pittsburgh Courier*—and they became the basis of this corpus. I also consulted the *Indianapolis Recorder*, a paper digitized by the libraries of Indiana University-Purdue University Indianapolis that is freely accessible to researchers.[34]

Using these seven digitized African American newspapers from the first three decades of the twentieth century, I searched for articles published between 1900 and 1929 that included the term "ghetto," "ghettos," or "ghettoes."[35] The search returned 134 total articles, which ranged from news reports to editorials, reports from travel abroad, and quite a few summaries of boxing matches about "ghetto" (Jewish) boxers.[36] I individually downloaded each article and used ABBYY FineReader optical character recognition (OCR) software to "transcribe" the PDF image into searchable plain text that I could copy and paste into a document. I then had to read through and check each article, because the OCR software often struggled with the older newsprint and with articles that hadn't been clearly digitized. Once I was confident that the text of each article accurately reflected the original, I compiled the articles into plain text file (PTF) documents organized by newspaper and decade of publication (i.e., in a single PTF document, I bundled all of the articles published in the *Chicago Defender* in the 1920s). I named the finished product The Ghetto in the African American Press Corpus (The GAAP Corpus). The corpus consists of 134 articles, containing 154 uses ("hits") of the word "ghetto" or its variants, out of 113,238 total words ("tokens").

Although I read each article as part of the process of cleaning the data, I took care not to analyze, interpret, or draw conclusions from these texts during the review process. I resisted examining how the term "ghetto" was being used in context, where and by whom it was being used, and how it contributed to the word's transition from a descriptor of Jewish urban neighborhoods to a descriptor of black neighborhoods. I sought to review the quantified data of the corpus without consciously or subconsciously reinforcing findings discovered through close reading.

In constructing the corpus, several of its limitations became clear. First, I relied on the accuracy of the OCR initially done on these articles by their digitizers, and I suspect that a number of articles employing the term "ghetto" were not found because of the inability of the OCR to correctly recognize them. Second, by narrowly selecting only those articles including the term "ghetto" or "ghetto(e)s," the corpus is not representative of all articles in the black press during these decades— I cannot claim that the language used in these ghetto articles is unique from or almost identical to other articles published in the black press during these years. As such, my arguments are limited to claims about the kind of language used in articles that include the term "ghetto." Finally, while the corpus is large enough to study patterns in how "ghetto" was used, it is not large enough to make broad claims about patterns of language usage. Despite these limitations, a brief review of the corpus revealed that the data were representatively distributed across the newspapers and across time. The corpus could thus be analyzed to show change over time in national, rather than local, black discourse.

With the corpus complete, I used the concordance software AntConc to analyze the texts.[37] AntConc is a set of tools to analyze any texts supported by the unicode standard. The various functions within AntConc can create visualizations that map the concordance of certain terms within the corpus (Key Word in Context and Concordance Plot), as well as quantify the dataset to measure the frequency of words (Word List) and the statistical relationship between certain words (Collocation and Corpus Keywords). I will further explain these functions in my description of my findings.

Finding the ghetto in the African American press corpus

In 1912, the usage of "ghetto" in the black press began, haltingly, to rise (Figure 11.1).[38] This coincided with a period in which cities in border and Northern states began trying to pass segregated housing ordinances akin to Southern Jim Crow legislation.[39] AntConc's Concordance Plot tool creates a visualization of the distribution of hits (uses of the term) across the various newspapers and across the decades, making it possible to compare when and where the frequency of the term increased. To condense the data, I created a table summarizing the distribution of the hits, both as a raw number and a percentage of the total number of

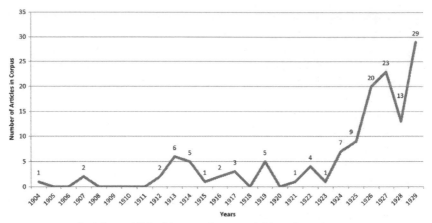

FIGURE 11.1 Articles published by year in seven African American newspapers

TABLE 11.1 Summary of concordance plot data

Decade	Newspaper	Number of hits	% of total hits
1900s	Afro American	2	1.3
TOTAL			**1.3**
1910s	Afro American	14	9.1
	Defender	7	4.5
	Recorder	8	5.2
	Tribune	1	0.6
TOTAL			**19.5**
1920s	Afro American	21	13.6
	Defender	16	10.4
	Recorder	2	1.3
	Tribune	9	5.8
	Amsterdam News	23	14.9
	Courier	36	23.4
	New Journal	15	9.7
TOTAL			**79.2**

hits (Table 11.1). The Concordance Plot reveals that in addition to the increasing frequency with which articles in the African American press in the 1920s used the word "ghetto," it was also used more frequently *within* articles in the 1920s. The term was also included in some newspapers more frequently than in others. Without accounting for the content of the articles, the computational analysis of the corpus thus demonstrates that something changed in the second decade of the twentieth century that made "ghetto" a more popular or compelling term than before.

The distribution of "ghetto" among the seven newspapers points to the national scope of the discussions of segregation in the black press. Incidents of the use of "ghetto" were not limited to a single paper and thus a single locale's metropolitan issues. The *Pittsburgh Courier* seemed to write especially frequently about ghettos, and it nearly tied the *Baltimore Afro-American* in number of uses despite only beginning to publish in the 1920s. It is likely that the higher incidence of hits in the *Courier* and *Amsterdam News* was due more to the strength of these newspapers during these years than to geography or local politics—these two papers, in particular, were distributed nationally and wrote for a wider audience than the black communities of New York and Pittsburgh.[40] Indeed, these papers viewed segregation and the ghettoization of African Americans as a national concern.

Despite these efforts on the part of the white ruling elite to create compulsory segregated black urban neighborhoods, "ghetto" was nonetheless used sporadically in the African American press. The articles in the corpus represent only 0.02 per cent of the total number of articles in these newspapers, a seemingly insignificant number of mentions. By contrast, however, variants of the words "segregate" appeared approximately 50 times more commonly than variants of "ghetto," and yet "segregate" only appeared in one per cent of the total number of newspaper articles.[41] Certainly, "ghetto" was not used frequently in the black press, and the black press did not strategically compare African American neighborhoods and the Jewish ghetto every time that the topic of segregation was discussed, but "ghetto" was nevertheless mentioned once for every five times that the topic of segregation occurred in the corpus.

The analogy may not have been used commonly in black discourse overall, but it was specifically deployed in discussions of racialized residential patterns. While the Plot Concordance tool measures the change in the frequency of a word's use over time, it cannot measure the frequency of a term relative to the other words used within the corpus. In order to find how often "ghetto" was used in comparison to other words in the corpus, I used AntConc's Word List tool to compile the number of times each word in the GAAP corpus was used and to sort them from highest (most frequent) to lowest (least frequent). The word list generated from the GAAP corpus demonstrates that "ghetto" was used with similar frequency as words related to the nation, government institutions, and color discrimination, reflecting that "ghetto" was associated in black discourse with a more national critique of segregation policy and was not solely used in local discussions of residential covenant ordinances.

Throughout the 1920s, the ghetto was still associated with Jews or discussed as a Jewish phenomenon. The first noun to appear in the GAAP corpus word list (Table 11.2) is "negro," and the nouns that appear in quick succession are "white," "people," and "colored."[42] Although it is not unexpected that these words would appear frequently in a corpus compiled from African American newspapers, it is notable that in a corpus constructed of articles that use the word "ghetto," the terms "negro," "negroes," "colored," and "black" occur more frequently (1215 times) than any variant of the word "Jew" (Jew, Jews, and Jewish). Variants of "Jew" are used 168 times throughout the corpus, just slightly more frequently than variants of the word "ghetto" (154).

TABLE 11.2 GAAP corpus word list, top 150

Rank	Times used	Word	Rank	Times used	Word	Rank	Times used	Word
1	8493	the	51	267	no	101	126	may
2	4695	of	52	259	its	102	126	now
3	3341	and	53	248	these	103	123	over
4	3061	to	54	240	other	104	121	t
5	2779	in	55	236	more	105	119	being
6	2477	a	56	234	if	106	119	states
7	1511	is	57	230	out	107	118	because
8	1375	that	58	230	so	108	116	very
9	967	for	59	230	when	109	116	while
10	964	it	60	229	negroes	110	115	ghetto
11	823	as	61	215	them	111	114	much
12	755	are	62	211	segregation	112	114	well
13	743	was	63	207	would	113	109	made
14	710	by	64	204	can	114	109	same
15	680	be	65	200	than	115	108	law
16	640	with	66	196	man	116	108	life
17	613	this	67	195	men	117	108	me
18	609	he	68	190	any	118	107	among
19	585	on	69	186	york	119	107	like
20	575	have	70	185	only	120	106	business
21	546	not	71	183	many	121	106	mr
22	532	at	72	183	some	122	105	just
23	519	i	73	183	up	123	104	make
24	507	negro	74	180	harlem	124	103	should
25	490	from	75	180	you	125	101	even
26	486	his	76	178	what	126	101	good
27	483	they	77	172	into	127	100	part
28	478	but	78	167	most	128	100	then
29	456	which	79	164	country	129	100	us
30	452	one	80	161	time	130	98	property
31	448	or	81	159	such	131	98	world
32	447	their	82	159	two	132	97	upon
33	417	we	83	159	where	133	96	after
34	406	has	84	155	those	134	96	united
35	396	will	85	154	about	135	94	also
36	395	all	86	152	every	136	92	america
37	391	who	87	149	court	137	92	before
38	383	white	88	149	do	138	92	better
39	375	s	89	148	black	139	92	jews
40	375	there	90	146	must	140	90	day
41	375	were	91	144	my	141	89	public
42	337	people	92	142	great	142	88	own
43	331	colored	93	141	years	143	88	still
44	323	our	94	140	said	144	87	dr
45	320	an	95	134	him	145	87	under
46	295	new	96	132	against	146	85	get
47	286	had	97	131	american	147	85	her
48	279	been	98	131	here	148	85	whites
49	277	city	99	127	street	149	84	cities
50	274	race	100	126	first	150	84	little

Despite the frequency of references to Jews within the total corpus (as seen in the word list), within the context of the discussion of ghettos the comparison had already clearly been drawn between Jewish and black segregated areas. The Word List tool does not account for the relationship of any word to another, either in terms of proximity or co-occurrence.[43] Words that are used frequently within the total corpus may be clustered in a small number of articles and may not be integral to discussions of the ghetto. The Concordance tool corrects for the bluntness of the word list by compiling a set range of words to the left and right (the "context") of an identified search term (the key word).[44] The benefit of the Concordance tool is that it allows researchers to sort the context horizon to find patterns in the way the key word is used. I created a context horizon with a range of seven, which captured the words located seven to the left and seven to the right of the key word "ghetto." By sorting the context so that the words directly to the left (1L) of "ghetto" are arranged in alphabetical order, the tool identifies that the phrase "black ghetto" is used eight times, "colored ghetto" is used two times, "Jewish ghetto" is used four times, and "negro ghetto" is used ten times in the GAAP corpus. That is a 5:1 ratio of black to Jewish references to the ghetto, indicating that "ghetto" already had a black connotation in African American discourse.

The black press was publishing news and commentary that identified segregation as a national phenomenon that was maintained in the North by legally sanctioned (if not legal) mechanisms. "Ghetto" was not being used to draw a parallel between the decrepit internal conditions of early-modern European Jewish and contemporary urban American black neighborhoods, but rather the term was being strategically applied to compare how these conditions were created by state control and the political enforcement of compulsory segregation. Considering that the word "ghetto" is the one constant throughout each article in the GAAP corpus, it is notable that "segregation" (used 211 times) occurs almost 50 per cent more commonly than ghetto. The appearance of other words associated with the state, governing, and justice also demonstrate that the ghetto was discussed in a national context. "Country," "state," "supreme" and "court," "American," "law," "right" "case," "national," "Washington," "citizen," "President," "policy," "government," and "united" "states" [of] "America" all appear within the top 300 most frequent words within the corpus. By contrast, the only local place names that appear in this range are New York City, Harlem, Washington, Baltimore, and Philadelphia. Uses of the former terms are more than twice as frequent as the latter. An examination of the words that occur seven to the left and right of "ghetto" and its variants reinforces the findings of the Word List that in the African American press, the term was used in close proximity to words like "restricted," "enforced," and "system," which evoked similarities between the state control of black neighborhoods and early-modern European Jewish ghettos.

More interestingly, a sorting of the words that occur directly to the right (1R) of ghetto reveals seven uses of the phrase "ghetto system." Unlike how social scientists would come to use the term following World War II, in the African American press the ghetto analogy *was* being used to demonstrate that segregated black neighborhoods were created so that the American state and/or society could control the black population. The use of the phrase "ghetto system" conveyed that these urban spaces were compulsory and enforced, and not voluntary, suggested, or a product of convenience.

Additionally, within the seven-word context horizon of the key word ghetto, certain themes emerged that reinforce the relationship between the ghetto's formation and the external control of black Americans by white power brokers: segregation, legality, violence, urbanity, environmental conditions and hygiene, and communal solidarity. To quantify and test the significance of these themes, I counted and compared the number of words associated with each. Variations of the words "segregation," for example, occur nine times, and variations of the words "restricted" and "force" or "enforce" occur eight times. Variants of "slum" appear within the proximity of "ghetto" four times, while "disease," "unsanitary," "lynching," "mob violence," and "crime" each appear three times. In addition, many words like "confined," "ordinance," "massacred," and "congested" appear fewer times, but contribute to these themes; for example, 34 (1.5 per cent) of the total of 2156 word tokens making up the Concordance context are related to segregation and 39 (1.8 per cent) are related to violence.[45]

"Ghetto" was being used in black discourse to describe a growing problem, that black neighborhoods were coming more and more to "veritably" resemble Jewish ghettos. Whereas the Concordance tool examines the relationship of words as a measure of proximity, AntConc's Collocation tool measures the relationship as a statistical measure of co-occurrence. Running the Collocation tool on the GAAP corpus revealed that the words "widespread" and "veritable" were more strongly associated with "ghetto" than any other word. "Tumbledown" and "tenement," two other words strongly correlated with ghetto, confirm its association with deteriorating health and environmental conditions.[46]

Analyzing the GAAP corpus thus reveals that the transmission of the term "ghetto" occurred at a particular historical moment—what the first generation of American urban historians would refer to as the "Ghetto synthesis." "Ghetto" was used with increasing frequency in black discourse in the 1920s, and the black press printed the words of speakers and writers who realized that the historical oppression of another American minority group yielded a politically effective metaphor. The comparison had already clearly been drawn between Jewish and black segregated areas, because although reference was made to Jewish ghettos, it was much more common for "ghetto" to occur in these African American newspapers proceeded by a racial qualifier. The "ghetto" was used when discussing a national trend towards residential racial segregation, particularly to compare how segregated conditions were created by state control and the political enforcement of compulsory segregation, and not voluntarily, from pathological resignation or as product of convenience.

Conclusions

An analysis of the GAAP corpus provides evidence indicating that as segregation became a national concern and housing patterns in the North increasingly came to resemble Southern *de jure* segregation, the term ghetto was used in black discourse in a way that evoked the definitional aspects of early-modern European ghettos: compulsory, segregated, and enclosed. Although this definition had dissipated in Jewish usage by the 1920s, as Daniel Schwartz shows, these findings reveal that it endured in 1920s black discourse because it paralleled the segregation ordinances being attempted in American cities. In this way, the early-modern Italian ghettos were chosen as the analogous symbol of segregation, and not the shtetls and Jewish settlements of the Pale or the Jewish neighborhoods of American cities.

Duneier, by focusing only on the social sciences, overstates the influence of the Nazi ghetto metaphor on the academics and public intellectuals who popularized the term "ghetto" in the American context. Cayton, Drake, and Clark may have found more rhetorical power in comparing white hostility against blacks in American cities to the persecution of Jews in Nazi ghettos, but there were other scholars who found a more compelling parallel between the control that Christians had over Jews in early-modern European ghettos and the restrictions that white city-dwellers placed on their black neighbors. More importantly, my research shows that this latter comparison was consistent with how "ghetto" was used in black discourse in the 1920s. As "ghetto" was adopted from Jewish political discourse and adapted to the specificities of the black urban experience, it was used to denote a national trend towards greater restriction and control over black lives.

In conjunction with close reading, corpus analysis can provide both a confirmation of findings and additional insight about broader patterns in language use that might subvert expectations. Historians do not often discuss trial and error, false positives, or experimentation, as is done in the science, technology, engineering, and mathematics (STEM) disciplines, but they are essential parts of the process of historical research. The GAAP corpus was not able to demonstrate when, where, how, why, or by whom "ghetto" was adopted to describe African American urban neighborhoods in the early twentieth century. It did prove instructive, however, in revealing the growing frequency of the word's use over time, in demonstrating the national scope of the word's use, and in identifying how speakers and writers in the black press understood segregation to be the result of systemic racially biased policies enforced by the state. It indicates that further qualitative research must be done to understand how African Americans in the 1920s negotiated their belonging in American society in relation to Jews and by evoking historical Jewish oppression.

Notes

1 K. Miller, "Kelly Miller Says," *Philadelphia Tribune*, May 24, 1928.
2 I am using the definition of discourse presented in B. Martin and F. Ringham, *Dictionary of Semiotics*, New York: Cassell, 2000, p. 51. I use the concept of black discourse instead of referring to black writers, journalists, or speakers for two reasons. First, white people both wrote for and were quoted in the black press – particularly public figures such as Supreme Court Justice Louis Marshall and NAACP leader Oswald Garrison Villard. Secondly, I am interested in the rhetoric that African Americans would have read and discussed, not only what they wrote.

3   H. Diner, *In the Almost Promised Land: American Jews and Blacks: 1915–1935*, Contributions in American History, no. 59, Westport, CT: Greenwood Press, 1977, p. 4.

4   I. Berlin, *The Making of African America: The Four Great Migrations*, New York: Viking, 2010, pp. 154–155; J. Gregory, "The Second Great Migration: A Historical Overview," in K. Kusmer and J. Trotter (eds) *African American Urban History Since World War II*, Chicago: University of Chicago Press, 2009, pp. 19–38.

5   For an overview of the literature describing Black-Jewish relations in the early twentieth century, see J. Trotter, "African Americans, Jews, and the City: Perspectives from the Industrial Era, 1900–1950," in V. Franklin et al. (eds) *African Americans and Jews in the Twentieth Century: Studies in Convergence and Conflict*, Columbia, MO: University of Missouri Press, 1998, pp. 193–207.

6   Diner, *In the Almost Promised Land*, p. xiii.

7   Ibid., pp. 74–75.

8   Ibid., p. 31.

9   Ibid., p. 49.

10   D. Schwartz, "What's in a Name? The 'Ghetto' Comes to America," unpublished paper, n.d., p. 4.

11   B. Ravid, "From Geographical Realia to Historiographical Symbol: The Odyssey of the Word Ghetto," in D. Ruderman (ed.) *Essential Papers on Jewish Culture in Renaissance and Baroque Italy*, New York: New York University Press, 1992.

12   Ibid., p. 10.

13   Schwartz, "What's in a Name?"

14   For the classic elaboration on this historiography, see appendix 7 of J. Trotter, *Black Milwaukee: The Making of an Industrial Proletariat, 1915–45*, Urbana, IL: University of Illinois Press, 2007.

15   M. Duneier, *Ghetto: The Invention of a Place, the History of an Idea*, New York: Farrar, Straus and Giroux, 2016, p. ix. See also: D. Michman, *The Emergence of Jewish Ghettos during the Holocaust*, Cambridge: Cambridge University Press, 2011.

16   Duneier, *Ghetto*, pp. 23–24.

17   Ibid., pp. 71–73.

18   Ibid., p. 115.

19   Ibid., pp. 142–148.

20   Ibid., p. 184.

21   Ibid., pp. 82–84.

22   Ibid., p. 24.

23   Ibid., pp. 73–114.

24   Trotter, *Black Milwaukee*, pp. 271–275.

25   A. Spear, *Black Chicago: The Making of a Negro Ghetto 1890–1920*, Chicago: University of Chicago Press, 1974, p. 229.

26   Duneier, *Ghetto*, p. 66.

27   Ibid., p. 71.

28   Ibid., p. 73.

29   Duneier admits as much, arguing that Drake and Cayton attempted to push back against Gunnar Myrdal's interpretation in *An American Dilemma*—that stronger commitment by whites to Christian-democratic ideals could lead to racial equality—by showing that despite Northerner's purported ideals of equality, the North was no more equal than the South. Ibid., p. 67.

30   S. Drake and H. Cayton, *Black Metropolis: A Study of Negro Life in a Northern City*, New York: Harcourt, Brace and Company, 1945, pp. 198–199.

31   For an excellent explanation of corpus linguistics for historians, see M. Moravec, "Corpus Linguistics for Historians," *History in the City*, December 23, 2013, online, available at: <http://historyinthecity.blogspot.com/2013/12/corpus-linguistics-for-historians.html> (Accessed March 22, 2017). For a general overview of corpus linguistics, see T. McEnery and A. Hardie, *Corpus Linguistics: Method, Theory and Practice*, Cambridge: Cambridge University Press, 2012.

32 H. Baker, "Language Surrounding Poverty in Early Modern England: Constructing Seventeenth-Century Beggars and Vagrants," Briefing, CASS: Briefings, Lancaster, UK: ESRC Center for Corpus Approaches to Social Science, Lancaster University, 2014, online, available at: <http://cass.lancs.ac.uk/wp-content/uploads/2015/04/09-CASS-Beggars-RL- FINISHED.pdf>, (Accessed March 22, 2017); A. Pionke, "Excavating Victorian Cuba in the British Periodicals Database," *Victorian Periodicals Review*, vol. 47, no. 3, 2014, pp. 369–397.

33 A diachronic corpus is assembled from texts published over a long span of time, not from a single moment (like a month, year, or decade) and is intended to show change in language over time. For Americanists, the most accessible general corpora of American English have been created by Dr. Mark Davies, Professor of Linguistics at Brigham Young University, which can be viewed online at <http://corpus.byu.edu/overview.asp>. The Google Ngram corpus is the other major corpus of American English, available at: <https://books.google.com/ngrams>.

34 *Indianapolis Recorder*, available at: <http://www.ulib.iupui.edu/collections/IRecorder>.

35 I filtered results to articles, front page articles, editorials, editorial cartoons, letters to the editor, reviews, and photo standalones because I was looking for language used in context and did not want to consider advertisements or classified ads. This was largely unnecessary, because the filters only eliminated 12 items from the search.

36 My searches initially turned up 156 results, several of which were eliminated because they were syndicated columns or wire-service articles and were thus duplicated across multiple papers. I included the first one that emerged in the search listing for inclusion in the corpus. Occasionally, the individual newspapers would make their own edits or add local commentary to newswire articles—in such cases, I would not count them as duplicates even if the majority of the articles' text was the same. I also eliminated a few which mistakenly recognized another word as "ghetto."

37 In addition to being available for free online download, AntConc has the advantage of many online tutorials to learn from. H. Froelich, "Corpus Analysis with Antconc," *Programming Historian*, June 19, 2015, available at: < http://programminghistorian.org/lessons/corpus-analysis-with-antconc>. I also thank Tony McEnery and the many advisors who taught the FutureLearn course Corpus Linguistics: Method, Analysis, Interpretation in the fall of 2015; they provided me with an invaluable introduction to the topic, methods, and practical skills necessary to conduct this research.

38 The earliest article in the GAAP corpus was published in 1904, one of only three that appear in the first decade of the twentieth century.

39 D. Massey and N. Denton, *American Apartheid: Segregation and the Making of the Underclass*, Cambridge: Harvard University Press, 2003, pp. 41–42.

40 W. Michaeli, *The Defender: How the Legendary Black Newspaper Changed America From the Age of the Pullman Porters to the Age of Obama*, Boston: Houghton Mifflin Harcourt, 2016, p. 164.

41 Maintaining all the filters used with my "ghetto*" search, as noted in an earlier footnote, I conducted a search of the six ProQuest newspapers sans a keyword. This search returned 614,245 items. That means that the 126 articles including a variant of "ghetto" from these six newspapers (134 minus the eight articles from the Indianapolis Recorder) represent only 0.02 per cent of the total [(126/614245) × 100]. By contrast, searching for "segregat*" (again maintaining the same filters) returns 6076 articles—which is 48 times greater than the 126 articles including a variant of "ghetto," and yet still only makes up 0.99 per cent of the total number of articles from the ProQuest newspapers.

42 Unsurprisingly, in almost every corpus, the top of this list is dominated by parts of speech. The five most common words in the GAAP Corpus, for example, are "the," "of," "and," "to," and "in." AntConc permits the use of a "stop list," which instructs the Word List tool to ignore specified terms. Researchers can construct stop lists that identify parts of speech and consequently remove them from the results. I chose not to employ a stop list, favoring the opportunity to compare the frequency of all words in the corpus.

43 Co-occurrence, known in corpus linguistics as "collocation," describes when two or more words appear together more commonly than random probability would indicate they should.

44 The Concordance tool is often referred to as the Key Word in Context, or KWIC.

45 The sum of seven words to the left and seven words to the right of the 154 uses of "ghetto" in the corpus equals 2156 (154 × 14). If 1.5 per cent seems small, consider that "and" and "the" together make up barely 12 per cent of the total (274 of 2156) and they are by far the most frequently used words within the Concordance context.

46 The Collocation tool nonetheless reveals the limitations of a medium-sized, tailored dataset. The sample is too small for any one term to distinguish itself as more highly correlated with "ghetto" than another, and so it is unclear whether the association of one word with "ghetto" is more significant than its association with another.

12

CONSTRAINED BUT NOT CONTAINED

Patterns of everyday life and the limits of segregation in 1920s Harlem

Stephen Robertson

In 1966, in the first major historical study of twentieth-century Harlem, Gilbert Osofsky told the story of the neighborhood in the 1920s as the making of a ghetto. What he described was the emergence of a large, segregated community, and the transformation of the area it occupied into a slum from which black residents could not escape.[1] The demographic evidence of segregated housing is clear. In an expanding area that by 1930 had reached the Harlem river, 155th Street, and Central Park West and begun to spill over 125th Street toward Central Park, the residents were almost exclusively African American migrants and West Indian immigrants. However, the black settlement in Harlem was not enclosed in the way that it was in Chicago. Efforts by whites to enforce boundaries quickly failed, the result, Kevin McGruder recently argued, of the diversity of white residents and their relatively short residence in Harlem.[2] Nor was Harlem characterized by the old, dilapidated housing found in other northern black neighborhoods that drove residents who could afford to, to look to the suburbs.[3] Relatively few black businesses and more limited black property ownership also distinguished Harlem from other black neighborhoods.[4] Yet evidence of residential segregation, however it spread and whatever its character, offers at best only a partial picture of the nature of the neighborhood. To determine if a neighborhood is a place apart also requires evidence of where residents went when they left their homes and who spent time in the neighborhood.

Evidence of lived experience in black neighborhoods is fragmentary, and so historians have not used everyday life as an organizing framework for understanding the character of such places. Instead, recent studies have explored specific threads of experience previously marginalized by studies focused on black organizations, writers, and intellectuals: nightlife, numbers gambling, sexual commerce, religion, sports, and consumption.[5] This project weaves these threads together with additional dimensions to reveal the patterns of everyday life across the week and the year. In doing so, it places an emphasis on exactly where residents spent their daily lives, which is only fitfully present in those studies. New digital mapping tools offer a means of combining fragmentary evidence and visualizing the spatial dimensions of everyday life to create maps comparable to those based on population censuses that are central to perceptions of Harlem as a segregated neighborhood. With a team at the University of Sydney, I created *Digital Harlem*, an online map-based visualization of both events and places in Harlem that we identified from a variety of sources: the case files of the Manhattan district attorney; the two major newspapers published in Harlem, the *New York Age* and the *New York Amsterdam News*; probation files; prison records; undercover investigations; social surveys; and material collected by the Federal Writers Project for the 1939 New York City Guide.[6] Our maps of those sources show that 1920s Harlem was not only a racially variegated place, in which whites as well as blacks were present, but also a place in which the rhythms of everyday life carried residents into white spaces within and beyond the neighborhood.

During waking hours, many adult residents of Harlem were absent from the neighborhood, at work. While the limited employment options of black New Yorkers are well known, how the location of that work shaped life in the neighborhood has not been explored. White business owners and staff, and whites working in Harlem's schools, hospitals, buses, streetcars, subways, and the police and fire departments were a presence in Harlem both when its workers were absent, and in many cases, after they returned. While clashes between residents and white police have attracted the attention of scholars, the myriad other interactions and clashes with whites that formed an unavoidable part of daily life have only begun to be explored, in important new work on black consumption by Shannon King.[7] But missing from that account are interracial interactions at sporting events, such as those discussed in Chicago by Davarian Baldwin, and involving children, which are features of daily life before and after the increased white presence in nightlife in the 1920s that King claims as a turning point.[8] Also missing are residents' experiences in non-commercial forms of leisure offered by churches, fraternal organizations, community organizations, and social clubs; and at places like beaches and summer camps. This wider fabric of activities is a key context for understanding the place of commercialized leisure in life in Harlem. Adults also ventured beyond the neighborhood's border for leisure as well as work, going even further afield in the summer. Even as Harlem became a neighborhood of segregated housing, then, it did not become an area from which whites and white authority were absent to a sufficient extent to justify King's claim that "all of Harlem … belonged to blacks."[9] Nor was the everyday life of its residents contained within Harlem, with many working and playing beyond its boundaries.

Out to work

As a *New York Times* journalist noted in 1935, "Harlem, in a manner of speaking, is a residential rather than a commercial or industrial city, self-maintained in its social aspects but reaching out into every section of New York in its economic life. 95 percent of Harlem's working population travels to its job. Every morning sees an exodus of workers filling subways, surface cars and elevated trains and every evening sees them returning to their homes."[10] White control of the neighborhood's businesses, and their exclusion of black men and women from most trades and professions, contributed to those journeys beyond Harlem. In 1916, the *New York Age* found that whites owned 75 percent of the 503 businesses in the area where blacks lived. That proportion remained the same in 1921, even as the area of black settlement spread. By 1929, another survey reported even greater white control: 81.51 percent of the 10,319 businesses in black Harlem were in the hands of whites. Few of those businesses employed black staff in their stores, and the deliverymen, insurance salesmen, and rent and bill collectors they sent into the neighborhood were likewise rarely black.[11]

Unlike their counterparts in other northern cities, Harlem's residents did not find work in New York City's major industries, kept out by white employers and unions. As a result, two-thirds of Harlem's male workers were employed in manual labor, as longshoremen, janitors, elevator and switchboard operators, porters, day laborers, and waiters.[12] Very few jobs in those fields could be found in Harlem. Morgan Thompson, a married West Indian father of two who turned forty years of age in 1929, worked as a construction laborer. Between 1928 and 1933, he found employment on fifteen different constructions sites, in downtown Manhattan and on the Upper East Side, and in the outer boroughs of Brooklyn, Queens, and the Bronx. Only once did he work in Harlem, on the new YMCA on 135th Street. Perry Brown, a married man aged in his 40s who came to Harlem from Pennsylvania, found better-paying work than Thompson, as an elevator operator and building superintendent, all in buildings in downtown Manhattan, at the opposite end of the island from Harlem.[13]

Harlem's women had even fewer employment options than men. Almost three-quarters worked in domestic and personal service, as laundresses, hairdressers, domestic day workers (general housework and laundry), and maids. A small number did secure some factory work, a field not open to black men.[14] Domestic work generally took women to different parts of the city than those to which men traveled for laboring jobs. Annie Dillard, for example, an 18-year-old West Indian, first found work as a servant on the Upper West Side, on West 102nd Street. In private homes, domestic servants usually performed a multitude of tasks, such as laundry, ironing, cooking, cleaning, and serving. The hours were long, the status low, and the supervision tight. Later, Dillard switched to work as a chambermaid in the McAlpin Hotel in midtown and in a boarding house on West 75th Street. Both jobs offered shorter hours than work in private homes: 9 am to 4.30 pm at the hotel and part-time at the boarding house. She also worked at Park West Hospital on West 76th Street, probably cleaning. In addition, she had a job in a laundry on Cherry Street in Lower Manhattan. A commercial steam laundry was mechanized and organized like a factory, and a job there is best thought of as industrial work. Only that last position took her into a neighborhood where Harlem's men were likely to find employment.[15]

Limited work could be found in Harlem. Roger Walker, a 19-year-old native of North Carolina, worked as a kitchen hand, counterman, or soda dispenser in restaurants and drug stores in a variety of different locations the length of Lenox and Seventh Avenues. He often worked 12 or 13 hours a day in these positions, and even overtime beyond those hours; in other cases, he worked the night shift. That employment offered little stability. Walker changed jobs repeatedly, holding nine different positions in a four-year span. He lost some of those positions due to cutbacks, but more often he quit or was fired as a result of disputes about unpaid or inadequate wages and taking days off.[16] Women could find laundry work in Harlem, which was home to at least fifteen laundries like those that operated in downtown Manhattan. With a little capital, and an apartment, women could open a beauty parlor. At least 200 beauty parlors operated in Harlem, making the beauty industry the neighborhood's largest legitimate black enterprise.[17] Operating a day nursery in their homes required even less capital, especially if a woman did not seek a license.[18] Both occupations had the advantage of not involving work under the gaze of whites, as domestic service did.

Growing up in Harlem

While most employed adults traveled outside Harlem to work six days a week, children remained in the neighborhood. An Urban League study of 2,400 families published in 1927 found that more than half of the mothers were in paid employment. Those women reported a variety of means of providing care for the youngest of their children. Most commonly, they put them in the care of relatives or friends, or the father. A much smaller proportion relied on paid childcare, in private homes, or, less often, in day nurseries.[19] Harlem had only six day nurseries in the 1920s, run by community and church groups, providing places for approximately 200 children a day.[20] The more extensive home-based nurseries varied widely in quality. *Amsterdam News* columnist Edgar Grey investigated 123 nurseries that advertised in local newspapers during a five-month period in 1927. Finding that only 19 of the operators had the permits required by New York law, and that most were located in unsanitary situations, he labeled them "baby farms."[21] Grey's polemic likely exaggerated the state of the homes he saw, but day nurseries that advertised in the *Amsterdam News* were clustered in areas of tenement housing, rather than in the more upscale and respectable districts that housed much of the beauty trade.[22]

Older children spent from 8.30 am to 3.00 pm in one of Harlem's schools, white-controlled spaces in contrast to black-controlled day care. Six public elementary schools served Harlem's black community in the 1920s, together with three Catholic elementary schools and two new public junior high schools built in 1924 and 1925. Although the numbers of white pupils in those schools quickly dwindled as black settlement spread, the teachers remained overwhelmingly white.[23] Nonetheless, the black press, which was certainly on the lookout for racial conflict, reported none within the schools. Controversy did flare in 1926 over claims that the principal of the girls' junior high school was steering her pupils toward vocational

programs rather than college preparatory courses.[24] An incident at an elementary
school two years later, in which a white teacher threatened to flog a black boy like
they did in the South, was reported as the first instance of children being molested
by white teachers since that incident.[25] To continue on to high school required navigating discriminatory admission processes that limited access and steered students
to vocational training, and then, except for the boys attending the industrial school
on West 138th Street, traveling beyond black Harlem to schools with overwhelmingly white student bodies. Few Harlem students made that journey.[26]

After school hours, with their parents still at work, Harlem's school-age children
were largely left to find their own place in the neighborhood. The 1927 Urban
League survey reported that some parents told their children to remain around
their school, and a slightly smaller group sent their children to the public library
branch on 135th street. By far the largest group of parents reported that their children were able to take care of themselves, or were in the streets.[27] By 1930, with
somewhere around 20,000 school-age children in Harlem, descriptions of them
as swarming the street after school hours hardly seems an exaggeration.[28] Some
children spent time on the major avenues: there, they swung on moving trolley
cars, auto trucks, and other fast-running vehicles. More often, children occupied
residential side streets for games of baseball, basketball, and punchball. The "reckless
way in which youngsters dart about in playing" made it difficult for automobiles
to negotiate those streets, and accidents frequently resulted.[29] In the mid-1920s, an
average of two children a day suffered injuries in automobile accidents between
130th and 155th Streets. Those accidents often led to clashes between drivers and
neighborhood residents; in Harlem, such conflicts had an added racial dimension,
as most of those driving its streets were white.[30]

Harlem's leaders lobbied white-controlled city agencies for traffic police posts
and traffic lights to mitigate the danger posed by traffic on the avenues, and for playgrounds to keep children off the streets. It took until 1923 for the Parks Department
to open the first playground in Harlem, long after facilities had appeared throughout the city. The Board of Education provided additional playgrounds as part of the
two new junior high schools and a public baths, and leased land for an additional
playground in 1928. In 1930, the Children's Aid Society purchased ten lots for a
playground in the block between West 133rd and West 134th and Lenox and Fifth
Avenues, demolishing most of the buildings and adding two additional lots with
funds provided by Rockefeller. All these playgrounds employed supervisors, a mix
of white and black adults who directed what black children could do in those
spaces.[31] For all the crowds that filled the playgrounds, the space to play off the
street never amounted to enough to remove more than a small proportion of the
growing population of children from the streets.

A weeknight out in Harlem

When men and women returned to Harlem from work in the evenings, a variety of
different tasks and activities sent them through the neighborhood. Residents used

the evening to shop and seek services. In the spring of 1920, Mrs. Jennie Taylor was among the witnesses to a shooting on Fifth Avenue near 137th Street just before 11 o'clock at night. She had left her home at half past nine to shop at Solomon's, the butcher, and having stopped several times to speak to friends and family, was still on her errand when the shooting took place. As well as butchers, businesses ranging from beauty salons and barbers to music shops and dentists remained open until as late as midnight. At 11 pm, the shops of Seventh Avenue "were still open, brightly lighted and doing a rushing business. The streets were full of people. Seventh Avenue had all the aspects of a lively Saturday afternoon."[32]

Shopping drew residents into interactions with whites. Although some white businessmen "were shrewd enough to hold prejudice in restraint for the sake of trade," as columnist Kelly Miller put it, ordinary transactions could erupt into conflicts that drew in other blacks.[33] The screams of a black customer, for example, attracted an angry crowd of several hundred to a hat-cleaning and shoe-shining establishment on Lenox Avenue in July 1930. The customer had been arguing with the white proprietor, Philip Nasselbaum, over ribbon missing from a hat that she had had him clean, when he allegedly struck her. With the crowd besieging the shop, a police officer on the scene had to summon a squad in order to arrest Nasselbaum and protect his store.[34] Poor service, a lack of respect, cheating, and racist jibes all provoked black customers into similar angry challenges to white control of Harlem's retail spaces. However, in most cases, residents did not respond to objectionable behavior with confrontations. The *New York Age* lamented that instead most customers "meekly accepted" their treatment. Characteristically more biting in its judgment, the *Interstate Tattler* noted that, aside from the occasional West Indian woman or housewife fresh from the South, "the rest of us seem to glory in being victimized," believing that "to insist on getting what they ask for or to protest against short weight would not be ladylike."[35] More was at work in the continued patronage of white businesses than a lack of fortitude or a concern with respectability. Some residents actually preferred them, choosing not to spend their money in stores run by members of their own race, and refusing to make payments to black collectors, to be served by black waiters or taxi drivers, or to be examined by black physicians. In explaining their behavior, those residents claimed white businesses carried more stock, provided better service, and charged lower prices, and that white professionals had greater skill. And in many cases, thanks to the refusal of whites to provide blacks with capital and access to training, they were correct.[36]

Residents also sought leisure on weekday evenings. Mostly they did so within the boundaries of black Harlem, which offered an extensive range of commercial and non-commercial activities, some of which were shared with whites. As happened in communities across the nation in the 1920s, many black residents of Harlem headed to the movies. Waiter Roger Walker attended four or five movie screenings a week through the 1920s and 1930s, even as he struggled to pay rent. A weekly visit to the movies with his wife was the one form of leisure that former building superintendent Perry Brown held on to as his economic situation deteriorated in the 1930s.[37] Five theaters could be found within black Harlem, open daily from 2 pm to 11 pm.

They all screened second- and third-run features, with supporting bills of comedies and novelties. You could also watch movies at the Lincoln and Lafayette theaters, which had presented live shows until the early 1920s, when small crowds led them to become combination movie theaters and vaudeville houses. The signature of the Lafayette became its midnight revue on Friday nights, which ran until around 4 am and drew white as well as black patrons. To see first-run movie features, residents of Harlem had to go to one of the half-dozen large cinemas on 125th Street. More than just their size and program differentiated those venues. Those on 125th Street still drew largely white patrons. So while theaters in central Harlem had desegregated before the 1920s, when the population of the neighborhood changed, those on 125th Street only did so gradually across the 1920s. In fact, those theaters only began advertising in the black press in 1930.[38]

A range of other commercialized leisure could be found without leaving Harlem. Poolrooms could be found along the commercial streets. Larger-scale venues with twenty to thirty tables often labeled themselves billiard halls to claim more respectability.[39] At least one billiard hall also featured a bowling alley. In 1930, the miniature golf craze reached Harlem, with two courses opening in July.[40] Harlem's nightclubs, as they became a regular destination for whites, drew few blacks by the second half of the 1920s. From 1926, blacks wanting to dance went instead to the Savoy Ballroom, a public dance hall. For those seeking liquor, speakeasies were ubiquitous in Harlem. They clustered on the avenues, many located within businesses, and attracted a mix of whites and blacks.[41] Those seeking more privacy and to avoid whites went to buffet flats that black residents operated in their apartments, away from the avenues where other forms of commercialized leisure were concentrated. The location of buffet flats was spread by word of mouth, allowing them to host prostitutes, gambling, and dancing as well as providing liquor.[42]

Residents did not only spend their weekday evenings in commercial venues. Churches and fraternal lodges also drew residents out of their homes for activities that rarely, if ever, involved whites. All the major churches held Friday evening prayer meetings, and most held at least one night of Bible study classes. Four churches advertised a weekly discussion meeting or lyceum; others almost certainly held such events.[43] In addition to these activities, church members formed clubs for educational, social, and financial purposes, most of which had a weekly meeting. These clubs reflect the concern with the material conditions of their congregants and the lived experiences of those in the surrounding community that Wallace Best has argued characterized many churches' response to the waves of migrants coming from the South.[44] One study estimated that the large churches each had 25 to 40 clubs. Salem M.E., with a congregation of more than 3,000 members, had over 40 groups including boxing, running, and basketball clubs; Brotherhood and Sisterhood clubs; Ladies Aid; home and Foreign Missionary; Men's and Women's Usher Boards; Phyllis Wheatley Club; Social Club; Historical, Junior, and Senior Sunshine Clubs; a Floral Circle; and a series of groups that were likely social clubs, the Confidential Club, Morning Star, Silver Leaf, Morning Glory, Willing Workers, Pilgrim Program, and Gold Leaf.[45] Members of Harlem's fraternal lodges also had a weekly meeting to attend, as did women in their affiliated temples. Like churches, lodges also had a web of additional clubs that met on other evenings. Whereas the lodge met in its hall, most of the clubs met in a member's residence.[46]

A full spectrum of these activities could also be found under a single roof in the very heart of Harlem, at the YMCA and YWCA. They hosted speakers, discussions, social clubs, and sporting contests similar to those found in churches and lodges, as well as offering bowling alleys and swimming pools. However, the two organizations had a different character than churches and lodges. The YMCA and YWCA were non-denominational, and part of a white-led organization. Although all the officers of the Harlem branches were black, white speakers and visitors were a more regular presence than in churches or lodges. In addition to providing accommodation, both the YMCA and YWCA gave a more central place to vocational education.[47] By 1927, residents could also attend free vocational evening classes in three of Harlem's public schools, P.S. 89, 90, and 136. In the schools, the instructors were more likely to be white than at the YMCA and YWCA. For men, the city's evening classes provided a path to white-collar work; by contrast, they equipped women for industrial work.[48]

Clubs and societies without connections to any institutions also proliferated in Harlem, just as they did across the nation in the 1920s. They differed from institutional groups in being local in character, and often existed for only a short time, no more than two or three years. Black organizations whose sole purpose was social or recreational appear to have outnumbered the women's clubs concerned with causes such as orphanages, girls' homes, nurseries, and hospitals. Social clubs certainly claimed more space in Harlem's two major black newspapers, thanks to the society columns that both ran as a regular feature. Clubs with names such as Harmony Exclusive Club, Conthex Bridge Club, Aeolian Girls' Club, and the Hunter Comets met in members' homes for musical entertainment and refreshments or card games throughout the week, with Mondays and Thursdays the favored evenings. Some clubs existed primarily to organize one or two social events each year, typically an event at one of the dancehalls for hire in Harlem. Those dances often took place on weeknights, when a venue cost less. Although commonly associated with the black elite, social clubs in the 1920s increasingly drew members from the black middle class.[49] The locations of meetings confirm that shift, revealing members residing the length of Harlem rather than concentrated in elite sections like Strivers Row and Sugar Hill. So too does the appearance of social clubs among those who made use of meeting spaces at the YWCA and YMCA.

Weekends of worship and sport

Saturday evenings offered distinctive forms of leisure that drew racially mixed crowds, with many of Harlem's sporting contests taking place on that night. College fraternities, lodges, YMCAs, YWCAs, churches, Sunday schools, public schools, and military units competed among themselves in athletics, bowling, and especially basketball. These contests largely, but not exclusively, featured men. Several girls' and women's basketball leagues did compete throughout the 1920s. Games took place in the gyms and halls attached to churches; the YMCA and YWCA, and the public schools; in the armory; and in dancehalls. Basketball games between athletic clubs affiliated with Harlem's churches became popular enough in the early 1920s to require a larger venue than was available in black Harlem, the Manhattan Casino, north of the neighborhood. Seeking to capitalize on that popularity, the white McMahon brothers established a black professional basketball team in 1922, to play at their venue, the Commonwealth Casino to the east of black Harlem. When that team failed to attract sufficient crowds and folded after two years, the New York Renaissance, or Rens, a black-run team that played at the Renaissance Ballroom in the heart of the neighborhood, became Harlem's team, displacing the amateur athletic clubs. Playing white teams, which local amateur teams did not, in a commercial venue more accessible to white fans than the halls of black organizations, helped the Rens attract crowds of whites as well as blacks. They also took to the road to play around the country, competing against both black and white opponents. Harlem's residents could also attend boxing contests at the Commonwealth Casino. Again, it was bouts between black and white fighters that drew large, and interracial, crowds to that white-owned venue. More racial tension seems to have existed in the crowds watching boxing than basketball, with fans trading insults and black fans pelting white referees with peanuts and pieces of hot dog when they felt a black fighter had been cheated of a win. But those outbursts never developed into the full-fledged conflicts that flared around traffic accidents, policing, or the behavior of white shopkeepers.[50]

On Sundays, churches became a central hub of activity. As a *Pittsburgh Courier* reporter observed, "avenues and cross streets are filled with throngs of worshippers wending their way to their respective churches."[51] Although Harlem's Protestant churches were black-controlled and dominated spaces, a small number of whites could be found in the congregation at Abyssinian Baptist Church, and likely some other churches. The Catholic parishes, by contrast, were led by white priests and retained significant numbers of white members into the 1930s.[52] A morning service was only one of the day's activities at most churches. All the churches taught Sunday Schools, in the early afternoon at churches like Abyssinian Baptist and St Marks ME, or prior to the morning service at Williams, adding children to the throngs traveling to church.[53] Methodist churches like St Marks and Williams also held early evening meetings of the Epworth League, an organization for young adults aged 18 to 35 years. In the late afternoon, a number of churches held a lyceum, or public meeting, usually addressed by a speaker. All Harlem's churches ended the day with a second service, beginning at 7.30 pm or 7.45 pm.[54]

Sunday afternoon was the time for cricket and baseball. The two sports had shared the same fields in Harlem, but those venues were no longer available by 1920, requiring players and spectators to travel further afield. Cricket was the sport of West Indians, played mostly at Van Cortlandt Park in the Bronx, where by the late 1920s up to six games took place at the same time in front of small crowds. Games against touring teams from the West Indies, and against white teams, were played at venues with larger capacities such as New York Oval on East 145th St and the Harlem River, Innisfail Park and Starlight Park in the Bronx, and Dyckman Oval in Washington Heights, and attracted several thousand spectators.[55] Such crowds were more typical at baseball games. Harlem had its own black professional base-ball team, the Lincoln Giants, controlled by a series of white owners. In the 1920s, watching the Giants required a long journey by subway to 177th Street and then a streetcar trip to get to the Catholic Protectory Oval, at East Tremont Avenue and Unionport Road in the Bronx. The team also played occasional games at other stadiums in Washington Heights and Upper Manhattan, and in the homes of white major league teams, Ebbets Field in Brooklyn and Yankee Stadium in the Bronx. Thousands of blacks journeyed to watch baseball in the early 1920s, but crowds waned later in the decade as disputes bedeviled the Eastern Colored League in which the Lincoln Giants competed, the team enjoyed limited on-field success, and basketball grew in popularity in Harlem. As with basketball, professional base-ball drew white spectators as well as black, around a quarter of the crowd in most estimates. They came particularly for contests between black and white teams, but also for Colored League games. Again, any racial antagonism that existed between fans did not rise to the level of actual clashes.[56] In the mid-1920s, as baseball drew smaller crowds, the Rens, the neighborhood's professional basketball team, shifted its regular games from Saturday evenings to Sunday evenings. Promoters had hit on the idea of combining games with dances, a formula that made the team viable (and became a template followed by others organizing basketball games).[57]

In addition to heading to church services, club meetings, and sporting events on Sundays, Harlem's residents simply took to the streets. Columnist Edgar Grey described the scene in the *Amsterdam News* in 1927: "On Saturday evenings and all Sundays the streets are filled with the residents of the community, and on every corner may be seen oceans of them milling about each other and drifting into the shops and stores, stopping to converse, blocking the sidewalk traffic, laughing, shouting merrily without worry or awareness of their plight." Some of those taking to the street Grey described as "out on dress parade."[58] This was the stroll, the use of the streets "as performative sites, readily accessible urban stages for prideful or leisurely strolling and creative sartorial display," and as venues for interacting with friends and strangers.[59] Such crowds made the daylight hours of Sundays and holi-days immediately distinguishable from other days of the week, when children, not adults, filled the streets.

Taking to the streets, moving around Harlem, put black residents into contact with white police, a ubiquitous presence patrolling posts and wandering its streets in plainclothes. Policing that was both "too vigorous and too lax" often made those encounters tense. On the one hand, blacks faced arrest without cause and "on suspicion," and, when in police hands, suffered random beatings, including the offi-cially sanctioned abuse of suspects that in the 1920s acquired its label as "the third degree." On the other hand, officers turned a blind eye toward vice in Harlem, ignoring speakeasies, numbers gambling, and prostitutes (or at least those who paid to be overlooked, who were mostly white). There were many occasions when residents were so riled by police activity that crowds took direct action against officers, particularly on the neighborhood's heavily populated arteries, Lenox and Seventh Avenues, and 135th Street.[60]

Residents not only strolled Harlem's sidewalks on Sundays, they also took to its streets to parade. A handful of parades associated with major events or conventions, such as the return of the 369th Regiment from World War I, the early United Negro Improvement Association (UNIA) conventions, and the Elks convention in 1927, traveled outside the boundaries of black settlement. In doing so, they claimed wider recognition for the activities of blacks, wove black life into the larger city, and sent a message to white New Yorkers. Only rarely did they address whites as directly as did the parade of the 1922 UNIA convention, which once it had crossed into white neighborhoods switched to a different set of banners, bearing slogans such as, "White man rules America, black man shall rule Africa," "We want a black civilization," and "God and Negro Shall Triumph." Most of Harlem's parades involved the neighborhood's fraternal organizations, and remained within black Harlem. Lodges marched from their headquarters to local churches to mark their anniversaries, and participated in parades to mark the groundbreaking of major institutional buildings, and holidays such as July 4th. The typical route took them from their lodge building up and down Seventh and Lenox Avenues, and across 135th Street. Lodges also turned out for parades on the occasion of a member's funeral, bearing the coffin from the undertakers to the site of the funeral and then out of Harlem for burial, usually in Woodlawn Cemetery in the Bronx. Pallbearers took the lead, followed by the hearse and other vehicles.[61] In parading on the streets rather than strolling on the pavement, blacks displaced whites who drove the buses, trams, and most of the taxis and private cars that traversed Harlem's streets. When a few thousand members of the New York UNIA paraded on August 1, 1925, a group larger than the typical parade but far short of the size of major marches, the *Amsterdam News* reported that, "Traffic along the streets and avenues on which the 'faithful' marched was at a standstill for over an hour."[62] As this and almost all the parades in Harlem occurred on a Sunday, traffic would have been relatively light, but the disruption would nonetheless have been significant. Lodges typically included their bands in a parade, extending their appropriation of the street by also interjecting themselves into the sounds of the neighborhood. For all the traffic delays and commotion they produced, parades did not set off clashes between residents and police. Instead, a permit from the city brought officers to accompany a march and facilitate the black takeover of the streets.

Summer breaks

While blacks could be found parading on Harlem's streets and strolling its sidewalks throughout the year, those activities occurred most often in the summer, when the weather reshaped everyday life. Summer moved life in Harlem outside, and pushed residents beyond the boundaries of the neighborhood. Children no longer attended school, but many did spend part of their summer in the school grounds, where the city operated vacation playgrounds. Staffed by city employees, usually public school teachers who were more often black later in the 1920s, vacation playgrounds offered physical training, baths, music, and special entertainments, as well as excursions around the city.[63] Community groups such as Utopia House, the Urban League, and the Children's Aid Society offered similar programs in their playgrounds.[64] Vacation Bible schools at the Abyssinian Baptist Church and Salem M.E. Church offered programs of art, athletics, and outings.[65]

Summer camps provided small numbers of children the chance to go beyond Harlem and spend extended time outside the city. The Urban League worked with the Fresh Air Fund to establish the first summer camp for Harlem residents in 1919, making it possible for one hundred and fifty boys to spend two weeks in Litchfield, Connecticut. Others followed in their footsteps each summer through the 1920s.[66] The YWCA offered the other longest-running summer camp, beginning in 1920, at Fern Rock, on the shore of Lake Tiorati in the Palisades Interstate Park.[67] By 1930, St Philips P. E. Church sent several hundred children aged eight to 18 years to the 314-acre Camp Guilford Bower, in New Paltz, New York, 85 miles from Harlem; the North Harlem Community Council Camp sent 100 children every two weeks to Livingston Manor, Sullivan County, an 86-acre camp; and the Harlem's Children's Fresh Air Fund sent 50 girls to spend two weeks at Camp James A. Farley, an 87-acre property five miles east of Poughkeepsie, New York.[68]

Adults also departed Harlem for summer camps. The YWCA's Fern Rock camp hosted young women as well as children. Beginning in 1929, the New York Business Academy sponsored Camp Swastika, also on Lake Tiorati, offering business and professional people the opportunity for boating, hiking, fishing, camp fires, high diving, swimming across the lake, and "night parties with ukes and guitars and tin pans." The camp proved most popular with nurses and post office clerks, many of whom went for weekends rather than the longer period typical for children.[69] However, the men of Harlem's 369th New York Infantry Regiment went to camp for two full weeks each summer. Their destination was Camp Smith, in Peekskill, New York, for practice on the rifle range, maneuvers in the mountains, and evenings of parades and band concerts. Just over one thousand men made this trip in 1930. The 369th announced their departure and return by parading between their armory at 143rd Street and the train depot at East 125th.[70]

Day trips to destinations closer to Harlem were a more widely shared summer activity. Social clubs gave up their weekly gatherings in favor of trips outside the neighborhood, and, particularly by the late 1920s, to the beach.[71] Beginning in the early 1920s, Rockaway in Long Island became Harlem's beach resort. Individuals traveled by train and bus, and church groups, Sunday schools, and social clubs chartered buses, typically on Thursdays, Sundays, and holidays.[72] By 1928, as visitors from New Jersey and Westchester County joined those from Harlem, blacks dominated the crowds bathing and playing games, displacing the white groups who had previously vacationed at Rockaway. In the process, they claimed a black place amid a landscape in which the *New York Age* saw "the various racial groups in New York … segregating themselves at separate beaches—the Jewish and Italian-Americans are the largest patrons of Coney Island, with the Irish and native American stock predominating at Brighton Beach … the Germans have the beaches at Throgg's Neck and City Island in the Bronx, with Rye Beach on Long Island Sound becoming the rendezvous of the upper-class native whites."[73] However, while blacks dominated the crowds at Rockaway, whites owned the businesses, replicating the situation—and the interracial tensions—that occurred in Harlem.[74]

The concern of whites in Rockaway to keep out black visitors is a reminder that the character of a place is defined not simply by who lives in its housing, but also by who spends time there. Segregated housing alone does not create a segregated community. Looking at patterns of everyday life shows the permeability of black Harlem's borders in the 1920s. Residents left to work and play, and whites entered to work and visit a range of institutions and patronize various forms of commercialized leisure. Exploring the nature of the interracial encounters that resulted highlights the limits to the black control of the community within the neighborhood. Residents experienced white economic and government power and violence in their daily lives, even as they created a range of places and institutions apart from whites. If not contained, black life in 1920s Harlem was constrained, neither entirely separate from whites nor free of their authority. As a result, Harlem in the 1920s was too racially variegated and contested a place to warrant the label of ghetto.

Notes

1 G. Osofsky, *Harlem: The Making of a Ghetto: Negro New York, 1890–1930*, 2nd ed., New York: Harper & Row, 1971. His concept of the ghetto reflects those being developed by social scientists in the 1960s. See M. Duneier, *Ghetto: The Invention of a Place, the History of an Idea*, New York: Farrar, Straus and Giroux, 2016.

2 K. McGruder, *Race and Real Estate: Conflict and Cooperation in Harlem, 1890–1920*, New York: Columbia University Press, 2015, pp. 11–12.

3 J. Ford, *Slums and Housing*, vol. 1, Cambridge, Harvard University Press, 1936, pp. 317–320.

4 K. Miller, "The Causes of Segregation," *Current History* 25, 1927, 827–831.

5 W. Best, *Passionately Human, No Less Divine: Religion and Culture in Black Chicago, 1915–1952*, Princeton: Princeton University Press, 2005; D. Baldwin, *Chicago's New Negroes: Modernity, the Great Migration, and Black Urban Life*, Chapel Hill: University of North Carolina Press, 2007; S. White, S. Garton, S. Robertson, and G. White, *Playing the Numbers: Gambling in Harlem Between the Wars*, Cambridge: Harvard University Press, 2010; C. Hicks, *Talk with You Like a Woman: African American Women, Justice, and Reform in New York, 1890–1935*, Chapel Hill: University of North Carolina Press, 2010; and L. Harris, *Sex Workers, Psychics, and Numbers Runners: Black Women in New York City's Underground Economy*, Urbana: University of Illinois Press, 2016.

6 S. Robertson, S. White, S. Garton, G. White, and D. Evans, *Digital Harlem: Everyday Life, 1915–1930*, <http://digitalharlem.org> (accessed August 31, 2016); S. Robertson, "Putting Harlem on the Map," in K. Nawrotzki and J. Dougherty (eds) *Writing History in the Digital Age*, Ann Arbor: University of Michigan Press, 2013, pp. 186–197; and S. Robertson, "Digital Mapping as a Research Tool: *Digital Harlem: Everyday Life, 1915–1930*," *American Historical Review* 121, 2016, 156–166. The *Digital Harlem Blog* posts cited in this chapter contain images of maps created in *Digital Harlem*. Readers can also go to *Digital Harlem* and create interactive maps of the places and events referred to in this chapter.

7   S. King, *Whose Harlem Is This, Anyway? Community Politics and Grassroots Activism during the New Negro Era*, New York: New York University Press, 2015.

8   Baldwin, *Chicago's New Negroes*, pp. 193–232.

9   King, *Whose Harlem Is This, Anyway?* pp. 32–33.

10 *New York Times*, March 24, 1935, E11.

11 S. Robertson, S. White, and S. Garton, "Harlem in Black and White: Mapping Race and Place in 1920s Harlem," *Journal of Urban History* 39, 2013, 867–868.

12 King, *Whose Harlem Is This, Anyway?* pp. 53–54, 59–67; and M. Sacks, *Before Harlem: The Black Experience in New York City Before World War 1*, Philadelphia: University of Pennsylvania Press, 2006, pp. 108–114.

13 S. Robertson, S. White, S. Garton, and G. White, "This Harlem Life: Black Families and Everyday Life in the 1920s and 1930s," Journal of Social History 44, 2010, 97–122; S. Robertson, "Morgan Thompson – A West Indian Laborer's Life in Harlem," *Digital Harlem Blog*, 2009, <https://digitalharlemblog.wordpress.com/2009/12/01/morgan-thompson/> (accessed August 31, 2016); and S. Robertson, "Perry Brown: A Lodge Member's Life in Harlem," *Digital Harlem Blog*, 2010, <https://digitalharlemblog.word-press.com/2010/07/15/perry-brown-lodge-member/> (accessed August 31, 2016).

14 King, pp. 64–67; Sacks, pp. 115–119.

15 S. Robertson, "Annie Dillard: Domestic Service & Single Motherhood in Harlem," *Digital Harlem Blog*, 2011, <https://digitalharlemblog.wordpress.com/2011/03/31/domestic-servant-harlem-1920s/> (accessed August 31, 2016).

16 Robertson et al., "This Harlem Life," 113–116; and S. Robertson, "Roger Walker – A Lodger's Life in 1920s Harlem," *Digital Harlem Blog*, 2010, <https://digitalharlemblog.wordpress.com/2010/06/15/roger-walker-lodger/> (accessed August 31, 2016).

17 T. Gill, *Beauty Shop Politics: African American Women's Activism in the Beauty Industry*, Urbana: University of Illinois Press, 2010; S. Robertson, "Harlem's Beauty Parlors," *Digital Harlem Blog*, 2010, <https://digitalharlemblog.wordpress.com/2010/09/10/beauty-parlors/> (accessed August 31, 2016); K. Phillips, *Daily Life During African American Migrations*, Santa Barbara: Greenwood, 2012, pp. 69, 85.

18 Arthur Crosby, *New Code of Ordinances of the City of New York*, New York: Banks Law Publishing Company, 1922, pp. 408, 457, <http://babel.hathitrust.org/cgi/pt?id=uc2.ark:/13960/t7kp7xw87;view=1up;seq=415> (accessed September 1, 2016).

19 New York Urban League, *Twenty-Four Hundred Negro Families in Harlem: An Interpretation of the Living Conditions in Harlem* (May 1927) (Schomburg Center for Research in Black Culture, New York Public Library), pp. 26–27.

20 S. Robertson, "Childcare in 1920s Harlem," *Digital Harlem Blog*, 2016, <https://digitalharlemblog.wordpress.com/2016/09/09/childcare-in-1920s-harlem/> (accessed September 10, 2016).

21 *Amsterdam News (AN)*, September 7, 1927, 15.

22 Robertson, "Childcare in 1920s Harlem."

23 D. Ment, "Patterns of Public School Segregation, 1900–1940: A Comparative Study of New York City, New Rochelle, and New Haven," in R. Goodenow and D. Ravich (ed.), *Schools in Cities: Consensus and Conflict in American Educational History*, New York: Holmes and Meier, 1983, pp. 71–95; and *World*, July 1, 1928, 7.

24 *New York Age (NYA)*, May 29, 1926, 1, 2; and *NYA*, June 5, 1926, 1, 2.

25 *Afro American*, June 23, 1928, 5.

26 Ment, "Patterns of Public School Segregation," pp. 86–92; and T. Harbison, "Part of the Problem or Part of the Solution? Harlem's Public Schools, 1914–1954," PhD dissertation, City University of New York, 2011, pp. 93, 170–181.

27 New York Urban League, *Twenty-Four Hundred Negro Families in Harlem*, 26–27.

28 Ment, "Patterns of Public School Segregation, 1900–1940," p. 72.

29 *NYA*, September 8, 1928, 10; O. Lovejoy, *The Negro Children of New York*, New York: Children's Aid Society, 1932, 33–34.

30 Robertson et al., "Harlem in Black and White," 871; S. Robertson, "Traffic Accidents in 1920s Harlem," *Digital Harlem Blog*, 2010, <https://digitalharlemblog.wordpress.com/2010/04/01/traffic-accidents-in-1920s-harlem/> (accessed August 31, 2016).

31 *NYA*, 8 September 1923, 2; *NYA*, 7 July 1928, 1; and *AN*, 16 April 1930, 14.
32 *People v. Otis Wilson*, 1921, p. 344, *Trial Transcripts of the County of New York 1883–1927*, Case 2974, Roll 358 (John Jay College of Criminal Justice); *Afro-American*, 14 July 1928, 5.
33 *AN*, March 25, 1925, 16.
34 *AN*, July 23, 1930, 2.
35 *NYA*, 28 July 28, 1928, 3; *Interstate Tattler*, January 4, 1929, 1.
36 Robertson et al., "Harlem in Black and White," 873–874.
37 Robertson et al., "This Harlem Life," 103, 115.
38 W. Thurman, *Negro Life in New York's Harlem*, Girard, Kansas: Haldemen–Julius Publications, 1927, pp. 35–38; Jervis Anderson, *This Was Harlem, 1900–1950*, New York: Farrar Straus, Giroux, 1981, pp. 110–111; and *Pittsburgh Courier*, December 3, 1927, 2. Similar patterns of movie exhibition and segregation were found in Chicago at this time. See M. Carbine, "'The Finest Outside the Loop': Motion Picture Exhibition in Chicago's Black Metropolis, 1905–1928," *Camera Obscura* 8, 1990, 8–41.
39 *NYA*, April 28, 1923, 1.
40 *AN*, July 30, 1930, 13.
41 Thurman, *Negro Life in New York's Harlem*, pp. 24–32; Rudolph Fisher, "The Caucasian Storms Harlem," *American Mercury*, 1927, 393, 395–396.
42 S. Robertson, S. White, S. Garton, and G. White, "Disorderly Houses: Residences, Privacy, and the Surveillance of Sexuality in 1920s Harlem," *Journal of the History of Sexuality* 21, 3, 2012, 460–465.
43 For example, see *NYA*, April 4, 1925, 5; *NYA*, April 5, 1930, 5. See also S. Robertson, "Churches," *Digital Harlem Blog*, 2009, <https://digitalharlemblog.wordpress.com/2009/04/17/churches/> (accessed September 9, 2016).
44 Best, *Passionately Human, No Less Divine*, pp. 71–93.
45 M. Pollard, "Harlem as Is," MA dissertation, College of the City of New York, 1936, pp. 173–176, 187–199 (Schomburg Center for Research in Black Culture, New York Public Library).
46 See, for example, *AN*, April 30, 1930, 14.
47 For the YWCA, see J. Weisenfeld, *African American Women and Christian Activism: New York's Black YWCA, 1905–1945*, Cambridge: Harvard University Press, 1997; *NYA*, November 15, 1924, 1, 5. For the YMCA, see *NYA*, January 3, 1920, 1, 2.
48 *NYA*, October 22, 1927, 3.
49 W. Gatewood, *Aristocrats of Color: The Black Elite, 1880–1920*, Bloomington: Indiana University Press, 1990, pp. 210–247; Pollard, "Harlem as Is," pp. 83–148.
50 Robertson et al., "Harlem in Black and White," 872–873; and S. Robertson, "Basketball in 1920s Harlem," *Digital Harlem Blog* (2011), <https://digitalharlemblog.wordpress.com/2011/06/03/basketball-in-1920s-harlem/> (accessed September 9, 2016). For parallels in 1920s Chicago, see Baldwin, *Chicago's New Negroes*, pp. 207–232.
51 *Pittsburgh Courier*, January 17, 1925, 8.
52 A. Powell, *Upon This Rock*, p. 39; S. Robertson, "Catholics in 1920s Harlem," *Digital Harlem Blog*, 2010, <https://digitalharlemblog.wordpress.com/2010/07/01/catholics-in-1920s-harlem/> (accessed September 4, 2016).
53 G. Hobart, *The Negro Churches of Manhattan*, New York: Greater New York Federation of Churches, 1930, pp. 24–25.
54 See, for example, *NYA*, April 4, 1925, 5; *NYA*, April 5, 1930, 5.
55 *NYA*, May 30, 1925, 6; *AN*, July 15, 1925, 5; *AN*, June 27, 1928, 7; *AN*, July 11, 1928, 6.
56 Robertson et al., "Harlem in Black and White," 869, 872–873; S. Robertson "Harlem and Baseball in the 1920s," *Digital Harlem Blog* (2011), <https://digitalharlemblog.wordpress.com/2011/07/27/baseball-1920s-harlem/> (accessed September 9, 2016).
57 S. Robertson, "Basketball in 1920s Harlem."
58 *AN*, August 25, 1927, 4.
59 S. White and G. White, *Stylin': African American Expressive Culture, from Its Beginnings to the Zoot Suit*, Ithaca: Cornell University Press, 1999, p. 161.

60 Robertson et al., "Harlem in Black and White," 869–871; and King, 173–186.
61 S. Robertson, "Parades in 1920s Harlem," *Digital Harlem Blog* (2011), <https://digitalharlemblog.wordpress.com/2011/02/01/parades-in-1920s-harlem/> (accessed September 9, 2016).
62 *AN*, August 5, 1925, 3.
63 See, for example, *NYA*, July 25, 1925, 2; *NYA*, September 5, 1925, 10.
64 *NYA*, June 16, 1928, 9; *NYA*, September 6, 1930, 2; *AN*, July 9, 1930, 9.
65 *NYA*, 14 August 1926, 10; *AN*, July 9, 1930, 9.
66 *NYA*, June 28, 1919, 2; *NYA* January 17, 1920, 2; *NYA* July 10, 1920, 6; *NYA* July 23, 1921, 8; *NYA* July 19, 1924, 10; *NYA*, February 15, 1930, 2.
67 *NYA*, June 23, 1923, 8; *NYA*, June 16, 1923, 8; *NYA*, August 4, 1923, 8; *AN*, June 24, 1925; *AN*, July 1, 1925.
68 *AN*, July 9, 1930, 5; Pollard, "Harlem as Is," p. 196.
69 *NYA*, June 22, 1929, 2; *NYA*, July 13, 1929, 2; *NYA*, August 30, 1930, 2.
70 *AN*, September 24, 1930, 3; Robertson, "Parades in 1920s Harlem."
71 See, for example, *NYA* July 5, 1930, 5; *AN*, July 9, 1930, 10.
72 *AN*, August 17, 1927, 15; *AN*, August 9, 1931, 9.
73 *NYA*, August 25, 1928, 7; *NYA*, August 3, 1929, 10.
74 *AN*, May 13, 1925, 1; *AN*, August 10, 1927, 15; *AN*, August 17, 1927, 15; *AN*, August 31, 1927, 9.

13

THE AMERICAN GHETTO AS AN INTERNATIONAL HUMAN RIGHTS CRISIS

The fight against racial restrictive covenants, 1945–1948

Jeffrey D. Gonda

A knock at the front door of their modest bungalow on Detroit's Seebaldt Avenue signaled trouble for Orsel and Minnie McGhee in early January 1945. The soft-spoken African American couple had moved in just days earlier, and while Seebaldt was only five blocks away from their previous residence, the peculiar geography of urban segregation made them into outsiders and targets in their new neighborhood. The McGhees had crossed north of Tireman Avenue, an unofficial dividing line between the races in northwest Detroit. They knew the neighbors standing on their porch were not there to welcome them.[1]

Led by Benjamin Sipes, a blue-collar auto factory worker who lived next door, the group of ten white homeowners asked to be let in from the blistering cold. The McGhees responded cautiously. Detroit was one of many cities with a lengthy history of vandalism and violence against black homebuyers who had breached residential color lines. Black residents still told stories of Dr. Ossian Sweet and his family, who had faced murder charges in 1925 after defending their home against a white mob determined to drive them out. An explosive race riot in the summer of 1943 had left memories still raw and troubling throughout the city. On this day, however, the McGhees sensed something other than violence was in the air and allowed their neighbors to step inside. Sipes sauntered through the front door and announced: "We are a group of taxpayers in the neighborhood ... and we are asking you to kindly vacate the property." "We also wish to inform you," he continued, "unless you move out, the Civic Association will take you to court."[2]

The Northwest Civic Association, a local white homeowners' group, had partnered with Sipes and his neighbors ten years earlier during the throes of the Great Depression to create a racially restrictive covenant along Seebaldt. The covenant was a legal agreement that prohibited white homeowners in the area from allowing African Americans to rent or occupy any of the homes on the block and empowered white residents to sue for the eviction of any homebuyer who violated the agreement. Restrictive covenants like this one had become an entrenched and ubiquitous feature of segregated cities across the country. "Nobody really knows how much land is covered by covenants," declared one leading publication, "but all students of it agree that the practice is widespread and growing fast." Indeed, many civil rights activists and scholars considered covenants the single greatest obstacle to African Americans' efforts to secure adequate housing in increasingly overcrowded urban areas and a key pillar of the modern American ghetto. In the words of contemporary experts, covenants were "the most dangerous," "the most discouraging," and "the most effective modern method," of residential segregation. Sipes's threat of legal action was therefore an ominous one. The McGhees knew the weight of the law stood against them.[3]

Buying the house on Seebaldt had not been a political act for the McGhees, but they immediately recognized that their decision about whether to stay and fight carried broader implications. When one of their furious neighbors demanded to know why they could not find "any other place to move rather than over here," Mr. McGhee shot back that perhaps he "could find another place." "But," he continued, "how about the other fourteen million black Americans that have no place to live but in the ghetto or doubling up?" Here, in the world's self-proclaimed "Arsenal of Democracy," the McGhees knew all too well the unrequited yearnings for justice and equality that lingered in the black community south of Tireman Avenue and others like it across Detroit and around the nation. They asked Sipes and his associates to leave, and steeled themselves for the impending legal battle. Their struggle would be both deeply personal and one that bespoke the aspirations of millions of black citizens who felt the walls of America's ghettos hardening fast around them.[4]

Through three years of appeals, civil rights litigators who fought on the McGhees' behalf launched a fullfledged counterattack on the enforcement of restrictive covenants in the nation's courts. These attorneys hoped to break through two decades of judicial intransigence that had treated racial restrictions on the use of property to be entirely permissible and almost completely immune from constitutional scrutiny. Time and again, American jurists had approved the eviction of black families by insisting that covenants were simply private contracts without any larger issues of legal relevance at stake. This narrow perspective ensured that residential desegregation efforts routinely faltered against the solid bulwark of white resistance and gave the patina of legal legitimacy to the discriminatory desires of white homeowners. Covenants thus played a critical role in the early legal architecture of America's developing ghettos, offering white residents a relatively straightforward means of harnessing the sanction and power of the state to exclude black home-seekers through formal channels.[5]

One of the chief tasks facing anti-covenant advocates in the aftermath of World War II, then, was how to force American courts to look past the immediate question of private property rights and consider the broader implications of housing segregation in American law, politics, and society. By 1948, local attorneys and activists at the National Association for the Advancement of Colored People (NAACP) had successfully brought the McGhees' case and three others like it from

St. Louis and Washington, D.C. to the United States Supreme Court. To do so, they crafted an array of experimental arguments that recast the stakes of the covenant fight and eventually secured a landmark victory. The Supreme Court ultimately declared in May 1948 that judges could no longer uphold racially restrictive agreements to evict families like the McGhees. Local courts' enforcement of covenants constituted discriminatory state action prohibited by the Fourteenth Amendment. This decision, known as *Shelley v. Kraemer* after the St. Louis case that stood first on the Supreme Court docket, held out the tantalizing promise of a new hope and trajectory for urban black communities. For a time, civil rights activists believed that this success might signal the impending doom of segregation in America's cities. Although their victory never became the forceful weapon against residential exclusion for which they had hoped, the campaign against covenants nonetheless offers a unique window into how activists understood and attacked the issue of housing discrimination following World War II. Pushing past what the cases failed to accomplish in order to examine what activists had hoped to achieve reveals the ideas and efforts fueling the first national postwar battle over the future of the American ghetto.[6]

One of the more fascinating elements of the anti-covenant fight was a set of arguments that never gained much traction in the courts, but that represented the innovation, urgency, and evolving political dynamics that shaped urban civil rights activism after the war. Throughout *Shelley*, the attorneys seized upon an emergent language of human rights and framed the hardships of residential segregation in an international context. This marked the first concerted effort by civil rights litigators to employ the dramatic transformations in postwar international politics and law for the purposes of racial equality in the United States. These attorneys drew on historical connotations and recent incarnations of the ghetto, the fresh memories of Nazi Germany's racial attitudes and atrocities, the creation of the United Nations, America's new treaty obligations, and looming tensions with the Soviet Union to broaden the scope of their arguments and to galvanize political coalitions that would provide crucial support for their cases. Legal activists sensed, in these years, an important opportunity to frame the nation's racial ghettos as an international human rights crisis and this interpretive framework played an important but under-appreciated role in the success of the anti-covenant campaign.

Activists' use of a global human rights perspective in these cases affords valuable insights into their efforts to contest the further entrenchment of urban segregation and how this struggle helped shape the process of litigating racial justice at mid-century. Firstly, these arguments reveal how the campaign against American ghettos spurred legal innovation and tactical dynamism that aided not only the work of lawyers in these cases, but the larger courtroom struggle for racial equality. The attorneys' human rights claims helped to build a broader coalition in support of civil rights, strengthened a key partnership between Jewish advocacy groups and the NAACP, challenged traditional applications of American law, and deepened the interest of federal authorities in the question of segregation's future. Secondly, an accounting of where these arguments succeeded and where they failed helps shed light on how various actors in American law and politics engaged with the powerfully disruptive image of the ghetto on a global stage. The transnational impact of the ghetto as a concept and the human rights framework that flowed from it revealed how activists, jurists, and federal officials negotiated the evolving impact of foreign affairs and particularly the experience and legacy of World War II in domestic civil rights law.

Unjust deeds: Restrictive covenants and the racial ghetto

In many respects, the fight against restrictive covenants offered a uniquely compelling vehicle for the human rights claims that movement lawyers ultimately crafted. To countless activists, the fates of covenants and the segregated metropolis were inextricably linked. The use of these instruments dated back to the 1890s, but had remained sparing until World War I when the Supreme Court invalidated a more popular tool of housing segregation: discriminatory municipal zoning ordinances. Covenants offered a ready alternative that skirted most constitutional vulnerabilities by keeping the mechanisms of exclusion in the hands of private citizens. By 1926, the Supreme Court had declared that it lacked jurisdiction to interfere with restrictive agreements and covenants quickly spread throughout northern cities. They multiplied anew in the 1940s as a wave of black migrants arrived in the urban North and West, searching for wartime employment. Soon, each new train from points south seemed to carry with it the seeds of an impending reckoning over the destiny of America's metropolitan areas. Housing would be at the heart of those contested futures.[7]

In the Gordian knot of discriminatory actors and tactics that kept neighborhood color lines in place, covenants held both a practical and symbolic significance. From a practical standpoint, racial restrictions provided a legal means of intimidation and eviction. They became powerful social signals, promoting cooperation and conformity among white property-owners and discouraging black home-seekers. Even when racial barricades faltered, covenants offered a respectable and relatively straightforward instrument to effect the removal of black families who had circumvented the obstacles arrayed against them and purchased covenanted homes. In city after city, these agreements made reaching beyond the boundaries of existing black neighborhoods – even by just a single block – a costly and humiliating endeavor.[8]

On a symbolic level, covenants exemplified the magnitude of the challenges that black home-seekers faced. More than any other tool of exclusion, restrictive agreements fostered and highlighted the collusion that existed between the major agents of housing discrimination: white homeowners, realtors, mortgage lenders, and governmental agencies. Covenants simultaneously relied upon individual enforcement, enjoyed the approval and promotion of the banking and real estate industries, and spread with the sanction of both local and federal housing agencies, especially the Federal Housing Administration (FHA). No other enforcement mechanism attained the same sheer level of cooperation between these various categories of actors.

In cities like Detroit, this meant that black families like the McGhees confronted a housing market where covenants blanketed an estimated 80 per cent of residences outside of the city's oldest areas. The local black press lamented that "today there is hardly an acre of unrestricted land in Wayne County." A detailed investigation in the 1940s confirmed these evaluations and found that "new restrictive agreements [came] into force almost daily." During that decade, another commentator noted, "not a single new subdivision has been established without a race restriction." Though Detroit was among the most extreme cases, cities across the country experienced the growing prevalence of covenants throughout their neighborhoods.[9]

Civil rights lawyers thus saw covenants as an urgent target in their litigation efforts. In the summer of 1945, the NAACP Legal Defense and Education Fund (LDF) – helmed by Thurgood Marshall and a small team of talented black attorneys – had declared their intention to attack the legal instruments of residential exclusion. Eighteen months later, after some contentious wrangling, the LDF petitioned the Court to hear the McGhee family's case, which Justices agreed to review late in 1947, granting *certiorari* to the McGhees, a St. Louis case brought without the LDF's involvement, and two suits from Washington, D.C. helmed by veteran NAACP activist and legal strategist Charles Hamilton Houston. The attorneys approached the Court believing that this might be their last real chance to stave off the permanent establishment of segregation in America's neighborhoods.[10]

The ghetto's global reach: Urban segregation's international implications

As the appeals in the restrictive covenant cases moved forward, LDF attorneys experimented with a broad array of claims – employing numerous legal, moral, social, and political arguments in their briefs. While the case rested primarily on the provocative contention that courts who enforced covenants were not simply neutral arbiters of private contractual disputes but instead state agents engaged in deliberate acts of discrimination, anti-covenant activists also steadily deployed the language and law of human rights that had emerged, newly invigorated, from World War II. These experiments sought to redefine the standards of postwar civil rights litigation and strengthen a revolutionary set of international principles that promised a more egalitarian future. The attorneys embraced these arguments for a number of reasons and in a variety of forms, testing to see just how far the lessons of the war would reach in the shifting sands of the postwar political climate.

The concept of human rights was not a new one in America's political ideology, but as historian Elizabeth Borgwardt has indicated, the experience of World War II profoundly shaped practical understandings of what the term signified and encompassed. For the first time, "human rights" now entered into more common parlance in the United States. In its reimagined form, the term drew from the aspirational politics found in documents like President Franklin Roosevelt's heralded "Four Freedoms," but also responded to the atrocities and exterminatory policies of Nazism. Human rights came to delineate a broad set of fundamental freedoms and egalitarian principles that deserved global attention, promotion, and protection. The creation of the United Nations (UN) soon offered a vehicle for the attainment of these goals, one that held a special resonance for many African American activists. In particular, the UN's Charter – a document that purported to define the priorities and values of a new global community – contained language pledging its members to promote "universal respect for, and observance of, human rights and fundamental freedoms for all without distinction as to race, sex, language, or religion."[11]

The NAACP and other advocacy organizations saw this wave of egalitarian sentiment as a compelling tool to strengthen a domestic civil rights movement that had already connected the international campaign against fascism to the struggle against Jim Crow at home. Appeals for racial justice couched in the language of human rights extended the most promising rhetorical, ideological, and political threads of the Allied war effort to touch critical issues on the home front. The LDF's anti-covenant campaign blended these idealistic aims with a cautionary emphasis on the repugnance of the racial ghetto as an institution of exclusion and isolation. Parallels with Nazi Germany's treatment of Jewish communities further underscored the urgency of the urban activists' cause. The language of human rights seemed ideally suited to both the moment and the issue at hand.

Yet civil rights lawyers found no fully-formed legal weapon to wield in their defense when they began exploring the utility of this framework. The vocabulary of human rights, the issues encompassed by the term, and understandings of America's national obligations under an emerging body of treaties were all evolving concepts in the aftermath of the war. Though American jurisprudence had its precedents for the proper application of international law in a domestic context, the novelty and expansiveness of the accords and ideas to which the United States now supposedly ascribed made human rights advocacy a malleable field. Legal activists deploying these claims therefore did more than find a finished instrument and put it to work in a well-defined process. Instead, they manned the forges themselves, attempting to craft new facets, sharpen particular edges, and explore innovative applications for this developing tool of resistance. Brandishing these concepts in courtrooms across the nation, anti-covenant litigators hoped to shape a new body of law and a new rationale for racial justice.[12]

The arguments they offered typically fell into three categories of use. The first was perhaps the simplest and yet the most problematic for American courts and federal officials to embrace. By casting the UN Charter and other international agreements as self-executing treaties rather than mere rhetorical pronouncements, anti-covenant lawyers insisted that the accords were binding legal obligations that superseded state laws or private contractual rights. This was an inventive attempt to federalize the question of civil rights enforcement in an era that typically left matters of racial discrimination in the hands of local jurisdictions. American courts and many state officials, however, strongly resisted this interpretation, believing it could drastically transform the nation's current legal system. Consistently, the courts rejected the idea that the UN Charter or similar documents were self-executing. Nevertheless, anti-covenant activists repeatedly pressed this question forward.[13]

A second category of human rights-based arguments tied international accords to the question of public policy. Even if courts denied the binding nature of these treaties, the attorneys reasoned, at a minimum they reflected the nation's overarching policy objectives. Federal officials and agencies had repeatedly and publicly affirmed that egalitarian treatment and the protection of human rights were critical priorities that the courts had some obligation to protect. The public policy argument gave attorneys added maneuverability by focusing on specific issues of law in a broader legal and political context. Local courts might find that restrictive covenants held to the letter of the law, but this finding ought to be counterbalanced by whether the consequences of continued enforcement might harm the health and objectives of the state itself.[14]

Public policy arguments connected closely with the third category of human rights claims that anti-covenant activists offered. More than ever before, the LDF's litigators integrated social scientific data about the consequences of racial discrimination into their legal briefs. Through reams of statistics and sociological findings on the dire state of African Americans' housing conditions, the attorneys dramatized the social, economic, moral, and human costs of urban segregation. They portrayed these communities in crisis as racial ghettos, denied access to the sort of fundamental freedoms that should have been theirs by virtue of their citizenship and their basic humanity. These arguments stretched beyond the confines of traditional legal claims and struck at the conscience of the judges who heard them while amplifying the public policy implications of continued covenant enforcement. Human rights arguments, in their relative novelty and uncertain legal footing, appealed to a sense of equity and justice that the attorneys hoped would supplant conventional precedents and shake the intransigence that had often made the law an obstacle in the pursuit of full citizenship rather than a means of its realization.[15]

Even before the LDF brought the McGhees' case to the Supreme Court in January 1948, civil rights lawyers at the local level had sensed the potential power of international human rights claims in their battles against covenants. Prominent Los Angeles attorney Loren Miller – perhaps the nation's most successful covenant fighter and an adept tactician – had caught the eye of the NAACP Board of Directors in February 1946 when he won a local housing case by using "as the basis for his arguments against such restrictions provisions of the United Nations Charter." Later in 1946, Miller expanded these claims in a brief to the California Supreme Court. He argued that the campaign against covenants endeavored to realize "the libertarian and equalitarian ideas embodied in our great state documents from the Declaration of Independence to the Charter of the United Nations." To Miller, the Charter was a modern incarnation of America's founding principles and he urged the treaty's use as a guiding basis for judicial reasoning. The egalitarianism of the Charter obligated courts to seek an end to the practices of residential discrimination. "The ghetto has no place in American life," Miller went on to write. The world had witnessed the consequences of a society governed by racial and religious prejudice and had borne a heavy cost to extinguish its spread. Few institutions could jeopardize the enduring purpose of America's sacrifice more than the racial ghetto, Miller warned.[16]

Anti-covenant arguments referencing the Charter and other international accords made their way into other courtrooms across the nation in the year ahead. The McGhee family's lawyers at the Detroit NAACP had lost their case in the Wayne County Circuit Court and hurriedly prepared an appeal to the Michigan Supreme Court that reflected the new components of human rights advocacy. Attorneys Francis Dent and Willis Graves argued that "the intervention of a World War and the declarations of statesmen and international deliberative bodies" had fomented an egalitarian public policy that ought to invalidate earlier precedents upholding covenants in Michigan. Additionally, they insisted upon the binding nature of recent foundational human rights documents, including the Atlantic Charter and the UN Charter, and maintained that American jurists could no longer support the existence of racial ghettos by sanctioning the instruments that helped make and sustain them.[17]

The Michigan Supreme Court's reaction to these claims, however, revealed the difficulties that civil rights activists faced with human rights arguments. As the court reaffirmed the McGhees' eviction, it took notice of the international dimensions to the case. Declaring that treaties between sovereign nations could not be understood to interfere with the contractual rights of individual citizens, the court dismissed postwar international human rights treaties as "merely indicative of a desirable social trend and an objective devoutly to be desired by all well-thinking peoples," rather than a controlling body of law.[18]

The court also expressed its discomfort at the way in which human rights claims pushed beyond the traditional boundaries of legal analysis. "These arguments," the court continued, "are predicated upon a plea for justice rather than the application of the settled principles of established law." Pleas rooted in a language of human rights seemed too nebulous and new to hold much legal merit, especially when they conflicted so clearly with the larger body of precedent. The court felt bound to emphasize continuity rather than an ostensibly abstract and malleable conception of justice.[19]

Dent and Graves understandably refused to back down. In a motion for the court to rehear the case, the attorneys insisted that the court rethink its priorities and weigh the extent of suffering created by residential discrimination and the growth of America's ghettos against the property rights of white homeowners. "This court," they urged bluntly, "should put human rights above property rights." The moral urgency of the issue demanded such a shift. Though the court remained unmoved, Dent and Graves never wavered in their belief that international human rights claims should be a central theme as the courtroom campaign against ghettos moved ahead.[20]

Part of what drove this determination was a resilient hope that these arguments might finally bear fruit when they reached the right ears. Once again, the attorneys looked beyond American borders for inspiration as a restrictive covenant case in the Canadian province of Ontario fueled their hopes. In *Re Drummond Wren* (1945), the Ontario High Court declared a covenant against "Jews or persons of objectionable nationality" void and used as its primary rationale a public policy argument rooted in international agreements and pronouncements including the Atlantic Charter, UN Charter, and speeches by former American president Franklin Roosevelt and British prime minister Winston Churchill. The court made its human rights emphasis even more apparent when it explicitly decried the fact that the covenant targeted Jews. This, the court argued, lent "poignancy to the matter when one considers that anti-Semitism has been a weapon in the hands of our recently-defeated enemies, and the scourge of the world." The experience of World War II cast racial discrimination with a newly objectionable meaning and demanded a greater degree of egalitarianism. Practices that perpetuated the humiliation and physical isolation of ethnic minorities could no longer enjoy the sanction of courts in the postwar world.[21]

American anti-covenant activists heralded the Canadian case as a beacon on the path forward. They cited it frequently, adopted many of the arguments that had proven successful therein, and encouraged wide dissemination of the decision. The court's ruling represented, in the words of a sympathetic commentator from the *Harvard Law Review*, "a keen realization that law must never be divorced from social needs." The *Wren* case offered "a method whereby the effects of local prejudice may be overcome, important social interests secured, and an additional flexibility imparted to the common law." Civil rights lawyers held fast to the belief that an international human rights framework might eventually lead to the sort of sweeping changes that would be needed to surmount the long history of legalized racial exclusion in the United States.[22]

When the LDF took the reins from Dent and Graves and began preparing *McGhee* for the Supreme Court in 1947, its written brief advanced an array of arguments devoted to restrictive covenants' international implications. Though the bulk of the brief revolved around the Fourteenth Amendment and the issue of discriminatory state action, the final section focused squarely on the relevance of the UN Charter to the case at hand. Using both public policy and self-executing treaty arguments, the attorneys pointed to "the right of colored persons to own and use property" as an essential human right protected by the Charter. Enforcement of covenants was "utterly destructive" to the nation's treaty obligations and ought to be struck down, they insisted. To ignore this fact would leave the United States to "stand before the world repudiating the human rights provisions of the United Nations Charter and saying of them that they are meaningless platitudes for which we reject responsibility." Doing so would not only jeopardize America's image in the eyes of the world, but risked condemning the new global spirit of concern for human rights to irrelevance.[23]

The LDF devoted even greater attention to mounting a social scientific case against the ghetto. In an extensive discussion, the attorneys cast the deprivations and inequalities that characterized residential segregation as a social catastrophe in the making. Forty pages of text and citations detailed in various ways the "nation-wide destruction of human and economic values," resulting from housing discrimination. The brief left no doubt as to the stakes of the fight. "This case," the attorneys concluded, "is not a matter of enforcing an isolated private agreement." Instead, they argued, "it is a test as to whether we will have a united nation or a country divided into areas and ghettos solely on racial or religious lines." Calling non-discriminatory access to decent housing a "basic human freedom" essential to the functioning of a democracy, the LDF attorneys invoked human rights concerns as a counterbalance to the property rights claims of white homeowners.[24]

McGhee's companion cases from Washington and St. Louis each offered variations of these same claims in their briefs and their oral arguments. They railed against the enormity of the human suffering and the various indignities that covenants forced upon black citizens. In an especially passionate argument before the Court, Charles Hamilton Houston's co-counsel from Washington, World War II veteran Phineas Indritz, described two recent cases in which judges evicted individual members of interracial families from their homes in order to enforce covenants. "The Nazi 'Nuremberg' laws," he seethed, "never went so far." Houston and Indritz were explicit in their use of the terrible lessons of Nazism and World War II in their brief as well, concluding with a declaration that: "To uphold this racial restrictive covenant would nullify the victories won by the United States and the allied nations at such great cost … and deliberately ignore the tensions and misery which the exaltation of racism has imposed on the entire world." Recreating the ghetto in the United States, they implied, would mean that although they had won the war, Americans might well lose the peace. Supreme Court Justice Harold Burton, who most observers believed to be against the LDF's cause, scrawled in his private notes that the two lawyers' arguments had been "excellent."[25]

In the end, Justice Burton joined his colleagues in a unanimous opinion that determined judicial enforcement of restrictive covenants to be unconstitutional. Anti-covenant activists heralded the decision in *Shelley v. Kraemer* as a milestone victory in pursuit of civil rights – one that led Thurgood Marshall to write privately of his conviction that now, "ghettos will be broken." To those who championed a human rights perspective, however, the decision sounded a sour note. The Court failed to address the attorneys' human rights claims, remaining, as legal scholar Bert Lockwood has argued, "thunderously silent" on the issue. *Shelley* earned the unmitigated ire of contemporary human rights scholar Paul Sayre, who minced no words in calling the Court's decision "inexcusable" and a "betrayal morally." While the anti-covenant cause prevailed, human rights arguments appeared to have faltered as an instrument of protest against the American ghetto. Though the LDF would keep these kinds of claims as part of its litigation strategy for a few years longer, the Court's unsympathetic stance in *Shelley* signaled that these arguments might be limited in their reach.[26]

Stirrings in the silence: *Shelley*'s human rights legacy

A deeper consideration, however, reveals a more substantive role for these claims, both in the anti-covenant campaign and in the broader trajectory of postwar black freedom struggles. While a human rights framework seemingly failed in the most obvious sense in *Shelley*, its use left important fingerprints on the outcome.

Anti-covenant activists used the transnational concepts of human rights and the ghetto to highlight the urgency, broaden the appeal, and test the capacities of their campaign. These largely unacknowledged stirrings beneath *Shelley's* "thunderous silence" provide a richer history of how the specter of America's racial ghettos offered a uniquely significant – albeit tenuous and contested – moment of opportunity that LDF litigators eagerly seized. They fought, without the relative caution and gradualism that characterized much of their litigation strategy, for dramatic changes to American law and the future of the nation's cities and genuinely believed for a time that their pursuit of the former had helped achieve the latter. While backlash, intransigence, and the shifting postwar international political climate would soon push the NAACP and LDF towards compromise and moderation of these more radical aims, *Shelley's* innovative attacks on urban segregation left a lasting impact on the legal struggle for racial justice.[27]

One of the largely unseen benefits that the attorneys derived from the power of the ghetto's human rights implications was an increasing receptiveness by judges at the state and federal appellate levels. The most important of these jurists, who acknowledged the moral exigencies that housing discrimination created, was D.C. Federal Circuit Court of Appeals Judge Henry Edgerton. Edgerton's rousing dissent in one of *Shelley's* companion cases explicitly embraced America's recent treaty obligations and egalitarian proclamations. Quoting the UN Charter, the *Wren* decision from Ontario, and leading public figures, Edgerton cast the fight against covenants as a repudiation of Nazism and stridently denounced restrictive agreements and "the ghetto system they enforce." His decision to use the term "ghetto" when describing the "scandalous housing conditions" in Washington was in itself a provocative move, one that he had refrained from making in a similarly vigorous anti-covenant dissent just two years earlier. By 1947, Edgerton recognized the global parallels and the moral freight that the term bore. His colleagues, no doubt aware of these connotations, delicately avoided the language. Although Edgerton stood alone in this case, his ideas had an outsized influence, especially upon his former colleague, U.S. Supreme Court Chief Justice Fred Vinson, who would write the Court's opinion in *Shelley*. Vinson's clerk later confirmed that the Chief Justice gave special attention to Edgerton's dissent as he evaluated the merits of the case. Regardless of what impact Edgerton's human rights claims had on Vinson's thinking behind the scenes, the anti-covenant campaign had already gathered momentum and encouragement from the victories – and even the impassioned defeats – that attention to human rights concerns had inspired in lower courts.[28]

The injustice of American ghettos also helped build a remarkable coalition supporting the LDF's litigation efforts. *Shelley* ultimately brought together the largest collection of *amicus curiae* briefs the Supreme Court had ever seen. More than nineteen different advocacy organizations representing a variety of racial, religious, and political groups, along with the American Federation of Labor and Congress of Industrial Organizations, supported the LDF's case. Many were deeply attuned to the human rights implications of the issue at hand and among the most enthusiastic supporters were five Jewish interest groups that drew direct links between historical iterations of the European ghetto and the emergence of ghettos in the United States. The American Jewish Congress, American Jewish Committee, the Anti-Defamation League, Jewish Labor Committee, and Jewish War Veterans of the United States of America each joined the pleadings as interested parties. Though they refrained from making arguments directly rooted in international treaty law – primarily to avoid repetition across the large number of briefs – their filings revealed how global connotations of the ghetto loomed large in America's postwar sociopolitical milieu.[29]

Calling restrictive covenants "instruments of bigotry," Jewish activists reminded the Court that their organizations were "peculiarly alert to the dangers" that covenants posed. "Jewish experience under European despotism," they continued, "gave rise to the word 'ghetto.' The threat of revival of that institution – implicit in the mushroom growth in almost every major American city of racial restrictive covenants – demands intercession in these cases." These groups saw the moral and human cost of allowing ghettos to survive in America as a threat that no one could afford to take lightly. As a result, they provided not only supporting briefs, but also financial contributions that underwrote a significant portion of the litigation's costs and they worked closely with LDF attorneys to refine courtroom strategies and gather other coalition members. This cooperation helped to cement a lasting alliance that lived on well after *Shelley*.[30]

The LDF's human rights arguments also furthered shifts underway within the organization itself. Anti-covenant lawyers embarked upon a new pattern of making social scientific data a much more prominent component of their litigation strategy, emphasizing the lived experiences of African American communities and more expansive notions of justice as grounds for courts to move beyond the judicial orthodoxies of decades past. This strategic transition began with *Shelley*, in part because of the volume of social scientific literature that had emerged on urban segregation and the uniquely powerful moral claims that the racial ghetto as a transnational historical concept made possible.[31]

Invoking the American ghetto as an international human rights crisis played a key part in another significant development affecting the outcome of the anti-covenant campaign: the intervention of the Department of Justice (DOJ) on behalf of the LDF's clients. Though the DOJ had taken steps to facilitate civil rights litigation in preceding years, its intercession in *Shelley* marked a significant and promising departure from standard practice, one that likely would not have occurred at this moment without the long shadow cast by the specter of racial ghettos in America. Indeed, *Shelley* became the first time in history that the DOJ participated in a civil rights case between private parties. This portended the growth of a new partnership between the LDF and the federal government and evidenced the impact of human rights arguments on official attitudes towards the domestic civil rights protest.[32]

Human rights claims and fears about the growth of ghettos figured prominently in the LDF's efforts to enlist the DOJ's aid. This extensive lobbying also coincided with the circulation of *An Appeal to the World*, the NAACP's petition for UN intervention in American race relations. Here, the NAACP and LDF each experimented with new ways to wield the instrument of postwar international human rights law in pursuit of racial justice. The *Appeal* did not beget the Justice Department's intervention in *Shelley*; in fact, federal officials fumed about the potential embarrassment it could cause and the perceived irresponsibility of the NAACP's public plea. But the release of the document was part of the larger body of pressure on the Attorney General's office and likely encouraged the DOJ to address the LDF's human rights concerns more explicitly in its arguments to the Court.[33]

The government's brief was composed primarily by a group of Jewish attorneys who volunteered their services from various divisions in the DOJ. Though they removed their names from the finished product – fearing that anti-Semitism might color the public reception of their arguments – their work unequivocally condemned ethnic discrimination in housing and depicted urban segregation as an urgent social and moral crisis with international ramifications. Covenants were the products of "ignorance, bigotry and prejudice," posed an imminent danger to America's "free institutions," and were "abhorrent to the law of the land." The brief pointed to the crisis state of many segregated urban communities and the "peculiarly disintegrating acid which enforced segregation distills." Individuals barred from access to decent homes, the authors wrote, found "there is no life in the accepted sense of the word; liberty is a mockery, and the right to pursue happiness a phrase without meaning, empty of hope and reality." In the postwar world, they argued, racial isolation and exclusion were simply un-American practices. Mirroring the LDF's public policy claims, the brief also insisted that perpetuating racial inequality through judicial acts of the state would serve only to embarrass the nation and exacerbate the destructive consequences of bigotry on a global stage. The DOJ's zealous intervention carried considerable weight in the Supreme Court's deliberations and played a key role in the LDF's victory.[34]

Still, the DOJ's approach reflected some of the tensions swirling around the novelty of postwar human rights obligations. The brief embodied both the enthusiastic egalitarianism that fueled the campaign against American racial ghettos and the anxious uncertainties of international law in this moment. The authors at the Justice Department made calculated concessions to the more cautious members of President Harry Truman's administration. Historian Rowland Brucken has detailed the efforts of State Department officials to temper the brief's tone regarding the applicability of international treaties to America's domestic legal concerns and the brief purposefully avoided any discussion of these accords as self-executing obligations. Additionally, the DOJ authors trod lightly in their use of the term "ghetto" to describe conditions in American cities, preferring instead less charged expressions such as "slum areas." In contrast to anti-covenant litigators who regularly employed this language, the "ghetto" appeared only a single time in the 130-page DOJ brief – as part of a quote from another source – and just once in the hour-long oral argument by the Solicitor General. This sparing use likely reflected a conscious restraint and an awareness of the disruptive symbolic power of the term. The authors believed the concept applied to American cities, but apparently felt compelled to curb their language strategically to afford a greater chance of consensus within the Truman administration and success in Court. This modeled the type of compromise and moderation that historian Carol Anderson has argued the NAACP and LDF increasingly pursued as a means of strengthening their relationship with federal officials in the years ahead.[35]

Shelley, however, marked a crucial moment before the LDF abandoned its more expansive human rights claims. LDF litigators carried the lessons of World War II and the historical costliness of the ghetto into American courtrooms and fashioned a fairly radical set of demands for change and challenges to legal tradition from these legacies. The attorneys' insistence that courts ought to treat urban segregation as a human rights crisis and apply the principles of international law to domestic acts of discrimination, while not the centerpiece of their campaign, nonetheless helped to strengthen a civil rights coalition, build a partnership between the LDF and the Justice Department, shape the LDF's use of social scientific data in the courtroom, and shake loose some of the intransigence that had stymied progress towards legal equality for decades. In short, this campaign helped to transform and revolutionize the legal sphere of the civil rights movement, even as it failed to stop the racial ghetto from becoming a fixture of American life.[36]

The restrictive covenant cases embodied the optimism and creativity of men and women who dared to imagine a future without ghettos, who challenged the injustice and indignity of America's segregated cities, and who believed that they might make racial inequality into a dying vestige of a bygone era. They seized upon the idea of human rights and fought to bring considerations of justice to the forefront of American jurisprudence. Their portrayal of the American ghetto as a human rights crisis would be one tool among many in this fight, but it was a more powerful and consequential tactic than historians have generally appreciated.

Still, one of the most significant legacies of this campaign against urban segregation would be found not in any office or agency or advocacy group, but instead in the homes of those individuals who risked so much to stay and fight for a more just future. The experiences of those like Orsel and Minnie McGhee offered eloquent testimony to the fact that the human rights claims pervading the anti-covenant campaign were far more than rhetorical tactics or legal ploys. In the aftermath of the Supreme Court's decision, Mr. McGhee spoke about what it meant to know that at last he could lay undisputed claim to this home of his choosing. He reflected the resolve and sacrifice that the battle had taken, but he also hinted that something greater had been at stake. To him, the Court's decision meant that now he could "feel that life is worth living and that eventually true democracy will be a reality in the United States." The McGhees had always understood their struggle as one not just for equality and opportunity, but for a recognition of their basic human dignity. And they had won. It was a victory they carried with them every day over the decades they would spend living in that same little bungalow on Seebaldt Avenue.[37]

Notes

1   Minnie McGhee Interview with Margaret Ward (27 October 1978) in Burton Historical Collection, Detroit Public Library, Detroit, Mich.

2 *McGhee v. Sipes* 334 U.S. 1 (1948), Transcript of Record, 22; McGhee interview; Kevin Boyle, *Arc of Justice: A Saga of Race, Civil Rights, and Murder in the Jazz Age* (New York: Holt, 2004).

3 *McGhee* (1948), Transcript of Record, 21–23; *U.S. News & World Report*, January 30, 1948; W.E.B. Du Bois, "Civil Rights Legislation Before and After the Passage of the 14th Amendment," January 25, 1947, in Francis Dent Collection, Box 10, Folder 3 Charles Wright Museum, Detroit, Mich.; Robert Weaver, *The Negro Ghetto* (New York: Harcourt Brace, 1948), 232; President's Committee on Civil Rights, *To Secure These Rights* (Washington, DC U.S. Government Printing Office, 1947), 68. On covenants: Wendy Plotkin, *Deeds of Mistrust: Race, Housing, and Restrictive Covenants in Chicago, 1900–1953* (Ph.D. Dissertation: University of Illinois Chicago, 1999); Michael Jones-Correa, "Origins and Diffusion of Racial Restrictive Covenants," *Political Science Quarterly* 115.4 (2000–2001): 541–568; Richard Brooks and Carol Rose, *Saving the Neighborhood: Racially Restrictive Covenants, Law, and Social Norms* (Cambridge: Harvard University Press, 2013).

4 McGhee interview.

5 Clement Vose, *Caucasians Only: The Supreme Court, the NAACP, and the Restrictive Covenant Cases* (Berkeley: University of California Press, 1959), 50–73.

6 The four cases were *McGhee v. Sipes, Shelley v. Kraemer* 334 U.S. 1 (1948), *Hurd v. Hodge* 334 U.S. 24 (1948), and *Urciolo v. Hodge* 334 U.S. 24 (1948). Although the state cases *Shelley* and *McGhee* were decided separately from *Hurd* and *Urciolo*, all four cases are often discussed in concert. On the litigation, see Vose, *Caucasians Only* and Jeffrey D. Gonda, *Unjust Deeds: The Restrictive Covenant Cases and the Making of the Civil Rights Movement* (Chapel Hill: UNC Press, 2015). See also Leland Ware, "Invisible Walls: An Examination of the Legal Strategy of the Restrictive Covenant Cases," *Washington University Law Quarterly* 67 (1989): 768–771; Carol Rose, "Property Stories: *Shelley v. Kraemer*" in *Property Stories*, eds. Gerald Korngold and Andrew Morriss (New York: Foundation Press, 2004): 169–200; Wendell Pritchett, "*Shelley v. Kraemer:* Racial Liberalism and the U.S. Supreme Court" in *Civil Rights Stories*, eds. Myriam Gilles and Risa Goluboff (New York: Foundation Press, 2008): 5–23.

7 Jones-Correa, "Origins"; *Corrigan v. Buckley* 271 U.S. 323 (1926); Isabel Wilkerson, *The Warmth of Other Suns: The Epic Story of America's Great Migration* (New York: Random House, 2010).

8 On covenants as social signals, see Brooks and Rose, *Saving*.

9 Lester Velie, "Housing: Detroit's Time Bomb," *Collier's* 118.21 (1946), 15; *Michigan Chronicle* 25 January 1947; Harold Black, "Restrictive Covenants in Relation to Segregated Negro Housing in Detroit" (M.A. thesis: Wayne University, 1947), 5–6.

10 Jeffrey D. Gonda, "Litigating Racial Justice at the Grassroots," *Supreme Court History* 39.3 (2014): 329–346.

11 Elizabeth Borgwardt, *New Deal for the World: America's Vision for Human Rights* (Cambridge: Harvard University Press, 2005), 53–61; Elizabeth Borgwardt, "FDR's Four Freedoms and Wartime Transformations in American's Discourse of Rights," in *Bringing Human Rights Home: A History of Human Rights in the United States, Vol. 1*, eds. Cynthia Soohoo et al. (Westport: Praeger, 2008), 41–67; Kenneth Cmiel, "The Recent History of Human Rights," *American Historical Review* 109 (2004): 117–135. See also UN Charter, Art. 55.

12 Bert Lockwood, "The UN Charter and U.S. Civil Rights Litigation: 1946–1955," *Iowa Law Review* 69 (1984): 901–956; Carol Anderson, *Eyes Off the Prize: The United Nations and the African American Struggle for Human Rights, 1944–1955* (New York: Cambridge University Press, 2003).

13 Lockwood, "UN Charter," 916.

14 "Anti-discrimination Legislation and International Declarations," *University of Chicago Law Review* 13.4 (1946): 477–486.

15 On sociological arguments, see Gonda, *Unjust Deeds*, 135–150.

16 "Feb. 1946 Meeting of the Board" in NAACP Papers (microfilm) – Part 1, Reel 7; Respondent's Brief, *Anderson v. Auseth* (1946) in Loren Miller Papers, Box 42, Folder

2, Huntington Library, San Marino, Calif. On Miller, see Kenneth Mack, *Representing the Race: The Creation of the Civil Rights Lawyer* (Cambridge: Harvard University Press, 2012), 181–206; Amina Hassan, *Loren Miller: Civil Rights Attorney and Journalist* (Norman: University of Oklahoma Press, 2015).

17 *McGhee* (1948), Transcript of Record, 16–17; "Restrictive Covenants Violate UN Charter," 14 February 1947 in NAACP – Part 5, Reel 21.

18 *McGhee* (1948), Transcript of Record, 67.

19 Ibid., 67–69; Vose, *Caucasians Only*, 148–150.

20 *McGhee* (1948), Transcript of Record, 75–76.

21 *Re Drummond Wren*, 4 D.L.R. 674 (1945).

22 "Discriminatory Covenant on Ontario Land Held Invalid," *Harvard Law Review* 59.5 (1946): 804–805. A *University of Chicago Law Review* note was more pessimistic, but hoped that *Wren* might be "an invitation to those state courts which are unsympathetic to restrictive covenants to limit the influence of the *Corrigan* decision." "Antidiscrimination Legislation," 485–486. See also Arthur Banks, "International Law and the Fourteenth Amendment," *Phylon* 9.1 (1948): 57–59.

23 *McGhee* (1948), Brief for Petitioners, 84–90.

24 Ibid., 47, 90–91.

25 Oral Presentation by Phineas Indritz, 16 January 1948 in Phineas Indritz Papers, Box B21, Folder 12, Howard Law Library, Washington, D.C. *Hurd* (1948), Brief for Petitioners, 131; Harold Burton Diary, 1948 in Harold H. Burton Papers (Microfilm Reel 2, Manuscripts Division, Library of Congress, Washington, D.C.).

26 Thurgood Marshall to James Bush, 24 May 1948 in NAACP – Part 5, Reel 22; Lockwood, "UN Charter," 935; Paul Sayre, "*Shelley v. Kraemer* and United Nations Law," *Iowa Law Review* 34.1 (1948): 11. Lockwood muses that perhaps the Justices addressed the UN Charter in conference or in draft opinions. A review of the Justices' papers reveals that no such references appeared in the draft opinions and indicates that the topic did not come up in conference. Lockwood maintains, however, that regardless of the Court's silence on the issue, the Charter's principles likely helped to shape the Court's new approach to the Fourteenth Amendment that emerged in the postwar period. Lockwood, "UN Charter," 936.

27 On shifting political climate: Azza Salama Layton, *International Politics and Civil Rights Policies in the United States, 1941–1960* (New York: Cambridge University Press, 2000); Mary Dudziak, *Cold War Civil Rights: Race and the Image of American Democracy* (Princeton: Princeton University Press, 2000).

28 *Hurd v. Hodge* 162 F.2d. 233, 244–245 (D.C. Circuit, 1947, Edgerton Dissent); Francis Allen, "Remembering *Shelley v. Kraemer*," *Washington University Law Quarterly* 67 (1989): 719–720. For other examples, see *Fairchild v. Raines* 24 Cal.2d 818, 831–835 (Cal. Supreme Court, 1944, Traynor Concurrence); *Mays v. Burgess* 147 F.2d 869, 873–878 (D.C. Circuit, 1945, Edgerton Dissent).

29 Vose, *Caucasians Only*, ix, 163–167.

30 *Shelley* (1948), Consolidated Brief of American Jewish Committee, et al. as *Amici Curiae*, 2–5. On Jewish activists' contributions, see Will Maslow to Thurgood Marshall, 6 February 1947 in NAACP – Part 5, Reel 22; Methods of Attacking Restrictive Covenants, 6 September 1947 in NAACP – Part 5, Reel 22; Newman Levy to Phineas Indritz, 15 August 1947 in NAACP – Part 5, Reel 22; Stuart Svonkin *Jews Against Prejudice: American Jews and the Fight for Civil Liberties* (New York: Columbia University Press, 1997), esp. chapter 4.

31 Gonda, *Unjust Deeds*, 194–218.

32 Layton, *International Politics*, 111–113.

33 Walter White to Tom Clark, 12 September 1947 in NAACP – Part 5, Reel 21; Anderson, *Eyes Off*, 78–112 and 140–153; NAACP, *Appeal to the World* (New York: NAACP, 1947); Layton, *International Politics*, 48–57.

34 *Shelley* (1948), Brief for the United States as *Amicus Curiae*, 4, 97–123; Tom Clark and Philip Perlman, *Prejudice and Property: An Historic Brief Against Racial Covenants*

(Washington: Public Affairs Press, 1948), 14; Argument Prepared by Philip Perlman, 15 January 1948 in NAACP – Part 5, Reel 21; Philip Elman and Norman Silber, "The Solicitor General's Office," *Harvard Law Review* 100.4 (1987): 818–819.

35 Clark and Perlman, *Prejudice*, 18; Argument Prepared by Philip Perlman, 15 January 1948 in NAACP – Part 5, Reel 21. Rowland Brucken, *A Most Uncertain Crusade: The United States, The United Nations, and Human Rights, 1941–1953* (Dekalb: Northern Illinois University Press, 2014), 119–121. Brucken appears to misstate the NAACP's attitude towards claims involving the UN, suggesting that the NAACP's "aggressive litigation strategy" operated "without any reference to the United Nations." On NAACP's relationship with human rights arguments, see Anderson, *Eyes Off* and Carol Anderson, "A Hollow Mockery: African Americans, White Supremacy, and the Development of Human Rights in the United States," in *Bringing Human Rights Home*, 68–99.

36 It was a testament to the revolutionary potential of these claims that they would live on in the hands of other organizations in the decades ahead, enduring and evolving just as the ghetto itself did. See the Black Panthers' appeals for UN oversight in Joshua Bloom and Waldo Martin, Jr., *Black Against Empire: The History and Politics of the Black Panther Party* (Berkeley: University of California Press, 2013), 122–124, and similar claims from Malcolm X in Nikhil Singh, *Black is a Country: Race and the Unfinished Struggle for Democracy* (Cambridge: Harvard University Press, 2004), 187–189.

37 *Michigan Chronicle* 8 May 1948; McGhee interview.

14

UNMAKING THE GHETTO

Community development and persistent social inequality in Brooklyn, Los Angeles, and Philadelphia

Brian Purnell

Introduction

In the 1950s and 1960s, Elsie Richardson, economic development director of the Central Brooklyn Coordinating Council, a consortium of over 90 community-based organizations in predominantly black and Latino communities in north-central Brooklyn, argued that all the books and studies and tours of the ghetto by outsiders perpetuated political inaction. When faced with giving another tour of Bedford-Stuyvesant, Brooklyn's largest black community, in February 1966 – this time to the junior U.S. senator from New York, Robert F. Kennedy – Richardson scoffed, "What, another tour? Are we to be punished by being forced again to look at what we look at all the time? We've been studied to death. The writers of sociology books have milked us of all the information." Her colleague, Ruth Goring, an assistant to the Brooklyn Borough President, concurred. "You know what, I'm tired, Mr. Kennedy," she said. "We got to have something concrete now, not tomorrow, yesterday."[1]

Goring and Richardson's frustrations extended to scholars. Decades of research uncovered how ghettos formed. They provided theories on the people who lived in America's ghettos, their cultures and behaviors, how they dealt with the many social problems in their communities. But if ghettos could be *made*, if they could come into existence at certain times and in certain places, could they then be *unmade*? Could the "something concrete" that Ruth Goring demanded of Senator Kennedy actually come to ghettos in America?

Answers to this question often depend on how one thinks about ghettos' histories. People's actions in time and space, and social relations of power that shaped their policies, created ghettos. Ghettos did not come into existence because of the culture and behavior of their residents, nor have ghettos remained fixed, frozen in time. Like any other social space, over the years they have experienced social and economic changes. And when ghettos change, they reconfigure along shifting applications of social power that stem from the wider political, economic, and cultural worlds in which ghettos exist. As the historian Arnold Hirsch wrote, "The real tragedy surrounding the emergence of the modern ghetto is not that it has been inherited but that it has been periodically renewed and strengthened. Fresh decisions, not the mere acquiescence to old ones, reinforced and shaped the contemporary black metropolis."[2] If certain applications of social power made ghettos, then alternative power relations can unmake ghettos.

The histories of those alternative power relations in ghettos must move beyond the race–class–space analytical trinity that shapes so much of how scholars, journalists, and politicians understand the existence of ghettos in American life. Most often, analysts of American ghettos have focused on race, especially blackness; class, especially extreme poverty; and spatial mismatches that grew between laborers who lived in ghettos and industries and capital that relocated away from cities, first to suburbs, then to the "Sunbelt South," then to nations overseas. Race, class, and space have served as the most important indicators of social inequality in American ghettos.[3] In order to develop a fuller understanding of how activists tried to *unmake* ghettos, historians must also add analyses of gender to this trinity.

Stereotypes about pervasive "matriarchies" that promoted social instability in ghettos promoted arguments for increasing black male leadership as the most important way to expand political and economic power in American ghettos. Indeed, the trope of the black matriarchy and policy makers' devotion to manpower development and training job sectors traditionally dominated by men had inestimable influence over past attempts to unmake ghettos.[4] But as Annelise Orleck, Rhonda Y. Williams, Premilla Nadesen, and others have shown, from the mid-to-late 1960s up through the 1980s, black women led some of the most successful social, economic, and political activism that, in part, worked to unmake the power dynamics that had sustained ghettos for decades.[5] When historians, social scientists, and policy makers ignore, or dismiss, these women, we further imperil our knowledge of dynamic efforts to unmake black ghettos.

After a brief overview of the history that made American ghettos, this essay presents case studies to show how three black activist communities worked in the mid-to-late 1960s to unmake ghettos. In each case, activists directly attacked the social relations of power race, space, and class that perpetuated economic and social inequality in their communities. The Brooklyn case study specifically shows the important work that black women did in unmaking the ghetto, and what was lost when men diminished their leadership roles.

Making the ghetto

For nearly 120 years, sociologists and historians have focused research on black people in American cities. Black people in cities became a cornerstone of American scientific sociology as early as 1899.[6] U.S. historians did not develop a significant subfield in African American urban history until the mid 1960s.[7] This changed after 1968. African American urban history blossomed throughout the 1970s; flagged a bit during the 1980s; rejuvenated in 1983 with the publication of *Making the Second Ghetto*, by Arnold Hirsch, and in 1985 with Joe William Trotter, Jr.'s *Black Milwaukee*; and since then has produced some of the best scholarly work in the field of U.S. history.[8]

The ghetto, both as a physical place and an idea, looms large in historical research on blacks in U.S. cities.[9] With few exceptions, much of the scholarship on African American urban history that appeared between the 1960s and the 1980s concerned itself with "ghetto formation."[10] These studies emphasized the political, economic, and social processes that created "compulsory, segregated, and enclosed" black urban communities in the United States.[11]

Histories of ghetto formation begin in the late-nineteenth century when the first significant cohort of black migrants moved to cities in the northeast and Midwest. When an even larger wave of black migrants hit northeastern and Midwestern cities during the 1910s, discernable black metropolises emerged. Gilbert Osofsky and other historians writing in the 1960s called these black urban communities ghettos. Like Jews forced by anti-Semitism to live in enclosed areas of European cities, racial discrimination and poverty forced black people in American cities into specific residential areas and made black renters and homeowners into captives of the ghetto.

Exploitative power imbalances sustained ghettos. Landlords charged black people a "race tax": higher rents compared to what whites paid to live in older, inferior housing. Over time, public institutions and services, like schools and sanitation, declined. Poor, working, and middle-class residents in ghettos sustained local black civic institutions like churches, benevolent societies, fraternal organizations, civil rights groups, and neighborhood-based businesses. Black-owned businesses co-existed with white ones. An institutional ghetto formed where black people from diverse class backgrounds lived together. They could access a variety of goods and services. Even in a racist jobs sector, most black people worked.[12]

Over time, the institutional ghetto changed. Arnold Hirsch identified that a "second ghetto" phase began during the New Deal and lasted through the early 1960s. Public housing developed along racial lines when planners adhered to the federal government's "neighborhood composition rule," which prevented public housing developments from changing an area's racial demography. White residents policed these lines with violence.[13]

Suburbanization accelerated ghettoization. Racially exclusive suburbs drew whites out of cities. Automation pushed urban jobs away from the city. In urban housing markets, racially restrictive covenants confined blacks to ghettos. Redlining practices underdeveloped black ghettos when they directed private and public investments into homes away from "undesirable" areas and channeled them into "safe," "stable" areas. Urban homeownership through contract buying became a predatory practice that fleeced black people of their savings and their ability to build wealth through home equity.[14] These exercises of social power deposited economic insecurity and material want into black ghettos.

Starting in the 1940s, but increasing from the 1960s–1990s when many metropolitan suburbs desegregated, middle-class blacks moved out of ghettos.[15] Urban working-class blacks suffered job losses brought on by de-industrialization. Police brutality and harassment sparked several uprisings during the mid-to-late 1960s. Vigorous protest movements emerged, but protest alone could not stem the tide of ghettoization and joblessness. By the late-1970s and into the 1980s and 1990s, black ghettos became "distressed black neighborhoods," or "jobless ghettos." Churches, fraternal organizations, block associations, political clubs, and activists' organizations in ghettos became overwhelmed by poverty, crime, health hazards, insufficient municipal services, and declining public institutions, especially in the areas of housing, police, education, health, and sanitation. Black civil society never disappeared from ghettos, but in the late-twentieth century, it fought for its life.[16]

Scholars who extended the black ghetto's historical timeline past the 1960s broke away from analytical narratives of "ghetto formation." Gilbert Osofsky's argument that an "enduring ghetto" shaped by a "tragic sameness" of racism and misery defined a century of black urban life and froze ghettos in time.[17] Is it any wonder that Americans understood the black ghetto as primarily a trope, metaphor, and signifier for urban black people? But when historians moved past the formation stage, they brought the black ghetto back into history. They returned analysis of how power operated in specific contexts to the ghetto. They argued that black residents of American ghettos were more than an "underclass." They were "city-makers," too.[18]

In Craig Wilder's book, *A Covenant with Color*, race shaped four centuries of social power in an American city. Wilder argued against the idea of black ghettos as synonyms for America's urban black culture, or as a synonym for the black urban neighborhood. "The ghetto is not so much a place," he wrote, "as it is a relationship – the physical manifestation of a perverse imbalance in social power."

> The ghetto is not the cause of social pathology, it is its destination (...) It cannot be defined by the people who occupy it but by the struggles that place them there. It is not social inequality but the attempt to predetermine the burden of social inequality. Thus ghettos are different sizes, have different demographics, and suffer different conditions. They have in common only the lack of power that allows their residents to be physically concentrated and socially targeted."[19]

Black people did not make ghettos, at least not by themselves. Power inequities that shaped black urban life made ghettos places that harbored specific historical conditions – widespread joblessness, high levels of crime, crumbling public infrastructures – in which all different kinds of black people had to live. "The ghetto gave color an unmistakable, undeniable, and unavoidable daily reality," Wilder concluded, "a reality that black people were accused of creating."

The ghetto was – and is – a product of historical relations of power that exist in housing, employment, policing, education, electoral politics, finance, banking, insurance, consumerism, taxation, credit markets, debt markets, health care, child care, welfare, environmental conditions, and discursive control of public and private spaces. Power flows through these social practices, away from the ghetto. The waste of this transfer of power becomes the social struggles that urban blacks confront in their everyday lives. Citizens in ghettos, Marcus Hunter argues, "might also be seen as *citymakers*," people whose diverse forms of agency shape urban life in multiple ways. If we only see ghettos as a metaphor, or a trope, for black people, then we mask the relations of power that created and, over time, maintained black ghettos. Tropes about ghettos serve to blame the ghetto's victims for their very existence.[20]

Unmaking the ghetto

Different forms of black protest rocked American ghettos in the decades after World War II. Local people organized to open jobs, desegregate schools, increase municipal services, end police brutality, improve neighborhood conditions, integrate housing, and strengthen their political and economic powers. By the middle of the 1960s, despite activists' best efforts, too few structural changes had occurred in the power dynamics that controlled education, housing, policing, and employment. American ghettos rose up in rebellion. The smoldering buildings and pitched battles with police and national guardsmen indicated that, one way or another, people who lived in American ghettos would fight for the ghetto's "ultimate dissolution as an enforced state of existence."[21]

Comprehensive development initiatives designed to unmake black ghettos started in the mid-to-late 1960s. They involved everything from housing rehabilitation to capital infrastructure projects, to health and wellness, to promotion of the arts, to youth organizing. In theory, these early stages of unmaking the ghetto happened through community involvement and resident empowerment.

The history of Community Development Corporations (CDCs) from the mid-1960s through the late-1970s reveals how the hopefulness engendered by the War on Poverty, and the massive investment of money into ghetto development projects, began to unmake some, but not all, of the social inequalities, economic disinvestment structures, and political disconnections that constructed and maintained black ghettos. Local people, mostly from the middle class, experienced as organizers and powerbrokers, led these institutions. For a time, they administered comprehensive development programs. Public and private funding from the federal government and from philanthropies like the Ford Foundation sustained these programs with tens of millions of dollars (see Figures 14.1 and 14.2). CDCs strengthened civil society in America's ghettos by bringing together internal institutions, like churches and community improvement associations, and powerful external institutions, like banks and philanthropies. Early CDCs funneled power into the ghetto, and channeled power that already existed in the ghetto, in order to transform these places from destinations of social inequity into the beautiful, vibrant, dynamic places their residents and leaders always knew existed.[22]

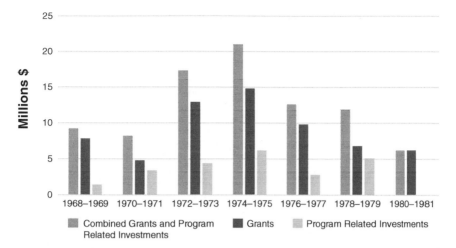

FIGURE 14.1 Ford Foundation Biennial CDC Grant total, 1968–1980. Data compiled from Sol Chafkin, "Some observations on Ford Foundation Community Development Corporations and their significance for implementation of government policies and programs," October 1977, in Rockefeller Archives Center, Ford Foundation Records, National Affairs, Office Files of Thomas Cooney, FA 653, Box 9

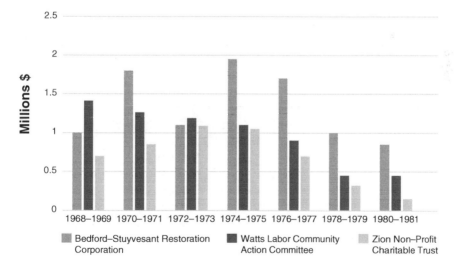

FIGURE 14.2 Ford Foundation Biennial Grants. Data compiled from Sol Chafkin, "Some observations on Ford Foundation Community Development Corporations and their significance for implementation of government policies and programs," October 1977, in Rockefeller Archives Center, Ford Foundation Records, National Affairs, Office Files of Thomas Cooney, FA 653, Box 9

CDCs originated during an early "war on the War on Poverty."[23] The promise of poor people's "maximum feasible participation" in anti-poverty work was part of the Economic Opportunity Act.[24] As one scholar summarized, the CDC as a poverty-fighting institution "evolved as a reaction to the promise, the accomplishments, and the disappointments" of community action agencies (CAAs). From 1966 to 1968, the efforts of New York Senators Robert F. Kennedy and Jacob Javitz and leaders at the Ford Foundation created CDCs. In 1967, Kennedy and Javitz co-sponsored an amendment to the Economic Opportunity Act that funded place-based, "locally initiated community corporations," designed to solve the most pressing problems in poor communities. The Ford Foundation and the federal government became the CDCs' most significant funders. One scholar has argued that the Ford Foundation used urban CDCs as a way to manufacture a white, elite, liberal takeover of the Black Power Movement's demand for "community control" of political and economic institutions in black ghettos. "Under government and foundation auspices," writes Alice O'Connor, "CDCs were de-radicalized and professionalized and they developed a keener eye for the bottom line. It was in this form that the CDC movement expanded and diversified in the 1970s and became a central institution for economic development in black ghettos."[25]

The first generation of CDCs lasted until roughly 1980. It is worth looking at well-funded, politically connected, first-generation urban CDCs, ones that used their big budgets or influential leaders to initiate dynamic and comprehensive community development programs in black ghettos. Three early CDCs stand out for the amount of funding they received, the types of comprehensive development projects they initiated to unmake ghettos, and the diverse types of women and men who led them. The Bedford-Stuyvesant Restoration Corporation, located in Brooklyn, New York, was one of the first and largest CDCs in the country. It was an exemplar of the possibilities of comprehensive community development in an American ghetto. The Watts Labor Community Action Committee, located in Los Angeles, CA, began in early 1965 as a way to channel black residents' connections to the traditions and resources of the labor movement into dynamic community redevelopment initiatives. It grew like a phoenix from the rubble of the 1965 uprising, and remade the area's built environment. The Zion Non-Profit Charitable Trust, located in Philadelphia, PA, mobilized one of the most powerful forms of social capital in black urban communities, black church members, into a force of economic development. The early history of these CDCs reveals a time when bold approaches to community development in American ghettos happened. It seemed possible that concrete actions would unmake the inequality that created and perpetuated ghettoization.

Three aspects these early CDCs shared were community organizing roots, comprehensive development plans, and large amounts of political and financial support. During the golden age of CDCs, these institutions worked to unmake the maldistribution of power that defined ghettos with bottom-up and top-down leadership. They would tackle many different issues – housing, jobs, health, the arts, infrastructure – at once. They enjoyed generous and continuous financial support. The more these CDCs drifted away from those three characteristics, the less effective they became as institutions that could unmake ghettos.

"Everything that we do has to be in order to improve this community": The Watts Labor Community Action Committee in Los Angeles

Many narratives of the Watts Labor Community Action Committee (WLCAC) begin with the violence that erupted in Los Angeles in 1965, but it would probably be more accurate to situate the WLCAC in a longer and broader history of the black community in Los Angeles and the labor movement's organizing traditions. In the 1910s and 1920s, whites' housing discrimination practices forced blacks into two small ghettos in the Central Avenue district and in Watts, a residential area seven miles south of downtown Los Angeles. African American Angelinos formed civil rights groups and their own newspaper to protest against racial discrimination. Most blacks in LA were poor and working class, but wartime migration and job opportunities in defense industries ballooned the black population to 70,000 in 1946. A class of black homeowners arose. Civil rights activism after the 1940s fought to integrate schools, jobs, and housing, but many of those efforts failed, or achieved only partial victories. Black civil rights activists failed to defeat a state-wide ban on open housing, but they gained some seats on the city council. When the War on Poverty created opportunities for local black leaders to shape community action projects, black Angelinos fought with the mayor – and each other – to create an independent development agency that could control anti-poverty government funds.[26]

Black leaders in Los Angeles found their independent anti-poverty institution in the WLCAC. In the spring of 1965, the United Auto Workers (UAW) wanted to take the industrial trade union organizing model, which centered on the workplace, and adjust it to organize poor communities in Los Angeles. During World War II, the need for manpower in defense industries and Roosevelt's executive order mandating nondiscrimination practices in businesses under contract with the government gave black workers inroads into unionized manufacturing and industrial labor. Black union workers became a solid backbone of the post-war black leadership class in Los Angeles. Ted Watkins was one of those workers. He eventually became an organizer with the UAW, and the leader of the WLCAC.

Born in Meridian, Mississippi, in 1923, Watkins moved west in 1938 and eventually went to work at a Ford plant in Pico Rivera in 1949. Watkins brought skills and experience to Ford. "I had been working on automobiles since I was almost seven years old, I guess, one way or the other," Watkins remembered, "and the job that I had when I went in the army was being an automobile repair man, body and fender and painting." He became a leader in his UAW local, first as a way to fight against racial discrimination in his union and his shop. Blacks were only 8% of the shop, Watkins recalled. He became leader of the recreation committee and helped break down some of the social barriers that separated the workers by organizing "successful recreational activities, Christmas parties, picnics and all of that." Watkins earned his fellow workers' respect. He became a member of the bargaining committee. In the 1960s, he was appointed by the UAW president to serve as a representative on the international union's board. And when the UAW wanted to turn its attention to community-organizing efforts, Watkins was ready to lead. "Because of the kind of conditions that existed in the community where we lived," Watkins remembered, "we felt that some of the same organizing capabilities and concessions and bargaining arrangements could be made with some of the politicians who supposedly represented this area."[27] By March 1966, the small WLCAC group assembled by the UAW elected Watkins chairman.

Watkins said that the WLCAC's purpose was to "change the face of Watts."[28] He saw the WLCAC's purpose for existing as "to demonstrate that it cares about Watts and its residents." That sense of care would spread from WLCAC and promote what Watkins called "community moral discipline." When residents cared for the entire community – their homes, their streets, the empty lots scattered throughout an area – and when they strengthened the moral discipline in the community, they then had a strong foundation upon which to build new physical structures. From there, economic development would prosper. In a time of heightened calls for radicalism and militancy, Watkins stressed that the WLCAC was "not political or psychological." "The most militant thing you can do is economic," Watkins argued. "Economic power is what counts."[29]

To foster economic power in Watts, however, the WLCAC had to counteract structures of power that undermined the residents' ability to build moral discipline. Housing demolition and human dislocation threatened the community's stability and cohesiveness. Urban renewal initiatives, which had advanced progress for the larger metropolis, had adverse effects on many black communities. One of the WLCAC's first grants from the Ford Foundation was for $25,000, to start a relocation plan for homeowners who would be displaced by new highway construction. The California State Division of Highways planned for two major projects that would displace more than 1,700 families in Watts and cut down on the area's viable development land. The WLCAC knew it could not stop these projects, and put its energies into working with state and federal government, as well as the Ford Foundation, to develop entire new residential areas for these affected families. The WLCAC and the Highway Division would use this opportunity "for the development of a viable and healthy community… with attractive homes for relocatees and other residents, a sound industrial and commercial base and the necessary supportive facilities."[30]

The $25,000 seed money started the WLCAC on the road to becoming a major housing developer in the area.[31] The WLCAC became a dynamic generator of jobs, housing, commerce, and much-needed infrastructure. Watkins's first major initiative was to organize the community to support a campaign for a new hospital in Watts. To build the hospital required voters to approve a 12.3 million dollar bond. WLCAC organized over 80 community organizations and hundreds of volunteers. Opponents tainted the project as an effort to appease black militants and radicals. The bond issue did not pass; the vote fell 3% short of the two-thirds necessary to pass. Still, the WLCAC organizing effort continued. Federal and state funds supported construction, which began on April 10, 1968. Four years later, South Central, Los Angeles, received its first major health-care facility when the Dr. Martin Luther King, Jr. General Hospital opened. "The hospital campaign converted WLCAC from a small group of Watts Unionists to a community organization composed of several hundred members."[32]

The WLCAC's leaders were mostly middle-class people, many of whom had ties to organized labor. As we will see in other CDCs, the poorest of the poor in black ghettos did not exercise a great deal of power over institutions that operated in their name and in their interests. This was a constant battle within many CDCs, and in the larger War on Poverty. The mandate for "maximum feasible participation of the poor" in community development initiatives stressed the *feasible* part more than it did the *maximum*; oftentimes, middle-class power brokers did not think it feasible to allow poor people to run these influential, bureaucratic organizations. Despite this shortcoming, the WLCAC, like many CDCs, always kept the people at the heart of its mission. In one of its early reports, the WLCAC summarized its vision for the role that Watts' residents should play in the CDC's work:

> The citizens most affected by the social and economic health of an area — in short, its residents — are those persons with the greatest natural interest in directing and carrying out social and economic improvements that better their community. WLCAC has worked and continues to work for the establishment of permanent economic bases within the Watts area, providing training and employment opportunities for its citizens and promising the gradual transformation of the area into a healthy, self-sustaining section of Los Angeles County.[33]

Or, as Ted Watkins said in an oral history interview, "Everything that we do has to be in order to improve this community."[34]

In short, the WLCAC used development projects that altered the structures of social power in LA's black ghetto, namely its housing volume, community-based infrastructure, negotiations with municipal elected officials, and flows of capital into and throughout Watts. For over three decades it worked to transform both the ghetto's spatial and economic characteristics and to strengthen its residents' "moral discipline" through structural, economic development. From 1968 to 1981, it received well over $6.7 million from the Ford Foundation to advance these efforts (see Figure 14.2).

"Four hundred thousand dollars makes a difference in race relations in America": The Zion Non-Profit Charitable Trust in Philadelphia

Similar to the WLCAC, the early success of the Zion Non-Profit Charitable Trust in Philadelphia stemmed from its combination of leaders who possessed wide, influential social networks and its roots in the Philadelphia black community's needs. The Zion Non-Profit Charitable Trust was connected in very material and economic ways to people for whom the ghetto was not an abstraction or a meta-phor, but a set of social relations that shaped their everyday lives. Through their churches, black Philadelphians created strong community development initiatives. They pioneered some of the most dynamic "self-help" economic development programs to come out of black communities in over a century.

Similar to ghettos across the country, the black ghetto in North Philadelphia emerged from decades of racial discrimination in housing and jobs and disinvest-ment in the area's housing stock, infrastructure, and services. By 1960, 529,240 black people lived in Philadelphia, 26% of the total population, and had doubled since 1940. Over the next decade, by 1970, another 126,000 black people moved to Philadelphia, pushing the black population to a third of the city's total. From 1950 to 1970, the white population declined by over 400,000 people. In North Philadelphia alone, from 1930 to 1960, the black population increased to over 215,000 people. In 1930, blacks were 22% of the area's population; in 1960, they were 69%. Demographics for one North Philadelphia census tract show the cor-relation between race, housing, and rent costs: as whites left and blacks arrived, the overall population increased, but occupied housing did not increase enough to accommodate all the newcomers; owner-occupancy percentages decreased, tene-ments' conditions became worse, but rent prices increased. By 1950, over 9,500 people lived in this one census tract, up from 5,944 in 1930. 97% of the population was black, up from 43%. The average rent in 1950 was $30, up from $20 in 1940. Meanwhile, just under 3,000 dwelling units were occupied in 1950, an increase of only 600 from the previous decade, and 80% of these tenement apartments were classified as dilapidated, or without a private bathroom.[35]

The Zion Trust's history often centers on its charismatic leader, the Rev. Leon L. Sullivan. His leadership of a selective buying campaign in the early 1960s opened his eyes to the economic power of black Philadelphians. 227 members of his Mt. Zion Baptist church joined his initial "10-36 Plan," which asked participants to invest $10 a month for thirty-six months. By 1964, the program was able to place a down payment on a $75,000 apartment building in an all-white neighborhood. In 1965, it started construction on a brand new apartment complex in the heart of North Philadelphia.[36]

Eventually, Sullivan's community-based support was so strong that the Mt. Zion Non-Profit Charitable Trust and its affiliate organizations initiated projects designed to bring new resources to North Philadelphia. It developed a for-profit investment wing. Sullivan eventually established the Opportunities Industrial Centers (OICs) all around the country. Sullivan called the OIC "the largest, fastest-growing, and most successful skills training program in the United States, a program that through the years has helped millions of African American people get training and jobs."[37] The Zion Trust, however, set the stage for success. Its first major project to unmake the black ghetto in North Philadelphia was Progress Plaza. Sullivan characterized this as the first shopping center in America that blacks built themselves. He remem-bered this story of how Zion secured a $1.7 million loan from Philadelphia's First Pennsylvania Bank and Trust Company:

I went to see the chairman of the bank. And I said that I want a construction loan. He said, well Reverend, you need some equity for something like this. He said, we like you. You've done some good things for the community. You're a wonderful preacher. But to build something like this you need some money. I said, how much equity do you need? He said, you need a couple of hundred thousand dollars. I told one of my people, give me the sack. (Laughter) I opened the sack, and four hundred thousand dollars' worth of equities came out. The man's eye glasses fell off his eyes. He came around the table and told me, Reverend we can work together. I found that four hundred thousand dollars makes a difference in race relations in America (Laughter).[38]

Progress Plaza combined investments from Zion Trust, loans from private banks, and grants from the Ford Foundation to produce a one-of-a-kind black institution in North Philadelphia. "The first black managers in Philadelphia came out of Progress Plaza," Sullivan remembered. "The first managers of super chains came out of Progress Plaza. Some of the first business by blacks came out of Progress Plaza. I develop an entrepreneurial training program that trained a thousand blacks in Philadelphia, how to run their own business and all that kind of thing at Progress Plaza."[39]

Zion Trust went on to initiate numerous housing, jobs, and health programs. Over thirteen years, it received $4,863,000 from the Ford Foundation (see 14.2). It sought to expand quality food and meat supermarkets throughout Philadelphia. Its initial success, however, was built upon a few hundred parishioners giving $10 a month from their hard-earned salaries. The best part about it, according to Sullivan, was that black people, "own it. We have the keys to get the door ourselves, and (all) in a couple of years (because) these people put up their ten dollars, and by faith. I would say to them not in your day but in the day of your children and your children's children. They will benefit not only psychologically from this, but also economically because you are owing a share."[40]

"What we need is brick and mortar": The Bedford-Stuyvesant Restoration Corporation in Brooklyn

The community-organizing roots of the Bedford-Stuyvesant Restoration Corporation (BSRC) began during the mid-1950s. Beginning in 1954, the Central Brooklyn Coordinating Council organized all the different community-based organizations in and around Bedford-Stuyvesant. Eventually, it grew to have over ninety affiliated groups. Elsie Richardson was one of its leaders. It hosted annual conferences on social conditions in Central Brooklyn, organized city-funded youth programs, sponsored health seminars and block clean-ups, and printed a monthly newsletter.

North-central Brooklyn slowly became an all-black ghetto in ways that mirrored North Philadelphia and Watts. During the New Deal, the area became redlined. Home improvement loans and refinancing options to shore up home equity during the Depression flowed into other areas of Brooklyn, areas that neighborhood assessors deemed "safe" for investments, and away from Bedford-Stuyvesant. White people moved out in droves and black people – African Americans from the South as well as Harlem, along with English- and Spanish-speaking Caribbean immigrants – flooded into the neighborhoods of Bedford-Stuyvesant, Brownsville, Crown Heights, and East Flatbush. Black people could buy homes, often at higher mortgage rates than whites. And the homes they purchased were old and in need of repairs after so many generations of Brooklynites living in them. Black homeowners had to turn two or three-family homes into spaces for boarders and tenants, which stressed the housing stock even more. And yet more and more black people came into the area, so that by 1960 over 300,000 people lived in Bedford-Stuyvesant: 71% black, 18% white, and 10% Puerto Rican.

The novelist Paule Marshall captured the transition in her coming-of-age novel, *Brown Girl, Brownstones*, when she described how, as white Brooklynites moved away, "the West Indians slowly edged their way in. Like a dark sea nudging its way onto a white beach and staining the sand, they came. The West Indians, especially the Barbadians who had never owned anything perhaps by a few poor acres in a poor land, loved the houses with the same fierce idolatry as they had the land on their obscure islands."[41] Most black Brooklynites were renters. In one 1971 estimate, decades of overcrowding and limited access to home improvement loans had made 60% of north-central Brooklyn's 125,000 housing units deteriorated or dilapidated. By 1974, one-third of local properties in Bedford-Stuyvesant required "substantial rehabilitation."[42]

The Central Brooklyn Coordinating Council (CBCC) had worked on issues related to overcrowding, health and wellness, and youth organizing for over ten years before it received substantial outside attention. The story of how Robert Kennedy worked with, and then replaced, the mostly female leaders of the Coordinating Council when he set up his flagship antipoverty program in Bedford-Stuyvesant is one of many instances where bureaucrats and power brokers, who were almost always men, replaced community leaders, many of who were women, as the heads of newly created urban CDCs.[43] Kennedy visited the CBCC, toured the ghetto in Bedford-Stuyvesant, and then promised to have his office do a full study of the area's needs. Elsie Richardson told him they did not need another study. "What we need," she informed the senator, "is brick and mortar."[44]

North-central Brooklyn needed power to build and develop on a massive scale. The CDC that grew in Brooklyn gave it that type of power, for a time. Women like Richardson – middle-class, Bedford-Stuyvesant homeowners, with a great deal of community organizing leadership and experience – were pushed out of BSRC's leadership. They were replaced by male power brokers. Money and development projects became commonplace in the community. The male leaders represented the community's best interests, but very few women or men from the community's working class or working poor exercised control or power in the organization.

Still, Restoration accomplished countless diverse programs during its first decade of existence. Of all the CDCs that the Ford Foundation funded around the country, Restoration received the most amount of money (see Figure 14.2). With that money, Restoration redeveloped abandoned space. It turned an abandoned milk bottling plant in the center of the community into a multi-use commercial plaza, which housed the neighborhood's first supermarket and even had an ice-skating rink. Restoration courted corporations to locate plants in the area. For a time, IBM operated a manufacturing plant in Bedford-Stuyvesant. Restoration built an arts and theater center, the Billie Holiday Theatre. It financed mortgage lending funds that channeled millions of dollars in home improvement loans and mortgages for first-time buyers into Bedford-Stuyvesant. Restoration's most successful programs, its satellite neighborhood service centers, where community residents went for help in navigating municipal bureaucracies, and its home improvement program, which refurbished the facades of hundreds of homes in the community, had their roots in community organizing traditions.[45]

Conclusion

In these brief vignettes, one can see the potential for CDCs' broad, comprehensive approaches to have beneficial effects for residents of black ghettos. This came about from tremendous financial and political support. It also emerged from diverse sources of leadership: labor unions, black church, women community organizers. The WLCAC had the full backing of the UAW. The union initially paid Ted Watkins's salary to lead the organization. The Zion Non-Profit Charitable Trust benefitted from its incredibly capable leader and its enormous grassroots support, which was rooted in the black community's strongest institution, the church. Bedford-Stuyvesant Restoration also had large networks of local leadership, which included dynamic women leaders, and the involvement of U.S. senators, as well as leaders of major corporations. Up to 1980, each of these CDCs received large financial support from the Ford Foundation (see Figure 14.1). But money alone did not define this first generation of CDCs as a golden age of community development in the American ghetto. The class and gender diversity of the leadership and involvement brought the very best of black urban communities to the forefront of efforts to unmake ghettos. It seemed like community organizers, anti-poverty professionals, philanthropists and government, men and women, working and middle classes, could work together in unprecedented ways to unmake America's ghettos.

Unfortunately, black ghettos and their CDCs suffered during the 1980s and 1990s. Many first-generation CDCs struggled to survive budget cutbacks, shifting policies, and changed attitudes toward antipoverty work. CDCs narrowed their focus. They trained people for unavailable jobs. They spearheaded small-scale housing developments. They morphed into "Empowerment Zones," which brought big-box business development and their low-wage jobs to black urban communities. Connections to community organizing efforts practically vanished. In the 1980s and 1990s, the government replaced the war on poverty with a war on drugs. It focused more on jails, not jobs, for poor people in cities. Urban black women, a foundation of community leadership in many black ghettos, were depicted nationally as irritants and liabilities rather than intellectuals and leaders.[46]

Ultimately, structural constraints imposed by political and economic policies, and limited political vision about the possibilities of urban community development, narrowed the focus and work of many CDCs to limited, market-based initiatives. In 2009, I found an advertisement flyer that showed one face of Restoration's contemporary affordable housing program in Bedford-Stuyvesant: $300K condos with $500 monthly maintenance fees for families with annual incomes of just under $127K.[47] On the one hand, this can help two middle-class, working people, each earning roughly $65K, to become property owners in the community; but chances are those potential homeowners did not come from the census tract where the homes were located. (In the census tract where the condos were located, 89% of the households in 2009 earned less than $125K; in the other census tract, the figure stood at 92%.[48]) On the other hand, Restoration no longer had the power to invest in businesses, the arts, and massive rehabilitation projects of existing housing and vacant space.

The comprehensive approach to development used by first-generation CDCs, which encouraged participation by local residents – women, church leaders, union members – or at least drew inspiration from community organizing roots, had a brief moment in the sun. Then, in order to survive, urban CDCs in black neighborhoods marched away from economic development initiatives that served ghetto residents, and embraced economic development initiatives that, in part, might be responsible for displacing ghetto residents. Contemporary CDCs might still be working to unmake black ghettos, but how, and for whom, are they doing this?

The history of first-generation urban CDCs reminds us that gentrification does not need to be the end result of unmaking the ghetto. With different political will, changed ideas about poor urban black people, and comprehensive, broad approaches to community development work, their greatness can return, albeit in different forms. We can already see this happening in some contemporary urban development initiatives that mirror the broad, comprehensive, community-oriented, place-based approach that first-generation CDCs pioneered.[49] If urban CDCs are to once again become institutions working to unmake ghettos, not just promote capitalist development; if they want to unmake ghettos for ghetto residents, not merely advance gentrification for newcomers with money and credit; then their leaders, funders, and political backers need to develop methods, finances, and will to revolutionize the power dynamics that created, and maintained, a century of black ghettos in America.

After all, "ghettos do not lend themselves to reform."[50]

Notes

1   Ralph Blumenthal, "Brooklyn Negroes Harass Kennedy," *New York Times,* February 5, 1966, 17.
2   Arnold Hirsch, *Making the Second Ghetto: Race and Housing in Chicago, 1940–1960* (Chicago: University of Chicago Press, 1983), 9.
3   An excellent summary of this analysis is William Julius Wilson, *When Work Disappears: The World of the New Urban Poor* (New York: Alfred A. Knopf, 1999). See also important

studies such as N.D.B. Connolly, *A World More Concrete: Real Estate and the Remaking of Jim Crow South Florida* (Chicago: University of Chicago Press, 2014); Andrew Kahrl, "Capitalizing on the Urban Fiscal Crisis: Predatory Tax Buyers in 1970s Chicago," *Journal of Urban History* (May, 2015); Andrew Kahrl, "Investing in Distress: Tax Delinquency and Predatory Tax Buying in Urban America," *Critical Sociology*, 43 (March 2017), 199-219; Matthew Lassiter, *The Silent Majority: Suburban Politics in the Sunbelt South* (Princeton: Princeton University Press, 2007); Robert O. Self, *American Babylon: Race and the Struggle for Postwar Oakland* (Princeton: Princeton University Press, 2005).

4   The most infamous example of this idea in a policy paper was Daniel P. Moynihan, *The Negro Family: The Case for National Action*, Washington, D.C., Office of Policy Planning and Research, U.S. Department of Labor, 1965. See also James T. Patterson, *Freedom Is Not Enough: The Moynihan Report and America's Struggle over Black Family Life – from LBJ to Obama* (New York: Basic Books, 2010).

5   Annelise Orleck, *Storming Caesars Palace: How Black Mothers Fought Their Own War on Poverty* (New York: Beacon, 2005); Rhonda Y. Williams, *The Politics of Public Housing: Black Women's Struggles Against Urban Inequality* (New York: Oxford University Press, 2004); Premilla Nadasen, *Welfare Warriors: The Welfare Rights Movement in the United States* (New York: Routledge, 2005); Premilla Nadasen, *Household Workers Unite: The Untold Story of African American Women who Built a Movement* (Boston, MA: Beacon, 2016); Lisa Levenstein, *A Movement Without Marches: African American Women and the Politics of Poverty in Postwar Philadelphia* (Chapel Hill, NC: University of North Carolina Press, 2009); Tamar W. Carroll, *Mobilizing New York: AIDS, Antipoverty, and Feminist Activism* (Chapel Hill, NC: University of North Carolina Press, 2015).

6   W.E.B. DuBois, *The Philadelphia Negro: A Social Study* (Philadelphia: University of Pennsylvania Press, 1899, 1996). See also St. Clair Drake and Horace R. Cayton, *Black Metropolis: A Study of Negro Life in a Northern City* (Chicago: University of Chicago Press, 1945, 1993).

7   Kenneth Kusmer, "The Black Urban Experience in American History," in Darlene Clark Hine, ed., *The State of Afro-American History: Past, Present, and Future* (Baton Rouge: Louisiana State University Press, 1986), 91–122, esp. 96–98; Joe William Trotter, Jr., "Appendix 7 – Afro-America Urban History: A Critique of the Literature," and "State of the Field," in *Black Milwaukee: The Making of an Industrial Proletariat, 1915–45* (Urbana, IL: University Press of Illinois, 2007), 264–282, 311–318.

8   Gilbert Osofsky, *Harlem: The Making of a Ghetto – Negro New York, 1890–1930* (New York: Harper & Row Publishers, 1963); and "The Enduring Ghetto," *Journal of American History* 55:2 (September 1968), 243–255; Elliot Rudwick, "Black Urban History in the Doldrums," *Journal of Urban History,* 9:2 (February 1983), 251–260; Thomas J. Sugrue, *The Origins of the Urban Crisis: Race and Inequality in Postwar Detroit* (Princeton: Princeton University Press, 1998).

9   Mitchell Duneier, *Ghetto: The Invention of a Place, the History of an Idea* (New York: Farrar, Straus and Giroux, 2016). On space, place and urban anthropology of black communities, see Steven Gregory, *Black Corona: Race and the Politics of Place in an Urban Community* (Princeton: Princeton University Press, 1998), 3–19. Here, Gregory reviews different ways "the trope of the black ghetto" has distorted social scientific and historical approaches to understanding twentieth-century black communities in cities. On page 10, Gregory writes that his book "is not a book about a 'black ghetto' or an 'inner-city' community. Whatever service these categories might have once rendered toward heightening recognition of the ferocity of racial segregation and urban poverty, they today obscure far more than they reveal. These concepts have become (and perhaps always were) powerful tropes conflating race, class, and place in a society that remains organized around inequalities in economic resources and political power that stretch beyond the imagined frontiers of the inner city."

10 See also Joe William Trotter Jr., *Black Milwaukee,* op. cit., 271 for a list of key books in this genre.

11   See Benjamin Ravid, "Ghetto: Etymology, Original Definition, Reality, and Diffusion," in this volume.

12   On the "institutional ghetto," see Alan H. Spear, *Black Chicago: The Making of a Negro Ghetto, 1890–1920* (Chicago: University Press of Chicago, 1967), 91–110; and William Julius Wilson, *When Work Disappears: The World of the New Urban Poor* (New York: Alfred A. Knopf, 1999), 3–24. On the "race tax," see Keeanga-Yamahtta Taylor, "Back Story to the Neoliberal Moment," *Souls* 14:3–4, 185–206.

13   See Arnold R. Hirsch, *Making the Second Ghetto*, 14; Arnold R. Hirsch, "Massive Resistance in the Urban North: Trumbull Park, Chicago, 1953–1966, *Journal of American History* 82:2 (September 1995), 522–550.

14   On automation, see Thomas Sugrue, *The Origins of the Urban Crisis*, op. cit. On redlining and housing discrimination, see Kenneth T. Jackson, "Race, Ethnicity, and Real Estate Appraisal: The Home Owners Loan Corporation and the Federal Housing Administration," *Journal of Urban History*, 6:4 (August 1980), 419–452; and Craig Steven Wilder, *A Covenant with Color: Race and Social Power in Brooklyn* (New York: Columbia University Press, 2000), 175–217. On contract buying, see Beryl Satter, *Family Properties: How the Struggle Over Race and Real Estate Transformed Chicago and Urban America* (New York: Metropolitan Books, 2009).

15   Andrew Wiese, *Places of Their Own: African American Suburbanization in the Twentieth Century* (Chicago: University of Chicago Press, 2005); Mary Pattillo, *Black on the Block: The Politics of Race and Class in the City* (Chicago: University of Chicago Press, 2007), and *Black Picket Fences: Privilege and Peril Among the Black Middle Class* (Chicago: University of Chicago Press, 1999).

16   The term "distressed black neighborhoods" comes from the work of Henry Louis Taylor, Jr., especially his lecture, "Rise of the Urban Metropolis: The City as Nightmare, Color-Blind Ideology and Black Community Development," University of Pennsylvania, A Race in the Academy Lecture, March 20, 2012. On jobless ghettos, see William J. Wilson, *When Work Disappears*, op. cit.

17   Gilbert Osofsky, "The Enduring Ghetto," opt. cit.

18   Marcus Hunter: *Black Citymakers: How the Philadelphia Negro Changed Urban America* (New York: Oxford University Press, 2013).

19   Craig Wilder, *Covenant*, 234.

20   *Ibid.*, 216. Marcus Hunter: *Black Citymakers*, op. cit., 214.

21   This phrase comes from *Black Metropolis*, 213. On the civil rights movement outside the South, see Thomas Sugrue, *Sweet Land of Liberty: The Forgotten Struggle for Civil Rights in the North* (New York: Random House, 2008); Jason Sokol, *All Eyes Are Upon Us: Race and Politics from Boston to Brooklyn* (New York: Basic Books, 2014); Jeanne Theoharis and Komozi Woodard, eds., *Freedom North: Black Freedom Struggles Outside the South, 1940–1980* (New York: Palgrave, 2003). For an overview of the historiography of the northern Black Freedom Movement, see Brian Purnell, "Freedom North Studies, the Long Civil Rights Movement and Twentieth-Century Liberalism in American Cities," *Journal of Urban History*, 42:3 (May 2016), 634–640.

22   Before the 1970s, there were fewer than 100 CDCs. During the 1970s, between 500 and 1,000 CDCs were formed. Federal funding for CDCs ballooned to over $500 million between 1966 and 1980. In the 1980s, the number of CDCs expanded to as many as 2,000. See Randy Stoecker, "The CDC Model of Urban Redevelopment: A Critique and an Alternative," *Journal of Urban Affairs*, 19:1 (1997), 2. The classic study of CDCs remains Avis Vidal, *Rebuilding Communities: A National Study of Urban Community Development Corporations* (Community Development Research Center, Graduate School of Management and Urban Policy, New School for Social Research, 1992).

23   Annelise Orleck, "Introduction: The War on Poverty from the Grass Roots Up," in Annelise Orleck and Lisa Gayle Hazirjian, eds., *The War on Poverty: A New Grassroots History, 1964–1980* (Athens, GA: University of Georgia Press, 2011), 14.

24   Orleck, op. cit., 10–14. On tensions between community activists and local and national powerbrokers over leadership of anti-poverty institutions, see essays in Orleck and

Hazirjian, eds., *The War on Poverty: A New Grassroots History*; Brian Purnell, "'What We Need is Brick and Mortar': Race, Gender, and Early Leadership of the Bedford-Stuyvesant Restoration Corporation," in Laura Warren Hill and Julia Rabig, eds., *The Business of Black Power: Community Development, Capitalism, and Corporate Responsibility in Postwar America* (Rochester, NY: University of Rochester Press, 2012), 217–244; Annelise Orleck, *Storming Caesars Palace: How Black Mothers Fought Their Own War on Poverty* (New York: Beacon, 2005), chapters 5–8, esp. 7–8; Robert Bauman, *Race and the War on Poverty: From Watts to East L.A.* (Norman, OK: University of Oklahoma Press, 2008), chapters 3–4; Robert Bauman, "The Black Power and Chicano Movements in the Poverty Wars in Los Angeles," *Journal of Urban History*, 33:2 (January 2007), 277–295. Perhaps the most well-known criticism of the idea that the Economic Opportunity Act gave poor people control over community action agencies, and of the CAAs in general, is in Daniel Patrick Moynihan, *Maximum Feasible Misunderstanding: Community Action in the War on Poverty* (New York: The Free Press, 1969).

25 Alice O'Connor, "Swimming Against the Tide: A Brief History of Federal Policy in Poor Communities," in Ronald F. Ferguson and William T. Dickens, eds., *Urban Problems and Community Development* (Washington, D.C.: Brookings Institution Press, 1999), 99–104, quote, on 106. On the 1967 amendment to the Economic Opportunity Act (1964) which created the SIP, see Kimberley Johnson, "Community Development Corporations, Participation and Accountability: The Harlem Urban Development Corporation and the Bedford-Stuyvesant Restoration Corporation," *The Annals of the American Academy of Political and Social Science*, 594 (2004), 111; On the Ford Foundation and Black Power see Karen Ferguson, *Top Down: The Ford Foundation, Black Power and the Reinvention of Racial Liberalism* (Philadelphia, PA: University of Pennsylvania Press, 2013), and "Organizing the Ghetto: The Ford Foundation, CORE, and White Power in the Black Power Era, 1967–1969," *Journal of Urban History*, 34:1 (November 2007), 67–100.

26 Robert Bauman, *Race and the War on Poverty: From Watts to East L.A.* (Norman, OK: University of Oklahoma Press, 2008).

27 James Briggs Murray interview with Ted Watkins, Community Development Corporation Oral History Project (December 11, 1990), transcript page 8, Schomburg Center for Research in Black Culture, New York.

28 Ford Foundation, National Affairs, Grant, PA 68–378, "Request for Grant Action," *Community Sponsored Relocation Program* (April 1968), p. 2, Reel 5477, Rockefeller Archives Center.

29 Ibid., "Grant Correspondence," p. 2–3.

30 Ibid., "Request for Grant Action," p. 4.

31 See Watts Labor Community Action Committee, *Greater Watts Model Neighborhood Housing Study, Presented to Los Angeles Community Analysis Bureau,* September 22, 1970; Watts Labor Community Action Committee, *WLCAC King Center Study, Prepared for an Urban Land Institute Panel Study,* March 8–11, 1972; Ford Foundation, "Far From Enough, But Enough to Be Important: An Assessment of Grants to the Watts Labor Community Action Committee (WLCAC), a Community Development Corporation Engaged in a Wide Range of Activities" (December 1976), 74–80, Rockefeller Archives Center, Ford Foundation Records, National Affairs, Office Files of Thomas Cooney, FA 653, Box 8, Folder: Community Development Corporations – Assessment, 1971–1976.

32 "Far from Enough, But Enough to Be Important," 4–8. See also Robert Bauman, *Race and the War on Poverty,* 69–89. For an expansive overview of the policies behind this effort, see Merlin Chowkwanyun's unpublished paper, "Beyond Medicare and Medicaid: The War on Poverty and Health Reform," presented at "The War on Poverty at 50: Its History and Legacy," a conference sponsored by the University of Pennsylvania's Social Science and Policy Forum, September 19, 2014; presentation available at: https://www.youtube.com/watch?v=a77dh539WB8&list=PLbdYmEXIEvkqTaGIdG0YU6iLjv_JCme6m&index=3 (accessed February 26, 2017).

33 Letter, Hortence Gabel to Louis Winnick, March 26, 1968, with "Watts Community Labor Action Committee Background," in Ford Foundation, National Affairs, Grant,

PA 68–378, Reel 5477, Rockefeller Archives Center, quote from page 9 of the document on background.

34 James Briggs Murray interview with Ted Watkins, op. cit., pp. 27–28.

35 Matthew Countryman, *Up South: Civil Rights and Black Power in Philadelphia* (Philadelphia: University of Pennsylvania Press, 2006), 51–52, 69.

36 Matthew Countryman, *Up South,* 111–112. See also, Guian A. McKee, *The Problem of Jobs: Liberalism, Race, and Deindustrialization in Philadelphia* (Chicago: University of Chicago Press, 2008); and Ford Foundation, "The Philadelphia Prototype: An Evaluation of the Rev. Leon Sullivan's Economic Development Enterprise," December 1969, Rockefeller Archives Center, Ford Foundation Records, National Affairs, Office Files of Thomas Cooney, FA 653, Box 10.

37 Leon Sullivan, *Moving Mountains: The Principles and Purposes of Leon Sullivan* (Valley Forge, PA: Judson Press, 1998), 3, 15–24.

38 *Building Hope: The CDC Oral History Project,* (21:28–22:40), available at: http://vimeo. com/5977553.

39 James Briggs Murray interview with Leon Sullivan, Community Development Corporation Oral History Project (November 23, 1990), transcript pages 6–10, Schomburg Center for Research in Black Culture, New York, NY.

40 Ibid.

41 Paule Marshall, *Brown Girl, Brownstones* (New York: Feminist Press, 1981), 4.

42 Craig Wilder, *Covenant with Color,* 175–217.

43 Purnell, "What We Need is Brick and Mortar," op. cit; Orleck, "Introduction: The War on Poverty from the Grass Roots Up," 18–19.

44 Interview with Elsie Ricardson, January 22, 2008, BSRC-OHP, Brooklyn Historical Society, quote at 08:14–08:20

45 Kimberley Johnson, "Community Development Corporations, Participation and Accountability," op. cit. See also, Tom Adam Davies, *Mainstreaming Black Power* (Oakland, CA: University of California Press, 2017), 58–117. The most comprehensive study to date of the history of the Bedford-Stuyvesant Restoration Corporation is Jason T. Bartlett, "The Politics of Community Development: A History of the Bedford-Stuyvesant Restoration Corporation," (unpublished PhD dissertation, Temple University, 2014).

46 Orleck, "Introduction: The War on Poverty from the Grass Roots Up," 18–19. On mass incarceration, see Wacquant, op. cit.; Heather Ann Thompson, "Why Mass Incarceration Matters: Rethinking Crisis, Decline, and Transformation in Postwar American History," *Journal of American History,* 97:3 (December 2010), 703–734;

47 Bedford Stuyvesant Restoration Corporation, "4 Affordable Homes for Sale," Flyer in author's possession. Also available for viewing: https://www.restorationplaza.org/ about/news/4-affordable-homes-for-sale.

48 Social Explorer Tables: ACS 2009 (5-Year Estimates)(SE), ACS2009_5yr, Social Explorer; U.S. Census Bureau.

49 See essays in Nancy O. Andrews and David J. Erickson, eds., *Investing in What Works for American's Communities: Essays on People, Place & Purpose*; for an excellent case study of a contemporary example, see Henry Louis Taylor, Jr., Linda McGlynn, and Gavin Luter, "Back to the Future: Public Schools as Neighborhood Anchors Institutions— The Choice Neighborhood Initiative in Buffalo, New York," in Kelly L. Patterson, Robert Mark Silverman (eds.), *Schools and Urban Revitalization: Rethinking Institutions and Community Development* (New York and London: Routledge, 2013), 109–135. The term "unmaking the ghetto" comes from Camilo José Vegara, *Harlem: The Unmaking of a Ghetto* (Chicago: University of Chicago Press, 2013). See also Josh Sides, ed., *Post-Ghetto: Reimagining South Los Angeles* (University of California Press, 2012).

50 Wilder, op. cit., 234.

PART IV
Urban locations, apartheid, and the ghetto in South Africa

Soweto, a South African township. © Kevin James

15

"THEIR WORLD WAS A GHETTO"

Space, power, and identity in Alexandra, South Africa's squatters' movement, 1946–1947

Dawne Y. Curry

On a sultry summer day (24 November 1946), businessman Schreiner Baduza began protesting the housing shortage that paralyzed Johannesburg from 1944 to 1947. During those three years, approximately 63,000 to 92,000 people[1] "... overflowed out of the backyards, the passages, the verandahs, outhouses and lavatories for which they were paying ridiculous rents. [T]hey spilled onto the veld, [and] into ... [places],"[2] such as Benoni, Alberton, Alexandra, and Soweto. Consisting of tenants (leasers of rooms owned by landlords), subtenants (leasers of rooms occupied by renters), rural migrants, and families, Baduza and his initial 700 constituents left the northeastern Johannesburg township of Alexandra following the government's decision not to extend the area's square mile. Under the auspices of the Bantu Tenants Association (BTA), a body formed by Alexandran activist and print shop owner A. E. P. Fish in 1938,[3] Baduza sought land to build homes as the body's banner militantly demanded. Baduza eyed land along Alexandra's western quadrant, an area encompassing the neighboring White suburb of Lombardy East and West and the industrial site of Marlboro to the township's north. "As an alternative to seeking sub-tenancies in the towns, [leaders such as Baduza] chose to squat on white small-holdings in the peri-urban areas."[4]

Burdened with their meager belongings, they littered Marlboro with shanties. News of their "invasion" quickly reached the police department's hallowed walls, where the wheels of justice viciously turned. In a matter of minutes, authorities dispatched Sergeant Piet Badenhorst to the scene. Badenhorst confiscated their membership cards, and ordered these "property owners" to dismantle their crudely constructed "homes."[5] He even arrested Baduza. While warned for the unlawful occupation of White-owned land, the squatters refused to relent. On 25 November, 100 of the landless built eighty shacks and began occupying fifty acres dotting an area in Lombardy East known as "the Homestead Block."[6] Like the other eviction, the police arrived, made 200 arrests, and forced the squatters to take down their shacks. On 29 November, four days later, Baduza and his troops returned to Alexandra, where 100 families squatted on the Number 3 Square, one of three public spaces within the township. After this move and following an address made by the Native Commissioner K. D. Morgan and the township's local authority, the Alexandra Health Committee (AHC), Baduza, instead of retreating, regrouped and ultimately joined James "Sofasonke" Mpanza and his two-year old shantytown in Orlando West, Soweto.[7] With Soweto's numbers mushrooming, the Johannesburg City Council (JCC), under an Emergency Regulation issued on 31 December, ordered the squatters to return to Alexandra and occupy that community's squares.

The day after receiving the eviction notice, the landless left Soweto and moved to Alexandra where they began their six-month (January–June 1947) occupation of its squares. They received anything but a hero's welcome. Instead of Alexandran residents accepting the squatters, dwellers opposed their presence, ostracized them, issued threats, and complained. Their discontent reached the public's discerning eye. One member of the AHC was interviewed by a *Rand Daily Mail* correspondent. Angered over the JCC's decision to remove the Alexandran squatters from Orlando, an unidentified member complained that the body had "… dumped them on the township's doorstep."[8] A group of property owners also chimed in when they urged the AHC "to dump its filth where it dumps its filth."[9]

Tensions between these parties erupted over how the squatters arrived in Alexandra, over the struggle for basic amenities, over health and sanitation concerns, and over the squatters' occupation of the township's public squares. Each side drew a solid line in the political sand. Alexandra became a contested site as the ideologies and the needs of the subordinate (squatters) and the dominant (township residents) violently collided. Divided into four parts: "Territory within a Territory," "Complaints against the Squatters," "From Crowded Alexandra to Moroka Emergency Camp," and "Conclusion," this chapter explores how the politics of geography and subordination intertwined. Alexandra not only fits into the traditional definition of a ghetto as a racialized space, it also shows how two spaces mirrored each other.

Because these groups competed and opposed each other, they created a different form of sequestration than that mandated by the government. Instead of segregation between Black and White, it existed between Alexandra's permanent dwellers and its temporary ones. Throughout its over 100-year existence, Alexandra proper occupied a subordinate liminal space within Johannesburg's urban areas. But with the squatters taking up dwelling, it became the dominant community that Baduza and his entourage, Abner Kunene (magistrate), Lucas Bokaba (treasurer), and Marks Rammitloa (secretary) dared to defy. Of Baduza's lieutenants, most information exists on Rammitloa, who after being a petty hawker, trade unionist, and squatter leader turned to writing short stories and poems under the pseudonym Modikwe Dikobe.[10] Alexandra's backdrop of protest – a consumer boycott in 1917, and a series of bus strikes in the 1940s – made the township highly attractive as a literary subject. Alexandra had other things going for it. The township maintained its own local authority, the Health Committee; ran a sewage disposal system; operated a skeleton staff clinic; and offered a bus line. Compared to Alexandra proper, the squatter encampment was a slum of epic proportions. But that did not stop Baduza from making Alexandra a significant spoke in the wheel of land dispossession and excessive poverty.

Drawing on his leadership skills as the president of the BTA and his involvement with the South African Communist Party (SACP), Baduza devoted himself full on to addressing housing, one of the subsistence issues that dominated politics in the 1940s.[11] While scholar Dominic Fortescue shows how the SACP gained momentum from their involvement in the black union trade movement and its influence in the urban areas by 1945, he writes that the body failed to address "… the undeveloped nature of class or even 'race' consciousness, and because of this the Party was unable to tailor its ideology to the predilections of the African working class."[12] Realizing the SACP's weakness, Baduza renounced his membership the same year he began leading the squatters' movement in 1946.

Baduza's creation of a "territory within a territory" spawned the development of competing and intersecting ghettoes within densely populated and infrastructure-deprived Alexandra. Each site shared the conditions of squalor: poverty, raw sewage, dimly lit streets, vermin, and overcrowding, among other signs of inferior living. So prevalent were these conditions in Johannesburg's townships that, for many Africans reduced to social marginalization on the outskirts of South Africa's cities, their world was a ghetto. Typically, scholars, laypersons, and government officials apply the term slum to discuss African townships and their geographical depravity rather than the word ghetto, which was often reserved for the country's Indian population. Indians began arriving when the Dutch controlled Cape Town from 1652 to 1684. Initially, Indians came to the country to work as slaves on Cape Town's farms or in the Lodge, the site where Dutch East India Company (VOC) officials lived and carried out business.[13] Other streams of Indian migrants came later in the eighteenth and nineteenth centuries to serve as indentured workers on Natal's sugar plantations or simply paid their way ("free" or passenger Indians) to visit South Africa.[14] While immigration ended in 1914, the year of the First World War, the Indian population had reached 219,000 people by 1936.[15]

Feeling the weight of their commercial and numerical threat, as many Indians owned businesses and competed with Whites,[16] the government enacted the 1946 Asiatic Land Tenure and Indian Representation Act. Colloquially known as the "Ghetto Act," this law designated areas within Natal for Indian occupation. This concept was not anything new. In 1848, the Diplomatic Agent for Native Tribes Theophilus Shepstone had set aside ten reserves for African occupation in the British-colonized Natal.[17] Years later in 1899, segregation's illogical application continued during the South African War when the British created concentration camps for the Afrikaner (Dutch-descended) population. Mirroring early policy initiatives, the "Ghetto Act," like the Jewish ghettos that emerged in Europe under German leader Adolph Hitler, revealed several things about how the state constructed and deconstructed race in terms of its buffering of difference and its containment of sameness. Like Benjamin Ravid in this volume, this chapter adopts the definition of a ghetto as a compulsory, segregated, and enclosed space,[18] while at the same time offering an interesting twist to this ongoing conversation.

In the beginning, the construction and composition of Alexandra's ghetto resided with race, but that changed to incorporate other identity markers such as permanent and temporary, resident and squatter, dominant and subordinate, perforated space and political exclave, and legal and illegal. By applying the term ghetto to Alexandra's case study, this chapter diverges from an increasing number of scholars who insert the word apartheid in its place to examine America's inner cities. In particular, Douglas S. Massey and Nancy Denton's analysis not only illustrates how segregated conditions gave rise to ghettos, but also shows how this policy fostered a culture of poverty.[19] Massey and Denton's interpretation raises key questions that this discussion on Alexandra's squatter movements addresses: how do subordinate groups negotiate inferior living conditions; how does a subordinate space emerge into a dominated one; and lastly, how do competing groups create other forms of ghettos within a similar structure of segregation?

Earlier work on the squatters' movements throughout Johannesburg examine the different leaders, discuss the economic push and pull factors, and address housing and the geographical spaces in which these historic protests occurred;[20] however, except for my 2006 PhD dissertation[21] and a 2008 study by Philip Bonner and Noor Nieftagodien,[22] the intra-relations between and among permanent and temporary dwellers in the township have escaped exploration. While Bonner and Nieftagodien address the conflict among Alexandra's dwellers, they fail to highlight the importance of geography in the analysis of resistance. Instead, they conceal the geographical relationship that the subordinate dominator (Alexandra proper dwellers) and the land-deprived squatters had.[23]

The main residential and temporary living areas mirrored each other spatially and because of this parallelism, they reveal the following: how the ghetto formed, how the ghetto regenerated, and how the ghetto created a symbiotic geographical relationship. Because of the squatters' presence in Alexandra, three types of ghettos emerged: the traditional, the intersected, and the temporary. Alexandra proper represented *the traditional ghetto* because it satisfied the government's desire to sequester a racial group to a confined area. Alexandra's geographical insulation made it easy for officials to monitor the township and to contain the population within its borders. Residents left Alexandra to find employment or to perform labor only to return to their racial enclave by the 9 pm curfew hour, at the end of their 72-hour employment permit or after their work day.

While creating an alternate and parallel community that differed from and was like Alexandra proper,[24] Baduza and his leadership also created an *intersecting ghetto*. Intersection occurred through geography and through power. Because Alexandra proper surrounded the squares, these spaces were in geographical terms perforated, and the main site an exclave because White suburbs totally encircled it. In June 1947, the government tried to address the squatter question when it began moving people to Hammanskraal, and to Klipspruit and other places around the country. Officials also established an emergency camp in Moroka. These sites served as *temporary ghettos* because the idea behind their formation was neither long-lasting nor did they promote the development of familyhood. Rather, they stood as places where single migrants could transition before going to more permanent locations.

"Territory within a territory"

Hemmed in by Sandton, Kew, Bramley, Kelvin, Orange Grove, and Wynberg, among other areas, Old Alexandra, which stretches a square mile from the Pretoria Main Road to its east to the M1 highway to its west, is one of South Africa's most iconic townships. Founded in 1912, two years after South Africa formed a union in 1910, the sloping hills of Alexandra became a Freehold of propertied Africans and Coloureds only. This was an important privilege as many Africans, by pains of the 1913 Natives Land Act, were deprived of land ownership rights in the city center.[25] Possibly named after Papenfus' love child,[26] his wife or that of King Edward VI, Alexandra sat nine miles northeast of Johannesburg's growing metropolis.

Bustling because of gold's discovery in 1888, Johannesburg's size mushroomed almost as if overnight. Worried White officials feared an encroaching African majority. While African workers dislodged gold, that elusive, shiny metal from the earth's belly, Africans, in the eyes of many Whites, presented a perceived economic and social threat. As long as Africans maintained parity with Whites, they could compete for the same jobs and seek the same arable land. Poor Whites faced the stiffest challenge, especially on farms where Africans squatted. But this was all outlawed with the 1913 Natives Land Act.[27]

To control African mobility, and to allow migrant laborers and participants in a cash economy, this law set aside a mere seven percent of land for African occupation. Alexandra remained unaffected as its Freehold status, along with that of Sophiatown, Newclare, and Martindale, precluded these areas from the law's tenets. This also made them highly sought after areas to live in. In 1923, segregation's proponents enacted the Natives Urban Areas Act (NUAA).[28] Promulgated twenty-five years before apartheid began in 1948, the NUAA established separate urban residential areas called townships.[29] Alexandra already existed as a racially sequestered space, going back to its conversion from a Whites-only area in 1905 to an African and Coloured Freehold in 1912.

Because Freehold status allowed Africans and Coloureds to own land in the city center, Alexandra attracted a highly diverse community clamoring for the township's close proximity to Johannesburg and its affordable accommodations. It also welcomed Asians, and to an even smaller extent Whites. Twenty-three avenues, seven perpendicular streets, and 2,525 stands accommodated Alexandra's diverse population. Divided into the "upstairs" and "downstairs," because of the steep gradient the township rested on, Alexandrans followed a distinct pattern of residency. Occupying both the lower- and higher-numbered streets, Asians lived sprinkled among Africans and Coloureds or congregated on First Avenue, where they owned a plethora of stores. Coloureds dwelled in the upper half from Second Avenue to Fourth Avenue while Sotho, Tswana, and other indigenous Africans predominated on the bottom's remaining nineteen streets.[30]

Not only did these roads and demographics define Alexandra, so did the community's three public squares. The No. 1 Square stretched from First to Third Avenues. The No. 2 Square extended from Twelfth to Fifteenth Avenues and bordered the No. 3 Square, which faced the township's southern portion near Twelfth and Thirteenth Avenues.[31] Traditionally, these public spaces, owned by everyone, served as sites where political bodies met, churches held gatherings, and township residents attended sporting or cultural events.[32] But as time went on, these spaces, as sociologist Belinda Bozzoli argues, took on a different meaning than originally intended.[33] While Baduza carried on the custom of using the squares as a space of protest, he also made the public areas private. The squatter leader created a "territory within a territory" "… [when he attempted] to influence or control objects, people and relationships in a delimited area."[34]

Because Baduza understood the relationship between the natural environment and human organization, he mimicked Alexandra proper rather than the White community for the following reasons. He sought the same meager services that the main area provided through its Health Committee rather than the state because the area lacked indoor plumbing and electricity and therefore had to offer its own social services. The squares served as a "territory within a territory" rather than as a "state within a state"[35] because Baduza understood the symbiotic geographical relationship that the two places shared. These intertwined spaces became replicas of the other as they each represented their own forms of an alternative and parallel community. Power, therefore, resided reciprocally – the subordinate dominators (proper residents) owned most of the township's square mile and had access to the White world, while the squatters ruled the squares and prevented their "geographical oppressors" from expanding onto the public areas.

Located on the No. 2 (175 × 350 feet) and the No. 3 (50 × 350 feet) Squares, "Shantytown" stretched from the middle of the township to its southern outskirts, from Twelfth to Fifteenth Avenues.[36] Seven thousand squatters and their families inundated Alexandra's public grounds with 1,000 shacks.[37] After paying 5s for membership to the BTA, squatters received their identity cards, numbered plates, and assigned plots. To ensure that they remained on their 50 × 50 allotment, they paid a weekly 1s 6d ($.25) subscription charge to the camp secretary.[38] In the squatters' land-seeking eyes, this option, while smaller than Alexandra's stands of 140 × 80 feet, was cheaper than paying for a regular room which cost up to £2 ($3.36) a month.[39] Alexandra's overcrowding hampered residents who lived "like mealie bags … with seven persons to a room" or they amounted up to twenty-two in a single-housed structure.[40] These conditions forced many to squat and erect "new homes."

A *Star* correspondent covering the mass housing campaign reported that the squatters' "… huts of split poles and hessian, cardboard, corrugated iron and pieces of motor cars, … [were] crowded with broken-down sofas, tables, chairs, beds, blankets, oil lamps, babies, dogs, and blue budgerigars in cages."[41] On the shanties' exteriors appeared weather-paned doors, and chiseled windows, which provided ventilation and sunlight. Hessian or other sackcloth blinds covered them nightly or during episodes of rain. Shacks stood no more than a yard a part. Corners appeared to represent the most coveted locations. Their diagonal angles lent themselves to greater levels of privacy, if not the illusion of that. Even still, these residents endured the encampment's crowded conditions, and because of this, its interior space was not as legible as Alexandra's gridiron pattern, but as equally undesirable as an emerging ghetto.

Because the squares existed as perforated spaces with Alexandra proper engulfing them, Baduza and his troops secured the perimeters. They posted guards, and fenced in traditionally open spaces. In a further attempt to protect their constituency from threats leveled by Alexandra proper residents, and the desire to run them out, squatter commanders used the shanties as dividing markers. A cluster of shacks stood on each side of the No. 2 Square. Posts of wattle and wood provided further divisions. The encampment's own police patrolled during the evenings, and refused to allow proper Alexandrans admittance, especially since some of them had threatened to burn down the shelters within a matter of days after their arrival from Orlando West in early January.[42]

With fifty civil guards patrolling the camps, leaders ran operations from a dilapidated corrugated iron office.[43] In that suite of hessian shacks, Baduza and his team assigned stands, collected social service fees, and conducted other business. That was not the only site of officialdom. A dimly lit enclosure of accumulated scrap material housed the Magistrate's office where Kunene presided over cases involving theft, assault, insubordination, and domestic disputes, among other issues that lined this court's docket. Wanting to avoid the tribalism that the government purposely stoked, Baduza promoted Sesotho and isiZulu, languages from two different families, the Sotho and the Nguni, as the encampment's official tongues. Like Mpanza, Baduza believed that the constituents he represented "[preferred] to call themselves Africans because it [avoided] unpleasant distinctions and [made] for [ethnic] harmony."[44] When it came to commerce, English "infiltrated" the encampment as the lingua franca.

Instead of advertising different price structures to compete or lure prospective customers, signage alone conveyed an item's salability. "Again and Again Butchery," "Fresh Meat Every Day," and "Eat More Fish for Less," and other posts decorated the shanties, and provided another form of recognition aside from the Baduza-imposed numbered plates. Music flooded throughout the squares. "Men sang … as if their own voices had the power to carry them out of the desolation of Alexandra into the clean veld [sic]."[45] Sometimes people sang songs "straight out of Hollywood."[46] Children played within the narrow lanes,[47] while an "old man [was] bundled up like discarded rags in a pool of sun outside of his tent."[48] Women also took advantage of the encampment's vibrant culture, as many of them relaxed and drank mareu from a jam jar while chatting about the latest news, or possibly culinary delights.[49]

Consumables came from the outside. After paying a fee to enter, vans supplied items[50] for the 422 shops[51] that existed in the permanent area, and the hundred or so that existed in the temporary one. Alexandra proper had clothing stores, funerary homes, and food shops, among a host of other options, and it also had a thriving but monopolistic transit company. While not replicating bussing services, many squatters availed themselves of bicycles. In fact, one of its shops catered to owners of the two-wheeled transport and music aficionados, as this quote reveals: "… bicycles and gramophones [were] being … repaired in an improvised open-air workshop."[52] Hair was also featured, with stylists offering their barbering and cosmetology skills. Amblers had no worries, especially with "Quick Service Boots and Repairs" committed to mending their worn-out shoes. Signage not only served as pleas to buy commodities, it also provided a road map into the world of squatter commerce. For instance, those signs advertised the vocational and artisanal skills of a dispossessed people. They also highlighted the salability of items and their limited and abundant supply and/or their waning and increasing demand. How much inhabitants trafficked through these cottage industries failed to appear in the written records, and thus negates the opportunity to analyze even further the impact of their self-contained economy.

With some squatters still paying rents in Alexandra proper, they needed money to maintain their permanent and nomadic homes, even if it meant remaining on the squares and paying for sanitation services cruder than Alexandra's bucket system. Performing a bi-weekly service, nightsoil workers picked up pail upon pail of human excrement that they deposited at a cemetery that doubled as a makeshift septic tank. Oftentimes, before the scheduled pickups, buckets overflowed and their contents seeped onto the ground. The stench filled the air, and the squalor reached staggering levels. But they provided something the squatters did not have, and possibly wanted, considering that they relieved themselves publicly in two pit latrines covered with hessian and wattle. "Pitched on unsuitable sites, [their] hessian huts crowd[ed] up against the fence around the crèche [daycare] … [and stood] within a few yards of the township's only clinic."[53] Even when squatter leaders ordered new holes dug up, they, per a government document dated 21 May 1947, "only had room to construct six additional toilets."[54]

Figuratively piled on top of each other, tent city not only challenged the constraints of the earth, but also Baduza's cultural geographer skills, as he and his inhabitants nearly faced an empty tank. Despite this challenge, Baduza had, by all estimations, successfully created an alternate and parallel community replete with social services, law and order, governance, an informal economy, and sanitation. His victory, in this regard, taunted the dominant population, whose displeasure was noted. By May 1947, Alexandrans had petitioned for the government to enforce its Emergency Regulations to remove the squatters from their public grounds. With their discontent reaching discerning eyes, a host of Alexandra proper residents weighed in on the heavyweight battle that loomed large over the shortage of housing, and the competition for scarce resources.

Complaints against the squatters

Medical practitioners and Alexandra proper residents compiled a laundry list of complaints against these perceived unlawful tenants. Rising to the top of the "dirty" pile was health, financial burden, illegal occupation, and safety. Health has always been a sensitive subject for Alexandrans, especially since they were repeatedly not given a clean bill. In fact, based on Alexandra's squalid conditions, its crime rate, and raw sewage, the predominately White North Eastern Districts Protection League (NEDPL) had petitioned for the township's abolition as early as 1938. In a very frank statement, the body declared, "There is an ever growing uncontrolled population of natives and coloured herded together, in the majority of cases under most unsanitary conditions, thus creating a breeding ground for disease."[55]

In the NEDPL's eyes, Alexandra was "[the] only uncontrolled native township near the Main Reef Towns, … [that] [served] [a]s the gathering place for the scum of the Reef, for the criminals of the Union, the brewers of skokiaan, the vendors of illicit liquor, and all that is bad in native life."[56] These conditions also threatened encroaching White populations, whose residents sought to further their expansion into Johannesburg's industrial north where a vulnerable, geographically insulated Alexandra sat. The NEDPL felt that "The time [had] … arrived when abolition of the Township as a non European [sic] residential area [was] the only possible solution to the problem from every point of view."[57]

Having the squatters on the township's formerly open spaces poured fuel onto a growing fire.[58] A slew of news articles and government documents publicly condemned the landless, as these do; "the squatters are a menace to health not only to Alexandra but Johannesburg," "[the squatter settlements] [are] ripe for disease," or "the unhygienic conditions of the Squatters' Camp [creates] … [a] menace … to the health of the Township."[59] Perpetuated by the media, residents, and even doctors, the menace-to-health argument[60] gained full steam when an unidentified medical professional proclaimed, "This [camp] is foul. It is ripe for disease. Under these conditions anything can strike – smallpox, typhoid, enteric or venereal disease. The whole township could be exposed."[61] This physician had put one nail into the squatters' coffins, while Alexandra's permanent dwellers kept on hammering in the others. With no checks and balances system, such as a trade association that issued licensure like Alexandran business people had, health standards on these public grounds fell by the dangerous wayside. During the dismantlement of one structure, cockroaches and other vermin flooded its hessian walls. This not only caused a problem for the inhabitants but also for a neighboring meat shop, whose freshness, cleanliness, and purity it compromised. The push for social hygiene appeared even further when inspectors closed the doors of four butcher shops after proprietors chose to sell the unstamped meat of a freshly slaughtered ox.

When a group of female visitors conducted an independent tour of the squatters' camp, they found, "sick people [lying] in the narrow open spaces between the shacks, while puddles of water and open garbage befouled the 'streets.'"[62] These images led them to include that "disease and death [were] gaining ground," not only on the squares but also in the permanent area. In December 1946 alone, forty cases of smallpox inflicted the original settlement, compared to Baduza's shantytown which had registered only four incidences. Because of the mass vaccination campaign, the rates of diseases such as typhoid, enteric, and others had declined throughout their six-month tenure in Alexandra. This success rested a lot with health professionals who administered preventive medicine, and consulted regularly with the squatters and vaccinated them. While medical officials gave the squatters a clean bill of health, they also jeopardized their constitution by using the Jukskei River.

Flowing from the Hartebeesport Dam to Alexandra, the Jukskei River served as the site where women socialized and washed clothes.[63] The use of this water-way, however, failed to quell the rising anxiety of the NEDPL, whose members argued that there was a danger "… in the widespread practice of European wash-ing being taken into the Township." The body further asserted, "Water used by natives … [was] taken mainly from surface wells, or from dongas, which [were] also used as latrines," "and [therefore] [was] [also possibly contaminated]."[64] The League had every reason to worry about impure water. The Jukskei River harbored more than a fabled snake that allegedly devoured children swimming within its reach.[65] Remains of rotting corpses floated within its currents.[66]

Decomposed bodies attracted unwanted bacteria, insects, and other health threats, making the river an unviable option for drinking water. Therefore, the Health Committee found other ways to supply water to meet its residents' needs. Because of the deficiency in modern conveniences, the body authorized the con-struction of public faucets to appear in yards that often housed four to five fami-lies. Their installation, however, lay with the Standowners, many of who viewed their costs as prohibitive. Water was so dear that Baduza's tapping into this precious pipeline placed an even further burden on the township's supply and demand. Approximately 90,000 people shared the taps, including the ones that the squatter leaders had secured on the No. 2 Square and the communal taps that they shared with township residents.[67] For that reason, water, its acquisition, and its expenses became a hotly contested issue.

Barely able to sustain the limited social services that it offered, the Health Committee relied on the meager taxes it imposed on dog licenses, property hold-ings, business certificates, water, bicycles, ambulances, and sanitation removal.[68] To incur the squatters' additional expense in water services would not only strain the Health Committee's scarce resources, it also made the body liable for their usage from January until April 1947. During this four-month period, the squatters racked up quite a bill, totaling to the amount of £352.56.7d or roughly $600, even when figures ebbed and flowed.[69] The following chart details the breakdown:[70]

Water usage by squatters

Account number	Date	Usage
4081	January, 1947	£79.18.3d
4083	February, 1947	£88.1.0d
4085	March, 1947	£97.16.9d
4086	April, 1947	£95. 0.9d
		£449.7.6d

Peaking in March and April, where usage reached its highest level, squatters spent an average of £96 ($161.78). This translated into 532,700 gallons of water out of a total of 4,528,000 gallons expended by the entire Alexandran community.[71] These figures possibly reflected three scenarios: an increase in the number of squatters inhabiting the squares, and/or signs of wasteful practices, and/or mismanagement of subscription fees. When a beleaguered Baduza appeared in court to address charges of extortion and assault, he also had to respond to questions of finance. Although the magistrate had acquitted the squatter leader of all charges, Alexandra proper dwellers had raised an important question regarding where the weekly subscription and the initial fees went. The squatters, after all, were not paying for their water usage, and proper inhabitants lost money from not being able to capitalize on typical income generators. The squatters' residence on the No. 2 Square prevented the Health Committee and others from renting stalls during their Saturday markets. Acting secretary for the AHC W. C. T. Pratt substantiates this sentiment. He wrote, "The squatters [have] literally engulfed this Committee's market, and thus interfered with the business carried on there."[72]

Several stallholders, including the national self-help group the Daughters of Africa (DOA), a body formed in 1932 by Lillian Tshabalala in Durban which used its funds to raise revenue for the Second World War to set up afterschool programs, and to hold national and regional conferences, had refused to renew their leases.[73] This made a huge dent in the Health Committee's intake of revenue. The body also had to compete with the squatters who allegedly engaged in illicit trading. On top of everything else, crime reared its ugly head as the rivaling Spoilers and Msomi gangs, often brandished knives and other weaponry to garnish the weekly pay of hardworking Alexandrans. These two factions, which had instrumentally divided the township into warring turfs, wreaked havoc on Alexandra and unleashed a reign of terror the township had never seen before. Even though the squares did not replicate this spate of unprecedented violence, these spaces did call the permanent residents' security into question.

Safety was not only a major concern for inhabitants, it also impacted students, and government officials daring to tread inside or near the squares. Native Commissioner K. D. Morgan weighed in on the discussion, writing "[there is] the danger to personal safety … scholars and other people passing through the camp are continually molested and threatened."[74] The lack of security rested on the shoulders of the "self-appointed rulers of the camp" who so badly beat up several members of the sanitation squad that they required medical attention. Attacking government employees seemed to have been the norm as another case made it into the official record. When distributing workers' wages, squatters allegedly molested Health Inspector A. C. Pelser who had come for a visit from the headquarters in Bothaville to supervise sanitation in the squatters' camp. Because Pelser's "boys" had protected him, the government employee had escaped unscathed on several occasions.[75]

While cases of abuse flooded the newspapers and filled the government files, many Africans chose not to provide corroborating evidence for fear of retribution or in case the squatters went unprosecuted. Located in nearby Wynberg, an area sandwiching Alexandra to its east and divided from the township by Watts Street and First Avenue, the only police station provided abysmal protection. Not only did the police address Alexandra's needs, they also answered the calls from six White suburbs. Policing was made even harder by the illegibility of the shacks, which did not appear on the landscape in clear, straight lines.[76] In addition to the geographical problem that the city of tents presented, there was also Baduza's own security force and the authority it commanded. Per Native Commissioner Morgan, the problem lay there, as the government " [Needed] "To suppress the bogus 'magistrate' and … illegal 'police force' [that] [the] [squatters] [had] set up …"[77] Morgan failed to address why the squatter police had existed in the first place.

Contrary to a *Bantu World* news article dated 18 January 1947, ill feelings existed between the squatters and the residents.[78] Standholders "were dead against [tenants] taking part in any activities … [they] were even prohibited from holding meetings on the square."[79] Baduza's BTA had already gone several rounds with the Standowners when the body had protested increasing rents in 1944. When the Rent Board sided with the property owners, it ultimately greenlighted the Standholders to raise rents even higher.[80] A joint body of the Alexandra General Council (AGC), the Alexandra Standholders Protection and Vigilance Association (ASPVA), and the Alexandra Coloured Associated Association (ACAA) refused to negotiate with the squatters because the bodies, believing that they had usurped the law, had called for the JCC to dismiss them by invoking further emergency regulations.[81] The male propertied elite failed to stop there. In a definitive statement, they proclaimed "[we] are strongly against the squatters. Fear bloodshed at any time."[82] The Alexandra Township Council of Women (ACTW) threatened to flood Johannesburg's sports fields if the squatters continued to remain in Alexandra.[83] The women, who marched throughout the township, also waited outside the Health Committee offices while the body deliberated on the squatter question.[84] All of this acrimony failed to treat the inherent problem: geographical impoverishment.

From crowded Alexandra to Moroka emergency camp

While Alexandra stood as one of the country's oldest townships, it languished far behind its counterparts, many of which had the luxuries of police, running water, and electricity. The move to another place also came at an opportunity cost because the township's social and human geography incurred drastic changes as people left simply because it ". . . was better than squatting in Alexandra."[85] Relocation began in late June (the 24th) and concluded in mid-July (11th) 1947. Fifty-five Defence Department vehicles transported the dispossessed, covering a total of 99,912 miles at an average of 3,300.4 miles per truck and an astounding cost of £623.15.11, to their new and old homes throughout Johannesburg and beyond.[86] That process not only involved physically removing people and their belongings, but also screening them for potential disease, as evictees underwent a thorough physical examination. Other variables such as age, marital status, length and place of employment, and previous residence also came into play.

Documenting the subtractions, the additions, the dividends, and the deficits, the government created a paper trail to show how this major geographical initiative transpired. Morgan noted the pattern of dispersal by enumerating it into these six categories with the following counts: (a) accepted by the municipality (4), (b) returned to Alexandra Township (47), (c) removed to Hammanskraal (55), (d) repatriated (3), and (e) absconded (17).[87] While basing everything on a numbers game, official letters and records failed to go far enough in elaborating on their decisions regarding the sites chosen for relocation. For example, Klipspruit (in Soweto), neighboring Alexandra, and Lombardy Estates served as transit camps while the hosting town of Elandsdoorn took in the elderly and the decrepit. Hammanskraal absorbed fifty-five people, which included squatter leader Baduza, who hailed from there. Standing on mine heaps and encompassing 425 acres, Moroka took in the most people. Of the 55,000 people comprising 11,000 families, at least 1,474 units came from Alexandra's squares.[88]

Squatters paid for the privilege to live in this emergency camp. For 15s a month, they received a 20 × 20 plot of land to erect their temporary shelters.[89] They also lived under very precise rules. These regulations were so disturbing that Baduza spoke out. He stated, "The squatters cannot accept the Nazi Plan which has been hatched by the City Council. They have not been asked for their opinion, [therefore] they are expressing their rejection of it by the only means open to them by refraining from co-operation to implement it."[90] Entitled, "Squatters Reject Nazi Rules," this article, appearing in the Communist Party organ, *Inkululeko*, captured the sentiment of Baduza's response. The cartoon shows a barricaded wooden fence that housed a main building where prospective tenants tendered their fees and received their respective plots of land.

Signage screamed of the very restrictions that Baduza and his squatters challenged. "No Trespassing," "No Houses," "No Dogs," "No Agitators," "No Hawkers," "No Democracy," and "No Bachelors" warned violators, inhabitants, and visitors as much as the two posts, "Keep In," and "Keep Out"[91] did. When the government encouraged family dwelling, it also promoted ghetto-like conditions by having inhabitants build temporary structures instead of more permanent ones such as homes. Moroka's emergency camp represented a project of racial engineering; like the squatters and the squares they inhabited, it too became an exercise in segregation between Blacks and Whites, and Africans with each other.

Conclusion

Alexandra's squatters' movement conveys a powerful story of the dominant and the subordinate and the intra-tensions that simmered and erupted between them. Threatened both by Baduza's success in creating a "territory within a territory," opponents felt the sting when the squatter leader successfully established an alternate and parallel community that competed with the permanent population for social services and geographical space. In his discussion of how a state sees, anthropologist and political scientist James C. Scott offered examples from Asia and Africa to explore how the legibility of the landscape allowed the state's apparatuses to monitor the subaltern.[92] The Alexandran case study presents an example of this type of sight, while also showing how the gaze occurred on multiple levels. While officials kept a close watch on the permanent population, the subordinate dominator also used its power to observe the squatters. The landless eyed their "geographic oppressors," the White minority regime and the predominant Alexandran community. In the ready-made ghetto (Alexandra proper) and the manufactured one (the squares), a geographic symbiosis existed.

As a political exclave, Alexandra engulfed the squares in terms of size and breadth. Its squalor and high density created the ghettoized conditions that existed there. When the squatters descended upon the squares, they created an *intersecting ghetto* based on its geographical link to Alexandra proper. This fluctuation within spaces did not end at Alexandra's darkened doorsteps – it continued to elasticize in Moroka. Moroka served as a *temporary ghetto* because it allowed the state to provide an emergency camp before transferring people to more permanent locations. Alexandra's squatters and residents also took advantage of natural demarcations. Like the Jukskei River, the township's steep gradient carved Alexandra into different topographical spheres that intersected with Alexandra proper, the *traditional ghetto*.

Both the dominant subordinator and the marginalized subordinate utilized the landscape to empower themselves and to destabilize the other. These groups not only saw like a state, they also mimicked it. In *Location of Culture*, scholar Homi K. Bhaba argues that the colonized imitate the culture of the dominant group[93] . When Alexandra proper residents issued their menace-to-health argument, they took on the role of the White community by discrediting the squatters and their movement, just like the NEDPL had done in the late 1930s. This imitation, however, was not one-sided. The squatters turned their perforated geographical spaces into a reflection of the dominant Alexandran community. With this mirroring, the landless replicated the social services and the governance of Alexandra proper within the squares they occupied. Because the squares contained the dispossessed into an enclosed, subordinate space, their world, and that of Alexandra proper, was a ghetto.

Notes

1   Alfred Stadler, "'Birds in the Cornfield': Squatter Movements in Johannesburg, 1944–47," *Journal of Southern African Studies*, 6, 1 (1979): 93.
2   Olive Schreiner, "The People Overflow: The Story of the Johannesburg Shanty Towns," pamphlet, 1947, 46.
3   Philip Bonner and Noor Nieftagodien, *AleXandra: A History* (Johannesburg: Witwatersrand University Press, 2008), 89.
4   Philip Bonner, "The Politics of Black Squatter Movements on the Rand, 1944–1952," *Radical History Review*, 46, 7 (1990): 92.
5   From Native Commissioner K. D. Morgan to the Director of Native Labour: Squatters Camp, Orlando West: ex Alexandra Township, dated December 28, 1946 (hereafter letter to Director of Native Labour).
6   Philip Bonner and Noor Nieftagodien, *AleXandra*, 91.

7   Ibid., 92.
8   "5,000 Squatters Erect Shelters in Alexandra: Health Committee Condemns Action of Council," *Rand Daily Mail*, January 8, 1947.
9   Letter to the Director of Native Labour.
10   Tim Couzens, "Nobody's Baby: Modikwe Dikobe and Alexandra, 1942–46, University of the Witwatersrand, History Workshop, 1978.
11   Alfred Stadler, "The Politics of Subsistence: Community Struggles in War-Time Johannesburg: Inaugural Lecture, (Johannesburg: Witwatersrand University Press, 1981).
12   Dominic Fortescue, "The Communist Party in South Africa and the African Working Class," The *International Journal of African Historical Studies*, 24, 3 (1991): 481.
13   Anahita Mukherji, "Durban largest 'Indian' city outside India," http://timesofindia. indiatimes.com/city/mumbai/Durban-largest-Indian-city-outside-India/article-show/9328227.cms, date accessed 29 August 2016.
14   Ibid.
15   Ibid.
16   Maynard Swanson, "'The Asiatic Menace': Creating Segregation in Durban, 1870–1900," *The International Journal of African Historical Studies*, 16, 3 (1983), 401–421.
17   "The Ghetto Act," http://www.sahistory.org.za/dated-event/ghetto-act-or-asiatic-land-tenure-and-indian-representation-act-no-28-1946-passed, date accessed 6 September 2016, 24.
18   Benjamin Ravid, "Ghetto: Etymology, Original Definition, Reality, and Diffusion," in (eds.) Wendy Z. Goldman and Joe William Trotter, Jr. *The Ghetto in Global History* (New York: Routledge, 2018).
19   Douglas S. Massey and Nancy Denton, *American Apartheid: Segregation and the Making of the Underclass* (Cambridge: Harvard University Press, 1993).
20   See Alfred Stadler, "'Birds in the Cornfield': Squatter Movements in Johannesburg, 1944-47" and Philip Bonner, "The Politics of Black Squatter Movements on the Rand."
21   Dawne Y. Curry, "Class, Community and Culture in Alexandra, South Africa 1912–1985," PhD dissertation, Michigan State University, East Lansing, Michigan, 2006, 79–90.
22   Philip Bonner and Noor Nieftagodien, *AleXandra*.
23   Ibid.
24   Kim D. Butler, *Freedoms Given, Freedoms Won* (Trenton: Rutgers University, 1998), 120–122. This theory comes from Kim D. Butler's work, *Freedoms Given, Freedoms Won*, in which she compares Sao Paulo and Salvador, Brazil, to explore how Africans living in these communities created alternate and parallel spaces that both differed from and were like the mainstream community.
25   Philip Bonner and Noor Nieftagodien, *AleXandra*, 18.
26   Ibid.
27   Leonard Thompson, *A History of South Africa* (New Haven: Yale University, 1990).
28   Aran S. Mackinnon, *The Making of South Africa: Culture and Politics* (New Jersey: Pearson Prentice Hall, 2004), 194. T. R. H. Davenport, "The Beginnings of Urban Segregation in South Africa: The Natives (Urban Areas) Act of 1923 and Its Background," Occasional Papers, Institute for Economic Research, Rhodes University, (1971), 15.
29   Dawne Y. Curry, *Apartheid on a Black Isle: Removal and Resistance in Alexandra, South Africa*, (New York: Palgrave, 2012), 1–30.
30   Ibid., 55.
31   Dan Mokonyane, *Lessons of Azikwelwa* (London: Nakong ya Rena, 1994), 21.
32   Ibid.
33   Belinda Bozzoli, "Space, Identity in Rebellion: Power, Target, Resource," Seminar paper, Institute for Advanced Social Research, 18 May 1996, 5.
34   David Sacks, *Conceptions of Space in Social Thought: A Geographic Perspective* (Minneapolis: University of Minnesota, 1980), 167–168
35   Alfred Stadler, "Birds in the Cornfield: Squatter Movements in Johannesburg, 1944–47," African Studies Seminar Paper, University of the Witwatersrand African Studies Institute, 64.

36   Dan Mokonyane, *Lessons of Azikwelwa*, 22.
37   Letter to the Director of Native Labour from K. D. Morgan, Native Commissioner, 31 March 1947. Alexandra.
38   Correspondence between Native Commissioner and the Department of Labour, Sanitation Files, April 1947, N2/10/3, National Archives of South Africa, Pretoria, South Africa. Primary documents do not reveal the rationale behind the configuration and measurement that the squatter leaders dispensed. The allotments differed from and were smaller than those granted in Alexandra.
39   Luli Callinicos, *A Place in the City: The Rand on the Eve of Apartheid*, Volume 3 (Johannesburg: Raven Press, 1995), 44.
40   Mike Sarakinsky, "From 'Freehold' to 'Model Township,'A Political History of Alexandra, 1905–1983," unpublished Honours Thesis, University of Witwatersrand, 1984, 22–25.
41   "Thousands of Native Squatters Form City's Gravest Problem," *Star*, March 3, 1947.
42   Letter to Chief Native Commissioner, Alexandra Standholders & Residents General Council, 19 February 1947. "Alexandra Squatters Put Guard on Their Camps," *Rand Daily Mail*, January 23, 1947.
43   Mike Sarakinsky, "From 'Freehold' to 'Model Township,'" 85.
44   "Squatters at Alexandra Cluster in Squalor: 7,000 Families Now Inhabit City of Shacks," *Johannesburg Star*, February 2, 1947. Baduza and Mpanza agreed ideologically on this issue.
45   "Squatters in Alexandra Cluster in Squalor."
46   Ibid.
47   Josiah Jele, interview conducted by Dawne Y. Curry, Pretoria, South Africa, 2 May 2002.
48   "What They Saw in the Squatters' Camp," *Rand Daily Mail*, March 19, 1947.
49   Ibid.
50   Baruch Hirson, *Yours for the Union: Class and Community Struggles in South Africa* (London: Zed, 1989), 149.
51   Peter Tourikis, "The 'Political Economy' of Alexandra Township, 1905–1958," dissertation, honours degree in Industrial Sociology, Faculty of Arts, University of Witwatersrand, 1981, 35.
52   "Squatters at Alexandra Cluster in Squalor."
53   "Thousands of Native Squatters."
54   Ibid.
55   Northeastern Districts Protection League, "Submission for Removal of Non Europeans," GES 353/13A, National Archives of Pretoria, Pretoria, South Africa, 1.
56   Ibid., 2.
57   Ibid.
58   Philip Bonner and Noor Nieftagodien, *AleXandra*, 92.
59   Letter to Director of Native Labour, from Acting Native Commissioner, 10 May 1947.
60   Philip Bonner and Noor Nieftagodien, *AleXandra*, 93.
61   Mike Sarakinsky, "From 'Freehold' to 'Model Township,'" 24.
62   "What They Saw in the Squatters' Camp."
63   Dawne Y. Curry, *Apartheid on a Black Isle*, 55.
64   John Nauright, "'Black Island in a White Sea': Black and White in the Making of Alexandra Township, South Africa," PhD Thesis, Queens University, 1992, 103.
65   Dawne Y. Curry, *Apartheid on a Black Isle*, 55–61.
66   John Nauright, "Black Island in a White Sea," 103.
67   "Alexandra Squatters" N2/10/3 Squatters Camp KJB-424. National Archives of South Africa, Pretoria, South Africa.
68   Dawne Y. Curry, "Class, Community, and Culture," 30.
69   Letter sent from the Alexandra Health Committee to the Magistrate re: Water Account, Squatters Camps Nos. 2 and 3 Squares, Alexandra Township, Squatters Alexandra Township, 353/13 Sanitation, National Archives of South Africa, Pretoria, South Africa.
70   Ibid.

71 "Alexandra Health Committee," to Magistrate from W. C. T. Pratt, Acting Secretary, 26 March 1947, National Archives of South Africa, Pretoria, South Africa.

72 Northeastern Districts Protection League, "Submission for Removal," 2.

73 Dawne Y. Curry, "'A Nation She Defined': Lillian Tshabalala and the Threat of An Apocalypse in Segregated South Africa, 1930–1948," unpublished paper.

74 John Nauright, "Black Island in a White Sea," 103.

75 "Alexandra Health Committee," to Magistrate.

76 James C. Scott, *Seeing Like a State: How Certain Schemes to Improve the Human Condition Have Failed* (New Haven: Yale, 1999).

77 "Letter to the Director of Native Labour".

78 "Rain Falls on Squatters' Town," *Bantu World*, January 18, 1947.

79 Philip Bonner and Noor Nieftagodien, *AleXandra*, 92.

80 Ibid.

81 "Deputation from Alexandra Standholders Association," 353/13 Sanitation Files, undated, National Archives of South Africa, Pretoria, South Africa.

82 Ibid.

83 "Threaten to Squat on Sports Fields," *Daily Dispatch*, January 1, 1947. Dawne Y. Curry, "Class, Community and Culture," 81.

84 "Inquiry into Alexandra Squatting: Women Parade Outside Meeting," *Star,* January 28, 1947.

85 "Better Than Squatting in Alexandra," *Umteteli waBantu*, June 14, 1947.

86 Letter from L. I. Venables, Manager to Mr. Kockett dated January 23, 1948, 158/9 Non-European Affairs Department, 353 Sanitation Files, National Archives of South Africa, Pretoria.

87 "Annexure "A" City Council of Johannesburg: Outline History of Squatter Movement submitted to Fagan Commission: September 1947, 59–60.

88 Ibid.

89 "New Laws Will End All Uncontrolled Squatting," *Umteteli waBantu*, March 15, 1947. "Better than Squatting in Alexandra," *Umteteli waBantu*, June 14, 1947.

90 "Squatters Reject Nazi Rules," *Inkululeko*, May 1947.

91 Ibid.

92 James C. Scott, *Seeing Like a State*, 2–3

93 Homi K. Bhaba, *The Location of Culture* (London: Routledge, 1990), 85–92.

16

CITIZENS, NOT SUBJECTS

Spatial segregation and the making of Durban's African working class

Alex Lichtenstein

Introduction: The African working class

Writing in the 1950s, Marxist anthropologist Max Gluckman voiced his impatience with his fellow Africanists' tendency to "make the tribe and the tribesman the starting point of analysis," even when studying urbanized Africans. To the contrary, Gluckman argued, "the moment an African crosses his tribal boundary, he is 'detribalized'." As soon as Africans "engage in industrial work," he continued, they will begin to form social relationships appropriate to their new situation," including trade unions.[1]

When applied to South Africa, at stake in this formulation is the role the African industrial working class played in the anti-apartheid movement. After 1960, in an economy increasingly dominated by manufacturing, Black workers began to shed their identity as oscillating rural migrants, oriented towards advancing their fortunes back in their regions of origin. Instead, tied ever more to urban residence in a segregated area, regular wage labor in a factory, and social life in the city, they became proletarianized, and thus ripe for organization. Nothing drove home this truth to employers, labor organizers, and the state more than the mass strikes of African factory workers that whipped through Natal province during 1973. From January 9th, the date of the first walkout by 1,500 Zulu migrant workers at the Coronation Brick factory, until the time 1973 came to an end, nearly 100,000 African workers engaged in illegal industrial actions—more than twice the number that had struck over the entire previous decade combined.[2]

The urban residential status of African workers in this crucial period is deeply implicated in the question of working-class consciousness in South Africa.[3] In his influential book *Citizen and Subject* (1996), Mahmood Mamdani suggests that enduring divisions between rural and urban dwellers, migrant peasants and settled proletarians, those whose political loyalties clung to tribal authorities based in rural areas and those whose civic identities embraced life in the urban townships, can be traced back to the 1973 Durban strikes of "mostly migrant" workers. Mamdani deploys this rupture between "citizen and subject" to explain the explosion of violence during apartheid's dying days between hostel-dwellers loyal to the Zulu nationalist organization (Inkatha) and working-class African National Congress (ANC) partisans living in the surrounding townships.[4] He contends that in South Africa "the key social link between the two social spheres, Native Authority and civil society, is migrant labor."[5] Strictly speaking, this is true. But in practice such an assertion rests heavily on a *particular* notion of migrant labor: long distance, oscillating movement by male workers who retain deep cultural, material, and patriarchal ties in the native reserves. Whether they still could claim their "customary right" to land in the tribal reserves or not, the conservative consciousness of these workers remained imprinted with patterns of "indirect rule" dating back to the colonial era. In short, in Mamdani's view, theirs was not a proletarian consciousness oriented towards workplace rights, class solidarity, and an urban-industrial future.

But by the 1970s, the rift between "citizens" and "subjects" no longer adequately described the experience of enormous numbers of "migrants" living and working in the sprawling Durban metropolitan area, many of whom lived with their families or, indeed, were female. The term "migrant worker" or "peasant-proletarian" does not characterize those Africans who permanently resided inside the city, or the far more numerous residents of the peri-urban townships like KwaMashu, Umlazi, or Clermont, some of which by the 1970s actually fell within the physical territory and under the political authority of the KwaZulu "homeland," governed by tribal authorities. These settled areas, in turn, spawned their own "informal settlements", shantytowns nominally within the homeland, but housing "spillover" of urban Africans unable to find adequate or legal lodging inside Durban. In the specific social and industrial geography of Durban, *pace* Mamdani, the new Black unions that sprung up in the wake of the 1973 strikes did not depend on a "migrant social base" of hostel-dwelling "free [male] peasant[s] in an urban industrial setting." The history of labor conflict and urban segregation in Durban militates against conflating "migrants", with male workers on temporary contract, dwelling in hostels, whose residential rights evaporated when their contract came to an end. Indeed, by the 1980s, the largest hostel in the Durban area was Kranskloof, on the edge of Clermont township. Here, half of the 11,000 residents were women who worked in the textile plants in nearby Pinetown, and who constituted the most militant section of the working class and the backbone of the National Union of Textile Workers during a series of strikes in the early 1980s.[6]

While it is clear that the brick workers who initiated the 1973 strike wave were hostel-dwelling Zulu migrants from rural areas—the classic migrant laborer associated with apartheid in South Africa—there is little consensus about the identity of the workers who subsequently built trade unions with the capacity to challenge apartheid.[7] Were they long-time legal urban residents in Durban with what were known as "Section 10" residential rights? Daily or weekly "commuters" from nearby KwaZulu? Illegal urban squatters residing in the shantytowns ringing the city? Or contract migrant workers living in hostels, like the strikers at Coronation Brick? Investigating the composition of Durban's African working class during and after the strikes reveals the connection between "ghettoized" urban residential patterns and labor relations at this crucial juncture in South African history.

Defining the South African "ghetto"

The term "ghetto" has never been widely used to describe the patterns of racial segregation scarring South African history, either by apartheid planners, their contemporaries, or by historians. The word's association with the Nazi persecution of the Jews made the term unpalatable after the 1948 election brought Afrikaner Nationalists and their policy of apartheid to power. Before then, the term had been deployed by South African Indians against the restrictive Asiatic Land Tenure and Representation Act of 1946, denounced by protestors as "the Ghetto Act."[8] Subsequently, South African metropolitan neighborhoods segregated by the 1950 Group Areas Act were referred to as "townships", as "locations", even sometimes as "suburbs". The sprawling, impoverished, and non-contiguous rural areas set aside for Africans by the apartheid state were designated as "homelands", or in a neologism designed to thinly disguise internal colonialism, "Bantustans", slated for an ersatz "independence" from the surrounding territory of "white" South Africa. Meanwhile, the unauthorized neighborhoods that increasingly sprang up around expanding urban industrial areas like Durban during the 1960s and 1970s were known as shantytowns, shack settlements, or, more politely, "informal settlements." Grasping the constantly shifting and frequently overlapping nature of these diverse forms of urban settlement and racial segregation in the second half of South Africa's twentieth century is essential to understanding the composition of Durban's African proletariat.

In South African historiography, the terms "segregation" and "apartheid" delineate different historical periods, divided by the electoral victory of the Afrikaner nationalists in 1948 and the National Party's subsequent extension of existing racial laws and imposition of a battery of new ones.[9] I deliberately use the terms in tandem to signal the overlapping and interlocking nature of several projects of racial engineering that came together in postwar Durban. A coastal and port city that developed within the heartland of "native reserves" set aside for the Zulu in the colonial period, Durban's post-1948 racial order represented a confluence of local segregation policy and the national project of apartheid. In the latter case, it was in Zululand that the *territorial* segregation based on the older colonial system of indirect rule found its purest modern expression in the "Bantustan" policy, stripping homeland residents of all residential rights within South Africa. At the same time, during the 1950s, the city of Durban served as a laboratory for urban segregation as mandated by the national apartheid state. Finally, the decentralized rapid growth of secondary manufacturing in postwar Durban represented the quintessential form of *industrial* apartheid, drawing on migrant African labor while attempting to shed the costs of its social reproduction, as mining had done in the pre-war period. Only in

Durban did these three forms of segregation come into perfect alignment. The city's unusual economic geography made a deep imprint on the nature of the segregated African workforce. The close proximity of the KwaZulu Bantustan allowed a growing concentration of secondary industry to draw on large pools of so-called "migrant" labor without relying on the long-distance contract system; many workers were daily or weekly commuters.

The racial division of South African urban areas may have been "compulsory" and "segregated", in the definitional sense of the ghetto described by Benjamin Ravid in his essay, but by no means were they "enclosed." Quite the contrary—like the original Venetian ghetto itself, apartheid "ghettos" were permeable. Segregated areas in South Africa served as labor reservoirs, especially for migrant workers. Usually located at a distant remove from industrial enclaves and urban areas reserved for whites, these areas shifted social costs to African rural residents and tribal authorities, and away from municipalities and white employers. Nevertheless, the African workers essential to the expansion of secondary industry maintained myriad forms of living and working arrangements. Some were indeed migrant laborers from distant homelands, employed under contract for most of the year, housed in hostels or compounds and repatriated to rural areas for intermittent periods between their services of employment. Others, however, found surreptitious residential niches in or on the edge of cities like Durban. Still others navigated the narrow "gates" of apartheid law to secure the right to urban residence under "Section 10" of the 1952 Native Laws Amendment Act, a "right" tightly linked to employment. In Durban, as "homelands" territory and peri-urban settlement increasingly melded into one another during the 1970s, more and more Black workers commuted across the artificial border daily from their designated "tribal" area to factories located in "white" South Africa only a dozen miles away.

Who were the strikers?

Available sources on the 1973 strikes offer little information about striking African workers' urban status. In part, this is because employers themselves remained ignorant of their own workers' legal residence. The most comprehensive study at the time, *The Durban Strikes*, noted that "most of the firms [we interviewed] seemed to have little idea of how many of their workers were migrants." The one company that offered figures indicated that 85 per cent of its 1,000-person work force was made up of "contract workers," but that nearly half of them had worked for the company for more than five years. "Their urban status is different" than legal Durban residents, the report concluded, "but their position as workers is the same." *The Durban Strikes* surmised that while "about one in two of the Africans working in Durban are probably migrants … most of these are 'permanent migrants' who in fact work all their lives in the city on regularly renewed contracts but are legally considered to be rural, and have no permanent residential rights in the urban areas." Many strikers resided in the township of Umlazi, on the southern edge of Durban, which remained part of the area designated as the KwaZulu homeland;

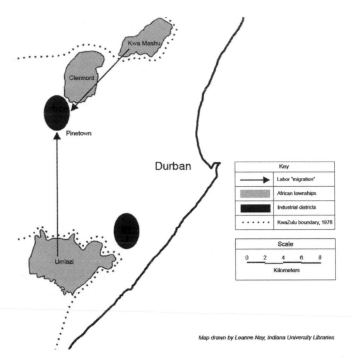

FIGURE 16.1 "Migrant" labor from African townships to Durban industrial districts, 1970s. Map drawn by Leanne Nay, Indiana University Libraries

in KwaMashu, to the north, a similar African township, still part of Durban in 1973 but envisioned as a future part of the KwaZulu Bantustan; or in Clermont, a freehold African township next to the industrial belt to the west of the city and adjacent to the KwaZulu "border" (Figure 16.1).

The researchers for the *Durban Strikes* interviewed a small sample of 91 workers: of those, two-thirds had lived in Durban for more than a decade and 42 per cent had worked for the same employer for more than five years.[10] Length of residence and employment were, in fact, key components of the Section 10 exception to the otherwise stringent restriction on African's urban residential rights. Even Hendrik Verwoerd, who as Minister of Native Affairs in the 1950s crafted apartheid's intransigent influx control policy for Africans, admitted that long-term city dwellers and "those who are such good workers that they have stayed for a long time with one employer" should be considered urbanized. As Deborah Posel points out, "The final version of section 10(1) introduced two important loopholes into the official influx control policy of the 1950s ... which seriously impeded the state's capacity to control African urbanisation in the ways it had originally intended": continuous residence in an urban area for 15 years, or continuous employment with one single employer for a decade, entitled one to permanent urban residential status.[11] Thus the apartheid state's conditions for seeking permanent urban residency status may have helped contribute to long-term solidarities in the workplace, even for putatively "migrant" workers from nearby Bantustan areas reserved for rural African residency. Another study concluded that "the African worker who lives in a homeland but crosses every day into the 'white' area to undertake work" is "most secure" in status, and thus most likely to engage in militant labor action."[12] At the same time, by the 1970s, industrial employers themselves preferred these more "stabilized" workers to the long-distant migrants recruited from deep in the KwaZulu hinterland.

Who is a "migrant worker"?

Evidence drawn from sociological studies and urban surveys done in the wake of the strikes suggests that hostel-dwelling long-distant migrants did not represent the majority of the African working class in the Durban area in the 1970s. The growth of manufacturing in and around Durban, and the growing militancy of the city's African proletariat, coincided with the rapid expansion of a ring of permanent African urban communities surrounding the city's core. Driven by a combination of forced relocation imposed by stricter segregation within Durban, the transfer of peri-urban areas to the homeland authorities of KwaZulu, the lack of adequate housing for African workers already in the city, and continued rural in-migration, these areas saw explosive population growth during the 1970s. In the aftermath of the labor upheaval of 1973, these segregated communities became an urban social laboratory, akin perhaps to Chicago in the 1920s–1940s (progenitor of the term "ghetto" in American urban sociology).[13] Indeed, this is one of the reasons we have so much data about African urban life in Durban in this era. Faced with an expanding population pressing on the city's space and resources, social scientists from the University of Natal (UND) fanned out across the African urban settlements that had sprung up over the past two decades. Many of their social surveys, conducted under the auspices of the university's Centre for Applied Social Science (CASS), sought to determine if urban residents, whether migrants living in hostels, settled township dwellers, or squatters in shantytowns, were "rural" or "urban" in their orientation. Key measures of this turned on their origins, continued ties to the countryside, aspirations, employment status, commitment to permanent urbanization, and familial living arrangements.

Residents of these communities worked in every sector of Durban's economy, from domestic service, to transport, to manufacturing, to the growing "informal sector." Unfortunately, it is impossible to determine how many *industrial workers* in the Durban area in 1973—or how many of the strikers—lived in long-term, semi-autonomous shack settlements on the edge of the city, old pockets of freehold areas where African workers could rent or own property, growing peri-urban townships like KwaMashu, were short-term commuters from the surrounding Bantustan of KwaZulu (e.g., Umlazi), or long-term migrant contract workers housed in hostels, like the brickworkers who initiated the strikes. Nevertheless, there is no reason to characterize them all as "migrants," as subjects "in civil society, but not of civil society." Instead, their growing urban stability coupled with their attenuating rural ties was one of the central features of worker identity and industrial citizenship in the Durban area at the time of the strikes, and certainly over the decade that followed.

A preliminary breakdown of "settled" and migrant workers in the Durban area comes from the records of the Central District Labour Bureau of the Port Natal Administration Board (PNAB). In the late 1970s, R.H. Scharff, a researcher at UND's Economics Department, used over 1,000 employee cards held by the PNAB to record workers' employment and legal residency status for 1978. The results are revealing. "Requisitioned" workers, that is, those who were not a "permanent resident of one of Durban's African townships," and "imported" into the Durban workforce by an employer who had convinced the labor bureau that "no suitable local labor was available," represented less than 40 per cent of the cards sampled. These workers, classified under segregation legislation as falling under Section 10(1)(d), had very limited urban residential rights, linked only to their temporary labor contracts.[14]

These requisitioned workers stood out from the majority of Africans in Durban's complex labor market. Many fell into the categories of "Stabilized Workers" with "some [Section 10] rights within the urban area and labour market," including "those who are township householders and their working families and dependents." As Scharff explained, many of these workers were "contract commuters," residents of the "dormitory townships of KwaMashu, Ntizuma, and Umlazi, near Durban." Their status as permitted work-seekers depended on their identity as "actual or intended citizens of KwaZulu," yet the Labour Board treated them "exactly as if they were resident in a [municipal] township managed by the [PNAB]." Others were considered "Settled Workers", who resided permanently in the townships and "could obtain permits-to-seek work on demand and could work for anyone they chose," as could their dependents. Finally, some workers held "Open Permits" under Section 10(1)(d), having acquired the right to reside in the Durban area and legally seek work there.[15] Table 16.1 shows the breakdown of the 1,000 workers sampled into categories provided by Scharff and puts this diverse labor force in perspective.

Of the stabilized workers, 18.8 per cent were women, as opposed to only 4.6 per cent of the requisitioned workers. Not surprisingly, nearly all the requisitioned workers came from Natal and the adjoining Transkei, but even about 30 per cent of them lived close enough to Durban "to commute to their work places" rather than

TABLE 16.1 Migrant status of workers, Durban, 1977

Requisitioned workers	38.4%
Contract commuters	10.1%
Settled workers	19.3%
Dependents	15.4%
Stabilized workers, total	61.6%

From R.H. Scharff, "A profile of the African workforce in Durban," Black/White income gap project, final research report no. 3 (Durban: UND Department of Economics, 1981), p. 9.

reside in urban hostels. Unfortunately, less than 30 per cent of the cards surveyed indicated workers' exact addresses, and even these proved unreliable, suggesting the fluidity of residential life for urbanized Africans, many of who may have lived in informal shack settlements. Nevertheless, of the cards that indicated address, residence in the outer townships of KwaMashu, Umlazi, and Ntuzuma was by far the most common, at 86.5 per cent (see Fig. 16.1). Notwithstanding their actual residence, two-thirds of the stabilized workers appeared to be limited to Section 10(1)(d) rights; only a minority had achieved more "permanent" residential status through the complex legal exceptions allowed under Section 10. Yet as Scharff showed, this undercounted dependents who had obtained residential rights. With this revision in mind, he estimated that only 43.8 per cent of stabilized workers were actually classified as Section d. Moreover, as Scharff noted, regardless of Section 10 status, "there is little to prevent the worker from moving his family to a shanty town …, and even less to prevent his offering his services illegally on the informal sector's labour market." Thus it was possible even for "a requisitioned worker to achieve a certain degree of residential stabilization."[16]

The case against proletarianization rests not just on an unexamined notion of migrancy, but on the persistence of Zulu ethno-political ties and cultural identity. In Scharff's sample, 85.8 per cent of workers were indeed of Zulu ethnicity, not surprising given Durban's location. But it is striking to note that, in fact, the proportion of Zulu workers was actually slightly *higher* (87.8 per cent) among stabilized than requisitioned (82.5 per cent) workers, with the latter consisting of a larger proportion of Xhosa workers, presumably because the location of the Transkei made long-distant contract work more likely for them than for Zulus residing nearer to Durban.

Most significantly, in Durban's manufacturing sector in particular, stabilized far outnumbered requisitioned workers; one-third of all stabilized workers labored in manufacturing, far more than in any other sector. Requisitioned workers were concentrated in domestic service and construction, and only 10.6 per cent worked in the manufacturing plants at the center of the 1973 strikes and the independent Black unions. Finally, the Durban labor force was surprisingly stable, at least in this survey. Fully half of the stabilized workers had held their jobs for five years or more (and thus had been present during the strikes), and 25 per cent had worked in the same place for more than ten years; remarkably, thanks to the call-in-card system, even 30 per cent of migrant workers showed similar employment persistence. Another 30 per cent had been in the same job for more than 2.5 years, that is, they had renewed their contracts at least twice.

Durban's "racial ecology"

The sociological studies generated at UND during the 1970s, and remaining PNAB records in the Durban Archives Repository, can supplement Scharff's data. This material reveals how the dual imposition of urban and territorial segregation shaped the nature of Durban's African working class. As Scharff's research suggests, an abstracted notion of "migrant labor" obscures the complex nature of segregation in Durban. The spatial arrangement of the close proximity of Durban's industrial core to an African labor force living in the reserves had deep historical roots. As Paul Maylam argues, at the moment that Durban's secondary industry began to grow in earnest during the late 1940s, the high proportion of "migrant" African workers (75 per cent) disguised the fact that "Durban's relative proximity to reserve areas ... makes the classification of people into migrant or non-migrant categories highly problematic." As he points out, even then many African workers commuted on a weekly basis between urban-industrial and rural-reserve areas, rather than working as 11-month contract laborers confined to urban hostels. Maylam concludes that "a definite trend towards stabilization [was] apparent" by the 1950s, with, by one estimate, half of the city's African population residing permanently in the urban area. Apartheid sought to reverse this trend.[17]

Of course, white residents in Durban, notwithstanding their reputation as English-speaking "liberals", had segregated urban social space long before the 1948 triumph of the Afrikaner National party. But until the 1940s, the relatively small number of African residents (only 70,000 in 1940), their residence in hostels, limited local state capacity, an abundance of open space, and an overwhelming focus on protecting white neighborhoods from the city's large Indian population kept full-scale segregationist policy at bay. It was in this era that an African freehold township like Clermont and an inner city shack settlement like Cato Manor established a firm foothold as part of Durban's urban geography. By the 1970s, Clermont remained the residential locus for African textile workers, but Africans in Cato Manor had been forcibly relocated by the municipality and formed the initial core of the townships of Umlazi and KwaMashu, which provided tens of thousands of daily commuters to the city's labor pool. A thorough 1958 study of Durban's "racial ecology" indicated that while in the census tracts of the original urban core African residents "consist[ed] mainly of single men or married men, living away from their families," this was not the case in the city's outer fringes, where the sex ratio in the African population had decreased to 1.38:1. Twenty-five years before the strikes, near the very sections of Durban where secondary industry concentrated, African workers lived in family units.[18]

Empowered by apartheid's 1950 Group Areas Act, and faced with an African population over twice the size of its pre-war numbers, the Durban City Council (DCC) embarked on a program of comprehensive urban segregation during the 1950s. Between 1958 and 1963, the city removed 120,000 Africans from Cato Manor, despite active resistance. But they were not "endorsed out" to rural Zululand; instead, still dependent on their labor for its growing manufacturing base, the city moved them to the large buffer zones with the native territory immediately to the south and north of the city, "close to cheap rail transport." These areas, adjacent to Native Reserves, proved ideal spots for relocating the African urban working class.[19]

KwaMashu, for instance, was first established in 1956, and removals of Cato Manor residents to this area on the edge of the city began two years later. By 1962, a rail line between KwaMashu and Durban went into service, and by 1970 it carried 44,000 African commuters to work daily (another 46,000 commuted from Umlazi).[20] In this segregated liminal zone between urban-industrial Durban and rural KwaZulu, the city's African working class increasingly found a home between 1950 and 1970, forced there by the government, often with the encouragement of factory owners.[21] One study shows, for example, that in 1911, 89 per cent of Africans resided in the inner district of Durban; by 1970, the proportion had been reversed, with 91 per cent consigned by law to the outer ghettos. This inversion coincided with the *decline* of migratory rural labor, and the urbanization of Native Reserve labor. The inner-city Africans in 1911 were single men living in barracks; the peripheral residents of 1970s were families, permanently located to Durban, and living in places like KwaMashu and Umlazi.[22]

The local concentration of manufacturing drew on this growing African labor pool. As early as 1954, Africans represented 57 per cent of all wage earners in private industry in Natal.[23] Moreover, industries clustered in the districts outside of Durban's original urban core—Pinetown/New Germany to the west, and Mobeni/Jacobs to the south. But as Kuper's 1958 study of the city's "racial ecology" suggested, even before then, these sections housed African families "with a young age structure and a fairly balanced sex composition," many of whom were Christianized and married "or simply living together." Between 1921 and 1951, for example, Durban's African population increased by 100,000 (300 per cent); the nearby Pinetown magisterial district by 20,000 (150 per cent); Umlazi, inside the Native Reserves but adjoining the city, by 26,000 (100 per cent); and Inanda, just to the North of Durban, by 8,000.[24] By the 1950s, many of these people worked in Durban's newly established plants in the textile, chemical, and metal industries, the epicenters of the strikes two decades later. In Pinetown and New Germany, adjacent to the African freehold township of Clermont, new textile plants clustered. Similarly, between 1948 and 1954, the number of metal and machine shops in Durban and Pinetown went from 144 to 207, and African employment in this sector increased significantly. Between 1946 and 1951, overall African employment in secondary industry in Durban increased by 87 per cent; one regional planner concluded that between 1925 and 1954 the most important change in industry had been "the rapid rise of the Native worker as the predominant industrial worker."[25]

Because of a lack of housing for Africans, many of these workers lived in impromptu shack dwellings. Indeed, Kuper drew an explicit contrast between this growing sector of Durban's African population and those who continued to reside in hostels in the center, "characterized by migrant labour, high masculinity rates, lobola marriage, ancestor-worship and affiliation to minor Christian and separatist sects." The latter, while a decreasing proportion of the African labor force in Durban, remained "subjects" of traditional authorities established by indirect rule in surrounding "Native Reserves." But as Kuper accurately predicted, Africans would "continue to enter the city" to look for work, "whatever regulations are passed to control their influx, and they will find accommodation where they can."[26]

After two decades of sustained economic growth and forced removals from inside the city, by the 1970s the number of migrant workers in the Durban area living in single-sex hostels had shrunk to a very small percentage of the overall African workforce, as low as 4 per cent according to one study. Between 1957 and 1970, nearly all the growth in the area's African population came in the form of families living together, rather than the expansion of single-sex hostels. Similarly, in a count done in 1977, Clermont had 95,000 residents in households (many in shacks), but only 6,000 living in hostels. KwaMashu, by then a border community of over 150,000 people, and, like Umlazi, legally part of the KwaZulu Bantustan rather than the city of Durban, had only 17,000 hostel residents. And Umlazi itself had grown to a "ghetto" of over 270,000 people, with only 8,400 people living in single-sex hostels.[27]

Incorporating the Bantustan

What made the evolution of this form of urban segregation in Durban distinctive was the overlap with the *territorial* segregation of "grand apartheid" in Natal province during the 1960s and 1970s. The expulsion of Africans from the inner precincts of Durban worked symbiotically with the second pillar of apartheid, embodied in the 1959 Promotion of Bantu Self Government Act, and its 1971 successor, the Bantu Homelands Constitution Act. These laws sought to "find room under the African sun for both the irresistible force of Bantu nationalism and the immovable object of White nationalism," as one of its ideologists put it. Apartheid promoted "independence" for the former "Native Territories," while continuing to draw on African "citizens" of these supposedly sovereign Bantustans in a kind of perverse guest worker program.[28] Of the ten regions designated as "Bantu nations" by the 1959 and 1971 Acts, KwaZulu, which covered a third of the province of Natal, was the most fragmented, consisting of ten non-contiguous pieces of land scattered across the province. Much of this territory was carved from the rural hinterland, but the most densely populated sections of it—the peri-urban enclaves of Umlazi and KwaMashu—directly abutted the city line of Durban.[29] In Durban and Natal, the "grand" policy of separate development across the total landscape and the "petty" policy of continued urban segregation mandated by the Group Areas Act worked in tandem without a major disruption to the African labor force required for the expansion of manufacturing.

Mahmood Mamdani contrasts the "decentralized despotism" of indirect rule, reproduced as apartheid planners devolved authority to tribal authorities in the rural areas during the 1960s and 1970s, to the "centralized despotism" of urban segregation, carried out under apartheid through national policy grafted under municipal control.[30] This important insight ignores how these two forms of segregated governance increasingly *intersected and overlapped* in the spatial organization of the Durban Metropolitan Area (DMA). If relocating urbanized Africans to distant Bantustans in the name of a counterfeit tribal identity spearheaded national apartheid policy, its local embodiment in Durban and KwaZulu was the removal of Africans from Cato Manor after 1958 to the nearby communities of KwaMashu and Umlazi. These large African townships, unlike their close kin, Johannesburg's Soweto, were annexed as part of the KwaZulu "sovereign" territory during the 1970s, even while integrating more fully into metropolitan Durban through transport links, a growing labor market, and a settled urban African population. As the PNAB, charged with overseeing influx control to the Durban labor market, pointed out, by the 1970s, 94 per cent of the African population in the DMA resided *within* the territory of Kwazulu. Meanwhile, in the decade after 1970, the population of KwaZulu living in urban townships went from 11 to 22 per cent of the Bantustan's "official" population, reaching 750,000 by 1980 (the widespread practice of illegal urban residence no doubt led to an undercount). In order to facilitate a regional labor market, Umlazi and KwaMashu residents were permitted to "work in Durban and may seek work there freely," even though, technically, they lived in KwaZulu, the PNAB admitted. As one sociological study noted, after 1977, "Homeland city or not, KwaMashu is still a 'black township'" of Durban.[31]

From migrants to proletarians

By the 1970s, many employers had concluded that long-distance migrancy might not be compatible with their production needs. Yet they faced the problem of the state's desire to retain a labor system that radically separated the sphere of social reproduction from the site of productive labor. The solution, especially in KwaZulu and Natal, was to continue to shift social burdens to the Bantustan authorities, while bringing ghettoized territory into closer proximity to production facilities. In some instances, this meant the encouragement of so-called "border industries" located in the hinterland. But in the expansion and then incorporation into KwaZulu of Umlazi and KwaMashu, it meant passing administrative control of the territory of peri-urban working-class districts to the recently constituted Homeland authorities. The goal was to make urban-industrial segregation compatible with apartheid's radical separation of territory into allegedly sovereign spheres.

Paradoxically, apartheid simultaneously tightened the laws governing the flow of labor from districts newly governed by Tribal Authorities to "prescribed" (i.e., segregated) areas of white urban, commercial, and industrial character. The 1965 and 1968 Bantu Labour Regulations Acts, along with the 1971 Bantu Administration Act, created a dense network of over 1,000 labor bureaus across the country, designed to articulate urban labor needs with Bantustan labor control. In Durban and KwaZulu, for example, from 1973, the PNAB oversaw the *influx* of labor into the "white" areas of the city—the location of industrial plants—while over 100 tribal labor bureaus located *inside* KwaZulu in theory regulated the flow from the source.[32] But the regulation of labor "efflux" was not applied in Umlazi, KwaMashu, or other urbanized areas of the homelands adjacent to Durban; African residents there were treated as "administrative section 10s," that is, allowed certain urban residential rights by default. Urban segregation, Bantustan policy, and control of labor flows thus came together not in the person of the hostel-dwelling rural migrant, but in the "commuter", known in Afrikaans as the *pendelaar*—an African worker

TABLE 16.2 Estimated annual number of "border crosses" between KwaZulu and
bordering white areas, by transport, 1976–1981

Year	Bus	Train	Other	TOTAL
1976	56,800	40,000	14,200	111,000
1977	58,000	40,000	14,700	113,500
1978	70,000	45,000	17,000	132,000
1979	77,000	50,000	19,500	147,000
1980	84,000	56,000	21,000	161,000
1981	89,000	60,000	23,000	172,000

"Estimates of migrants and commuters 1976–1981," Urban–rural workshop report, University of Natal,
Durban. 1982, from F. Christensen, "Pondo migrant workers in Natal – rural and urban strains," M.A.
thesis, Department of Sociology, UND, 1988, p. 70.

who technically only had residential rights within a designated homeland, but was
permitted to work in a prescribed area by commuting to work there daily.[33]

The number of *pendelaars* grew rapidly during the 1970s. The 1980 Buthelezi
Commission, charged with making an "independent" KwaZulu economically sus-
tainable, discovered that the gross earnings of long-distance migrants were twice
those of these daily "commuters" in 1970, but by 1976, earnings by commuters had
multiplied seven-fold, and surpassed migrant earnings. One study of daily border
crossings from KwaZulu into Natal determined that between 1976 and 1981, these
figures increased by 50 per cent, from 111,000 to 172,000 (Table 16.2).[34]

Moreover, in KwaZulu, thanks to the urban geography of Durban, commuters outstripped the numbers of requisitioned migrant workers by the early 1980s
(Figure 16.2). Finally, at the recruitment end of the urban labor market, of the

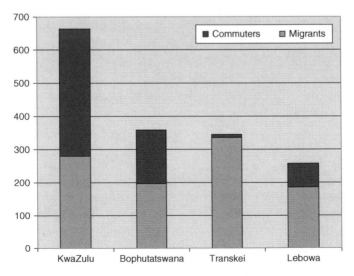

FIGURE 16.2 Long-distance migrants and short-term commuters sent from four
homelands to South Africa, 1981. Derived from SAIRR, 137–138, 1982.

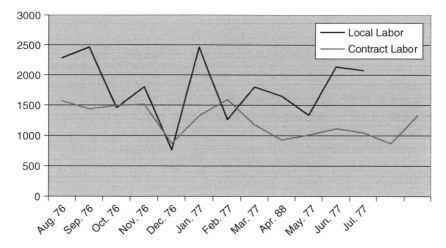

FIGURE 16.3   Vacancies filled in PNAB area, 1976–1977. Derived from PNAB: Returns, registers, reports, central. 1/1/1/274. Durban Archives Repository.

380,000 workers requisitioned by the PNAB in 1982, commuters outnumbered migrant workers 2:1.[35]

"The state is simply 'moving' whole populations of people (e.g., KwaMashu outside Durban) by re-defining the borders of the 'homelands' and incorporating townships [into them]," critics charged. More than half of all African commuters in South Africa came from KwaZulu, "where the homeland areas border directly on the industrial areas, thus making them perfect for 'commuting,'" a student "wages commission" observed. "The state has paved the way for including these people under controls applicable to 'outsiders' while industry retains the benefits of having a stable, close urban pool to draw from for their needs," they concluded.[36]

A measure of the relative prevalence of "migrants" and "commuters" in the Durban labor market are the monthly requisition records kept by the PNAB. These records allow comparison of the "vacancies filled" in the Durban/Pinetown district by long-distance contract (or "introduced") and by "local" labor over the course of a 12-month period (allowing for seasonal variation) in 1976–1977 (see Figure 16.3).

Manufacturing employers preferred the stability of employing "local" commuters to the uncertainty of long-distant migrant workers, who were expected to return to their homelands and re-sign an annual contract rather than develop residence rights.[37] "The average employer … has had the most unfortunate experience with local [contract] labour," wrote Pinetown's Bantu Affairs Commissioner (BAC). "In industry and commerce local labour under contract has shown a complete indifference to his work and has no qualms about breaking his contract," he complained. As a result, he observed, "many employers refuse local contract labour and ask for labour *with residential qualifications* for whom no labour fee is payable" (emphasis added). Particularly onerous for employers was the fee they remitted to tribal labor bureaus for each worker the Bantustan authorities sent their way.

The enormous textile plants in Pinetown/New Germany complained to the local commissioner that contract labor proved unreliable, prone to smoking dagga, sleeping on the job, or outright desertion, melting away into the surrounding townships or informal settlements. "A concern like [Consolidated Frame Cotton Company] employs 8000 Bantu in New Germany and have a turnover of 50% and more … the financial loss on labour fees would in a twelve month period reach considerable proportions," the textile conglomerate's labor officer complained. As the local Bantu Affairs officer wrote to his superior, the labor recruitment system "is being defeated by the attitude of the Bantu … There is no sanctity of contract."[38] Faced with these complaints, by the mid-1970s, the PNAB created employment service centers that transformed the peri-urban regions of Durban into labor ghettos for "border" industries that happened to be located inside municipal Durban. The priority areas consisted of Umlazi, Clermont, and Ntuzuma (adjacent to KwaMashu), because of their "closeness to industrial centres and the concentration of workers."[39]

Umlazi had long been part of the "Native Territories" adjoining the city to the south. To the north, KwaMashu became part of the KwaZulu Homeland—overnight converting commuters who worked inside the Durban city line into "migrant workers"—on April 1, 1977. By the 1970s, KwaMashu supplied almost 50,000 workers to the Durban area, and by one estimate nearly 9,000 of these labored in manufacturing.[40] Only 12 miles north of Durban city hall, and 15 miles from the industrial enclave of Pinetown/New Germany, served by commuter rail lines and home to 30 schools and more than 50 churches, KwaMashu, while perhaps a "ghetto" was, in the view of the PNAB, a modern, urban community. The township had a balanced sex ratio, and most people lived in family dwellings. A library study done on the eve of its transfer to KwaZulu indicated that the 150,000 residents of KwaMashu showed a 69 per cent literacy rate, far greater than KwaZulu's rural areas.[41]

Residents appeared to share the view of the PNAB authorities. When researchers asked people living in KwaMashu what they would do if their income tripled, less than 5 per cent claimed they would invest back in the countryside. Indeed, only a quarter of the sample even had "access to land in the rural areas" and only 17.3 per cent made use of this land. Nor did "visits to the rural homeland" crop up in the residents' list of favored leisure activities. The study observed that by the mid-1970s, even for those residents whose integration into urban-industrial life appeared blocked by apartheid, and who thus might "fall back on 'landed' independence" in the reserves, a fully urban orientation remained the norm. "If [return to the reserves] were the case in former days, for most workers of today there will be no going back," the study concluded. As UND sociologists noted, "The majority of migrant workers interviewed [in Durban townships] expect to remain in town for a considerable period of time—usually for the duration of a working lifetime."[42]

The other source of African labor in the Durban area by the 1970s was the expanding number of shack-dwellers who crowded both established areas like Clermont and growing settlements on the urban fringe, like Malukazi, a large "spontaneous settlement" adjacent to Umlazi.[43] The 1968 law requiring annual contract renewals in the Homelands, halting any process of permanent urban settlement by Africans, had the unintended consequence of pushing them instead to seek informal—and illegal—housing in the poorly administered territory that lay at the urban fringes where Durban and Bantustan met.[44] By one estimate, by the 1970s, over a third of African residents of the hilly Durban area—300,000 people—lived in these shantytowns, "often hidden in valleys where they cannot be easily seen" between built-up areas. Natal's Black Sash, an organization long engaged in contesting the pass laws and redressing the problem of urban housing insecurity, reported in 1979 that 60,000 African squatters lived in Clermont alone, twice as many as the residents living there in official dwellings. The ability of Africans to own land in the township adjacent to the textile mills meant that "spontaneous dwellings in Clermont are built on private land with the land-owner's consent for which payment is made."[45]

Another study of these shack-dwellers determined that while slightly more than half had migrated directly from rural areas, a full 70 per cent "were strongly committed to permanent urban living," and a majority did not even maintain ties with their rural families. These workers joined the shack settlement because they had been unable to obtain residential rights close enough to work. A UND study of "squatters" living in "informal settlements" on the fringes of Durban disclosed much the same dynamic. Many of them lived with extended families, and 65 per cent worked in "industry and commerce in the metropolitan area." Since many of these squatters resided within the territory controlled by KwaZulu authorities but worked in Durban, legally they constituted "migrant" workers. Yet, as the study noted, "as social types, the people in the informal [housing] sector bear little resemblance to rural people or to migrant contract workers."[46]

One of the most revealing social surveys of the late 1970s looked at the recently established "informal settlement" of Malukazi. Although on the verge of being annexed to Umlazi, at the time of the study Malukazi remained under tribal authority, so that "land is held by kraal-heads by virtue of allocation by a tribal chief." Yet, despite this "rural" social characteristic, the study concluded that "the population of Malukazi is substantially an urban one seeking refuge in informal settlement" because of the lack of adequate services, a trend the study regarded as prevalent in Durban. The sex ratio in the settlement was almost even across age cohorts, and only 3.4 per cent of households comprised one person; marriage was widespread; school attendance was "unusually high," as was literacy. Much to the researchers' surprise, over half of the population in Malukazi had been born in Durban or a nearby peri-urban settlement rather than in the countryside. Less than a quarter "recorded a clear rural origin as place of prior residence," and 57 per cent "have spent all their lives in or near town." Those with jobs commuted to the center of Durban, or to industrial enclaves in nearby Jacobs and Isipingo. "There can be little doubt," the study concluded, "that employment … links the people of Malukazi to the Durban Metropolitan Area." Yet, on paper, every single one of these workers was a "migrant laborer" travelling from "rural" KwaZulu to work in an "urban" area. Above all, the study demonstrated that such peri-urban shantytowns grew not from the presence of long-distant migrants who previously would have resided in single-sex hostels and then returned to the countryside. Rather, they were populated by "spillover" from permanent urban dwellers unable to find adequate housing in town. In other words, Malukazi—and by extension, the other ghettos ringing the city—did not represent Mamdani's "rural in the urban", but the reverse, as urbanized African commuters encroached on rural territory overseen by KwaZulu authorities rather than the Durban municipality.[47]

Conclusion

While the 1950 Group Areas Act imprinted segregation on Durban and its outskirts, it left large peri-urban enclaves in place for Africans, governed as "Native Reserves" and then Bantustans. Given their proximity to employment, African workers drawn from these areas became, both structurally and legally, "commuters" rather than "migrants"; in some cases, they might even have been able to walk to work. Despite the fact that a third of its African laborers could be classified as "migrants" from the Homelands, by the 1970s, Durban's African working class appeared remarkably stable. Its social composition consisted primarily of daily commuters from Umlazi and KwaMashu, long-term residents of the few remaining African enclaves inside Durban city limits, shack dwellers in Clermont and on the urban fringe, and a very few long-distant rural migrants living in sex-segregated hostels. Increasing numbers of even these workers were young female textile workers bunking in the Kranskloof Hostel on the edge of Clermont. Informal settlements ringed the urban core of the city, even while some had been incorporated into the KwaZulu Bantustan. Squeezed between the central city and these communities lay the industrial belt that underlay the region's wealth, employed its growing African working class, and became the epicenter of the 1973 strikes. The same areas housed the social base of the new trade unions that sprang up in the strikes' wake. Although many Africans retained some semblance of rural ties, all the sociological data collected at this moment suggest that the vast majority of them oriented themselves towards a future of urbanism and full-time engagement with the city's labor market. In Durban, by the 1970s, the hostel-dwelling male migrant, with a deep attachment to his rural homestead and loyalty to tribal authorities in a distant Homeland, represented a tiny minority of the working class. Instead, peri-urban African working-class communities constituted the extension of the urban ghetto out into the "rural", rather than the temporary sojourn of rural residents in the proletarianized world of Durban's factories.

This is not to deny the attraction of Zulu nationalism to large sections of Natal's working class during the 1980s. There was, after all, a violent civil war pitting trade unionists affiliated with the left-wing ANC-aligned unions against Inkatha partisans whose political loyalties ultimately lay with Mangosuthu Buthelezi, the leader of the KwaZulu Homeland and by the 1980s the main rival to the ANC in the townships surrounding Durban. Yet the idea that the Durban strikes and their aftermath helped crystallize a hostel-dwelling, migrant Zulu labor force whose primary identity lay in their ethnic loyalty to their rural homeland does not hold up against the evidence. For if we had to choose between these workers as rural or urban, peasant or proletarian, subject or citizen, it is clear from all the data that they had become a ghettoized urban proletariat struggling for industrial citizenship in a segregated society.

Notes

1 M. Gluckman, "Anthropological Problems Arising from the African Industrial Revolution," in A. Southall, ed., *Social Change in Modern Africa*, London: Oxford University Press, 1961, pp. 68–70.

2 Institute of Industrial Education, *The Durban Strikes, 1973*, Johannesburg: Ravan Press, 1974, pp. 9–38, 98–99; South African Institute of Race Relations (SAIRR), "A View of the 1973 Strikes," RR 151/73, Appendix A, for a list of strikes and dates; SAIRR, *A Survey of Race Relations, 1973*, Johannesburg: SAIRR, 1974, pp. 284–286.

3 D. Hemson and K. Cox, "Mamdani and the Politics of Migrant Labor in South Africa: Durban Dockworkers and the Difference that Geography Makes," *Political Geography*, 27(2008), pp. 194–212.

4 A. Minnaar, ed., *Patterns of Violence: Case Studies of Conflict in Natal*, Pretoria: HSRC, 1992.

5 M. Mamdani, *Citizen and Subject: Contemporary Africa and the Legacy of Late Colonialism*, Princeton: Princeton University Press, 1996, p. 218.

6 Ibid., pp. 218–220; J. Copelyn, *Maverick Insider: A Struggle for Union Independence in a Time of National Liberation*, Johannesburg: Picador, 2016, pp. 96–118.

7 A. Lichtenstein, "'A Measure of Democracy': Works Committees, Black Workers, and Industrial Citizenship in South Africa, 1973– 1979," *South African Historical Journal*, 67 (June 2015), pp. 113– 138.

8 G. Shirli, "Jews and the Racial State: Legacies of the Holocaust in Apartheid South Africa, 1945–60," *Jewish Social Studies*, 16, no. 3 (2010): 32–64, p. 39.

9 W. Beinart and S. Dubow, *Segregation and Apartheid in Twentieth-Century South Africa*, New York: Routledge, 1995.

10 *Durban Strikes*, pp. 78, 8, 48.

11 D. Posel, *The Making of Apartheid: Conflict and Compromise*, New York: Oxford, 1991, p. 112.

12 L. Douwes Dekker, D. Hemson, J.S. Kane-Berman, J. Lever, and L. Schlemmer, "Case Studies in African Labour Action in South Africa and Namibia," in R. Sandbrook and R. Cohen, eds., *The Development of an African Working Class: Studies in Class Formation and Action*, London: Longman, 1975, 207–238, p. 24.

13 Mitchell Duneier, *Ghetto: The Invention of a Place, the History of an Idea*, New York: Farrar, Strauss and Giroux, 2016, pp. 34– 37.

14 R.H. Scharff, "A Profile of the African Workforce in Durban," Black/White Income Gap Project, Report No. 3, Durban: UND Department of Economics, 1981, p. 3.

15 Ibid., pp. 6– 7.

16 Ibid., pp. 10–13, 27, 8.

17 P. Maylam, "The Struggle for Space in Twentieth-Century Durban," in Maylam and I. Edwards, eds., *The People's City: African Life in Twentieth-Century Durban*, Pietermaritzburg: University of Natal Press, 1996, 1–30, p. 17.

18 Ibid., pp. 4, 12–22; L. Kuper, *Durban: A Study in Racial Ecology*, London: Jonathan Cape, 1958, pp. 24-34, 117–118.

19 Maylam, pp 22–26; Kuper, pp. 186–187.

20 G. Maasdorp and A.S.B. Humphreys, eds., *From Shantytown to Township: An Economic Study of African Poverty and Rehousing in a South African City*, Cape Town: Juta, 1975, p. 91.

21 Kuper, pp. 184–186, 190–191; A. Manson, "From Cato Manor to KwaMashu," *Reality* 13(March 1981), pp. 10–15; I. Edwards, "Cato Manor: Cruel Past, Pivotal Future," *Review of African Political Economy*, Vol. 21, No. 61 (Sep., 1994), pp. 415–427, p. 419.

22 R.J. Davies, "The Spatial Formation of the South African City," *GeoJournal*, Supplementary Issue 29(1981), 59–72, table 5, p. 68.

23 M. Katzen, *Industry in Greater Durban*, part 1, Pietermaritzburg: Natal Town & Regional Planning Commission, 1961, pp. 4, 8, 20.

24 Kuper, p. 142; J. Burrows, *The Population and Labour Resources of Natal*, Pietermaritzburg: Natal Town & Regional Planning Commission, 1959, pp. 82–83.

25 Ibid., pp. 167, 179–181; Katzen, pp. 165, 178.

26 Kuper, pp. 142, 214.

27 T.R.H. Davenport, "The Beginnings of Urban Segregation in South Africa: The Natives (Urban Areas) Act of 1923, and its Background," Grahamstown: Institute of Social and Economic Research, 1971; Maasdorp, *Shantytown*, pp. 68–69; Durban Facts and Figures, J. Maree papers, A3.S, African Studies Library, University of Cape Town.

28 S. Dubow, *Apartheid, 1948–1994*, Oxford: Oxford University Press, 2014, pp. 105–107; J. Butler, *The Black Homelands of South Africa*, Berkeley: University of California Press, 1977; S. Pienaar and A. Sampson, *South Africa: Two Views of Separate Development*, Oxford: Oxford University Press, 1960, p. 21.

29 Maasdorp, *Shantytown*, pp. 135–136, 138.

30 Mamdani, *Citizen and Subject*, pp. 96, 101.

31 "Report on the Labour Administration in the Durban Metropolitan Area," n.d. (c. 1969), PNAB records, 1/1/5/2, Durban Archives Repository (DAR); D. Bonnin, G. Hamilton, R. Morrell, and A. Sitas, "The Struggle for Natal and Kwazulu: Workers, Township Dwellers and Inkatha, 1972–1985," in R. Morrell, ed., *Political Economy and Identities in Kwazulu-Natal*, Durban: Indicator Press, 1996, p. 143; V. Moller et al., *A Black Township in Durban: A Study of Needs and Problems*, Durban: CASS, 1978.

32 UCT Wages Commission, "Riekert: Don't Worry, Everything's Okay," Cape Town: SRC, 1980, pp. 20–24; SAIRR, *A Survey of Race Relations*, 1968, pp. 159–161; *KwaZulu Ekonomiese – Economic Review, 1975*, Pretoria: Benbo, 1975, p. 75; S. Greenberg, *Legitimating the Illegitimate: State, Markets, and Resistance in South Africa*, Berkeley: University of California Press, 1987, pp. 45–46, 99; M. Horrell, *Legislation and Race Relations: A Summary of the Main South African Laws Which Effect Race Relations*, Johannesburg: SAIRR, 1971, p. 43, for the 1968 Act.

33 A. Lemon, *Apartheid: A Geography of Separation*, Westmead: Saxon House, 1976, pp. 196–197; Greenberg, *Legitimating the Illegitimate*, p. 99; Scharff, pp. 5–6.

34 Greenberg, *Legitimating the Illegitimate*, p. 95; The Buthelezi Commission, *The Requirements for Stability and Development in KwaZulu and Natal*, vol. 2, Durban: H + H Publications, 1982, pp. 154–155; F. Christensen, "Pondo Migrant Workers in Natal – Rural and Urban Strains," M.A. thesis, Department of Sociology, UND, 1988, p. 70; SAIRR, *A Survey of Race Relations*, 1971, p. 169.

35 SAIRR, *Survey of Race Relations*, 1982, pp. 138–139.

36 UCT Wages Commission, "Riekert," p. 41.

37 Horrell, *Legislation and Race Relations*, p. 43; D. Hemson, "Breaking the Impasse, Beginning the Change: Labour Market, Unions and Social Initiative in Durban," in B. Freund and V. Padayachee, *(D)urban Vortex: South African City in Transition*, Pietermaritzburg: University of Natal Press, 2002, pp. 195–221, 203–04.

38 BAC to Chief BAC, 12 August 1969, Bantu Labour, 2/PTN N/3/11/2/95, DAR; Chief Labour Officer of CFCC to BAC, Durban, October 29, 1971, 2/PTN N3/11/2/97, Pinetown Mag. District, Bantu Labour, 1971–1982, DAR; E.F. Ashwell to BAC, 13 May 1969, 16 June 1969, 2/PTN N/3/11/2/95, DAR; BAC Pinetown to Chief BAC, 29 October 1971, 2/PTN N3/11/2/97, DAR.

39 PNAB Executive Committee, Minutes, Oct. 7, 1975, 2/3/7/1, Minutes, Subcommittee, Transport & Labour, DAR, pp. 5–6.

40 J. Maree, "An Analysis of the Independent Trade Unions in South Africa in the 1970s," Ph.D. thesis, University of Cape Town, 1986, p. 141; Republic of South Africa, Department of Statistics, *Population Census 1970, Metropolitan Area of Durban*, p. 214, reports that of 58,000 male residents in KwaMashu, 8,500 worked in manufacturing, the largest number in any sector.

41 "Some notes on Bantu housing in Durban, with special reference to kwaMashu, 30 March 1977," and L. Schlemmer, "Commuting from Kwa Mashu," *Sunday Tribune*, May 28, 1978, PNAB, Statistics, 1/1/5/2, DAR.

42 Moller et al., *A Black Township*, pp. 33, 113, 81, 39; L. Schlemmer and V. Moller, "The Situation of African Migrant Workers in Durban: Brief Report on a Preliminary Survey Analysis," CASS, UND, 1977, p. 17.

43 Black Sash, "Some Factors Relating to Squatter Settlements in Durban with Specific Reference to Malukazi and Clermont," March 1979.

44 Schlemmer and Moller, "Black Urbanisation," pp. 1–2.

45 Maasdorp, *From Shantytown to Township*, p. 71; Black Sash, "Some Factors Relating to Squatter Settlements," pp. 2–3.

46 G. Maasdorp and N. Pillay, *Informal Settlements: Socio-Economic Profiles*, Durban: Economic Research Unit, UND, p. 147; L. Schlemmer, "Squatter Communities: Safety Valves in the Urban Rural Nexus," in H. Giliomee and L. Schlemmer, eds., *Up Against the Fences: Poverty, Passes, and Privilege in South Africa*, Cape Town: David Philip, 1985, pp. 167–192.

47 P. Stopforth, "Profile of the Black Population of a Spontaneous Urban Settlement Near Durban," Fact Paper No. 3, CASS, UND, 1978, pp. 1, 39, 44, 50, 54; V. Moller, "Mobility on the Urban Fringe: Some Observations Based on Seventy-Two African Households in the Inanda Peri-Urban Area," CASS, UND, 1978.

17

LOCATION CULTURE IN SOUTH AFRICA

Gavin Steingo

Introduction

This chapter examines contemporary Soweto—South Africa's largest black peri-urban area—through the comparative lens of the ghetto. My primary aim is to elucidate some of the cultural forms that have developed in Soweto since the end of apartheid in 1994, but in the context of a much longer history. My approach is historical, but also ethnographic: I have conducted extensive fieldwork in Soweto over the past eight years and, as an ethnomusicologist, have focused primarily on popular music practices associated with a genre known as *kwaito*.[1] This chapter includes discussions of music but extends more generally to cultural practices in contemporary Soweto.

Describing Soweto as a 'ghetto' immediately raises a number of issues. On the one hand, Soweto certainly *is* a ghetto in the normative use of the term, as articulated for example by Benjamin Ravid: it is segregated (almost entirely black), enclosed (it has clear borders), and to some extent it is 'compulsory' (one cannot simply choose to leave it).[2] Furthermore, Soweto is occasionally referred to as a 'ghetto' by its own inhabitants, particularly by those who view themselves as part of a Black Atlantic culture extending from Johannesburg and Nairobi to Kingston, New York, London, and beyond. On the other hand, 'ghetto' is by no means the most common term for segregated spaces such as Soweto. In English, such areas have since the early days of apartheid been referred to either as 'locations' (sometimes 'Native Locations') or 'townships'. The latter term is somewhat surprising, especially considering the very different way this term has been used in other countries, such as in the United States.[3] For residents of these segregated, enclosed, and compulsory areas, vernacular terminology is typically derived from the Afrikaans word *lokasie*: the most common vernacular terms are *kasie*, *loxion*, and *lokshini*.

Along with these vernacular terms, Soweto has developed a distinctive 'location culture'—a form of aesthetics, sensibility, and sociality that extends from sartorial style and music to interpersonal interaction, exchange, and caregiving. Despite the aggressively top-down construction of South African townships in the mid-twentieth century, people living in these ghetto (or at the very least, 'ghetto-like') areas have developed rich cultural forms. Such cultural forms lie at the nexus of multiple intersecting histories: of 'ethnicity' (such as in the case of apartheid's 'ethnic zoning'), of race (both in terms of apartheid and in the affirmative terms of Black Power), of spatial politics, and of mobility or immobility. In this chapter, I examine these intersecting lines both in material (or structural) terms *and* in the terms used by residents themselves.

A culture of immobility

When I first began fieldwork in Soweto in 2008, I was immediately struck by how immobile many people were. Movement is particularly restricted for the approximately 40% of unemployed adults with whom I spent most of my days. My musician friends would hardly leave their own homes, in part because they feared that their equipment would be stolen in their absence. Several musicians told me, with a mix of frustration and resignation: 'I am always here. I am always at home'.

More generally speaking, it is possible to identify three interrelated types of immobility in Soweto: immobility between individual townships, immobility between townships and other parts of the greater Johannesburg area, and difficulties leaving the home. These three forms of immobility are hierarchically related. If someone cannot leave her house, then clearly she also cannot visit another township or another part of the city. On the other hand, immobility is not simply a matter of scale. Indeed, the reasons for immobility between houses are not the same as those for the immobility between townships or between township and city.

In previous years, apartheid policies limited the movement of human bodies between township, city center, and suburb through curfews imposed on the black populace, raids, and 'passbooks'. During apartheid, police raids were a serious impediment to both movement and social gatherings. It is not surprising, then, that the apartheid police force played a large role in the cultural *imaginaire* of South Africans during apartheid. For example, the popular pennywhistle-based genre of the 1950s, *kwela*, was named after the term township residents used to warn each other that a police van was approaching.[4] The popular vocal genre *isicathamiya*, moreover, involved quietly dancing on tip-toes, ostensibly to avoid attracting the attention of mine bosses or police. Indeed, the word *isicathamiya* itself is derived from the Zulu verb *–cathama*, which means 'tread carefully'.

The infamous Group Areas Act (1950–1991, with many revisions and amendments) assigned racial groups to different residential areas and denied black South Africans access to the city center after working hours. In addition, the period between 1985 and 1989 was marked by a series of 'states of emergency', during which time strict curfews were instated arbitrarily and without justification. My friend Mike, now in his early 40s, told me that in the 1980s he and his friends carefully analyzed police raid patterns and had 'informants' in the police force through which he learned when raids would take place. He would attend clubs in the city center until about 9 pm and would return to Soweto just before police raids. At midnight, he would return to town to resume partying. This was not a sure strategy and many young men and women found themselves in jail for the night.

In the post-apartheid period, the boundary separating township and city center is far more porous, and all South Africans are legally entitled to move about freely in any public space. In fact, mobile fluidity has become something of a trope in academic writings about post-apartheid Johannesburg. Lindsey Bremner, for example, contrasts townships during apartheid—which she calls 'places of non-life, urban warehouses for black bodies'—with townships in the post-apartheid period: 'Now that apartheid has ended, these townships are, in a sense, no longer there. They have slipped out, leaked and scattered. The city, Johannesburg in particular, has become a Township–Metropolis'.[5] Similarly, Xavier Livermon argues that in the post-apartheid period new connections are revealed between city and township, especially through a genre of electronic music called kwaito, which he sees as 'the music of this new black mobility'.[6]

Bremner and Livermon are not incorrect. It is impossible to underestimate the importance of the fact that there are no longer political mandates preventing black people from leaving the township at night without permission, as was the case during apartheid. However, the mobility that scholars such as Bremner and Livermon describe is limited almost exclusively to the black middle class. Livermon goes to great lengths to illustrate that the Bohemian area of Melville, near to the city center, has become a type of Soweto out of Soweto. However, when I took a friend from Soweto to a bar in Melville one night, it was the first time he had ever been there. I realized then that going without my car would have been unthinkable. Thus, while I acknowledge that the black middle class is certainly very important in contemporary South Africa, one should not forget that the vast majority of Soweto residents are not middle class and so find it very difficult to move about the city of Johannesburg without access to personal vehicles.[7]

Getting home from Melville at night can be very difficult for workers, who often have to hustle. As Achal Prabhala has noted:

> [T]he walking classes have their own ways of making nightlife safe. When, for instance, people need to get back home—after working the kitchens and tables in Midrand, Melville, and Norwood, or just enjoying a good night out—they take South Africa's safest form of late-night transport: the Armed Response Taxi. Security company employees, driven to boredom on their late-night patrols and eager for a quick buck, will pick you up and take you home for the same price as a taxi.[8]

But the 'Armed Response Taxi' service cannot serve the entire working force of the hundreds of restaurants and bars in Midrand, Melville, and Norwood. Another popular, although precarious, form of transport hustling is the sugar daddy.[9] Many young women rely on boyfriends with cars to get them home at night – for this reason, sugar daddies are often known as 'Ministers of Transport'.[10] For most township residents, however, working in or going to Melville is simply not a viable option.

In brief, the city center and areas like Melville that surround it are considered inaccessible by many Soweto residents. A member of the Soweto Electricity Crisis Committee, an organization that protests against the privatization of electricity in the area, succinctly describes how most Sowetans view the city center of Johannesburg: 'Johannesburg is a different place. It is where the municipal offices are located … It requires transport money to reach, which is not a reality for most people here [i.e., in Soweto]'.[11]

Bremner and Livermon exaggerate the extent to which Soweto has merged with other parts of the greater Johannesburg area. In fact, for most residents of Soweto, the townships still feel fairly isolated. Most Sowetans spend much of their time during the day in their own township and much of their time at night isolated at home.

The amount of money and time invested in acquiring home audiovisual entertainment systems in Soweto is striking. In a study of 59 houses in Orlando West, Soweto, Helen Meintjes found that although 'virtually no labor-saving domestic cleansing appliances' such as washing machines or irons were owned, in almost all houses, 'hi-fis sporting all the available bells and whistles took their place in wall-units, [and] large televisions blared America soap opera melodrama daily'.[12] In the neighborhood of Soweto where I stayed during my first stint of fieldwork, I knew many people who had monthly subscriptions to satellite television. As I noted at the time, subscription rates in 2008 ranged between R150 (approximately $19) and R400 (approximately $50). Considering that the rent of a two-bedroom house is generally about R400, this means that TV subscriptions alone make up at least 15% of monthly household expenses.[13]

The post-apartheid dispensation has therefore resulted in a very limited form of movement between township, city center, and suburb. Most people do not feel safe in the streets at night. Moreover, very few people in Soweto own cars. Travel, especially at night, is extremely difficult for the 'walking class' in the enormous cluster of townships called Soweto.

Tracing the roots of immobility in Soweto

Since its inception, Soweto has been governed by principles of segregation and movement control. Soweto was originally created by the ruling white minority of South Africa as a collection of contiguous areas to the south-west of Johannesburg with the purpose of housing black workers. Areas housing non-whites came to be known as locations or townships. Note that although Soweto is usually described as *a* township, it is actually a *collection* of several contiguous townships. During apartheid, Soweto was a separate municipality, but today it is part of the City of Johannesburg Metropolitan Municipality.

The history of Johannesburg and, by extension Soweto, is intimately related to the process of capital accumulation. Johannesburg—also known as eGoli, or 'place of gold'—sprang up almost overnight, and quickly became a magnet for luck-hunters around the world. Migration intensified following the Second Anglo-Boer War (1899–1902), when rural economic collapse and the advent of taxation forced thousands of black South Africans to move in search of mine work. Nonetheless, in 1904, only about 22% of mineworkers came from South Africa. The majority flooded in from surrounding countries, as far away as Zambia. Initially, only black men went in search of work: in 1911, a mere 5% of the total black population on the Reef was made up of women.

Residential segregation along racial lines began in 1908, when municipal authorities ruled that only black servants could live in white areas. Segregation policies were often carried out in the name of 'sanitation',[14] as is evidenced by the fact that residential planning in Johannesburg's early years was the responsibility of health authorities. Maud observes that until 1927, non-residential aspects of 'native' life were administered by the same committee responsible for the zoological gardens.[15]

White anxieties about living in close proximity to black people can be clearly observed in the history of domestic servants. While most black workers were only permitted entrance into the 'white areas' during the day for work, domestic workers—who needed to be constantly at hand and were thus given permission to live in white areas—posed a particular problem. Between 1890 and 1940, several experiments were carried out to find the most suitable arrangement for these 'proletarian Trojan horse[s]'.[16] Until about 1910, it was standard practice to employ a black 'houseboy'—in reality, an adult man—as a domestic servant in white homes. This arrangement did not last long, however, and black men were soon replaced by female domestic workers, in large part because of anxieties surrounding black male sexuality.[17] In the 1930s, female domestic workers were replaced with young Pedi and Tswana boys. The notion that young boys would not be troublesome proved wrong again: the derogatorily-labeled 'piccaninnies' assembled themselves into gangs that terrorized white families, committing numerous acts of robbery and assault. As this brief historical sketch illustrates, the problems of multi-racial areas were simply impossible to resolve in a context where non-whites were violently oppressed. The anxieties borne out of this impossibility were symptomatic of severe structural inequality.

Although blacks were forbidden to live in white areas after 1908, the law was impossible to implement: mixed neighborhoods were convenient for workers and profitable for property owners. The first black township (Klipspruit) was established in 1905, but the population in this area remained small for decades, while slum yards in or adjacent to white areas continued to mushroom. Initially a failure, the first township nonetheless signaled the onset of a process that would accelerate in the next several decades. Built about 12 miles from the city, adjacent to a municipal sewage farm, Klipspruit was renamed Western Native Township in 1918. In the 1930s, two further 'locations' were built to the south-west of Johannesburg: Pimville (in 1934) and Orlando (in 1935). This was the beginning of the *south-west townships*, later named Soweto.

With the advent of apartheid in 1948, the state was no longer willing to tolerate multi-racial residential areas—even for the 'economic' reasons often provided by slumlords in the city. The government began brutally implementing laws prohibiting mixed areas, most notably with a series of forced removals of blacks from white areas. Several new locations to the south-west of Johannesburg were created, including Zondi, Chiawelo, and Senaoane. In addition to these locations, migrant workers evicted from the city were housed in a hostel in Dube. Apartheid, however, was not satisfied with merely dividing people along racial lines. Using a classic divide-and-rule strategy, the state categorized black people into ten subdivisions or 'national units' based on linguistic families. These divisions were not entirely arbitrary, and conformed—at least in some basic sense—to cultural patterns and geographical origins. Nonetheless, apartheid sought to purify and rigidify the distinctions, ultimately encouraging each ethnicity to develop separately along its own course. In 1956, new townships built in Soweto were sorted by ethnicity: five townships were built to house those falling under the Sotho language group, while another seven were built for Nguni speakers. Venda speakers were assigned to Chiawelo. Older townships like Orlando and Pimville, by contrast, remained ethnically mixed.

The apartheid policy of 'ethnic zoning' was at once spatial, cultural, and sensory. On the level of race, black South Africans were permitted access only to certain forms of labor (manual or menial) and a certain form of education ('Bantu education'). The literal valorization of the black body and denigration of the black intellect were tied to the *spatial* logic of apartheid, which denied blacks access to the city outside the context of labor. On the level of ethnicity, black South Africans were forced to live within their language group. As such, language and culture were tied directly to labor and space. President Verwoed was well aware of apartheid's sensible distributions. He declared that 'those who belong together naturally want to live near one another, and the policy of ethnic grouping will lead to the development of an intensified community spirit'.[18] In time, and with the careful application of apartheid logic, this statement gained some credence. Sibongile Mkhabela, who grew up in Zola, had this to say about her childhood: 'Zola is a Zulu area so, somehow, you were forced to unite on the basis of your language. A street away from my street in Naledi, a Sotho area. As long as I was walking in the streets of Zola, I was perfectly safe. But if I crossed the street into Naledi, then I'd have problems. As soon as I walked there I'd be a stranger to every kid and therefore a target'.[19] In this way, apartheid was not only a physical or spatial regime—it was also a sensory arrangement. It defined how and where one could speak and listen.

Mhoze Chikowero makes a similar observation about mid-twentieth century Rhodesia (now Zimbabwe), which was also dominated by a white settler minority, and which had deep political and economic ties to apartheid South Africa. Chikowero comments on weekly dance performances in a so-called 'Native Location' outside Salisbury (now Harare):

> Colonial officials and industrialists hailed the dances for distracting Africans from disruptive behaviors like fighting, drinking, and stealing. But they also

promoted the dances for their utility in constituting templates of intra-African difference and collective African distance from whites; their imagined belonging to 'tribes' rather than the nation; and their reinforcement of Africans' sense of migrancy, loyalty to the state as the supreme political authority, and respect for the 'dignity of labor'.[20]

As Chikowero notes, Rhodesia's white settler minority was interested in 'capturing, stultifying, and promoting these performances as "native administration"'.[21] So-called 'tribal dances', he continues, 'were an aspect of the colonial "traditions" that colonists and Africans cocreated in reactionary ways at the moment of colonization. The colonial state harnessed them into a cultural technology of domination'.[22]

On the one hand, these 'technologies of domination' worked at the level of sensory-perception rather than ideology *per se*. As Jacques Rancière has argued, and as I have elaborated elsewhere, domination does not require that the oppressed 'be convinced in the depths of their being'.[23] 'It is enough for them to act on an everyday basis', argues Rancière, 'as though this were the case: it is enough that their arms, their gaze and their judgment make their know-how [*savoir-faire*] and the knowledge of their condition accord with one each other, and vice-versa. There is no illusion here, nor any misrecognition'.[24] In other words, apartheid functioned largely through what Rancière has famously called 'distributions of the sensible'. This would explain Mkhabela's 'feeling of safety' when walking in a Zulu area; it would also explain how a 'tribal dance'—even if newly invented and bogus—might function in a context of colonial domination.

On the other hand, the very fact that apartheid domination was to a large extent 'sensory' meant that it was liable to sensory resistance. One very common way of resisting apartheid's 'stultifying' and tribalist sensory partitioning was to participate in black cosmopolitan forms of musicking, such as jazz. As anti-apartheid activist Albie Sachs once noted, the music of Hugh Masekela and Abdullah Ibrahim 'bypasses, overwhelms, ignores apartheid, establishes its own space'.[25] Indeed, there is a long apartheid history (some of it recounted earlier in this chapter) of black South Africans going to extreme and even dangerous lengths merely to dance or simply listen to jazz and other popular musics.

But apartheid's sensory distributions were not so easily undone. Instead, they were aggressively produced by connecting urban apartheid to two other forms: 'grand apartheid' which sought to partition the country into discrete racial locations, and 'petty apartheid' which sought to reduce personal contact between people of different races or ethnicities.[26] The forced removals of blacks to the townships in the 1950s and 1960s—urban apartheid—was complemented by the grand apartheid design of 'homelands' or 'Bantustans'. Bantustans were rural areas and were purportedly the true homes of the various black ethnic groups in South Africa. Blacks working in the city were considered 'temporary residents' in the townships and were forced to return 'home' to the Bantustans annually. The apartheid notion of 'separate development'—through which, it was believed, each ethnicity should develop separately along its own course—fully materialized in 1959, with the Bantu Self-Government Act. Under this

Act, blacks were not regarded as legitimate South Africans and instead were considered citizens of homelands. James Ferguson notes: 'Even South Africans born and raised in so-called white areas would be assigned citizenship on the basis of their ethnicity in one of the Bantu states, thus becoming foreigners in their own land'.[27]

It is worth emphasizing that during apartheid the discourse of *racial* domination was translated into one of *national* difference. This shift was strategic in two ways. First, it divided a large black population into much smaller groups, thereby thwarting a unified insurrection. Second, it sneakily erased race from the equation at a time when 'discrimination on the basis of color' was 'rapidly losing legitimacy both inside and outside South Africa'.[28] Writes Ferguson: 'Through this sinister and ingenious plan, the race problem (so-called) would be solved at a stroke, for there would *be* no more black South Africans'.[29] The problem of race, in other words, was replaced with the seemingly less anachronistic notion of independent nation-states.

Even so, apartheid policies continually crisscrossed the boundaries between race and nationality, either by blurring those boundaries or by sharpening them. Although blacks were divided into different ethnic groups, no similar division existed for white South Africans. A.J. Christopher points out that, while white South Africans were certainly outnumbered by black South Africans, no single ethnic group of blacks was significantly larger than the white population.[30] By dividing the black population into ethnic groups, the white population was no longer, by definition, outnumbered. This is why, despite the decades-old rift between English and Afrikaans speakers, the apartheid government ensured that whites from all backgrounds officially fell under a single 'ethnicity'.

The physical construction of Johannesburg and its surrounding townships reflects the apartheid regime's concern with segregation and bodily regulation. Soweto in particular was built in a highly structured way, with each township comprising rows of identical 'matchbox' houses on a plot of about 260 square meters.[31] Two types of matchbox houses were built. The first, and more common, model was a house of 40 square meters consisting of two bedrooms, a kitchen, and a living room. A tap and flushable lavatory were built in the backyard. The second and later model was slightly larger at 44 square meters and included a small bathroom with sink, lavatory, and bath.

Although houses were built in a highly structured way, their layout was intentionally 'extraordinarily inefficient'.[32] For the security of the regime, roads were constructed to make internal circulation difficult. All major roads led directly to centers of employment or retail. Within the townships, roads circle, stop in a dead end, and make travel generally quite frustrating. In fact, circulation within a *single* township is not always particularly difficult. However, to move from one township to the next—even when the two townships are directly adjacent to one another—is often extremely cumbersome and frustrating. Christopher summarizes this spatial logic in his *Atlas of Apartheid*:

> The [urban planning] guidelines proposed that group areas be drawn on a sectoral pattern with compact blocks of land for each group, capable of

extension onwards as the city grew. Group areas were separated by buffer strips of open land at least 30 meters wide, which were to act as barriers to movement and therefore restrict local contact. Accordingly, rivers, ridges, industrial areas, etc., were incorporated into the town plan. Links between different group areas were to be limited, preferably with no direct roads between the different group areas, but access only to commonly used parts of the city, for example, the industrial or central business district.[33]

These 'buffer strips' became a crucial feature of the apartheid landscape. In certain, very limited instances, a person could walk from a Zulu zone directly to a Sotho zone, as Mkhabela recounts (see above). More commonly, though, zones were separated by buffer strips that were extremely difficult to traverse. The original apartheid layout of Soweto can still be clearly felt, where a distance of one mile as the crow flies often requires that one traverses several miles. Consider, for example, the journey from Levubu Street in Naledi Extension 1 to Halolo Street in Mapetla (see Figure 17.1). The journey is 3.6 miles, although the distance between the streets is only 0.6 miles.

Soweto has, of course, experienced dramatic changes since the demise of apartheid. The nature of these changes is best articulated through Manuel DeLanda's observation that there are two main ways that urban areas are constructed: either as pre-planned assemblages organized from the top down, or as self-organizing systems with no central decision maker.[34] Clearly, Soweto's early development was determined by the former method. That is to say, the apartheid state designed

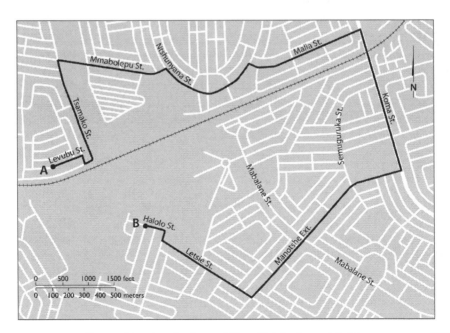

FIGURE 17.1 Route from Levubu Street (A) to Halolo Street (B). Map courtesy of Bill Nelson

Soweto very rigidly, incorporating modernist planning principles, including a unique interpretation of the work of Le Corbusier.[35] However, although Soweto was originally planned and built in a very top-down manner, it soon yielded to processes of immanent self-organizing. As early as the 1970s, housing shortages led to overcrowding and the construction of shacks in backyards. At this time, however, Soweto was still closely monitored by apartheid police and informal housing remained limited. In 1978, only 1% of properties had backyard shacks. During the 1980s, however, shack life exploded when Soweto became far more difficult to monitor and control because of increased protest in the townships. By 1987, 40% of formal houses had at least one backyard shack and 23% had a formally built 'garage' that was inhabited by subtenants.[36]

In 1997, there were nearly as many backyard shacks as there were formal houses in Soweto. In his ethnography of Soweto, Adam Ashforth observes: 'The severe crenellations of the original streetscape, bare but for the symmetrical rows of 70,000 "matchbox" houses, softened as trees grew, outhouses sprang up, and, after the administrators lost control, the mass-produced dwellings were expanded to fit the comfort and means of their occupants'.[37] What is interesting about these organic processes is that they have not eclipsed the basic regular structure of the original Soweto. Shacks are built onto the highly organized scaffold, but the scaffold remains. Informal, bottom-up organization is radicalized *within* and *on top of* the framework of formal modernist planning. Today, each original township has a three to four times higher population density than was intended, but the matchbox houses remain, as do their backyards.

Music production and the conditions of creativity

The specific mix of self-organization, embedded in the original rigid construction of Soweto, has led to a complex space that is very conducive to creativity. Although Soweto has developed fairly 'chaotically' in the post-apartheid period, these immanent processes are carefully hinged to the basic original structure. Thus, although each township has dozens of musicians and other creative workers, these people are still—to a certain extent—trapped in their respective areas. In what follows, I draw on over eight years of fieldwork in Soweto to offer some insights into contemporary 'location culture', with a focus on music.

In contemporary Soweto, each area is densely populated with musicians, many of whom are fairly immobile. Because most people in Soweto are not formally employed, they generally spend most of their day wandering around the neighborhood and visiting friends. In such a context, individual houses become nodes of communal creativity. On any day of the week, at least ten musicians pass by the house of a producer named Sizwe who resides in the township of Chiawelo in Soweto. People from the neighborhood come by to borrow equipment, play a bass line over something Sizwe is working on, write some lyrics, or exchange music. On some days, people will stay for six or seven hours at a time; on other days, they drop by for only a few minutes.

Communal creativity is largely the result of the three forms of immobility outlined earlier in this chapter. On the largest scale, few musicians can afford transport out of Soweto. On the scale of the township, it is easier for musicians to remain within their own township since movement to another township is often cumbersome. On the micro-level, musicians such as Sizwe seldom leave their homes. Musicians often own computers, amplifiers, speakers, and musical instruments. Because leaving expensive goods unattended is risky, it is difficult to go out for long periods of time—this is an issue to which I will later return. The highly sedentary nature of musicians has important consequences for knowledge exchange and creativity in Soweto. Put simply, musicians in Chiawelo know that Sizwe is usually home. For this reason, appointments and phone calls are unnecessary. When I lived in Soweto, if I wanted to see Sizwe I could simply go to his house. If he was not home, I was assured that he would be back shortly.

When Sizwe does leave, he does not go far. Generally, he only walks to a local grocery store or to a nearby friend's house. When people are walking outside and are asked, 'Wenzani?' ('What are you up to?'), they almost invariably respond: 'Ngishaya e-round' ('I am walking around'), or: 'Ngiya lapha no lapha' ('I am going here and here'). Notice that the latter expression is not 'lapha no lapho'—'here and *there*'—but 'lapha no lapha': 'here and *here*'.

Sizwe lives in a formally constructed room, adjacent to a main house, on a typical 260 square meter plot owned by his mother. His mother, sister, and two nieces live in the main house. The main house and Sizwe's room share a gate leading to the street, which is locked only at night. It is generally considered discourteous to lock one's gate during the day, as friends and neighbors may want to stop by. In most cases, at least when residents are home, house doors are also left unlocked or even standing open. Sizwe's house is therefore not properly speaking a 'private space'. In many ways, it is a central node of Chiawelo's musical and informational network.

Like most Sowetans, Sizwe makes music with whoever lives across the street or down the road. Because of the conditions of immobility and sedentariness, each township is a musical topology, a space of musical possibilities. But this space is circumscribed and narrow; one might say that it is aggressively partitioned, or even claustrophobic.

In brief, one might say that music performance in Soweto is constituted by a tension between creativity (or generativity) and privation.

I mentioned earlier that one of the reasons that a musician such as Sizwe seldom leaves his home is that he needs to protect his musical equipment. This observation implies that in Soweto, private property is configured in a particular way. A musician's computer is almost a kind of prosthesis—it exists as a veritable extension of his or her body. In the absence of rigorous state protection in the form of police, and with the 'deregulation of monopolies over the means of legitimate force, of moral orders, of the protection of persons and properties',[38] people tend to relate to their property *directly*. In other words, private property is seldom mediated by the force of law. Instead, there is an unmediated relationship between a person and a thing, where the thing is 'owned' through physical use. Thus, Sizwe can only be certain that a thing (such as a computer) is in his possession for the duration that he is actively engaging with it. The moment he leaves his room or even falls asleep, his relationship to property disintegrates.

Of course, the situation is even more extreme since property is often pried from individuals through robbery and mugging. In these situations, too, things have a prosthetic quality: since a thing 'belongs' to an individual only when it is somehow attached to the human body (for example, when it is in a pocket or grasped tightly in the palm of a hand), that thing is configured as an extension of the body. Things, then, do not belong to *citizens* in the form of private property as much as they belong to human *bodies* that grip onto things or else protect them with physical force.

Surprisingly, although people go to extreme measures to safeguard their belongings, they often *lend* things out easily, without a second thought. In fact, people do not only lend things out easily, they often freely *give* them away. The reason for this apparent contradiction is actually quite simple: lending is a social obligation. Adam Ashforth notes that in Soweto, 'people survive because others feel obliged to share and support them as members of their families, as neighbors, and as friends'.[39] There is an almost ubiquitous assumption, in fact, that resources will be distributed 'equitably and according to need'.[40] This does not mean that people lend things or give them away happily or unbegrudgingly. But it is uncommon to refuse a genuine request if one can reasonably meet it.

On the one hand, then, property is treated as a kind of bodily prosthesis, but on the other hand a person's relationship to his or her property is understood as fragile, provisional, or temporary. A Sowetan might guard a phone, a hard drive, or a wad of cash with her life but then only a moment later give all of these things away without a second thought when a friend knocks on the door and makes a simple request. The giver might depart with her belongings begrudgingly, but she will usually depart with them nonetheless because she knows—or at the very least trusts—that she will receive the same treatment at a later date.

It is important to recognize the profound tensions within any community that functions through intensive mutual dependence. As Carol Stack notes in her seminal study of a mid-size African-American ghetto community, 'Close kin who have relied upon one another over the years often complain about the sacrifices they have made and the deprivation they have endured from one another'.[41] One of Stack's interlocutors stated the following about the incessant demands of her mother:

> A mother should realize that you have your own life to lead and your own family. You can't come when she calls all the time, although you might want to and feel bad if you can't. I'm all worn out from running from my house to her house like a pinball machine. That's the way I do. I'm doing it 'cause she's my mother and 'cause I don't want to hurt her. Yet, she's killing me.

In Soweto, I have often been struck by a similar collision of incredible generosity and crushing resentment that characterizes material exchange. Hence, if the African principle of *ubuntu* is typically defined as 'a person is a person through other people' (*ubuntu ngubuntu ngabantu*), then perhaps Ashforth is correct that in contemporary Soweto this principle acquires a dark twist. If 'a person is a person through other people', this is indeed because other people can sustain your life—but it is also because they can kill you.[42]

But let us briefly return to equipment, and to musical equipment in particular. In terms of information storage, the situation in Soweto is extremely delicate. Musicians are often obligated to lend storage technologies such as external hard drives and memory sticks to friends. But external hard drives are not plentiful in Soweto. It is more common, in fact, for people to lend hard drives from their own computers or even to lend the computer itself. For example, Sizwe removed the chassis of his desktop computer years ago. When a friend wants to copy information from Sizwe's computer, or when Sizwe wants to transport information, he removes the hard drive from his computer. There have been many days during my fieldwork when I arrive at Sizwe's house to make music only to find that a friend had borrowed his hard drive for an undetermined period of time.

When storage technologies are lent to friends, and then to friends of friends, they often get lost along the way. Furthermore, hard drives are more susceptible to theft when they are being carried about than when they at the home of their owner and under his or her watchful eye. Finally, hard drives that circulate among an always-expanding network of people are liable to break or get viruses. Thus, recording—and not only performance—is transient. Music is hardly ever stockpiled or successfully archived; rather, it exists as a series of relays between 'live' performed music and *temporary* recordings. This musical form, as well as the cultural form surrounding it, is of course largely a result of the history and infrastructure of Soweto.

Concluding thoughts on Soweto as a ghetto

I conclude with a few remarks about 'location (i.e., township) culture' in relation to the transnational history of the ghetto. Certainly, apartheid-era Soweto was a ghetto in Ravid's sense of being segregated, enclosed, and compulsory—this much is not difficult to illustrate. But what about post-apartheid era Soweto? If Soweto's inhabitants continue to be segregated and enclosed, and if this segregation and enclosure is compulsory, this is clearly in a very different sense than during the apartheid period. Indeed, contemporary Soweto compels us to rethink and conceptually clarify the terms 'segregated', 'enclosed', and 'compulsory'. While Soweto certainly remains racially segregated from other parts of the greater metropolitan area of Johannesburg, the processes sustaining this segregation are not exclusively or even primarily top-down. We have seen in the course of this chapter some of the reasons that a large portion of Soweto's residents remains 'enclosed': recall the three forms of immobility outlined above. I have also noted the various reasons that immobility in Soweto is 'compulsory'—at least if we take this word literally, that is, as derived from the Latin *compulsus* (part participle of *compellere*, 'to compel'). For a variety of reasons, including the physical layout of the townships and the various expenses and dangers of transportation, many Sowetans are compelled to remain in Soweto.

Two other points are worth emphasizing vis-à-vis Soweto *qua* ghetto.

First, it is interesting to note the manner in which Soweto *mixes* top-down construction with bottom-up self-organization, or rather, the manner by which post-apartheid Soweto is constituted by a layering of 'chaotic' self-organization over an extremely rigid top-down design. Unlike most shantytowns or slums, Soweto's layout is defined by apartheid's obsessive rigidity. It is just that now, more than twenty years after the end of apartheid, that rigidity undergirds a highly complex set of social structures that are no longer restrained by explicit centralized control.

The second point concerns precisely the culture that has emerged through the unleashing of self-organization on top of a rigidly planned urban environment. In the recent groundbreaking book, *Ghetto*, sociologist Mitchell Duneier argues for the conceptual coherence of the term 'ghetto' across geographical space and over a long historical durée.[43] But he also insists on recognizing the stark *differences* between the medieval Jewish ghetto, for example, and the Jewish ghettos of the Third Reich—in large part because the former often allowed for cultural flourishing while the latter were essentially spaces of misery and death.[44] While this distinction is of course important, a place such as Soweto forces a considerable amount of blurring. In this chapter, I have examined the history of Soweto's contemporary 'location culture', a culture that remains firmly embedded within the location. Is this culture a flourishing? Or is it a kind of misery, a kind of social death? Who gets to decide?

In contemporary Soweto, the answer to these questions is being played out through a heated debate over one particular term: ghetto. On the one hand, there are those who affirm their 'ghetto fabulousness', that is to say, 'the willful retention of values and behaviors that oppose bourgeois middle-class sensibility'.[45] As Livermon observes, while the notion of 'ghetto fabulousness grew from a particular aesthetic centered in New York', it is today a central expression amongst South Africa's township youth.[46] On the other hand, however, there is a growing movement to indict 'the ghetto' *de natura*. Consider, for example, a song by the professional musician Simphiwe Dana, who—largely through her success as a musician—lives in a middle-class suburb of Johannesburg. Dana's song 'Sizophum' Elokishini' (2006) is a direct call for people to leave the townships *en masse*. For Dana, notes cultural theorist Pumla Gqola,

> townships are both the geographical ghettos that have come to define 'authentic' Blackness and the mentality that polices legitimate forms of Blackness. Townships are a white supremacist construction, and although they have been shaped by vibrancy, defiance and counter-cultures, the time to claim the world beyond township borders has long been with us.[47]

On her website, Dana adds the following quote before a transcription of the lyrics for the song: 'But townships were never our homes, Mandingo! This is where the butchers that were the architects of the horror that was apartheid sent us to die of disease, filth and self-hate'.[48] And yet, there is also a deep and obvious irony in Dana's 'Sizophum' Elokishini', for this song is stylistically an effervescent, 'retro' performance of apartheid-era, pre-kwaito township music (*marabi*, jazz, and township 'jive')—an elaborate sounding of all the suffering and all the hope that location culture has prohibited and afforded.

Notes

1   I would like to thank Joe William Trotter, Jr. and Wendy Goldman for excellent conversations about and comments on this chapter. See G. Steingo, *Kwaito's Promise: Music and the Aesthetics of Freedom in South Africa*, Chicago: University of Chicago Press, 2016. Portions of this chapter appeared as 'Sound and circulation: immobility and obduracy in South African electronic music', *Ethnomusicology Forum*, 2015, vol. 24.1, 102–123.

2   B. Ravid, 'Ghetto', in *Oxford Bibliographies* in Renaissance and Reformation, http://www.oxfordbibliographies.com.pitt.idm.oclc.org/view/document/obo-9780195399301/obo-9780195399301-0085.xml (accessed 11 July, 2016).

3   Consider the following intellectual lineage. In *On Revolution*, Hannah Arendt (1964: 235) noted: 'Lewis Mumford recently pointed out how the political importance of the township was never grasped by the founders, and that the failure to incorporate it into either the federal or the state constitutions was [in Mumford's own words] "one of the tragic oversights of post-revolutionary political development"'. In the paragraph before the phrase quoted by Arendt, Mumford (1961: 332) writes: 'But the New England towns added a new feature that has never been sufficiently appreciated nor as widely copied as it deserved: the township. The township is a political organization which encloses a group of towns, villages, hamlets, along with the open country area that surrounds them: it performs the functions of local government, including the provision of schools and the care of local roads, without accepting the long established division between town and country'. See Arendt, *On Revolution*, London: Penguin, 1964 [1963], p. 235; Mumford, *The City in History*, London: Harcourt, 1961, p. 332.

4   C.A., Muller, *Focus: Music of South Africa*, 2nd ed., New York: Routledge, 2008.

5   L. Bremner, 'The geography of exile', paper presented at the conference Urban Traumas, 7–11 July, 2004, Barcelona, Spain.

6   X. Livermon, 'Sounds in the city', in S. Nuttall and A. Mbembe (eds.) *Johannesburg: The Elusive Metropolis*, Durham: Duke University Press, 2008, 271–284, p. 282.

7   Rates of personal car ownership in Soweto are as low as 5% (although this is a very rough estimate). See http://www.nab.co.za/press-releases/carownership/ (accessed February 20, 2014) for more information. See also Steingo, *Kwaito's Promise*, p. 258, n 17.

8   Prabhala, 'Yeoville confidential', in *Johannesburg*, 307–316, pp. 309–310.

9   C.E. Kaufman and S.E. Stavrou, '"Bus fare please": the economies of sex and gifts among young people in urban South Africa', *Culture, Health & Sexuality*, 2004, vol. 6.5, 377–391, p. 379.

10 Ibid., p. 384.

11 As quoted in A. Wafer, 'Scale and identity in post-apartheid Soweto', *Transformation*, 2008, vols. 66–67, 98–115, p. 103.

12 See Meintjes, '"Washing machines make lazy women": domestic appliances and the negotiation of women's propriety in Soweto', *Journal of Material Culture*, 2001, vol. 6.3, 345–363, p. 347. Meintjes argues that appliances that would make 'women's work' easier were not prioritized in the homes she studied. While she may be correct in some sense, my own experience is that the gendered division of labor is not straightforward in Soweto.

13 See G. Steingo, 'After Apartheid: kwaito music and the aesthetics of freedom', PhD diss., University of Pennsylvania, 2010.

14 M. Swanson, 'The sanitation syndrome: bubonic plague and urban native policy in the Cape Colony, 1900–1909', *Journal of African History*, 1977, vol. 18.3, 387–410.

15 J.P.R. Maud, *City Government: The Johannesburg Experiment*, Oxford: Clarendon, 1938; as cited in A. Mbembe and S. Nuttall, 'Introduction: afropolis', *Johannesburg*, 1–33, p. 20.

16 I borrow this phrase from Alain Corbin's discussion of 'maids' in nineteenth-century Paris. See his *Time, Desire and Horror: Towards a History of the Senses*, trans. J. Birrell, Cambridge: Polity Press, 1995, p. 64.

17 B. Bozzoli reports that although male domestics did not dominate domestic service after 1920, men were 'still preponderant in the occupation'. See her *Women of Phokeng: Consciousness, Life Strategy, and Migrancy in South Africa, 1900–1983*, London: James Currey, 1991, p. 99.

18 As quoted in P. Bonner and L. Segal, *Soweto: A History*, Cape Town: Maskew Miller Longman, 1998, p. 43.

19 As quoted in ibid., p. 44.

20 Chikowero, *African Music, Power, and Being in Colonial Zimbabwe*, Bloomington: Indiana University Press, 2015, p. 131.

21 Ibid., p. 132.

22 Ibid.

23 J. Rancière, 'Thinking between the disciplines: an aesthetics of knowledge', *Parrhesia*, 2006, vol. 1, 1–12, pp. 3–4. See also Steingo, *Kwaito's Promise*.

24 Ibid.

25 'Preparing ourselves for freedom: culture and the ANC constitutional guidelines', *TDR*, 1991, vol. 35.1, 187–193, p. 188.

26 A.J. Christopher, *The Atlas of Apartheid*, New York: Routledge, 1994, p. 7. Note that the various forms of apartheid were implemented, with various degrees of intensity, on different temporal axes.

27 Ferguson, *Global Shadows: Africa in the Neoliberal World Order*, Durham: Duke University Press, 2006, p. 56.

28 Ibid.

29 Ibid., 54, original emphasis.

30 *Atlas of Apartheid*, p. 66.

31 J. Beall, O. Crankshaw, and S. Parnell, 'Social differentiation and urban governance in greater Soweto: a case study of postapartheid Meadowlands', in R. Tomlinson et al. (eds.), *Emerging Johannesburg: Perspectives of the Postapartheid City*, New York: Routledge, 2003, 197–214, p. 200.

32 R. Tomlinson et al., 'The postapartheid struggle for an integrated Johannesburg', in *Emerging Johannesburg*, 3–20, p. 6.

33 *Atlas of Apartheid*, pp. 105–106.

34 M. DeLanda, *A Thousand Years of Non-Linear History*, New York: Zone, 1997.

35 See E. Haarhoff, 'Appropriating Modernism: apartheid and the South Africant ownship', Paper presented at the conference Urban Transformation, 12–15 July, 2010, Istanbul, Turkey.

36 Beall et al., 'Social differentiation and urban governance', p. 200.

37 A. Ashforth, *Witchcraft, Violence, and Democracy in South Africa*, Chicago: University of Chicago Press, 2005, p. 23.

38 J.L. Comaroff and J. Comaroff (eds.), 'Law and disorder in the postcolony: an introduction', *Law and Disorder in the Postcolony*, Chicago: University of Chicago Press, 2008, 1–56, p. 2.

39 Ashforth, *Witchcraft*, p. 32.

40 Ibid.

41 C.B. Stack, *All Our Kin: Strategies for Survival in a Black Community*, New York: Harper & Row, 1974, p. 36.

42 Ashforth, *Witchcraft*, p. 1.

43 M. Duneier, *Ghetto: The Invention of a Place, the History of an Idea*, New York: Farrar, Straus, and Giroux, 2016.

44 Indeed, Duneier refers to the conceptual conflation of medieval ghettos and the ghettos during the Third Reich as a form of 'Nazi *deception*'. He shows how the Nazis claimed that their treatment of the Jewish population was nothing new.

45 X. Livermon, "'Si-ghetto fabulous" ("We are ghetto fabulous"): kwaito musical performance and consumption in post-apartheid South Africa', *Black Music Research Journal*, 2014, vol. 34.2: 285–303, p. 295.

46 Ibid.

47 *A Renegade Called Simphiwe*. Auckland Park: MF Books, 2013, p. 85.

48 See https://simphiwedana.wordpress.com/2013/12/10/lyrics-for-one-love-movement-on-bantu-biko-street-album/, accessed August 11, 2016. The quote is from Eric Miyeni's novel, *O'Mandingo! The Only Black at a Dinner Party*.

CONCLUSION

Common themes and new directions

Wendy Z. Goldman and Joe William Trotter, Jr.

The Ghetto in Global History deepens our understanding of residential segregation, politics, and social change across five centuries and three continents. It treats ghettoization as a dynamic historical process of growth, development, dissolution, and reformulation of space in transnational perspective. The volume not only documents extraordinary forms of human volition behind ghetto walls, but also accents the ongoing interpenetration of ghetto life with the larger surrounding urban world. It also reveals striking commonalities among ghettos that resonate across time and place. The volume provides us with a platform that allows us to survey a long history and to compare the findings and debates of scholars in fields that often have little contact with each other. The themes which emerge from such a comparative approach suggest not only some striking parallels among our four cases, but also new areas for future research. Among the most important themes shared by the cases are first, the ongoing struggle between the creators and the inhabitants of the ghetto; second, the degree of permeability of ghetto boundaries; third, intra ghetto inequalities and divisions; and fourth, the transnational linkages between the early modern Jewish ghetto and its subsequent iterations.

Ghetto residents organize: Struggle for control over space

From the outset of ghettoization, ghetto residents organized to give meaning to their own lives. Even more so than other areas of research, the politics of liberation and the quest for survival among ghetto residents will require multiple generations of scholarship to fully fathom. During the early modern era, Jewish governing councils played a major role in organizing and channeling the self-activity of ghetto residents. These governing bodies (rooted in earlier forms of Jewish governance and politics) often fragmented as well as unified the Jewish people. As noted elsewhere, the establishment of the Venetian ghetto entailed significant negotiation between

Jews, particularly merchants, and municipal authorities. Following the erection of ghetto walls, however, merchants, bankers, and, increasingly, realtors contended for influence over the course of ghettoization. In 1541, on the complaint of visiting Levantine Jewish merchants, Venetian authorities "assigned twenty dwellings in the adjacent Ghetto Vecchio" to alleviate overcrowding and insufficient space for the expanding Jewish population. Moreover, as Benjamin Ravid notes, "preemancipation Jewish communities, whether or not confined to a ghetto, were treated as corporate bodies and granted internal autonomy." They controlled their own religious practices and communal activities, "with assemblies and committees whose complexity depended on the size and nature of the specific community." Kenneth Stow, however, sees the sphere of Jewish autonomy and control as far more circumscribed by external control. He contends that Jews were never permitted primary jurisdiction over their own affairs. Stow does note, however, that Jews in Rome made every effort to contain disputes within the community and to gain some measure of power over their own affairs. They sought to litigate through Jewish notaries, thus creating an eventual base for a Roman Jewish "civil society."

As increasing numbers of Jews departed the ghettos in the wake of the democratic revolutions of the nineteenth century, the politics of Jewish liberation varied considerably from place to place. Although the essays differ over how much influence ghetto inhabitants were capable of wielding, even our contributors to the Nazi case, the most brutal iteration of the ghetto, stress that the Nazis never exercised total control over the ghettos. In the Nazi ghettos, where external authorities maintained power over life and death and ruled with extreme violence, Anike Walke and Zvi Gitelman/Lenore Weitzman demonstrate that ghetto inhabitants transformed forced labor into a means of resistance at every opportunity. The daily exit of Jewish workers from the ghetto became a conduit for escape and for smuggling food and weapons. Gali Mir-Tibon shows that even under life-threatening pressure, Jewish Committees tried to ameliorate conditions, keep order, and save as many people as possible. Helene J. Sinnreich, Walke, and Gitelman/Weitzman all describe activities that small self-organized groups within the ghettos undertook to subvert Nazi rule. They created social services and soup kitchens, engaged in smuggling, organized schools and cultural programs, and exploited every possible opening for survival.

Resistance also found its place in the transnational spread of the ghetto to the United States. In *Ghetto: The History of a Place, the Invention of an Idea*, Mitchell Duneier captures these dynamics of ghetto coercion and resistance in his descriptive phrase, "flourishing and control." While sociologist Kenneth Clark advanced the idea of the ghetto as the "institutionalization of powerlessness," sociologists St. Clair Drake and Horace R. Cayton described a robust "world within a world" of families, churches, and voluntary associations.[1] Both Avigail Oren and Jeffrey D. Gonda highlight the efforts of ghetto residents, journalists, and civil rights activists to undermine the legal foundations of segregation. Historian Jeffrey D. Gonda shows how interwar and early-post-World War II African American activists and their white allies defined the African American ghetto as a destructive form of human habitation that violated the United Nations charter on human rights. By treating the ghetto as "an international human rights crisis," civil rights attorneys astutely harnessed the increasing national and international condemnation of Nazi ghettos to their spirited and ultimately successful campaign to strike down racially restrictive housing covenants in the U.S. Supreme Court case of *Shelley v. Kraemer* (1948). Moreover, they did so by consciously deploying the word "ghetto" and the experience of European Jews. Brian Purnell discusses the effort of the Community Development Corporations to "unmake" the ghetto by empowering its inhabitants.

Our contributors to the South African case also demonstrate how township residents actively remade the constraints imposed upon them. Alex Lichtenstein describes how the concentration of black rural migrants into "ghettos" or urban locations forged groups with new identities, power, and aims. The labor demands of employers created new spatial forms that in turn gave rise to massive strikes and resistance. Ultimately, the needs of the factories for labor proved at odds with the aims of the apartheid state to maintain the cities for whites only. Gavin Steingo details how musicians developed "practices of immobility," imposed by larger spatial constraints that both nurtured and limited the development of their music, as a form of self-activity.

The permeability of ghetto boundaries

The question of permeability resonates throughout all four case studies. While some scholars stress the ubiquity of "walls" throughout early modern cities, they also invariably acknowledge varying degrees of permeability. As David Harvey points out, there can be no center without a periphery, and each helps to define the other.[2] Samuel Gruber stresses that Venice was a collection of walled enclosures. The Jewish ghetto, in his view, must be understood as one example among many, part of a larger culture of separation and control that affected many groups as well as the relationships among them. Yet, as Ravid notes, even walls had "holes, or more accurately, gates." The ghetto gates were open during daylight hours: Jews could leave and Christians enter. Jews maintained their own religious identity but shared the "general outlooks and interests" of their Christian neighbors. Stow, on the other hand, emphasizes the effect of enclosure. Although he acknowledges breaches in the walls that separated Christians and Jews, he nonetheless reinforces images of the ghetto as set apart from the surrounding non-Jewish world and vulnerable to immanent violence and even threats of extermination by Christian authorities.

According to Sinnreich, Walke, and Gitelman/Weitzman, even Nazi ghettos proved porous despite brutal efforts by the authorities to exercise complete control over movement. Even under the most totalizing attempts at control, ghetto inhabitants found ways to move food, people, and necessary items in and out. Tim Cole challenges the notion of ghetto enclosure in another way. Describing the ghettoization of Jews in Budapest in 1944, he notes that the Hungarian authorities designated specific buildings and even apartments as "Jewish ghettos." These ghettos were dispersed throughout the city and Jews continued to live side by side with Christians. Indeed, Jews often relied on their Christian neighbors to help them negotiate the severe restrictions on movement. Both Stephen Robertson and Cole note the ways in which ghettos, enclosed not by walls but rather by legal restrictions and discrimination, affected movement as well as access to goods and services.

In comparison with their European counterparts, scholars of North American ghettos accent their permeability. Notions of ghetto formation in North America emphasized its voluntary and fluid rather than coerced and enclosed character. In this scholarship, the ghetto was a staging environment for upward mobility for large numbers of Jews, non-Jewish European immigrants, and, to some extent, African Americans. But people of African descent soon encountered the most stringent and least permeable neighborhood boundaries in the urban industrial environment. An entire generation of postwar urban historians described African Americans as the target of the same coercive features associated with medieval and early modern Jewish ghettos. These ghetto formation studies repeatedly described early twentieth-century black urban communities as compulsory, segregated, and enclosed spaces that offered "no escape." Yet in line with later scholarship on the African American urban experience, our contributors eschew such iron-clad portrayals. Stephen Robertson, examining Harlem, takes up the case for extreme permeability. Indeed, he notes that the community's boundaries were so porous and crossed so often by those within and without that Harlem, often seen as the quintessential ghetto, was in fact nothing of the kind. Employing innovative digital mapping techniques, Robertson charts the day-to-day and seasonal ebb and flow of Harlem's "ordinary people not just the cultural elite." In accenting the myriad ways that blacks and whites continued to interact (in schools, small businesses, hospitals, law enforcement offices, and transit facilities) within and beyond the boundaries of an increasingly majority-black community, Robertson counters scholarship that posits the near impermeability of the color line in early twentieth-century Harlem. And while the system of strict residential segregation in South Africa created far less porous boundaries than in North America, as historian Alex Lichtenstein notes, authorities repeatedly made exceptions for African workers to take up residence in the white city to serve the labor needs of urban political and economic elites.

Contributors thus differ on the effects of segregation and enclosure, and they place different emphasis on the degree of porosity at any given site. Yet the issues they raise – human relationships across boundaries, the ability of elites to impose totalizing enclosure, and the challenge of structural processes and resistance movements to fixed boundaries – all suggest new avenues for research. Taken together, they make a persuasive argument that no wall can ever be totally impermeable, and no boundary so marked that it cannot be crossed.

Intra ghetto inequality, divisions, and conflict

All ghetto residents were subjected to external oppression, which united them in a community of shared suffering and identity. At the same time, our contributors reveal that divisions also flourished among them, and that, moreover, these were often exacerbated by the spatial limits they inhabited. Within the early modern Jewish ghettos, Bernard Dov Cooperman notes that restrictions on expansion "favored a concentration of power in a narrowing oligarchy based on property." As populations grew, limited real estate assumed ever greater value, yet the presence of a captive market provided little incentive to owners to invest in the buildings. Centuries later, similar problems characterized urban locations in South Africa and African American ghettos in the United States. As limited space became increasingly overcrowded, landlords both within and outside the ghetto realized enormous profits from tenants who had little choice about where to live. Even the poorer ghetto residents engaged in a robust market based on the subdivision of existing space. Indeed, subdivision is common to all four cases where too many people were confined in too small a space. Dawne Y. Curry vividly demonstrates the sharp tensions between squatters and residents in Alexandra, and shows how residents rented yards, sheds, and rooms, using and profiting from every available inch of unoccupied space. Curry illuminates the complicated process by which a subset of African people was segregated by class and condition within what she describes as "the bowels" of Alexandra's apartheid system. Squatters created their own "alternate and parallel community," culture, and politics (replete with their own system of governance, justice, and injustice, including police brutality) within their limited segment of the city. They created a ghetto within a ghetto. For his part, Brian Purnell demonstrates conflict over funding among poorer and more prosperous groups in black urban communities in the United States.

Even in Nazi ghettos, where the entire population was marked for death, there were sharp divisions between the poor and the rich, those of high status and low, and refugees and original tenants. Under the deadly food rations imposed by the Germans, refugees lacking material goods to barter were often the first to die of starvation. Mir-Tibon shows that in the Mogilev district, wealth and status influenced the Jewish Committees that were forced by Romanian authorities to meet quotas of people for shipment out of the ghetto to starvation camps. Wealthier Jews who were from the area escaped the shipments, while poorer refugees, especially single mothers with children, were selected for death.

These essays all deal with painful issues, and caution us against any approach to the ghetto that fails to consider the divisions within it. Although we must never lose sight of the external constraints that ghetto inhabitants suffered, the ways in which class, status, and stratification within the ghetto interact with those constraints provide new and challenging areas for research.

Historical connections and transnational linkages

Finally, by placing these four case studies in comparative perspective, connections among them that were hitherto obscured or ignored begin to emerge. One of the volume's most valuable findings is that both the makers and the inhabitants of ghettos drew on previous practices and experiences. Indeed, the linkages between the successive iterations of ghettos over time and place suggest some of the most interesting new directions for future research. The issue of iteration or, more specifically, antecedent, arises in the very first case. As Ravid notes, the disagreements among early modern historians have their origin to some extent in the blurring of two related but different notions of Jewish life, namely, the distinction between the long history of identifiable "Jewish quarters" before the rise of the ghetto and the later development of the "ghetto" as a distinctive form of segregated Jewish living arrangements in early modern cities. The most enduring and best-known of the early pre-ghetto Jewish quarters was Frankfurt am Main in Germany. But it was not considered a ghetto until well after the creation of the Venetian ghetto in 1516.

What were the antecedents of the first "getto" that was created in Venice in 1516? Here we find that our contributors differ. On the one hand, ghettoization supplanted a previous history of Jewish expulsion from Christian-dominated territories, and some historians deem the Venetian ghetto a victory over earlier forms of exclusion and hostility. On the other hand, Stow notes that the next iteration of the ghetto, in Rome, differed in fundamental respects from Venice. In 1555, Pope Paul IV seized upon the example of Venice to institute ghettoization throughout the Papal States with the aim of exclusion and segregation, not inclusion. As Stow points out, previously to the Papal Bull, Jews in Rome lived freely throughout the city. Unlike Venice, subsequent ghettos could hardly be considered a form of inclusion. In *The Emergence of Jewish Ghettos during the Holocaust*, historian Dan Michman weds the Venetian word to the Roman practice. He contends that the early modern ghetto was an amalgam of "the Venetian word plus the Roman content."[3] Yet the differences among our contributors raise critical issues that cannot be so easily resolved. They rest on different antecedents to explain the first ghetto in Venice and its subsequent iterations throughout the Papal States. These antecedents – medieval merchant quarters, Jewish streets and villages, the Papal Bull – lead our contributors to different conclusions about the purpose and nature of the early modern ghetto. Their differences suggest that much is still unknown about the Jewish quarters that predated the ghetto, and the relationship between the creation of the Venetian ghetto and the ways in which the Church chose to repurpose the concept to segregate and exclude.

The issue of how one set of practices affects the next raises issues not just for the early modern case, but for each new, successive iteration of the ghetto. The ongoing quest to unravel the tightly intertwined socioeconomic, demographic, religious, and political roots of segregated spaces presents a promising line of inquiry for the next generation of scholarship. Based on a systematic examination of published book titles, Ravid argues that until the 1840s, references to the ghetto applied to segregated spaces on the Italian peninsula. Thereafter, however, as German Jews gradually entered the modernizing and assimilating middle class, the designation "ghetto" took on new meaning as a way to describe large numbers of so-called "unassimilated" Jews in Eastern Europe. Under the impact of the French Revolution and the Napoleonic Wars, Jews gradually left "compulsory, segregated, and enclosed" living spaces. Increasing numbers (particularly in Germany) entered mainstream European culture and society. Yet even as some Jews sought to put the ghetto behind them, new forms of anti-Semitism emerged and intensified during the late nineteenth and early twentieth century. Social-scientific ideologies increasingly displaced earlier forms of religious exclusion. Whereas the latter aimed at conversion to Christianity, the former targeted "all Jews" for proscription and ostracism as part of a despised "race." As Gitelman and Weitzman note, "Religious texts that had defined Jews were replaced by racist theories that determined who was a Jew by 'blood' or descent." Under the Nazis, even Jewish converts to Christianity were marked for death. Yet how did the demise of the early modern ghettos and the incorporation of Jews into new nation states give rise to the vicious anti-Semitic practices of the Nazi era? What happened to ideas of the ghetto in Europe within the period bookended by the fall of the ghetto gates in Rome and the rise of Hitler? What new tensions produced the eliminationist anti-Semitism that both drew on and transformed earlier practices of exclusion? These questions still remain to be answered.

This volume also raises numerous questions about the links between early modern ghettos and their Nazi counterparts. Michman uncovered one such link in the work of Peter-Heinz Seraphim, an anti-Semitic ideologue of the 1930s. Seraphim argued that Jewish residential districts in cities or "ghettos," particularly in Eastern Europe, were the source of Jewish unity, expansion, and strength. His thinking drew on and inverted current debates among German Jews and Zionists who were also deeply preoccupied with the sources of Jewish strength and difference. Based on the work of Seraphim, the Nazis initially concluded that ghettoization of the Jews would create a Jewish power base that would be difficult to police and control. Yet with the invasion of Poland, dislodging the Jews and creating *lebensraum* for the Germans "played a prominent role," in Michman's words, "in this great colonialist project."[4] Michman's insight into the ideological linkage with Seraphim reveals how shifting understandings of the early modern ghetto influenced Nazi policy as it unfolded in Eastern Europe and the Soviet Union.

Michman's detailed examination of ideology, history, and policy suggests that additional significant transnational linkages between early modern ghettos and other colonial forms may yet be uncovered.[5] During the late nineteenth and early twentieth centuries, Germany, Belgium, France, Britain, and Italy all engaged in the colonization of Africa. European states competed to carve up the continent into spheres for the extraction of raw materials and agricultural products. Native peoples were forcibly dispossessed of their land and put to work on vast coffee and rubber plantations, mining gold, and in brutal extractive industries. The practices of rule all drew heavily on profoundly racialist ideologies, notions of purity and "pollution," and forms of spatial segregation that echoed early segregationist practices towards the Jews in Europe. How did these colonial practices develop? To what extent were they informed by earlier experiences with the exclusion, segregation, and containment of the early modern ghettos?

Moreover, our volume reveals that the transnational circulation of the ghetto not only impacted various colonial models, but that colonial models influenced

Nazi practices. Indeed, the practices of colonization had an important effect on the Nazi's understanding of their own mission. Modeled in part on the immensely profitable colonies that Europe created in Africa, the Nazis aimed to create their own vast colony in Eastern Europe and the Soviet Union that would provide *lebensraum* for the German people as well as a powerful resource base for grain and raw materials. The Slavs were expected to become slaves. What were the ideological and policy linkages between Nazi practices of rule and colonial forms of exploitation and spatial segregation? If the Nazis understood their project as the creation of a vast colony in the East, what techniques and experiences of European colonization in Africa did they overtly reference? Here, our volume raises a host of questions to be explored by a new generation of scholars interested in the transnational circulation of technologies of rule and administration.

Drawing upon the scholarship of leading black urban sociologists, Mitchell Duneier notes that the term ghetto may have occasionally surfaced among early twentieth century observers of African American urban life, but the abiding connection with the Jewish ghetto (particularly its Nazi iteration) only gained currency in the years after World War II. Yet our contributors, notably Avigail S. Oren, demonstrate that the comparison between the Jewish and African American experiences was recognized and employed by both communities even earlier. African American and Jewish journalists invoked medieval and early modern European experiences at a time when the Nazi ghetto was still more than a decade away. The linkages between these two sets of experiences have only begun to be explored. Much research remains to be done, not only on the work of earlier sociologists and historians, but also that of journalists and activists – black, white, and Jewish – in understanding how experience is shared, understood, and resisted from below.

Throughout this volume, we have explored not only the ways in which policy makers imposed the ghetto on subject populations, but also how the term traveled and was used in turn by scholars and activists seeking to understand or challenge its constraints. Just as the ghetto as concept and practice may have figured in colonial projects, so too was the concept of colonization applied to African American ghettos. Deeply influenced by the strong liberation struggles in the 1960s and 1970s in Africa, the Black Power movement in the United States moved away from the concept of ghetto to understand African American segregation and oppression. Left-wing movements throughout the world were strongly influenced by anti-colonial resistance in Africa, Vietnam, and Latin America. As Duneier notes, Kenneth Clark and radical activists, including the Black Panther Party, came to understand black oppression in the United States through a colonial lens that emphasized systemic and structural forms of exploitation.[6] The colonial model, however, was deeply rooted in the global impact of armed anti-colonial struggles for independence. Over time, its explanatory power for theorists of the ghetto gradually faded along with the movements that once provided its impetus.

Yet the transnational circulation of ideas continues. The colonial model was not the only idea that U.S. scholars and activists borrowed from southern Africa. Following the fall of apartheid during the 1990s, some scholars of the African

American experience adopted the notion of "racial apartheid" to describe the process of ghettoization on U.S. soil.[7] In the words of sociologists Douglas Massey and Nancy Denton, "As in South Africa, residential segregation in the United States provides a firm basis for a broader system of racial injustice … [American] apartheid not only denies blacks their rights as citizens but forces them to bear the social costs of their own victimization."[8] In the meantime, in a new and fascinating switch in direction, contributors to this volume have begun to invoke the notion of ghetto to explain urban segregation in South Africa. Curry references the internationally popular song by African American funk band War, "The World Is a Ghetto" (1972) to make her case for rethinking apartheid through the prism of ghettoization, defined as "a racialized," disfranchised, and "infrastructure-deprived" space. Likewise, both Lichtenstein and Steingo reinforce the utility of "ghettoization" for understanding the experiences of South Africans. Lichtenstein places the city's increasingly segregated "urban proletariat" and its struggle for full citizenship at the center of his analysis. He argues that this unique ghettoization process underlay the emergence of the strike wave and ultimately undermined the larger edifice of the apartheid system itself. Focusing on Soweto, "South Africa's largest urban ghetto, and a site of anti-apartheid activism," Steingo's extensive ethnographic fieldwork on the recent period shows that residents themselves describe Soweto as a ghetto, particularly those who closely identify with a larger "Black Atlantic culture extending from Johannesburg and Nairobi, to Kingston, New York, London, and beyond." As the idea, practice, and lived experience of the ghetto continues to move around the world, this very fruitful interchange of conceptualizations for understanding its many iterations suggest fresh new possibilities for research in the years ahead.

Conclusion

This volume enables us to comprehend processes of ghettoization and spatial segregation across several centuries of time and space. It also establishes the intellectual foundation for a new generation of scholarship. Fertile fields for future research include more systematic theoretical and empirical studies of the diverse and shifting meanings, sources, and politics of ghettoization. Over the course of nearly 500 years, ghettos moved from their early modern beginnings as compulsory, segregated, and enclosed spaces to segregated areas without walls, from killing fields to labor extraction, and from sites of labor to high concentrations of poverty and unemployment. *The Ghetto in Global History* opens the door to a broader and more inclusive transnational historical perspective on racially and ethnically divided cities. As we enter a new global era in which the prospects for steady employment become increasingly precarious, as racism and religious hatreds intensify, elites invoke new walled forms of "protection" as solutions to pressing inequalities, and the United States continues to erect prison walls to house predominantly poor urban people of color (Latino/Latina and African Americans). History suggests that we can expect the ghetto to take new forms in new places. And, as current leaders in Europe and the United

States move to build both literal and figurative walls around the nation state, it is clear that studies of ghettos and ghetto formation will take on ever greater significance in the twenty-first century.

Notes

1 Mitchell Duneier, *Ghetto: The Invention of a Place, The History of an Idea*, New York: Farrar, Straus and Giroux, 2016, pp. 221, 69.
2 David Harvey, *Social Justice and the City*, Athens and London, University of Georgia Press, 2009, p. 16.
3 Dan Michman, *The Emergence of Jewish Ghettos during the Holocaust*, Cambridge: Cambridge University Press, 2011, p. 23.
4 Michman, pp. 45–60, 63, 63–67.
5 On the transnational spread of the ghetto to the United States, see Duneier, pp. 217–237. Also see Carl H. Nightingale, *Segregation: A Global History of Divided Cities*, Chicago: University of Chicago Press, 2012, pp. 1–16. Unlike Duneier, Nightingale focuses primarily on the rise of "racially" divided cities under the impact of what he calls capitalist colonial empires, particularly Britain, France, and the United States.
6 Duneier, pp. 115, 129–131.
7 Douglas Massey and Nancy Denton, *American Apartheid: Segregation and the Making of the Underclass,* Cambridge: Harvard University Press, 1993.
8 Massey and Denton, pp. 15–16.

BIBLIOGRAPHY

Adams, Luther. *Way Up North in Louisville: African American Migration in the Urban South, 1930–1970*, Chapel Hill: University of North Carolina Press, 2010.

Amartya, Sen. *Poverty and Famines: An Essay on Entitlement and Deprivation*, Oxford: Oxford University Press, 1986.

Ancel, Jean. *The History of the Holocaust in Romania*, Jerusalem: Yad Vashem 2002.

Arad, Yitzhak. *Ghetto in Flames: The Struggle and Destruction of the Jews of Vilna in the Holocaust*, Jerusalem: Yad Vashem, 1980.

Aschheim, Stephen E. *Brothers and Strangers: The East European Jew in German and German Jewish Consciousness, 1800–1923*, Madison: University of Wisconsin Press, 1982.

Ashforth, Adam. *Witchcraft, Violence, and Democracy in South Africa*, Chicago: University of Chicago Press, 2005.

Atkins, Keletso. *The Moon is Dead! Give Us Our Money! The Cultural Origins of an African Work Ethic in Natal, South Africa, 1843–1900*, Portsmouth: Heinemann, 1993.

Baldwin, Davarian. *Chicago's New Negroes: Modernity, the Great Migration and Black Urban Life*, Chapel Hill: University of North Carolina Press, 2007.

Beavon, Kevin. *Johannesburg: The Making and Shaping of the City*, Pretoria: University of South Africa Press, 2004.

Beinart, William and Saul Dubow, eds. *Segregation and Apartheid in Twentieth-Century South Africa*, New York: Routledge, 1995.

Bender, Sara. *The Jews of Bialystok During World War II and the Holocaust*, Waltham: Brandeis University Press, 2008.

Benocci, Carla and Enrico Guidoni. *Il Ghetto*, Rome: Bonsignori Editore, 1993.

Bonfil, Robert. *Jewish Life in Renaissance Italy*, Berkeley: University of California Press, 1994.

Bonner, Philip and Lauren Segal. *Soweto: A History*, Cape Town: Maskew Miller Longman, 1998.

Brinkmann, Tobias. *Sundays at Sinai: A Jewish Congregation in Chicago*, Chicago: University of Chicago Press, 2012.

Brooks, Richard R.W. and Carol M. Rose. *Saving the Neighborhood: Racially Restrictive Covenants, Law, and Social Norms*, Cambridge: Harvard University Press, 2013.

Broussard, Albert S. *Black San Francisco: The Struggle for Racial Equality in the West, 1900–1954*, Lawrence: University of Kansas, 1993.

Browning, Christopher. "Introduction." In *The United States Holocaust Memorial Encyclopedia of Camps and Ghettos, 1933–45. Vol. II: Ghettos in German-Occupied Eastern Europe*, edited by Martin Dean and Geoffrey P. Megargee, xxxiii–xxxvi, Bloomington: Indiana University Press, 2012.

Carp, Mattatias. *Cartea Neagră, Suferintele evreilor din Romania, 1940–1944* (The Black Book of the Sufferings of Romanian Jews), Bucuresti: Societatea Nationala de Editura si Arte Gratice "Dacia Traiana," 1947 (Romanian), vol. 3.

Christopher, A.J. *The Atlas of Apartheid*, London: Routledge, 1994.

Cole, Tim. *Holocaust City: The Making of a Jewish Ghetto*, London: Routledge, 2003.

Cole, Tim. *Holocaust Landscapes*, London: Bloomsbury, 2016.

Cole, Tim. *Traces of the Holocaust: Journeying in and Out of the Ghettos*, London: Continuum, 2011.

Concina, Ennio, Ugo Camerino and Donatella Calabi. *La citta degli Ebrei. Il Ghetto di Venezia: architettura e urbanistica*, Venice: Abrizzi, 1991.

Connolly, N. D. B. *A World More Concrete: Real Estate and the Remaking of Jim Crow South Florida*, Chicago: University of Chicago Press, 2014.

Cooper, Frederick. *From Slaves to Squatters: Plantation Labor & Agriculture in Zanzibar & Coastal Kenya, 1890–1925*, London: Heinemann, 1997.

Cozzi, Gaetano, ed. *Gli Ebrei e Venezia*, Milan: Edizioni di Comunita, 1987.

Curiel, Roberta and Bernard D. Cooperman. *The Venetian Ghetto*, New York: Rizzoli, 1990.

Davis, Robert C. and Benjamin Ravid, eds. *The Jews of Early Modern Venice*, Baltimore: John Hopkins University Press, 2001.

Dean, Martin and Geoffrey P. Megargee, eds. *The United States Holocaust Memorial Encyclopedia of Camps and Ghettos, 1933–45. Vol. 2: Ghettos in German-Occupied Eastern Europe*, Bloomington: Indiana University Press, 2012.

Deletant, Dennis. "Transnistria and the Romanian Solution to the 'Jewish Problem.'" In *The Shoah in Ukraine: History, Testimony, Memorialization*, edited by Ray Brandon and Wendy Lower, 156–189, Bloomington: Indiana University Press, 2010.

Dieckmann, Christoph. *Deutsche Besatzungspolitik in Litauen, Vol. 1–2*, Göttingen: Wallstein Verlag, 2011.

Drake, St. Clair and Horace Cayton, *Black Metropolis: A Study of Negro Life in a Northern City*, New York: Harcourt, Brace and Company, 1945.

Dubow, Saul. *Apartheid, 1948–1994*, Oxford: Oxford University Press, 2014.

Duneier, Mitchell. *Ghetto: The Invention of a Place, the History of an Idea*, New York: Farrar, Straus and Giroux, 2016.

Ehrenburg, Ilya, Vasily Grossman and David Patterson, eds. *The Complete Black Book of Russian Jewry*, New Brunswick: Transaction, 2002.

Ferguson, James. *Global Shadows: Africa in the Neoliberal World Order*, Durham: Duke University Press, 2006.

Ferguson, Karen. *Top Down: The Ford Foundation, Black Power and the Reinvention of Racial Liberalism*, Philadelphia: University of Pennsylvania Press, 2013.

Ferguson, Ronald F. and William T. Dickens, eds. *Urban Problems and Community Development*, Washington, D.C.: Brookings Institution Press, 1999.

Flamming, Douglas. *Bound for Freedom: Black Los Angeles in Jim Crow America*, Berkeley: University of California Press, 2005.

Fredrickson, George M. *White Supremacy: A Comparative Study in American and South African History*, Oxford: Oxford University Press, 1981.

Freund, David. *Colored Property: State Policy and White Racial Politics in Suburban America*, Chicago: University of Chicago Press, 2007.

Friedman, Philip. "The Jewish Ghettos of the Nazi Era," *Jewish Social Studies*, Vol. 16, 1 (Jan 1954): 61–88.

Gandhi, Mahatma. *Collected Works of Mahatma Gandhi*, https://en.wikisource.org/wiki/The_Collected_Works_of_Mahatma_Gandhi/Volume_II/1899#Indians_in_the_Transvaal_.2817-5-1899.29, accessed April 8, 2017.

Geissbuhler, Simon, ed. *Romania and the Holocaust*, Stuttgart: Ibidem Press, 2016.

Gerlach, Christian. *Kalkulierte Morde: Die deutsche Wirtschafts- und Vernichtungspolitik in Weißrussland 1941–1944*, Hamburg: Hamburger Edition, 1999.

Giccaria, Paolo and Claudio Minca, eds. *Hitler's Geographies: The Spatialities of the Third Reich*, Chicago: Chicago University Press, 2016.

Gitelman, Zvi. *Bitter Legacy: Confronting the Holocaust in the USSR*, Bloomington: Indiana University Press, 1997.

Gold, Michael. *Jews Without Money*, New York: Horace Liveright, 1930.

Gonda, Jeffrey D. *Unjust Deeds: The Restrictive Covenant Cases and the Making of the Civil Rights Movement*, Chapel Hill: University of North Carolina Press, 2015.

Gregory, Steven. *Black Corona: Race and the Politics of Place in an Urban Community*, Princeton: Princeton University Press, 1998.

Gutman, Israel. *Resistance: The Warsaw Ghetto Uprising*, New York: Houghton Mifflin, 1994.

Harbe, Anton. *Diepsloot*, Cape Town: Jonathan Ball, 2011.

Harvey, David. *Social Justice and the City*, Athens: University of Georgia Press, 2009.

Higginson, John. *Agrarian Origins of South African Apartheid, 1900–1948*, Cambridge: Cambridge University Press, 2014.

Hirsch, Arnold. *Making the Second Ghetto: Race and Housing in Chicago, 1940–1960*, Chicago: University of Chicago Press, 1983.

Huchzermeyer, Marie. *Unlawful Occupation: Informal Settlements and Urban Policy in South Africa and Brazil*, Lawrenceville: Africa World Press, 2008.

Hutchinson, Ray and Bruce D. Haynes, eds. *The Ghetto: Contemporary Global Issues and Controversies*, Boulder: Westview, 2011.

Jones, Will P. *The March on Washington: Jobs, Freedom, and the Forgotten History of Civil Rights*, New York: W.W. Norton & Company, 2013.

Kanogo, Tabitha. *Squatters & the Roots of Mau Mau, 1905–63*, Columbus: Ohio University Press, 1997.

Kassow, Samuel D. *Who Will Write our History? Emanuel Ringelblum, the Warsaw Ghetto, and the Oyneg Shabbos Archive*, Bloomington: Indiana University Press, 2007.

Knowles, Anne Kelly, Tim Cole and A. Giordano, eds. *Geographies of the Holocaust*, Bloomington: Indiana University Press, 2014.

Legassick, Martin. "British Hegemony and the Origins of Segregation in South Africa, 1901–1914." In *Segregation and Apartheid in Twentieth Century South Africa*, edited by William Beinart and Saul Dubow, 43–59, New York: Routledge, 1995.

Lewis, Earl. *In Their Own Interests: Race, Class, and Power in Twentieth-Century Norfolk, Virginia*, Berkeley: University of California Press, 1991.

Malkiel, David Joshua. *A Separate Republic. The Mechanics and Dynamics of Venetian Jewish Self-Government, 1607–1624*, Jerusalem: Magnes Press, 1991.

Mamdani, Mahmood. *Citizen and Subject: Contemporary Africa and the Legacy of Late Colonialism*, Princeton: Princeton University Press, 1996.

Massey, Douglas S. and Nancy Denton. *American Apartheid: Segregation and the Making of the Underclass*, Cambridge: Harvard University Press, 1993.

Maylam, Paul and Iain Edwards, eds. *The People's City: African Life in Twentieth-Century Durban*, Pietermaitzburg: University of Natal Press, 1996.

Michman, Dan. *The Emergence of Jewish Ghettos during the Holocaust*, New York: Cambridge University Press, 2011.

Michman, Dan. *Holocaust Historiography: A Jewish Perspective*, Elstree, UK: Vallentine Mitchell, 2003.

Michney, Todd M. *Surrogate Suburbs: Black Upward Mobility and Neighborhood Change in Cleveland, 1900–1980*, Chapel Hill: University of North Carolina Press, 2017.

Milano, Attilio. *Il Ghetto di Roma (Le Ghetto de Rome)*, Rome: Staderini, 1966.

Moore, Shirley Ann Wilson. *To Place Our Deeds: The African American Community in Richmond, California, 1910–1963*, Berkeley: University of California Press, 2000.

Nepi, Serena Di. *Sopravvivere al ghetto: Per una storia sociale della comunità ebraica nella Roma del Cinquecento*, Rome: Viella, 2013.

Nightingale, Carl H. *Segregation: A Global History of Divided Cities*, Chicago: University of Chicago Press, 2012.

Nuttall, Sarah and Achille Mbembe, eds. *Johannesburg: The Elusive Metropolis*, Durham: Duke University Press, 2008.

O'Connor, Alice. *Poverty Knowledge: Social Science, Social Policy, and the Poor in Twentieth-Century U.S. History*, Princeton: Princeton University Press, 2001.

Ofer, Dalia and Lenore Weitzman, eds. *Women in the Holocaust*, New Haven: Yale University Press, 1999.

Orleck, Annelise and Lisa Gayle Hazirjian, eds. *The War on Poverty: A New Grassroots History, 1964–1980*, Athens: University of Georgia Press, 2011.

Osofsky, Gilbert. *Harlem: The Making of a Ghetto, Negro New York, 1890–1930*, Chicago: Ivan R. Dee Publisher, 1963.

Pullan, Brian. *Rich and Poor in Renaissance Venice: The Social Institutions of a Catholic State, to 1620*, Cambridge: Harvard University Press, 1971.

Ravid, Benjamin "Curfew Time in the Ghetto of Venice." In *Medieval and Renaissance Venice*, edited by Ellen E. Kittelland and Thomas F. Madden, 237–275, Urbana-Champaign: University of Illinois Press, 1999.

Ravid, Benjamin. *Studies on the Jews of Venice, 1382–1797*, Farnham: Ashgate, 2003.

Rothstein, Richard. Interview with Terry Gross. "Historian Says Don't 'Sanitize' How Our Government Created Ghettos," National Public Radio, March 5, 2015.

Ruderman, David. "The Cultural Significance of the Ghetto in Jewish History." In *From Ghetto to Emancipation: Historical and Contemporary Reconsiderations of the Jewish Community of Scranton*, edited by David N. Myers and William V. Rowe, 1–16, Scranton: Scranton University Press, 1997.

Schwartz, Daniel. *The Ghetto and Jewish Modernity*, Boston: Harvard University Press, in progress.

Shachan, Avigdor. *Burning Ice: The Ghettos of Transnistria (East European Monographs)*, New York: Columbia University Press, 1996.

Shapiro, Paul, Alvin Rosenfeld and Sara Bloomfield. "Preface." In *Encyclopedia of Camps and Ghettos, 1933–1945, Vol. II: Ghettos in German-Occupied Eastern Europe*, edited by Geoffrey P. Megargee and Martin Dean, xxvi, Bloomingdale: Indiana University Press, 2012.

Siegmund, Stefanie B. *The Medici State and the Ghetto of Florence: The Construction of an Early Modern Jewish Community*, Stanford: Stanford University Press, 2005.

Spear, Allan H. *Black Chicago: The Making of a Negro Ghetto 1890–1920*, Chicago: University of Chicago Press, 1967.

Steingo, Gavin. *Kwaito's Promise: Music and the Aesthetics of Freedom in South Africa*, Chicago: University of Chicago Press, 2016.

Stow, Kenneth R. *Theater of Acculturation: The Roman Ghetto in the Sixteenth Century*, Seattle: University of Washington Press, 2001.

Strickland, Arvarh E. and Robert E. Weems, Jr., eds. *The African American Experience: A Historiographical and Bibliographical Guide*, Westport: Greenwood Press, 2001.

Sugrue, Thomas J. *The Origins of the Urban Crisis: Race and Inequality in Postwar Detroit*, Princeton: Princeton University Press, 1996.

Taylor, Quintard. *The Forging of a Black Community: Seattle's Central District from 1870 through the Civil Rights Era*, Seattle: University of Washington Press, 1994.

Tooze, Adam. *The Wages of Destruction: The Making and Breaking of the Nazi Economy*, New York: Viking Penguin, 2006.

Trivellato, Francesca. *The Familiarity of Strangers: The Sephardic Diaspora, Livorno, and Cross-Cultural Trade in the Early Modern Period*, New Haven: Yale University Press, 2009.

Trotter, Jr., Joe William. *Black Milwaukee: The Making of an Industrial Proletariat, 1915–1945*, Champaign-Urbana: University of Illinois Press, 2006.

Vieira, Jose Luandino. *Our Musseque*, Sawtry: Dedalus, 2016.

Vose, Clement E. *Caucasians Only: The Supreme Court, the NAACP, and the Restrictive Covenant Cases*, Berkeley: University of California Press, 1959.

Wale, Kim. *South Africa's Struggle to Remember: Contested Memories of Squatter Resistance in the Western Cape*, New York: Routledge, 2016.

Walke, Anike. *Pioneers and Partisans: An Oral History of Nazi Genocide in Belorussia*, Oxford: Oxford University Press, 2015.

Weaver, Robert C. *The Negro Ghetto*, New York: Harcourt, Brace and Company, 1948.

Wilder, Craig Steven. *A Covenant with Color: Race and Social Power in Brooklyn*, New York: Columbia University Press, 2000.

Wilson, William J. *When Work Disappears: The World of the New Urban Poor*, Chicago: University of Illinois Press, 1996.

Wirth, Lewis. *The Ghetto*, Chicago: University of Chicago, 1928.

Wolpe, Harold. "Capitalism and Cheap Labour Power in South Africa: From Segregation to Apartheid." In *Segregation and Apartheid in Twentieth-Century South Africa*, edited by William Beinart and Saul Dubow, 60–90, New York: Routledge, 1995.

Wright, George C. *Life Behind a Veil: Blacks in Louisville, Kentucky, 1865–1930*, Baton Rouge: Louisiana State University Press, 1985.

Zangwill, Israel. *Children of the Ghetto: A Study of a Peculiar People*, London: W. Heinemann, 1892.

Zangwill, Israel. *Dreamers of the Ghetto*, Freeport, NY: Books for Libraries Press, [1893], 1970.

Zangwill, Israel. *Ghetto Tragedies*, New York: Macmillan, [c. 1899], 1919.

INDEX

Note: page numbers in bold are cross-referencing terms found in figures; page numbers in italics are cross-referencing terms found in tables.